P9-DCX-977

6698419

always up to date

The law changes, but Nolo is on top of it! We offer several
ways to make sure you and your Nolo products are up to date:

1 **Nolo's Legal Updater**
We'll send you an email whenever a new edition of this book is
published! Sign up at **www.nolo.com/legalupdater**.

2 **Updates @ Nolo.com**
Check **www.nolo.com/update** to find recent changes
in the law that affect the current edition of your book.

3 **Nolo Customer Service**
To make sure that this edition of the book is the most
recent one, call us at **800-728-3555** and ask one of
our friendly customer service representatives.
Or find out at **www.nolo.com**.

please note

We believe accurate, plain-English legal information should help you solve many of your own legal problems. But this text is not a substitute for personalized advice from a knowledgeable lawyer. If you want the help of a trained professional—and we'll always point out situations in which we think that's a good idea—consult an attorney licensed to practice in your state.

8th edition

Your Rights in the Workplace

by Attorney Barbara Kate Repa

EIGHTH EDITION	JULY 2007
Legal research	TRISH KEADY
	TERRY McGINLEY
	ALAYNA SCHROEDER
Cover design	SUSAN PUTNEY
Book design	TERRI HEARSH
Proofreading	ELAINE MERRILL
Index	THÉRÈSE SHERE
Printing	CONSOLIDATED PRINTERS, INC.

Repa, Barbara Kate
  Your rights in the workplace / by Barbara Kate Repa. -- 8th ed., [rev.]
     p. cm.
  Includes index.
  ISBN-13: 978-1-4133-0643-9
  ISBN-10: 1-4133-0643-8
  1. Labor laws and legislation--United States--Popular works. 2. Employee rights--
United States--Popular works. I. Title.
KF3455.Z9R47 2007
344.7301--dc22

                              2007002196

For information on bulk purchases or corporate premium sales, please contact the Special Sales Department. For academic sales or textbook adoptions, ask for Academic Sales. Call 800-955-4775 or write to Nolo, 950 Parker Street, Berkeley, CA 94710.

Acknowledgments

Many people—both outside and inside Nolo—gave their time, expertise, and wise counsel to help make this tome possible initially.

This eighth edition is made possible by the many workers since then who have shared their stories, their pains and gains.

My heartfelt thanks to all.

Table of Contents

Appendix

Index

Your Rights in the Workplace

Maybe you're just curious. Or maybe you're the cautious type of soul who likes to think ahead and prevent a wrong before it happens. But the best bet is that you are reading this book because you already have a work-related problem:

- You were not hired for a job and you have good reason to suspect it was because of your race. Or your disability.
- Your employer promoted a less-qualified person to fill a position you were promised.
- You want to know your legal rights if you consistently work overtime. Or if you want to take a leave to care for a sick parent. Or if you are called to serve on a jury.
- You have just been laid off and you're wondering if you have the right to get your job back. Or to get unemployment payments in the meantime. Or whether your employer owes you severance pay.
- You want to help evaluate a new job you've been offered. Or you want to find out your legal rights as a jobseeker.

This book will help you understand the legal rights that apply to your situation. It explains federal workplace laws—such as those guaranteeing your rights to be paid fairly and on time and to work free from discrimination. It also explains the twists state law may place on your workplace rights—regulating, for example, both your right to smoke and your right to work in a smoke-free place, or whether or not you are entitled to time off work to vote or to care for a sick child.

Tackling a potential workplace problem can feel difficult, so heed that noble adage: Simplify, simplify. Better still: Simplify. Woe unto the reader whose concerns span every chapter. Proceed to the chapters that discuss the substance of your problem and skip the rest for now.

Also, be aware that there are many public and private agencies, groups, and organizations that specialize in workplace issues, and many of them provide free—or low-cost—counseling, support, or referrals. You will find information on these organizations peppered throughout the book, and a comprehensive listing in the appendix.

Analyzing Your Options

If something is amiss in your workplace and you have turned to watercooler wisdom, commuter train tales, or locker room skinny, you may have come away with the same urging: Sue.

For most people, that is bad advice. The courtroom is usually the worst place to resolve workplace disputes. Most of them can be handled more efficiently and much more effectively in the workplace itself—through mediation, arbitration or, most often, by honest conversation.

If you have suffered an insult, an injury, or a wrong at work, you are probably feeling angry or hurt. If you have lost your job, you may be hurting financially, too. All of this is likely to cloud your ability to make well-reasoned decisions. So go slowly. Decide what you want to gain. If an apology from your employer would suffice, save yourself the time and expense of filing a legal action.

Talking It Over With Your Employer

Do not overlook the obvious: First try talking over your workplace problem with your employer. An intelligent discussion can resolve most wrongs—or at least get your differences out on the table. Most companies want to stay within the law and avoid legal tangles. So the odds are that your problem is the result of an oversight, a misunderstanding, or a lack of legal knowledge.

Here are a few tips on how to present your concerns to your employer or former employer:

Know your rights. The more you know about your legal rights in the workplace—to be paid fairly and on time, to do your job free from discrimination and retaliation, to labor in a safe and healthy place—the more confident you will be in presenting your problem. This book offers a wealth of information about the basic laws of the workplace—and tells you where to turn if you need more specific information to clarify your rights.

Also, the book contains a number of charts summarizing state laws on various workplace rights, including specific penalties that may be imposed on employers who violate them. Your best course is probably not to sue your employer over a violation of a law requiring paid time off for jury duty or a single miscalculation of overtime pay. But knowing

whether a particular transgression can be punished with a fine, a criminal conviction, or an order to rehire you is the kind of information that can make your employer take your complaint more seriously in the bargaining process.

Stick to the facts. Keeping your legal rights firmly in mind, write a brief summary of what has gone wrong and your recommendation for resolving the problem. It often helps to have someone who is more objective than you are, such as a friend or family member, review the facts of your workplace problem with you and discuss possible approaches to resolving it.

Check the facts again. The human memory is not nearly as accurate as we like to think it is—particularly when it comes to remembering numbers and dates. Before you approach your employer with a complaint about your pay, check to be sure your math is correct. If your beef is about a discriminatory remark, be sure you can quote it verbatim. Review all of your written records to make sure you have not overlooked a past event or pivotal memo.

Do not be overly emotional. Recognize that dealing with a workplace problem can be stressful. After all, if you are like most workers, you spend about half of your waking hours on the job. But you also know friends, relatives, and acquaintances who are out of work—and who are having hard times finding new jobs. Acknowledge that these pressures of time and money can make it more difficult to deal with a workplace problem. Then vow to proceed as calmly and rationally as possible.

Stay on the job if possible. If your job is on shaky ground, try not to jeopardize it further by losing your temper and getting fired as a result. A calm presentation of a complaint is always better than an emotional confrontation. Remember the common wisdom that it is easier to find a new job while you still have your old one. At the very least, it's easier to blaze a new career trail if you leave no muddy tracks behind you.

Be discreet. Discussions of workplace problems are often very personal and should take place privately—not in front of coworkers. Employment problems can be divisive not only for those involved, but for an entire workplace. You don't want to be justly accused of poisoning the workplace atmosphere or of filling it with disgruntled workers forming pro and con camps. Ask for an appointment to discuss your complaint privately with your supervisor or another appropriate manager. If you give that person a chance to resolve your problem rationally and privately, he or she will be more apt to see things your way.

Documenting the Problem

Most employers now embrace the workplace mantra reinforced by thousands of court cases: Document, document, document. If your good working situation has gone bad— or you have recently been fired—you, too, must heed the call: Make a record, preferably a written one, of all that happened. You are nowhere, legally, without evidence of how and when things went wrong.

A little bit of workplace paranoia may later prove to be a healthy thing. Even if everything seems fine now, take the extra seconds to create a paper trail. Collect in one place all documents you receive on the job: initial work agreements, employee handbooks, management memos, performance reviews. To be safe, keep your file at home, away from the office.

If you have what seems to be a valid complaint, it is crucial to gather evidence to bolster your claim. From the start, beware of deadlines for filing specific types of legal claims. The deadlines may range from a few weeks to a few years but will likely signal that you have to act quickly.

CAUTION

Watch what you grab. While it's true that you are in the best position to gather evidence while you are still working, you must be wary of what you take in hand. Confidential information, such as evidence of the company's finances, and other documents that the employer has clearly indicated should not be disclosed, are off limits. If you take these kinds of documents out of the workplace, that may actually become a legal ground for the company to fire you—or for a court to limit or deny your remedies for wrongful treatment you suffered while on the job.

There are several kinds of evidence you should collect as soon as possible.

Company policies. Statements of company policy, either written or verbal, including job descriptions, work rules, personnel pamphlets, notices, or anything else that either indicates or implies that company policy is to treat workers unfairly may be the most meaningful evidence you can amass. A straightforward company policy can also help bolster your case or complaint if you can show that the policy promised something the company didn't deliver.

Written statements by management. Statements by supervisors, personnel directors, or other managers about you are also important. Save any written statements and note when and from whom you received them. If you have not received any written reasons for a job decision you feel is discriminatory or otherwise wrongful, make a written request for a statement of the company's reasons.

Verbal comments. In many cases, employers and their managers do not write down their reasons for making an employment decision. In such cases, you may still be able to document your claim with evidence of verbal statements by supervisors or others concerning unwritten company policy or undocumented reasons for a particular action involving your job.

Make accurate notes of what was said as soon as you can after the statement is made. Also note the time and place the statement was made, who else was present, and the conversation surrounding it. If others heard the statement, try to get them to write down their recollections, and have them sign that statement. Or have them sign your written version of the statement, indicating that it accurately reflects what they heard.

We're All in This Together

Coworkers may be reluctant to help you with your workplace complaint, whether by giving statements of their own experiences or by backing up your story of what has occurred. You may run into the same common reaction: "I don't want to get involved."

People may be afraid they will lose their own jobs or suffer in some other way if they pitch in and create bad blood with the company. You may be able to persuade them to help you by reassuring them that the same law that prohibits the initial wrongful treatment also specifically prohibits the company or union from retaliating against anyone who helps in an investigation of your claim.

However, if your attempts to coax coworkers are unsuccessful, respect their rights to remain mum—and proceed with whatever other good evidence you can garner.

Considering Legal Action

Wipe the dollar signs from your eyes. While it's true that some workers have won multimillion dollar judgments against their employers, it's also true that such judgments are very few and very far between. There are several things to think about before you decide to launch a no-holds-barred legal challenge to your firing or wrongful workplace treatment.

Evaluate your motives. First, answer one question honestly: What do you expect to gain by a lawsuit? Are you angry, seeking some revenge? Do you hope to teach your former employer a lesson? Do you just want to make your former employer squirm? None of these provides a strong basis on which to construct a lawsuit. If an apology, a letter of recommendation, or a clearing of your work record would make you feel whole again, negotiate first for those things.

You will need good documentation. As this book stresses again and again, the success of your claim or lawsuit is likely to depend upon how well you can document the circumstances surrounding your workplace problem. If your employer claims you were fired because of incompetence, for example, make sure you can show otherwise by producing favorable written performance reviews or evidence that your employer circumvented the company's disciplinary procedures before firing you.

Before you discuss your case with a lawyer, look closely at your documentation and try to separate the aspects of your problem that you can prove from those you merely suspect. If you cannot produce any independent verification of your workplace problem, you will be in the untenable position of convincing a judge or jury to believe your word alone.

Taking action will require time and effort. You can save yourself some time and possibly some grief by using this book to objectively analyze your job loss or problem. If possible, do it before you begin talking with a lawyer about handling your case. Once again, the keys to most successful wrongful discharge lawsuits are good documentation and organized preparation—both of which must come from you.

Be mindful of the expense. Because many challenges to workplace problems are legal long shots, lawyers who specialize in this type of case often refuse to handle them. In fact, these days, many originally well-meaning employment lawyers have switched to where the money is: They now represent employers.

So your initial search for legal help is likely to be frustrating. And, if you do find a lawyer willing to take your case, you will probably have to pay dearly. If you hire a lawyer with expertise in wrongful discharge lawsuits and your case is less than a sure win, you can expect to deposit several thousands of dollars to pay for the lawyer's time if your lawsuit fails, plus thousands more to cover other costs. (See Chapter 17, "Hiring a Lawyer," for more advice on this.)

Wages and Hours

The French writer Voltaire once pointed out that work spares us from three great evils: boredom, vice, and need. Most of us can tolerate a little boredom, and some may even enjoy a small helping of vice. But need is something we would all rather avoid. Although most people would prefer their jobs to be fun and fulfilling, what they likely want most is to be paid—fairly and on time—so that they can enjoy the other aspects of their lives.

The Fair Labor Standards Act

The most important and most far-reaching law guaranteeing a worker's right to be paid fairly is the federal Fair Labor Standards Act, or FLSA. (29 U.S.C. §§ 201 and following.) The FLSA:

- defines the 40-hour workweek
- establishes the federal minimum wage
- sets requirements for overtime, and
- places restrictions on child labor.

Basically, the FLSA establishes minimums for fair pay and hours—and it is the single law most often violated by employers. An employer must also comply with other local, state, or federal workplace laws that set higher standards. So, in addition to determining whether you are being paid properly under the FLSA, you may need to check whether the other laws discussed in this chapter also apply to your situation.

The FLSA was passed in 1938 after the Depression, when many employers took advantage of the tight labor market to subject workers to horrible conditions and impossible hours. One of the most complex laws of the workplace, the FLSA has been amended many times. It is full of exceptions and exemptions —some of which seem to contradict one another. Most of the revisions and interpretations have expanded the law's coverage by, for example:

- requiring that male and female workers receive equal pay for work that requires equal skill, effort, and responsibility
- including in its protections state and local hospitals and educational institutions
- covering most federal employees and employees of states, political subdivisions, and interstate agencies
- setting out strict standards for determining, paying, and accruing compensatory or comp time—time given off work instead of cash payments, and
- establishing specific requirements for how and when employers must pay for overtime work.

Who Is Covered

The FLSA applies only to employers whose annual sales total $500,000 or more, or who are engaged in interstate commerce.

You might think that this would restrict the FLSA to covering only employees in large companies, but, in reality, the law covers nearly all workplaces. This is because the courts have interpreted the term interstate commerce very broadly. For example, courts have ruled that companies that regularly use the U.S. mail to send or receive letters to and from other states are engaged in interstate commerce. Even the fact that employees use company telephones or computers to place or accept interstate business calls or take orders has subjected an employer to the FLSA.

Who Is Exempt

A few employers, including small farms—those that use relatively little outside paid labor—are explicitly exempt from the FLSA.

In addition, some employees are exempt from FLSA requirements, such as pay for overtime and minimum wages, even though their employers are covered. For example, many airline employees are exempt from the FLSA's overtime provisions. And most companions for the elderly are exempt from both minimum wage and overtime provisions.

Exemption and partial exemption from the FLSA cuts both ways. For employees who are exempt, the often-surprising downside is that they are generally not entitled to wage extras such as overtime and compensatory time. The upside is that, at least theoretically, exempt employees are paid a salary that is handsome enough to compensate them for the extra duties and responsibilities they have taken on as part of their jobs. In addition, the paychecks of the exempt can be docked only for complete days of absence for vacation, personal business, illness, or partial initial or final weeks of employment.

Employers who attempt to have it both ways—for example, by denying workers overtime by claiming they're exempt but docking them for tardiness or time away for an occasional errand—risk violating wage and hour laws.

Executive, Administrative, and Professional Workers

This is the most confusing and most often mistakenly applied broad category of exempt worker.

Above all, bear in mind that you are not automatically exempt from the FLSA solely because you receive a salary; the work you do must be of a certain type as well.

The Department of Labor, not renowned for issuing succinct or comprehensible regulations, attempts some additional guidance on what type of work these employees must perform to qualify as exempt.

Executive exemption. The requirements for an exempt executive worker are most rigorous. He or she must:

- manage other workers as the primary job duty
- direct the work of two or more full-time employees
- have the authority to hire, fire, discipline, promote, and demote others or make recommendations about these decisions, and
- earn a salary of at least $455 per week. Employees who own at least 20% of the business are exempt only if they are "actively engaged" in its management.

Administrative exemption. An administrative employee generally must:

- primarily perform office or nonmanual work directly for company management or administration
- primarily use his or her own discretion and judgment in work duties, and
- earn a salary of at least $455 weekly.

Professional exemption. To qualify as an exempt professional, an employee must:

- perform work requiring invention, imagination, originality, or talent in a recognized creative field—such as music, writing, acting, and the graphic arts, or
- perform work requiring advanced knowledge—work that is predominantly intellectual, requires a prolonged course of instruction, and requires the consistent exercise of discretion and judgment, such as law; medicine; theology; accounting; actuarial computation; engineering; architecture; teaching; various types of physical, chemical, and biological sciences; and pharmacy, and
- earn a salary of at least $455 per week —although doctors, lawyers, teachers, and many computer specialists need not meet this minimal earning requirement.

Highly compensated employees. Employees who perform office or nonmanual work and are paid total annual compensation of $100,000 or more—which must include at least $455 per week paid on a salary or fee basis—are exempt from the FLSA if they regularly perform at least one of the duties of an exempt executive, administrative, or professional employee as described earlier.

Common problems. The Department of Labor has tagged a number of problems that commonly come up relating to the exemption for executive, administrative, and professional workers. The top contenders include workplaces in which:

- there is no formal sick leave policy, but salaried workers are docked for time missed due to illness

- allegedly exempt workers are paid less than full salary each week
- employees deemed exempt perform nearly exclusively routine work that has no bearing on setting management policies
- exempt employees with scholastic degrees perform exclusively unprofessional, unrelated work
- acquired job skills are confused with the need to use independent judgment and discretion, and
- salaried employees are all labeled exempt, without regard to actual work duties or the percentage of time spent on them.

RESOURCE

If you do not fit squarely within a particular definition of an exempt employee, following the nuances and semantic turns can be flummoxing. For more help, go to the Department of Labor's website at www.dol.gov or seek guidance from the DOL's toll-free helpline at 866-487-9243.

Outside Salespeople

An outside salesperson is exempt from FLSA coverage if he or she:

- regularly works away from the employer's place of business, and
- makes sales or obtains orders or contracts for services or facilities.

Typically, an exempt salesperson will be paid primarily through commissions and will require little or no direct supervision in doing the job. And, under the law, outside sales do not include those made by mail, by telephone, or over the Internet.

Computer Specialists

This exemption applies to computer systems analysts, computer programmers, software engineers, and or other similarly skilled workers in the computer field who are compensated either on a salary or fee basis at a rate not less than $455 per week or not less than $27.63 an hour.

If you work in such circles, you may well know who you are. But the law specifically requires that an exempt computer specialist's primary work duties must involve:

- applying systems analysis techniques and procedures—including consulting with users to determine hardware, software, or system functional specifications
- designing, developing, documenting, analyzing, creating, testing, or modifying computer systems or programs, including prototypes, based on and related to user or system design specifications
- designing, documenting, testing, creating, or modifying computer programs related to machine operating systems, or
- a combination of these duties.

Miscellaneous Workers

Several other types of workers are exempt from the minimum wage and overtime pay provisions of the FLSA. The most common include:

- employees of seasonal amusement or recreational businesses

- employees of local newspapers having a circulation of less than 4,000
- seamen or women on foreign vessels
- newspaper delivery workers
- workers on small farms, and
- personal companions and casual baby-sitters. Officially, domestic workers— housekeepers, child care workers, chauffeurs, gardeners—are covered by the FLSA if they are paid at least $1,000 in wages from a single employer in a year, or if they work eight hours or more in a week for one or several employers. For example, if you are a teenager who babysits only an evening or two each month for the neighbors, you probably cannot claim coverage under the FLSA; a full-time au pair would be covered.

Apprentices

An apprentice is a worker who's at least 16 years old and who has signed an agreement to learn a skilled trade. Apprentices are exempt from the requirements of the FLSA. But beware that your state may have a law limiting the number of hours you can work as an apprentice. State law may also require that, as an apprentice, you must be paid a certain percentage of the minimum wage. Check with your state labor department for more information. (See the Appendix for contact details.)

 RESOURCE

For detailed information on the FLSA, see *The Essential Guide to Federal Employment Laws,* by Lisa Guerin and Amy DelPo (Nolo).

Independent Contractors Are Exempt

The FLSA covers only employees, not independent contractors, who typically are hired to work on specific projects. However, whether a person is an employee for purposes of the FLSA generally turns on whether that worker is employed by a single employer.

The FLSA was passed to clamp down on employers who cheated workers of their fair wages. As a result, employee status is broadly interpreted so that as many workers as possible come within the protection of the law.

If nearly all of your income comes from one company, a court would probably rule that you are an employee of that company for purposes of the FLSA, regardless of whether other details of your work life would appear to make you an independent contractor.

In early cases determining close questions of employment status, most courts found workers to be employees rather than independent contractors, and the scales remain tipped that way. Key facts cited by the courts: The relationship appeared to be permanent, the workers lacked bargaining power with regard to the terms of their employment (*Martin v. Albrecht*, 802 F.Supp. 1311 (1992)), and the individual workers were economically dependent upon the business to which they gave service (*Martin v. Selker Bros., Inc.*, 949 F.2d 1286 (1991)).

But workers' skills and pay level can push courts to the opposite conclusion. Some courts are more likely to class workers with higher skills and higher pay as independent contractors rather than as employees. In three cases hailing from Texas, for example, three groups of workers—delivery service drivers, pipe welders, and topless dancers—all of which were classified as independent contractors, claimed they were really employees under the labor laws and so should be entitled to overtime pay. The courts, apparently reasoning that making deliveries and welding pipes take more skill than dancing topless, held that the drivers and welders were independent contractors, but the dancers were employees. (*Metzler v. Express 60-Minutes Delivery*, 1997 U.S. Dist. LEXIS 11217 (1997); *Carrell v. Sunland Constr., Inc.*, 998 F.2d 330 (5th Cir. 1993); *Reich v. Circle C. Investments, Inc.*, 998 F.2d 324 (5th Cir. 1993).)

Rights Under the FLSA

The FLSA guarantees a number of rights, primarily aimed at ensuring that workers get paid fairly for the time they work. (See "Enforcing Your Right to Be Paid Fairly" and "Filing a Complaint or Lawsuit," below, for an explanation of how to take action for FLSA violations.)

Minimum Wage

Employers must pay all covered employees not less than the minimum wage—currently set at $5.15 an hour.

Some states have established a minimum wage that is higher than the federal one—and you are entitled to the higher rate if your state allows for one. Employers not covered by the FLSA, such as small farm owners, are required to pay all workers the state minimum wage rate. (See "State Minimum Wage Laws for Regular and Tipped Employees," below.)

The FLSA does not require any specific system of paying the minimum wage, so employers may base pay on time at work, on piece rates, or according to some other measurement. In all cases, however, an employee's pay divided by the hours worked during the pay period must equal or exceed the minimum wage.

Many employers either become confused by the nuances and exceptions in the wage and hour law—or they bend the rules to suit their own pocketbooks. Whatever the situation, you would do well to double-check your employer's math. A few simple rules distilled from the law may help.

- **Hourly.** Hourly employees must be paid minimum wage for all hours worked. Your employer cannot take an average —or pay you less than minimum wage for some hours worked and more for others.
- **Fixed rate or salary.** Employees paid at a fixed rate can check their wages by dividing the amount they are paid in a pay period by the number of hours worked. The resulting average must be at least minimum wage.
- **Commissions and piece rates.** Your total pay divided by the number of hours you worked must average at least the minimum hourly wage rate.

Form of Pay

Under the FLSA, the pay you receive must be in the form of cash or something that can be readily converted into cash or other legal forms of compensation, such as food and lodging. Your employer cannot, for example, pay you with a coupon or token that can be spent only at a store run by the employer. Employee discounts granted by employers do not count toward the minimum wage requirement.

Pay for Time Off

Neither the minimum wage section nor any other part of the FLSA requires employers to pay employees for time off, such as vacation, holidays, or sick days. Although most employers provide full-time workers some paid time off each year, the FLSA covers payment only for time on the job.

Going Up: The Latest Rage on the Minimum Wage

While former debates over increasing the minimum wage revealed themselves to be so many tempests in teapots, the threat or promise—depending on your politics—to do just that.

The Fair Minimum Wage Act of 2007 amends the FLSA and gradually raises the federal minimum wage from $5.15 per hour to $5.85 per hour on July 24, 2007, to $6.55 per hour on July 24, 2008, and finally to $7.25 per hour on July 24, 2009.

The Act is a component of the 100-Hour Plan announced by Speaker Nancy Pelosi when the Democrats assumed congressional leadership in January 2007 after spending a long time on the outside looking in.

As is true of most wage measures, this controversial legislation had both vehement supporters and opponents. Workers' groups pointed out that the federal minimum wage has been frozen at $5.15 an hour since 1997, the longest stretch without an increase since the FLSA established a minimum in 1938. And that wage netted full-time minimum wage workers just $206 a week, $10,400 a year—far below the poverty line for even a small family.

Big business and conservative economists warned that a minimum wage increase would only increase unemployment and create inflationary pressures. But the proposal had some unlikely allies even among their ilk, including Wal-Mart, whose fund managers were lured by the extra cash for lower-income households that could be spent at their stores.

And some argued that setting a minimum wage is a state and local issue. "If Mississippi had the same minimum wage as San Francisco, it probably would cause a lot of unemployment," speculated Eric French, a senior economist specializing in labor and health issues at the Federal Reserve Bank of Chicago.

The legislation was introduced on January 5, 2007, by George Miller (D-CA) and passed by the House on January 10. All 233 House Democrats voted in its favor and 82 Republicans joined them; 116 Republican representatives voted "No," and four representatives did not vote.

The bill was eventually signed by President George W. Bush on May 25, 2007.

However, some state laws mandate that employees get paid time off for jury duty, for voting, as explained later in this chapter, and for family and medical leave (see Chapter 4, "State Laws on Family Leave"). And most state laws provide that, if employers offer paid vacation days off, employees are entitled to be paid for the portion they have already earned when they quit or are fired.

Tips

When employees routinely receive a minimum amount in tips as part of their jobs—commonly, $20 to $30 per month as set out in state law—their employers are allowed to pay less than the minimum wage and credit the tips received against the minimum wage requirement. However, the employee's hourly wage plus the tips the employee actually earns must add up to at least the minimum wage—or the employer has to make up the

---

A Possible Cure for Sick Leave: PTO

Recent studies have found that compared to alternative rewards, time off ranks near the top of employees' preferences—even above cash bonuses, raises, and future career advancement. Recognizing this, a growing number of workplaces give employees a certain amount of Paid Time Off, or PTO, without labeling it vacation, sick leave, or personal leave; all three types of traditional time off are rolled into one figure.

For example, say your company's traditional system specifies that employees receive ten vacation days, seven sick days, and three personal days. The system is revamped, creating a PTO bank for each employee that accrues at a rate of 12 hours a month. That's 18 days a year that employees can use however they want.

Proponents of PTO, now embraced in nearly two-thirds of all larger workplaces, praise its flexibility, as it allows employees to claim and schedule time off from work when it best suits their needs. They also point out that PTO helps keep everyone more honest, as it obviates a worker's human tendency to fake a bout of the flu when his or her favorite team is playing a day game on the home field. Many employers also claim that PTO relieves them of the meddlesome duties of tracking and policing workers' time off.

And there is often an unexpected advantage for employees who leave a job with PTO on their slates: Unlike personal or sick leave, employers must pay them for time that has accrued but not been taken.

There are possible disadvantages to the arrangement, however. Some research shows that workplaces with PTO policies give employees fewer days off, overall. And some lament that employees view PTO as a benefit and use all the time they are allotted—or regard PTO as vacation time and come to work when they are sick, jeopardizing their coworkers' health.

difference. (Some states have different rules, summarized in the chart on "State and Local Laws," below. And see "Jobs Involving Tips," below, for more on tips as wages.) Also, the employee must be allowed to keep all of the tips he or she receives.

EXAMPLE: Alfonse is employed as a waiter and earns more than $10 per hour in tips. The restaurant's owner, Denis, may use those tips as a partial credit to reach the minimum wage requirement. Denis is still required, however, to pay Alfonse at least the minimum amount set out by law per hour on top of his tips for the first 40 hours worked in each week.

During the two weeks or so following a negative review by a local newspaper columnist, the restaurant business slows to a crawl, and Alphonse's tips dip to $2 an hour. Denis must make up the full amount of minimum wage Alfonse is owed.

Commissions

When people are paid commissions for sales, those commissions may take the place of wages. However, if the commissions do not equal the minimum wage, the FLSA requires the employer to make up the difference.

EXAMPLE: Julia, a salesperson in an electronics store, is paid a percentage of the dollar volume of the sales she completes. During one slow week, she averaged only $2 in commissions per hour. Under the FLSA, her employer must pay her an additional amount for each hour she worked through the first 40 hours of that week to equal the minimum wage, and more for any overtime hours.

Finding Out More About the FLSA

FLSA exemptions for employers change often. Double-check any exemption your employer claims by calling the local U.S. Labor Department, Wage and Hour Division office, listed in the federal government section of your telephone directory and also available on the Department of Labor's website at www.dol.gov. Keep in mind, however, that the FLSA is so broadly written and so full of amendments and cross-references that it applies to most employers.

Most of the exemptions to FLSA coverage are listed in federal statute 29 U.S.C. § 213. The most direct way to become familiar with these exemptions is to read about them in an annotated edition of the code. You can also find the letter of the law on the DOL's website. Click on the topic "Wages," then "Fair Labor Standards Act (FLSA)," then "Applicable Laws and Regulations." (See Chapter 17, "Legal Research," for more information about how to do your own legal research.)

Equal Pay for Equal Work

Men and women who do the same job or jobs that require equal skill and responsibility must be compensated with equal wages and benefits under a 1963 amendment to the FLSA called the Equal Pay Act. (29 U.S.C. § 206.) Be aware, however, that some payment schemes that may look discriminatory at first glance do not actually violate the Equal Pay Act. The Act allows disparate payments to men and women if they are based on:

- seniority systems
- merit systems
- systems measuring earnings by quantity or quality of production, such as a piece goods arrangement, or
- any factor other than sex—for example, salary differentials that stem from unequal starting salaries based on differences in experience levels.

Although the Equal Pay Act basically covers the same employers and employees as the rest of the FLSA, there is one important difference: The Equal Pay Act also protects against discriminatory pay arrangements for executive, administrative, and professional employees—including administrators and teachers in elementary and secondary schools.

(Because the Equal Pay Act is enforced along with other antidiscrimination laws by the Equal Employment Opportunity Commission, illegal wage discrimination based on gender is discussed in detail in Chapter 7, "Illegal Discrimination.")

Pay for Overtime

The FLSA does not limit the number of hours an employee may work in a week—unless the employee is a minor. (See "Restrictions on Child Labor," below.) But it does require that any covered worker who works more than 40 hours in one week must be paid at least one and one-half times his or her regular rate of pay for every hour worked in excess of 40.

The math is simple if you are paid solely an hourly salary.

EXAMPLE: Raymond works for a software shipping company at the wage of $8 per hour. When he works 50 hours in one week filling back orders in preparation for a national exhibition, Raymond must be paid $12 per hour for the last ten hours he worked that week.

Jody, who is vice president of the software shipping company and also Raymond's boss, also worked 50 hours the same week. Since Jody qualifies as an executive and so is exempt from the FLSA (see "Who is Exempt," above), she is not entitled to overtime pay, but receives her regular weekly salary.

There is no legal requirement under the FLSA that workers must receive overtime pay simply because they worked more than eight hours in one day (although a few states require it). Nor is there anything that requires a worker to be paid on the spot for overtime. Under the FLSA, an employer is allowed to calculate and pay overtime by the week— which can be any 168-hour period made up of seven consecutive 24-hour periods.

It is custom, not law, that determines that a workweek begins on Monday. However, the FLSA requires consistency. An employer cannot manipulate the start of the workweek to avoid paying overtime.

Also, because of the nature of the work involved, common sense—and the law—both dictate that some jobs are exempt from the overtime pay requirements of the FLSA.

The most common of these jobs include:

- commissioned employees of retail or service establishments
- some auto, truck, trailer, farm implement, boat, or aircraft workers
- railroad and air carrier employees, taxi drivers, certain employees of motor carriers, seamen and women on American vessels, and local delivery employees
- announcers, news editors, and chief engineers of small nonmetropolitan broadcasting stations
- domestic service workers who live in their employer's residence
- employees of motion picture theaters, and
- farmworkers.

And, finally, some employees may be partially exempt from the Act's overtime pay requirements. The most common of this hybrid type is an employee who works in a hospital or residential care establishment who agrees to work a 14-day work period. However, these employees must be paid overtime premium pay for all hours worked over eight in a day or 80 in the 14-day work period, whichever is the greater number of overtime hours.

In addition to the FLSA overtime provisions, a number of state laws also define how and when overtime must be paid. Some states measure overtime on a daily, rather than weekly, basis. In these states, workers who put in more than eight hours a day are generally entitled to overtime, even if they work a total of 40 or fewer hours in a week. The chart that follows summarizes state overtime rules for private employers. Note that if the federal and state law conflict, your employer must obey the stricter law—that is, the law that provides the most expansive rights to you.

CAUTION

Additional laws may apply. If the chart below indicates that your state has no statute, this means that there is no law that specifically addresses the issue. However, there may be a state administrative regulation or local ordinance that does control overtime work and pay. Call your state labor department for more information. (See the Appendix for contact details.)

TIP

Is it a bonus or a bludgeon? Some employers have tried to skirt the overtime pay requirements by labeling part of the pay received as a bonus. In fact, bonuses have a strict legal definition, being reserved only for money paid in addition to wages because of some extra effort you have made on the job, as a reward for loyal service, or as a gift. While the term bonus has a grand ring to it, be skeptical if you receive one too often. And take the time to do the math to discover whether the bonus is an apt description for the sum you receive—or a ploy to circumvent the laws requiring overtime pay.

State Overtime Rules

This chart covers private sector employment only. The overtime rules summarized are not applicable to all employers or all employees. Occupations that generally are not subject to overtime laws include health care and attendant care, emergency medical personnel, seasonal workers, agricultural labor, camp counselors, nonprofits exempt under FLSA, salespeople working on a commission, transit drivers, babysitters, and other household workers, and many others. For more information, contact your state's department of labor and be sure to check its website, where most states have posted their overtime rules. (See Appendix A for contact details.)

Alabama

No state overtime rules that differ from FLSA.

Alaska

Alaska Stat. § 23.10.060

Time and a half after x hours per DAY: 8

Time and a half after x hours per WEEK: 40

Employment overtime laws apply to: Employers of 4 or more employees; commerce or manufacturing businesses.

Notes: Voluntary flexible work hour plan of 10-hour day, 40-hour week, with premium pay after 10 hours permitted.

Arizona

No overtime limits for private sector employers.

Arkansas

Ark. Code Ann. §§ 11-4-211, 11-4-203

Time and a half after x hours per WEEK: 40

Employment overtime laws apply to: Employers of 4 or more employees.

Employment excluded from overtime laws: Employment that is subject to the FLSA.

Notes: Employees in retail and service establishments who spend up to 40% of their time on nonexempt work must be paid at least twice the state's minimum wage ($572 per week).

California

Cal. Lab. Code §§ 500–511; Cal. Code Regs. tit. 8, §§ 11010 and following

Time and a half after x hours per DAY: 8; after 12 hours, double time.

Time and a half after x hours per WEEK: 40. On 7th day: time and a half for the first 8 hours; after 8 hours, double time.

Employment excluded from overtime laws: Computer software employees who design, develop, create, analyze, test, or modify programs using independent judgment, or who are paid at least $49.77/hour.

Notes: Alternative four 10-hour day workweek is permitted, if established prior to 7/1/99.

Colorado

7 Colo. Code Regs. § 1103-1(4)

Time and a half after x hours per DAY: 12

Time and a half after x hours per WEEK: 40

Employment overtime laws apply to: Employees in retail and service, commercial support service, food and beverage, health and medical industries.

Connecticut

Conn. Gen. Stat. Ann. §§ 31-76b, 31-76c

Time and a half after x hours per WEEK: 40; premium pay on weekends, holidays, or 6th or 7th consecutive day.

Notes: In restaurants and hotels, time-and-a-half pay required for the 7th consecutive day of work or for hours that exceed 40 per week.

State Overtime Rules (continued)

Delaware

No state overtime rules that differ from FLSA.

District of Columbia

D.C. Code Ann. § 32-1003(c); D.C. Mun. Regs. tit. 7, § 906

Time and a half after x hours per WEEK: 40

Notes: Employees must be paid one hour minimum wage for each day a split shift is worked.

Florida

No state overtime rules that differ from FLSA.

Georgia

No state overtime rules that differ from FLSA.

Hawaii

Haw. Rev. Stat. §§ 387-1, 387-3

Time and a half after x hours per WEEK: 40. Dairy, sugar cane, and seasonal agricultural work: 48 hours per week.

Employment excluded from overtime laws: Employees earning guaranteed compensation of $2,000 or more per month.

Idaho

No state overtime rules that differ from FLSA.

Illinois

820 Ill. Comp. Stat. §§ 105/3(d), 105/4a

Time and a half after x hours per WEEK: 40

Employment overtime laws apply to: Employers of 4 or more employees.

Indiana

Ind. Code Ann. § 22-2-2-4(j)

Time and a half after x hours per WEEK: 40

Employment excluded from overtime laws: Employment that is subject to the FLSA, movie theaters, seasonal camps and amusement parks, FLSA-exempt nonprofits.

Notes: Collective bargaining agreements ratified by the NLRB may have different overtime provisions. Domestic service work is not excluded from overtime laws.

Iowa

No state overtime rules that differ from FLSA.

Kansas

Kan. Stat. Ann. § 44-1204

Time and a half after x hours per WEEK: 46

Employment excluded from overtime laws: Employment that is subject to the FLSA.

Kentucky

Ky. Rev. Stat. Ann. §§ 337.050, 337.285

Time and a half after x hours per WEEK: 40

Employment excluded from overtime laws: Retail, hotel, and restaurant businesses.

Notes: 7th day, time and a half.

Louisiana

No state overtime rules that differ from FLSA.

Maine

Me. Rev. Stat. Ann. tit. 26, § 664(3)

Time and a half after x hours per WEEK: 40

Employment excluded from overtime laws: Auto mechanics, parts clerks, and salespersons; hotels, motels, and restaurants; canning, freezing, packing, and shipping produce and perishable foods.

Maryland

Md. Code Ann., [Lab. & Empl.] § 3-420

State Overtime Rules (continued)

Time and a half after x hours per WEEK:
40; 48 hours for bowling alleys and residential employees caring for the sick, aged, or mentally ill in institutions other than hospitals; 60 hours for agricultural work.

Massachusetts

Mass. Gen. Laws ch. 151, § 1A

Time and a half after x hours per WEEK: 40

Employment excluded from overtime laws: Agriculture, farming, fishing; hotel, motel, or restaurant; seasonal workers less than 5 months; hospital, nursing home, or rest home; public transit.

Notes: Sunday or holiday: Time and a half as overtime unless already paid that rate as part of regular compensation.

Michigan

Mich. Comp. Laws §§ 408.382, 408.384a

Time and a half after x hours per WEEK: 40

Employment overtime laws apply to: Employers of 2 or more employees.

Employment excluded from overtime laws: Employees not subject to state minimum wage laws.

Minnesota

Minn. Stat. Ann. § 177.25

Time and a half after x hours per WEEK: 48

Mississippi

No state overtime rules that differ from FLSA.

Missouri

Mo. Rev. Stat. §§ 290.500, 290.505

Time and a half after x hours per WEEK: 40; 52 hours for seasonal amusement or recreation businesses.

Employment excluded from overtime laws: Employment that is subject to the FLSA.

Montana

Mont. Code Ann. §§ 39-3-405, 39-3-406

Time and a half after x hours per WEEK: 40; 48 hours for students working seasonal jobs at amusement or recreational areas.

Notes: Some types of employment excluded from overtime laws; see *Mont. Code Ann. § 39-3-406.*

Nebraska

No state overtime rules that differ from FLSA.

Nevada

Nev. Rev. Stat. Ann. § 608.018

Time and a half after x hours per DAY: 8

Time and a half after x hours per WEEK: 40

Notes: Provisions apply only if employee's regular rate of pay is less than 1½ times the minimum wage. Employer and employee may agree to flextime schedule of four 10-hour days.

New Hampshire

N.H. Rev. Stat. Ann. § 279:21(VIII)

Time and a half after x hours per WEEK: 40

Employment excluded from overtime laws: Employees covered by the FLSA; employees in amusement, seasonal, or recreational business open 7 months or less a year.

New Jersey

N.J. Stat. Ann. §§ 34.11-56a4, 34.11-56a4.1

Time and a half after x hours per WEEK: 40

Employment excluded from overtime laws: June to September: Summer camps, conferences, and retreats operated by nonprofit or religious groups.

State Overtime Rules (continued)

New Mexico

N.M. Stat. Ann. § 50-4-22(C)

Time and a half after x hours per WEEK: 40

New York

N.Y. Lab. Law §§ 160(3), 161; N.Y. Comp. Codes R. & Regs. tit. 12, § 142-2.2

Time and a half after x hours per WEEK: 40 for nonresidential workers; 44 for residential workers.

Employment excluded from overtime laws: Same exemptions as FLSA.

North Carolina

N.C. Gen. Stat. §§ 95-25.14, 95-25.4

Time and a half after x hours per WEEK: 40; 45 hours a week in seasonal amusement or recreational establishments.

Employment excluded from overtime laws: Employment that is subject to the FLSA.

North Dakota

N.D. Admin. Code § 46-02-07-02(4)

Time and a half after x hours per WEEK: 40; 50 hours per week, cab drivers.

Employment excluded from overtime laws: Computer professionals who design, develop, create, analyze, test, or modify programs using independent judgment or who are paid at least $27.63/hour.

Ohio

Ohio Rev. Code Ann. §§ 4111.01, 4111.03

Time and a half after x hours per WEEK: 40

Employment overtime laws apply to: Employers who gross more than $150,000 a year.

Oklahoma

No state overtime rules that differ from FLSA.

Oregon

Or. Rev. Stat. §§ 653.261, 653.265

Time and a half after x hours per WEEK: 40

Notes: Time and a half required after 10 hours a day in canneries, driers, packing plants, mills, factories, and manufacturing facilities.

Pennsylvania

43 Pa. Cons. Stat. Ann. § 333.104(c); 34 Pa. Code § 231.41

Time and a half after x hours per WEEK: 40

Rhode Island

R.I. Gen. Laws §§ 28-12-4.1 and following, 5-23-2(h)

Time and a half after x hours per WEEK: 40

Notes: Time and a half for Sunday and holiday work is required for most retail businesses (these hours are not included in calculating weekly overtime).

South Carolina

No overtime provisions.

South Dakota

No overtime provisions.

Tennessee

No overtime provisions.

Texas

No overtime provisions.

Utah

No overtime provisions.

Vermont

Vt. Stat. Ann. tit. 21, §§ 382, 384(b); Vt. Code R. 24 090 003

Time and a half after x hours per WEEK: 40

State Overtime Rules (continued)

Employment overtime laws apply to: Employers of 2 or more employees.

Employment excluded from overtime laws: Retail and service businesses, hotels, motels, restaurants; some amusement or recreational establishments; transportation workers exempt under FLSA.

Virginia

No overtime provisions.

Washington

Wash. Rev. Code Ann. § 49.46.130

Time and a half after x hours per WEEK: 40

West Virginia

W. Va. Code §§ 21-5c-1(e), 21-5c-3

Time and a half after x hours per WEEK: 40

Employment overtime laws apply to: Employers of 6 or more employees at one location.

Employment excluded from overtime laws: Employees that are subject to the FLSA.

Wisconsin

Wis. Stat. Ann. §§ 103.01, 103.03; Wis. Admin. Code §§ DWD 274.01, 274.03, 274.04

Time and a half after x hours per WEEK: 40

Employment overtime laws apply to: Manufacturing, mechanical, or retail businesses; beauty parlors, laundries, restaurants, hotels; telephone, express, shipping, and transportation companies.

Wyoming

No overtime provisions.

Current as of February 2007

Piece Rates and Commissions

People who work on piece rates and commissions instead of by the clock have a more complicated task in calculating their rates of pay.

For piece rate workers, the regular wage rate may be calculated by averaging hourly piece rate earnings for the week. Calculating overtime is a bit trickier. Employees are entitled to an additional one-half times the regular rate of pay for each hour worked over 40, plus the full piece work earnings.

EXAMPLE: Max is an assembler in a photocopier factory who is paid a piece rate of 75 cents for each copier cover he installs. One week, he worked 40 hours and installed 400 covers, so his regular rate of pay for that week was $7.50 per hour (400 x .75, divided by 40).

One of two alternatives may be used to determine Max's overtime pay:

- Increase the piece rate by 50% during the overtime hours. For example, Max's employer could raise his piece rate to $1.13 per copier cover (150% of .75) for overtime hours.
- Estimate an average hourly wage and then use that estimated average to compute overtime.

Keep in mind that if the U.S. Labor Department investigates the legality of your pay rate, it may require proof that any estimates used to calculate your pay are in line with the piece rate pay you actually earned over a substantial time—usually several months.

The methods for calculating and paying commissions vary tremendously. If you have questions about whether your employer is complying with the wage laws on piece rates and commissions, call or visit the nearest office of the Labor Department's Wage and Hour Division; see the Appendix for contact details.

Jobs Involving Tips

If you regularly work for tips, the tips you receive are not counted as part of your regular rate of pay when calculating over-time pay. Only the wage that your employer has agreed to pay you counts; in most cases where people work for tips, that is the federal minimum wage. (See the chart on "State and Local Laws," below, for specialized state rules.) Of course, tip money that you receive beyond the minimum wage amount is still taxable to you as income.

> **EXAMPLE:** Lisa works as a waitress for wages plus tips. Because she receives a substantial amount in tips, her employer is allowed to take a setoff, the hourly minimum set out in the law for tipped employees. Nevertheless, her regular rate of pay for calculating overtime pay under the FLSA standards is still the minimum wage amount.
>
> One week, Lisa worked 41 hours—one hour of overtime. For that overtime hour, she must be paid one and one-half times

the minimum wage amount, regardless of the tips she received during that hour.

Split Payscales

If your job involves different types of work for which different payscales have been established, you must calculate your regular rate of pay for each category of work, then apply the appropriate rate to any overtime hours. The payscale that applies to the type of work you did during overtime hours is the one on which you calculate the time-and-a-half rule.

> **EXAMPLE:** Matt works for a company that manages a large apartment complex. For landscaping work, he is paid $8 per hour. When he works as a guard with the company's private security force for the complex, Matt gets $10 per hour. For payroll purposes, his workweek begins on Monday.
>
> During one week in the spring, he worked eight hours a day, Monday through Friday, for a total of 40 hours with the landscaping crew. But the landscaping crew does not work on weekends, and Matt needed some extra money, so he worked eight hours on Saturday with the security patrol. He took Sunday off.
>
> Because the FLSA's overtime pay rules take effect only after an employee works 40 hours in one week, the eight overtime hours Matt worked with the security force were at the security patrol rate of $10 per hour. His overtime pay for that week is $120 ($10 x 8 x 1½).

Exemption for Skills Training

Up to ten hours per week of otherwise payable time is exempt from the overtime rules for some types of skills training. To qualify, the extra hours must be used to provide employees who have not graduated from high school or otherwise demonstrated that they have attained at least an eighth grade education with general training in reading and other basic skills. To qualify for this exemption, the training cannot be specific to the worker's current job but must cover skills that could be used in virtually any job. (29 U.S.C. § 207(q).)

Multiple Employers

No matter how many jobs you hold, the overtime pay rules apply to each of your employers individually. If in one week you work 30 hours for one employer and 30 additional hours for another, for example, neither one owes you overtime pay.

Compensatory Time

Most workers are familiar with compensatory or comp time—the practice of employers offering employees time off from work in place of cash payments for overtime. What comes as a shock to many is that the practice is illegal in most situations. Under the FLSA, only state or government agencies may legally allow their employees time off in place of wages. (29 U.S.C. § 207(o).)

Even then, comp time may be awarded only:

- according to the terms of a collective bargaining unit agreement (see Chapter 15), or
- if the employer and employee agree to the arrangement before work begins.

When compensatory time is allowed, it must be awarded at the rate of one-and-a-half times the overtime hours worked—and comp time must be taken during the same pay period that the overtime hours were worked.

EXAMPLE: John, a state employee, is paid a fixed salary every two weeks. His standard workweek is made up of five shifts, each eight hours long. During the first week of a pay period, John works 44 hours, earning four hours of overtime pay. During the second week of that pay period, he can take six hours off as comp time (4 hours x 1½). In the second week of the pay period, he works only 34 hours but is paid his full salary as though he had worked 40 hours.

Many employers and employees routinely violate the rules governing the use of compensatory time in place of cash overtime wages. However, such violations are risky. Employees can find themselves unable to collect money due them if a company goes out of business or they are fired. And employers can end up owing large amounts of overtime pay to employees if they get caught by the labor department.

State Laws

Some states do allow private employers to give employees comp time instead of cash.

But there are complex, often conflicting, laws controlling how and when it may be given. A common control, for example, is that employees must voluntarily request in writing that comp time be given instead of overtime pay—before the extra hours are worked. Check with your state's labor department for special laws on comp time in your area. (See the Appendix for contact information.)

Alternative Arrangements

Employees who value their time off over their money may feel frustrated with the letter of the law preventing them from taking comp time. If you are in this boat, you may have a few options for getting an arrangement that feels like comp time but is still within the letter of the law.

You may be allowed to take time off by rearranging your work schedule. This is legal if both of the following are true:

- The time off is given within the same pay period as the overtime work.
- You are given an hour and a half of time off for each hour of overtime worked.

One way is to subtract the time during a single workweek.

> **EXAMPLE:** Josh, an editorial assistant at a publishing company, normally works eight hours a day, Monday through Friday. One week, Josh and some of the editors need to meet a deadline on a book due at the printer. So, that week, Josh works ten hours a day, Monday through Thursday. The publishing company gives Josh Friday off and pays him for a 40-hour week at his regular rate of pay. This is legal

because Josh hasn't worked any overtime as defined by the FLSA; only the hours over 40 hours a week count as overtime hours.

But you are not confined to an hour-for-hour trade. You can also take time-and-a-half pay in one week, then reduce your hours the next week so that your paycheck remains constant.

> **EXAMPLE:** Christi works at Wholey Soles, a shop that specializes in handmade shoes, and earns $600 at the close of each two-week pay period. Because she needs to prepare an inventory of shoes to have on hand during a street fair, the shop's owner wants Christi to work longer hours one week. However, the owner doesn't want to increase Christi's paycheck, and Christi does not want to habitually work long hours. Christi works 50 hours the week before the fair but takes 15 hours off the next week (ten hours of overtime x 1½ per hour = 15 hours). Since Christi is paid every two weeks, Wholey Soles may properly reduce Christi's hours the second week to keep her paycheck at the $600 level.

Restrictions on Child Labor

Minors under 18 years old may not work in any jobs that are considered to be hazardous —including those involving mining, wrecking and demolition, logging, and roofing. The Secretary of Labor defines what jobs are deemed hazardous and so out-of-bounds for young workers. To find out which jobs are currently considered hazardous for the purposes of the FLSA, call the local office of the U.S. Labor Department's Wage and Hour Division; see the Appendix for contact details. The Department of Labor's website, at www. dol.gov, has a listing of local offices—and also has information about child labor restrictions.

To encourage youngsters to stay in school rather than become beholden to the dollar too soon, there are additional restrictions on when and how long workers between ages 14 and 16 may be employed in nonhazardous jobs:

- They may work no more than three hours on a school day and no more than 18 hours in a school week.
- They may work no more than eight hours on a nonschool day and no more than 40 hours in a nonschool week.
- During the period that starts with the day after Labor Day and ends at midnight May 31, their workday may not begin earlier than 7 a.m. or end later than 7 p.m.
- From June 1 through Labor Day, their workday may not begin earlier than 7 a.m., but it can end as late as 9 p.m.

Some industries have obtained special exemptions from the legal restrictions on child labor. Youths of any age may deliver newspapers, for example, or perform in television, movie, or theatrical productions.

The farming industry has been fighting the child labor restrictions as well as the rest of the FLSA ever since the law was first proposed in the 1930s, so less-strict rules apply to child farmworkers. For example, children as young as 12 may work on their parents' farms. And workers as young as ten years old may work for up to eight weeks

as hand harvest laborers as long as their employers have obtained a special waiver from the U.S. Labor Department.

CAUTION

Watch for state law twists. Many states also have restrictions on child labor. A number of them are more restrictive than the federal law—requiring, for example, more frequent meal or rest breaks for younger workers. Check with your state labor department for specific laws that may apply to your situation. (See the Appendix for contact details.)

Calculating Your Pay

To resolve most questions or disputes involving the FLSA, you must first know the regular rate of pay to which you are legally entitled.

Whether you work for hourly wages, salary, commissions, or a piece rate, the courts have ruled that your regular rate of pay typically includes your base pay plus any shift premiums, hazardous duty premiums, cost of living allowances, bonuses used to make otherwise undesirable worksites attractive, and the fair value of such things as food and lodging that your employer routinely provides as part of your pay.

Obviously, there is much room here for individual interpretation and arbitrary decisions. But the overriding concept is that everything that you logically consider to be a routine part of your hourly pay for a routine day is a part of your regular rate of pay.

The courts have often ruled that the regular rate of pay does not include contributions that an employer makes to benefit plans, paid vacations and holiday benefits, premiums paid for working on holidays or weekends, and discretionary bonuses. And some employee manuals clarify what is included in your regular rate of pay by specifying that some benefit programs are regarded by the company to be extra compensation that is not part of an employee's regular pay.

The regular rate of pay for people who work for hourly wages is their hourly rate including the factors just mentioned.

For salaried workers, the hourly rate is their weekly pay divided by the number of hours in their standard workweek.

If you are paid a salary that covers a period longer than a week, it may be a bit trickier to compute your wage rate. Department of Labor regulations attempt to shed light on this by requiring that all salaries must be reduced to a weekly equivalent to determine the rate of pay.

If you are paid a monthly salary, for example, you can determine your weekly wage rate by multiplying your total monthly salary by 12 (the number of months in a year), then dividing that sum by 52 (the number of weeks in a year).

Calculating Workhours

When a work pay period begins and ends is determined by a law called the Portal-to-Portal Pay Act. (29 U.S.C. § 251.) This amendment to the FLSA and several other workplace laws requires that an employee must be paid for any time spent that is controlled by and that benefits the employer.

This aspect of wage and hour law has generated a tremendous number of clashes—and cases in which the courts have attempted to sharpen the definition of payable time.

Work time for which you must be paid includes all the time you must be on duty or at the workplace. However, the courts have ruled that on-the-job time does not include the time employees spend washing themselves or changing clothes before or after work, unless a workplace requires specialized uniforms or other garb that is impractical to don off the premises; nor does it include time spent in a regular commute to the workplace.

Employers are not allowed to circumvent the Portal-to-Portal Pay Act by simply "allowing" you to work on what is depicted as your own time. You must be paid for all the time you work—voluntary or not. This issue has come up frequently in recent years because some career counselors have been advising people that volunteering to work free for a company for a month or so is a good way to find a new job. Although working for free may be legal in situations where the job being sought is exempt from the FLSA—for example, a professional fundraising position with a nonprofit organization—it is not legal when the job involved is governed by the Act. (See "Who is Exempt," above, for details on FLSA exemptions.)

For ease of accounting, employers are allowed to round off records of work time to the nearest five-minute mark on the clock or the nearest quarter hour. But rounding off becomes illegal if it means employees will get paid for less time than they actually worked. In practice, this means that your employer will usually round up your work time to add a few minutes each day to the time for which you are paid.

In calculating on-the-job time, most concerns focus on how to deal with specific questionable situations, such as travel time, time spent at seminars, meal and coffee breaks, waiting periods, on-call periods, and sleeping on the job.

Travel Time

The time you spend commuting between your home and the place you normally work is not considered to be on-the-job time for which you must be paid. But it may be payable time if the commute is actually part of the job.

If you are a lumberjack, for example, and you have to check in at your employer's office, pick up a chainsaw, and then drive ten miles to reach the cutting site for a particular day, your workday legally begins when you check in at the office.

Even if the commute is not part of your job, circumstances may allow you to collect for the odd trip back and forth. You can claim that you should be paid for your time in commuting only when you are required to go to and from your normal worksite at odd hours in emergency situations.

EXAMPLE: Ernest normally works 9 to 5 as a computer operator and is paid hourly. One day, about two hours after he arrived home from work, he got a call from his office notifying him that the computer was malfunctioning and that he was needed there immediately to help correct the problem. It took him one-half hour to drive back to the office, two hours to get the computer back on track, and one-half hour to drive home again.

The company must pay Ernest for three extra hours—two of them workhours and the third for the extra hour of commuting time that he was required to put in because of the company's emergency.

Lectures, Meetings, and Training Seminars

Generally, if you are a nonexempt employee and your employer requires you to attend a lecture, meeting, or training seminar, you must be paid for that time—including travel time if the meeting is away from the worksite.

The specific exception to this rule is that you need not be paid if all of the following are true:

- You attend the event outside of regular working hours.
- Attendance is voluntary.
- The instruction session isn't directly related to your job.
- You do not perform any productive work during the instruction session.

When It's Unclear Whether You're Coming or Going

Questions about whether workers can be considered on the job while enroute to it or from it often make it to courtrooms when there is possible liability for an accident. For example, a worker who gets in a car crash on the way home from work may claim the employer should foot the bill for medical costs and property damages.

Courts and employers usually invoke the Going and Coming Rule, which generally absolves employers from liability by holding that an employee is "not acting within the scope of employment" when going to or coming from the workplace.

There are, however, specific exceptions to this rule. Courts have found employers liable where they:

- get some benefit from the trip—such as new clients or business contacts
- pay the employee for the travel time and travel expenses such as gasoline and tolls, and
- request that the employee run a special errand while traveling to or from work—such as picking up supplies or dropping off a bank deposit—although carpooling with coworkers and taking classes as encouraged by an employer do not count here.

Meal and Break Periods

Contrary to the laws of gastronomy, federal law does not require that you be allotted or paid for breaks to eat meals.

However, many states have laws specifically requiring that employees be allowed a half hour or so in meal and rest breaks during each workday. (See the chart below.) Your employer generally does not have to pay you for meal breaks of 30 minutes or more—as long as you are completely relieved of work duties during that time. Technically, however, if your employer either requires that you work while eating—or allows you to do so—you must be paid for time spent during meals. Also, you must be paid for break periods that are less than 20 minutes.

CAUTION

Additional laws may apply. If the chart below indicates that your state has no statute, this means there is no law that specifically requires private employers to provide meal and rest breaks. However, there may be a state administrative regulation or local ordinance that does control breaks. Call your state labor department for more information. (See the Appendix for contact details.) Also, some states require employers to provide meal and rest breaks only to younger workers, or require that younger workers receive longer or more frequent breaks. Those rules are not covered here.

State Meals and Rest Breaks

Note: The states of Alabama, Alaska, Arizona, Arkansas, District of Columbia, Florida, Idaho, Indiana, Iowa, Louisiana, Maryland, Michigan, Mississippi, Missouri, Montana, New Jersey, New Mexico, North Carolina, Ohio, Oklahoma, South Carolina, South Dakota, Texas, Utah, Virginia, and Wyoming are not listed in this chart because they do not have laws or regulations on rest and meal breaks for adults employed in the private sector. Many states also exclude professional, administrative, and executive employees from these rules.

Other exceptions may apply. For example, many states have special break rules for specific occupations or industries, which are beyond the scope of this chart. Check the statute or check with your state department of labor if you need more information. (See this appendix for contact information.)

California

Cal. Code Regs. tit. 8, §§ 11010, 11160; Cal. Lab. Code §§ 512, 1030

Applies to: Employers in most industries.

Exceptions: Motion picture and other occupations. See wage orders, Cal. Code Regs. tit. 8, §§ 11010 to 11160, for additional exceptions.

Meal Break: 30 minutes, unpaid, after 5 hours, except when workday will be completed in 6 hours or less and employer and employee consent to waive meal break. Employee cannot work more than 10 hours a day without a second 30-minute break, except, if workday is no more than 12 hours, second meal break may be waived if first meal break was not waived.

On-duty paid meal period permitted when nature of work prevents relief from all duties and parties agree in writing.

Rest Break: Paid 10-minute rest period for each 4 hours worked or major fraction thereof; as practicable, in the middle of the work period. Not required for employees whose total daily work time is less than 3½ hours.

Breastfeeding: Reasonable time to breastfeed infant or to express breast milk; paid if taken concurrent with other break time; otherwise, unpaid.

Colorado

Colo. Code Regs. tit. 7 § 1103-1(7)-(8)

Applies to: Retail and service, food and beverage, commercial support service, and health and medical industries.

Exceptions: Numerous exceptions are listed in the regulation.

Meal Break: 30 minutes, unpaid, after 5 hours of work. On-duty paid meal period permitted when nature of work prevents break from all duties.

Rest Break: Paid 10-minute rest period for each 4 hours or major fraction worked; if practical, in the middle of the work period.

Connecticut

Conn. Gen. Stat. Ann. §§ 31-51ii, 31-40w

Applies to: All employers, except as noted.

Exceptions: Employers who pay for rest breaks as described below, those with a written agreement providing other break rules, and those granted an exemption for reasons listed in statute.

Meal Break: 30 minutes, unpaid, after first 2 hours of work and before last 2 hours for employees who work 7½ or more consecutive hours.

Rest Break: As alternative to meal break, a total of 30 minutes paid in each 7½-hour work period.

State Meals and Rest Breaks (continued)

Breastfeeding: Employee may use meal or rest break for breastfeeding or expressing breast milk.

Delaware
Del. Code Ann. tit. 19, § 707

Applies to: All employers, except as noted.

Exceptions: Employers with alternative written agreement and those granted exemptions specified in statute. Law does not apply to teachers.

Meal Break: 30 minutes, unpaid, after first 2 hours and before the last 2 hours, for employees who work 7½ consecutive hours or more.

Georgia
Ga. Code Ann. § 34-1-6

Applies to: All employers.

Breastfeeding: Reasonable unpaid break time to breastfeed infant or to express breast milk.

Hawaii
Haw. Rev. Stat. § 378-2

Applies to: All employers.

Breastfeeding: Allowed during any break required by law or collective bargaining agreement.

Illinois
820 Ill. Comp. Stat. §§ 140/3, 140/3.1, 260/10

Applies to: All employers.

Exceptions: Employees whose meal periods are established by collective bargaining agreement. Employees who monitor individuals with developmental disabilities or mental illness, or both, and who are required to be on call during an entire 8-hour work period; these employees must be allowed to eat a meal while working.

Meal Break: 20 minutes, no later than 5 hours after the beginning of the shift, for employees who work 7½ or more continuous hours. Hotel room attendants in Cook County get two 15-minute rest breaks and a 30-minute meal period per 7-hour shift.

Breastfeeding: Reasonable unpaid break time to breastfeed infant or express breast milk.

Kansas
Kan. Admin. Reg. 49-30-3(b)(2)(A)

Applies to: Employees not covered under FLSA.

Meal Break: Not required, but if less than 30 minutes is given, break must be paid.

Kentucky
Ky. Rev. Stat. Ann. §§ 337.355, 337.365; Ky Admin. Regs. tit. 803, 1:065 § 4

Applies to: All employers, except as noted.

Exceptions: Written agreement providing different meal period; employers subject to Federal Railway Labor Act.

Meal Break: Reasonable off-duty period close to the middle of the shift; can't be required to take it before the third or after the fifth hour of work.

Rest Break: Paid 10-minute rest period for each 4-hour work period. Rest period must be in addition to regularly scheduled meal period.

Maine
Me. Rev. Stat. Ann. tit. 26, § 601

Applies to: Most employers.

Exceptions: Small businesses with fewer than 3 employees on duty who are able to take frequent breaks during the workday. Collective bargaining or other written agreement between employer and employee may provide for different breaks.

Meal or Rest Break: 30 minutes, unpaid, after 6 consecutive hours of work, except in cases of emergency.

State Meals and Rest Breaks (continued)

Massachusetts

Mass. Gen. Laws ch. 149, §§ 100, 101

Applies to: All employers, except as noted.

Exceptions: Excludes iron works, glass works, paper mills, letterpresses, print works, and bleaching or dyeing works. Attorney general may exempt businesses that require continuous operation if it won't affect worker safety. Collective bargaining agreement may also provide for different breaks.

Meal Break: 30 minutes, if work is for more than 6 hours.

Minnesota

Minn. Stat. Ann. §§ 177.253, 177.254, 181.939

Applies to: All employers.

Exceptions: Excludes certain agricultural and seasonal employees.

A collective bargaining agreement may provide for different rest and meal breaks.

Meal Break: Sufficient unpaid time for employees who work 8 consecutive hours or more.

Rest Break: Paid adequate rest period within each 4 consecutive hours of work to utilize nearest convenient restroom.

Breastfeeding: Reasonable unpaid break time to breastfeed infant or express milk.

Nebraska

Neb. Rev. Stat. § 48-212

Applies to: Assembly plant, workshop, or mechanical establishment.

Exceptions: Other written agreement between employer and employees.

Meal Break: 30 minutes off premises.

Nevada

Nev. Rev. Stat. Ann. § 608.019

Applies to: Employers of two or more employees.

Exceptions: Employees covered by collective bargaining agreement; exemptions for business necessity.

Meal Break: 30 minutes for 8 continuous hours of work.

Rest Break: Paid 10-minute rest period for each 4 hours or major fraction worked; as practicable, in middle of the work period. Not required for employees whose total daily work time is less than 3½ hours.

New Hampshire

N.H. Rev. Stat. Ann. § 275:30-a

Applies to: All employers.

Meal Break: 30 minutes after 5 consecutive hours, unless the employer allows the employee to eat while working and it is feasible for the employee to do so.

New York

N.Y. Lab. Law § 162

Applies to: Factories, workshops, manufacturing facilities, mercantile (retail and wholesale) establishments.

Meal Break: Factory employees, 60 minutes between 11 a.m. and 2 p.m.; mercantile employees, 30 minutes between 11 a.m. and 2 p.m. If a shift starts before 11 a.m. and ends after 7 p.m., every employee gets an additional 20 minutes between 5 and 7 p.m. If a shift starts between 1 p.m. and 6 a.m., a factory employee gets 60 minutes, and a mercantile employee gets 45 minutes, in the middle of the shift. Labor commissioner may permit a shorter meal break; the permit must be in writing and posted

State Meals and Rest Breaks (continued)

conspicuously in the main entrance of the workplace.

North Dakota

N.D. Admin. Code § 46-02-07-02(5)

Applies to: Applicable when two or more employees are on duty.

Exceptions: Waiver by employee or other provision in collective bargaining agreement.

Meal Break: 30 minutes for each shift over 5 hours. Unpaid if employee is completely relieved of duties.

Oregon

Or. Admin. R. § 839-020-0050

Applies to: All employers except as noted.

Exceptions: Agricultural workers and employees covered by a collective bargaining agreement.

Meal Break: 30 minutes, unpaid if relieved of all duties; paid time to eat if employee cannot be relieved of duty; a 20-minute paid break, if employer can show that it is industry practice or custom. If shift of 7 hours or less, meal break must occur between hours 2 and 5; if shift longer than 7 hours, meal break must be between hours 3 and 6.

Rest Break: Paid 10-minute rest period for each 4 hours or major fraction worked; if practical, in the middle of the work period.

Rest period must be in addition to usual meal break and taken separately; can't be added to meal period or deducted from beginning or end of shift to reduce length of total work period.

Rest period is not required for certain solo adult employees serving the public, although they must be allowed to use rest room.

Pennsylvania

43 Pa. Cons. Stat. Ann. § 1301.207

Applies to: Employers of seasonal farm workers.

Meal Break: 30 minutes after 5 hours.

Rhode Island

R.I. Gen. Laws §§ 28-3-8, 28-3-14, 23-13.2-1

Applies to: Employers with 5 or more employees.

Exceptions: Employers of health care facility or employers with fewer than 3 employees on any shift.

Meal Break: 20 minutes, unpaid, within a 6-hour shift or 30 minutes, unpaid, within an 8-hour shift.

Breastfeeding: Reasonable unpaid break time to breastfeed infant or express breast milk.

Tennessee

Tenn. Code Ann. §§ 50-2-103(h), 50-1-305

Applies to: Employers with 5 or more employees.

Meal or Rest Break: 30 minutes unpaid for employees scheduled to work 6 consecutive hours or more unless work is such that there is ample time for breaks throughout the day.

Breastfeeding: Reasonable unpaid break time to breastfeed infant or express breast milk.

Vermont

Vt. Stat. Ann. tit. 21, § 304

Applies to: All employers.

Meal Break: Employees must be given reasonable opportunities to eat and use toilet facilities during work periods.

Washington

Wash. Admin. Code §§ 296-126-092, 296-131-020

Applies to: All employers except as noted.

Exceptions: Newspaper vendor or carrier, domestic or casual labor around private

State Meals and Rest Breaks (continued)

residence, sheltered workshop. Separate provisions for agricultural labor.

Meal Break: 30-minute break, if work period is more than 5 consecutive hours, not less than 2 hours nor more than 5 hours from beginning of shift. This time is paid if employee is on duty or is required to be at a site for employer's benefit. Employees who work 3 or more hours longer than regular workday are entitled to an additional half hour, before or during overtime.

Agricultural employees: 30 minutes if working more than 5 hours; additional 30 minutes if working 11 or more hours in a day.

Rest Break: Paid 10-minute rest break for each 4-hour work period, scheduled as near as possible to midpoint of each work period. Employee cannot be required to work more than 3 hours without a rest break.

Scheduled rest breaks not required where nature of work allows employee to take intermittent rest breaks equivalent to required standard.

Agricultural employees: 10-minute paid rest break for each 4 hours worked.

West Virginia

W.Va. Code § 21-3-10a; W.Va. Code St. R. § 42-5-2(2.6)

Applies to: All employers.

Meal Break: At least 20-minute break for each 6 consecutive hours worked, unless employees are allowed to take breaks as needed or to eat lunch while working.

Rest Break: Rest breaks of 20 minutes or less must be counted as paid work time.

Wisconsin

Wis. Admin. Code § DWD 274.02

Applies to: All employers.

Meal Break: Recommended but not required: 30 minutes close to usual meal time or near middle of shift. Shifts of more than 6 hours without a meal break should be avoided. If employee is not free to leave the workplace, meal period is considered paid time.

Current as of February 2007

Waiting Periods

Time periods when employees are not actually working but are required to stay on the employer's premises or at some other designated spot while waiting for a work assignment are covered as part of payable time. For example, a driver for a private ambulance service who is required to sit in the ambulance garage waiting for calls must be paid for the waiting time.

On-Call Periods

A growing number of employers are paying on-call premiums—or sleeper pay—to workers who agree to be available to be reached outside regular work time and respond by phone or computer within a certain period. Some plans pay an hourly rate for the time spent on call; some pay a flat rate.

If your employer requires you to be on call but does not require you to stay on the company's premises, then the following two rules generally apply:

- On-call time that you are allowed to control and use for your own enjoyment or benefit is not counted as payable time.
- On-call time over which you have little or no control and which you cannot use for your own enjoyment or benefit is payable time.

Questions of pay for on-call hours have become stickier—and more common—as a burgeoning number of technological gadgets such as cell phones, pagers, and mobile email trumpet that they can keep their owners in touch 24/7 and as more employees opt for more flexible arrangements that allow them to work outside of the office.

In cases of close calls as to whether on-call time is work time that must be compensated, courts will often perform a balancing act, weighing:

- whether the worker is constrained to stay in a particular spot while on call
- the frequency of the calls received
- the length of time the employee must work when called
- any specific agreement as to whether the on-call time is work time, and
- whether the employee is limited in how he or she may use the on-call time.

EXAMPLE: Jack works in an office, 9 to 5, Monday through Friday, as a client services representative for a funeral director. His employer also requires him to be on call at all times in case a business question arises—and furnishes

him with a message beeper. Jack can spend his free time any way he wants. All his employer requires him to do is to call the office as soon as is convenient after his beeper registers a message, so Jack's on-call time is not payable time.

EXAMPLE: Elizabeth is a rape crisis counselor with a social service agency. The agency that employs her must constantly have someone with her expertise available. During weekends when Elizabeth is the on-call counselor, she is allowed to stay at home but must remain near her telephone at all times. Elizabeth generally receives three to five calls during a 24-hour period—most of which she handles through counseling sessions on the telephone, each of which lasts between 30 to 70 minutes. She cannot leave her apartment except in response to a rape report, and she cannot drink any alcohol. Practically speaking, she cannot even throw a little dinner party because, if a call were to come in, she would have to leave her guests immediately. Elizabeth's on-call time is not hers to control and enjoy, so it is payable time.

Unless there's an employment contract that states otherwise, employers are generally allowed to pay a different hourly rate for on-call time than they do for regular work time, and many do. The employer need only make sure that the employees are paid at least the minimum amount required under wage and hour regulations.

EXAMPLE: A hospital emergency room has a policy of paying medical technicians a high hourly rate when they are actually working on a patient, and just the minimum wage when they are merely racking up on-call time on the hospital's premises. If such a technician were to record 20 hours active time and 20 hours on-call time in one week, the FLSA requires only that he or she receive the minimum wage for the 20 on-call hours.

The courts have generally approved such split-rate pay plans for the purposes of both the minimum wage and overtime requirements if there are marked differences in the types of work performed and the employer has clearly informed employees that different wages are paid for different types of work. (See the discussion of "Split Payscales," above.)

Sleep Time

If you are required to be on duty at your place of employment for less than 24 hours at a time, the U.S. Labor Department allows you to count as payable any time that you are allowed to sleep during your shift of duty. If you are required to be at work for more than 24 hours at a time—for example, if you work as a live-in housekeeper—you and your employer may agree to exclude up to eight hours per day from your payable time as sleep and meal periods.

However, if the conditions are such that you cannot get at least five hours of sleep during your eight-hour sleep-and-eat period, or if you end up working during that period,

then those eight hours revert to being payable time.

EXAMPLE: Bill works on an offshore oil rig for two days at a time. At the start of each shift, the boat takes him out to the platform, and does not come back for him until two days later. Bill and his employer have an agreement that requires that Bill gets an unpaid eight-hour sleep period each day, so his payable time for each 48-hour period he spends on the platform totals 32 hours. During one of Bill's shifts, a storm blew up and caused so much trouble that he had to keep working through the night. That reduced one of his sleep periods to only two hours. Bill must be paid for the sleep period that was cut short, so his payable time at the end of that shift would be 40 hours, or 32 + 8 hours payable sleep time.

State and Local Laws

Although the niggling matters of wage and hour requirements are not among the most scintillating workplace topics, disputes over either tend to hit employees hard and fast. In addition to broad controls over wages and hours that are set out in federal law, a number of state and local regulations are thrown into the fray. If your dispute involves a wage and hour issue, check all these sources of legal controls to get a clear picture of your possible rights and remedies. (See "Payroll Withholding and Deductions," below, for a discussion and state listing of wage garnishment laws.)

In particular, check the discussions of laws and charts below on:

- minimum wages
- time off for jury duty
- time off for voting, and
- military leave.

Pay Interval Laws: How Often Is Often Enough?

The question of how often you must be paid is most often addressed by state wage and hour laws. The FLSA states only that the pay period must be no longer than once a month, but state laws controlling pay intervals often require that most employees be paid at least every two weeks or twice a month.

Like state wage and hour laws, state laws governing how often you must be paid are complex, usually covering only certain types of companies and employees. If you have a question about how often you must be paid under your state's laws, consult the local office of your state's labor department. (See the Appendix for contact details.)

Minimum Wage Laws

All but a few states have laws specifying wage and hour standards. Some of these laws are virtually meaningless because they set standards less stringent than those set by federal law. Some state laws set lower minimum wages for groups of employees such as young workers or apprentices—and this is legally permissible.

On the other hand, some state wage rates are higher than the federal minimum. (See the chart below.) And, in recognition that the federal minimum wage increases from time to time, a number of states specify that the state minimum is a certain amount above the current minimum wage. If the federal minimum increases, the state minimum will automatically rise. The District of Columbia is a good example. Its minimum wage is $1 higher than the federal minimum. And Nevada recently amended its constitution to guarantee residents this dollar-more wage, both after hard battles.

Each state has its own rules about who is covered by its minimum wage law, and these rules are usually complex. The best way to determine whether your job is covered by a state wage and hour law that has a standard higher than the FLSA is to call the local office of your state's labor department. (See the Appendix for contact details.)

Whenever the FLSA sets a standard higher than one at the state or local level, the FLSA rules. When a state or local law sets standards higher than the FLSA, the state or local law is the one that applies.

> **CAUTION**
>
> **Check local controls.** In the last few years, some counties, cities, and towns have also passed their own wage laws. Such local wage laws are still rare and controversial, but you may want to check with the law department of the county or municipality in which you work if you have reason to think that it has passed a wage and hour law covering your job.

State Minimum Wage Laws for Tipped and Regular Employees

The chart below gives the basic state minimum wage laws. Depending on the occupation, the size of the employer's business, or the conditions of employment, the minimum wage may vary from the one listed here. Minimum wage rates in a number of states change from year to year and because of the recent increase in the federal minimum wage rate, many state laws will likely be modified, too; to be sure of your state's current minimum, contact your state department of labor or check its website, where most states have posted the minimum wage requirements. (See the Appendix for contact information.) Also, some local governments have enacted ordinances that set a higher minimum wage—contact your city or county government for more information.

"Maximum Tip Credit" is the highest amount of tips that an employer can subtract from the employee's hourly wage. The employee's total wages minus the tip credit cannot be less than the state minimum wage. If an employee's tips exceed the maximum tip credit, the employee gets to keep the extra amount.

"Minimum Cash Wage" is the lowest hourly wage that an employer can pay a tipped employee.

State and Statute	Notes	Basic Minimum Hourly Rate (*=tied to federal rate)	Maximum Tip Credit	Minimum Cash Wage for Tipped Employee	Minimum Tips to Qualify as a Tipped Employee (monthly unless noted otherwise)
United States *29 U.S.C. § 206* *29 U.S.C. § 203*	This is the current federal minimum wage	$5.85; $6.55 effective 7/24/08; $7.25 effective 7/24/09	$3.02	$2.13	More than $30
Alabama	No minimum wage law				
Alaska *Alaska Stat. § 23.10.065*		$7.15	No tip credit	$7.15	N/A
Arizona *Ariz. Rev. Stat. § 23-363*	Applies to employers with greater than $500,000 in gross revenue	$6.75	$3.00	$3.75	Averaged total of actual tips and cash minimum must equal minimum wage for each pay period
Arkansas *Ark. Code Ann. §§ 11-4-210 to -213*	Applies to employers with 4 or more employees	$6.25	58%	$2.63	Not specified
California *Cal. Code Regs. tit. 8, § 11000*		$7.50 $8 effective 1/1/08	No tip credit	$6.75	N/A

State Minimum Wage Laws for Tipped and Regular Employees (continued)					
State and Statute	**Notes**	**Basic Minimum Hourly Rate** (*=tied to federal rate)	**Maximum Tip Credit**	**Minimum Cash Wage for Tipped Employee**	**Minimum Tips to Qualify as a Tipped Employee** (monthly unless noted otherwise)
Colorado *Colo. Rev. Stat. § 8-6-109; 7, Colo. Code Regs. § 1103-1*	Minimum wage applies to these industries: retail and service, commercial support service, food and beverage, and health and medical	$6.85	$3.02	$3.83	More than $30
Connecticut *Conn. Gen. Stat. Ann. § 31-58(j)* *Conn. Admin Code § 31-60-02, § 31-62-E1ff*		greater than $7.65 or FLSA rate + ½%	29.3% waiters; 8.2% bartenders; $0.35 others	$5.41 waiters; $7.03 bartenders; $7.30 others	$10/week
Delaware *Del. Code Ann. tit. 19, § 902(a)*		$6.65 or FLSA rate if higher	$4.42	$2.23	More than $30
Dist. of Columbia *D.C. Code Ann. §§ 32-1003 to 32-1004*		$7 or FLSA rate + $1.00	$4.23	$2.79	Not specified
Florida *Fla. Const., Art X § 24 Fla. Stat Ann. § 448.110*		$6.67	$3.02	$3.65	More than $30
Georgia *Ga. Code Ann. § 34-4-3*	Applies to employers with 6 or more employees and more than $40,000 per year in sales	$5.15	Minimum wage does not apply to tipped employees	N/A	N/A
Hawaii *Haw. Rev. Stat. §§ 387-1 to 387-2*		$7.25	$0.25	$7.00	More than $20; employee's cash wage plus tips must be at least $0.50 higher than the minimum wage
Idaho *Idaho Code § 44-1502*		$5.15	35%	$3.35	More than $30

State Minimum Wage Laws for Tipped and Regular Employees (continued)

State and Statute	Notes	Basic Minimum Hourly Rate (*=tied to federal rate)	Maximum Tip Credit	Minimum Cash Wage for Tipped Employee	Minimum Tips to Qualify as a Tipped Employee (monthly unless noted otherwise)
Illinois *820 Ill. Comp. Stat. § 105/4; Ill. Admin. Code tit. 56, § 210.110*	Applies to employers with 4 or more employees	$7.50; $7.75 effective 7/1/08; $8.00 effective 7/1/09	40%	$4.50	At least $20
Indiana *Ind. Code Ann. § 22-2-2-4*	Applies to employers with 2 or more employees	$5.15	$3.02	$2.13	Not specified
Iowa *Iowa Code § 91D.1*	Minimum wage does not apply to first 90 calendar days of employment	$6.20 or FLSA rate if higher	40%	$3.09	At least $30
Kansas *Kan. Stat. Ann. § 44-1203*	Applies to employers not covered by the FLSA	$2.65	40%	$1.59	More than $20
Kentucky *Ky. Rev. Stat. Ann. § 337.275*		Same as FLSA rate	$3.02	$2.13	More than $30
Louisiana	No minimum wage law				
Maine *Me. Rev. Stat. Ann. tit. 26, §§ 663(8), 664*		$6.75; $7.00 effective 10/1/07	50%	$3.38 $3.50 effective 10/1/07	More than $20
Maryland *Md. Code Ann., [Lab. & Empl.] §§ 3-413, 3-419*		$6.15 or FLSA rate if higher	$2.77	$2.38	More than $30
Massachusetts *Mass. Gen. Laws ch. 151, § 1; Mass. Regs. Code tit. 455, §§ 2.02 & following*		$7.50	$4.37	$2.63	More than $20

State Minimum Wage Laws for Tipped and Regular Employees (continued)

State and Statute	Notes	Basic Minimum Hourly Rate (*=tied to federal rate)	Maximum Tip Credit	Minimum Cash Wage for Tipped Employee	Minimum Tips to Qualify as a Tipped Employee (monthly unless noted otherwise)
Michigan *Mich. Comp. Laws §§ 408.382 to 408.387a*	Applies to employers with 2 or more employees. Excludes all employers subject to the FLSA, unless state minimum wage is higher than federal	$7.15; $7.40 effective 7/01/08	$4.50	$2.65	Not specified
Minnesota *Minn. Stat. Ann. § 177.24*	$5.25 for small employer (business with annual receipts of less than $625,000)	$6.15	No tip credit	$6.15	N/A
Mississippi	No minimum wage law				
Missouri *Mo. Rev. Stat. §§ 290.502, 290.512*	Doesn't apply to retail or service business with gross annual sales of less than $500,000	$6.50	Up to 50%	$3.25	Not specified
Montana *Mont. Code Ann. §§ 39-3-404, 39-3-409; Mont. Admin. R. 24.16.1508 & following*	$4.00 for businesses with gross annual sales of $110,000 or less	$6.15	No tip credit	$6.15	N/A
Nebraska *Neb. Rev. Stat. § 48-1203*	Applies to employers with 4 or more employees	$5.15	$3.02	$2.13	Not specified
Nevada *Nev. Rev. Stat. Ann. §§ 607.160, 608.018, 608.160, 608.250, 608.270, 233B.0613 Nev. Admin Code ch. 608 § 110; NV Const. Art. 15 § 16*	Voters approved $1 increase in 2006; to be adjusted annually	$5.15 if employer provides health benefits $6.15 if no health benefits provided	No tip credit	$5.15	N/A

State Minimum Wage Laws for Tipped and Regular Employees (continued)				
State and Statute	**Notes**	**Basic Minimum Hourly Rate** (*=tied to federal rate)	**Maximum Tip Credit**	**Minimum Cash Wage for Tipped Employee**	**Minimum Tips to Qualify as a Tipped Employee** (monthly unless noted otherwise)
New Hampshire N.H. Rev. Stat. Ann. § 279:21		FLSA rate	$2.57	$2.38 or 45% of minimum wage, if higher	More than $20
New Jersey N.J. Stat. Ann. § 34:11-56a4; N.J. Admin. Code tit. 12, §§ 56-3.1 & following, 56-14.4		$7.15*	Depends on occupation	Depends on occupation	Not specified
New Mexico N.M. Stat. Ann. § 50-4-22		$5.15; $6.50 effective 01/01/08; $7.50 effective 01/01/09	$3.47	$2.13	More than $30; tipped employees must make at least $5.60 an hour with tips
New York N.Y. Lab. Law § 652; N.Y. Comp. Codes R. & Regs. tit. 12, §§ 137-1.4, 138-2.1		$7.15 or FLSA rate if higher	Depends on occupation	Depends on occupation $4.60 for waiters and busboys $5.40 for other tipped employees	Depends on occupation
North Carolina N.C. Gen. Stat. §§ 95-25.2(14), 95-25.3		$6.15	$3.02	$3.13	More than $20
North Dakota N.D. Cent. Code § 34-06-03; N.D. Admin. Code R. 46-02-07-02 to -03		$5.15	33%	$3.45	More than $30

State Minimum Wage Laws for Tipped and Regular Employees (continued)

State and Statute	Notes	Basic Minimum Hourly Rate (*=tied to federal rate)	Maximum Tip Credit	Minimum Cash Wage for Tipped Employee	Minimum Tips to Qualify as a Tipped Employee (monthly unless noted otherwise)
Ohio *Ohio Rev. Code Ann. § 4111.02* *Ohio Const. art. II § 34a*	Employer definitions same as FLSA	$6.85	50%	$3.83	More than $30
Oklahoma *Okla. Stat. Ann. tit. 40, §§ 197.2, 197.4, 197.16*	Applies to employers with 10 or more full-time employees OR gross annual sales over $100,000; $2.00 for all other employers who are not subject to the FLSA	Same as FLSA	50% for tips, food, and lodging combined	$2.58	Not specified
Oregon *Or. Rev. Stat. §§ 653.025, 653.035(3)*	Adjusted annually for inflation; posted at www.boli.state.or.us	$7.80	No tip credit	$7.25	N/A
Pennsylvania *43 Pa. Cons. Stat. Ann. §§ 333.104 & following; 34 Pa. Code § 231.1*	Employers with more than 10 employees; if less than 10, then $6.65	$7.15	$2.32	$2.83	More than $30
Rhode Island *R.I. Gen. Laws §§ 28-12-3 & following*		$7.40	$4.31	$2.89	Not specified
South Carolina	No minimum wage law				
South Dakota *S.D. Codified Laws Ann. §§ 60-11-3 to -3.1*		$5.15	$3.02	$2.13	More than $35
Tennessee	No minimum wage law				

State Minimum Wage Laws for Tipped and Regular Employees (continued)

State and Statute	Notes	Basic Minimum Hourly Rate (*=tied to federal rate)	Maximum Tip Credit	Minimum Cash Wage for Tipped Employee	Minimum Tips to Qualify as a Tipped Employee (monthly unless noted otherwise)
Texas Tex. Lab. Code Ann. §§ 62.051 & following	Applies to employers not covered by the FLSA	Same as FLSA rate	$3.02	$2.13	More than $20
Utah Utah Code Ann. §§ 34-40-102 to -103; Utah Admin. R. 610-1	Applies to employers not covered by the FLSA	Same as FLSA rate	$3.02	$2.13	More than $30
Vermont Vt. Stat. Ann. tit. 21, § 384(a); Vt. Code R. 24 090 003	Applies to employers with 2 or more employees	$7.53 increases by 5% or CPI on January 1st of each year	$3.88 for employees of hotels, motels, restaurants, and tourist places; no tip credit otherwise	$3.65	More than $30
Virginia Va. Code Ann. §§ 40.1-28.9(D) to 28.10	Applies to employers with 4 or more employees	Same as FLSA rate	Tips actually received	Minimum wage less tips actually received	Not specified
Washington Wash. Rev. Code Ann. § 49.46.020; Wash. Admin. Code § 296-126-022	Adjusted annually for inflation; posted at www.lni.wa.gov	$7.93	No tip credit	$7.65	N/A
West Virginia W.Va. Code §§ 21-5C-2, 21-5C-4	Applies to employers with 6 or more employees at one location who are not covered by the FLSA	$6.55; $7.25 effective 7/01/08	20%	$5.24	Not specified
Wisconsin Wis. Admin. Code DWD 272.03		$6.50	$4.17	$2.33	Not specified
Wyoming Wyo. Stat. § 27-4-202		$5.15	$3.02	$2.13	More than $30

Current as of July 2007

CAUTION

Additional laws may apply. If the chart above indicates that your state has no statute, this means there is no law that specifically addresses the issue. However, there may be a state administrative regulation or local ordinance that does control. Call your state labor department for more information. (See the Appendix for contact details.)

Time Off for Jury Duty

Most states have some specific requirements that apply to employees who are called to serve on juries. Most of these laws fall under the broad rubric of wage and hour controls.

Some employers doggedly resist the idea of allowing employees time off from work—and apply subtle or not-so-subtle pressure on them to do what they can to squirm out of jury service. Employees are easy targets for this form of coercion, since most people think of themselves as indispensable workers, and many have a natural fear and loathing of serving on a jury, anyway. Recognizing this, many state laws contain an antidiscrimination twist —baldly stating that employees called to serve on juries may not be fired for doing so. And a few laws broadly restrict employers from attempting to intimidate employees into not serving on juries.

A number of state laws impose picayune obligations on employees before they can claim legal protections. California protection, for example, applies only if an employee has given advance notice of the jury summons. In Tennessee, you must show the summons to your employer the day after you receive it.

A few states have gone through gyrations in an attempt to reach a balance between the court systems that sorely need jurors to serve and the reality of workplaces that need to remain productive. Illinois, for example, protects night shift employees, who cannot be required to work nights and do jury duty during the day. And Michigan specifies that the number of hours of jury duty plus work time must not exceed employees' regular number of working hours for that day.

But, these days, when employees labor under the fear of losing their jobs and employers labor under the pressure of increasing their bottom lines, the issue of taking time off for jury duty looms ever larger. The two major concerns are:

- whether employers must pay employees who are called as jurors, and
- what the penalties are for employers who violate statutes setting out obligations for employees on jury duty.

Pay Requirements

Unless employee handbooks or other published policies state otherwise, employees are not generally entitled to be paid by their employers for time off work spent responding to a summons or serving on a jury.

However, a number of states are exceptions to this rule. In Colorado, for example, employers must pay workers—including those who are part time and temporary—up to $50 daily for their first three days of jury services. (See "State Laws on Jury Duty," below, for additional restrictions and requirements in state laws.)

Penalties for Employer Violations

Most of the statutes specify what penalties can be imposed upon employers who do not live up to their legal rights and responsibilities when it comes to employee-jurors.

However, unless you have an exceptionally high tolerance for legal minutiae, you will not likely want to end up in court because an employer has violated your rights to time off for jury duty. But, as a practical matter, laws that set out penalties for employers who violate them can speak more loudly during your negotiations to resolve a wrong. Some laws specifically allow discharged employees to file lawsuits for back wages. Presumably, employees would be free to file such lawsuits even in states with laws that are mum on the issue. A few state laws specify that an employee who is fired specifically for taking jury duty must be reinstated.

Many states make a violation a misdemeanor, so that employees who are discriminated against or fired in violation of a jury duty law need only complain to the district attorney or other local prosecuting authority, who will decide whether to prosecute the case. A prosecutor who is successful and creative should be able to get back pay and even reinstatement for employees who are fired. But keep reality in mind. Prosecutors are not required to bring charges—and in areas where serious crime is rampant, a district attorney may well decide to put his or her energy elsewhere.

South Carolina is an example of a state with a harsh consequence: Employers who fire an employee because of jury duty may be liable for up to one year of the discharged employee's salary, or the difference between the original and the lessened salary if the employee is demoted. But New York's law is the toughest on employers who break jury duty laws; it leaves the employer open to criminal contempt charges.

State Laws on Jury Duty

The chart below summarizes state laws on jury duty. If you wish to read the complete text of the law, you can track it down through the citation at the end of each entry. (See Chapter 17, "Legal Research," for help.)

CAUTION

Additional laws may apply. If the chart below indicates that your state has no statute, this means there is no law that specifically addresses the issue. However, there may be a state administrative regulation or local ordinance that does control it. Call your local court administrator or your state labor department for more information. (See the Appendix for contact details.) Also, consider talking to the judge who is overseeing the case for which you have been called. He or she might have something to say about your employer not giving you time off to do your civic duty—and might be able to point you to a specific local law or regulation that can help.

Ignoring the Jury Duty Laws:
'Not One of His Smarter Management Decisions'

A Texas employer was arrested recently after firing a worker who insisted on honoring her civic duty of responding to a call for jury duty.

Jennifer Sutton, an executive assistant at Dallas-based computer company Affiliated Computer Services, claims she reminded her boss, Warren Edwards, about the jury duty summons several times in advance. She even confided that she was looking forward to serving on a jury for the first time.

Edwards response was to give her a reprimand and an additional work assignment, which she came to work early to finish on the morning her jury duty was to begin. He then demanded she stay to finish the task.

"I was in tears and told Mr. Edwards that I needed to go to jury duty," Sutton recalls. "He said for me to pack up my stuff, consider this my last day, that I was fired." The verbal pink slip was delivered ten days before Christmas.

Sutton's tale so incensed District Judge John M. Marshall that he issued a warrant for Edwards's arrest and ordered Dallas deputies to bring him in at once.

"I made it clear to him that this was not one of his smarter management decisions," opined the judge.

"It was a mistake," a computer company official later conceded of the firing.

Sutton seconded that emotion, refusing the company's offer of another job. Her final demand was getting her former job back—or six months' pay.

The final settlement terms are undisclosed. But the story of the ill-decided firing was writ large in newspapers nationwide.

State Laws on Jury Duty

Alabama

Ala. Code §§ 12-16-8 to 12-16-8.1

Paid leave: Full-time employees are entitled to usual pay minus any fees received from the court.

Notice employee must give: Must show supervisor jury summons the next working day; must return to work the next scheduled hour after discharge from jury duty.

Employer penalty for firing or penalizing employee: Liable for actual and punitive damages.

Alaska

Alaska Stat. § 09.20.037

Unpaid leave: Yes.

Additional employee protections: Employee may not be threatened, coerced, or penalized.

Employer penalty for firing or penalizing employee: Liable for lost wages and damages; may be required to reinstate the fired employee.

Arizona

Ariz. Rev. Stat. § 21-236

Unpaid leave: Yes.

Additional employee protections: Employee may not lose vacation rights, seniority, or precedence. Employer may not require employee to use annual, sick, or vacation hours.

Employer penalty for firing or penalizing employee: Class 3 misdemeanor, punishable by a fine of up to $500 or up to 30 days' imprisonment.

Note: Employers with 5 or fewer full-time employees: Court must postpone an employee's jury service if another employee is already serving as a juror.

Arkansas

Ark. Code Ann. § 16-31-106

Unpaid leave: Yes.

Additional employee protections: Absence may not affect sick leave and vacation rights.

Employer penalty for firing or penalizing employee: Class A misdemeanor, punishable by a fine of up to $1,000.

California

Cal. Lab. Code §§ 230, 230.1

Unpaid leave: Employee may use vacation, personal leave, or comp time.

Additional employee protections: Victims of crime, domestic violence, or sexual assault are protected against discharge, discrimination, or retaliation for attending a court proceeding or seeking judicial relief.

Notice employee must give: Reasonable notice.

Employer penalty for firing or penalizing employee: Employer must reinstate employee with back pay and lost wages and benefits. Willful violation is a misdemeanor.

Colorado

Colo. Rev. Stat. §§ 13-71-126, 13-71-133 to 13-71-134

Paid leave: All employees (including part-time and temporary who were scheduled to work for the 3 months preceding jury service): regular wages up to $50 per day for first 3 days of jury duty. Must pay within 30 days of jury service.

Additional employee protections: Employer may not make any demands on employee which will interfere with effective performance of jury duty.

Employer penalty for firing or penalizing employee: Class 2 misdemeanor, punishable by a fine of $250 to $1,000 or 3 to 12 months' imprisonment, or both. May be liable to employee for triple damages and attorney's fees.

State Laws on Jury Duty (continued)

Connecticut

Conn. Gen. Stat. Ann. §§ 51-247 to 51-247c

Paid leave: Full-time employees: regular wages for the first 5 days of jury duty; after 5 days, state pays up to $50 per day.

Employer penalty for firing or penalizing employee: Criminal contempt: punishable by a fine of up to $500 or up to 30 days' imprisonment, or both. Liable for up to 10 weeks' lost wages for discharging employee. If employer fails to pay the employee as required, may be liable for treble damages and attorney's fees.

Delaware

Del. Code Ann. tit. 10, § 4515

Unpaid leave: Yes.

Employer penalty for firing or penalizing employee: Criminal contempt: punishable by a fine of up to $500 or up to 6 months' imprisonment, or both. Liable to discharged employee for lost wages and attorney's fees and may be required to reinstate the fired employee.

District of Columbia

D.C. Code Ann. §§ 11-1913, 15-718

Paid leave: Full-time employees: regular wages for the first 5 days of jury duty.

Employer penalty for firing or penalizing employee: Criminal contempt: punishable by a fine of up to $300 or up to 30 days' imprisonment, or both, for a first offense; up to $5,000 or up to 180 days' imprisonment, or both, for any subsequent offense. Liable to discharged employee for lost wages and attorney's fees and may be required to reinstate the fired employee.

Florida

Fla. Stat. Ann. § 40.271

Unpaid leave: Yes.

Additional employee protections: Employee may not be threatened with dismissal.

Employer penalty for firing or penalizing employee: Threatening employee is contempt of court. May be liable to discharged employee for compensatory and punitive damages and attorney's fees.

Georgia

Ga. Code Ann. § 34-1-3

Unpaid leave: Yes.

Additional employee protections: Employee may not be discharged, penalized, or threatened with discharge or penalty for responding to a subpoena or making a required court appearance.

Notice employee must give: Reasonable notice.

Employer penalty for firing or penalizing employee: Liable for actual damages and reasonable attorney's fees.

Hawaii

Haw. Rev. Stat. § 612-25

Unpaid leave: Yes.

Employer penalty for firing or penalizing employee: Petty misdemeanor: punishable by a fine of up to $1,000 or up to 30 days' imprisonment. May be liable to discharged employee for up to 6 weeks' lost wages and may be required to reinstate the fired employee.

Idaho

Idaho Code § 2-218

Unpaid leave: Yes.

Employer penalty for firing or penalizing employee: Criminal contempt: punishable by a fine of up to $300. Liable to discharged employee for triple lost wages.

State Laws on Jury Duty (continued)

Illinois

705 Ill. Comp. Stat. § 310/10.1

Unpaid leave: Yes.

Additional employee protections: A regular night shift employee may not be required to work if serving on a jury during the day. May not lose any seniority or benefits.

Notice employee must give: Must give employer a copy of the summons within 10 days of issuance.

Employer penalty for firing or penalizing employee: Employer will be charged with civil or criminal contempt, or both; liable to employee for lost wages and benefits.

Indiana

Ind. Code Ann. §§ 32-28-4-1, 35-44-3-10

Unpaid leave: Yes.

Additional employee protections: Employee may not be deprived of benefits or threatened with the loss of them.

Employer penalty for firing or penalizing employee: Class B misdemeanor: punishable by up to 180 days' imprisonment; may also be fined up to $1,000. Liable to discharged employee for lost wages and attorney's fees and may be required to reinstate the fired employee.

Iowa

Iowa Code § 607A.45

Unpaid leave: Yes.

Employer penalty for firing or penalizing employee: Contempt of court. Liable to discharged employee for up to 6 weeks' lost wages and attorney's fees and may be required to reinstate the fired employee.

Kansas

Kan. Stat. Ann. § 43-173

Unpaid leave: Yes.

Additional employee protections: Employee may not lose seniority or benefits. (Basic and additional protections apply to permanent employees only.)

Employer penalty for firing or penalizing employee: Liable for lost wages and benefits, damages, and attorney's fees and may be required to reinstate the fired employee.

Kentucky

Ky. Rev. Stat. Ann. §§ 29A.160, 29A.990

Unpaid leave: Yes.

Employer penalty for firing or penalizing employee: Class B misdemeanor: punishable by up to 89 days' imprisonment or fine of up to $250, or both. Liable to discharged employee for lost wages and attorney's fees. Must reinstate employee with full seniority and benefits.

Louisiana

La. Rev. Stat. Ann. § 23:965

Paid leave: Regular employee entitled to one day full compensation for jury service. May not lose any sick, vacation, or personal leave or other benefit.

Additional employee protections: Employer may not create any policy or rule that would discharge employee for jury service.

Notice employee must give: Reasonable notice.

Employer penalty for firing or penalizing employee: For each discharged employee: fine of $100 to $1,000; must reinstate employee with full benefits. For not granting paid leave: fine of $100 to $500; must pay full day's lost wages.

Maine

Me. Rev. Stat. Ann. tit. 14, § 1218

Unpaid leave: Yes.

State Laws on Jury Duty (continued)

Additional employee protections: Employee may not lose or be threatened with loss of health insurance coverage.

Employer penalty for firing or penalizing employee: Class E crime: punishable by up to 6 months in the county jail or a fine of up to $1,000. Liable for up to 6 weeks' lost wages, benefits, and attorney's fees.

Maryland
Md. Code Ann., [Cts. & Jud. Proc.] § 8-502

Unpaid leave: Yes.

Additional employee protections: An employee may not be required to use annual, sick, or vacation leave. Employer penalty for violating this provision is a fine up to $1,000.

Massachusetts
Mass. Gen. Laws ch. 234A, §§ 48 and following

Paid leave: All employees (including part-time and temporary who were scheduled to work for the 3 months preceding jury service): regular wages for first 3 days of jury duty. If paid leave is an "extreme financial hardship" for employer, state will pay. After first 3 days state will pay $50 per day.

Michigan
Mich. Comp. Laws § 600.1348

Unpaid leave: Yes.

Additional employee protections: Employee may not be threatened or disciplined; may not be required to work in addition to jury service, if extra hours would mean working overtime or beyond normal quitting time.

Employer penalty for firing or penalizing employee: Misdemeanor, punishable by a fine of up to $500 or up to 90 days' imprisonment,

or both. Employer may also be punished for contempt of court, with a fine of up to $7,500 or up to 93 days' imprisonment, or both.

Minnesota
Minn. Stat. Ann. § 593.50

Unpaid leave: Yes.

Employer penalty for firing or penalizing employee: Criminal contempt: punishable by a fine of up to $700 or up to 6 months' imprisonment, or both. Also liable to employee for up to 6 weeks' lost wages and attorney's fees and may be required to reinstate the fired employee.

Mississippi
Miss. Code Ann. §§ 13-5-23, 13-5-35

Unpaid leave: Yes.

Additional employee protections: Employer may not threaten or intimidate, persuade, or attempt to persuade employee to avoid jury service. As of January 1, 2008, employee may not be required to use annual, sick, or vacation leave for jury service.

Notice employee must give: As of January 1, 2008, reasonable notice is required.

Employer penalty for firing or penalizing employee: If found guilty of interference with the administration of justice: at least one month in the county jail or up to 2 years in the state penitentiary, or a fine of up to $500, or both. May also be found guilty of contempt of court, punishable by a fine of up to $1,000 or up to 6 months' imprisonment, or both.

Note: Employers with 5 or fewer full-time employees: Court must postpone an employee's jury service if another employee is already serving as a juror.

State Laws on Jury Duty (continued)

Missouri

Mo. Rev. Stat. § 494.460

Unpaid leave: Yes.

Additional employee protections: Employer may not take or threaten to take any adverse action. Employee may not be required to use annual, sick, vacation, or personal leave.

Employer penalty for firing or penalizing employee: Employer may be liable for lost wages, damages, and attorney's fees and may be required to reinstate the fired employee.

Montana

Mont. Admin. R. 24.16.2520

Paid leave: No paid leave laws regarding private employers.

Nebraska

Neb. Rev. Stat. § 25-1640

Paid leave: Normal wages minus any compensation (other than expenses) from the court.

Additional employee protections: Employee may not lose pay, sick leave, or vacation or be penalized in any way; may not be required to work evening or night shift.

Notice employee must give: Reasonable notice.

Employer penalty for firing or penalizing employee: Class IV misdemeanor, punishable by a fine of $100 to $500.

Nevada

Nev. Rev. Stat. Ann. § 6.190

Unpaid leave: Yes.

Additional employee protections: Employer may not recommend or threaten termination; may not dissuade or attempt to dissuade employee from serving as a juror.

Notice employee must give: At least one day's notice.

Employer penalty for firing or penalizing employee: Terminating or threatening to terminate is a gross misdemeanor, punishable by a fine of up to $2,000 or up to one year's imprisonment, or both; in addition, employer may be liable for lost wages, damages equal to lost wages, and punitive damages to $50,000 and must reinstate employee. Dissuading or attempting to dissuade is a misdemeanor, punishable by a fine of up to $1,000 or up to 6 months in the county jail, or both.

New Hampshire

N.H. Rev. Stat. Ann. § 500-A:14

Unpaid leave: Yes.

Employer penalty for firing or penalizing employee: Employer may be found guilty of contempt of court; also liable to employee for lost wages and attorney's fees and may be required to reinstate the fired employee.

New Jersey

N.J. Stat. Ann. § 2B:20-17

Unpaid leave: Yes.

Employer penalty for firing or penalizing employee: Employer may be found guilty of a disorderly persons offense, punishable by a fine of up to $1,000 or up to 6 months' imprisonment, or both. May also be liable to employee for economic damages and attorney's fees and may be ordered to reinstate the fired employee.

New Mexico

N.M. Stat. Ann. §§ 38-5-18 to 38-5-19

Unpaid leave: Yes.

Additional employee protections: An employee may not be required to use annual, sick, or vacation leave.

State Laws on Jury Duty (continued)

Employer penalty for firing or penalizing employee: Petty misdemeanor, punishable by a fine of up to $500 or up to 6 months in the county jail, or both.

New York

N.Y. Jud. Ct. Acts Law § 519

Unpaid leave: Yes.

Paid leave: Employers with more than 10 employees must pay first $40 of wages for the first 3 days of jury duty.

Notice employee must give: Must notify employer prior to beginning jury duty.

Employer penalty for firing or penalizing employee: May be found guilty of criminal contempt of court, punishable by a fine of up to $1,000 or up to 30 days in the county jail, or both.

North Carolina

N.C. Gen. Stat. § 9-32

Unpaid leave: Yes.

Additional employee protections: Employee may not be demoted.

Employer penalty for firing or penalizing employee: Liable to discharged employee for reasonable damages; must reinstate employee to former position.

North Dakota

N.D. Cent. Code § 27-09.1-17

Unpaid leave: Yes.

Additional employee protections: Employee may not be laid off, penalized, or coerced because of jury duty, responding to a summons or subpoena, serving as a witness, or testifying in court.

Employer penalty for firing or penalizing employee: Class B misdemeanor, punishable

by a fine of up to $1,000 or up to 30 days' imprisonment, or both. Liable to employee for up to 6 weeks' lost wages and attorney's fees, and may be required to reinstate the fired employee.

Ohio

Ohio Rev. Code Ann. § 2313.18

Unpaid leave: Yes.

Additional employee protections: An employee may not be required to use annual, sick, or vacation leave.

Notice employee must give: Reasonable notice. Absence must be for actual jury service.

Employer penalty for firing or penalizing employee: May be found guilty of contempt of court, punishable by a fine of up to $250 or 30 days' imprisonment, or both, for first offense; a fine of up to $500 or 60 days' imprisonment, or both, for second offense; a fine of up to $1,000 or 90 days' imprisonment, or both, for third offense.

Note: Employers with 25 or fewer employees: Court must postpone an employee's jury service if another employee is already serving as a juror.

Oklahoma

Okla. Stat. Ann. tit. 38, §§ 34, 35

Unpaid leave: Yes.

Additional employee protections: Employee can't be required to use annual sick or vacation leave.

Notice employee must give: Reasonable notice.

Employer penalty for firing or penalizing employee: Misdemeanor, punishable by a fine of up to $5,000. Liable to discharged employee for actual and exemplary damages; actual damages include past and future lost wages, mental anguish, and costs of finding suitable employment.

State Laws on Jury Duty (continued)

Oregon

Or. Rev. Stat. § 10.090

Unpaid leave: Yes (or according to employer's policy).

Additional employee protections: Employee may not be threatened, intimidated, or coerced.

Employer penalty for firing or penalizing employee: Employer must reinstate discharged employee with back pay.

Pennsylvania

42 Pa. Cons. Stat. Ann. § 4563; 18 Pa. Cons. Stat. Ann. § 4957

Unpaid leave: Yes (applies to retail or service industry employers with 15 or more employees and to manufacturers with 40 or more employees).

Additional employee protections: Employee may not lose seniority or benefits. (Any employee who would not be eligible for unpaid leave will be automatically excused from jury duty.) Employee who must appear in court as a victim or witness, or as a family member of a victim or witness, must also be given unpaid leave.

Employer penalty for firing or penalizing employee: Liable to employee for lost benefits, wages, and attorney's fees; may be required to reinstate the fired employee.

Rhode Island

R.I. Gen. Laws § 9-9-28

Unpaid leave: Yes.

Additional employee protections: Employee may not lose wage increases, promotions, length of service, or other benefit.

Employer penalty for firing or penalizing employee: Misdemeanor punishable by a fine of up to $1,000 or up to one year's imprisonment, or both.

South Carolina

S.C. Code Ann. § 41-1-70

Unpaid leave: Yes.

Additional employee protections: Employee may not be demoted or dismissed for responding to a subpoena to testify.

Employer penalty for firing or penalizing employee: For discharging employee, liable for one year's salary; for demoting employee, liable for one year's difference between former and lower salary.

South Dakota

S.D. Codified Laws Ann. §§ 16-13-41.1, 16-13-41.2

Unpaid leave: Yes.

Additional employee protections: Employee may not lose job status, pay, or seniority.

Employer penalty for firing or penalizing employee: Class 2 misdemeanor, punishable by a fine of up to $500 or up to 30 days in the county jail, or both.

Tennessee

Tenn. Code Ann. § 22-4-108

Paid leave: Regular wages minus jury fees.

Additional employee protections: Night shift employees are excused from shift work during and for the night before the first day of jury service.

Notice employee must give: Employee must show summons to supervisor the day after receiving it.

Employer penalty for firing or penalizing employee: Violating employee rights or any provisions of this law is a Class A misdemeanor, punishable by up to 11 months, 29 days' imprisonment or a fine up to $2,500, or both. Liable to employee for lost wages and benefits

State Laws on Jury Duty (continued)

and must reinstate employee.

Note: Does not apply to employers with fewer than 5 employees or to temporary employees who have worked less than 6 months.

Texas

Tex. Civ. Prac. & Rem. Code Ann. §§ 122.001, 122.002

Unpaid leave: Yes.

Notice employee must give: Employee must notify employer of intent to return after completion of jury service.

Employer penalty for firing or penalizing employee: Liable to employee for not less than one year's nor more than 5 years' compensation and attorney fees. Must reinstate employee.

Note: Only applies to permanent employees.

Utah

Utah Code Ann. § 78-46-21

Unpaid leave: Yes.

Additional employee protections: Employee may not be threatened or coerced and may not be requested or required to use annual or sick leave or vacation.

Employer penalty for firing or penalizing employee: May be found guilty of criminal contempt, punishable by a fine of up to $500 or up to 6 months' imprisonment, or both. Liable to employee for up to 6 weeks' lost wages and attorney's fees and may be required to reinstate the fired employee.

Vermont

Vt. Stat. Ann. tit. 21, § 499

Unpaid leave: Yes.

Additional employee protections: Employee may not be penalized or lose any benefit available to other employees; may not lose seniority,

vacation credit, or any fringe benefits. Protections also apply to an employee appearing as a witness in court or testifying before a board, commission, or tribunal.

Employer penalty for firing or penalizing employee: Fine of up to $200.

Virginia

Va. Code Ann. § 18.2-465.1

Unpaid leave: Yes.

Additional employee protections: Employee may not be subject to any adverse personnel action and may not be forced to use sick leave or vacation. Employee who has appeared for 4 or more hours cannot be required to start a shift after 5 p.m. that day or before 3 a.m. the next morning. Protections also apply to an employee summoned or subpoenaed to appear, except criminal defendants.

Notice employee must give: Reasonable notice.

Employer penalty for firing or penalizing employee: Class 3 misdemeanor, punishable by a fine of up to $500.

Washington

Wash. Rev. Code Ann. § 2.36.165

Unpaid leave: Yes.

Additional employee protections: Employee may not be threatened, coerced, harassed, or denied promotion.

Employer penalty for firing or penalizing employee: Intentional violation is a misdemeanor, punishable by a fine of up to $1,000 or up to 90 days' imprisonment, or both; also liable to employee for damages and attorney's fees and may be required to reinstate the fired employee.

State Laws on Jury Duty (continued)

West Virginia
W.Va. Code § 52-3-1

Unpaid leave: Yes.

Additional employee protections: Employee may not be threatened or discriminated against; regular pay cannot be cut.

Employer penalty for firing or penalizing employee: May be found guilty of civil contempt, punishable by a fine of $100 to $500. May be required to reinstate the fired employee. May be liable for back pay and for attorney's fees.

Wisconsin
Wis. Stat. Ann. § 756.255

Unpaid leave: Yes.

Additional employee protections: Employee

may not lose seniority or pay raises; may not be disciplined.

Employer penalty for firing or penalizing employee: Fine of up to $200. May be required to reinstate the fired employee with back pay.

Wyoming
Wyo. Stat. § 1-11-401

Unpaid leave: Yes.

Additional employee protections: Employee may not be threatened, intimidated, or coerced.

Employer penalty for firing or penalizing employee: Liable to employee for up to $1,000 damages, costs, and attorney's fees. May be required to reinstate the fired employee with no loss of seniority.

Current as of February 2007

Time Off for Voting

Another set of state laws that falls under the broad category of wages and hours regulates the time off employers must allow for employees to vote.

Some state laws set out a specific amount of time that employees must be allowed off from work to cast their ballots. In some states, the time off must be paid; not in others. Some states require employers to provide leave only if the employee won't have enough time before or after work, when the polls are open, to vote. And most state laws prohibit employers from disciplining or firing employees who take time off work to vote.

Finally, some states impose hardball restrictions on employees who want to claim

protection under the voter laws, requiring them to show proof that they actually cast a ballot before they can claim the time off. In nearly half the states, employees must give employers previous notice that they intend to take time off work to vote.

 CAUTION

Additional laws may apply. If the chart below indicates that your state has no statute, this means there is no law that specifically addresses the issue. However, there may be a state administrative regulation or local ordinance that does control. Call your local board of elections or your state labor department for more information. (See the Appendix for contact details.)

State Laws on Taking Time Off to Vote

Note: The states of Connecticut, Delaware, District of Columbia, Florida, Idaho, Indiana, Louisiana, Maine, Michigan, Mississippi, Montana, New Hampshire, New Jersey, North Carolina, Oregon, Pennsylvania, Rhode Island, South Carolina, Vermont, and Virginia are not listed in this chart because they do not have laws or regulations on time off to vote that govern private employers. Check with your state department of labor if you need more information. (See Appendix A for contact list.)

Alabama
Ala. Code § 17-1-5

Time off work for voting: Necessary time up to one hour. The employer may decide when hours may be taken.

Time off not required if: Employee has 2 nonwork hours before polls open or one nonwork hour after polls are open.

Time off is paid: No.

Employee must request leave in advance: "Reasonable notice."

Alaska
Alaska Stat. § 15.56.100

Time off work for voting: Not specified.

Time off not required if: Employee has 2 consecutive nonwork hours at beginning or end of shift when polls are open.

Time off is paid: Yes.

Arizona
Ariz. Rev. Stat. § 16-402

Time off work for voting: As much time as will add up to 3 hours when combined with nonwork time. Employer may decide when hours are taken.

Time off not required if: Employee has 3 consecutive nonwork hours at beginning or end of shift when polls are open.

Time off is paid: Yes.

Employee must request leave in advance: One day before election.

Arkansas
Ark. Code Ann. § 7-1-102

Time off work for voting: Employer must schedule work hours so employee has time to vote.

Time off is paid: No.

California
Cal. Elec. Code § 14000

Time off work for voting: Up to 2 hours at beginning or end of shift, whichever gives employee most time to vote and takes least time off work.

Time off not required if: Employee has sufficient time to vote during nonwork time.

Time off is paid: Yes (up to 2 hours).

Employee must request leave in advance: 2 working days before election.

Colorado
Colo. Rev. Stat. § 1-7-102

Time off work for voting: Up to 2 hours. Employer may decide when hours are taken, but employer must permit employee to take time at beginning or end of shift, if employee requests it.

Time off not required if: Employee has 3 nonwork hours when polls are open.

Time off is paid: Yes (up to 2 hours).

Employee must request leave in advance: Prior to election day.

Georgia
Ga. Code Ann. § 21-2-404

Time off work for voting: Up to 2 hours. Employer may decide when hours are taken.

State Laws on Taking Time Off to Vote (continued)

Time off not required if: Employee has 2 nonwork hours at beginning or end of shift when polls are open.

Time off is paid: No.

Employee must request leave in advance: "Reasonable notice."

Hawaii

Haw. Rev. Stat. § 11-95

Time off work for voting: 2 consecutive hours excluding meal or rest breaks. Employer may not change employee's regular work schedule.

Time off not required if: Employee has 2 consecutive nonwork hours when polls are open.

Time off is paid: Yes.

Employee required to show proof of voting: Yes (voter's receipt). If employer verifies that employee did not vote, hours off may be deducted from pay.

Illinois

10 Ill. Comp. Stat. §§ 5/7-42, 5/17-15

Time off work for voting: 2 hours. Employer may decide when hours are taken.

Time off is paid: Yes.

Employee must request leave in advance: One day in advance (for general or state election). Employer must give consent (for primary).

Iowa

Iowa Code § 49.109

Time off work for voting: As much time as will add up to 3 hours when combined with nonwork time. Employer may decide when hours are taken.

Time off not required if: Employee has 3 consecutive nonwork hours when polls are open.

Time off is paid: Yes.

Employee must request leave in advance: In writing "prior to the date of the election."

Kansas

Kan. Stat. Ann. § 25-418

Time off work for voting: Up to 2 hours or as much time as will add up to 2 hours when combined with nonwork time. Employer may decide when hours are taken, but it may not be during a regular meal break.

Time off not required if: Employee has 2 consecutive nonwork hours when polls are open.

Time off is paid: Yes.

Kentucky

Ky. Const. § 148; Ky. Rev. Stat. Ann. § 118.035

Time off work for voting: "Reasonable time," but not less than 4 hours. Employer may decide when hours are taken.

Time off is paid: No.

Employee must request leave in advance: One day before election.

Employee required to show proof of voting: No proof specified, but employee who takes time off and does not vote may be subject to disciplinary action.

Maryland

Md. Code Ann. [Elec. Law] § 10-315

Time off work for voting: 2 hours.

Time off not required if: Employee has 2 consecutive nonwork hours when polls are open.

Time off is paid: Yes.

Employee required to show proof of voting: Yes; also includes attempting to vote. Must use state board of elections form.

State Laws on Taking Time Off to Vote (continued)

Massachusetts

Mass. Gen. Laws ch. 149, § 178

Time off work for voting: First 2 hours that polls are open. (Applies to workers in manufacturing, mechanical, or retail industries.)

Time off is paid: No.

Employee must request leave in advance: Must apply for leave of absence (no time specified).

Minnesota

Minn. Stat. Ann. § 204C.04

Time off work for voting: May be absent during the morning of election day.

Time off is paid: Yes.

Missouri

Mo. Rev. Stat. § 115.639

Time off work for voting: 3 hours. Employer may decide when hours are taken.

Time off not required if: Employee has 3 consecutive nonwork hours when polls are open.

Time off is paid: Yes (if employee votes).

Employee must request leave in advance: "Prior to the day of election."

Employee required to show proof of voting: None specified, but pay contingent on employee actually voting.

Nebraska

Neb. Rev. Stat. § 32-922

Time off work for voting: As much time as will add up to 2 consecutive hours when combined with nonwork time. Employer may decide when hours are taken.

Time off not required if: Employee has 2 consecutive nonwork hours when polls are open.

Time off is paid: Yes.

Employee must request leave in advance: Prior to or on election day.

Nevada

Nev. Rev. Stat. Ann. § 293.463

Time off work for voting: If it is impracticable to vote before or after work: Employee who works 2 miles or less from polling place may take 1 hour; 2 to 10 miles, 2 hours; more than 10 miles, 3 hours.

Time off not required if: Employee has sufficient nonwork time when polls are open.

Time off is paid: Yes.

Employee must request leave in advance: Prior to election day.

New Mexico

N.M. Stat. Ann. § 1-12-42

Time off work for voting: 2 hours. (Includes Indian nation, tribal, and pueblo elections.)

Time off not required if: Employee's workday begins more than 2 hours after polls open or ends more than 3 hours before polls close.

Time off is paid: Yes.

New York

N.Y. Elec. Law § 3-110

Time off work for voting: As many hours at beginning or end of shift as will give employee enough time to vote when combined with nonwork time. Employer may decide when hours are taken.

Time off not required if: Employee has 4 consecutive nonwork hours at beginning or end of shift when polls are open.

Time off is paid: Yes (up to 2 hours).

Employee must request leave in advance: Not more than 10 or less than 2 working days before election.

State Laws on Taking Time Off to Vote (continued)

North Dakota

N.D. Cent. Code § 16.1-01-02.1

Time off work for voting: Employers are encouraged to give employees time off to vote when regular work schedule conflicts with times polls are open.

Time off is paid: No.

Ohio

Ohio Rev. Code Ann. § 3599.06

Time off work for voting: "Reasonable time."

Time off is paid: Yes.

Oklahoma

Okla. Stat. Ann. tit. 26, § 7-101

Time off work for voting: 2 hours, unless employee lives so far from polling place that more time is needed. Employer may decide when hours are taken or may change employee's schedule to give employee nonwork time to vote.

Time off not required if: Employee's workday begins at least 3 hours after polls open or ends at least 3 hours before polls close.

Time off is paid: Yes.

Employee must request leave in advance: One day before election.

Employee required to show proof of voting: Yes.

South Dakota

S.D. Codified Laws Ann. § 12-3-5

Time off work for voting: 2 consecutive hours. Employer may decide when hours are taken.

Time off not required if: Employee has 2 consecutive nonwork hours when polls are open.

Time off is paid: Yes.

Tennessee

Tenn. Code Ann. § 2-1-106

Time off work for voting: "Reasonable time" up to 3 hours.

Time off not required if: Employee's workday begins at least 3 hours after polls open or ends at least 3 hours before polls close.

Time off is paid: Yes.

Employee must request leave in advance: Before noon on the day before the election.

Texas

Tex. Elec. Code Ann. § 276.004

Time off work for voting: Employer may not refuse to allow employee to take time off to vote, but no time limit specified.

Time off not required if: Employee has 2 consecutive nonwork hours when polls are open.

Time off is paid: Yes.

Utah

Utah Code Ann. § 20A-3-103

Time off work for voting: 2 hours at beginning or end of shift. Employer may decide when hours are taken.

Time off not required if: Employee has at least 3 nonwork hours when polls are open.

Time off is paid: Yes.

Employee must request leave in advance: "Before election day."

Washington

Wash. Rev. Code Ann. § 49.28.120

Time off work for voting: Employer must either arrange work schedule so employee has enough nonwork time (not including meal or rest breaks) to vote, or allow employee to take off work for a "reasonable time," up to 2 hours.

State Laws on Taking Time Off to Vote (continued)

Time off not required if: Employee has 2 nonwork hours when polls are open or enough time to get an absentee ballot.

Time off is paid: Yes.

West Virginia

W.Va. Code § 3-1-42

Time off work for voting: Up to 3 hours. (Employers in health, transportation, communication, production, and processing facilities may change employee's schedule so that time off doesn't impair essential operations but must allow employee sufficient and convenient time to vote.)

Time off not required if: Employee has at least 3 nonwork hours when polls are open.

Time off is paid: Yes (if employee votes).

Employee must request leave in advance: Written request at least 3 days before election.

Employee required to show proof of voting: None specified, but time off will be deducted from pay if employee does not vote.

Wisconsin

Wis. Stat. Ann. § 6.76

Time off work for voting: Up to 3 consecutive hours. Employer may decide when hours are taken.

Time off is paid: No.

Employee must request leave in advance: "Before election day."

Wyoming

Wyo. Stat. § 22-2-111

Time off work for voting: One hour, other than a meal break.

Time off not required if: Employee has at least 3 consecutive nonwork hours when polls are open.

Time off is paid: Yes (if employee votes).

Employee required to show proof of voting: None specified, but pay contingent on employee voting.

Current as of February 2007

Time Off for Military or National Guard Duty

In the wake of America's invasion of Iraq in 2003, workplaces around the nation were jolted to heed some laws many had forgotten or ignored, as thousands of members of the National Guard and reserves were called away and pressed into duty.

A federal law, the Uniformed Services Employment and Reemployment Rights Act, or USERRA, sets out some broad guidelines that all employers must follow. That law, which applies to employers of all sizes and types, requires them to provide up to five years of unpaid leave to those called to the military services. The law generally prohibits discriminating against workers who serve and assures that they can reclaim their jobs after a stint of duty or training. USERRA also mandates that employers continue and pay for health benefits for the first 30 days of military leave and protects employees' pension rights upon return. To take advantage of this law, employees must provide their employers with oral or written notice of the need for leave, if possible, and must return to work within a set period of time after their service ends. Special rules apply to employees who are disabled by their military service.

In addition, most states have laws requiring employers to give time off for National Guard or state militia members or reservists to serve, most of which expand upon the basic rights provided in USERRA. A number of laws set a minimum amount of paid or unpaid time off that must be given. And most laws include a provision preventing discrimination against employees who take military leave.

When leave is required, the employer must usually reemploy service member employees without loss of benefits, status, or reduction in pay. These reemployment guarantees usually contain a number of additional conditions. Typical rights and restrictions are that:

- the employee must not have been dishonorably discharged
- the employee must present proof that he or she has satisfactorily completed service
- the employee must request reinstatement within a specified time
- if the employee is not able to do the job he or she left, the employer must offer an appropriate substitute position, and
- the employer need not reinstate the serviceperson if changes in the workforce have made that unreasonable.

Taking Aim at USERRA

The war in Iraq has brought about the greatest mobilization of National Guard and Reserve troops since World War II, with duty call-ups as long as two years and several units mobilizing more than once. This activity has strained the bounds and utility of the USERRA, revealing problems in the law that its drafters never contemplated.

In response, members of the American Bar Association's Standing Committee on Legal Assistance for Military Personnel, many of them current or retired military attorneys, undertook a year-long study of USERRA and other legal provisions for military. In August 2004, it issued a fairly scathing report—highlighting problems with USERRA's provisions and its enforcement. Specifically, it found that:

- civil service employees who miss promotion examinations while away on military duty were potentially missing out on promotion eligibility for several years
- employees for whom performance bonuses comprise a substantial portion of their compensation were being effectively penalized upon their return as a result of their absence while in military service
- the Department of Labor had not promulgated regulations on implementation of USERRA, despite a requirement in the 1994 statute that it do so
- the Department of Labor Veterans' Employment and Training Service was not seen as an aggressive advocate for the returning veteran
- the Office of Special Counsel in the Office of Personnel Management did not function as USERRA had contemplated that it would.

- when the Department of Justice brings an action on behalf of a veteran, the local United States Attorneys offices are not generally receptive to acting as counsel for the veteran
- few private attorneys take USERRA cases against private employers, because they generally do not involve substantial sums, and
- the USERRA requirement to accommodate returning veterans who have suffered service-connected disabilities was yet to be tested.

Response to the report and criticisms from other quarters was swift, if scattershot.

In March 2005, the DOL issued a rule requiring employers to provide those entitled to USERRA rights and benefits with notice of the law's provisions—by posting them in workplaces or mailing or emailing them to individual employees.

In December 2005, the DOL issued 70 pages of regulations intended to clarify USERRA, a law that a Department of Labor spokesman acknowledged was "very complicated" and its enforcement spotty because of "a lack of awareness and understanding."

In October 2006, the DOL launched an enhanced data management system aimed at tracking and resolving job-related complaints by National Guard members, reservists, and veterans.

And in August 2006, the Attorney General joined in the USERRA revival efforts by launching a website (www.servicemembers.gov) to provide service members and veterans information and resources on enforcing their legal rights.

State Laws on Military Leave

Alabama

Alabama Stat. §§ 31-12-1 to 31-12-4

State national guard and militia members called to active duty for at least 30 consecutive days or for federally funded duty for service other than training have the same leave and reinstatement rights and benefits guaranteed under USERRA.

Alaska

Alaska Stat. § 26.05.075

Employees called to active service in the state militia are entitled to unlimited unpaid leave and reinstatement to their former or a comparable position, with the pay, seniority, and benefits the employee would have had if not absent for service. Employee must return to work on next workday, after time required for travel. Disabled employee must request reemployment within 30 days of release; if disability leaves the employee unable to do the job, employee must be offered a position with similar pay and benefits.

Arizona

Ariz. Rev. Stat. §§ 26-167, 26-168

Members of the national guard called to active duty have the same leave and reinstatement rights and benefits guaranteed under USERRA. Members of the national guard called to participate in maneuvers or drills are entitled to unlimited unpaid leave and reinstatement to their former or a higher position with the same seniority and vacation benefits. Employer may not dissuade employees from enlisting in state or national military forces by threatening economic reprisal.

Arkansas

Ark. Code Ann. § 12-62-413

Employees called by the governor to active duty in the Arkansas National Guard or the state

militia have the same leave and reinstatement rights and benefits guaranteed under USERRA.

California

Cal. Mil. & Vet. Code §§ 394, 394.5, 395.06

Members of the state national guard called to active duty are entitled to unlimited unpaid leave and reinstatement to their former position or to a position of similar seniority, status, and pay without loss of retirement or other benefits, unless the employer's circumstances have so changed as to make reinstatement impossible or unreasonable. Employee must apply for reinstatement within 40 days of discharge, and cannot be terminated without cause for one year. Employees in the U.S. uniformed services, national guard, or naval militia are entitled to 17 days' unpaid leave per year for training or special exercises. Employer may not terminate employee or limit any benefits or seniority because of a temporary disability resulting from duty in the national guard or naval militia (up to 52 weeks). Employer cannot discriminate against employee because of membership in the military services.

Colorado

Colo. Rev. Stat. §§ 28-3-609, 28-3-610.5

Employees who are members of Colorado National Guard or U.S. uniformed services reserves are entitled to 15 days' unpaid leave per year for training and reinstatement to their former or a similar position with the same status, pay, and seniority. Employees called to active service in the Colorado National Guard are entitled to unlimited unpaid leave and reinstatement to their former or comparable position, with the pay, seniority, and benefits the employee would have had if not absent for service.

State Laws on Military Leave (continued)

Connecticut

Conn. Gen. Stat. Ann. §§ 27-33a, 27-34a

Members of the Connecticut National Guard ordered into active duty are entitled to the same rights and benefits guaranteed under USERRA, except those pertaining to life insurance. Employees who are active or reserve members of the state militia or national guard are entitled to take leave to attend meetings or drills that take place during regular work hours, without loss or reduction of vacation or holiday benefits. Employer may not discriminate in terms of promotion or continued employment.

Florida

Fla. Stat. Ann. §§ 250.482, 627.6692(5)(h) to (j)

Employees who are members of the Florida National Guard and are called into active duty by the governor may not be penalized for absence from work. Employees not covered by COBRA whose employment is terminated while on active duty are entitled to a new 18-month benefit period beginning when active duty or job ends, whichever is later.

Georgia

Ga. Code Ann. § 38-2-280

Members of U.S. uniformed services or Georgia National Guard called into active federal or state service are entitled to unlimited unpaid leave for active service and up to 6 months' leave in any 4-year period for service school or annual training. Employee is entitled to reinstatement with full benefits unless employer's circumstances have changed to make reinstatement impossible or unreasonable. Employee must apply for reinstatement within 90 days of discharge or within 10 days of completing school or training.

Hawaii

Haw. Rev. Stat. § 121-43

Members of the national guard are entitled to unlimited unpaid leave and reinstatement to the same or a position comparable in seniority, status, and pay. If an employee is not qualified for his or her former position because of a disability sustained during service but is qualified for another position, the employee is entitled to the position that is most similar to his or her former position. Employee cannot be terminated without cause for one year after reinstatement. Employer cannot discriminate against employee because of any obligation as a member of the national guard.

Idaho

Idaho Code §§ 46-224, 46-225, 46-407

Members of state national guard ordered to active duty by the governor may take up to one year of unpaid leave and are entitled to reinstatement to former position or a comparable position with like seniority, status, and pay. If an employee is not qualified for his or her former position because of a disability sustained during service but is qualified for any another position, the employee is entitled to the position that is most similar to his or her former position in seniority, status, and pay. Employee must apply for reinstatement within 30 days of release. Returning employees may not be fired without cause for one year. Members of the U.S. National Guard and reserves may take up to 15 days' leave per year for training without affecting the employee's right to receive normal vacation, sick leave, bonus, advancement, and other advantages of employment. Employee must give 90 days' notice of training dates.

State Laws on Military Leave (continued)

Illinois

20 Ill. Comp. Stat. §§ 1805/30.1 to 1805/30.20; 330 Ill. Comp. State. § 60/4

Members of the state national guard are entitled to unlimited leave and reinstatement with the same increases in status, seniority, and wages that were earned during the employee's military duty by employees in like positions, or to a position of like seniority, status, and pay, unless employer's circumstances have changed so that reinstatement would be unreasonable or impossible or impose an undue hardship. If employee is no longer qualified for the position because of the military service but is qualified for any other position, then the employee is entitled to the position that will provide like seniority, status, and pay. If reasonably possible, employee must give advance notice of military service. Members of the national guard must submit request for reemployment the day after finishing duty if duty lasted less than 31 days, within 14 days if duty lasted longer than 30 days, or within 90 days if duty lasted longer than 180 days. Members of the U.S. uniformed services must submit request for reemployment within 90 days. Employee can't be discharged without cause for one year.

Indiana

Ind. Code Ann. §§ 10-17-4-1 to 10-17-4-5

Members of U.S. uniformed services reserves may take up to 15 days' unpaid (or paid at employer's discretion) leave per year for training. Employee must provide evidence of dates of departure and return, and proof of completion of the training upon return. Leave does not affect vacation, sick leave, bonus, or promotion rights. Employee must be reinstated to former or a similar position with no loss of seniority or benefits.

Iowa

Iowa Code § 29A.43

Members of the U.S. National Guard, reserves, or the civil air patrol called into temporary duty are entitled to reinstatement to former or a similar position. Leave does not affect vacation, sick leave, bonuses, or other benefits. Employee must provide proof of satisfactory completion of duty and of qualifications to perform the job's duties.

Kansas

Kan. Stat. Ann. §§ 48-517, 48-222

Members of state military forces called into active duty by the state are entitled to reinstatement to the same position or a comparable position with like seniority, status, and pay. If an employee is not qualified for his or her former position because of a disability sustained during service but is qualified for any another position, the employee is entitled to the position that is most similar to his or her former position in seniority, status, and pay. Employee must report to work within 72 hours of release from duty or recovery from service-related injury or illness. In addition to unlimited leave for active duty, employees are entitled to 5 to 10 days' leave each year to attend state national guard training camp.

Kentucky

Ky. Rev. Stat. Ann. § 38.238

Members of Kentucky National Guard are entitled to unlimited unpaid leave for active duty or training and reinstatement to former position with no loss of seniority or benefits. Employer may not in any way discriminate against employee or threaten to prevent employee from enlisting in the Kentucky National Guard or active militia.

State Laws on Military Leave (continued)

Louisiana

La. Rev. Stat. Ann. §§ 29:38, 29:38.1

Employees called into active duty in any branch of the state military forces are entitled to the same leave and reinstatement rights and benefits guaranteed under USERRA. Employees on leave are entitled to the benefits offered to employees who take leave for other reasons. Employee must report to work within 72 hours of release or recovery from service-related injury or illness and cannot be fired, except for cause for one year after reinstatement. Employees in the U.S. National Guard are entitled to 15 days of paid leave annually for training. Employer cannot discriminate against employee because of any obligation as a member of the state military forces.

Maine

Me. Rev. Stat. Ann. tit. 37-B, § 342(5)

Employer may not discriminate against employee for membership or service in state military forces.

Maryland

Md. Code Ann. [Public Safety] § 13-705

Members of the state national guard and Maryland Defense Force ordered to military duty have the same leave and reinstatement rights and benefits guaranteed under USERRA.

Massachusetts

Mass. Gen. Laws ch. 149, § 52A

Employees who are members of U.S. uniformed forces reserves or the state armed forces may take up to 17 days per year for training. Leave does not affect vacation, sick leave, bonus, or promotion rights. Employee who is qualified must be reinstated to former or a similar position. Employee must give employer notice of departure and anticipated return date.

Michigan

Mich. Comp. Laws §§ 32.271 to 32.274

Members of state or U.S. uniformed services called into active state or federal duty may take unpaid leave; employee may also take unpaid leave to take a physical, enlist, be inducted, or attend training. Returning employee must generally be reinstated to former position. Employee must apply for reinstatement within 15 days of release from service. Employer may not in any way discriminate against employee or threaten to prevent employee from enlisting in the state armed forces.

Minnesota

Minn. Stat. Ann. § 192.34

Employer may not discharge employee, interfere with military service, or dissuade employee from enlisting by threatening employee's job. Applies to employees who are members of the U.S., Minnesota, or any other state military or naval forces.

Mississippi

Miss. Code Ann. § 33-1-19

Members of U.S. uniformed services and Mississippi armed forces are entitled to unpaid leave for active state duty or state training duty. If still qualified to perform job duties, employee entitled to reinstatement to previous or similar position. Employee must give evidence of completion of training.

Missouri

Mo. Rev. Stat. § 41.730

Employer may not discharge employee, interfere with employee's military service, or threaten to

State Laws on Military Leave (continued)

dissuade employee from enlisting in the state militia or U.S. armed forces.

Montana
Mont. Code Ann. §§ 10-1-1005, 10-1-1006, 10-1-1007

Members of the state-organized militia called to active service during a state-declared disaster or emergency are entitled to unpaid leave for duration of service. Leave may not be deducted from sick leave, vacation, or other leave, although employee may voluntarily use that leave. Returning employee is entitled to reinstatement to same or similar position with the same seniority, status, pay, health insurance, pension, and other benefits. Employer may not in any way discriminate against employee or dissuade employee from enlisting.

Nebraska
Neb. Rev. Stat. § 55-161

Employees who are members of the Nebraska National Guard and are called into active state duty have the same leave and reinstatement rights and benefits guaranteed under USERRA.

Nevada
Nev. Rev. Stat. Ann. §§ 412.139, 412.606

Employers may not discriminate against members of the Nevada National Guard and may not discharge any employee because he or she is called into active service.

New Hampshire
N.H. Rev. Stat. Ann. §§ 110-B:65(II), 110-C:1

Members of the state national guard or militia called to active duty have the same leave and reinstatement rights and benefits guaranteed under USERRA. Employer may not discriminate against employee because of connection or service with national guard; may not dissuade employee from enlisting by threatening job.

New Jersey
N.J. Stat. Ann. § 38:23C-20

An employee is entitled to take unpaid leave for active service in the U.S. or state military services. Upon return, employee must be reinstated to the same or a similar position, unless employer's circumstances have changed to make reinstatement impossible or unreasonable. Employee must apply for reinstatement within 90 days of release from service. Employee may not be fired without cause for one year after returning from service. Employee is also entitled to take up to 3 months' leave in 4-year period for training or assemblies relating to military service. Employee must apply for reinstatement within 10 days.

New Mexico
N.M. Stat. Ann. §§ 28-15-1, 28-15-2

Members of the state national guard, militia or U.S. armed forces may take unpaid leave for service. Employee who is still qualified must be reinstated in former or similar position with no loss of status or seniority. Employee may not be fired without cause for one year after returning from service. Employee must request reinstatement within 90 days. Employer may not discriminate against or discharge employee because of membership in the national guard; may not prevent employee from performing military service.

New York
N.Y. Mil. Law § 317

Members of the state military forces called up by governor and members of U.S. uniformed services are entitled to unpaid leave for active service; reserve drills or annual training; service school; initial full-time or active duty training.

State Laws on Military Leave (continued)

Returning employee is entitled to reinstatement to previous position, or to one with the same seniority, status, and pay, unless the employer's circumstances have changed and reemployment is impossible or unreasonable. Employee must apply for reinstatement within 90 days of discharge from active service, 10 days of completing school or annual training, or 60 days of completing initial training.

North Carolina
N.C. Gen. Stat. §§ 127A-201, 127A-201.1, 127B-14

Members of the North Carolina National Guard called to active duty by the governor are entitled to take unpaid leave. Returning employee must be restored to previous position or one of comparable seniority, status, and salary; if no longer qualified, employee must be placed in another position with appropriate seniority, status, and salary, unless the employer's circumstances now make reinstatement unreasonable. Employee must apply for reinstatement, in writing, within 5 days of release or recovery from service-related injury or illness. Employer may not discriminate against or discharge an employee because of membership in the national guard or discharge an employee called up for emergency military service.

Ohio
Ohio Rev. Code Ann. §§ 5903.01, 5903.02

Employees who are members of the Ohio militia or national guard called for active duty or training; members of the commissioned public health service corps; or any other uniformed service called up in time of war or emergency have the same leave and reinstatement rights and benefits guaranteed under USERRA.

Oklahoma
Okla. Stat. Ann. tit. 44, §§ 71, 208.1

Employees called to state active duty in the Oklahoma National Guard have the same leave and reinstatement rights and benefits guaranteed under USERRA. Members of the national guard may take leave to attend state national guard training, drills, or ceremony.

Oregon
Or. Rev. Stat. § 399.230

Members of state organized militia called into active duty may take unpaid leave for term of service. Returning employee is entitled to reinstatement with no loss of seniority or benefits including sick leave, vacation, or service credits under a pension plan. Employee must return to work within 7 calendar days of release from service.

Pennsylvania
51 Pa. Cons. Stat. Ann. §§ 7302 to 7309

Employee who enlists or is drafted during a time of war or emergency called by the president or governor is entitled to unpaid military leave along with reservists called into active duty. Returning employee must be reinstated to same or similar position with same status, seniority, and pay. Employers may not discharge or discriminate against any employee because of membership or service in the military. Employees called to active duty are entitled to 30 days' health insurance continuation benefits at no cost.

Rhode Island
R.I. Gen. Laws §§ 30-11-2 to 30-11-9, 30-21-1

Members of state military forces and national guard members on state active duty have the same leave and reinstatement rights and benefits

State Laws on Military Leave (continued)

guaranteed under USERRA. Members of the national guard are entitled to unpaid leave for training and are entitled to reinstatement with the same status, pay, and seniority. Employees in the U.S. armed forces are entitled to reinstatement to the same position or a position with similar seniority, status, and pay unless the employer's circumstances make reinstatement impossible or unreasonable. Employee must request reinstatement within 40 days. Employer may not discriminate against or discharge employee because of membership in the military, interfere with employee's military service, or dissuade employee from enlisting by threatening employee's job.

South Carolina

S.C. Code Ann. §§ 25-1-2310 to 25-1-2340

Members of the South Carolina National Guard and State Guard called to state duty by the governor are entitled to unpaid leave for service. Returning employee must be reinstated to previous position or one with same seniority, status, and salary; if no longer qualified, must be given another position, unless employer's circumstances make reinstatement unreasonable. Employee must apply for reinstatement in writing, within 5 days of release from service or related hospitalization.

South Dakota

S.D. Codified Laws Ann. § 33-17-15.1

Members of the South Dakota National Guard ordered to active duty by the governor or president have the same leave and reinstatement rights and benefits guaranteed under USERRA.

Tennessee

Tenn. Code Ann. § 58-1-604

Employer may not refuse to hire or terminate an employee because of national guard membership or because employee is absent for a required drill or annual training.

Texas

Tex. Gov't. Code Ann. § 431.006

Members of the state military forces called to active duty or training are entitled to unpaid leave. Returning employee is entitled to reinstatement to the same position with no loss of time, efficiency rating, vacation, or benefits unless employer's circumstances have changed so that reemployment is impossible or unreasonable.

Utah

Utah Code Ann. § 39-1-36

Members of U.S. armed forces reserves who are called to active duty, active duty for training, inactive duty training, or state active duty may take up to 5 years of unpaid leave. Upon return, employee is entitled to reinstatement to previous employment with same seniority, status, pay, and vacation rights. Employer may not discriminate against an employee based on membership in armed forces reserves.

Vermont

Vt. Stat. Ann. tit. 21, § 491

Employees who are members of an organized unit of the national guard or the ready reserves and are called to active state duty or training with the U.S. uniformed services are entitled to unpaid leave. Employee must give 30 days' notice for U.S. training and as much notice as is practical for state duty. If still qualified, returning employee must be reinstated to former position with the same status, pay, and seniority, including any seniority that accrued during the leave of

State Laws on Military Leave (continued)

absence. Employer may not discriminate against an employee who is a member or an applicant for membership in the state or federal national guard.

Virginia
Va. Code Ann. §§ 44-93.2 to 44-93.4

Members of the Virginia National Guard, Virginia State Defense Force, or naval militia called to active state duty by the governor are entitled to take unpaid leave and may not be required to use vacation or any other accrued leave (unless employee wishes). Returning employee must be reinstated to previous position or one with same seniority, status, and pay if position no longer exists, then to a comparable position unless employer's circumstances would make reemployment unreasonable. Employee must apply for reinstatement, in writing, within 5 days of release from service or related hospitalization. Employer cannot discriminate against employees because of membership in state military service.

Washington
Wash. Rev. Code Ann. §§ 73.16.032 to 73.16.035

Members of the uniformed services are entitled to reinstatement to the same position or a position of like seniority, status and pay; unless the employer's circumstances have changed so that reinstatement is impossible or unreasonable or would be an undue hardship. If the employee is no longer qualified for the position because of a disability sustained during service in the uniformed services, but is qualified for any another position, the employee is entitled to a position with the same seniority, status, and pay. Employer cannot discriminate against employees because of membership in state military service.

West Virginia
W.Va. Code § 15-1F-8

Employees who are members of the organized militia in active state service have the same leave and reinstatement rights and benefits guaranteed under USERRA.

Wisconsin
Wis. Stat. Ann. § 21.79

Employees who enlist, are inducted, or are called to serve in the uniformed services, or civilians requested to perform national defense work during an officially proclaimed emergency, may take up to 4 years' leave for military service and/or training unless period of service is extended by law. Returning employee is entitled to reinstatement to previous position, or to one with the same seniority, benefits, and pay, unless the employee is no longer qualified or the employer's circumstances have changed and reemployment is impossible or unreasonable. Employee must apply for reinstatement within 90 days of release or 6 months of release from service-related hospitalization and must present evidence of completion of training or service. Employee may not be fired without cause for one year after returning from service.

Wyoming
Wyo. Stat. §§ 19-11-103, 19-11-110,19-11-111

Employees who are members of, or who apply for membership in, the uniformed services; employees who report for active duty, training, or a qualifying physical exam; or who are called to state duty by the governor, may take up to 5 years' leave of absence. Employee must give advanced notice of service. Employee may use vacation or any other accrued leave but is not required to do so. Returning employee is entitled to reemployment with the same seniority, rights, and benefits, plus any additional seniority and benefits that employee would have earned if there had been no absence, unless employer's circumstances have changed so that reemployment is impossible or unreasonable or would impose an undue hardship. Employee is

entitled to complete any training program that would have been available to employee's former position during period of absence. Employee may not be terminated without cause for one year after returning to work. Employer cannot discriminate against applicant or member of the uniformed services.

Current as of February 2007

Payroll Withholding and Deductions

Since the end of the Depression of the 1930s, the right and responsibility of employers to withhold a portion of your pay has become a virtually undisputed part of American culture. The laws that created the income tax and Social Security programs, for which funds are withheld, typically authorize payroll withholding to finance those programs.

But a growing number of additional deductions are now also authorized.

What Can Be Deducted or Withheld

In addition to Social Security and local, state, and federal taxes, an employer may also make several other deductions from minimum wages: costs of meals, housing and transportation, loans, debts owed the employer, child support and alimony, payroll savings plans, and insurance premiums. As in most other workplace laws, there are exceptions to these rules. There are often

limitations on how much may be withheld or deducted from a paycheck.

Meals, Housing, and Transportation

Employers may legally deduct from an employee's paycheck the "reasonable cost or fair value" of meals, housing, fuel, and transportation to and from work.

But to deduct any of these amounts from a paycheck, an employer must show that it customarily paid these expenses and that:

- they were for the employee's benefit
- the employee was told in advance about the deductions, and
- the employee voluntarily accepted the meals and other accommodations against minimum wage.

EXAMPLE: Jane accepted a job as a guide at a remote wilderness ski resort after the employer told her that the job paid $10 per hour plus room and board. But when she got her first paycheck, Jane saw that charges for housing and meals had been deducted from her pay. And the charges were so high that she really was earning only $3 per hour, far less than the minimum wage.

Asking around among other employees at the resort, Jane learned that the exorbitant meal charges were billed to her payroll account by a catering service owned by the resort owner's brother-in-law. Jane's employer had violated several of the FLSA's rules governing noncash compensation, so Jane filed a complaint with the U.S. Labor Department's Wage and Hour Division.

Loans

An employer that has loaned you money can withhold money from your pay to satisfy that loan. However, it is illegal to make any such deduction if it would reduce your pay to below the minimum wage.

EXAMPLE: Bruce works 40 hours a week at $8 per hour making deliveries for an auto parts store. He is paid each Saturday. One Monday morning, the battery in his car went dead. His employer authorized Bruce to replace his car's battery with a new one out of the store's stock—if he agreed that the price of the new battery, $100, would be deducted from his pay.

However, it took three weeks for the store to be fully paid for the battery. Under the FLSA, Bruce's employer could not deduct an amount during any week that would drop Bruce's pay rate to below the required minimum hourly wage x 40 hours.

Additional Guidance on Payroll Withholding

The Internal Revenue Service rules for payroll withholding and reporting vary greatly among the legal categories of work: employee, statutory employee, statutory nonemployee, and independent contractor. (See "The Fair Labor Standards Act," above.)

You can obtain a detailed explanation of those rules free by calling the IRS forms distribution center at 800-829-3676 and requesting Publication 15-A, entitled *Employer's Supplemental Tax Guide.* This booklet is also available at your local IRS office and can be downloaded from the agency's website at www.irs.gov. The guide provides a thorough employers'-eye view of requirements for classifying workers and withholding required.

State and local payroll withholding taxes usually parallel the IRS rules, but the taxing authorities in your state and city should be able to provide you with publications outlining their payroll withholding rules.

Debts and Wage Garnishments

If you owe someone money and do not pay, that person might sue you and obtain a court judgment against you. If you do not pay the judgment, the creditor may try to collect by taking a portion of your paycheck until the judgment is paid in full. This is called a wage attachment or wage garnishment. Except in a few situations—student loans, child support, alimony, and taxes, which are all discussed below—a creditor must sue you and obtain a court judgment before he or she can garnish your wages.

A wage garnishment works simply. A creditor who has obtained a judgment against you delivers a copy of it to a sheriff or marshal, who in turn sends a copy to your employer. Your employer must immediately:

- notify you of the garnishment
- begin withholding a portion of your wages, and
- give you information on how you can protest the garnishment.

In most states, the employer can also charge you a modest fee to cover the costs of garnishing your wages. (See the chart below.)

Protesting is straightforward. You file a paper with the court and obtain a hearing date. At the hearing, you can present evidence showing that your expenses are very high and that you need all of your paycheck to live on. The judge has the discretion to terminate the wage garnishment or let it remain.

A federal law, the Consumer Credit Protection Act (15 U.S.C. §§ 1673 and following), prohibits judgment creditors from taking more than 25% of your net earnings through a wage garnishment to satisfy a debt. A few states offer greater protection, however, limiting judgment creditors to a lower percentage of your wages.

The Consumer Credit Protection Act also prohibits your employer from firing you because your wages are garnished to satisfy a single debt. If two judgment creditors garnish your wages or one judgment creditor garnishes your wages to pay two different judgments, however, you can be fired. Again, some state laws offer employees stronger job protection. In Washington, for example, an employer cannot fire you unless your wages are garnished by three different creditors or to satisfy three different judgments within a year.

RESOURCE

For more information on debts, getting sued, and wage garnishments, see *Solve Your Money Troubles: Get Debt Collectors Off Your Back & Regain Financial Freedom*, by Robin Leonard (Nolo).

There are several types of statutes that prohibit employers from retaliating against an employee for being subject to a wage garnishment. (See the chart below.) They differ in how many garnishments an employee is allowed each year without retaliation.

Most state laws have a general provision protecting employees who have their wages garnished. Some states prohibit retaliation if the employee has one garnishment per year; some laws apply to more than one garnishment. To heap on a little legal intrigue, many state statutes simply do not specify whether the protection extends to one garnishment per year or to multiple garnishments for one debt or to something else. If you run up against this confusion, contact your state's consumer protection agency for help.

Another type of anti-retribution for wage garnishment statute is one that applies to cases in which income is withheld to satisfy child support obligations. (See also "Child Support, Medical Support, and Alimony," below.) Employers may not fire employees merely because they are subject to this type of order, regardless of the quantity of garnishments.

Of course, none of these statutes prohibit firing for just cause. They only prohibit firing an employee solely because of the wage garnishment.

! **CAUTION**

Additional laws may apply. If the chart below indicates that your state has no statute, this means there is no law that gives employees more protection than the Consumer Credit Protection Act. However, there may be a state administrative regulation or local ordinance that does control. Call your state labor department for more information. (See the Appendix for contact details.)

Student Loans

The federal Emergency Unemployment Compensation Act of 1991 extended unemployment insurance for Americans who are out of work. (20 U.S.C. § 1095a.) A 2006 amendment to that bill authorizes the U.S. Department of Education or any agency trying to collect a student loan on behalf of the Department of Education to garnish up to 15% of a former student's net pay if he or she is in default on a student loan.

The Department of Education does not have to sue you before garnishing your wages. But at least 30 days before the garnishment is set to begin, you must be notified in writing of:

- the amount the Department believes you owe

- how you can obtain a copy of records relating to the loan
- how to enter into a voluntary repayment schedule, and
- how to request a hearing on the proposed garnishment.

The law includes only one specific ground upon which you can object to the garnishment: that you returned to work within the past 12 months after having been fired or laid off.

Child Support, Medical Support, and Alimony

The federal Family Support Act of 1988 (102 Stat. § 2343) requires that all new or modified child support orders include an automatic wage withholding order. If child support is combined with alimony and paid as family support, the wage withholding applies to the payment. It is not required for orders of alimony only.

In an automatic wage withholding order, a court orders you to pay child support; then the court or your child's other parent sends a copy of the order to your employer. At each pay period, your employer withholds a portion of your pay and sends it on to the parent who has custody. Currently, about $23 billion a year in child support payments are collected through income withholding by employers. In addition, medical support orders, which require noncustodial parents to include their children under their health insurance coverage, are established and enforced by state child support enforcement agencies, if necessary. A National Medical

Support Notice, modeled on the standard income withholding form, works the same way as child support orders to facilitate making the health insurance deductions from paychecks.

In most states where there is not an automatic wage attachment, employers must withhold wages if you are one month delinquent in paying support. But an employer cannot discipline, fire, or refuse to hire you because your pay is subject to a child support wage withholding order. If an employer does discriminate against you, the employer can be fined by the state. (See the chart above for specific state law provisions.) Federal law also prohibits employers from firing, disciplining, or refusing to hire someone because he or she is subject to wage withholding to pay child support.

Back Taxes

If you owe the IRS and do not pay, the agency can grab most—but not all—of your wages. The amount that you get to keep is determined by the number of your dependents and the standard tax deduction to which you are entitled.

If the IRS wants your wages, it sends a wage levy notice to your employer, who must immediately give you a copy. On the back of the notice is an exemption claim form. You should fill out, sign, and return this simple form to the IRS office that issued it within three days after you receive it. Your employer should not pay anything to the IRS until you have your chance to file your exemption claim.

If you do not file the claim form, your employer must pay you a minimal amount per week, based on your filing status and exemptions claimed, and give the rest to the IRS. An employer who ignores the IRS wage levy notice and pays you anyway is liable to the IRS for whatever amounts were wrongly paid. Once the wage levy takes effect, it continues until either the taxes are paid in full or the collection period expires—ten years from when the taxes are assessed.

Most state and some municipal taxing authorities also have the power to seize a portion of your wages—and some act even more quickly than the IRS does when you owe back taxes. State laws vary, however, as to the maximum amount of wages that the state can take. In California, for example, the state taxing authority cannot take more than 25% of your net pay.

What Cannot Be Deducted or Withheld

State laws generally control what may be deducted or withheld from an individual paycheck. Commonly, only a few things are off-limits for an employer to deduct:

- the value of time taken for meal periods (see "Meal and Rest Break Periods," above)
- the cost of broken merchandise
- tools and materials used on the job
- required uniforms, and
- cash register shortages and losses due to theft.

State Laws on Administering Wage Garnishments

This chart describes state laws for administering wage garnishments, including permissible fees employers may charge to administer garnishments, as well as laws prohibiting employer discrimination or retaliation because of wage garnishments. Other state statutes may apply.

Alabama

Ala. Code §§ 15-18-142, 15-18-143, 30-3-70, 30-3-71

Applies to: Child support garnishments and restitution to victims of crime.

Employer's fee: $2 per payment (child support only).

Employer penalties: Contempt of court. For garnishments for restitution for crime victims, employer may not discharge employee solely because of garnishment, and in addition to contempt of court, may be required to reinstate the employee.

Alaska

Alaska Stat. § 25.27.062

Applies to: Child support garnishments only.

Employer's fee: $5 per payment.

Employer penalties: If employer discharges, disciplines, or refuses to hire someone because of having child support withholding orders, may be fined up to $1,000 and be required to reinstate or provide restitution to the employee.

Arizona

Ariz. Rev. Stat. §§ 23-722.02, 25-505.01

Applies to: Child support or spousal maintenance garnishment.

Employee protections that exceed federal law: Newly hired, rehired, or returning employees may be asked to disclose any child support wage assignment orders but may not be discriminated against, fired, or disciplined because of having them.

Employer penalties: Employer who refuses to hire, discharges, or disciplines employee because of having child support withholding orders is subject to contempt of court and fines. Employer who fails without good cause to comply with income withholding order may be liable for amounts not paid, reasonable attorney fees and costs, and may be subject to contempt of court. Employee wrongfully refused employment, wrongfully discharged, or otherwise disciplined may recover damages and may be reinstated, if appropriate, and be entitled to recovery of attorney fees and costs.

Arkansas

Ark. Code Ann. §§ 9-14-226, 9-14-227, 9-14-515

Applies to: Child support garnishments and child's health care coverage.

Employer's fee: $2.50 per payment.

Employer penalties: If employer fails to withhold, contempt of court or fine of up to $50 per day.

California

Cal. Fam. Code §§ 5235, 5241; Lab. Code § 2929

Employee protections that exceed federal law: Employee may not be fired or discriminated against for being threatened with a wage garnishment.

Employer's fee: $1.50 per payment.

Employer penalties: In child support cases, if employer willfully fails to withhold, can be held in contempt of court. If employer does not withhold or does not forward payments, liable for amount of payments plus interest.

State Laws on Administering Wage Garnishments (continued)

Colorado

Colo. Rev. Stat. §§ 5-5-107, 13-54.5-110, 14-14-111.5(4), (16.7), 14-14-112 (4), 26-13-121.5

Employee protections that exceed federal law: Employee may not be discharged because a consumer creditor garnishes or attempts to garnish wages (no limit on number of garnishments).

Employer's fee: Up to $5 per month for child support garnishments.

Employer penalties: Liable to discharged employee for up to six weeks' wages, reinstatement, court costs, and attorney fees (applies to general wage garnishments, child support, and child national medical support order and health insurance withholding).

Connecticut

Conn. Gen. Stat. Ann. §§ 46b-88, 52-361a(j), 52-362(j)

Employee protections that exceed federal law: Employee may not be disciplined, suspended, or discharged for having wages garnished unless there are more than seven within a calendar year.

Employer penalties, general wage garnishment: Liable to employee for all wages and benefits from time of discipline or discharge to reinstatement.

Employer penalties, child support withholding: Fine of up to $1,000 for discharging, refusing to employ, disciplining, or discriminating against an employee because of a withholding order. Also applies to child health care coverage.

Delaware

Del. Code Ann. tit. 10, § 3509; tit. 13, § 513(b)(10)

Employee protections that exceed federal law: Employer may not dismiss employee because

employer was summoned to appear in court in a garnishment proceeding. Employer can only withhold 15% of employee's wages.

Employer penalties, child support withholding: For failing to comply with law or terminating employee, fine of up to $1,000 or up to 90 days' imprisonment, or both, for first offense; for each subsequent offense, fine of up to $5,000 or up to one year's imprisonment, or both. For refusing to employ because of a support withholding order, fine of up to $200 for each offense. Corporations are subject to criminal charges. Also applies to child health care coverage and spousal support.

District of Columbia

D.C. Code Ann. §§ 16-573, 46-212(d), 46-219

Employee protections that exceed federal law: In any month, employer can not withhold more than 10% of gross wages until at least $200 of the employee's wages have been withheld that month; can not collect more than 20% until at least $500 has been withheld. Employee may not be discharged because a creditor garnishes or attempts to garnish wages (no limit on number of garnishments).

Employer's fee: $2 for each child support payment.

Employer penalties, child support withholding: Employer who discharges, refuses to employ, takes disciplinary action against, or otherwise discriminates against employee is subject to a penalty of up to $10,000, which employee may use to offset support obligations. Any adverse action employer takes within 90 days of receiving notice to withhold wages is presumed to be in violation of law.

State Laws on Administering Wage Garnishments (continued)

Florida
Fla. Stat. Ann. §§ 61.12(2), 61.1301(2)(e)

Applies to: Child or spousal support garnishments.

Employee protections that exceed federal law: Employer may not fire, refuse to hire, or discipline employee who has wages garnished for child or spousal support.

Employer's fee: $5 for first deduction, $2 for each subsequent deduction.

Employer penalties: Fine of up to $250 for first violation and up to $500 for each subsequent violation; employer may also be held in contempt of court.

Georgia
Ga. Code Ann. § 19-11-20

Applies to: Child support garnishments.

Employer's fee: $25 for first child support deduction, $3 for each subsequent deduction.

Hawaii
Haw. Rev. Stat. §§ 378-2(5), 378-32(1), 571-52(b), 576E-16(5), 710-1077

Employee protections that exceed federal law: Employer may not fire, suspend, or discriminate against employee for having wages garnished or because employer was summoned as a garnishee in an action or proceeding where the employee is the debtor. Employer who refuses to hire or discharges an employee who has wages garnished for child support is guilty of unlawful discrimination.

Employer's fee: $2 for each deduction.

Employer penalties, child support withholding: Employer who discriminates against employee is guilty of criminal contempt of court.

Idaho
Idaho Code §§ 28-45-105, 32-1210(7), 32-1211

Employee protections that exceed federal law: Employee may not be discharged because a consumer creditor garnishes or attempts to garnish wages (no limit on number of garnishments). In child support cases, garnishment plus the employer's processing fee can not exceed 50% of the employee's disposable income.

Employer's fee: $5 for each deduction (child support).

Employer penalties, child support withholding: For discharging, disciplining, or refusing to hire an employee: liable for double lost wages and other damages, costs and attorneys' fees; and may be fined up to $300 and ordered to hire or reinstate employee.

Illinois
735 Ill. Comp. Stat. §§ 5/12-818, 5/12-814; 740 Ill. Comp. Stat. § 170/10; 750 Ill. Comp. Stat. §§ 28/35, 28/50

Employee protections that exceed federal law: May not discharge or suspend employee for any indebtedness or for one wage garnishment.

Employer's fee: $12 or 2% of entire amount withheld, whichever is greater, for general wage garnishment; $5 per month for child support.

Employer penalties, general wage garnishment: Discharging or suspending employee because wage garnishment for one indebtedness or one wage garnishment is a class A misdemeanor, which carries a fine of up to $2,500 and imprisonment for up to one year.

Employer penalties, child support withholding: Liable for amount of wages not withheld or paid; if employer discriminated

State Laws on Administering Wage Garnishments (continued)

against employee, may be fined up to $200 and ordered to hire or reinstate employee.

Indiana

Ind. Code Ann. §§ 24-4.5-5-105 to 24-4.5-5-106

Employee protections that exceed federal law: Employer may not discharge employee because creditor has garnished or attempted to garnish wages (no limit on number of garnishments).

Employer's fee: $12 or 3% of entire amount withheld, whichever is greater, for general wage garnishment, 50% paid by employee and 50% by creditor; $2 per deduction for child support.

Iowa

Iowa Code § 252D.17

Employer's fee: $2 for each child support deduction.

Employer penalties, child support withholding: Employer who fails to withhold or remit payment for the first offense is guilty of a misdemeanor, and a serious misdemeanor for each subsequent offense, and in either case may have to pay costs, interest, and attorneys' fees for collection. An employer who discharges, refuses to employ, or takes disciplinary action against an employee because of a wage garnishment is guilty of a simple misdemeanor and may be subject to contempt of court proceedings.

Kansas

Kan. Stat. Ann. §§ 23-4,108(e),(j), 60-2311

Employer's fee: $5 per pay period or $10 per month for income withheld for child or spousal support, whichever is less.

Employer penalties, general wage garnishment: Illegal to discharge employee because of wage garnishment of any type.

Employer penalties, child support withholding: For not withholding and remitting payments, or discharging, refusing to employ, or taking disciplinary action against an employee because of garnishment, subject to a fine of up to $500.

Kentucky

Ky. Rev. Stat. Ann. §§ 405.465, 405.991

Employer's fee: $1 per payment for child or spousal support withholding.

Employer penalties, child support withholding: Fine of up to $500 or up to one year in the county jail, or both.

Louisiana

La. Rev. Stat. Ann. §§ 13:3921(B), 23:731

Employee protections that exceed federal law: Employee can not be discharged or denied employment because of a single wage garnishment. Employee may not be fired for a wage garnishment unless there are three or more garnishments for unrelated debts in a two-year period. However, employee may not be fired if garnishment resulted from an accident or illness that caused employee to miss ten or more consecutive workdays.

Employer's fee: $3 per pay period for as long as garnishment is in effect

Employer penalties, general wage garnishment: Discharged employee is entitled to reinstatement and back pay, but not damages. A person denied employment solely because of garnishment is entitled to reasonable damages.

Maine

Me. Rev. Stat. Ann. tit. 9-A, § 5-106; tit. 14, § 3127-B; tit. 19-A, §§ 2306, 2652, 2662

State Laws on Administering Wage Garnishments (continued)

Employee protections that exceed federal law: Employee can not be fired because creditor garnishes or attempts to garnish wages (number of garnishments not specified).

Employer's fee: $1 per check issued to creditor for general wage garnishment; $2 per week for child support withholding payment.

Employer penalties, child support withholding: For knowingly failing to withhold or remit payments, fine of up to $100. For discharging, refusing to employ, or disciplining employee, fine of up to $5,000; liable for actual and punitive damages plus attorneys' fees and court costs.

Maryland

Md. Code Ann. [Com. Law] § 15-606; [Fam. Law] § 10-129

Employee protections that exceed federal law: Employer cannot discharge employee for having one garnishment in a single year.

Employer's fee: $2 per child support withholding order.

Employer penalties, general wage garnishment: For discharging employee, subject to $10,000 fine and imprisonment of up to one year, or both.

Employer penalties, child support withholding: Employer who fails to withhold or remit payments is liable for amount of wages not withheld or paid. Employer may not use garnishment as reason to discriminate, discharge, refuse to hire, or refuse to promote employee.

Massachusetts

Mass. Gen. Laws ch. 119A, § 12(f)

Applies to: Child and spousal support garnishments only.

Employee protections that exceed federal law: Employer may not discipline, suspend, discharge, or refuse to hire an employee because of having child support withholding orders.

Employer's fee: $1 per pay period.

Employer penalties, child support withholding: For violating employee rights, liable for lost wages and benefits plus a fine of up to $1,000; for failing to comply with a withholding order, liable for amount not withheld or fine of up to $500, whichever is greater.

Michigan

Mich. Comp. Laws §§ 552.623, 600.4012, 600.4015

Employee protections that exceed federal law: Employer may not refuse to hire, discharge, take disciplinary action against, or impose a penalty against an employee because of a wage garnishment, including using the fact that the employee had an occupational, recreational, or driver's license suspended under child support laws, unless license is legally required for employee's job.

Employer's fee: $6 per writ of garnishment.

Employer penalties, general wage garnishment: Must reinstate employee and pay back all lost wages and benefits.

Employer penalties, child support withholding: Guilty of a misdemeanor punishable by a fine of up to $500; must reinstate employee with back pay.

Minnesota

Minn. Stat. Ann. §§ 518A.53, 571.927

Employee protections that exceed federal law: Employer shall not discharge or otherwise discipline an employee as a result of an earnings garnishment (no number specified).

State Laws on Administering Wage Garnishments (continued)

Employer's fee: $1 for each child support payment.

Employer penalties, general wage garnishment: Employee entitled to reinstatement and employer liable to employee for double wages lost.

Employer penalties, child support withholding: For intentional failure to withhold or remit funds, liable for amount not paid, plus interest from the time payments were due, and attorneys' fees, and may be subject to sanctions for contempt; for violating employee protection laws, liable for double lost wages and subject to a fine of no less than $500.

Mississippi

Miss. Code Ann. § 93-11-111

Applies to: Child support garnishments.

Employee protections that exceed federal law: Employer may not discharge, discipline, refuse to hire or otherwise penalize the employee because of the duty to withhold income (number of garnishments not specified).

Employer's fee: $2 per payment inside Mississippi. If support payments administered by state agency, additional $15 per month (which employer then pays to the agency).

Missouri

Mo. Rev. Stat. §§ 452.350, 454.505(3),(10), 525.230

Employer's fee: 2% or $8, whichever is greater, for general wage garnishment; up to $6 per month per payment for child support withholding.

Employer penalties, child support withholding: For failing to withhold or remit payments, employer is liable for support not withheld; may be fined up to $500 for not complying with a court order to correct or stop unlawful action.

For discharging, refusing to hire, or disciplining an employee because of garnishment, liable for fine of up to $150, order to reinstate employee, and payment of back wages, costs, and attorneys' fees, plus support which should have been withheld during time employee was wrongfully discharged. (Discharge within 30 days of receipt of support order is presumed wrongful.)

Montana

Mont. Code Ann. §§ 39-2-302, 40-5-416(c), 40-5-422

Employee protections that exceed federal law: Employee may not be discharged or laid off because of wage garnishment (number not specified).

Employer's fee: $5 per month for child support payments.

Employer penalties, child support withholding: If employer discharges, disciplines, or refuses to hire employee because of garnishment, subject to a fine of $150 to $500; must reinstate employee with full restitution, including back pay.

Nebraska

Neb. Rev. Stat. §§ 42-364.01, 42-364.12, 43-1725

Employee protections that exceed federal law: Employer may not fire, demote, discipline, or penalize employee because of any proceeding to collect child support.

Employer's fee: $2.50 per month for child support payments.

Employer penalties, child support withholding: For failing to remit payments, liable for entire amount owed plus interest, costs, and attorneys' fees; for violating employee rights, liable for damages plus interest, costs, and attorneys' fees. If support payments administered by the state, may also be liable for a fine of up to $500

State Laws on Administering Wage Garnishments (continued)

and may be required to make full restitution, including reinstatement and back pay.

Nevada

Nev. Rev. Stat. Ann. §§ 31.296, 31.298, 31A.090, 31A.120

Employee protections that exceed federal law: It is unlawful to discharge, discipline, or refuse to hire an employee because employer required to withhold earnings because of a garnishment (no number specified).

Employer's fee: $3 per pay period up to $12 per month for general wage garnishments; $3 per child support payment withheld.

Employer penalties, general wage garnishment: For willfully refusing to withhold payments or misrepresenting employee's income, must pay entire amount not withheld; may be liable to employee for punitive damages of up to $1,000 per pay period.

Employer penalties, child support withholding: For violating employee rights, employer must reinstate employee and is liable for any payments not withheld plus a $1,000 fine; if employee wins in court, employer liable for not less than $2,500, plus costs and attorney's fees. For willfully refusing to withhold payments or misrepresenting employee's income, must pay entire amount not withheld; may be liable to person to whom support owed for punitive damages of up to $1,000 per pay period.

New Hampshire

N.H. Rev. Stat. Ann. §§ 161-H:5, 458-B:6

Applies to: Child support and child's medical support garnishments.

Employer's fee: $1 per support payment.

Employer penalties, child support withholding: For discharging, refusing to employ, or taking any

disciplinary action against an employee, guilty of a misdemeanor with a fine of up to $1,000; for failing to withhold payments, a fine up to $100 per pay period.

New Jersey

N.J. Stat. Ann. §§ 2A:17-56.11, 2A:17-56.12, 2C:40A-3

Employee protections that exceed federal law: Employer may take no disciplinary action against employee because of wage garnishment (no number specified).

Employer's fee: $1 per garnishment (child support).

Employer penalties, general wage garnishment: For discharging or disciplining an employee because of a wage garnishment, guilty of a disorderly person offense; must rehire and compensate employee for damages.

Employer penalties, child support withholding: For discharging, failing to employ, or disciplining an employee because of a wage garnishment, employer liable for a fine and civil damages and must reinstate employee; if employee wins in court, liable for attorneys' fees, twofold compensatory damages, including court costs, and lost income. For failing to withhold child support payments, liable for a fine or for amount not withheld as well as interest and attorneys' fees. For failing to withhold payments under a medical support order, liable for children's medical expenses and any other amount that should have been withheld.

New Mexico

N.M. Stat. Ann. §§ 40-4A-8, 40-4A-11

Applies to: Child support garnishments.

Employer's fee: $1 per payment.

Employee protections that exceed federal law: Employer may not discharge, discipline, or

State Laws on Administering Wage Garnishments (continued)

otherwise penalize the employee because of the duty to withhold income under a child or spousal support order (number of garnishments not specified).

Employer penalties, child support withholding: Employer who willfully fails to pay liable to a fine for total amount not withheld. For discharging, disciplining, refusing to hire, or otherwise penalizing an employee because of a wage garnishment, liable for reinstatement and damages; subject to action for contempt of court.

New York

N.Y. C.P.L.R. Law §§ 5241, 5252

Employee protections that exceed federal law: Current employee may not be fired, laid off, refused promotion, or disciplined, and prospective employee may not be refused employment because of one or more current, past, or pending garnishments.

Employer penalties, general wage garnishment: Liable to employee for reinstatement and up to six weeks' lost wages, plus fine of up to $500 for first offense and up to $1,000 for each additional offense. May also be liable for civil contempt of court.

Employer penalties, child support withholding: Liable to employee for reinstatement and up to six weeks' lost wages, plus fine of up to $500 for first offense and up to $1,000 for each additional offense.

North Carolina

N.C. Gen. Stat. §§ 110-136(c),(e), 110-136.8, 110-136.13, 131E-49, 131E-50

Employee protections that exceed federal law: Employee may not be discharged or disciplined for having wages garnished to pay a public hospital debt. An employer who violates this provision

may be liable for damages, including back pay, reinstatement, costs, and attorneys' fees.

Employer's fee: $1 per child support payment; $1 per payment to public hospital.

Employer penalties, child support withholding: If employer fails to employ, discharges, or takes disciplinary action against employee because of garnishment, liable to employee for reinstatement and reasonable damages. May also be liable for a fine of $100 for first offense; $500 for second; and $1,000 for third (also applies to child medical support orders). For violating the terms of an order, may be liable for contempt.

North Dakota

N.D. Cent. Code §§ 14-09-08.11, 14-09-09.3, 14-09-09.6, 32-09.1-18

Employee protections that exceed federal law: Employee may not be discharged because of wage garnishment (no number specified).

Employer's fee: $3 per month for child support (voluntary garnishment).

Employer penalties, general wage garnishment: For discharging employee because of a garnishment, liable for twice lost wages and reinstatement.

Employer penalties, child support withholding: For failing or refusing to deliver income, may be punished for contempt of court. May be liable for payment as well as costs, interests, and attorneys' fees. If employer fails or refuses to deliver income for seven days, may result in late fees of $25 to $75 per business day. If more than 14 business days, court shall award at least $200 in damages plus costs, interest, and attorneys' fees. Employer who refuses to employ, dismisses, demotes, disciplines, or in any way penalizes the employee because of a wage garnishment or a

State Laws on Administering Wage Garnishments (continued)

proceeding to collect child support is liable for damages, costs, interest, and attorneys' fees, and may be required to make restitution, including reinstatement and back pay.

Ohio

Ohio Rev. Code Ann. §§ 2716.041(C)(4)(e), 2716.05, 3121.18, 3123.99

Employee protections that exceed federal law: Employee may not be discharged because of wage garnishments by a single creditor in a 12-month period.

Employer's fee: $3 per pay period that earnings withheld for general wage garnishment; $2 per support order or 1% of amount withheld, whichever is greater, for child support.

Employer penalties, child support withholding: For discharging employee, subject to fine of $50 to $200, and ten to 30 days in jail.

Oklahoma

Okla. Stat. Ann. tit. 12, §§ 1171.3, 1190; tit. 14A, § 5-106; tit. 56, § 240.2

Employee protections that exceed federal law: Employee may not be discharged because of a garnishment to collect on a consumer credit transaction, unless the employee has more than two such garnishments in one year.

Employer's fee: $5 per payment (up to $10/month) for child support; $10 for each general wage garnishment.

Employer penalties, child support withholding: For discharging or disciplining employee, liable for wages and benefits lost from time of discharge or discipline to time of reinstatement or promotion. For failing to withhold or remit payments, liable for amount not withheld, plus fine of up to $200 for each payment not made.

Oregon

Or. Rev. Stat. §§ 18.385, 25.414(6), 25.424, 659A.885

Employee protections that exceed federal law: Employer may not discharge employee because of a wage garnishment (no number specified).

Employer's fee: $5 per month for child support withholding.

Employer penalties, child support withholding: For failure to withhold, liable for all amounts not paid as well as a fine of $250 for each willful failure to pay. For discharging, refusing to hire, or discriminating or retaliating against employee, may be liable for reinstatement, back pay, compensatory damages or $200 (which is greater), punitive damages, costs, and attorneys' fees.

Pennsylvania

23 Pa. Cons. Stat. Ann. § 4348(j),(k),(l)

Applies to: Child support garnishments only.

Employee protections that exceed federal law: Employer may not refuse to employ, discharge, discipline, or demote employee because of a wage garnishment (no number specified).

Employer's fee: 2% of amount withheld per support payment.

Employer penalties, child support withholding: For violating employee rights, liable for damages and subject to a fine of up to $1,000. For failing to withhold payment, may be jailed and fined for contempt of court.

Rhode Island

R.I. Gen. Laws §§ 10-5-8, 15-5-24(i), 15-5-26, 15-5-29

Employer's fee: $5 per general garnishment order; $2 per child support payment.

Employer penalties, child support withholding: For dismissing, demoting, disciplining, or penalizing employee, liable for damages, interest,

State Laws on Administering Wage Garnishments (continued)

court costs, and attorneys' fees, and may be required to reinstate employee with back pay; subject to a fine of up to $100. For discharging, demoting, or disciplining an employee because of a wage garnishment for child medical support, or failing to withhold for the same, liable for a $100 fine.

South Carolina

S.C. Code Ann. §§ 20-7-1315(F),(I), 37-5-106

Employee protections that exceed federal law: Employee may not be discharged because of wage garnishment (no number specified).

Employer's fee: $3 per child support payment.

Employer penalties, child support withholding: For violating employee rights, liable for a fine of up to $500.

South Dakota

S.D. Codified Laws Ann. §§ 21-18-9, 25-7A-46, 25-7A-59

Applies to: Child support and children's health garnishments only.

Employee protections that exceed federal law: Employer may not discharge, refuse to employ, discipline, or penalize an employee because of a wage garnishment (child support; no number specified).

Employer's fee: $15 for preparing a garnishment disclosure.

Employer penalties, child support withholding: For violating employee rights or failing to withhold or pay garnishment, guilty of petty offense.

Tennessee

Tenn. Code Ann. §§ 36-5-501(i),(l), 40-35-111(e)(3)

Applies to: Child and spousal support garnishments only.

Employee protections that exceed federal law: Employee whose wages are ordered withheld for either child or spousal support may not be fired or disciplined (no number specified).

Employer's fee: Up to 5% of amount withheld (no more than $5/month) for child support and spousal orders.

Employer penalties, child support withholding: Refusing to employ, discharging, or taking disciplinary action against an employee, or refusing to withhold is a class C misdemeanor, which carries a fine of up to $50 or up to 30 days' imprisonment, or both.

Texas

Tex. Civ. Prac. & Rem. Code Ann. § 63.006; Fam. Code §§ 8.204 to 8.209, 158.204, 158.209, 158.210

Employee protections that exceed federal law: Employee may not be fired, disciplined, or refused employment because of wage withholding orders for spousal support.

Employer's fee: Actual cost or up to $10 per month, whichever is less, for general wage garnishments under state or federal law; $10 per month for child support payments; $5 per month for spousal support payments.

Employer penalties, child support withholding: For violating employee rights, employer must reinstate employee with full benefits and seniority and is liable for wages plus court costs and attorneys' fees. For knowingly failing to withhold or remit child or spousal support payments, liable for the amount withheld but not paid as well as attorneys' fees and costs, $200 for each instance.

Utah

Utah Code Ann. §§ 62A-11-316, 62A-11-406, 62A-11-410, 78-7-44; Utah R. Civ. Proc. Rule 64D

State Laws on Administering Wage Garnishments (continued)

Applies to: Child support garnishments.

Employee protections that exceed federal law: Employer may not discharge or prejudice an employee because of any garnishment (child support).

Employer's fee: $10 for a single garnishment and $25 for a continuing garnishment (child support only).

Employer penalties, child support withholding: For discharging, refusing to hire, or disciplining because of a garnishment, liable to employee for damages; liable to state child support enforcement agency for amount of garnishment or $1,000, whichever is greater, plus interest, costs, and attorneys' fees.

Vermont

Vt. Stat. Ann. tit. 12, §§ 3171, 3172; tit. 15, §§ 787, 790

Employee protections that exceed federal law: If employee is discharged within 60 days of a garnishment order, presumed to be in violation of law (Vermont uses term "trustee process").

Employer's fee: $5 per month for child support withholding.

Employer penalties, general wage garnishment: Liable to discharged employee for reinstatement, back wages, and damages; if employee wins in court, also liable for costs and reasonable attorneys' fees. For failure to withhold, liable for amount of garnishment plus interest, costs, and attorneys' fees.

Employer penalties, child support withholding: Liable to discharged employee for reinstatement, back wages, and damages; if employee wins in court, also liable for costs and reasonable attorneys' fees. Employers failing to forward payments may be subject to penalties of $100 to $1,000.

Virginia

Va. Code Ann. §§ 8.01-512.2, 20-79.3, 63.1-271

Employee protections that exceed federal law: Employee who voluntarily assigns earnings to settle a support debt may not be discharged because of assignment.

Employer's fee: $10 for each general wage garnishment summons; $5 per child support withholding payment.

Employer penalties, child support withholding: For discharging, taking disciplinary action against, or refusing to employ an employee, fine of up to $1,000 for violating employee rights.

Washington

Wash. Rev. Code Ann. §§ 6.27.170, 26.18.110, 26.23.090, 74.20A.080, 74.20A.230, 74.20A.240

Applies to: Child and spousal support garnishments.

Employee protections that exceed federal law: Employee may not be discharged unless there are garnishments for three or more separate debts within a 12-month period. Employee may not be fired, disciplined, or refused employment because of wage withholding orders for spousal support.

Employer's fee: $10 for first payment, $1 for each successive payment for child or spousal support withholding; $15 for first payment, $1 for each successive payment for processing earnings assignment issued by department of social and health services.

Employer penalties, support withholding: For discharging, disciplining, or refusing to hire, liable to employee for double lost wages, damages, costs, and attorneys' fees; may also be required to reinstate or hire employee. Liable for a civil fine up to $2,500 per violation. For failing to withhold,

State Laws on Administering Wage Garnishments (continued)

liable for full payment plus costs, interests, and attorneys' fees (includes child health care support). Also applies to spousal support.

West Virginia

W. Va. Code §§ 46A-2-131, 46B-6-5, 48-14-406(c), 48-14-407, 48-14-418

Employee protections that exceed federal law: Employer may not take any form of reprisal against employee because of wage garnishment to pay judgment for consumer credit or rent-to-own transaction (no number specified).

Employer's fee: $1 per child support withholding order.

Employer penalties, child support withholding: Employer who discharges, refuses to employ, or takes disciplinary action against an employee because of a garnishment is guilty of a misdemeanor, punishable by a fine of $500 to $1,000.

Wisconsin

Wis. Stat. Ann. §§ 425.110, 767.75(3)(h)(6)(c); 812.43

Employee protections that exceed federal law: Employer may not charge a fee or take any adverse action because of a general wage garnishment (no number specified).

Employer's fee: Up to $3 per child or spousal support payment.

Employer penalties, general wage garnishment: Discharged employee may sue for reinstatement, back wages and benefits, restoration of seniority, and attorneys' fees.

Employer penalties, child support withholding: For denying employment, fine of up to $500 (also applies to child health and support).

Wyoming

Wyo. Stat. §§ 1-15-509, 20-6-212(c), 20-6-218, 40-14-506

Employee protections that exceed federal law: Employee may not be discharged for having wages subject to continuing garnishment for any judgment or for a judgment from a consumer credit transaction (no number specified).

Employer's fee: $5 per child support payment.

Employer penalties, general wage garnishment: Employee may sue for reinstatement, 30 days' lost wages, costs, and attorneys' fees.

Employer penalties, child support withholding: For discharging, disciplining, or otherwise penalizing employee, subject to fine of up to $200. For failing to withhold, liable for amount that should have been withheld.

Current as of February 2007

Enforcing Your Right to Be Paid Fairly

Your first step in enforcing your right to be paid fairly should be to decide whether your complaint involves a violation of a law or is simply a matter of disagreement or misunderstanding between you and your employer.

If, for example, your employer refused to pay you time and a half for five hours of overtime that you worked, then the issue would be covered by the FLSA. But if you had been working under the impression that you would get a raise every year—a matter not covered by the FLSA—and your employer will not give you one, then the issue is left for you to resolve with your employer, without the clout that a law can lend.

Once you have refined your complaint, try discussing it with your employer or former employer before filing any official action. Some companies have dispute resolution programs—usually outlined in their employee manuals—that can help you resolve a pay dispute without resorting to legal action. (See Chapter 17, "Mediation and Arbitration.")

Filing a Complaint or Lawsuit

If your complaint involves what you believe is a violation of the FLSA—for example, you have not been paid fairly or on time—contact your local office of the Wage and Hour Division of the U.S. Department of Labor (see the Appendix for contact details).

If you call, visit, or write to your local Wage and Hour Division office, workers there will take down the information you provide and transcribe it onto a complaint form. You can request one of these forms and fill it out yourself. But, because the staff members are familiar with which details are legally pertinent, they usually prefer to fill it out themselves. They will probably ask you to provide photocopies of documents relevant to your dispute, such as pay stubs.

Review the completed complaint form and attached documents to be sure they are correct and as complete as possible. If you are assigned to a staff person who seems particularly unsympathetic or unhelpful, calmly and politely ask to speak with someone else. Also, keep in mind that a huge dollop of patience is required. The process—from filing a complaint through investigation and the final outcome—typically takes from one to three years.

Once your complaint has been put together, U.S. Labor Department investigators will take over the job of gathering additional data that should either prove or disprove your complaint.

If the thought of reporting your employer to the authorities frightens you, take some comfort in knowing that Labor Department investigators must keep the identities of those who file such complaints confidential. Also, it is illegal for an employer to fire or otherwise discriminate against an employee for filing a complaint under the FLSA or for participating in a legal proceeding related to its enforcement. Many state laws also provide protection for employees who file state wage and hour complaints.

Where the federal investigators find violations of the FLSA, the action that they then take will depend upon the severity of the violations and whether or not the employer appears to have been violating the law willfully.

When the violations are severe and apparently willful, the Labor Department may ask the Justice Department to bring criminal charges against the employer. Government lawyers will handle the matter for you. If convicted, a first-time violator of the FLSA may be fined by the courts; subsequent convictions can result in both fines and imprisonment.

If the violations are not too severe, or if the Labor Department investigators feel the infractions were not willful, one of the following steps may be taken:

- The Labor Department may set up and supervise a plan for your employer to pay back wages to you and anyone else injured by the violations.
- The Secretary of Labor may file a lawsuit asking the court to order your employer to pay you the wages due, plus an equal amount as damages. The court may also issue an injunction or order preventing your employer from continuing the illegal behavior.
- You may file your own lawsuit under the FLSA to recover the wages you're owed, plus other damages, attorneys' fees, and court costs. You will probably need to hire a lawyer to help with this type of lawsuit. (See Chapter 17, "Hiring a Lawyer.")

When You Cannot Sue Under the FLSA

You cannot file an FLSA lawsuit if your employer has already paid back wages to you under the supervision of the Labor Department. This amounts to an incentive system for employers: An employer who cooperates in correcting any violations discovered by the Wage and Hour Division investigators must pay only the back wages that are due. An employer who refuses to cooperate by paying back wages stands the chance of having to pay double the wages, plus your attorneys' fees and costs, plus the cost of its own defense.

You cannot bring a lawsuit under the FLSA if the Secretary of Labor has already done so on your behalf. And, if you file a lawsuit and then the Secretary of Labor files a lawsuit over the same violations, your right to sue ends and the Labor Department takes over.

Violations of State and Local Laws

The laws of each state and municipality specify which branch of government is responsible for enforcing state and local wage and hour laws, and what remedies—criminal, civil, or both—are available. In most states, the Labor Department is authorized to take action on your behalf to recover unpaid wages. (See the Appendix for contact information.)

The History of Payroll Withholding

The Social Security Act of 1935, a part of President Franklin D. Roosevelt's New Deal, was the first law to sink its teeth firmly into the typical paycheck. Intended only to save industrial and commercial hourly workers of the Depression era from poverty in old age, the original Social Security program required employers to withhold a mere 1% of workers' pay.

Since then, the Social Security Act has been amended many times. The age of eligibility has been lowered from 65 to 62, and coverage has been extended to people unable to work because of physical disabilities, government employees, self-employed people, and a number of other groups not covered by the original act. Consequently, the amount withheld from most wages to pay for Social Security programs now is more than 7%.

Public debate is again abuzz with talk of the Social Security Act, prompted by statistics of aging and survival and what it means for the changing workforce. Baby boomers will begin retiring in less than a decade, and life expectancy is rising. By 2025, the number of people age 65 and older will grow by an estimated 74%. In contrast, the number of workers supporting the system in its current incarnation would grow by 14%, which some see as a threat to deplete its coffers completely. Sharply divided politicians are urging a potpourri of reforms, offering everything from restoring solvency with minimal changes to scrapping the system entirely.

The federal income tax, the other major cause of paycheck shrinkage, was created when the 16th Amendment to the U.S. Constitution was passed in 1913. The original federal income tax rates ranged from 1% to 7% of annual income above $3,000—a lot of money back then.

To pay for World War II, however, the government raised the income tax rates so dramatically that the tax on the top income level bracket hit a record of 94% in 1944 and 1945. The minimum income subject to taxation was lowered so that most working people were for the first time subject to some income tax.

Politicians, hoping to assuage the public angst over paying a large yearly lump sum, decided to lessen the trauma by making employers withhold the income tax, little by little, from workers' pay each week.

By the 1970s, employees had become so accustomed to having large sums of money withheld from their pay that most states and cities—as well as nongovernment groups such as health insurance companies and pension fund managers—instituted additional withholding programs.

Today, it is common for employees to have more than a third of their pay withheld by their employers on behalf of government, with still more withheld to finance private benefit plans.

If you are dissatisfied with the action taken by the government agency responsible for enforcing state or local wage and hour laws, consider resolving your problem in small claims court. Because of the relatively small amounts of money typically involved, disputes over wages, commissions, or other forms of compensation can often be pursued quickly and inexpensively in small claims courts without requiring help from a lawyer.

RESOURCE

For a complete explanation of small claims court—from preparing a case through collecting a judgment—see *Everybody's Guide to Small Claims Court,* by Ralph Warner (Nolo).

Health Insurance

Despite sweeping reforms proposed and reproposed by politicians, health insurance remains an expensive necessity. Long-term treatment of a medical condition or even a short hospital stay can quickly bankrupt most Americans. To help foot the bills, most employers offer their employees some type of group insurance plan.

The specifics of insurance coverage are dictated by the terms of individual policies. This chapter discusses the broader state and federal legal controls on health insurance and will help you evaluate whether any insurance you have meets the minimum legal standards.

No Legal Right to Coverage

Offering health insurance to employees is purely voluntary—a matter of tradition, not law. This truth flies in the face of many firmly held beliefs about workplace benefits. But, in fact, there is no federal law that requires employers to provide or pay for health insurance coverage for all current employees, or even full-time employees. In 2006, only 61% of all working employers received health insurance coverage from their employers— and less than half were offered any type of dental care coverage, and only about 20% offered coverage for vision care.

No federal legal scheme requires every employer to offer insurance coverage. However, an employer who promises to provide health insurance—in an employee manual, for example—must follow through on the promise. And benefits must be provided without discriminating against any employee or group of employees. That includes employees who are statistically more likely to incur high medical costs. For example, federal laws specifically provide that women workers and older workers must be provided with the same coverage as other workers. (See Chapter 7, "The Equal Pay Act" and "The Older Workers Benefit Protection Act.") One grand exception to this general rule is that many state laws now allow employers to offer health plans that offer higher premiums to smokers. (See Chapter 6, "Tobacco Smoke in the Workplace.")

In recent years, some companies have discontinued or cut back on insurance coverage they offer employees, simply because of the expense. The legal rule emerging is that of evenhandedness: Employers cannot offer insurance coverage to some employees and deny it to others.

But because health insurance is a job benefit that is not regulated by law, employers are otherwise free to fashion a plan of any stripe. They may:

- require employees to contribute to or even over the cost of premiums
- offer reduced reimbursement or pro rata coverage to part-time employees
- limit options to one insurance plan or offer a variety of choices, or
- give employees a sum of money earmarked for insurance coverage that may be applied to any chosen plan.

As anyone who has read the fine print on a health insurance policy can attest, insurers, too, place conditions on the coverage they provide. The most nettling of these limitations is on preexisting conditions. Under these provisions, if you have had a recent illness or have a chronic medical condition, you may be denied coverage, be made to wait a specific time period until your condition will be covered, or be forced to pay high premiums for specialized coverage. The greatest headway on doing away with the preexisting condition denial of coverage has been made in the federal law requiring continuing coverage for former employees, as described below.

Traditionally, employers that have provided health care coverage have done so through an indemnity or reimbursement plan that pays the doctor or hospital directly or reimburses the employee for medical expenses he or she has already paid.

While traditional coverage allowing employees to seek out their preferred medical provider is still widely used, a growing number of employers today provide coverage through the alternatives of a health maintenance organization (HMO) or a preferred provider organization (PPO).

An HMO is made up of hospitals and doctors who provide specified medical services to employees for a fixed monthly fee. Within the HMO service area, covered employees must use the HMO hospitals and doctors unless it's an emergency or they receive permission to go elsewhere.

A PPO is a network of hospitals and doctors who agree to provide medical care for specified fees. Often the network is put together by an insurance company that also administers it. Employees usually can choose between using the network's hospitals and doctors or going elsewhere.

There are two main categories of employee health insurance: coverage for current employees and coverage for former employees.

But Wait—There's More

Insurance—and all its crafty permutations—has insinuated itself into many aspects of workplace law. You will find discussions of other insurance-related issues peppered throughout the book, including:

- privacy issues, such as employers' access to medical records (see Chapter 5, "Your Personnel Records")
- coverage for unemployed workers provided by state unemployment insurance programs (see Chapter 11)
- coverage for sick or disabled workers provided by state workers' compensation programs (see Chapter 12), by the Social Security disability system (see Chapter 13), and by private and state disability programs (see Chapter 10, "Replacing Your Income")
- coverage or time off provided for family and medical leave (see Chapter 4), and
- continuing coverage after retirement (see Chapter 14).

Coverage for Current Employees

No law mandates insurance coverage in every workplace. But employees can take some insurance aid and comfort from a number of state laws—and from a federal law imposing some fundamental fairness in coverage.

> **CAUTION**
>
> **Independent contractors need not apply.** If you work as an independent contractor—a term used to describe people who are in business for themselves, such as consultants, freelancers, the self-employed, entrepreneurs, and business owners—you are covered by neither federal nor state laws that require health insurance coverage or continuation. To become insured, you must proceed on your own through the often mind-numbing process of procuring insurance—and the often wallet-draining process of paying for it. If you have questions about your work status as an independent contractor or employee, consult your local department of labor. (See the Appendix for contact details.)

State Laws

A few states, counties, and cities now require some employers to provide health insurance coverage for some employees who work there. For example, Hawaii requires employers to provide coverage to employees earning a set amount or more per month. (Haw. Rev. Stat. § 393-11.)

In addition, some state laws require that employers who offer insurance to employees must provide certain minimum coverage. The state requirements vary considerably, but typical minimums include coverage for medical and surgical benefits, treatment of mental illness, alcoholism and drug abuse, and preventative testing such as mammograms and PAP smears. Check with your state's health commissioner to find out whether there is any minimum mandated coverage in your area.

Some states impose additional restrictions on workplace health insurance. For example, a growing number of them make it illegal for employers to fire employees because they file a legitimate claim against their company's health insurance.

Why Do You Think They Call Them Premiums?

A recent analysis of the cost of workplace health benefits revealed the following harrowing costs:

Average annual cost of worker contribution for single coverage:	$ 627
Average annual cost of employer contribution for single coverage:	$ 3,615
Average annual cost of worker contribution for family coverage:	$ 2,973
Average annual cost of employer contribution for family coverage:	$ 8,508

And it showed the following harrowing effects:

Increase in cost of employer-sponsored health insurance, from 2005 to 2006:	7.7%
Increase in overall inflation during that time:	3.5%
Increase in wage gains during the same period:	3.8%
Increase in cost of premiums for family coverage since 2000:	87%

Sources: Health Care in America 2006 Survey by ABC News, Kaiser Foundation, and USA Today; California Employer Health Benefits Survey by the California HealthCare Foundation and The Center for Studying Health System Changes, 2006 .

The Health Insurance Portability Act

The Health Insurance Portability and Accountability Act, or HIPAA (Pub. Law 104-191), a federal law that took effect in July of 1997, made it easier for employees to change jobs without losing insurance coverage—and to get coverage in the first place.

The law's biggest promise is to improve the portability of health insurance coverage. But in addition, it purports to:

- take aim against health care discrimination, fraud, and abuse, and
- promote the use of tax-favored insurance plans.

Increased Portability

Group insurers now face limits when attempting to restrict enrollment because of preexisting medical conditions.

Under HIPAA, for example, pregnancy is not considered a preexisting condition—and newborns or newly adopted children cannot be excluded if they are enrolled within 30 days of birth or adoption.

The maximum amount of time a group health insurance plan, HMO, or self-insured plan may exclude someone on the basis of a preexisting condition is 12 months. This exclusion period is reduced by the amount of time an employee previously had continuous coverage through other private insurance or public insurance programs.

Insurers must offer individual coverage to a person who loses group coverage if the individual:

- was continuously covered for 18 months under a group health plan
- has exhausted COBRA coverage (see "Coverage for Former Employees," below), or
- is ineligible for coverage through government programs such as Medicare or Medicaid.

Discrimination Protection

Group health plans and employers cannot deny coverage for an individual and his or her dependents based on health status, physical or mental medical condition, claims experience, genetic information, disability, or domestic violence.

The Inspector General and U.S. Attorney General are charged with establishing a program to coordinate federal, state, and local programs to control health plan fraud and abuse—and criminal penalties can be imposed for defrauding any health benefits program.

Tax-favored Insurance Plans

The Medicare Prescription Drug, Improvement, and Modernization Act of 2003, which became effective January 1, 2004, made a number of programs available with the aim of giving employees tax advantages to offset health care costs.

Health Savings Accounts. A Health Savings Account permits some workers to save for, and pay, health care expenses for themselves, a spouse, and dependents, free of taxes.

HSAs may be established by any individual who is covered by a qualified high-deductible health plan—those with an annual deductible of at least $1,050 for individuals or $2,100 for families. Contributions can be made into these accounts—by either individual employees or their employers, up to a maximum of $2,700 for individuals and $5,450 for families. They operate much the same way as the now-familiar Individual Retirements Accounts (IRAs) do for saving retirement money.

Medical Savings Accounts (MSAs) were the precursor to HSAs—and money put in them can be rolled over into an HSA.

Possible benefits of HSAs include:

- You can claim a tax deduction for contributions you make, even if you do not itemize your deductions on Form 1040.
- Interest or other earnings on the assets are tax-free.
- Distributions may be tax-free if you pay qualified medical expenses.
- Contributions remain in from year to year until you use them.
- They are portable; they stay with you if you change employers or leave the work force.

Flexible Spending Arrangements. A Flexible Spending Arrangement (FSA), offered at an employer's discretion, allows employees to be reimbursed for medical expenses. FSAs are usually funded through voluntary salary reduction agreements with your employer. No employment or federal income taxes are deducted from your contribution—and you are also free to contribute.

Possible benefits of an FSA include:

- Your employer's contributions can be excluded from your gross income.
- No employment or federal income taxes are deducted from the contributions.
- Withdrawals may be tax-free if you pay qualified medical expenses.
- You can withdraw funds from the account to pay qualified medical expenses even if you have not yet placed the funds in the account.

Health Reimbursement Arrangements. A Health Reimbursement Arrangement (HRA) must be funded solely by an employer. The contribution cannot be paid through your own voluntary salary reduction agreement. Employees are reimbursed tax-free for qualified medical expenses up to a maximum dollar amount for a coverage period. An HRA may be offered with other health plans.

Possible benefits of an HRA:

- You can exclude your employer's contributions from your gross income.
- Reimbursements may be tax-free if you pay qualified medical expenses.
- Any unused amounts in the HRA can be carried forward for reimbursements in later years.

RESOURCE

For more information on all of these tax-deferred accounts, see IRS Publication 969, *Health Savings Accounts and Other Tax-Favored Health Plans*, at www.irs.gov. Or order it from the IRS by calling 800-829-3676.

Explaining the 'Un' in 'Uninsured'

In a recent nationwide poll, Americans who identified themselves as uninsured gave the following as the main reasons:

Too expensive	54%
Refused due to illness, poor health, or age	15%
Not eligible for employer coverage	9%
Employer doesn't offer it	5%
Don't need it	4%
Don't know how to get it	1%

Source: Health Care in America 2006 Survey by ABC News, Kaiser Foundation, and *USA Today.*

Coverage for Former Employees

A federal workplace law, the Consolidated Omnibus Budget Reconciliation Act, or COBRA (29 U.S.C. § 1162), requires your employer to offer you—and your spouse and dependents—continuing insurance coverage in either of the following situations:

- You lose insurance coverage because your number of work hours is reduced.
- You lose your job for any reason other than gross misconduct. Because the law was a drastic change from Business as Usual, the courts are still grappling with the question of how egregious the workplace behavior must be to qualify as gross misconduct. So far, courts have ruled that inefficiency, poor performance, negligence, or errors in judgment on the job are not enough. There must be some deliberate, wrongful violations of workplace standards to qualify as gross misconduct.

COBRA was intended to extend access to group health insurance coverage to people who would otherwise be totally unprotected—and unlikely to be able to secure coverage on their own. The law applies to all employers with 20 or more employees. Under the law, employers need only make the insurance available; they need not pay for it. Employers may charge up to 102% of the base premium for continued coverage—the extra 2% thrown in to cover administrative costs.

Those covered under COBRA include:

- all individuals who are or were provided insurance coverage under an employer's group plan, and
- those individuals' beneficiaries—who typically include a spouse and dependent children.

Continuing Coverage

Qualified employees and former employees may elect to continue coverage up to 18 months after they quit or are fired or get laid off, or after a reduction in hours that makes them ineligible for coverage. Those who become disabled, however, can get COBRA coverage for 29 months—until Medicare payments typically kick in.

No one can choose to enroll in an insurance plan upon becoming ineligible for workplace coverage. COBRA extends only to those already enrolled when their health insurance coverage ceases.

In addition, COBRA provides that covered individuals must be given the right to convert to an individual policy at the end of the continuation period—although that coverage is usually significantly more expensive.

Coverage for Dependents

Beneficiaries or dependents may also elect to continue coverage for 18 months.

However, they may opt to have coverage continued for up to 36 months if any of the following occur:

- The covered employee dies.
- The covered employee becomes entitled to Medicare.
- They are divorced or legally separated from the covered employee.
- A minor dependent child turns 18 or otherwise ceases to be considered a dependent under the plan.
- They become disabled and eligible for Social Security disability insurance benefits. (See Chapter 13.)

Preexisting Conditions

COBRA addresses the most common health insurance bugaboo: denial of coverage for preexisting conditions.

Under COBRA, coverage must be offered regardless of any preexisting medical conditions. And, if an employee obtains new employment with coverage that contains exclusions or limitations for any

such conditions, the former employer may not terminate coverage before the end of the COBRA coverage period. However, the employer may end coverage if a beneficiary such as a spouse is covered by another group health plan—as long as there is no significant gap in benefits.

Coordination Is Key for Some Plans

Many group insurance plans contain coordination of benefits (COB) provisions in which two policies provide overlapping coverage—a common situation for families with two working spouses. A COB provision establishes a hierarchy for determining which policy provides primary coverage and which provides secondary coverage.

Most COBs provide that if the primary insurer's obligation is less than the amount of the total bill, the insured can then submit a claim to the secondary insurer, asking for coverage for the amount not paid. If only one policy has a COB provision, the policy that does not have a COB clause is primarily responsible for paying; if the same person is covered as an employee and a dependent, the employee policy coverage is primary.

In addition, for coverage of children of two working parents covered by insurance, most states now follow the Birthday Rule. That rule provides that the parent who has a birthday earlier in the year is the one whose insurance will cover the children.

Insurance From Continuing or Former Employment

Medicare is a federal government program that assists older and some disabled people with their medical costs. Many people who are eligible for Medicare continue to work and have health insurance through their own or their spouse's employer.

And many other people keep their job-related health insurance after they retire, as part of their retirement benefits package, although they usually have to pay much more than a current employee.

Employment-based health plans require you to sign up for Medicare when you turn 65, but most of them will cover you in conjunction with Medicare. The health benefits or human resources office at your work or union can explain the details of coordinating coverage.

Just because you are eligible for a work-related health plan, however, does not mean that you have to continue with it. You may find that

Medicare plus an additional limited policy—often called medigap—or Medicare through a health maintenance organization (HMO) provides you with better coverage at a better price than does your work's medical insurance combined with Medicare benefits.

Even if you decide not to participate in the regular health plan offered in your workplace, your employer's insurance company may offer you a different policy with limited coverage for some services Medicare does not cover at all, such as prescription drugs, dental care, or hearing aids. Compare such a policy with the medigap policies and managed care plans discussed in this chapter to see which one offers you the best coverage for your money.

Adapted from *Social Security, Medicare, & Government Pensions: Get the Most Out of Your Retirement and Medical Benefits*, by Joseph L. Matthews with Dorothy Matthews Berman (Nolo)

Enforcing COBRA

COBRA provides for a number of fines for employers and health insurance plan administrators who violate its requirements. However, the Act has so many complexities that no one can agree on exactly what circumstances release an employer from its requirements. And, frustratingly, there is no one place you can call to get help if you think your rights under COBRA have been violated.

Parts of the law are administered by the U.S. Labor Department and other parts fall under the Internal Revenue Service—and the two agencies frequently refer COBRA complaints back and forth to each other.

If you have a COBRA-related question or complaint, you can try calling your local office of either of those agencies, but neither has a track record of actively enforcing COBRA requirements. Your employer is required to provide you with an explanation of your

COBRA rights when you are enrolled in a group health care plan covering 20 or more employees. However, these materials are seldom well written or easy to understand.

In general, COBRA can be enforced only through an expensive lawsuit. That means that the statute typically can be used only by large groups of former employees who have been denied their rights to continue group health insurance coverage—and who can share the expense of hiring a lawyer and filing a lawsuit to enforce that right. (See Chapter 17, "Class Action Lawsuits.")

RESOURCE

For detailed information on COBRA, see *The Essential Guide to Federal Employment Laws* by Lisa Guerin & Amy DelPo (Nolo).

If you need advice or run into problems claiming COBRA benefits, contact the Older Women's League; 666 Eleventh Street, NW, Suite 700; Washington, DC 20001; 202-783-6686. The organization also assists younger women and men.

Individual Health Insurance

Even if your state does not have a law that gives you the right to continue group health care coverage after employment ends, it may have a law that requires health insurance companies to offer you the option of converting your group policy to individual coverage. (See the chart below.)

Individual coverage typically is much more expensive than group coverage—and

the coverage limits are usually much lower than those offered under group coverage. For example, a group health insurance policy often will not have any limit on total benefits paid during your lifetime, while individual coverage often limits total lifetime benefits to $500,000. However, laws that give you the right to convert to individual health coverage usually do not require you to lose your job to be eligible.

If your employer cancels your group health care coverage but continues to employ you—an increasingly common situation—these laws can give you the right to convert to individual coverage until you can find a better insurance deal or a job with better health insurance benefits. You can usually find the laws guaranteeing you the right to convert group health insurance coverage to individual coverage among the statutes governing your state's insurance industry. Some states have a consumer complaint section in their insurance departments that can help you with this.

State Laws on Insurance Continuation

Because COBRA generally cannot be enforced by any means other than a complex and expensive lawsuit, state laws that give former employees the right to continue group health insurance coverage after leaving a job are often a better alternative.

State laws often provide interesting twists that make it easier to get continued coverage. California, for example, provides for three

Diagnosis: Ailing—And Bound to Get Worse

Recent research reveals a sickening prognosis: We're seeing the most rapid rise in health care costs in more than a decade—with a current price tag of nearly $2 trillion.

According to a health insurance trade group, America's Health Insurance Plans (AHIP), the fingers of blame point in a number of directions, including at the health care and drug industries, government—and consumers who want expensive care and more of it. AHIP maintains that spending on health care costs is speeding up at a far faster rate than the rest of the economy for a number of reasons:

- Americans are demanding more health services and using them more frequently. While this can translate to longer, healthier lives, it also increases health care spending.

- People over 50 use twice as much health care as those in their 20s—and almost four times as much by the time they hit 60. So as the population ages, the cost of health care rises.

- Many of the state-of-the art technologies in vogue and in demand are also expensive to buy, maintain, and operate—significantly increasing costs.

- Hospitals are spending more, too—and because more of them are organized as networks, they have more power to bargain on the prices they charge.

- Spending on prescription drugs is rising at a double-digit rate—up more than 40% since 2000. The current craze of advertising directly to consumers puts added pressure on doctors to prescribe what patients request rather than cost-effective alternatives.

- State and federal governments keep passing new legal mandates requiring insurers to cover an increasing variety of services and items—not always in keeping with consumer's needs and preferences, but at a greater expense to all.

What you can do to help control the cost of health insurance premiums: Foremost, mind the common sense urgings to take care of yourself by exercising, eating a balanced diet, maintaining the correct weight, and not smoking. Make sure all the information you give to medical providers is correct and current—and review bills and statements for accuracy. Be aware of public policies that influence the cost of health care—and agitate against those you feel would raise it unnecessarily.

Source: America's Health Insurance Plans, www.ahip.org, 2005

months of group insurance coverage in addition to COBRA coverage, although, in most states, you must choose one or the other. A number of states—including California—provide special insurance protections for older workers, who are most likely to suffer in a staff cut. And, in Washington, the spouse and children of a worker who is fired even after severe misconduct may be entitled to continued coverage. (See the chart below.)

For an employee to be eligible for continued coverage, most state laws require that he or she must be covered for a certain time—three months is common—just before being terminated. In nearly all instances, any continuation of coverage will be at your expense—just as it would be under COBRA.

However, the specific requirements of these laws and how they are enforced vary tremendously. For more specific information, contact your state's insurance department, or read the controlling laws at a local law library. (See Chapter 17, "Legal Research.") In addition, the plant closing laws of a few states may give you the right to continue group health insurance coverage. (See Chapter 9, "Plant Closings.")

 CAUTION

Additional laws may apply. If the chart below indicates that your state has no statute, this means there is no law that specifically addresses the issue. However, there may be a state administrative regulation or local ordinance that does control. Contact your state insurance commission or state labor department for more information. (See the Appendix for state labor department contact details.)

State Health Insurance Continuations Laws

Alabama

Ala. Code § 27-55-3(4)

Coverage: 18 months for subjects of domestic abuse who have lost coverage they had under abuser's insurance and who do not qualify for COBRA.

Arizona

Ariz. Rev. Stat. §§ 20-1377, 20-1408

Employers affected: All employers who offer group disability insurance.

Length of coverage for dependents: Insurer must either continue coverage for dependents or convert to individual policy upon death of covered employee or divorce or legal separation. Coverage must be the same unless the insured chooses a lesser plan.

Time employer has to notify employee of continuation rights: No provisions for employer. Insurance policy must include notice of conversion privilege. Clerk of court must provide notice to anyone filing for divorce that dependent spouse entitled to convert health insurance coverage.

Time employee has to apply: 31 days after termination of existing coverage.

Arkansas

Ark. Code Ann. §§ 23-86-114 to 23-86-116

Employers affected: All employers who offer group health insurance.

Eligible employees: Continuously insured for previous 3 months.

Length of coverage for employee: 120 days.

Length of coverage for dependents: 120 days.

Time employee has to apply: 10 days.

California

Cal. Health & Safety Code §§ 1373.6, 1373.621; Cal. Ins. Code §§ 10128.50 to 10128.59

Employers affected: Employers who offer group health insurance and have 2 to 19 employees.

Eligible employees: Continuously insured for previous 3 months.

Qualifying event: Termination of employment; reduction in hours.

Length of coverage for employee: 36 months.

Length of coverage for dependents: 36 months.

Time employer has to notify employee of continuation rights: 15 days.

Time employee has to apply: 31 days after group plan ends; 30 days after COBRA or Cal-COBRA ends (63 days if converting to an individual plan).

Special situations: Employee who is at least 60 years old and has worked for employer for previous 5 years may continue benefits for self and spouse beyond COBRA or Cal-COBRA limits (also applies to COBRA employers). Employee who began receiving COBRA coverage on or after 1/1/03 and whose COBRA coverage is for less than 36 months may use Cal-COBRA to bring total coverage up to 36 months.

Colorado

Colo. Rev. Stat. § 10-16-108

Employers affected: All employers who offer group health insurance.

Eligible employees: Employees continuously insured for previous 6 months.

Length of coverage for employee: 18 months.

Length of coverage for dependents: 18 months.

State Health Insurance Continuations Laws (continued)

Time employer has to notify employee of continuation rights: Within 10 days of termination.

Time employee has to apply: 30 days after termination; 60 days if employers fails to give notice.

Connecticut

Conn. Gen. Stat. Ann. §§ 38a-538, 38a-554, 31-51o

Employers affected: All employers who offer group health insurance.

Eligible employees: Continuously insured for previous 3 months.

Length of coverage for employee: 18 months, or until eligible for Social Security benefits.

Length of coverage for dependents: 18 months, or until eligible for Social Security benefits; 36 months in case of employee's death or divorce.

Time employer has to notify employee of continuation rights: 14 days.

Time employee has to apply: 60 days.

Special situations: When facility closes or relocates, employer must pay for insurance for employee and dependents for 120 days or until employee is eligible for other group coverage, whichever comes first. (Does not affect employee's right to conventional continuation coverage, which begins when 120-day period ends.)

District of Columbia

D.C. Code Ann. §§ 32-731 to 32-732

Employers affected: Employers with fewer than 20 employees.

Eligible employees: All covered employees are eligible.

Length of coverage for employee: 3 months.

Length of coverage for dependents: 3 months.

Time employer has to notify employee of continuation rights: Within 15 days of termination of coverage.

Time employee has to apply: 45 days after termination of coverage.

Florida

Fla. Stat. Ann. § 627.6692

Employers affected: Employers with fewer than 20 employees.

Eligible employees: Full-time (25 or more hours per week) employees covered by employer's health insurance plan.

Length of coverage for employee: 18 months.

Length of coverage for dependents: 18 months.

Time employer has to notify employee of continuation rights: Carrier notifies within 14 days of learning of qualifying event (employer is responsible for notifying carrier).

Time employee has to apply: 30 days from receipt of carrier's notice.

Georgia

Ga. Code Ann. §§ 33-24-21.1 to 33-24-21.2

Employers affected: All employers who offer group health insurance.

Eligible employees: Employees continuously insured for previous 6 months.

Length of coverage for employee: 3 months plus any part of the month remaining at termination.

Length of coverage for dependents: 3 months plus any part of the month remaining at termination.

Special situations: Employee, spouse, or former spouse who is 60 years old and who has been covered for previous 6 months may continue coverage until eligible for Medicare. (Applies to companies with more than 20 employees; does

State Health Insurance Continuations Laws (continued)

not apply when employee quits for reasons other than health.)

Hawaii

Haw. Rev. Stat. §§ 393-11, 393-15

Employers affected: All employers required to offer health insurance (those paying a regular employee a monthly wage at least 86.67 times state hourly minimum—about $542).

Length of coverage for employee: If employee is hospitalized or prevented from working by sickness, employer must pay insurance premiums for 3 months or for as long as employer continues to pay wages, whichever is longer.

Illinois

215 Ill. Comp. Stat. §§ 5/367e, 5/367.2, 5/367.2-5

Employers affected: All employers who offer group health insurance.

Eligible employees: Employees continuously insured for previous 3 months.

Length of coverage for employee: 9 months.

Length of coverage for dependents: 9 months (but see below).

Time employee has to apply: 10 days after termination or reduction in hours or receiving notice from employer, whichever is later, but not more than 60 days from termination or reduction in hours.

Special situations: Upon death or divorce, 2 years' coverage for spouse under 55 and eligible dependents who were on employee's plan; until eligible for Medicare or other group coverage for spouse over 55 and eligible dependents who were on employee's plan. A dependent child who has reached plan age limit or who was not already covered by plan, is also entitled to 2 years' continuation coverage.

Iowa

Iowa Code §§ 509B.3 to 509B.5

Employers affected: All employers who offer group health insurance.

Eligible employees: Employees continuously insured for previous 3 months.

Length of coverage for employee: 9 months.

Length of coverage for dependents: 9 months.

Time employer has to notify employee of continuation rights: 10 days after termination of coverage.

Time employee has to apply: 10 days after termination of coverage or receiving notice from employer, whichever is later, but no more than 31 days from termination of coverage.

Kansas

Kan. Stat. Ann. § 40-2209(i)

Employers affected: All employers who offer group health insurance.

Eligible employees: Employees continuously insured for previous 3 months.

Length of coverage for employee: 6 months.

Length of coverage for dependents: 6 months.

Time employee has to apply: 31 days from termination of coverage.

Kentucky

Ky. Rev. Stat. Ann. § 304.18-110

Employers affected: All employers who offer group health insurance.

Eligible employees: Employees continuously insured for previous 3 months.

Length of coverage for employee: 18 months.

Length of coverage for dependents: 18 months.

Time employer has to notify employee of continuation rights: Employer must notify

State Health Insurance Continuations Laws (continued)

insurer as soon as employee's coverage ends; insurer then notifies employee.

Time employee has to apply: 31 days from receipt of insurer's notice, but no more than 90 days after termination of group coverage.

Louisiana
La. Rev. Stat. Ann. §§ 22:215.7, 22:215.13

Employers affected: All employers who offer group health insurance and have fewer than 20 employees.

Eligible employees: Employees continuously insured for previous 3 months.

Length of coverage for employee: 12 months.

Length of coverage for dependents: 12 months.

Time employee has to apply: Must apply and submit payment before group coverage ends.

Special situations: Surviving spouse who is 50 or older may have coverage until remarriage or eligibility for Medicare or other insurance.

Maine
Me. Rev. Stat. Ann. tit. 24-A, § 2809-A

Employers affected: All employers who offer group health insurance.

Eligible employees: Employees continuously insured for previous 3 months.

Length of coverage for employee: One year (either group or individual coverage at discretion of insurer).

Length of coverage for dependents: One year (either group or individual coverage at discretion of insurer). Upon death of insured, continuation only if original plan provided for coverage.

Time employee has to apply: 90 days from termination of group coverage.

Special situations: Temporary layoff or work-related injury or disease: Employee and employee's dependents entitled to one year group or individual continuation coverage. (Must have been continuously insured for previous 6 months; must apply within 31 days from termination of coverage.)

Maryland
Md. Code Ann., [Ins.] §§ 15-407 to 15-410

Employers affected: All employers who offer group health insurance.

Eligible employees: Employees continuously insured for previous 3 months.

Length of coverage for employee: 18 months.

Length of coverage for dependents: 18 months upon death of employee; upon change in marital status, 18 months or until spouse remarries or becomes eligible for other coverage.

Time employer has to notify employee of continuation rights: Must notify insurer within 14 days of receiving employee's continuation request.

Time employee has to apply: 45 days from termination of coverage. Employee begins application process by requesting an election of continuation notification form from employer.

Massachusetts
Mass. Gen. Laws ch. 175, §§ 110G, 110I; ch. 176J, § 9

Employers affected: All employers who offer group health insurance and have fewer than 20 employees.

Eligible employees: All covered employees are eligible.

Length of coverage for employee: 18 months; 29 months if disabled.

Length of coverage for dependents: 18 months upon termination or reduction in hours; 29 months if disabled; 36 months on divorce, death

State Health Insurance Continuations Laws (continued)

of employee, employee's eligibility for Medicare, or employer's bankruptcy.

Time employer has to notify employee of continuation rights: When employee becomes eligible for continuation benefits.

Time employee has to apply: 60 days.

Special situations: Termination due to plant closing: 90 days' coverage for employee and dependents, at the same payment terms as before closing.

Minnesota

Minn. Stat. Ann. § 62A.17

Employers affected: All employers who offer group health insurance and have 2 or more employees.

Eligible employees: All covered employees are eligible.

Length of coverage for employee: 18 months; indefinitely if employee becomes totally disabled while employed.

Length of coverage for dependents: 18 months for current spouse; divorced or widowed spouse can continue until eligible for Medicare or other group health insurance. Upon divorce, dependent children can continue until they no longer qualify as dependents under plan. Upon death of employee, spouse and/or dependent children can continue for 36 months.

Time employer has to notify employee of continuation rights: Within 10 days of termination of coverage.

Time employee has to apply: 60 days from termination of coverage or receipt of employer's notice, whichever is later.

Mississippi

Miss. Code Ann. § 83-9-51

Employers affected: All employers who offer group health insurance and have fewer than 20 employees.

Eligible employees: Employees continuously insured for previous 3 months.

Length of coverage for employee: 12 months.

Length of coverage for dependents: 12 months.

Time employer has to notify employee of continuation rights: Insurer must notify former or deceased employee's dependent child or divorced spouse of option to continue insurance within 14 days of their becoming ineligible for coverage on employee's policy.

Time employee has to apply: Employee must apply and submit payment before group coverage ends; dependents or former spouse must elect continuation coverage within 30 days of receiving insurer's notice.

Missouri

Mo. Rev. Stat. § 376.428

Employers affected: All employers who offer group health insurance.

Eligible employees: Employees continuously insured for previous 3 months.

Length of coverage for employee: 9 months.

Length of coverage for dependents: 9 months.

Time employer has to notify employee of continuation rights: No later than date group coverage would end.

Time employee has to apply: 31 days from date group coverage would end.

Montana

Mont. Code Ann. §§ 33-22-506 to 33-22-510

Employers affected: All employers who offer group disability insurance.

State Health Insurance Continuations Laws (continued)

Eligible employees: All employees.

Length of coverage for employee: One year (with employer's consent).

Time employee has to apply: 31 days from date group coverage would end.

Special situations: Insurer may not discontinue benefits to child with disabilities after child exceeds age limit for dependent status.

Nebraska

Neb. Rev. Stat. §§ 44-1640 and following, 44-7406

Employers affected: Employers not subject to federal COBRA laws.

Eligible employees: All covered employees.

Length of coverage for employee: 6 months.

Length of coverage for dependents: One year upon death of insured employee. Subjects of domestic abuse who have lost coverage under abuser's plan and who do not qualify for COBRA may have 18 months' coverage (applies to all employers).

Time employer has to notify employee of continuation rights: Within 10 days of termination of employment must send notice by certified mail.

Time employee has to apply: 10 days from receipt of employer's notice.

Nevada

Nev. Rev. Stat. Ann. §§ 689B.245 and following, 689B.0345

Employers affected: Employers with fewer than 20 employees.

Eligible employees: Employees continuously insured for previous 12 months.

Length of coverage for employee: 18 months.

Length of coverage for dependents: 36 months; insurer cannot terminate coverage for disabled, dependent child who is too old to qualify as a dependent under the plan.

Time employer has to notify employee of continuation rights: 14 days after receiving notice of employee's eligibility.

Time employee has to apply: Must notify employer within 60 days of becoming eligible for continuation coverage; must apply within 60 days after receiving employer's notice.

Special situations: While employee is on leave without pay due to disability, 12 months for employee and dependents (applies to all employers).

New Hampshire

N.H. Rev. Stat. Ann. §§ 415:18(VIIg), (VII-a)

Employers affected: Employers with 2 to 19 employees.

Eligible employees: All insured employees are eligible.

Length of coverage for employee: 18 months; 29 months if disabled at termination or during first 60 days of continuation coverage.

Length of coverage for dependents: 18 months; 29 months if disabled at termination or during first 60 days of continuation coverage; 36 months upon death of employee, divorce or legal separation, loss of dependent status, or employee's eligibility for Medicare.

Time employer has to notify employee of continuation rights: Within 15 days of termination of coverage.

Time employee has to apply: Within 31 days of termination of coverage.

Special situations: Layoff or termination due to strike; 6 months' coverage with option to extend for an additional 12 months. Surviving, divorced, or legally separated spouse who is 55 or older

State Health Insurance Continuations Laws (continued)

may continue benefits available until eligible for Medicare or other employer-based group insurance.

New Jersey

N.J. Stat. Ann. §§ 17B:27-51.12, 17B:27A-27

Employers affected: Employers with 2 to 50 employees.

Eligible employees: Employed full time (25 or more hours).

Length of coverage for employee: 18 months; 29 months if disabled at termination or during first 60 days of continuation coverage.

Length of coverage for dependents: 18 months; 29 months if disabled at termination or during first 60 days of continuation coverage; 36 months upon death of employee, divorce or legal separation, loss of dependent status, or employee's eligibility for Medicare.

Time employer has to notify employee of continuation rights: At time of qualifying event employer or carrier notifies employee.

Time employee has to apply: Within 30 days of qualifying event.

Special benefits: Coverage must be identical to that offered to current employees.

Special situations: Total disability: Employee who has been insured for previous 3 months and employee's dependents entitled to continuation coverage that includes all benefits offered by group policy (applies to all employers).

New Mexico

N.M. Stat. Ann. § 59A-18-16

Employers affected: All employers who offer group health insurance.

Eligible employees: All insured employees are eligible.

Length of coverage for employee: 6 months.

Length of coverage for dependents: May continue group coverage or convert to individual policies upon death of covered employee or divorce or legal separation.

Time employer has to notify employee of continuation rights: Insurer or employer gives written notice at time of termination.

Time employee has to apply: 30 days after receiving notice.

New York

N.Y. Ins. Law §§ 3221(f), 3221(m)

Employers affected: All employers who offer group health insurance and have fewer than 20 employees.

Eligible employees: All covered employees are eligible.

Length of coverage for employee: 18 months; 29 months if disabled at termination or during first 60 days of continuation coverage.

Length of coverage for dependents: 18 months; 29 months if disabled at termination or during first 60 days of continuation; 36 months upon death of employee, divorce or legal separation, loss of dependent status, or employee's eligibility for Medicare.

Time employee has to apply: 60 days after termination or receipt of notice, whichever is later.

North Carolina

N.C. Gen. Stat. §§ 58-53-5 to 58-53-40

Employers affected: All employers who offer group health insurance.

Eligible employees: Employees continuously insured for previous 3 months.

Length of coverage for employee: 18 months.

State Health Insurance Continuations Laws (continued)

Length of coverage for dependents: 18 months.

Time employer has to notify employee of continuation rights: Employer has option of notifying employee as part of the exit process.

Time employee has to apply: 60 days.

North Dakota
N.D. Cent. Code §§ 26.1-36-23, 26.1-36-23.1

Employers affected: All employers who offer group health insurance.

Eligible employees: Employees continuously insured for previous 3 months.

Length of coverage for employee: 39 weeks.

Length of coverage for dependents: 39 weeks; 36 months if required by divorce or annulment decree.

Time employee has to apply: Within 10 days of termination or of receiving notice of continuation rights, whichever is later, but no more than 31 days from termination.

Ohio
Ohio Rev. Code Ann. §§ 3923.38, 1751.53

Employers affected: All employers who offer group health insurance.

Eligible employees: Employees continuously insured for previous 3 months who are entitled to unemployment benefits.

Length of coverage for employee: 6 months.

Length of coverage for dependents: 6 months.

Time employer has to notify employee of continuation rights: At termination of employment.

Time employee has to apply: Whichever is earlier: 31 days after coverage terminates; 10 days after coverage terminates if employer notified employee of continuation rights prior to termination; 10 days after employer notified employee of continuation rights, if notice was given after coverage terminated.

Oklahoma
Okla. Stat. Ann. tit. 36, § 4509

Employers affected: All employers who offer group health insurance.

Eligible employees: Employees insured for at least 6 months. (All other employees and their dependents entitled to 30 days' continuation coverage.)

Length of coverage for employee: Only for losses or conditions that began while group policy was in effect: 3 months for basic coverage; 6 months for major medical at the same premium rate prior to termination of coverage.

Length of coverage for dependents: Only for losses or conditions that began while group policy was in effect: 3 months for basic coverage; 6 months for major medical at the same premium rate prior to termination of coverage.

Special benefits: Includes maternity care for pregnancy begun while group policy was in effect.

Oregon
Or. Rev. Stat. §§ 743.600 to 743.610

Employers affected: Employers not subject to federal COBRA laws.

Eligible employees: Employees continuously insured for previous 3 months.

Length of coverage for employee: 6 months.

Length of coverage for dependents: 6 months.

Time employee has to apply: 10 days after termination or after receiving notice of continuation rights, whichever is later, but not more than 31 days.

State Health Insurance Continuations Laws (continued)

Special situations: Surviving, divorced, or legally separated spouse who is 55 or older and dependent children entitled to continuation coverage until spouse remarries or is eligible for other coverage. Must include dental, vision, or prescription drug benefits if they were offered in original plan (applies to employers with 20 or more employees).

Rhode Island

R.I. Gen. Laws §§ 27-19.1-1, 27-20.4-1 to 27-20.4-2

Employers affected: All employers who offer group health insurance.

Eligible employees: All insured employees are eligible.

Length of coverage for employee: 18 months (but not longer than continuous employment). Cannot be required to pay more than one month premium at a time.

Length of coverage for dependents: 18 months (but not longer than continuous employment). Cannot be required to pay more than one month premium at a time.

Time employer has to notify employee of continuation rights: Employers must post a conspicuous notice of employee continuation rights.

Time employee has to apply: 30 days from termination of coverage.

Special situations: If right to receiving continuing health insurance is stated in the divorce judgment, divorced spouse has right to continue coverage as long as employee remains covered or until divorced spouse remarries or becomes eligible for other group insurance. If covered employee remarries, divorced spouse must be given right to purchase an individual policy from same insurer.

South Carolina

S.C. Code Ann. § 38-71-770

Employers affected: All employers who offer group health insurance.

Eligible employees: Employees continuously insured for previous 6 months.

Length of coverage for employee: 6 months (in addition to part of month remaining at-termination).

Length of coverage for dependents: 6 months (in addition to part of month remaining at termination).

Time employer has to notify employee of continuation rights: At time of termination must clearly and meaningfully advise employee of continuation rights.

South Dakota

S.D. Codified Laws Ann. §§ 58-18-7.5, 58-18-7.12, 58-18C-1

Employers affected: All employers who offer group health insurance.

Eligible employees: All covered employees.

Length of coverage for employee: 18 months; 29 months if disabled at termination or during first 60 days of continuation coverage.

Length of coverage for dependents: 18 months; 29 months if disabled at termination or during first 60 days of continuation coverage; 36 months upon death of employee, divorce or legal separation, loss of dependent status, employee's eligibility for Medicare.

Special situations: When employer goes out of business: 12 months' continuation coverage available to all employees. Employer must notify employees within 10 days of termination of benefits; employees must apply within 60 days of

State Health Insurance Continuations Laws (continued)

receipt of employer's notice or within 90 days of termination of benefits if no notice given.

Tennessee

Tenn. Code Ann. § 56-7-2312

Employers affected: All employers who offer group health insurance.

Eligible employees: Employees continuously insured for previous 3 months.

Length of coverage for employee: 3 months (in addition to part of month remaining at termination).

Length of coverage for dependents: 3 months (in addition to part of month remaining at termination); 15 months upon death of employee or divorce.

Special situations: Employee or dependent who is pregnant at time of termination entitled to continuation benefits for 6 months following the end of pregnancy.

Texas

Tex. Ins. Code Ann. §§ 1251.252 to 1251.255

Employers affected: All employers who offer group health insurance.

Eligible employees: Employees continuously insured for previous 3 months.

Length of coverage for employee: 6 months.

Length of coverage for dependents: 6 months.

Time employee has to apply: 31 days from termination of coverage or receiving notice of continuation rights from employer or insurer, whichever is later.

Special situations: Layoff due to a labor dispute: Employee entitled to continuation benefits for duration of dispute, but no longer than 6 months.

Utah

Utah Code Ann. § 31A-22-722

Employers affected: All employers who offer group health insurance.

Eligible employees: Employees continuously insured for previous 6 months.

Length of coverage for employee: 6 months.

Length of coverage for dependents: 6 months.

Time employer has to notify employee of continuation rights: In writing within 30 days of termination of coverage.

Time employee has to apply: Within 30 days of receiving employer's notice of continuation rights.

Vermont

Vt. Stat. Ann. tit. 8, §§ 4090a to 4090c

Employers affected: All employers who offer group health insurance and have fewer than 20 employees.

Eligible employees: Employees continuously insured for previous 3 months.

Length of coverage for employee: 6 months.

Length of coverage for dependents: 6 months.

Time employee has to apply: Within 60 days (upon death of employee or group member); within 30 days (upon termination, change of marital status, or loss of dependent status) of the date that group coverage terminates, or the date of being notified of continuation rights, whichever is sooner.

Virginia

Va. Code Ann. §§ 38.2-3541 to 38.2-3452; 38.2-3416

Employers affected: All employers who offer group health insurance.

State Health Insurance Continuations Laws (continued)

Eligible employees: Employees continuously insured for previous 3 months.

Length of coverage for employee: 90 days.

Length of coverage for dependents: 90 days.

Time employer has to notify employee of continuation rights: 15 days from termination of coverage.

Time employee has to apply: Must apply for continuation and pay entire 90-day premium before termination of coverage.

Special situations: Employee may convert to an individual policy instead of applying for continuation coverage (must apply within 31 days of termination of coverage).

Washington

Wash. Rev. Code Ann. §§ 48.21.075, 48.21.250, 48.21.260

Employers affected: All employers who offer and pay for group health insurance.

Eligible employees: Insured employees on strike.

Length of coverage for employee: 6 months if employee goes on strike.

Length of coverage for dependents: 6 months if employee goes on strike.

Special situations: Former employees may continue benefits for a period of time agreed upon with the employer. At the end of that time, the employee may then convert to an individual policy unless terminated for misconduct—in that case, employee's spouse and dependents may convert, but not employee.

West Virginia

W.Va. Code §§ 33-16-2, 33-16-3(e)

Employers affected: Employers providing insurance for at least 2 employees.

Eligible employees: All covered employees are eligible.

Length of coverage for employee: 18 months in case of involuntary layoff.

Wisconsin

Wis. Stat. Ann. § 632.897

Employers affected: All employers who offer group health insurance.

Eligible employees: Employees continuously insured for previous 3 months.

Length of coverage for employee: 18 months (or longer at insurer's option).

Length of coverage for dependents: 18 months (or longer at insurer's option).

Time employer has to notify employee of continuation rights: 5 days from termination of coverage.

Time employee has to apply: 30 days after receiving employer's notice.

Wyoming

Wyo. Stat. § 26-19-113

Employers affected: Employers not subject to federal COBRA laws.

Eligible employees: Employees continuously insured for previous 3 months.

Length of coverage for employee: 12 months.

Length of coverage for dependents: 12 months.

Time employee has to apply: 31 days from termination of coverage.

Current as of February 2007

Utilization Review

If your health insurance coverage provider has joined the swelling ranks of those who use a process called utilization review, you may get caught in the crossfire of one of the greatest workplace legal feuds on record if you become ill.

The idea behind utilization review is simple: By having an objective eye, usually an independent agency, take a look at your medical problem and approve or disapprove the things your doctor recommends, insurance companies can cut down on treatments that are unnecessary and expensive. The savings can then be passed along to the employers and employees who are finding it ever more difficult to pay for health insurance coverage.

Most physicians hate utilization review—for different reasons. Some feel the pain in their wallets: Any process that prevents doctors from prescribing treatment significantly reduces the charges they can bill to your insurance company. And a number of doctors view utilization review as nettlesome bureaucratic padding—too often staffed with decision makers who know little about medical practice. But employers like utilization review. So lawyers have found a lucrative place for themselves in the middle of that opinion clash—routinely filing lawsuits on behalf of doctors, employers, and their insurance companies.

Utilization Review and Insurance Coverage

Unless the legal feud over utilization review is settled, you should be particularly careful in making sure you understand what role it would play in your health care coverage if you became ill and needed to file a claim.

Here are some questions to ask to help you evaluate coverage:

- Does my health insurance coverage include a provision for utilization review?
- If so, who will perform the review? Will it be someone on the company's staff? Someone on the insurance company's staff? An outside agency?
- What kind of professional credentials are required of the people who would review my doctor's recommendations for treating me?
- What methods does my health insurance coverage use to enforce its utilization review decisions? For example, some health insurance plans merely compile lists of doctors whose charges are habitually high and then try to talk them into exercising restraint. Others use more aggressive tactics, such as reducing by 25% the fees paid to doctors who fail to obtain permission from the insurance company before performing a treatment on a patient.

- Do I have the option of electing to participate in a health insurance plan that doesn't include utilization review? If so, will it cost me more to be covered by that plan?
- If my doctor or I disagree with a decision made by a reviewer, would I have the option of rejecting the utilization reviewer's decision?

Having this information is not likely to keep you completely out of the utilization review feud, but at least you will understand what is happening to you and what options you have if you get caught in it.

CHAPTER

4

Family and Medical Leave

The typical American household has changed dramatically in the decades since the 1950s, when most families were rigidly organized around a wage-earning father and a housekeeping, stay-at-home mother.

The workforce, too, has changed dramatically, as women, single parents, and two-paycheck couples have entered in droves.

And, due to the astronomical costs of medical care, more workers are yoked with the responsibility for providing at least some of the care for sick or injured family members and aging parents.

There have been some additions to workplace legal rights that recognize these grand changes. But, by and large, legislation has limped far behind societal shifts.

The Family and Medical Leave Act

The most sweeping federal law to help workers with the precarious balance between job and family is the Family and Medical Leave Act, or FMLA. (29 U.S.C. §§ 2601 and following.) Under the FMLA, an employee is eligible for up to 12 weeks of unpaid leave during a year's time for the birth or adoption of a child, family health needs, or the employee's own health needs.

The employer must not only allow an employee to take the leave, but must allow the employee to return to the same or a similar position to the one he or she held before taking it. And, during the leave, the employer must continue to make the same benefit contributions, such as paying insurance policy premiums, as the employee was receiving before going on leave. However, the FMLA does not require that employers pay any benefits that are not generally provided to employees—and seniority and pension benefits need not accrue during an employee's leave.

Employers who violate the Act, including its provisions against retaliating against those who take advantage of its protections (see "Penalties for Retaliation," below), may be required to pay back pay, damages, attorneys' and expert witnesses' fees—and, perhaps more important, for the cost of up to 12 weeks of caring for a child, spouse, or parent.

Who Is Covered

The FMLA applies to all private and public employers with 50 or more employees—an estimated one-half of the workforce.

To take advantage of this law, an employee must have:

- been employed at the same workplace for a year or more, and
- worked at least 1,250 hours—or about 24 hours a week—during the year preceding the leave.

At first glance, this length of work requirement seems straightforward. But questions about the math have surfaced. The Department of Labor, in an attempt to provide guidance on the issue, has stated that the requisite 12 months of employment must be measured as of the date the leave begins. But that still leaves murky whether a employee can roll into meeting the requirement if, for example, he or she is out on sick leave or vacation before being on the job for a full year.

Courts that have considered this issue have reached different conclusions. Most conclude that the date the leave began was prior to the 12-month anniversary and deny any entitlement to FMLA leave. However, a district court in Maine has held otherwise, relying on the regulation that states that being on the payroll, even if on leave, counts as employment, and therefore, once 12 months have been reached, an employee meets the eligibility prerequisite. (*Ruder v. Maine General Medical Center*, 204 F. Supp. 2d 16 (D. Me. 2002).)

Restrictions on Coverage

Anticipating that some of the leave provisions in the FMLA might cause a hardship for smaller and some specialized employers, Congress included a number of exceptions to its coverage. Some of the exceptions sound rather harsh and would likely result in dividing some workplaces—providing some employees with benefits that others are blanketly denied. So, to maintain morale and encourage company loyalty, many employers opt to adopt uniform standards for all employees rather than adhere slavishly to the exceptions allowed.

50 Employees Within 75 Miles

Companies with fewer than 50 employees within a 75-mile radius are exempt from the FMLA. This means that small regional offices of even the largest companies may be exempt from the law's requirements. However, the magic number of 50, for purposes of the FMLA, is computed by adding up all the employees on the payroll, so that those already on leave and those who work erratic schedules are tallied into the final count.

The Highest-paid 10%

The law allows companies to exempt the highest-paid 10% of their employees. This exception recognizes the theory that, in many companies, the highest-paid employees are the executives, the leaders, and the managers —the ones who must be around to keep workplaces running smoothly. Employers may choose to provide these employees with unpaid leave, however, and many do— recognizing that the standard is broader than the reality of most workplaces. For example, in a smallish workplace of 100 employees, it is highly unlikely that ten workers will be deemed top-level executives.

Teachers and Instructors

Those who work as schoolteachers or instructors are partially exempt from the FMLA—that is, they may be restricted from taking their unpaid leave until the end of a teaching period, commonly a quarter or semester, to avoid disrupting the continuity of the classroom. Teaching assistants and school staff, however, are fully covered under the FMLA.

Two Spouses, One Employer

Unless their need for leave is due to a personal medical problem, spouses who work for the same employer must aggregate their 12 weeks of leave time—that is, together, they are entitled to a total of 12 weeks off.

When Counting Employees, Use Both Hands

In a departure from most other federal workplace laws, the FMLA may extend coverage to workers by including contingent workers among those counted to meet the 50-employee threshold for coverage.

Workers generally cut out of other workplace benefits who may be able to take advantage of the FMLA include temp workers who customarily are placed with employers through agencies. The FMLA regulations specify that temp agencies and the workplaces accepting the workers may be considered their joint employers. The two must generally split duties under the FMLA. The temp agency is charged with informing workers about benefits, providing leave, and returning the worker to his or her job after a leave. The employer accepting the temp's services must also accept the temp back after a leave and cannot discriminate against a temp who has taken a leave. Time spent working at the temp agency and for the employer can be added to meet the FMLA requirement of 1,250 workhours—an especially important twist if an employer decides to hire the temp.

EXAMPLE: Macrotech, a computer software firm, has only 20 employees. It contacts the Placeright Agency, a midsized temp agency, to provide ten more programmers to help deliver a new software program. Since Macrotech and Placeright together have over 50 employees, both now must comply with FMLA requirements.

The expansive counting requirements of the FMLA may also extend coverage to other work arrangements. This includes:

- small corporate employers or joint venturers that share control over a business where the combined employee total is at least 50 employees, and
- business owners who buy out a business that was covered by FMLA regs in the past.

While small business owners loudly protested that this broad interpretation of the counting requirement was nothing more than a sleight of hand that would thwart their abilities to do business, their cries fell on the Department of Labor's selectively deaf ears.

Early Returns Show Tepid Results

The Family and Medical Leave Act is a newish law. Before it took effect in July of 1993, critics blasted the law as portending doom for small businesses forced to keep unproductive workers on staff. Supporters heralded the measure as the first real taste of family values palatable to workers of every political stripe.

But, in its short history, the law has delivered neither gloom nor glory. No one is quite sure why—and pollsters, for once, have avoided the issue of why no one showed up for the revolution.

In February of 1998, on the FMLA's fifth anniversary, then-Secretary of Labor Alexis Herman declared victory: "The past five years have proven that this law has worked exactly as it was intended," she said. "Millions of American workers have gained precious time to be with their families during medical emergencies. At the same time, their employers have not experienced the effects that some who opposed the law feared."

Herman's view of the glass is half full.

The Department of Labor, responsible for enforcing the law, investigated 6,000 FMLA complaints during its first five years or so in existence. About 90% of those were settled, usually after a quick call from the DOL explaining how to comply. Agency officials claim they have completed investigating and acting on about 95% of the complaints filed; it has taken legal action for violations in only 16 cases.

And a 2000 report by the Department of Labor also revealed other, more confounding numbers. Only 16.5% of all eligible workers took leave; an additional 3.5 million workers who

needed leave said they could not afford to take time off unpaid.

Of those who took FMLA leave:

- 7.9% used the time for a pregnancy-related disability.
- 18.5% used it to care for a newborn or adopted or foster child.
- 11% used it to care for an ill child.
- More than 50% used it to cover their own serious illnesses.

The time spent off work for parental leave was brief—usually less than ten days.

Perhaps most tellingly, there has been no similar survey of FMLA effectiveness since 2000. The Act's tenth anniversary passed, unmarked by the usual glowing proclamations from the Secretary of Labor—although Senators Christopher Dodd (D-Conn.) and Edward Kennedy (D-Mass.) did take the occasion to introduce a bill, The Family and Medical Leave Expansion Act, that included a pilot program that would allow six weeks of paid leave.

Why are so few employees taking advantage of the FMLA? One key reason is that the leave is unpaid—meaning that many workers cannot afford to take advantage of it. Among women who took time off for family care during the FMLA's first 18 months, one in eight was forced to go on public assistance to make ends meet.

Interestingly, a number of employees say they would hesitate to take the proffered leave because of more subtle psychological pressures: They think others would view them as less-serious workers. In a workplace that gives the greatest glories to those who have put in the most hours, perceived slackers do not make the grade.

Congress defends this exception in the FMLA as a way to counter an employer's unwillingness to hire a married couple. In reality, it forces a couple to choose who should be the caregiver in the family. Note, however, that because of the loophole allowing time off for medical problems, if a woman qualifies for a pregnancy leave, her husband may be entitled to family leave to care for her.

Scheduling Time Off

Theoretically, an employee and employer are required to agree in advance on scheduling leave time to be taken under the FMLA. The law requires the employee to give at least 30 days of notice for "foreseeable medical treatment."

But the reality is that the FMLA provides time off from work for events that are often unpredictable and impossible to schedule precisely: birth, adoption, sudden illness. In cases of medical emergencies, premature births, or surprise adoption placements, employee leave is allowed—even without the employer's advance approval.

Reasons for Time Off

The FMLA established what was long awaited in the workplace: a federal standard guaranteeing many workers the right to leave for the birth or adoption of a child and to care for their own or a family member's serious health condition.

When Is a Benefit Not a Benefit?

Your employer can count your accrued paid benefits—vacation, sick leave, and personal leave days—toward the 12 weeks of leave you are allowed under the FMLA, as long as that paid leave is taken for the same reason as family leave would be taken. If you use three weeks of vacation, for example, and another week of sick leave, you are left with only eight weeks of protected job leave under the FMLA.

To ease the strain, however, many employers let employees decide whether to include paid leave time as part of their family leave allotment.

Birth, Adoption, or Foster Care

The FMLA states that all covered employees must be given 12 weeks of unpaid leave for the birth, adoption, or foster placement of a child, as long as that leave is taken within a year of the child's arrival. Also, if the leave is for a new child, it must be taken in a 12-week chunk (unlike a leave for medical problems, which may be scheduled more flexibly).

Health Problems

The law is intended to allow workers to provide adequate care for children under 18 who are ill or injured and for children 18 and older who cannot take care of themselves because of a physical or mental disability. Leave is available to care for an employee's son or daughter—which is broadly defined to include biological, adopted, or foster children; stepchildren; and legal wards. Also covered are children for whom employees stand in the place of parents—such as cases in which a grandparent, aunt, or uncle has complete caretaking responsibilities.

The FMLA also provides for time off for health problems—physical and psychological —that affect either the employee or his or her spouse or parents. The required care need only limit the employee's ability to work or the employee's family member's ability to carry on with daily activities.

In the FMLA, the definition of spouse is limited to "a husband or wife, as the case may be"—overtly banning unmarried partners from the Act's coverage. In-laws are not included in the definition of parents.

The FMLA's definition of a medical condition entitling an employee to take a leave is quite liberal. It includes, for example, time off to care for a parent or spouse who has Alzheimer's disease or clinical depression, has suffered a stroke, is recovering from major surgery, or is in the final stages of a terminal disease. It also covers employees who need time off to recover from the side effects of a medical treatment—including chemotherapy or radiation treatments.

However, the employee's or family member's health condition or medical treatment must require either an overnight stay in the hospital or a three-day absence from work. For example, a one-time health problem that is expected to require a short recovery period, such as orthodontic treatments, is not covered under the FMLA.

Nor does the law cover requests for time off for routine physical, eye, or dental exams—except when required to diagnose a serious illness. In fashioning the law, Congress presumed, rightly or wrongly, that most workplace sick days or personal leave policies would be sufficient to cover these situations.

How Serious is Serious?

Noting that a number of courts had been stumped by the meaning of "serious health condition" in the FMLA, the DOL recently acknowledged that "the department itself has struggled with this definition."

It cited an earlier regulation it had issued that stated that "ordinarily, unless complications arise, the common cold, the flu, earaches, upset stomach, minor ulcers, headaches other than migraine, routine dental or orthodontia problems, periodontal disease, etc., are examples of conditions that do not meet the definition of a serious health condition and do not qualify for FMLA leave."

Just over a year and a half later, however, it changed its tune, stating that the earlier opinion letter expressed "an incorrect view, being inconsistent with the department's established interpretation of qualifying 'serious health conditions' under the FMLA regulations." Minor illnesses would not be expected to last more than three days, but if they did meet the regulatory criteria for a serious health condition, they would qualify for FMLA leave.

The DOL recently signaled that it might soon again revamp the definition.

Penalties for Retaliation

By passing the FMLA, Congress intended to signal that employers must foster employees' needs to preserve both family and job. As in other workplace laws prohibiting unfair practices, the FMLA prohibits employers from demoting or firing an employee solely because he or she took a legally sanctioned leave.

The law also provides that an employer may not use either a carrot or a stick in handling leave requests. That is, an employee may not be promised a raise or promotion as an inducement not to take a leave; nor may an employee be denied a raise or promotion because of taking a leave.

Returning to Work

When you return to work after taking a family leave, the FMLA requires that you be returned to your old position or to an equivalent one.

This is a strict requirement and, according to the Department of Labor, the single provision employers violate most often. Congress has intimated that it is not enough that the position to which you are returned be "comparable" or "similar." It has stated that the "terms, conditions, and privileges"—including the security of the position within the company—must be the same as the previous position.

EXAMPLE: A credit manager, responsible for supervising several employees, took a leave from her position due to pregnancy. When she returned to work, she was given a job with the same pay, the same benefits, and the same office as her previous position, but she no longer had a job title, she supervised fewer employees—and a fourth of her worktime was to be spent in clerical work. Focusing on the diminished responsibility and authority, a court held that the new position was not equivalent under the terms of the FMLA. (*Kelley Co., Inc. v. Marquardt*, 493 N.W. 2d 68 (1992).)

If You Do Not Return to Work

An interesting twist in the law provides that if an employee does not return to work after an FMLA-sanctioned leave, the employer may seek return of the benefits paid while he or she was away.

Although it has not yet been questioned in court, this recapture provision seems to be a mistake in the law, as it enables employers to set off benefit amounts from an employee's final paycheck or from a severance award. However, the setoff most often involves health insurance premiums, which the employer usually pays directly to the insurer.

TIP

Counting military time under the FLSA. The Department of Labor recently issued a memorandum that clarifies its position on the rights of returning uniformed service members to family and medical leave under the Uniformed Services Employment and Reemployment Rights Act, or USERRA. (See Chapter 2, "Time Off for Military or National Guard Duty.")

Under ordinary circumstances, a worker becomes eligible for leave under the FMLA after working for a covered employer for at least 12 months, during which he or she completed at least 1,250 hours of work. The memorandum clarifies that the months and hours that the employee would have worked, but for his or her military service, should be combined with the months employed and the hours actually worked to meet the 12 months and the 1,250 hours of employment required by the FMLA.

Enforcing Your Rights

You must file a claim under the FMLA within two years after an employer violates the Act—or within three years if the violation is willful. It is still unclear what conduct will be considered willful, but retaliation is likely to be such an offense.

As mentioned, employers found to violate the FMLA may be liable for a number of costs and benefits, including:

- wages, salary, employment benefits, or other compensation an employee has lost
- the cost of providing up to 12 weeks of care for a baby or ill family member
- reasonable attorneys' and expert witness fees, and
- interest on the amounts described above.

The employee may also win the right to be promoted or reinstated to a particular job.

The FMLA is now enforced by the U.S. Department of Labor, much the same as the Fair Labor Standards Act, which controls work hours and wages. (See Chapter 2, "Filing a Complaint or Lawsuit.") If you have specific questions about the FMLA, contact the Department of Labor at 866-487-2365. Or check the materials on the department's website, at www.dol.gov.

The Department of Labor recommends that you take the following commonsense steps if you are denied family and medical leave to which you are entitled:

- **Write down what happened.** Write down the date, time, and place. Include what was said and who was there. Keep a copy of these notes at home. They will be useful if you decide to file a complaint against your company or take legal action.
- **Get emotional support from friends and family.** It can be very upsetting to feel treated unfairly at work. Take care of yourself. Think about what you want to do. Get help to do it.
- **Talk to your union representative.** If you belong to a union, your union representative can help you file a grievance if you are denied family leave.
- **See what your company can do to help.** Your company may have a way for you to make a complaint. For instance, some companies offer ways to resolve problems, such as mediation. Check your employee handbook for procedures that may be available.
- **Find out if other workers have been denied leave.** Talk with anyone else who had the same problem. Join with them to try to work out the problem.
- **Keep doing a good job and keep a record of your work.** Keep copies at home of your job evaluations and any letters or memos that show that you do a good job at work. Your boss may criticize your job performance later on in order to defend what he or she did to you.

A Leave by Any Other Name Is Still FMLA Leave

In the first case it has decided on the FMLA, the U.S. Supreme Court sent a cloaked message to employees that they must be proactive about learning about their legal rights to medical leave rather than depending on their employers to educate them.

Ironically, the case arose over regulations that Congress had earlier urged the Department of Labor to issue to make it easier to administer the tangled rules that make up the FMLA. While the FMLA grants 12 weeks of unpaid medical leave, it urges employers to adopt more generous policies on their own. One of the companies that seemed to heed this call to generosity was shoe manufacturer Wolverine World Wide. It provided employees who had been on the job for at least six months with up to 30 weeks of disability leave.

One year after she began work at the shoe manufacturer Wolverine, Tracy Ragsdale was diagnosed with Hodgkin's disease. While she underwent surgery and radiation treatments, Wolverine held her job open, paid for six months of health insurance, and granted her repeated extensions of leave time. But after she had taken 30 weeks of leave, Wolverine denied Ragsdale's requests for more time off and to work part time. And, when she did not come back to work, she was fired.

Ragsdale sued, claiming that she was entitled to 12 additional weeks of leave because Wolverine had violated a procedural rule promulgated by the Department of Labor that required that she be informed in writing that the 30 weeks

of leave she took would be counted against her FMLA entitlement of 12 weeks.

In reviewing the case, the Supreme Court held that Ragsdale was right; the rule technically required employers to designate the time off as FMLA leave. But it shot down the DOL rule as an overly bureaucratic machination that would defeat the very purpose of the FMLA by dissuading employers from providing more generous leave on their own. Rather than dictate a guiding rule about categorizing leave, the Court opined that close FMLA questions must be weighed and decided individually—a signal that the courts will likely be littered with cases in the future as workplaces grapple with interpreting the FMLA.

The Court noted that 12 weeks' time off for FMLA is inviolate—a hotly contested compromise reached by employers who wanted fewer weeks and employees who wanted more.

And, finally, it intimated that in resolving future questions over whether damages or other relief should be given in FMLA cases, the focus should be on the reality of whether an employee would have:

- taken leave
- returned to work after taking the leave, or
- taken less leave or intermittent leave, if the employer had given the proper notice.

In this interesting twist, the Court noted that the DOL would exceed its authority by setting out categorical penalties in its regulations.

(*Ragsdale v. Wolverine World Wide, Inc.*, 535 U.S. 81 (2002).)

- **File a complaint.** Remember, the law has a time limit on how long you can wait to file a complaint against your company. You can file a complaint even if you do not work for your employer anymore. You can file a complaint through your local U.S. Department of Labor Wage and Hour office. Look in the telephone book under the heading Federal Government.

- **Contact community resources.** If you and several other workers are being denied rights to leave by the same boss, you may be able to file a formal complaint as a group. Call a women's or disability rights group. You may be able to help other people in the future.

- **Find out more about your legal rights.** You do not need a lawyer to file a legal claim. But you may want to call a free legal service or a lawyer who specializes in job rights. (See the Appendix and Chapter 17 for more information.

State Laws on Family Leave

The majority of states now have leave laws, but their provisions differ wildly—leaving a patchwork of protections, benefits, and loopholes that are often confusing to both employers and employees.

And on February 5, 2007, San Francisco became the first city in the nation to mandate that employers of all sizes provide paid sick leave for employees, including part-time and temporary workers. The city ordinance entitles every employee to one hour of paid sick leave, to be accrued in hourly increments for every 30 hours worked, with a cap of 40 hours for employers with fewer than ten employees and a cap of 72 hours for all other employers. Employers must allow employees to carry over accrued sick leave, as limited by these caps, but are not required to pay out unused sick leave upon termination of employment. A number of other locales are poised to follow this national precedent.

Leaves With Pay

In general, state family leave laws only require employers to grant an employee a leave without pay. Paid leaves are uncommon, but some companies—typically very large ones or very small ones that regard their employees as family members—do provide at least partial paid leave.

Check with your supervisor well before you anticipate needing a leave to determine your workplace's policy on paid leaves. Make sure that you fulfill all the requirements for receiving your regular pay during the time that you're away from work—such as giving your employer adequate notice of your need to take such a leave.

Choosing Protections

If your state also has some incarnation of a family leave law, you are free to seek benefits under the federal FMLA or your state law—whichever law offers you the greatest benefit. If you have a baby one year, you may use the leave allotted you by the state; if you

Labor The DOL Seeks Help in Understanding Itself

In a rare show of eating humble pie, the Department of Labor issued a "Request for Information From the Public" on December 1, 2006, acknowledging that many of the FMLA provisions and regulations are confused and confusing. The request was hailed by hopefuls as signaling that the DOL is getting serious about considering a major overhaul to the leave law.

In its missive the DOL seeks input "from interested parties having knowledge of, or experience with the FMLA" to submit their comments and other information to help the agency gauge the law's effectiveness.

As discussed above, it sought comment on how to define "serious health condition" to maintain the regulations' substantive standards while also upholding congressional intent that minor illnesses such as colds and earaches not be covered by the FMLA.

And it singled out a number of additional particularly flummoxing provisions.

Coordinating HIPAA claims. The DOL also noted that the enactment of the Health Insurance Portability and Accountability Act, or HIPAA (discussed in Chapter 3), has resulted in challenges about coordinating the two laws. Under HIPAA, a health care provider must first receive a valid authorization from the employee before sending the information to the employer. Yet under the FMLA, the DOL noted, "employers have the statutory right to obtain sufficient medical information to determine whether an employee's leave qualifies for FMLA protections."

In addition to asking about the possibility of simplifying the required certification form, the DOL asked whether the FMLA regulatory provision that permits an employer to contact an employee's health care provider for purposes of clarification and authentication only through the employer's health care provider results in unnecessary expenses for employers or delays the certification process.

Unscheduled intermittent leave. The DOL also acknowledged employers' concerns about unforeseen intermittent leave and the requirement that employees be allowed to take FMLA leave in increments. It stated: "Employers contend that one of the unintended consequences of the FMLA regulations has been that employers have little recourse to prevent those employees who take FMLA leave improperly from doing so under the current regulatory scheme." It asks for more information on the issue from different industries and employers, and about exempt and nonexempt employees.

Morale issues. Noting studies that reveal that employers tend to cover the work of employees out on FMLA leave with coworkers, the DOL also asked how the availability of FMLA leave affects employee morale and productivity.

become ill the next year, you may be entitled to benefits guaranteed by the FMLA. However, several states have recently amended their laws to provide that state and federal coverage cannot be piggybacked; you must choose coverage under one law or the other.

State Laws

State laws governing family leaves differ greatly as to:

- the size of workplace covered—varying from 4 to 100
- the reasons allowed for time off—some states provide leaves for birth and adoption only; others also provide it for family members' illnesses; the District of Columbia appears to be among the first to allow leave to care for domestic partners
- who is covered—a number of states specify that an employee must have worked for one employer for a minimum time before being entitled to a leave
- the length of leave allowed
- the length of notice that an employee must give before taking a leave
- whether or not benefits must be continued and at whose expense
- whether or not an employee is entitled to the same or an equivalent position after returning to work—in some states, this is required only if proper advance notice has been given
- how rights to parental leaves are divided when both parents are employed by the same company, and
- how the laws can be enforced.

Several states also provide that parents must be given a certain amount of unpaid leave to attend a child's school conferences.

On their faces, many state laws are more liberal than the federal law. But many state laws are rife with large loopholes, too. For example, the family leave laws in a number of states provide that an employer is free to replace a worker who has taken leave if the time off would burden the workplace.

Changing Your Mind

A common sore point with employers is that some employees officially state they are taking a parental leave of only a few months, but then decide to become full-time parents and quit their jobs outright.

This strategy is particularly popular among employees who are having their first baby because, at the very least, it seems to allow the option of going back to a job after experimenting with a few months of stay-at-home parenting.

But this strategy is far from new—and most employers have seen it before. Many companies now require employees who take paid parental leaves and then decide to leave their jobs permanently to pay back compensation received during the leave. And the FMLA specifically allows employers to recover the cost of maintaining health insurance coverage from employees who do not return after a leave. (See "If You Do Not Return to Work," above.)

State Family and Medical Leave Laws

States that are not listed below do not have laws that apply to private employers or have laws that offer less protection than the FMLA.

California

Cal. Gov't. Code § 12945; Cal. Lab. Code §§ 230 and following; Cal. Unemp. Ins. §§ 3300 and following

Employers Covered: Employers with 5 or more employees must offer pregnancy leave; employers with 25 or more employees must offer leave for victims of domestic violence or sexual assault and school activity leave; employers with 50 or more employees must offer leave for domestic partners; employers whose employees contribute to state temporary disability insurance ("SDI") fund must allow employees to participate in state's paid family leave benefits program.

Eligible Employees: All employees for pregnancy leave, domestic violence, or school activity leave; employees eligible for leave under federal FMLA for domestic partners leave; employees who contribute to SDI fund for paid family leave benefits program.

Family Medical Leave: Up to 4 months for disability related to pregnancy (in addition to 12 weeks under state or federal FMLA if the employee is eligible). Up to 12 weeks of leave per year to care for seriously ill registered domestic partner. Employees who contribute to SDI fund may receive paid family leave benefits for up to 6 weeks of leave per year to care for a seriously ill family member (including a registered domestic partner) or bond with a new child. This leave is paid through employee contributions to the SDI fund; the employee will receive approximately 55% of regular earnings. Does not provide job protection unless the employee is otherwise covered by the state or federal FMLA.

School Activities: 40 hours per year.

Domestic Violence: Reasonable time for issues dealing with domestic violence or sexual assault, including health, counseling, and safety measures. Family member or domestic partner of a victim of a felony may take leave to attend judicial proceedings related to the crime.

Colorado

Colo. Rev. Stat. §§ 19-5-211, 24-34-402.7

Employers Covered: All employers who offer leave for birth of a child for adoption leave; employers with 50 or more employees for domestic violence leave.

Eligible Employees: All employees for adoption leave; employees with one year of service for domestic violence leave.

Family Medical Leave: Employee must be given same leave for adoption as allowed for childbirth (doesn't apply to stepparent adoption).

Domestic Violence: Up to 3 days' leave to seek restraining order, obtain medical care or counseling, relocate, or seek legal assistance for victim of domestic violence, sexual assault, or stalking.

Connecticut

Conn. Gen. Stat. Ann. §§ 31-51kk to 31-51qq, 46a-51(10), 46a-60(7)

Employers Covered: Employers with 75 employees must offer childbirth, adoption, and serious health condition leave; with 3

State Family and Medical Leave Laws (continued)

employees, must offer maternity disability.

Eligible Employees: Any employee with one year and at least 1,000 hours of service in last 12 months.

Family Medical Leave: 16 weeks per any 24-month period for childbirth, adoption, employee's serious health condition, care for family member with serious health condition, or bone marrow or organ donation. "Reasonable" amount of maternity disability leave. May also use up to 2 weeks' accumulated sick leave.

Family Member: Includes parents-in-law.

District of Columbia

D.C. Code Ann. §§ 32-501 and following, 32-1202

Employers Covered: Employers with at least 20 employees.

Eligible Employees: Employees who have worked at company for at least one year and at least 1,000 hours during the previous 12 months.

Family Medical Leave: 16 weeks per any 24-month period for childbirth, adoption, pregnancy/maternity, employee's serious health condition, or care for family member with serious health condition.

School Activities: Up to 24 hours of leave per year.

Family Member: Includes anyone related by blood, custody, or marriage; anyone sharing employee's residence and with whom employee has a committed relationship (including a child for whom the employee assumes permanent parental responsibility).

Hawaii

Haw. Rev. Stat. §§ 398-1 to 398-11, 378-1, 378-71 to 378-74

Employers Covered: Employers with at least 100 employees must offer childbirth, adoption, and serious health condition leave; all employers must offer pregnancy leave and domestic violence leave.

Eligible Employees: Employees with 6 months of service are eligible for childbirth, adoption, and serious health condition benefits; all employees are eligible for pregnancy and maternity leave.

Family Medical Leave: 4 weeks per calendar year for childbirth, adoption, or care for family member with serious health condition; "reasonable period" of pregnancy/maternity leave required by discrimination statute and case law; may include up to 10 days' accrued leave or sick leave.

Family Member: Includes reciprocal beneficiary, parents-in-law, grandparents, grandparents-in-law, stepparents.

Domestic Violence: Employer with 50 or more employees must allow up to 30 days' unpaid leave per year for employee who is a victim of domestic or sexual violence or if employee's minor child is a victim. Employer with 49 or fewer employees must allow up to 5 days' leave.

Illinois

820 Ill. Comp. Stat. §§ 147/1 and following, 180/1 and following

Employers Covered: Employers with 50 or more employees.

Eligible Employees: Employees who have worked at least half-time for 6 months.

State Family and Medical Leave Laws (continued)

School Activities: 8 hours per year (no more than 4 hours per day); required only if employee has no paid leave available.

Domestic Violence: Up to 12 weeks' unpaid leave per 12-month period for employee who is a victim of domestic violence or sexual assault or for employee with a family or household member who is a victim.

Iowa
Iowa Code § 216.6

Employers Covered: Employers with 4 or more employees.

Eligible Employees: All.

Family Medical Leave: Up to 8 weeks for disability due to pregnancy, childbirth, or legal abortion.

Kentucky
Ky. Rev. Stat. Ann. § 337.015

Employers Covered: All.

Eligible Employees: All.

Family Medical Leave: Up to 6 weeks for adoption of a child under 7 years old.

Louisiana
La. Rev. Stat. Ann. §§ 23:341 to 23:342, 23:1015 and following, 40:1299.124

Employers Covered: Employers with more than 25 employees must offer pregnancy/maternity leave; with at least 20 employees must comply with bone marrow donation provisions; all employers must offer leave for school activities.

Eligible Employees: All employees are eligible for pregnancy/maternity or school activities leave; employees who work 20 or more hours per week are eligible for leave to donate bone marrow.

Family Medical Leave: "Reasonable period of time" not to exceed four months for pregnancy/maternity leave, if necessary for pregnancy or related medical condition; up to 40 hours' paid leave per year to donate bone marrow.

School Activities: 16 hours per year.

Maine
Me. Rev. Stat. Ann. tit. 26, §§ 843 and following

Employers Covered: All employers for domestic violence leave; employers with 15 or more employees at one location for family medical leave.

Eligible Employees: Employees with at least one year of service.

Family Medical Leave: 10 weeks in any two-year period for childbirth, adoption (for child 16 or younger), employee's serious health condition, or care for family member with serious health condition.

Domestic Violence: "Reasonable and necessary" leave for employee who is victim of domestic violence, sexual assault, or stalking, or whose parent, spouse, or child is a victim, to prepare for and attend court, for medical treatment, and for other necessary services.

Maryland
Md. Code Ann., [Lab. & Empl.] § 3-802

Employers Covered: Employers that allow workers to take leave for the birth of a child.

Eligible Employees: All employees.

Family Medical Leave: Employee must be given same leave for adoption as allowed for childbirth.

State Family and Medical Leave Laws (continued)

Massachusetts

Mass. Gen. Laws ch. 149, §§ 52D, 105D; ch. 151B, § 1(5)

Employers Covered: Employers with 6 or more employees must provide maternity and adoption leave; employers with 50 or more employees must offer leave for school activities.

Eligible Employees: Full-time female employees who have completed probationary period, or 3 months of service if no set probationary period, are eligible for maternity and adoption leave; employees who are eligible under FMLA are eligible for all other leave.

Family Medical Leave: 8 weeks total for childbirth/maternity or adoption of child younger than 18 (younger than 23 if disabled); additional 24 hours total per year (combined with school activities leave) to accompany minor child or relative age 60 or older to medical and dental appointments.

School Activities: 24 hours per year total (combined with medical care under "other").

Minnesota

Minn. Stat. Ann. §§ 181.940 and following

Employers Covered: Employers with at least 21 employees at one site must provide childbirth/maternity and adoption leave; with at least 20 employees must allow leave to donate bone marrow; all employers must provide leave for school activities.

Eligible Employees: Employees who have worked at least half-time for one year are eligible for maternity leave; at least 20 hours per week are eligible for leave to donate bone marrow; at least one year are eligible for school activities.

Family Medical Leave: 6 weeks for childbirth/maternity or adoption; up to 40 hours paid leave per year to donate bone marrow; parent can use accrued sick leave to care for sick or injured child.

School Activities: 16 hours in 12-month period; includes activities related to child care, preschool, or special education.

Montana

Mont. Code Ann. §§ 49-2-310, 49-2-311

Employers Covered: All.

Eligible Employees: All.

Family Medical Leave: "Reasonable leave of absence" for pregnancy/maternity and childbirth.

Nebraska

Neb. Rev. Stat. § 48-234

Employers Covered: Employers that allow workers to take leave for the birth of a child.

Eligible Employees: All employees.

Family Medical Leave: Employee must be given same leave as allowed for childbirth to adopt a child under 9 years old or a special needs child under 19. Does not apply to stepparent or foster parent adoptions.

Nevada

Nev. Rev. Stat. Ann. §§ 392.920, 613.335

Employers Covered: All.

Eligible Employees: Parent, guardian, or custodian of a child.

Family Medical Leave: Same sick or disability leave policies that apply to other medical conditions must be extended to pregnancy, miscarriage, and childbirth.

State Family and Medical Leave Laws (continued)

School Activities: Employers may not fire or threaten to fire a parent, guardian, or custodian for attending a school conference or responding to a child's emergency.

New Hampshire
N.H. Rev. Stat. Ann. § 354-A:7(VI)

Employers Covered: Employers with at least 6 employees.

Eligible Employees: All.

Family Medical Leave: Temporary disability leave for childbirth or related medical condition.

New Jersey
N.J. Stat. Ann. §§ 34:11B-1 to 34B:16

Employers Covered: Employers with at least 50 employees.

Eligible Employees: Employees who have worked for at least one year and at least 1,000 hours in previous 12 months.

Family Medical Leave: 12 weeks (or 24 weeks reduced leave schedule) in any 24-month period for pregnancy/maternity, childbirth, adoption, or care for family member with serious health condition.

Family Member: Includes civil domestic partners and parents-in-law; child includes legal ward; parent includes someone with visitation rights.

New York
N.Y. Lab. Law §§ 201-c, 202-a

Employers Covered: Employers that allow workers to take leave for the birth of a child must allow adoption leave; employers with at least 20 employees at one site must allow leave to donate bone marrow.

Eligible Employees: All employees are eligible for adoption leave; employees who work at least 20 hours per week are eligible for leave to donate bone marrow.

Family Medical Leave: Employees must be given same leave as allowed for childbirth to adopt a child of preschool age or younger, or no older than 18 if disabled; up to 24 hours' leave to donate bone marrow.

North Carolina
N.C. Gen. Stat. § 95-28.3

Employers Covered: All employers.

Eligible Employees: All employees.

School Activities: Parents and guardians of school-aged children must be given up to 4 hours of leave per year.

Oregon
Or. Rev. Stat. §§ 659A.030, 659A.150 and following, 659A.312

Employers Covered: Employers of 25 or more employees must provide childbirth, adoption, and serious health condition leave; all employers must allow leave to donate bone marrow.

Eligible Employees: Employees who have worked 25 or more hours per week for at least 180 days are eligible for childbirth, adoption, and serious health condition leave; employees who work an average of 20 or more hours per week are eligible for leave to donate bone marrow.

Family Medical Leave: 12 weeks per year for pregnancy/maternity, adoption, or childbirth; additional 12 weeks per year for serious health condition, care for family member with serious

CHAPTER 4 | FAMILY AND MEDICAL LEAVE | 139

State Family and Medical Leave Laws (continued)

health condition, or care for child who has an illness, injury, or condition that requires home care; up to 40 hours or amount of accrued paid leave (whichever is less) to donate bone marrow.

Family Member: Includes parents-in-law, same-sex domestic partner, and domestic partner's parent or child.

Rhode Island

R.I. Gen. Laws §§ 28-48-1 and following

Employers Covered: Employers with 50 or more employees.

Eligible Employees: Employees who have worked an average of 30 or more hours a week for at least 12 consecutive months.

Family Medical Leave: 13 weeks in any two calendar years for childbirth, adoption of child up to 16 years old, employee's serious health condition, or care for family member with serious health condition.

Family Member: Includes parents-in-law.

School Activities: Up to 10 hours a year.

South Carolina

S.C. Code Ann. § 44-43-80

Employers Covered: Employers with 20 or more workers at one site in South Carolina.

Eligible Employees: Employees who work an average of at least 20 hours per week.

Family Medical Leave: Up to 40 hours paid leave per year to donate bone marrow.

Tennessee

Tenn. Code Ann. § 4-21-408

Employers Covered: Employers with at least 100 employees.

Eligible Employees: Employees who have worked 12 consecutive months.

Family Medical Leave: Up to 4 months of unpaid leave for pregnancy/maternity and childbirth (includes nursing); employee must give 3 months' notice unless a medical emergency requires the leave to begin sooner; these laws must be included in employee handbook.

Vermont

Vt. Stat. Ann. tit. 21, §§ 471 and following

Employers Covered: Employers with at least 10 employees must provide parental leave for childbirth and adoption; with at least 15 employees must provide family medical leave to care for a seriously ill family member or to take a family member to medical appointments.

Eligible Employees: Employees who have worked an average of 30 or more hours per week for at least one year.

Family Medical Leave: 12 weeks per year for childbirth, adoption of child age 16 or younger, employee's serious health condition, or care for family member with a serious health condition; combined with school activities leave, additional 4 hours of unpaid leave in a 30-day period (up to 24 hours per year) to take a family member to a medical, dental, or professional well-care appointment or respond to a family member's medical emergency.

School Activities: Combined with leave described above, 4 hours' total unpaid leave in a 30-day period (but not more than 24 hours per year) to participate in child's school activities.

Family Member: Includes parents-in-law.

State Family and Medical Leave Laws (continued)

Washington

Wash. Rev. Code Ann. §§ 49.78.010 and following, 49.12.265 and following, 49.12.350 and following

Employers Covered: All employers must allow employees to use available paid time off to care for sick family members; employers with 50 or more employees must provide leave to care for newborn, adopted or foster child, or family member with serious health condition.

Eligible Employees: All employees who accrue paid leave can use it to care for sick family members; employees who have worked at least 1,250 hours in the previous year are eligible for parental leave to care for newborn, adopted or foster child; or leave to care for a family member with serious health condition.

Family Medical Leave: In addition to any leave available under federal FMLA, employee may take leave for the period of time when she is sick or temporarily disabled due to pregnancy

or childbirth; employers with 50 or more employees must allow up to 12 weeks during any 12-month period for the birth or placement of a child; all employees can use paid leave to care for a sick family member.

Family member: Includes parents-in-law, grand-parents, and stepparents.

Wisconsin

Wis. Stat. Ann. § 103.10

Employers Covered: Employers of 50 or more employees.

Eligible Employees: Employees who have worked at least one year and 1,000 hours in the preceding 12 months.

Family Medical Leave: 6 weeks per 12-month period for pregnancy/maternity, childbirth, or adoption; additional 2 weeks per 12-month period to care for family member with a serious health condition or for own serious health condition.

Current as of February 2007

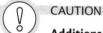 CAUTION

Additional laws may apply. If the chart above indicates that your state has no statute, this means there is no law that specifically addresses the issue. However, there may be a state administrative regulation or local ordinance that does control family and medical leave. Call your state labor department for more information. (See the Appendix for contact details.)

Parental Leave: Does Your State Make the Grade?

Researchers who recently analyzed and graded the state laws on parental leave quickly reached a sad conclusion: "Our nation's parental leave policies are among the worst in the world." It noted that a recent Harvard University study of 168 countries found that 163 guarantee paid leave to women in connection with childbirth, and 45 guarantee paid paternity or parental leave. By contrast, it found, "The United States guarantees no paid leave at all to new parents."

It also noted some new but enduring workplace trends. In 78% of today's families, both parents work for pay. More than half of pregnant women stay on the job until one month before the birth of their first child. And women are returning to work after childbirth at a faster rate than in previous decades.

Despite these realities, the study found that the nation lacks a valedictorian—and most states got lower than C averages. It used the following grading system:

- 25 points for a program that provides paid parental leave to new parents caring for newborns, newly adopted children or newly placed foster children. Benefits may also cover taking leave to care for a spouse or partner with a maternity-related disability.
- 25 points for a program providing additional job protection, broader than that provided by the federal FMLA, to new parents caring for infants.
- 20 points for giving job protection to women for pregnancy-related disabilities and recovery from childbirth that is more expansive than the federal FMLA.

- 20 points for a program that provides workers a longer period of job-protected leave to care for new babies or recover from maternity disability than the federal FMLA.
- 20 points for a program that provides paid medical leave for new birth moms placed on pregnancy disability leave, and for recovery after childbirth.
- 15 points for states that allow workers to use accrued paid leave to care for a new child or a spouse or partner with a maternity disability.
- 15 points for those that provide their own employees with paid family or medical leave that covers pregnancy disability and recovery from childbirth.
- 15 points were awarded to states with At-Home Infant Care (AHIC) programs. AHIC programs provide eligible, lower-income working parents with some wage replacement to provide care for their newborns or newly adopted children.
- 10 points for programs that have their own family and medical leave laws addressing parental leave. These laws give state residents additional rights to ensure their access to job-protected leave after the birth or adoption of a child.
- 10 points were awarded to states that provide their own employees with more than 12 weeks of job-protected parental leave.

The states, with final grades and scores, are listed below.

Parental Leave: Does Your State Make the Grade? (continued)

Report Card

A-		New York	30	F	
California	125	Tennessee	30	Federal Government	0
B+		C-		Alabama	0
Hawaii	90	Illinois	25	Arkansas	0
District of Columbia	85	Montana	25	Delaware	0
Oregon	85	Ohio	25	Georgia	0
B		D+		Idaho	0
Connecticut	75	Iowa	20	Kansas	0
New Jersey	75	South Carolina	20	Maryland	0
Washington	75	D		Mississippi	0
B-		New Mexico	15	Missouri	0
Maine	65	D-		Nebraska	0
Vermont	65	Alaska	10	Nevada	0
Minnesota	60	Arizona	10	North Carolina	0
Rhode Island	60	Colorado	10	Oklahoma	0
C+		Florida	10	Pennsylvania	0
Massachusetts	55	Indiana	10	South Dakota	0
Louisiana	50	Kentucky	10	Texas	0
C		Michigan	10	Virginia	0
Wisconsin	35	North Dakota	10	West Virginia	0
New Hampshire	30	Utah	10	Wyoming	0

Source: *Expecting Better: State-by-State Analysis of Parental Leave Programs*, 2005, by the National Partnership for Women and Families, www.nationalpartnership.org

Antidiscrimination Provisions

Some state laws also forbid workplace discrimination on the basis of gender. In states that have no specific family leave laws, antidiscrimination laws often can be used to establish a right for parents to take time off from work for pregnancy and childbirth.

The antidiscrimination laws of most states include marital status among the factors that may not be used as the basis for work-related discrimination. Some states, such as Alaska, for example, go a step farther, by specifically listing parenthood as an illegal basis for discrimination. (See the chart in Chapter 7, "State and Local Antidiscrimination Laws," for a complete listing.)

Enforcing Your Rights

Antidiscrimination laws often can be applied to such leaves only through slow-moving complaints to the Equal Employment Opportunity Commission or through complex and expensive lawsuits. But, in general, state laws that grant family leaves offer a clear basis for enforcing the right to take such a leave.

But, most often, the most direct and constructive way to exercise your right to take a family leave is to know your rights and to make sure your employer is aware of both your plans and the law well before you take a leave. Nearly all state family leave laws have been enacted fairly recently, and your employer may be sincerely unaware of them.

If you have made your employer aware of your right to take such a leave and the employer refuses to comply, the options available to you will vary with the situation.

- If your problem seems to be merely a matter of disagreement over interpretation of the law, suggest to your employer calling in a mediator or arbitrator to help settle the dispute. (See Chapter 17, "Mediation and Arbitration.")

- If your state is listed in this chapter as having a specific leave law, you may be able to have a state agency intervene in your case. To find the appropriate state agency, start with the one responsible for overseeing your state's antidiscrimination law. (See Chapter 7, "State and Local Antidiscrimination Laws.")

- If your case involves a violation of Title VII of the Civil Rights Act, you can file a complaint with the Equal Employment Opportunity Commission (EEOC). If the EEOC decides not to take action in your case, you may be able to file a federal lawsuit on your own. (See Chapter 7, "Title VII of the Civil Rights Act.")

- If your state has no agency to enforce its law, you may be able to file a lawsuit on your own behalf. (See Chapter 7, "Hiring a Lawyer.") In some states, those who sue under family leave laws are allowed to collect punitive damages, court fees, and the cost of hiring a lawyer to help.

When Parents' Rights Are Parents' Wrongs

According to many experts, the next wave of legal reform in the workplace is likely to be championed by an unexpected source: workers who have no children.

The backlash, ironically, may first be felt most strongly in companies that attempted to provide the most accommodations for workers. Corning, Inc., a large optical fiber and ceramics company based in New York, is one good example: The company recently began providing a number of innovative benefits for workers—child care programs, child care counseling, flexible work schedules for parents. "After the first couple of years, people who didn't have young children started quietly saying, 'What about us? Does my personal life count?'" recalls Sonia Werner, a workplace consultant at Corning. Corning recently righted its shortsightedness by offering flexible work schedules to workers who have no children, changing the name of its Family Support Program to Work Life, and offering employee seminars in assertiveness training and other general concerns.

The murmurs of resentment are becoming louder in many other workplaces, too. Many workers who feel the sting—and nearly two-thirds of U.S. workers do not have children under age 18—say this type of discrimination takes subtle forms, so it is often more difficult to document, speak up about, and correct. But an increasing number of childless workers are beginning to voice their grievances, including that they are customarily treated differently from their coworkers who have children. The childfree say they are:

- expected to work more hours
- made targets for frequent transfers and out-of-country assignments
- forced to absorb extra work to cover for parents who arrive late or leave early to drop off and pick up their children
- deprived of paid benefits such as child care and counseling offered only to traditional families, and
- exclusively called upon to cover weekend and after-hours assignments.

Some companies are beginning to get the message. For example, Quaker Oats, a food company based in Chicago, recently began to offer workers a more equitable benefits program, as masterminded by a team of workers in various ages and stages holding various positions throughout the company. Quaker's new Flexplan gives an additional $300 to employees who claim no dependents on company-reimbursed insurance coverage. Their employees can opt to take the $300 in cash or as an investment to their 401(k) plans—or they can use it to buy other employee benefits, such as vacation time.

The Pregnancy Discrimination Act

Additional workplace rights for new parents come from the Pregnancy Discrimination Act, or PDA (92 Stat. § 2076), passed in 1978 as an amendment to Title VII of the Civil Rights Act of 1964. The PDA outlaws discrimination based on pregnancy, childbirth, or any related medical condition.

Working Mothers Are Here to Stay

Even the most stalwart ostrich might be willing to concede that women continue to face a lopsided level of discriminatory treatment on the job.

Many people believe that the heart—or the womb—of the matter are antiquated images of both the U.S. workforce and the nature of pregnancy. Even in this day and this age, the term Working Mother still prompts strong reactions ranging from awe to disdain.

But figures show that moms on the job are the norm, not the aberration.

More than two-thirds of American women work for pay.

At least 80% of women who now work for pay are of childbearing age.

Of these women, 93% are likely to become pregnant at some point in their working lives.

Of the more than 80 million mothers in the United States, about 74% currently go back to work after having their first child.

Sources of statistics: *Equal Rights Advocates* and *Moms in Business Network*, 2005

Who Is Covered

Like other provisions of Title VII, the PDA applies to all workplaces that:

- engage in some type of interstate commerce—today, broadly construed to include all employers that use the mails, telephones, or computers, and
- have 15 or more employees for any 20 weeks of a calendar year. (See Chapter 7, "Title VII of the Civil Rights Act," for more on these protections.)

Available Protections

The PDA specifies that pregnant employees—and those recovering from an abortion—who need time off from work must be treated the same as other temporarily disabled employees. For example, a company that allows employees to return to work with full seniority and benefit rights after taking time off for a surgical operation and recovery must similarly reinstate women who take time off because of a pregnancy.

On the flip side, this law may also help sanction the denial of a benefit to a pregnant worker if that benefit has been denied any other temporarily disabled worker. If it is company policy, for example, to suspend seniority rights and benefits for employees who require extended medical leave, those work benefits must also be denied to pregnant workers on leave.

Also, while the PDA bars discrimination based on pregnancy, unlike the Family and Medical Leave Act (discussed earlier in this chapter), it does not require an employer to provide a pregnant employee with leave—and does not guarantee job security while a worker is out on leave.

The protections in the Act sound sensible and absolute. But, in truth, employers routinely shirk their legal duties when dealing with pregnant workers. The EEOC, which enforces complaints of pregnancy discrimination on the job, reports that the number of charges of this wrong increased by well over third in the last decade. And, with 20 million new pregnancies likely among working women in the decade kicked off by the year 2000, the problems and complaints are not likely to shrink without more definitive legislation, stronger workplace policies, or both.

Forced Leaves

The PDA bars mandatory maternity leaves— and those that are prescribed for a set time and duration. The focus instead is on individual work capabilities. A pregnant woman cannot be required to take a leave from work during her pregnancy as long as she remains able to do her job.

> **EXAMPLE:** Jody's pregnancy is proceeding without problems, and she has no difficulty performing her job as an office manager. Even though she is a week past her delivery due date according to her doctor's calculations, her employer cannot force her to take off work in anticipation of labor.

Hiring and Promotion Discrimination

In addition, an employer cannot refuse to hire or promote a woman solely because she is pregnant—or because of stereotyped notions of what work is proper for a pregnant woman to do or not to do.

> **EXAMPLE:** Marsha is the most qualified applicant for a job but is six months pregnant at the time of her job interview. The company cannot choose another applicant simply because it does not want to find a replacement for Marsha when she takes a leave to give birth.

Insurance Discrimination

The PDA also states that an employer cannot refuse to provide health care insurance benefits that cover pregnancy if it provides such benefits to cover other medical conditions.

> **EXAMPLE:** The Dumont Company provides complete hospitalization insurance to spouses of female employees but has a $500 cap on childbirth coverage for spouses of male employees. This policy is illegal under the PDA.

The sole exception here is that an employer need not pay for health insurance benefits for an abortion—except where the life of the pregnant woman would be endangered if the fetus is carried to term or where there are medical complications following the abortion.

Men's Rights to Leaves

Under Title VII, an employer must grant men the same options for taking leaves from their jobs to care for children as it grants to women. To do otherwise would constitute illegal discrimination based on gender.

Flexibility Is Key for Today's Workers—and Tomorrow's, Too

A study of corporate employees was recently conducted in an attempt to better understand what's driving today's job choices—and how those patterns affect companies' recruitment and retention efforts. The study identified the workplace factors most critical to job satisfaction and personal fulfillment, including the elusive one of workplace flexibility.

Importance of Workplace Flexibility by Gender and Job Category

	Overall	Exempt Women	Exempt Men	Non-Exempt Women	Non-Exempt Men
Extremely important	21%	30%	14%	27%	15%
Very important	31%	29%	37%	30%	25%
Important	32%	31%	36%	28%	33%
Slightly important	12%	10%	10%	10%	20%
Not at all important	4%	Less than 1%	4%	6%	7%

And researchers also note that the yen for flexibility on the job will likely become more important—and essential to workplaces—over the years. Workers under 50 are more likely than workers 50 and older to rate flexible work options as important, very important, or extremely important to their satisfaction with work.

And while 25% of respondents under 30 cited flexibility as extremely important, only 16% of respondents 60 and older felt as strongly about the importance of flexibility.

Source: *The New Career Paradigm: Flexibility Briefing,* 2006, by The American Business Collaboration for Quality Dependent Care and WFD Consulting

EXAMPLE: Steven works for a company that provides a 12-week unpaid leave for women who give birth to or adopt a child. If his employer refuses to allow Steven to take such a leave to adopt a child, he can file a complaint against his employer under Title VII, alleging gender discrimination.

For details about who is covered by Title VII and how to file a complaint under it, see Chapter 7, "Title VII of the Civil Rights Act." But first read "State Laws on Family Leave," earlier in this chapter, to see if your state offers a more direct approach. Also, see the Appendix for organizations that provide information on work and family issues.

Work/Life Balance

Some companies help employees juggle work and family responsibilities and help increase their health and enjoyment of life in various ways, including:

- allowing employees to work part time or to share a job
- allowing employees to put in some of their work hours at home
- allowing flexible on-site work hours
- allocating dependent care spending accounts
- providing specific child care benefits, including emergency care programs, on-site care centers, employer-arranged discounts with local care providers, and
- providing additional assistance to employees, such as counseling and seminars on work and family issues.

If you feel that one of these options is feasible in your workplace and would make your life more manageable, talk with your employer. Better still, come to the talk armed with success stories of similar set-ups in local companies. (See the Appendix for contact details.)

Work-at-Home Agreements

These days, many workers depend on computers as essential tools. And computers can easily be transported or hooked up to communicate with the main worksite from various locales. Many other kinds of work are also portable and may lend themselves well to work-at-home arrangements for employees.

These arrangements often involve an agreement between the worker and the company—best if it is in writing—that spells out who is responsible for any legal liabilities that arise from the work-at-home arrangement and how worktime will be measured.

For example, a work-at-home agreement may specify that you are responsible for any damage that occurs to a company-owned laptop computer while it is being used in your home. Most homeowners' and renters' insurance policies do not automatically cover business equipment, so you may have to purchase additional coverage.

Also, check the agreement against the wage and hour laws (discussed in Chapter 2) to make sure that neither you nor your employer would be breaking the Fair Labor Standards Act through your work-at-home plan. In general, if you are not an exempt employee, the wages and hours provisions of the Act still apply even when you are working at home.

Flexible Workhours

In many urban workplaces, where rush hour commuting makes for immense amounts of downtime, 9 to 5 workdays are all but extinct. In fact, a growing number of employers everywhere are putting less credence in the rigid Monday to Friday, 9 to 5 workweek and allowing employees to adopt more flexible work schedules.

When this idea was newer, it was referred to by the high-tech appellation of flextime. Flextime is not a reduction in hours, but simply a shift in the times employees are required to clock in and out of work. An increasingly popular flextime option, for example, is the ten-hour/four-day workweek, as it gives employees at least the illusion of a three-day weekend. Since flextime employees usually maintain 40-hour workweeks, they lose no benefits—such as health care coverage or vacation time—in the bargain.

Counseling and Other Benefits

Many employers now make employee counseling an integral part of their discipline procedures. That is, fewer employees are surprised by being fired from a company, since more have had the option of getting some form of counseling first—to improve their work performances, to help them conquer drug or alcohol abuse problems, to help raise awareness about potential sexual harassment.

And more enlightened employers now also offer employees a number of seminars and workshops more indirectly related to the workplace—workshops on building self-esteem, dealing with long-term health care for aging parents, and First Aid and CPR certification. These educational workshops not only train employees in more valuable skills, they also have the more nebulous value of improving morale.

At some workplaces, employees have taken the initiative in setting up their own workshops during lunchtimes or after work hours. Volunteers from local special interest groups—the Red Cross, stress management groups, battered women's shelters, self-defense trainers—are often available to present the training free or at a very low cost.

Whose Child Is This?

According to a recent AT&T study of working parents, 73% of men and 77% of women with children under 18 said they take time at work to deal with family issues. And 25% of men and 48% of women reported that they spend "unproductive time at work because of child care issues." Indeed, some workplace specialists posit that filling in for child care arrangements that have run awry is the biggest source of employee absenteeism and lack of workplace productivity.

Still, employers have done little to pitch in. Very few offer incentive compensation earmarked for child care. And fewer still provide the solution for which parents clamor loudest: onsite child care facilities.

Many businesses are hesitant to establish their own child care facilities simply because they represent a grand departure from business practices as usual. Others fear reprisals from the appearance of inequality—offering a service that cannot benefit workers without children.

And some cite start-up difficulties—picayune state regulations requiring separate kitchen facilities and per-child minimums on everything from space to caretakers to supervisors of caretakers.

But where the experiment has been tried—Stride Rite Corporation in Boston and Nyloncraft of Indiana were among the trendsetters—it has, by most accounts, succeeded. Employee turnovers, absenteeism, and tardiness plummet and peace of mind and company loyalty escalate. As one human resources director at a bank put it, their child care center is good for the bottom line: "Not only is this an excellent recruitment tool, but a phenomenal retention tool."

Breastfeeding on the Job: From Crime to Prime Time

Recently released pediatric guidelines again profess the historical wisdom that mothers can boost the health, development—and maybe even the smarts—of their babies if they breastfeed them for a year. But, for many moms, the urging is a tough act to follow. Public displays of breastfeeding are often met with sentiments from shock to scorn.

And, for mothers who return to work, the admonition to breastfeed is often downright unrealistic; very few employers provide working moms the time or place to nurse or express milk on the job. Some business managers fear repercussions from other employees who might decry that the moms are being given preferential treatment on the job. And others decry the very act, labeling it Unprofessional Workplace Behavior. In the face of this, few persevere: Only about 12% of full-time working mothers continue nursing for five months or longer.

But the picture is changing—egged on by recent legislative changes.

All but a small minority of states—Alaska, the District of Columbia, Idaho, Massachusetts, North Dakota, Pennsylvania, West Virginia, and Wyoming—have passed laws decriminalizing public breastfeeding, exempting the act from the indecent exposure laws on the books.

Most of these lactation accommodation moves took place within the last few years, prompted by intense public pressure, and subject to the whims of the legislators in situ. In California, for example, mothers are not protected by the breastfeeding provision if they deign to nurse in "the private home or residence of another." But, in several states—including California, Idaho, Iowa, Kansas, Nebraska, Oklahoma, and Oregon—nursing moms are given the added carrot of being exempted from the commonly dreaded civic obligation of jury duty.

And a growing number of states—now including California, Connecticut, Georgia, Hawaii, Illinois, Minnesota, Mississippi, New York, Oklahoma, Oregon, Tennessee, Texas, Virginia, and Washington—have passed legislation specifically addressing lactating moms on the job. Most of these laws require employers to provide "a reasonable amount of break time," usually unpaid, to express milk—and a place to do it—commonly, "a room, other than a toilet stall, in close proximity to the employees' work area."

Some state statutes begin with preachy prefaces, such as Georgia's, which proclaims breastfeeding to be "a basic act of nurture to which every baby has a right." And Louisiana calls loudly for "an end to the vicious cycle of embarrassment and ignorance that constricts women and men alike on the subject of breast-feeding."

And, in Texas and Washington, employers who adhere to the letter of the law in providing for breastfeeding on the job can promote their workplaces as state-sanctioned Mother Friendly or Infant Friendly.

For more specifics on breastfeeding and the latest on pending legislation, contact the La Leche League, 1400 North Meacham Road, Schaumburg, IL 60173, 847-519-7730, or visit its website at www.lalecheleague.org.

Privacy Rights

Technology has made it easier to pry into people's lives and psyches— through computerized record keeping, drug and alcohol testing, videotaping, and audiotaping. And that has caused more workers to want to protect something of themselves, to jealously guard their rights to privacy, to be left alone at work.

Theoretically, at least, employers sit on the other side of the fence. They are understandably concerned about stomping down on wrongdoing and waste in the workplace, such as drug and alcohol abuse, theft, incompetence, and low productivity. And, usually, their concerns center on finding and keeping the best-qualified employees. To that end, most employers want to learn as much as possible about what goes with workers on the job.

While there are some legal controls on what an employer and prospective employer can find out about you and on how they can use that information, there are still many ways an employer can invade your privacy—for example, by requiring you to take a drug test under some circumstances. But there are also some subtle limits on the extent to which your privacy can be invaded. In general, employers are entitled to intrude on your personal life no more than is necessary for legitimate business interests.

Most abuses of privacy rights occur when people are not aware of these legal constraints and how to enforce them. This chapter covers these rules and outlines some current workplace privacy issues: access to personnel records, medical and psychological testing, use of credit checks, and surveillance during work.

Your Personnel Records

Your employer is required by law to keep some tabs on you—including information on your wages and hours, workplace injuries and illnesses, and tax withholding, as well as records of accrued vacation and other benefits. That information is usually gathered together in one place: your personnel file. Your file will usually contain little information you did not know or provide to your employer in the first place.

But personnel files can sometimes become the catchalls for other kinds of information: references from previous employers, comments from customers or clients, employee reprimands, job performance evaluations, or memos of management's observations about an employee's behavior or productivity. When employment disputes develop, or an employee is demoted, transferred, or fired, the innards of his or her personnel file often provide essential information—often unknown to the employee—about the whys and wherefores.

A federal law, the Privacy Act (5 U.S.C. § 552a), limits the type of information that federal agencies, the military, and other government employers may keep on their workers.

However, private employers have a nearly unfettered hand when it comes to the kind of information they can collect. While many states now have some type of law regulating personnel files (see the following chart), most of these laws control not the content of the files, but:

- whether and how employees and former employees can get access to their personnel files
- whether employees are entitled to copies of the information in them, and
- how employees can contest and correct erroneous information in their files.

Getting Access to Your File

The best way to find out what a company knows about you, or what it is saying about you to outside people who inquire, is to obtain a copy of the contents of your personnel file from your current or former employer.

In some states, the only way you get to see those files is while collecting evidence after filing a lawsuit against the employer or former employer. And even then you might be in for a legal battle over what portions of the files are relevant to the case. But, in many states, you have the right to see the contents of your personnel file—or at least some of the documents in it—without filing a lawsuit.

State laws on employee access to personnel records generally cover technical matters, such as when your request must be made and how long the employer has to respond. Before you request your file, read the law on procedures for your state. In general, you must make your request to see your personnel file in writing to your employer or former employer as soon as you decide that you want to see it. If you send your request by certified mail, you will be able to prove when the request was submitted, should you need that evidence later.

If you live in a state that does not have a specific law ensuring you access to your personnel records, all is not lost. If you wish to see and copy your personnel files, ask to do so. If you meet with resistance, make a more formal request in writing. If that request is denied, and you genuinely believe your records may contain information that is critical to your position, you may need to consult with an expert such as a private investigator or experienced attorney.

Forcing an Employer to Keep Your Secrets

Employers are supposed to collect only information about you that is job related. And only those people with a proven need to know are supposed to have access to your personnel file. For example, your employer cannot tell your coworkers the results of a drug screening test you were required to take. But the truth is that employers frequently give out information about their employees to other people: other employers, unions, police investigators, creditors, insurance agents.

Job applicants or employees who want some personal information to remain private—address and phone number, for example, if they fear physical violence at the hands of a former spouse—should request in writing that the information be kept confidential. That request may end up being worth little more than the paper it is written on. But it may also be the strongest evidence of an employer's carelessness should problems develop later.

State Laws on Access to Personnel Records

This chart deals with only those states that authorize access to personnel files. Generally, an employee is allowed to see evaluations, performance reviews, and other documents that determine a promotion, bonus, or raise; access usually does not include letters of reference, test results, or records of a criminal or workplace-violation investigation. Under other state laws, employees may have access to their medical records and records of exposure to hazardous substances; these laws are not included in this chart.

Alaska
Alaska Stat. § 23.10.430

Employers affected: All.

Employee access to records: Employee or former employee may view and copy personnel files.

Conditions for viewing records: Employee may view records during regular business hours under reasonable rules.

Copying records: Employee pays (if employer so requests).

California
Cal. Lab. Code §§ 1198.5; 432

Employers affected: All employers subject to wage and hour laws.

Employee access to records: Employee has right to inspect at reasonable intervals any personnel records relating to performance or to a grievance proceeding. Employee also has a right to a copy of any personnel document employee has signed.

Conditions for viewing records: Employee may view records at reasonable times, during break or nonwork hours. If records are kept offsite or employer does not make them available at the workplace, then employee must be allowed to view them at the storage location without loss of pay.

Connecticut
Conn. Gen. Stat. Ann. §§ 31-128a to 31-128h

Employers affected: All.

Employee access to records: Employee has right to inspect personnel files within a reasonable time after making a request, but not more than twice a year. Employer must keep files on former employees for at least one year after termination.

Written request required: Yes.

Conditions for viewing records: Employee may view records during regular business hours in a location at or near worksite. Employer may require that files be viewed on the premises and in the presence of employer's designated official.

Copying records: Employer must provide copies within a reasonable time after receiving employee's written request; request must identify the materials employee wants copied. Employer may charge a fee that is based on the cost of supplying documents.

Employee's right to insert rebuttal: Employee may insert a written statement explaining any disagreement with information in the personnel record. Rebuttal must be maintained as part of the file.

Delaware
Del. Code Ann. tit. 19, §§ 730 to 735

Employers affected: All.

Employee access to records: Current employee, employee who is laid off with reemployment rights, or employee on leave of absence may inspect personnel record; employee's agent is not entitled to have access to records. Unless there is

State Laws on Access to Personnel Records (continued)

reasonable cause, employer may limit access to once a year.

Written request required: Yes. Employer may require employee to file a form and indicate either the purpose of the review or what parts of the record employee wants to inspect.

Conditions for viewing records: Records may be viewed during employer's regular business hours. Employer may require that employees view files on their own time and may also require that files be viewed on the premises and in the presence of employer's designated official.

Copying records: Employer is not required to permit employee to copy records. Employee may take notes.

Employee's right to insert rebuttal: If employee disagrees with information in personnel file and cannot reach an agreement with employer to remove or correct it, employee may submit a written statement explaining her position. Rebuttal must be maintained as part of the personnel file.

Illinois
820 Ill. Comp. Stat. §§ 40/1 to 40/12

Employers affected: Businesses with 5 or more employees.

Employee access to records: Current employee, or former employee terminated within the past year, is permitted to inspect records twice a year at reasonable intervals, unless a collective bargaining agreement provides otherwise. An employee involved in a current grievance may designate a representative of the union or collective bargaining unit, or other agent, to inspect personnel records that may be relevant to resolving the grievance. Employer must make records available within 7 working days after

employee makes request (if employer cannot meet deadline, may be allowed an additional 7 days).

Written request required: Yes. Employer may require use of a form.

Conditions for viewing records: Records may be viewed during employer's normal business hours at or near employee's worksite or, at employer's discretion, during nonworking hours at a different location. Employer may require that records be viewed on the premises.

Copying records: After reviewing records, employee may get a copy. Employer may charge only actual cost of duplication. If employee is unable to view files at worksite, employer, upon receipt of a written request, must mail employee a copy.

Employee's right to insert rebuttal: If employee disagrees with any information in the personnel file and cannot reach an agreement with employer to remove or correct it, employee may submit a written statement explaining his position. Rebuttal must remain in file with no additional comment by employer.

Iowa
Iowa Code § 91B.1

Employers affected: All employers with salaried employees or commissioned salespeople.

Employee access to records: Employee may have access to personnel file at time agreed upon by employer and employee.

Conditions for viewing records: Employer's representative may be present.

Copying records: Employer may charge copying fee for each page that is equivalent to a commercial copying service fee.

State Laws on Access to Personnel Records (continued)

Maine

Me. Rev. Stat. Ann. tit. 26, § 631

Employers affected: All.

Employee access to records: Within 10 days of submitting request, employee, former employee, or authorized representative may view and copy personnel files.

Written request required: Yes.

Conditions for viewing records: Employee may view records during normal business hours at the location where the files are kept, unless employer, at own discretion, arranges a time and place more convenient for employee. If files are in electronic or any other nonprint format, employer must provide equipment for viewing and copying.

Copying records: Employee entitled to one free copy of personnel file during each calendar year, including any material added to file during that year. Employee must pay for any additional copies.

Massachusetts

Mass. Gen. Laws ch. 149, § 52C

Employers affected: All. (Employers with 20 or more employees must maintain personnel records for 3 years after termination.)

Employee access to records: Employee or former employee must have opportunity to review personnel files within 5 business days of submitting request. (Law does not apply to tenured or tenure-track employees in private colleges and universities.)

Written request required: Yes.

Conditions for viewing records: Employee may view records at workplace during normal business hours.

Copying records: Employee must be given a copy of record within 5 business days of submitting a written request.

Employee's right to insert rebuttal: If employee disagrees with any information in personnel record and cannot reach an agreement with employer to remove or correct it, employee may submit a written statement explaining her position. Rebuttal becomes a part of the personnel file.

Michigan

Mich. Comp. Laws §§ 423.501 to 423.505

Employers affected: Employers with 4 or more employees.

Employee access to records: Current or former employee is entitled to review personnel records at reasonable intervals, generally not more than twice a year, unless a collective bargaining agreement provides otherwise.

Written request required: Yes. Request must describe the record employee wants to review.

Conditions for viewing records: Employee may view records during normal office hours either at or reasonably near the worksite. If these hours would require employee to take time off work, employer must provide another time and place that is more convenient for the employee.

Copying records: After reviewing files, employee may get a copy; employer may charge only actual cost of duplication. If employee is unable to view files at the worksite, employer, upon receipt of a written request, must mail employee a copy.

Employee's right to insert rebuttal: If employee disagrees with any information in personnel record and cannot reach an agreement with employer to remove or correct it, employee may submit a written statement explaining his position. Statement may be no longer than five 8½" by 11" pages.

State Laws on Access to Personnel Records (continued)

Minnesota

Minn. Stat. Ann. §§ 181.960 to 181.966

Employers affected: All.

Employee access to records: Current employee may review files once per 6-month period; former employee may have access to records once only during the first year after termination. Employer must be given 7 days' advance request (14 days' if personnel records kept out of state). Employer may not retaliate against an employee who asserts rights under these laws.

Written request required: Yes.

Conditions for viewing records: Current employee may view records during employer's normal business hours at worksite or a nearby location; does not have to take place during employee's working hours. Employer or employer's representative may be present.

Copying records: Employer must provide copy free of charge. Current employee must first review record and then submit written request for copies. Former employee must submit written request; providing former employee with a copy fulfills employer's obligation to allow access to records.

Employee's right to insert rebuttal: If employee disputes specific information in the personnel record, and cannot reach an agreement with employer to remove or revise it, employee may submit a written statement identifying the disputed information and explaining her position. Statement may be no longer than 5 pages and must be kept with personnel record as long as it is maintained.

Nevada

Nev. Rev. Stat. Ann. § 613.075

Employers affected: All.

Employee access to records: An employee who has worked at least 60 days, and a former employee within 60 days of termination, must be given a reasonable opportunity to inspect personnel records.

Conditions for viewing records: Employee may view records during employer's normal business hours.

Copying records: Employer may charge only actual cost of providing access and copies.

Employee's right to insert rebuttal: Employee may submit a reasonable written explanation in direct response to any entry in personnel record. Statement must be of moderate length; employer may specify the format.

New Hampshire

N.H. Rev. Stat. Ann. § 275:56

Employers affected: All.

Employee access to records: Employer must provide employees a reasonable opportunity to inspect records.

Copying records: Employer may charge a fee related to actual cost of supplying copies.

Employee's right to insert rebuttal: If employee disagrees with any of the information in personnel record and cannot reach an agreement with the employer to remove or correct it, employee may submit a written statement of her version of the information along with evidence to support her position.

Oregon

Or. Rev. Stat. § 652.750

Employers affected: All.

Employee access to records: Employer must provide employees a reasonable opportunity to inspect personnel records used to determine

State Laws on Access to Personnel Records (continued)

qualifications for employment, promotion, or additional compensation, termination, or other disciplinary action. Employer must keep records for 60 days after termination of employee.

Conditions for viewing records: Employee may view records at worksite or place of work assignment.

Copying records: Employer must provide a certified copy of requested record to current or former employee (if request made within 60 days of termination). May charge only actual cost of providing copy.

Pennsylvania

43 Pa. Cons. Stat. Ann. §§ 1321 to 1324

Employers affected: All.

Employee access to records: Employer must allow employee to inspect personnel record at reasonable times. (Employee's agent, or employee who is laid off with reemployment rights or on leave of absence, must also be given access.) Unless there is reasonable cause, employer may limit review to once a year by employee and once a year by employee's agent.

Written request required: At employer's discretion. Employer may require the use of a form as well as a written indication of the parts of the record employee wants to inspect or the purpose of the inspection. For employee's agent: Employee must provide signed authorization designating agent; must be for a specific date and indicate the reason for the inspection or the parts of the record the agent is authorized to inspect.

Conditions for viewing records: Employee may view records during normal business hours at the office where records are maintained, when there is enough time for employee to complete the review. Employer may require that employee or agent view records on their own time and may also require that inspection take place on the premises and in the presence of employer's designated official.

Copying records: Employer not obligated to permit copying. Employee may take notes.

Employee's right to insert rebuttal: The Bureau of Labor Standards, after a petition and hearing, may allow employee to place a counterstatement in the personnel file, if employee claims that the file contains an error.

Rhode Island

R.I. Gen. Laws § 28-6.4-1

Employers affected: All.

Employee access to records: Employer must permit employee to inspect personnel files when given at least 7 days' advance notice (excluding weekends and holidays). Employer may limit access to no more than 3 times a year.

Written request required: Yes.

Conditions for viewing records: Employee may view records at any reasonable time other than employee's work hours. Inspection must take place in presence of employer or employer's representative.

Copying records: Employee may not make copies or remove files from place of inspection. Employer may charge a fee reasonably related to cost of supplying copies.

Washington

Wash. Rev. Code Ann. §§ 49.12.240 to 49.12.260

Employers affected: All.

Employee access to records: Employee may have access to personnel records at least once a year within a reasonable time after making a request.

State Laws on Access to Personnel Records (continued)

Employee's right to insert rebuttal: Employee may petition annually that employer review all information in employee's personnel file. If there is any irrelevant or incorrect information in the file, employer must remove it. If employee does not agree with employer's review, employee may request to have a statement of rebuttal or correction placed in file. Former employee has right of rebuttal for two years after termination.

Wisconsin

Wis. Stat. Ann. § 103.13

Employers affected: All employers who maintain personnel records.

Employee access to records: Employee and former employee must be allowed to inspect personnel records within 7 working days of making request. Access is permitted twice per calendar year unless a collective bargaining agreement provides otherwise. Employee involved in a current grievance may designate a representative of the union or collective bargaining unit, or other agent, to inspect records that may be relevant to resolving the grievance.

Written request required: At employer's discretion.

Conditions for viewing records: Employee may view records during normal working hours at a location reasonably near worksite. If this would require employee to take time off work, employer may provide another reasonable time and place for review that is more convenient for the employee.

Copying records: Employee's right of inspection includes the right to make or receive copies. If employer provides copies, may charge only actual cost of reproduction.

Employee's right to insert rebuttal: If employee disagrees with any information in the personnel record and cannot come to an agreement with the employer to remove or correct it, employee may submit a written statement explaining his position. Employer must attach the statement to the disputed portion of the personnel record.

Current as of February 2007

○! **CAUTION**

Additional laws may apply. If the chart above indicates that your state has no statute, this means there is no law that specifically addresses the issue. However, there may be a state administrative regulation or local ordinance that does control access to personnel records. Call your state labor department for more information. (See the Appendix for contact details.)

Criminal Records

According to recent statistics collected by the Bureau of Justice, approximately one-third of the workforce has a criminal record, most commonly including theft. Despite this high proportion of workers with criminal records, many feel they are approached with wariness, or even subjected to abject discrimination, by employers who learn of their histories.

Arrest and conviction records are public records available to anyone, including an employer, who has the wherewithal and incentive to search for them. These records are also kept by a number of agencies—including police, prosecutors, courts, the FBI, probation departments, prisons, and parole boards. These record keepers are theoretically barred from releasing this information to anyone other than other criminal justice agencies and a few types of specialized employers (those who help manufacture controlled substances or run child care or elder care facilities for example.) In reality, however, slips of the tongue are made and persistent employers can generally find the ways and means to get their eyes on the information.

Most states now have laws that specifically bar employers and prospective employers from getting access to records of arrests that did not lead to convictions. And a growing number of states forbid employers from even asking job applicants about such arrests. But some states, including Hawaii and Wisconsin, expressly allow employers to inquire about past convictions that have rational relation-ships to the specific job the applicant seeks—a theft conviction, for example, for any person who has access to the company coffers.

Still, there are many exceptions to this Don't Ask, Don't Tell rule for specific categories of workers, including most bank employees, securities industry and commodities workers, and nuclear power employees.

Also, states are especially mindful of an employer's need and right to do thorough background checks when employees and volunteers will be working closely with children or adults who are ill or elderly and may be considered vulnerable. Many statutes specify that those working in schools, adult care homes, nursing homes, home care agencies, and facilities for those with mental and physical disabilities may—and often must—be subjected to criminal background checks before being allowed on the job.

Connecticut stands alone in offering employers overt statutory encouragement to hire qualified applicants who have criminal records.

Whatever the state of the law, the reality is that employers customarily bend and trample on the rules against asking about former arrests and convictions. And, in most states, private employers can check—and are often duty-bound to check—the conviction records of prospective employees. Since most records of criminal convictions are freely open to the public, there is usually little a job applicant or employee can do to stop an employer from discovering them.

Expunging Your Past

Many states have laws that allow individuals to expunge, or seal, their criminal records. When a record is expunged, it is usually not available to anyone other than criminal justice agencies and the courts. If your criminal record has been expunged, you are generally allowed to deny that you have one when a prospective employer asks about it.

But states have varying policies on this. In Massachusetts, for example, an employer that asks about criminal history must include on the application a statement that an applicant with a sealed record is entitled to answer "no record" about the underlying offenses. But in Ohio, an employer may question an applicant about an expunged record if the underlying incident relates to the type of job being sought.

Some states extend the expungement privilege only to a first arrest that did not result in a conviction. Other states are more generous, allowing a conviction for a petty offense to be expunged if probation was successfully completed. Some states limit the procedure to juvenile records. Usually, a request to seal your record will be granted only if you have remained clear of any contacts with the criminal justice system for a specified period of time following your arrest or conviction.

The bottom line: Only small-potato crimes can be easily expunged from your record—not the ones likely to derail you from most jobs. Records of truly serious offenses cannot be sealed and are with you for life.

Checking Up on Yourself

The FBI is charged with maintaining complete arrest records—or rap sheets—on every individual who is arrested. It may behoove you to look at the information in your file before an employer does.

You can obtain a copy of your FBI rap sheet by writing to:

Federal Bureau of Investigation
CJIS Division; Record Request
1000 Custer Hollow Road
Clarksburg, WV 26306

Along with your request, you must include your name, date and place of birth, and a set of rolled ink fingerprints obtainable at a local police department—along with an $18 certified check or money order payable to the United States Treasury. It will take about six to eight weeks to process your request.

You are allowed to correct inaccurate FBI records—although it requires substantial patience and good documentation.

 CAUTION

Additional laws may apply. If the chart below indicates that your state has no statute, this means there is no law that specifically addresses the issue. However, there may be a state administrative regulation or local ordinance that does control arrest and conviction records. Call your state labor department for more information. (See the Appendix for contact details.)

State Laws on Employee Arrest and Conviction Records

The following chart summarizes state laws and regulations on whether an employer can get access to an employee's or prospective employee's past arrests or convictions. It includes citations to statutes and agency websites, as available.

Many states allow or require private sector employers to run background checks on workers, particularly in fields like child care, elder care, home health care, private schools, private security, and the investment industry. Criminal background checks usually consist of sending the applicant's name (and sometimes fingerprints) to the state police or to the FBI. State law may forbid hiring people with certain kinds of prior convictions, depending on the kind of job or license involved.

Federal law allows the states to establish procedures for requesting a nationwide background check to find out if a person has been "convicted of a crime that bears upon the [person's] fitness to have responsibility for the safety and well-being of children, the elderly, or individuals with disabilities." (42 U.S.C.A. § 5119a(a)(1).)

If your state isn't listed in this chart, then it doesn't have a *general statute* on whether private sector employers can find out about arrests or convictions. There might be a law about your particular industry, though.

It's always a good idea to consult your state's nondiscrimination enforcement agency or labor department to see what kinds of questions you can ask. The agency guidelines are designed to help employers comply with state and federal law. For further information, contact your state's agency.

Alaska

Agency guidelines for preemployment inquiries: Alaska Department of Labor and Workforce Development, Alaska Employer Handbook, "Preemployment Questioning," at www.labor.state.ak.us/employer/aeh.pdf.

Arizona

Ariz. Rev. Stat. § 13-904(E)

Rights of employees and applicants: Unless the offense has a reasonable relationship to the occupation, an occupational license may not be denied solely on the basis of a felony or misdemeanor conviction.

California

Cal. Lab. Code § 432.7

Rules for employers:

- **Arrest records.** May not ask about an arrest that did not lead to conviction; may not ask about pretrial or posttrial diversion program. May ask about arrest if prospective employee is awaiting trial.
- **Convictions.** May ask about conviction even if no sentence is imposed.

Agency guidelines for preemployment inquiries: Department of Fair Employment and Housing, "Preemployment Inquiry Guidelines," DFEH-161 at www.dfeh.ca.gov/Publications/DFEH%20161.pdf.

Colorado

Colo. Rev. Stat. §§ 24-72-308 (II)(f)(I), 8-3-108(m)

Rules for employers: May not inquire about arrest for civil or military disobedience unless it resulted in conviction.

Rights of employees and applicants: May not be required to disclose any information in a sealed record; may answer questions about arrests or convictions as though they had not occurred.

Agency guidelines for preemployment inquiries: Colorado Civil Rights Division, Publications, "Preventing Job Discrimination," at

State Laws on Employee Arrest and Conviction Records (continued)

www.dora.state.co.us/civil-rights/Publications/JobDiscrim2001.pdf.

Connecticut

Conn. Gen. Stat. Ann. §§ 46a-79, 46a-80, 31-51i

Rules for employers: State policy encourages hiring qualified applicants with criminal records. If an employment application form contains any question concerning criminal history, it must include a notice in clear and conspicuous language that (1) the applicant is not required to disclose the existence of any arrest, criminal charge, or conviction, the records of which have been erased; (2) defining what criminal records are subject to erasure; and (3) any person whose criminal records have been erased will be treated as if never arrested and my swear so under oath. Employer may not disclose information about a job applicant's criminal history except to members of the personnel department or, if there is no personnel department, person(s) in charge of hiring or conducting the interview.

Rights of employees and applicants: May not be asked to disclose information about a criminal record that has been erased; may answer any question as though arrest or conviction never took place. May not be discriminated against in hiring or continued employment on the basis of an erased criminal record. If conviction of a crime has been used as a basis to reject an applicant, the rejection must be in writing and specifically state the evidence presented and the reason for rejection.

Delaware

Del. Code Ann. tit. 11, § 4374(e)

Rights of employees and applicants: Do not have to disclose an arrest or conviction record that has been expunged.

Florida

Fla. Stat. Ann. § 112.011

Rights of employees and applicants: May not be disqualified to practice or pursue any occupation or profession that requires a license, permit, or certificate because of a prior conviction, unless it was for a felony or first-degree misdemeanor and is directly related to the specific line of work.

Georgia

Ga. Code Ann. §§ 35-3-34, 42-8-62, 42-8-63

Rules for employers: In order to obtain a criminal record from the state Crime Information Center, employer must supply the individual's fingerprints or signed consent. If an adverse employment decision is made on the basis of the record, must disclose all information in the record to the employee or applicant and tell how it affected the decision.

Rights of employees and applicants: Probation for a first offense is not a conviction; may not be disqualified for employment once probation is completed.

Hawaii

Haw. Rev. Stat. §§ 378-2, 378-2.5, 831-3.2

Rules for employers:

- **Arrest records.** It is a violation of law for any employer to refuse to hire, to discharge, or to discriminate in terms of compensation, conditions, or privileges of employment because of a person's arrest or court record.
- **Convictions.** May inquire into a conviction only after making a conditional offer of employment, provided it has a rational relation to job. May not examine any convictions over 10 years old.

Rights of employees and applicants: If an arrest or conviction has been expunged, may state that

State Laws on Employee Arrest and Conviction Records (continued)

no record exists and may respond to questions as a person with no record would respond.

Agency guidelines for preemployment inquiries: Hawaii Civil Rights Commission, "What is Employment Discrimination?" at www.hawaii. gov/labor/hcrc/pdf/HCRCemploymdiscrim.pdf.

Idaho

Agency guidelines for preemployment inquiries: Idaho Human Rights Commission, "Preemployment Inquiries," at http://cl.idaho. gov/lawintvw3.pdf.

Illinois

775 Ill. Comp. Stat. § 5/2-103

Rules for employers: It is a civil rights violation to ask about an arrest or criminal history record that has been expunged or sealed, or to use the fact of an arrest or criminal history record as a basis for refusing to hire or to renew employment. Law does not prohibit employer from using other means to find out if person actually engaged in conduct for which they were arrested.

Kansas

Kan. Stat. Ann. §§ 22-4710

Rules for employers: Cannot require an employee to inspect or challenge a criminal record in order to obtain a copy of the record, but may require an applicant to sign a release to allow employer to obtain record to determine fitness for employment. Employers can require access to criminal records for specific businesses.

Agency guidelines for preemployment inquiries: Kansas Human Rights Commission, "Guidelines on Equal Employment Practices: Preventing Discrimination in Hiring," at www. khrc.net/hiring.html.

Louisiana

La. Rev. Stat. Ann. § 37:2950

Rights of employees and applicants: Prior conviction cannot be used as a sole basis to deny employment or an occupational or professional license, unless conviction is for a felony and directly relates to the job or license being sought.

Special situations: Protection does not apply to medical, engineering and architecture, or funeral and embalming licenses, among others listed in the statute.

Maine

Me. Rev. Stat. Ann. tit. 5, § 5301

Rights of employees and applicants: A conviction is not an automatic bar to obtaining an occupational or professional license. Only convictions that directly relate to the profession or occupation, that include dishonesty or false statements, that are subject to imprisonment for more than 1 year, or that involve sexual misconduct on the part of a licensee may be considered.

Agency guidelines for preemployment inquiries: The Maine Human Rights Commission, "Pre-employment Inquiry Guide," at www. maine.gov/mhrc/publications/pre-employment _inquiry_guide.html, suggests that asking about arrests is an improper race-based question, but that it is okay to ask about a conviction if related to the job.

Maryland

Md. Code Ann. [Crim. Proc.], § 10-109; Md. Regs. Code 09.01.10.02

Rules for employers: May not inquire about any criminal charges that have been expunged. May not use a refusal to disclose information as sole basis for not hiring an applicant.

State Laws on Employee Arrest and Conviction Records (continued)

Rights of employees and applicants: Need not refer to or give any information about an expunged charge. A professional or occupational license may not be refused or revoked simply because of a conviction; agency must consider the nature of the crime and its relation to the occupation or profession; the conviction's relevance to the applicant's fitness and qualifications; when conviction occurred and other convictions, if any; and the applicant's behavior before and after conviction.

Agency guidelines for preemployment inquiries: The Office of Equal Opportunity and Program Equity, "Guidelines for Preemployment Inquiries Technical Assistance Guide," at www.dllr.state.md.us/oeope/preep.htm.

Massachusetts

Mass. Gen. Laws ch. 151B, § 4; ch. 276, § 100A; Mass. Regs. Code tit. 804, § 3.02

Rules for employers: If job application has a question about prior arrests or convictions, it must include a formulated statement (that appears in the statute) that states that an applicant with a sealed record is entitled to answer, "No record."

- **Arrest records.** May not ask about arrests that did not result in conviction.
- **Convictions.** May not ask about first-time convictions for drunkenness, simple assault, speeding, minor traffic violations, or disturbing the peace; may not ask about misdemeanor convictions 5 or more years old.

Rights of employees and applicants: If criminal record is sealed, may answer, "No record" to any inquiry about past arrests or convictions.

Agency guidelines for preemployment inquiries: Massachusetts Commission Against Discrimination, "Discrimination on the Basis of Criminal Record," at www.mass.gov/mcad/crimrec.html.

Michigan

Mich. Comp. Laws § 37.2205a

Rules for employers: May not request information on any arrests or misdemeanor charges that did not result in conviction.

Rights of employees and applicants: Employees or applicants are not making a false statement if they fail to disclose information they have a civil right to withhold.

Agency guidelines for preemployment inquiries: Michigan Civil Rights Commission, "Preemployment Inquiry Guide," at www. michigan.gov/documents/pre-employment_inquery_guide_13019_7.pdf.

Minnesota

Minn. Stat. Ann. §§ 364.01 to 364.03

Rules for employers: State policy encourages the rehabilitation of criminal offenders; employment opportunity is considered essential to rehabilitation.

Rights of employees and applicants: No one can be disqualified from pursuing or practicing an occupation that requires a license, unless the crime directly relates to the occupation. Agency may consider the nature and seriousness of the crime and its relation to the applicant's fitness for the occupation. Even if the crime does relate to the occupation, a person who provides evidence of rehabilitation and present fitness cannot be disqualified.

Agency guidelines for preemployment inquiries: Minnesota Department of Human Rights, "Hiring, Job Interviews and the Minnesota

State Laws on Employee Arrest and Conviction Records (continued)

Human Rights Act," at www.humanrights.state.
mn.us/employer_hiring.html.

Missouri

**Agency guidelines for preemployment
inquiries:** Commission on Human Rights,
Missouri Department of Labor and Industrial
Relations, "Preemployment Inquiries," at www.
dolir.mo.gov/hr/interview.htm.

Nebraska

Neb. Rev. Stat. § 29-3523

Rules for employers: After one year from date
of arrest, may not obtain access to information
regarding arrests if no charges are completed or
pending.

Nevada

Nev. Rev. Stat. Ann. §§ 179.301, 179A.100(3)

Rules for employers: May obtain a prospective
employee's criminal history record only if it
includes convictions or a pending charge,
including parole or probation.

Special situations: State Gaming Board may
inquire into sealed records to see if conviction
relates to gaming.

**Agency guidelines for preemployment
inquiries:** Nevada Equal Rights Commission,
"Preemployment Inquiry Guide," at http://detr.
state.nv.us/nerc/nerc_preemp.htm.

New Hampshire

*N.H. Rev. Stat. Ann. § 651:5 (X)(c); N.H. Code Admin.
R. Hum. 405.03*

Rules for employers: May ask about a previous
criminal record only if question substantially
follows this wording, "Have you ever been
arrested for or convicted of a crime that has not
been annulled by a court?"

• **Arrest records.** It is unlawful discrimination
for an employer to ask about an arrest record,
to have a job requirement that applicant
have no arrest record, or to use information
about arrest record to make a hiring decision,
unless it is a business necessity. It is unlawful
discrimination to ask about arrest record if
it has the purpose or effect of discouraging
applicants of a particular racial or national
origin group.

New Jersey

*N.J. Stat. Ann. §§ 5:5-34.1, 5:12-89 to 5:12-91, 32:23-
86; N.J. Admin. Code tit. 13, §§ 59-1.2, 59-1.6*

Rules for employers: May obtain information
about convictions and pending arrests or charges
to determine the subject's qualifications for
employment. Employers must certify that they
will provide sufficient time for applicant to
challenge, correct, or complete record, and will
not presume guilt for any pending charges or
court actions.

Rights of employees and applicants: Applicant
who is disqualified for employment based on
criminal record must be given adequate notice
and reasonable time to confirm or deny accuracy
of information.

Special situations: There are specific rules for
casino employees, longshoremen and related
occupations, horse racing, and other gaming
industry jobs.

New Mexico

*Criminal Offender Employment Act, N.M. Stat.
Ann. § 28-2-3*

For a license, permit, or other authority to engage
in any regulated trade, business, or profession,
a regulating agency may consider convictions
for felonies and for misdemeanors involving

State Laws on Employee Arrest and Conviction Records (continued)

moral turpitude. Such convictions cannot be an automatic bar to authority to practice in the regulated field, though.

New York

N.Y. Correct. Law §§ 750 to 754; N.Y. Exec. Law § 296(16)

Rules for employers:

- **Arrest records.** It is unlawful discrimination to ask about any arrests or charges that did not result in conviction, unless they are currently pending.
- **Convictions.** Employers with 10 or more employees may not deny employment based on a conviction unless it relates directly to the job or would be an "unreasonable" risk to property or to public or individual safety.

Rights of employees and applicants: Upon request, applicant must be given, within 30 days, a written statement of the reasons why employment was denied.

Agency guidelines for preemployment inquiries: New York State Division of Human Rights, "Recommendations on Employment Inquiries," at www.nysdhr.com/employment.html.

North Dakota

N.D. Cent. Code § 12-60-16.6

Rules for employers: May obtain records of convictions or of criminal charges (adults only) occurring in the past three years, provided the information has not been purged or sealed.

Agency guidelines for preemployment inquiries: North Dakota Department of Labor, Human Rights Division, "Employment Applications and Interviews," www.state.nd.us /labor/publications/docs/brochures/005.pdf.

Ohio

Ohio Rev. Code Ann. §§ 2151.357, 2953.33, 2953.55

Rules for employers: May not inquire into any sealed convictions or sealed bail forfeitures, unless question has a direct and substantial relation to job.

Rights of employees and applicants: May not be asked about arrest records that are sealed; may respond to inquiry as though arrest did not occur.

Oklahoma

Okla. Stat. Ann. tit. 22, § 19(F)

Rules for employers: May not inquire into any criminal record that has been expunged.

Rights of employees and applicants: If record is expunged, may state that no criminal action ever occurred. May not be denied employment solely for refusing to disclose sealed criminal record information.

Oregon

Or. Rev. Stat. §§ 181.555 and 181.560, 659A.030

Rules for employers: Before requesting information, employer must notify employee or applicant; when submitting request, must tell State Police Department when and how person was notified. May not discriminate against an applicant or current employee on the basis of an expunged juvenile record unless there is a "bona fide occupational qualification."

- **Arrest records.** May request information about arrest records less than 1 year old that have not resulted in acquittal or have not been dismissed.
- **Convictions.** May request information about conviction records.

Rights of employees and applicants: Before State Police Department releases any criminal

State Laws on Employee Arrest and Conviction Records (continued)

record information, it must notify employee or applicant and provide a copy of all information that will be sent to employer. Notice must include protections under federal civil rights law and the procedure for challenging information in the record. Record may not be released until 14 days after notice is sent.

Pennsylvania

18 Pa. Cons. Stat. Ann. § 9125

Rules for employers: May consider felony and misdemeanor convictions only if they directly relate to person's suitability for the job.

Rights of employees and applicants: Must be informed in writing if refusal to hire is based on criminal record information.

Agency guidelines for preemployment inquiries: Pennsylvania Human Relations Commission at http://sites.state.pa.us/PA_Exec/ PHRC/publications/literature/Pre-Employ%20 QandA%208x11%20READ.pdf.

Rhode Island

R.I. Gen. Laws §§ 12-1.3-4, 28-5-7(7)

Rules for employers:

- **Arrest records.** It is unlawful to include on an application form or to ask as part of an interview if the applicant has ever been arrested or charged with any crime.
- **Convictions.** May ask if applicant has been convicted of a crime.

Rights of employees and applicants: Do not have to disclose any conviction that has been expunged.

South Dakota

Agency guidelines for preemployment inquiries: South Dakota Division of Human Rights, "Preemployment Inquiry Guide," at www.

state.sd.us/dol/boards/hr/preemplo.htm suggests that an employer shouldn't ask or check into arrests or convictions if they are not substantially related to the job.

Utah

Utah Admin. R. 606-2

Rules for employers: Utah Labor Division Anti-Discrimination Rules, Rule R606-2. "Preemployment Inquiry Guide," at www.rules. utah.gov/publicat/code/r606/r606-002.htm.

- **Arrest records.** It is not permissible to ask about arrests.
- **Convictions.** Asking about felony convictions is permitted but is not advisable unless related to job.

Vermont

Vt. Stat. Ann. tit. 20, § 2056c

Rules for employers: Only employers who provide care for children, the elderly, and the disabled or who run postsecondary schools with residential facilities may obtain criminal record information from the state Criminal Information Center. May obtain record only after a conditional offer of employment is made and applicant has given written authorization on a signed, notarized release form.

Rights of employees and applicants: Release form must advise applicant of right to appeal any of the findings in the record.

Virginia

Va. Code Ann. § 19.2-392.4

Rules for employers: May not require an applicant to disclose information about any criminal charge that has been expunged.

State Laws on Employee Arrest and Conviction Records (continued)

Rights of employees and applicants: Need not refer to any expunged charges if asked about criminal record.

Washington

Wash. Rev. Code Ann. §§ 43.43.815, 9.94A.640(3), 9.96.060(3), 9.96A.020; Wash. Admin. Code § 162-12-140

Rules for employers:
- **Arrest records.** Employer who asks about arrests must ask whether the charges are still pending, have been dismissed, or led to conviction that would adversely affect job performance once and the arrest occurred within the last ten years.
- **Convictions.** Employer who obtains a conviction record must notify employee within 30 days of receiving it and must allow the employee to examine it. May make an employment decision based on a conviction only if it is less than 10 years old and the crime involves behavior that would adversely affect job performance.

Rights of employees and applicants: If a conviction record is cleared or vacated, may answer questions as though the conviction never occurred. A person convicted of a felony cannot be refused an occupational license unless the conviction is less than 10 years old and the felony relates specifically to the occupation or business.

Special situations: Employers are entitled to obtain complete criminal record information for positions that require bonding, or that have access to trade secrets, confidential or proprietary business information, money, or items of value.

Agency guidelines for preemployment inquiries: Washington Human Rights Commission's "Pre-employment Inquiries Guide," at www.hum.wa.gov/employer/law-wac.htm.

West Virginia

Agency guidelines for preemployment inquiries: Bureau of Employment Programs, "Preemployment Inquiries Technical Assistance Guide," at www.wvbep.org/bep/Bepeeo/empinqu.htm. The state's website says that employers can only make inquiries about convictions directly related to the job. Consider the nature and recentness of the conviction and evidence of rehabilitation. Include a disclaimer that a conviction is not necessarily a bar to employment.

Wisconsin

Wis. Stat. Ann. §§ 111.31 and 111.335

Rules for employers: It is a violation of state civil rights law to discriminate against an employee on the basis of a prior arrest or conviction record.
- **Arrest records.** May not ask about arrests unless there are pending charges.
- **Convictions.** May not ask about convictions unless charges substantially relate to job.

Special situations: Employers are entitled to obtain complete criminal record information for positions that require bonding and for burglar alarm installers.

Agency guidelines for preemployment inquiries: Wisconsin Department of Workforce Development, Civil Rights Division Publications, "Fair Hiring & Avoiding Loaded Interview Questions," http://dwd.wisconsin.gov/dwd/publications/erd/pdf/erd_4825_pweb.pdf.

Current as of February 2007

Medical Records

Medical information about employees comes into the workplace a number of ways. It is volunteered by an employee who is calling in sick. It becomes general knowledge after filtering through the gossip mill. It is listed on the insurance application for a group policy, which your employer will likely have on file.

As a general legal rule, employers are not supposed to reveal medical information about employees unless there is a legitimate business reason to do so. Again, that nebulous standard, so often used as a fallback in workplace controversies, provides little guidance because it is so poorly defined.

In an attempt to curb witting and unwitting leaks of medical information in the workplace, the Americans With Disabilities Act, or ADA—the broad federal law prohibiting disability discrimination on the job—imposes strict requirements on how and where employers must keep medical information on employees.

Under the ADA, medical information must be kept in a secure location, separate from nonmedical information—and access to it should be limited to a designated individual.

The law also limits those entitled to learn about medical information in the workplace to:

- supervisors of employees whose work duties are limited or who require some accommodation because of a medical condition
- first aid and safety workers who may need to administer emergency treatment or respond during an evacuation, and
- government and insurance officials who require the information for official business purposes.

Still, despite the confidentiality measures imposed by the ADA, information leaks and abuses still occur. If you are concerned about keeping your medical information confidential and out of the workplace limelight, you must take active steps to do so. If you confide any medical information about yourself to coworkers, ask them not to tell others. Inform all doctors who treat you that they should not reveal anything about your health or treatment to another person without getting a release, or written permission, from you first. (See "Medical Examinations," below, for more on employee medical exams and records.)

Credit Information

This era of the computer is also the era of the ever-present personal credit rating. Credit bureaus—profit-making companies that gather and sell information about a person's credit history—have become a booming business. And the growing power and popularity of the computerized credit rating has found its way into the workplace, as well.

Many employers now use the same credit bureau files used by companies that issue credit cards and make loans to do routine credit checks on employees and job applicants. Unfortunately, there is very little you can do to prevent employers from evaluating your credit history in deciding whether to hire, promote, or even continue to employ you.

Employers' Access to Your Record

A federal law, the Fair Credit Reporting Act (15 U.S.C. §§ 1681 and following), requires credit agencies to share their data only with those who have a legitimate business need for the information, and employers generally qualify. Employers are given broad access to an individual's credit report, which they can use to evaluate eligibility for "employment, promotion, reassignment, or retention." In short, as far as your employer or prospective employer is concerned, your credit rating is an open book.

Credit bureaus typically track not only your bill-paying habits, but also all companies that have asked to see your credit rating when you apply for credit, insurance, a place to live, or a new job. The result is that employers increasingly use credit bureau files to find out whether an employee is job hunting with other companies. And prospective employers may use a shaky credit report to conclude that it is risky to welcome you aboard.

However, an amendment to the Fair Credit Reporting Act gives you some rights to know how and whether a current or prospective employer is using credit information about you. It requires an employer to get your written permission before peeping at your credit report. And the words granting permission can't be buried deep within a job application form or other word-laden document; you have to sign separately to signal your approval.

While this sounds like strong stuff at first, the truth is that, if you refuse to give approval to the employer's wondering eyes, you will leave the impression that you have something to hide—and that will likely kill your chances for getting or keeping the job.

Also, the amendment mandates that a prospective employer who rejects you for a job based "in whole or in part" on an item on your credit report must give you:

- a copy of the report before turning you down, and
- written instructions on how to challenge the accuracy of that report.

Again, while this smells at first whiff like strong consumer protection, the reality is that it is tough to track whether employers have followed the letter of the law. They remain free to claim that you were turned down for reasons entirely separate from the harsh marks on your credit report—and you will be hard pressed to prove otherwise.

How to Take Action

Amendments to the Fair Credit and Reporting Act at least theoretically give you some idea of whether you are up against an employer marauding for credit information that might cause you to lose out on a job.

And an employer who uses your credit information against you is not only supposed to fess up to it, but must also give you the name, address, and telephone number of the credit agency that provided the report about you. You are entitled to a free copy of the report from that agency.

You also have the right to correct any errors in credit reports compiled about you, and most experts recommend that you check and correct your file every few years, especially if you will be job hunting or applying for credit.

Call the nearest office of the Federal Trade Commission, listed in the federal government section of the telephone directory, for guidance on how to correct the report, or check the FTC's website, at www.ftc.gov. If you suspect a misuse of your credit report, you may want to contact your state consumer protection agency or attorney general to see whether state laws give you additional avenues for action.

RESOURCE

For more detailed information about how credit bureaus operate and how to deal with them, see *Solve Your Money Troubles: Get Debt Collectors Off Your Back & Regain Financial Freedom*, by Robin Leonard (Nolo).

Workplace Testing

Ostensibly, prospective employers and employees want the same thing: to match the best person with the most fitting job. These days, there are a number of tests that purport to take the guesswork out of the process. Ploughing through the Information Age and into the Biotech Century, many employers are quick to welcome outside evaluations of an individual's mental and physical fitness and integrity and to believe in their results—often at the risk of sacrificing individual privacy rights.

Medical Examinations

A number of insurers require employees to undergo medical evaluations before coverage will begin. Beyond that, and often in addition to that, employers may require specific physical and mental examinations to ensure a qualified workforce. However, there are strict rules on when those exams can be conducted and who can learn the results.

Courts have ruled that the constitutional right to privacy covers medical information and that honesty is the only policy when it comes to medical tests for prospective and existing employees. That is, employers must identify what conditions they are testing for—and get individual consent to perform the tests, first.

Examining Job Applicants

Employers may legally give prospective employees medical exams to make sure they are physically able to perform their jobs. However, timing is crucial. Under the federal Americans With Disabilities Act, or ADA (discussed in Chapter 7), covered employers cannot require medical examinations before offering an individual a job. They are, however, free to make an employment offer contingent upon a person's passing a medical exam.

The ADA also requires your employer to keep your medical history and exam results in a file separate from your other personnel records. Only a few individuals have the right to see your medical file:

- a supervisor who needs to know whether your medical condition or

Of Genes and Pink Slips

When it first became possible to test for the genetic risks of isolated diseases, the advance was widely hailed as a modern medical near-miracle, sure to improve preventative health care and treatment. People with the risk of contracting inherited conditions such as breast cancer, colon cancer, and Huntington's disease now commonly undergo genetic testing to gauge their chances. But testing can also pose a triple-edged threat to workers' jobs, health insurance, and privacy.

Privacy experts warn that genetic test results could be misused against employees who may run up health insurance costs. And, these problems can follow workers, hampering their chances of finding another job. The Council for Responsible Genetics claims it has documented hundreds of cases in which healthy individuals have suffered insurance and other workplace discrimination based on predictive genetic information.

Despite the hand-wringing, it's hard to get a true bead on how much genetic testing is really going on. Cynics fear that much of it is kept under wraps. And in the murkiness of definitions lies another rub: While legal experts generally agree that genetic tests may be permissible where they are "work related" and "business necessities," those terms, too, are hard to pin down and patrol.

Help from Congress on this politically charged issue has historically been slow. In the waning hours of his administration, Bill Clinton was able to push through a law banning testing of federal employees. And the Genetic Information Nondiscrimination Act, introduced in January 2007, is supported by more than 200 sponsors.

In the meantime, state legislatures have acted to pick up some of the slack: 34 states have passed laws prohibiting genetic discrimination in the workplace, most of them requiring informed consent from the person tested before results can be disclosed. Legislative proposals are pending in several more states.

And, in April of 2001, the EEOC settled the first case successfully challenging the use of workplace genetic testing. In that case, Burlington Northern Santa Fe Railroad fessed up to a testing program it had planned to perform on employees. While company attorneys defended that the testing was necessary to combat the "unusually high" number of Carpal Tunnel Syndrome claims filed, employees there protested the harm that might result to them. At least one worker was threatened with termination after refusing to submit a blood sample. In the settlement, which banned retaliation against anyone who opposed the testing, Burlington agreed to stop future genetic tests and halt analysis of all employee blood immediately.

According to then-EEOC Chair Ida Castro, the settlement "sends a message to all other companies that if they're thinking of using genetic testing to make employment decisions, they should understand they are delving into a very dangerous realm."

Perhaps employers heeded the warning. To date, no additional genetic employment discrimination lawsuits have been filed.

health requires that you be specially accommodated within the workplace

- First Aid or medical personnel who need to administer emergency treatment, and
- government officials who are checking to be sure your employer is complying with the ADA.

During the course of a medical exam, a company-assigned doctor may ask anything at all about an applicant's health and medical history. However, the final medical evaluation is supposed to include only a stripped-down conclusion: able to work, able to work with restrictions, not able to work.

Examining Existing Employees

Employees can be required to take a physical or psychological examination after they are hired only if there is a reason to believe they are jeopardizing the health and safety of others in the workplace. For example, several courts have opined that if an employee clearly appears to be homicidal or suicidal, then an employer may have the duty to require a psychological exam, or even inform coworkers of the condition, in the name of workplace safety.

Again, while an examining doctor or psychologist has freer reign to ask questions as part of the examination of these employees than of applicants, the final evaluation revealed to an employer is supposed to be succinct and free of detail: able to work, able to work with restrictions, not able to work.

Drug and Alcohol Testing

The abuse of alcohol and drugs such as cocaine has been widely publicized for many years—and many private employers now test for drug and alcohol use. The laws regulating drug abuse in the workplace and the testing of employees for such abuse, however, are relatively new and still being shaped by the courts. Currently, there is a hodgepodge of legal rules controlling drug testing—some in the Americans With Disabilities Act (see Chapter 7, "The Americans With Disabilities Act"), some set out in specific state laws (see the chart below), and a number arrived at through court decisions.

Testing is an institution rather than an aberration in many workplaces these days. About 71% of major U.S. companies regularly test for drugs and alcohol, according to a 2004 poll by the Institute for a Drug-Free Workplace based in Washington, D.C. Some of that is explained by the passage, in 1988, of the Drug-Free Workplace Act. (102 Stat. § 4181.) That law dictates that workplaces receiving federal grants or contracts must be drug-free or lose the funding, although it does not call for testing or monitoring workers.

Of late, some of the fervor over drug and alcohol abuse in the workplace has calmed somewhat, as concern and legislation have concentrated on testing illegal immigrants and students. In a 2005 Gallup poll, 37% of the 1,006 respondents said that substance abuse problems at work had increased in the last five years; 38% said they remained about the same.

But work-related drug tests are still common. And they take a number of forms. Analyzing urine samples is the method most commonly used, but samples of a worker's saliva, blood, hair, and breath can also be tested for the presence of alcohol or other drugs in the body. Typically, state laws set out the testing methods that may or must be used. Many statutes provide for retesting, at the employee's expense, if the initial results are positive.

Metabolics of illegal substances remain in urine for various periods: cocaine for approximately 72 hours, and marijuana from two weeks to two months, depending on frequency of use. Detectable residues apparently remain in hair samples for several months.

Testing Job Applicants

In general, employers have the right to test new job applicants for traces of drugs in their systems as long as all of the following are true:

- The applicant knows that such testing will be part of the screening process for new employees.
- The employer has already offered the applicant the job.
- All applicants for the same job are tested similarly.
- The tests are administered by a state-certified laboratory.

Today, most companies that intend to conduct drug testing on job candidates include in their job applications an agreement to submit to such testing. If, in the process of applying for a job, you are asked to agree to drug testing, you have little choice but to agree to the test or drop out as an applicant.

Testing Existing Employees

There are a number of employees who, because of their specialized positions or type of work, can be tested more freely for drugs and alcohol use. For example, the Department of Transportation requires drug testing for some critical positions, such as airline pilots. And a 2006 rule by the Federal Aviation Administration mandates testing of all airline maintenance employees. In addition, courts have routinely approved random drug testing for employees with national security clearances, prison officers, employees at chemical weapons and nuclear power plants, and police officers. Note, however, that while many laws allow such employees to be tested, they do not require automatic discharges if the results are positive.

But there are some legal constraints on testing existing employees for drug usage in most private employment jobs. Companies cannot usually conduct blanket drug tests of all employees or random drug tests; the testing must be focused on an individual. In some cases where employers have tested for drugs without good reason, the employees affected have sued successfully for invasion of privacy and infliction of emotional harm.

However, the courts have generally ruled that companies may test for drugs among employees whose actions could clearly cause human injury or property damage if their performances were impaired by drugs, and in cases where there is good reason to think that the employees are abusing drugs. For example, a bulldozer operator who swerved the machine illogically through a field crowded with workers could be the legal target of drug testing.

And a legal secretary found slumped at her desk, unable to respond cogently to questions asked of her, was also considered fair game for a drug test.

Challenging Drug Tests

As an employee, you can always refuse to take a workplace drug test. But, if you are fired because of your refusal, you may have little recourse. Your employer needs only to show that he or she had good reason to believe that you were a safety hazard on the job or that you seemed unable to perform the work required. You would be placed in the untenable position of proving that your employer knew no such thing. You may, however, be able to win your job back if you can show that you were treated differently from other employees in the same position.

If you have been given a drug test and unfairly suspended or demoted because of it, your best bet may be to argue that the testers did not meet with the strict requirements for form and procedure set out in your state law. (See the chart below.) And note that employers are free to add safeguards to protect against specimen tampering—requiring those taking the test to remove their own clothing and don hospital gowns, or providing a test monitor who checks the temperature of the urine and adds dye to toilet water, as examples. However, a modicum of discretion is required; while most courts have found it reasonable to have a monitor listen as a urine test is administered, a number have found it an unreasonable invasion of privacy for the monitor to watch.

In addition, many laws require employers to maintain workplace counseling and

---

When Is a Suspicion Reasonable?

In most situations, an employer may test you for drugs only if there is a reasonable suspicion that you are using them. What suspicion is reasonable and what is not is in the eye and mind of the beholder, which makes it a slippery standard indeed.

But some statutes and courts have attempted to set some guidelines that may be helpful if you are targeted for a test and you believe your employer's suspicions are less than reasonable. A reasonable suspicion of drug use must generally be based on actual facts and logical inferences such as:

- direct observation of drug use or its physical symptoms, including slurred speech, agitated or lethargic demeanor, uncoordinated movement, and inappropriate response to questions
- abnormal conduct or erratic behavior while at work, or significant deterioration in work performance
- a report of drug use provided by a reliable and credible source that has been independently corroborated
- evidence that the employee has tampered with current drug test results
- information that the employee has caused or contributed to an accident at work, or
- evidence that the employee has used, possessed, sold, solicited, or transferred drugs while working or at work.

outreach programs before they can test employees. While most employers these days are too savvy to slip up on procedural details, many of the laws are so picky and detailed that it may be worth your while to wade through and see whether your test made the grade.

State and Local Drug Testing Laws

As mentioned, a number of state courts have set out rulings defining when and why drug tests may be given. Some recent examples:

- Two employees at an electronic equipment manufacturer, a truck driver and an editor of the company's user manuals, challenged the company's random drug testing program. A Massachusetts court found that the employer's legitimate business interests justified the drug test of the driver, whose job involved safety and liability risks. However, the court held that testing the editor was impermissible and that the employee's privacy interests outweighed the employer's interests, because the company failed to show a sufficient connection between his job duties and any harms feared. It noted specifically that he did not have a security clearance at the company, nor did he work directly on matters of national security. (*Webster v. Motorola, Inc.*, 637 N.E. 2d 203 (1994).)
- An employee was required to submit to a drug test when she was hired at a Denver car dealer. Nearly a year later, her employer informed her that it had

overlooked the test result, which was positive for marijuana. When another test was inconclusive, she refused to take the test again and was terminated. A Colorado court held that the state did not have a clearly expressed employee right to refuse drug testing, rejecting the employee's contention that the testing invaded her privacy. (*Slaughter v. John Elway Dodge Southwest/AutoNation*, 107 P.3d 1165 (2005).)
- The city of Seattle required a preemployment urinalysis drug test for about half its positions. Several taxpayers challenged the constitutionality of this program, though none claimed to have applied to the city for employment. A Washington court likened drug testing to a warrantless search that could not be justified merely by concerns of cost and efficiency. It noted that Seattle's testing program was applied too broadly to positions, such as librarians and accountants, that did not implicate public safety issues. (*Robinson v. City of Seattle*, 102 Wn. App. 795 (2000).)

In addition, a number of states and several municipalities have laws that regulate work-related testing for substance abuse. Those that do also specify the scientific procedures to which testing labs must adhere. And many of these laws provide ways of dealing with overbroad or abusive workplace drug testing that are simpler, quicker, and less expensive than filing a lawsuit. Some states also require companies to distribute to employees written policies on drug testing and rehabilitation.

State Drug and Alcohol Testing

Note: The states of Colorado, Delaware, Kansas, Kentucky, Massachusetts, Michigan, Missouri, Nevada, New Hampshire, New Jersey, New Mexico, New York, Pennsylvania, South Dakota, Texas, Washington, West Virginia, Wisconsin, Wyoming, and the District of Columbia are not included in this chart because they do not have specific drug and alcohol testing laws governing private employers. Additional laws may apply. Check with your state department of labor for more information.

Alabama
Ala. Code §§ 25-5-330 to 25-5-340

Employers affected: Employers who establish a drug-free workplace program to qualify for a workers' compensation rate discount.

Testing applicants: Must test upon conditional offer of employment. Must test all new hires. Job ads must include notice that drug and alcohol testing required.

Testing employees: Random testing permitted. Must test after an accident that results in lost work time. Must also test upon reasonable suspicion; reasons for suspicion must be documented and made available to employee upon request.

Employee rights: Employees have 5 days to contest or explain a positive test result. Employer must have an employee assistance program or maintain a resource file of outside programs.

Notice and policy requirements: All employees must have written notice of drug policy. Must give 60 days' advance notice before implementing testing program. Policy must state consequences of refusing to take test or testing positive.

Drug-free workplace program: Yes.

Alaska
Alaska Stat. §§ 23.10.600 to 23.10.699

Employers affected: Voluntary for employers with one or more full-time employees. (There is no state-mandated drug and alcohol testing.)

Testing employees: Employer may test:
- for any job-related purpose
- to maintain productivity or safety
- as part of an accident investigation, or
- upon reasonable suspicion.

Employee rights: Employer must provide written test results within 5 working days. Employee has 10 working days to request opportunity to explain positive test results; employer must grant request within 72 hours or before taking any adverse employment action.

Notice and policy requirements: Before implementing a testing program employer must distribute a written drug policy to all employees and must give 30 days' advance notice. Policy must state consequences of a positive test or refusal to submit to testing.

Arizona
Ariz. Rev. Stat. §§ 23-493 to 23-493.05

Employers affected: Employers with one or more full-time employees.

Testing applicants: Employer must inform prospective hires that they will undergo drug testing as a condition of employment.

Testing employees: Employees are subject to random and scheduled tests:
- for any job-related purpose
- to maintain productivity or safety
- as part of an accident investigation, or
- upon reasonable suspicion.

Employee rights: Policy must inform employees of their right to explain positive results.

State Drug and Alcohol Testing (continued)

Notice and policy requirements: Before conducting tests employer must give employees a copy of the written policy. Policy must state the consequences of a positive test or refusal to submit to testing.

Drug-free workplace program: Yes.

Arkansas

Ark. Code Ann. §§ 11-14-105 to 11-14-112

Employers affected: Employers who establish a drug-free workplace program to qualify for a workers' compensation rate discount.

Testing applicants: Must test for drug use upon conditional offer of employment, may test for alcohol but not required. Job ads must include notice that testing required.

Testing employees: Employer must test any employee:
- upon reasonable suspicion
- as part of a routine fitness-for-duty medical exam
- after an accident that results in injury, or
- as follow-up to a required rehabilitation program.

Employee rights: Employer may not refuse to hire applicant or take adverse personnel action against an employee on the basis of a single positive test that has not been verified by a confirmation test and a medical review officer. An applicant or employee has 5 days after receiving test results to contest or explain them.

Notice and policy requirements: Employer must give all employees a written statement of drug policy and must give 60 days' advance notice before implementing program.

Drug-free workplace program: Yes.

California

Cal. Lab. Code §§ 1025, 1026

Employers affected: No provisions for private employer testing. An employer with 25 or more employees must reasonably accommodate an employee who wants to enter a treatment program. Employer is not, however, required to provide paid leave. Employer may fire or refuse to hire an employee whose drug or alcohol use interferes with job duties or workplace safety.

Employee rights: Employer must safeguard privacy of employee who enters treatment program.

Connecticut

Conn. Gen. Stat. Ann. §§ 31-51t to 31-51bb

Employers affected: All.

Testing applicants: Employer must inform job applicants in writing that drug testing is required as a condition of employment.

Testing employees: Employer may test:
- when there is reasonable suspicion that employee is under the influence of drugs or alcohol and job performance is or could be impaired
- when authorized by federal law
- when employee's position is dangerous or safety-sensitive, or
- as part of a voluntary employee assistance program.

Employee rights: Employer may not take any adverse personnel action on the basis of a single positive test that has not been verified by a confirmation test.

Florida

Fla. Stat. Ann. §§ 440.101 to 440.102

Employers affected: Employers who establish a drug-free workplace program to qualify for a workers' compensation rate discount.

State Drug and Alcohol Testing (continued)

Testing applicants: Must inform job applicants that drug and alcohol testing is required as a condition of employment.

Testing employees: Must test any employee:
- upon reasonable suspicion
- as part of a routine fitness-for-duty medical exam, or
- as part of a required rehabilitation program.

Employee rights: Employees who voluntarily seek treatment for substance abuse cannot be fired, disciplined, or discriminated against, unless they have tested positive or have been in treatment in the past. All employees have the right to explain positive results within 5 days. Employer may not take any adverse personnel action on the basis of an initial positive result that has not been verified by a confirmation test and a medical review officer.

Notice and policy requirements: Prior to implementing testing, employer must give 60 days' advance notice and must give employees written copy of drug policy. Policy must state consequences of a positive test result or refusal to submit to testing.

Drug-free workplace program: Yes.

Georgia
Ga. Code Ann. §§ 34-9-410 to 34-9-421

Employers affected: Employers who establish a drug-free workplace program to qualify for a workers' compensation rate discount.

Testing applicants: Applicants are required to submit to a substance abuse test after they have been offered employment.

Testing employees: Must test any employee:
- upon reasonable suspicion
- as part of a routine fitness-for-duty medical exam

- after an accident that results in an injury, or
- as part of a required rehabilitation program.

Employee rights: Employees have 5 days to explain or contest a positive result. Employer must have an employee assistance program or maintain a resource file of outside programs.

Notice and policy requirements: Employer must give applicants and employees notice of testing and must give 60 days' notice before implementing program. All employees must receive a written policy statement; policy must state the consequences of refusing to submit to a drug test or of testing positive.

Drug-free workplace program: Yes.

Hawaii
Haw. Rev. Stat. §§ 329B-1 to 329B-5

Employers affected: All.

Testing applicants: Same conditions as current employees.

Testing employees: Employer may test employees only if these conditions are met:
- employer pays all costs including confirming test
- tests are performed by a licensed laboratory
- employee receives a list of the substances being tested for
- there is a form for disclosing medicines and legal drugs, and
- the results are kept confidential.

Idaho
Idaho Code §§ 72-1701 to 72-1714

Employers affected: Voluntary for all private employers.

Testing applicants: Employer may test as a condition of hiring.

Testing employees: May test as a condition of

State Drug and Alcohol Testing (continued)

continued employment.

An employer who follows drug-free workplace guidelines may fire employees who refuse to submit to testing or who test positive for drugs or alcohol. Employees will be fired for misconduct and denied unemployment benefits.

Employee rights: An employee or applicant who receives notice of a positive test may request a retest within 7 working days. Employer may not take any adverse employment action on the basis of an initial positive result that has not been verified by a confirmation test. If the retest results are negative, the employer must pay for the cost; if they are positive, the employee must pay.

Notice and policy requirements: Employer must have a written policy that includes a statement that violation of the policy may result in termination due to misconduct, as well as what types of testing employees may be subject to.

Drug-free workplace program: Yes (compliance is optional).

Illinois

775 Ill. Comp. Stat. § 5/2-104(C)(3)

Employers affected: Employers with 15 or more employees.

Testing employees: Statute does not "encourage, prohibit, or authorize" drug testing, but employers may test employees who have been in rehabilitation.

Indiana

Ind. Code Ann. §§ 22-9-5-6(b), 22-9-5-24

Employers affected: Employers with 15 or more employees.

Testing employees: Employer may prohibit all employees from using or being under the influence of alcohol and illegal drugs.

Employer may test employees who have been in rehabilitation. Employee may be held to the same standards as other employees, even if the unsatisfactory job performance or behavior is due to drug use or alcoholism.

Iowa

Iowa Code § 730.5

Employers affected: Employers with one or more full-time employees.

Testing applicants: Employer may test as a condition of hiring.

Testing employees: Employer may test employees:

- as a condition of continued employment
- upon reasonable suspicion
- during and after rehabilitation, or
- following an accident that caused a reportable injury or more than $1,000 property damage.

Employee rights: Employee has 7 days to request a retest. Employers with 50 or more employees must provide rehabilitation for any employee testing positive for alcohol use who has worked for at least one year and has not previously violated the substance abuse policy. Employer must have an employee assistance program or maintain a resource file of outside programs.

Drug-free workplace program: Yes (compliance is optional).

Louisiana

La. Rev. Stat. Ann. §§ 49:1001 to 49:1012

Employers affected: Employers with one or more full-time employees. (Does not apply to oil drilling, exploration, or production.)

Testing applicants: Employer may require all applicants to submit to drug and alcohol test. Employer does not have to confirm a positive

State Drug and Alcohol Testing (continued)

result of a preemployment drug screen but must offer the applicant the opportunity to pay for a confirmation test and a review by a medical review officer.

Employee rights: Employees with confirmed positive results have 7 working days to request access to all records relating to the drug test. Employer may allow employee to undergo rehabilitation without termination of employment.

Maine

Me. Rev. Stat. Ann. tit. 26, §§ 681 to 690

Employers affected: Employers with one or more full-time employees. (Law does not require or encourage employers to conduct substance abuse testing.)

Testing applicants: Employer may require applicant to take a drug test only if offered employment or placed on an eligibility list.

Testing employees: Employer may test based upon probable cause but may not base belief on a single accident; must document the facts and give employee a copy. May test when:

- there could be an unreasonable threat to the health and safety of coworkers or the public, or
- an employee returns to work following a positive test.

Employee rights: Employee who tests positive has 3 days to explain or contest results. Employee must be given an opportunity to participate in a rehabilitation program for up to 6 months; an employer with more than 20 full-time employees must pay for half of any out-of-pocket costs. After successfully completing the program, employee is entitled to return to previous job with full pay and benefits.

Notice and policy requirements: All employers must have a written policy approved by the state department of labor. Policy must be distributed to each employee at least 30 days before it takes effect. Any changes to policy require 60 days' advance notice. An employer with more than 20 full-time employees must have an employee assistance program certified by the state office of substance abuse before implementing a testing program.

Maryland

Md. Code Ann., [Health-Gen.] § 17-214

Employers affected: Law applies to all employers.

Testing applicants: May use preliminary screening to test applicant. If initial result is positive, may make job offer conditional on confirmation of test results.

Testing employees: Employer may require substance abuse testing for legitimate business purposes only.

Employee rights: The sample must be tested by a certified laboratory; at the time of testing employee may request laboratory's name and address. An employee who tests positive must be given:

- a copy of the test results
- a copy of the employer's written drug and alcohol policy
- a written notice of any adverse action employer intends to take, and
- a statement of employee's right to an independent confirmation test at own expense.

Minnesota

Minn. Stat. Ann. §§ 181.950 to 181.957

Employers affected: Employers with one or more full-time employees. (Employers are not required to test.)

State Drug and Alcohol Testing (continued)

Testing applicants: Employers may require applicants to submit to a drug or alcohol test only after they have been given a job offer and have seen a written notice of testing policy. May only test if required of all applicants for same position.

Testing employees: Employers may require drug or alcohol testing only according to a written testing policy. Testing may be done if there is a reasonable suspicion that employee:

- is under the influence of drugs or alcohol
- has violated drug and alcohol policy
- has been involved in an accident, or
- has sustained or caused another employee to sustain a personal injury.

Random tests permitted only for employees in safety-sensitive positions. With two weeks' notice, employers may also test as part of an annual routine physical exam. Employer may test, without notice, an employee referred by the employer for chemical dependency treatment or evaluation or participating in a chemical dependency treatment program under an employee benefit plan. Testing is allowed during and for two years following treatment.

Employee rights: If test is positive, employee has 3 days to explain the results; employee must notify employer within 5 days of intention to obtain a retest. Employer may not discharge employee for a first-time positive test without offering counseling or rehabilitation; employee who refuses or does not complete program successfully may be discharged.

Notice and policy requirements: Employees must be given a written notice of testing policy which includes consequences of refusing to take test or having a positive test result. Two weeks'

notice required before testing as part of an annual routine physical exam.

Mississippi

Miss. Code Ann. §§ 71-7-1 to 71-7-13, 71-3-205 to 71-3-213

Employers affected: Employers with one or more full-time employees. Employers who establish a drug-free workplace program to qualify for a workers' compensation rate discount must implement testing procedures.

Testing applicants: May test all applicants as part of employment application process. Employer may request a signed statement that applicant has read and understands the drug and alcohol testing policy or notice. (Must test applicants if drug-free workplace.)

Testing employees: May require drug and alcohol testing of all employees:

- upon reasonable suspicion
- as part of a routinely scheduled fitness for duty medical examination
- as a follow-up to a rehabilitation program, or
- if they have tested positive within the previous 12 months.

Employee rights: Employer must inform an employee in writing within 5 working days of receipt of a positive confirmed test result; employee may request and receive a copy of the test result report. Employee has 10 working days after receiving notice to explain the positive test results. Employer may not discharge or take any adverse personnel action on the basis of an initial positive test result that has not been verified by a confirmation test. Private employer who elects to establish a drug-free workplace program must have an employee assistance program or maintain a resource file of outside programs.

State Drug and Alcohol Testing (continued)

Notice and policy requirements: 30 days before implementing testing program employer must give employees written notice of drug and alcohol policy which includes consequences:
- of a positive confirmed result
- of refusing to take test, and
- of other violations of the policy.

Drug-free workplace program: Yes.

Montana
Mont. Code Ann. §§ 39-2-205 to 39-2-211

Employers affected: Employers with one or more employees.

Testing applicants: May test as a condition of hire.

Testing employees: Employees may be tested:
- upon reasonable suspicion
- after involvement in an accident that causes personal injury or more than $1,500 property damage
- as a follow-up to a previous positive test, or
- as a follow-up to treatment or a rehabilitation program.

Employer may conduct random tests as long as there is an established date, all personnel are subject to testing, the employer has signed statements from each employee confirming receipt of a written description of the random selection process, and the random selection process is conducted by a scientifically valid method.

Employer may require an employee who tests positive to undergo treatment as a condition of continued employment.

Employee rights: After a positive result, employee may request additional confirmation by an independent laboratory; if the results are negative, employer must pay the test costs.

Notice and policy requirements: Written policy must be available for review 60 days before testing. Policy must state consequences of a positive test result.

Nebraska
Neb. Rev. Stat. §§ 48-1901 to 48-1910

Employers affected: Employers with 6 or more full-time and part-time employees.

Testing employees: Employer may require employees to submit to drug or alcohol testing and may discipline or discharge any employee who refuses.

Employee rights: Employer may not take adverse action on the basis of an initial positive result unless it is confirmed according to state and federal guidelines.

North Carolina
N.C. Gen. Stat. §§ 95-230 to 95-235

Employers affected: Law applies to all employers.

Testing employees: Employer must preserve samples for at least 90 days after confirmed test results are released.

Employee rights: Employee has right to retest a confirmed positive sample at own expense.

North Dakota
N.D. Cent. Code §§ 34-01-15, 65-01-11

Employers affected: Any employer who requires a medical exam as a condition of hire or continued employment may include a drug or alcohol test, but employer must pay for the test.

Testing employees: Employer may test following an accident or injury that will result in a workers' compensation claim, if employer has a mandatory policy of testing under these circumstances, or if employer or physician has reasonable grounds to

State Drug and Alcohol Testing (continued)

suspect injury was caused by impairment due to alcohol or drug use.

Ohio

Ohio Admin. Code §§ 4123-17-58, 4123-17-58.1

Employers affected: Employers who establish a drug-free workplace program to qualify for a workers' compensation rate discount.

Testing applicants: Must test all applicants and new hires within 90 days of employment.

Testing employees: Must test employees:
- upon reasonable suspicion
- following a return to work after a positive test
- after an accident which results in an injury requiring offsite medical attention or property damage over limit specified in drug and alcohol policy
- at random to meet requirements for greater discounts.

Employee rights: Employer must have an employee assistance plan. Employer must offer health care coverage which includes chemical dependency counseling and treatment. Not required for employers with few than 25 employees.

Notice and policy requirements: Policy must state consequences for refusing to submit to testing or for violating guidelines. Policy must include a commitment to rehabilitation.

Drug-free workplace program: Yes.

Oklahoma

Okla. Stat. Ann. tit. 40, §§ 551 to 565

Employers affected: Employers with one or more employees. (Drug or alcohol testing not required or encouraged.)

Testing applicants: Employer may test applicants as a condition of employment and may refuse to hire applicant who refuses to undergo test or has a confirmed positive result.

Testing employees: Before requiring testing, employer must provide an employee assistance program. Random testing is allowed. May test employees:
- upon reasonable suspicion
- after an accident resulting in injury or property damage over $500
- on a random selection basis
- as part of a routine fitness-for-duty examination, or
- as follow-up to a rehabilitation program.

Employee rights: Employee has right to retest a positive result at own expense; if the confirmation test is negative, employer must reimburse costs.

Notice and policy requirements: Before requiring testing employer must:
- adopt a written policy
- give a copy to each employee and to any applicant offered a job, and
- allow 30 days' notice.
  Policy must state consequences of a positive test result or refusing to submit to testing.

Oregon

Or. Rev. Stat. §§ 659.840, 659A.300, 438.435

Employers affected: Law applies to all employers.

Testing applicants: Unless there is reasonable suspicion that an applicant is under the influence of alcohol, no employer may require a breathalyzer test as a condition of employment. Employer is not prohibited from conducting a test if applicant consents.

Testing employees: Unless there is reasonable suspicion that an employee is under the

State Drug and Alcohol Testing (continued)

influence of alcohol, no employer may require a breathalyzer or blood alcohol test as a condition of continuing employment. Employer is not prohibited from conducting a test if employee consents.

Employee rights: No action may be taken based on the results of an on-site drug test without a confirming test performed according to state health division regulations. Upon written request, test results will be reported to the employee.

Rhode Island

R.I. Gen. Laws §§ 28-6.5-1 to 28-6.5-2

Employers affected: Law applies to all employers.

Testing employees: May require employee to submit to a drug test only if there are reasonable grounds, based on specific observations, to believe employee is using controlled substances that are impairing job performance.

Employee rights: Employee who tests positive may have the sample retested at employer's expense and must be given opportunity to explain or refute results. Employee may not be terminated on the basis of a positive result but must be referred to a licensed substance abuse professional. After referral, employer may require additional testing and may terminate employee if test results are positive.

South Carolina

S.C. Code Ann. §§ 41-1-15, 38-73-500

Employers affected: Employers who establish a drug-free workplace program to qualify for a workers' compensation rate discount.

Testing employees: Must conduct random testing among all employees. Must conduct a follow-up test within 30 minutes of the first test.

Employee rights: Employee must receive positive test results in writing within 24 hours.

Notice and policy requirements: Employer must notify all employees of the drug-free workplace program at the time it is established or at the time of hiring, whichever is earlier. Program must include a policy statement that balances respect for individuals with the need to maintain a safe, drug-free environment.

Drug-free workplace program: Yes.

Tennessee

Tenn. Code Ann. §§ 50-9-101 to 50-9-114

Employers affected: Employers who establish a drug-free workplace program to qualify for a workers' compensation rate discount.

Testing applicants: Must test applicants upon conditional offer of employment. Job ads must include notice that drug and alcohol testing is required.

Testing employees: Employer must test upon reasonable suspicion; must document behavior on which the suspicion is based within 24 hours or before test results are released, whichever is earlier; and must give a copy to the employee upon request. Employer must test employees:

- who are in safety-sensitive positions
- as part of a routine fitness-for-duty medical exam
- after an accident that results in injury, or
- as a follow-up to a required rehabilitation program.

Employee rights: Employee has the right to explain or contest a positive result within 5 days. Employee may not be fired, disciplined, or discriminated against for voluntarily seeking treatment unless employee has previously tested positive or been in a rehabilitation program.

State Drug and Alcohol Testing (continued)

Notice and policy requirements: Before implementing testing program, employer must provide 60 days' notice and must give all employees a written drug and alcohol policy statement. Policy must state consequences of a positive test or refusing to submit to testing.

Drug-free workplace program: Yes.

Utah

Utah Code Ann. §§ 34-38-1 to 34-38-15

Employers affected: Employers with one or more employees.

Testing applicants: Employer may test any applicant for drugs or alcohol as long as management also submits to periodic testing.

Testing employees: Employer may test employee for drugs or alcohol as long as management also submits to periodic testing. Employer may require testing to:

- investigate possible individual employee impairment
- investigate an accident or theft
- maintain employee or public safety, or
- ensure productivity, quality, or security.

Employee rights: Employer may suspend, discipline, discharge, or require treatment on the basis of a confirmed positive test result.

Notice and policy requirements: Testing must be conducted according to a written policy that has been distributed to employees and is available for review by prospective employees.

Vermont

Vt. Stat. Ann. tit. 21, §§ 511 to 515

Employers affected: Employers with one or more employees.

Testing applicants: Employer may not test applicants for drugs or alcohol unless there is a job offer conditional on a negative test result and applicant is given written notice of the testing procedure and a list of the drugs to be tested for.

Testing employees: Random testing not permitted unless required by federal law. Employer may not require testing unless:

- there is probable cause to believe an employee is using or is under the influence
- employer has an employee assistance program which provides rehabilitation, and
- employee who tests positive and agrees to enter employee assistance program is not terminated.

Employee rights: Employer must contract with a medical review officer who will review all test results and keep them confidential. Medical review officer is to contact employee or applicant to explain a positive test result. Employee or applicant has right to an independent retest at own expense. Employee who successfully completes employee assistance program may not be terminated, although employee may be suspended for up to 3 months to complete program. Employee who tests positive after completing treatment may be fired.

Notice and policy requirements: Must provide written policy that states consequences of a positive test.

Virginia

Va. Code Ann. § 65.2-813.2

Employers affected: Employers who establish drug-free workplace programs to qualify for workers' compensation insurance discount.

Drug-free workplace program: State law gives insurers the authority to establish guidelines and criteria for testing.

Current as of February 2007

Laws in a rapidly growing number of states include a kinder, gentler twist by protecting employees who seek treatment for a substance abuse problem from being discriminated against or fired.

Ironically, workers in states that have laws regulating the timing and procedures of drug and alcohol testing may actually have more protections than those living in states with no testing laws. Employees living in such lawless states, for example, may generally be tested without advance notice.

Statutes in nearly a quarter of the states set out provisions for establishing a drug-free workplace program. The programs, most of them optional, offer employers reduced workers' compensation costs. In return, employers must establish a written policy, testing program, and employee assistance and education component.

Drug and alcohol testing laws vary tremendously and are changing rapidly. The best way to get up-to-date details on laws in your state is to research them online or at a library near you. (See Chapter 17, "Legal Research.") Your state labor department may also have information on current testing laws. (See the Appendix for contact details.)

CAUTION

Additional laws may apply. If the chart above indicates that your state has no statute, this means there is no law that specifically addresses the issue. However, there may be a state administrative regulation or local ordinance that does control testing. Call your state labor department for more information. (See the Appendix for contact details.)

Psychological Testing

A number of people who label themselves as Workplace Consultants claim they have developed several series of written questions—integrity tests—that can predict whether a person would lie, steal, or be unreliable if hired for a particular job. And a number of other alleged experts claim to have perfected personality tests that allow employers to tell in advance whether an individual is suited by temperament and talent to a particular position. Employers are drawn to these tactics because they seem to short-circuit the process of interviewing—and because they seem to promise some insight into an applicant's personality, which can be tough to assess in an interview setting.

Psychological tests are not a new idea. They were first developed during World War I to help the military decide how to assign soldiers to various jobs. Some legal cutbacks to personality and psychological testing in the workplace began in the 1970s, when employers were banned from questioning prospective employees about age, race, or sex. The tests had a heyday again in the early '90s, shortly after lie-detector screening was curtailed by law. (See "Lie Detector Tests," below.) And, today, legions of test publishers have cropped up online—most of which claim they can forecast everything from a potential employee's likelihood of being honest and hardworking to his or her absence and injury rate on the job. And they promise an analysis fast—often within 48 hours of receiving responses to test questions. Critics say that is a suspiciously tall order to fill so

Target Learns What Not to Ask

The first major case to challenge psychological testing of job applicants yielded grand results: a $2 million settlement and a five-year ban on testing.

The settlement came in July 1993, in a class action brought by several people who had applied to the Target stores chain for work as security guards. As part of the application process, they had been asked to respond to over 700 true/false statements including:

- I am very strongly attracted by members of my own sex.
- I have never indulged in unusual sex practices.
- I believe my sins are unpardonable.
- I believe in the second coming of Christ.
- I have had no difficulty starting or holding my urine.

About 30% of the 2,500 test takers did not get jobs with Target—either because of the answers they gave or because the results were deemed inconclusive.

But the test made even successful applicants queasy. Robert Marzetta worked at Target for a year before becoming one of the main plaintiffs in the case. He said that while he felt the test questions were "out of line" and made him "uncomfortable," he didn't object at exam time because he needed the job.

Sue Urry joined in the case because, she said, as a Mormon, she found the religious questions particularly offensive.

Another plaintiff, Sibi Soroka, also got a guard job. Soroka found the test questions so unsettling that he copied all 700 of them before turning in his answers—then went to the American Civil Liberties Union and a number of attorneys seeking help. He was on the job only about a month because, he said, "it's kind of difficult to work for a person you're suing."

Target argued that the test, the Rodgers Condensed CPI-MMPI, helped weed out the emotionally unstable from the pool of those who would be subjected to the stressful task of apprehending shoplifting suspects.

The applicants challenged the test as violating their privacy rights and the state Labor Code, which bans questions about sexual orientation.

They shared in the $2 million in wealth Target lost.

This headline-grabbing case inspired hundreds of other workers around the nation to mount challenges to psychological tests they found offensive or intrusive. So far, the majority of courts have sided with the workers.

quickly. And there may be legal pitfalls to the tests as well. Despite the doubts that surround them, however, the employee screening tests remain popular with many employers, most of whom claim to temper their acceptance with a dollop of skepticism and to cast about for information in more subtle ways.

Today's prescreening questionnaires usually cover legally forbidden topics in roundabout ways. For example, employers may glean information about marital and family status by asking applicants to give information about hobbies and other interests. And many employers—about 40% of them, according to the American Management Association—use these questionnaires in the process of screening applicants for job openings. But even that temptation has been curbed of late by a number of cases that send a clear warning: Psychological tests cannot be used as an excuse to discriminate against prospective employees—and they must be limited to job-related questions.

Lie Detector Tests

For decades, lie detectors, or polygraphs, now more euphemistically referred to as "psychological stress evaluator tests," that purport to measure the truthfulness of a person's statements by tracking bodily functions such as blood pressure and perspiration, were routinely used on employees and job applicants.

Employers could—and often did—ask employees and prospective employees questions about extremely private matters such as sexual preferences, toilet habits, and family finances, while a machine to which they were hooked passed judgment on the truthfulness of the answers. Push the machine's needle too far by reacting to an offensive question and you could be labeled a liar and denied employment.

The federal Employee Polygraph Protection Act (29 U.S.C. § 2001), passed in 1988, virtually outlawed using lie detectors in connection with employment. That law covers all private employers in interstate commerce, which includes just about every private company that uses a computer, U.S. mail or the telephone system to send messages to someone in another state.

Under the Act, it is illegal for all private companies to:

- require, request, suggest, or cause any employee or job applicant to submit to a lie detector test
- use, accept, refer to, or inquire about the results of any lie detector test conducted on an employee or job applicant, or
- dismiss, discipline, discriminate against, or even threaten to take action against any employee or job applicant who refuses to take a lie detector test.

The law also prohibits employers from discriminating against or firing those who use its protections.

While government employees are not protected by this law, they are generally protected from lie detector tests by civil service rules.

When Lie Detector Tests Can Be Used

The Employee Polygraph Protection Act allows polygraph tests to be used in connection with jobs in security and handling drugs or in investigating a specific theft or other suspected crime. However, before you can be required to take such a test as part of an investigation of an employment-related crime, you must be given a written notice, at least 48 hours before the test, stating that you are a suspect. And there must be a provable, reasonable suspicion that you were involved in the theft or other conduct triggering the investigation.

The Act does not apply to employees of federal, state, or local government, nor to certain jobs that handle sensitive work relating to national defense.

Limitations on the Tests

In addition to the strict strictures on when and to whom the tests may be given, there are a number of restrictions on their format. Before a lie detector test can be administered, your employer must read to you and ask you to sign a statement that includes:

- a list of topics you cannot be asked about, including questions on religious beliefs, sexual preference, racial matters, lawful activities of labor organizations, and political affiliation
- information on your right to refuse to take the test
- the fact that you cannot be required to take the test as a condition of employment
- an explanation of how the test results can be used, and
- an explanation of your legal rights if the test is not given in keeping with the law.

While the test is being administered, you have the right:

- to stop it at any time, and
- to be asked questions in a way that is not "degrading or needlessly intrusive."

When the test is said and done, results can be disclosed only to the employer who ordered the test, the employee who was tested, a court or government agency, or an arbitrator or mediator if there is a related court order. The law specifically prohibits prospective employers from getting access to old test results.

How to Take Action

The Employee Polygraph Protection Act is enforced by the U.S. Department of Labor. If you have questions about whether the Act applies to your job or if you suspect that you have been subjected to illegal polygraph testing, call the office of the U.S. Labor Department's Wage and Hour Division nearest you. (See the Appendix for contact details.)

There is no official form for filing a complaint. If, after discussing your situation with a Wage and Hour Division investigator, you decide to file a complaint, do so as soon as possible by writing a letter addressed to your local Wage and Hour Division office. Include such details as the name and address of the employer, when the incident occurred, and the address and telephone number where an investigator can reach you. And keep a copy of your letter for your records.

If the labor department finds that your rights under the Act were violated, it can fine the offending employer up to $10,000 and issue an injunction ordering the employer to reinstate you to your job, promote you, compensate you for back wages, hire you, or take other logical action to correct the violation.

If the labor department's action on your complaint does not satisfy you, you can file a lawsuit against the employer to obtain whatever compensation or other remedy would be appropriate. Move quickly, because the lawsuit must be filed within three years. You will probably need to hire an attorney to help you if you decide to file a lawsuit under this Act. (See Chapter 17, "Hiring a Lawyer.") But the law allows the court to grant you attorneys' fees and other costs if you win.

State Laws on Lie Detector Tests

As noted in the chart, "Employee Polygraph Examination Laws," some states have laws prohibiting or restricting employers from using lie detectors in connection with employment, but most have been made obsolete by the federal antipolygraph statute. Some states go farther and prohibit employers from even suggesting such a test.

In addition, state coverage may be broader; while the federal law does not apply to state and local government employees, many of the state statutes do.

Note that the laws in several states provide that an employee who volunteers to take a lie detector test may be given one. But such laws have safeguards, requiring that the tests be administered under approved and supervised conditions and that employees be clearly informed about how and why test results may be used.

CAUTION

Additional laws may apply. If the chart below indicates that your state has no statute, this means there is no law that specifically addresses the issue. However, there may be a state administrative regulation or local ordinance that does control polygraph tests. Call your state labor department for more information. (See the Appendix for contact details.)

Employee Polygraph Examination Laws

Alaska

Alaska Stat. § 23.10.037

Employers covered: All

What's prohibited: Employer may not suggest, request, or require that employee or applicant take a lie detector test.

California

Cal. Lab. Code § 432.2

Employers covered: All

What's prohibited: Employer may not demand or require that employee or applicant take a lie detector test.

What's allowed: Employer may request a test, if applicant is advised in writing of legal right to refuse to take it.

Connecticut

Conn. Gen. Stat. Ann. § 31-51g

Employers covered: All, including employment agencies.

What's prohibited: Employer may not request or require that employee or applicant take a lie detector test.

Delaware

Del. Code Ann. tit. 19, § 704

Employers covered: All

What's prohibited: Employer may not suggest, request, or require that employee or applicant take a lie detector test in order to obtain or continue employment.

District of Columbia

D.C. Code Ann. §§ 32-901 to 32-903

Employers covered: All

What's prohibited: Employer may not administer, have administered, use, or accept the results of any polygraph examination.

Hawaii

Haw. Rev. Stat. § 378-26.5

Employers covered: All

What's prohibited: Employer may not require employee or applicant to take lie detector test.

What's allowed: Employer may request test if current or prospective employee is told, orally and in writing, that refusing to take test will not result in being fired or hurt chances of getting job.

Idaho

Idaho Code § 44-903

Employers covered: All

What's prohibited: Employer may not require an employee or applicant to take a lie detector test.

Illinois

225 Ill. Comp. Stat. § 430/14.1

Employers covered: All

What's prohibited: Unless directly related to employment, examination may not include questions about:

- political, religious, or labor-related beliefs, affiliations, or lawful activities
- beliefs or opinions on racial matters, or
- sexual preferences or activity.

Iowa

Iowa Code § 730.4

Employers covered: All

What's prohibited: Employer may not request, require, administer, or attempt or threaten to administer a lie detector test; may not request or require that employee or applicant sign waiver of any action prohibited by this law.

Maine

Me. Rev. Stat. Ann. tit. 32, § 7166

Employee Polygraph Examination Laws (continued)

Employers covered: All

What's prohibited: Employer may not request, require, suggest, or administer a lie detector test.

What's allowed: Employee may voluntarily request a test if these conditions are met:
- results cannot be used against employee
- employer must give employee a copy of the law when employee requests test, and
- test must be recorded or employee's witness must be present during the test, or both.

Maryland

Md. Code Ann. [Lab. & Empl.] § 3-702

Employers covered: All

What's prohibited: Employer may not require or demand that employee or applicant take a lie detector test.

What's required: All employment applications must include specified notice that no person can be required to take a lie detector test as a condition of obtaining or continuing employment; must include space for applicant to sign and acknowledge notice.

Massachusetts

Mass. Gen. Laws ch. 149, § 19B

Employers covered: All

What's prohibited: Employer may not request, require, or administer a lie detector test.

What's required: All employment applications must include specified notice that it is unlawful to require a lie detector test as a condition of obtaining or continuing employment.

Michigan

Mich. Comp. Laws §§ 37.203, 338.1719

Employers covered: All

What's prohibited: Employer may not request, require, administer, or attempt or threaten to administer a lie detector test; may not request or require that employee or applicant sign waiver of any action prohibited by this law.

What's allowed: Employee may voluntarily request a test if these conditions are met:
- before taking test employee is given copy of the law
- employee is given copies of test results and reports
- no questions asked about sexual practices; marital relationship; or political, religious, or labor or union affiliations, unless questions are relevant to areas under examination, and
- examiner informs employee
  - of all questions that will be asked
  - of right to accept, refuse, or stop test at any time
  - that employee is not required to answer questions or give information, and
  - that information volunteered could be used against employee or made available to employer, unless otherwise agreed to in writing.

Minnesota

Minn. Stat. Ann. §§ 181.75, 181.76

Employers covered: All

What's prohibited: Employer may not directly or indirectly solicit or require an applicant or employee to take a lie detector test.

What's allowed: Employee may request a test, but only if employer informs employee that test is voluntary. Results of voluntary test may be given only to those authorized by employee.

Montana

Mont. Code Ann. § 39-2-304

What's prohibited: Employer may not require an employee or applicant to take a lie detector test.

Employee Polygraph Examination Laws (continued)

Nebraska

Neb. Rev. Stat. § 81-1932

Employers covered: All

What's prohibited: Employer may not require an employee or applicant to take a lie detector test.

What's allowed: Employer may request that test be taken, but only if these conditions are met:

- no questions asked about sexual practices; marital relationship; or political, religious, or labor or union affiliations
- examinee is given written and oral notice that test is voluntary and may be discontinued at any time
- examinee signs form stating that test is being taken voluntarily
- prospective employees are asked only job-related questions and are not singled out for testing in a discriminatory manner
- employee requested to take test only in connection with a specific investigation
- results of test are not the sole reason for terminating employment, and
- all questions and responses are kept on file by the employer for at least one year.

Nevada

Nev. Rev. Stat. Ann. §§ 613.480 to 613.510

Employers covered: All

Exceptions: Manufacturers or distributors of controlled substances; providers or designers of security systems and personnel; ongoing investigation.

What's prohibited: Employer may not directly or indirectly require, request, suggest, or cause a lie detector test to be taken; may not use, accept, refer to, or ask about the results of any test. May not take adverse employment action solely on the basis of test results or a refusal to take test.

What's allowed: Nevada law allows testing in the same limited circumstances as the federal EPPA, with similar rules and restrictions on when and how the test is given.

New Jersey

N.J. Stat. Ann. § 2C:40A-1

Employers covered: All

Exceptions: Employers that deal with controlled, dangerous substances.

What's prohibited: Employer may not influence, request, or require applicant or employee to take a lie detector test.

What's allowed: Employers who are allowed to test must observe these rules:

- job must require direct access to controlled substance
- test limited to preceding five years
- questions must be work-related or pertain to improper handling, use, or illegal sale of legally distributed controlled dangerous substances
- test taker has right to legal counsel
- written copy of test results must be given to test taker upon request
- test information may not be released to any other employer or person, and
- employee or prospective employee must be informed of right to present results of a second independently administered test prior to any personnel decision being made.

New York

N.Y. Lab. Law §§ 733 to 739

Employers covered: All

What's prohibited: Employer may not require, request, suggest, permit, or use results of a lie detector test.

Employee Polygraph Examination Laws (continued)

Oregon

Or. Rev. Stat. Ann. §§ 659.840, 659A.300

Employers covered: All

What's prohibited: Employer may not require an employee or applicant to take a lie detector test.

Pennsylvania

18 Pa. Cons. Stat. Ann. § 7321

Employers covered: All

Exceptions: Employers with positions that have access to narcotics or dangerous drugs.

What's prohibited: Employer may not require an employee or applicant to take a lie detector test.

Rhode Island

R.I. Gen. Laws §§ 28-6.1-1 to 28-6.1-4

Employers covered: All

What's prohibited: Employer may not request, require, subject, nor directly or indirectly cause an employee or applicant to take a lie detector test.

Tennessee

Tenn. Code Ann. §§ 62-27-123, 62-27-128

Employers covered: All

What's prohibited: Employer may not take any personnel action based solely upon the results of a polygraph examination. No questions may be asked about:

- religious, political, or labor-related beliefs, affiliations, or lawful activities
- beliefs or opinions about racial matters
- sexual preferences or activities
- disabilities covered by the Americans With Disabilities Act, or
- activities that occurred more than five years before the examination, except for felony

convictions and violations of the state drug control act.

(Exception: Examination is part of an investigation of illegal activity in one of the above subject areas.)

What's required: Prospective examinee must be told if examiner is a law enforcement or court official and informed that any illegal activity disclosed may be used against examinee. Must receive and sign a written notice of rights including:

- right to refuse to take the test or to answer any question
- right to terminate examination at any time
- right to request an audio recording of examination and pretest interview, and
- right to request examination results within 30 days of taking it.

Vermont

Vt. Stat. Ann. tit. 21, §§ 494 to 494e

Employers covered: All

Exceptions: Employers whose primary business is sale of precious metals, gems, or jewelry; whose business includes manufacture or sale of regulated drugs and applicant's position requires contact with drugs; employers authorized by federal law to require a test.

What's prohibited: Employer may not request, require, administer, or attempt or threaten to administer a lie detector test. May not request or require that employee or applicant sign waiver of any action prohibited by state law. May not discriminate against employee who files a complaint of violation of laws.

When testing is allowed, no questions may be asked about:

- political, religious, or labor union affiliations

Employee Polygraph Examination Laws (continued)

- sexual practices, social habits, or marital relationship (unless clearly related to job performance), or
- any matters unrelated to job performance.

What's required: Prior to taking test examinee must receive a copy of state laws and a copy of all questions to be asked. Must be told that any information disclosed could be used against examinee or made available to employer, unless there is a signed written agreement to the contrary. Examinee must be informed of rights including:

- right to accept or refuse to take examination
- right to refuse to answer any questions or give any information
- right to stop examination at any time, and
- right to a copy of examination results and of any reports given to employer.

Virginia

Va. Code Ann. § 40.1-51.4:3

Employers covered: All

What's prohibited: Employer may not require an applicant to answer questions about sexual activities in a polygraph test, unless the sexual activity resulted in a conviction for violation of state law.

What's required: Any record of examination results must be destroyed or maintained on a confidential basis, open to inspection only upon agreement of the employee.

Washington

Wash. Rev. Code Ann. § 49.44.120

Employers covered: All

Exceptions: Applicant or employee who manufactures, distributes, or dispenses controlled substances, or who works in a sensitive position directly involving national security.

What's prohibited: Employer may not require, directly or indirectly, that an employee or applicant take a lie detector test.

West Virginia

W. Va. Code §§ 21-5-5a to 21-5-5d

Employers covered: All

Exceptions: Employees or applicants with direct access to controlled substances.

What's prohibited: Employer may not require or request, directly or indirectly, that an employee or applicant take a lie detector test; may not knowingly use the results of a lie detector test.

Wisconsin

Wis. Stat. Ann. § 111.37

Employers covered: All

Exceptions: Manufacturers or distributors of controlled substances; providers or designers of security systems and personnel; ongoing investigation.

What's prohibited: Employer may not directly or indirectly require, request, suggest, or cause an applicant or employee to take a lie detector test; may not use, accept, refer to, or inquire about the results of a test. May not take adverse employment action solely on the basis of test results or a refusal to take test. May not discriminate or retaliate against employee who files a complaint of violation of laws.

What's allowed: Wisconsin law allows testing in the same limited circumstances as the federal EPPA, with similar rules and restrictions on when and how the test is given.

Current as of February 2007

AIDS Testing

The disease of Acquired Immune Deficiency Syndrome (AIDS) was first identified in 1981. Fairly early on, researchers isolated its viral cause, the Human Immunodeficiency Virus (HIV), which suppresses the immune systems of those who carry it, making them easy targets for various other infections and diseases. Since then, while great strides have been made in treating AIDS symptoms, there still is no cure. Many of those who have the HIV infection live nearly symptom-free. But, ultimately, the disease is still considered fatal—and is spreading.

The impact on American workplaces has been and will continue to be enormous. Not only have hundreds of thousands of workers died, most of them have also suffered from the reactions of others—irrational fear and ostracism—that play in tandem with the AIDS epidemic: AFRAIDS. Many workplaces responded to the hysteria with more hysteria, developing intrusive policies of isolating workers suspected to have the disease. (See the section in Chapter 7, "Discrimination Against Workers With HIV or AIDS.")

Another offshoot of this hysteria is the practice of testing employees for the HIV virus. While a number of courts have struck down state and local efforts to screen employees for HIV, the practice continues in many workplaces.

Types of Tests

Although medical researchers may develop more methods of testing for HIV, the test first approved for commercial use by the Food and Drug Administration in 1985 is still in use today. Basically, the test measures antibodies in the blood that are stimulated by the virus. If a test is positive, indicating exposure to the deadly virus, a confirmation test is usually performed that uses a more complicated system of weighing molecular weights found in the blood.

However, there are a number of things the HIV antibody testing does not indicate. Tests do not identify people who have AIDS. AIDS is defined by the Centers for Disease Control (CDC), and the definition is still evolving. Currently, an individual is considered to have AIDS if he or she has any of the AIDS-related diseases specified by the CDC and has a T-count—or number of infection-fighting white corpuscles—of less than 200 in a cubic milliliter of blood.

Also, tests do not identify every person carrying the AIDS virus. The tests are aimed at measuring the antibodies stimulated by HIV, so they do not work effectively on individuals who have been exposed to the virus but have not developed antibodies to it—a period which usually takes about eight weeks, but may take up to a year or more.

Legal Controls on Testing

Originally, HIV blood tests were fashioned to screen blood, not people. But when prospective employees and employees are subjected to testing, the reality is that people are being screened—and sometimes labeled as unfit workers.

A federal law, the Americans With Disabilities Act (see Chapter 7,), prohibits testing job applicants to screen out people with

HIV or AIDS. Once an applicant is offered a job, however, the legal constraints on testing become a bit murkier. To avoid singling out any individual or group, which would be illegal discrimination, an employer would have to test all employees. Even then, to justify giving employees an HIV test, an employer would have to show that the test is necessary to determine whether applicants are fit to hold a job. This would be nearly an impossible task, as many people infected with HIV show no symptoms of ill health.

Most states have laws setting some controls on employers' uses of HIV tests. Test results may not be used to determine suitability for insurance coverage or employment according to the laws in a number of states, including Florida. (Fla. Stat. § 381.004.) And Massachusetts bans employers from requiring employees to take a test as a condition of employment. (Mass. Gen. Laws ch. 111, § 70f.)

Also, a number of cities have enacted ordinances that put additional limits on how and when employers may test for HIV and AIDS. A strict law in San Francisco, for example, states that employers cannot test for AIDS unless they can show that the absence of AIDS is an essential employment qualification. (San Francisco Police Code §§ Art. 38, 3801-16.)

This area of the law is changing very rapidly. Double check your local, state, and federal law for recent changes. A local clinic, support group, or AIDS hotline may be able to provide you with the most up-to-date local information. A number of organizations also offer information on the HIV virus, AIDS, and resources on AIDS in the workplace. (See the Appendix for organization contact details.)

Legal Actions Against Privacy Violations

There are specific laws that forbid employers from being overly invasive. However, your most powerful weapon may be to file a lawsuit against your employer claiming invasion of privacy. And the most likely way to win such a case is to show that, in the process of collecting information on you, the employer was guilty of one or more of the following.

Deception. Your employer asked you to submit to a routine medical examination, for example, but mentioned nothing about a drug test. However, the urine sample that you gave to the examining physician was analyzed for drug traces, and because drugs were found in your urine, you were fired.

Violation of confidentiality. Your former employer asked you to fill in a health questionnaire and assured you that the information would be held in confidence for the company's use only. But you later found out that the health information was divulged to a prospective employer that called to check your references.

Secret, intrusive monitoring. Installing visible video cameras above a supermarket's cash registers would usually be considered a legitimate method of ensuring that employees are not stealing from the company. But installing hidden video cameras above the stalls in an employee restroom would probably qualify as an invasion of privacy in all but the highest-security jobs.

Intrusion on your private life. Your employer hired a private detective, for example, to monitor where you go in the evening when you're not at work. When the company discovered that you are active in a gay rights organization, you were told to resign from that group or risk losing your job.

Surveillance and Monitoring

We have arrived at the place we long feared: Technological advances have made it easy for Big Brother—and anyone else who wants to join him—to watch us. In truth, most employers cannot properly be painted as paranoid Peeping Toms. And the law does require that most workplace monitoring—listening in on telephone calls, audiotaping, or videotaping conversations—must have some legitimate business purpose. Other than that, however, there are very few federal legal controls protecting workers from being watched and listened to while at work.

Some states set their own bounds on how much prying you must tolerate. For example, several states have laws specifically restricting searches and surveillance of employees, and some of those laws are quite powerful.

In Connecticut, for example, an employer that repeatedly uses electronic devices such as video cameras or audiotape recorders to monitor employees in restrooms, locker rooms, or lounges can be fined and sentenced to jail for 30 days. (Conn. Gen. Stat. § 31-48b 2006.)

Telephone Calls

In general, it is legal for employers to monitor business-related telephone calls to and from their own premises—for example, to evaluate the quality of customer service. However, a federal law, the Electronic Communications Privacy Act, or ECPA (18 U.S.C. §§ 2510 to 2720), puts some major limitations on that right. The ECPA restricts individuals and organizations, including employers, from intercepting wire, oral, or electronic communications.

Under the Act, even if a call is being monitored for business reasons, which is perfectly legal, if a personal call comes in, an employer must hang up as soon as he or she realizes the call is personal. An employer may monitor a personal call only if an employee knows the particular call is being monitored—and he or she consents to it.

While the federal law seems to put some serious limits on employers' rights to monitor phone calls, some state laws have additional safeguards. A number of them require, for example, that not only the employee but the person on the other end of the phone must know about and consent to the call's being monitored.

Despite these legal controls, however, the reality is that employers fairly freely listen in on employees' phone calls—and the number of such eavesdroppers is on the rise. The American Management Association in 2005 did a follow-up study to see how and whether workplace telephone monitoring had changed since 2001 when it first polled employers on the issue.

In 2005, 57% of employers said they blocked access to 900 lines and other unauthorized phone numbers—apparently, a newer-discovered method of monitoring. Employers who monitor the amount of time employees spend on the phone and track the numbers called jumped to 51%, up from 9% in 2001. And the percentage of companies that tape phone conversations also grew during those years. In 2001, 9% of companies recorded workers' phone calls. Four years later, 19% admitted they taped the calls of employees in selected job categories, and another 3% said they recorded and reviewed all employees' phone chats.

Caught Red-Lipped, She Got Away

A decade ago, the first test of the ECPA's bounds questioned an employer's right to secretly monitor workplace calls.

In the case, Newell and Juanita Spears, owners of a liquor store, tape-recorded and listened to the telephone calls of an employee they suspected of helping rig a burglary of the store. They first warned the employee, Sibbie Deal, to stop making personal calls and that her calls might be monitored. The Spearses recorded about 22 hours of phone calls. While the tapes mentioned not a peep about the burglary, they did reveal that Deal sold a keg of beer at cost in violation of store policy—and that she carried on long and salacious phone calls with her extramarital boyfriend while store customers presumably listened and waited.

The Spearses fired Deal—first playing her a snippet of the tapes to explain their beef. But the court held that the Spearses had violated the ECPA by taping and playing her calls and that warning her they might monitor the calls did not qualify as consent. It ordered Newell and Juanita Spears to each pay $10,000 to both Deal and her lover. A while later, nearly 30 additional plaintiffs, most of whom had been recorded during Deal's workplace phone chats, also sued for the wrongful recording; in their case, however, the court held their claims were barred by the statute of limitations. (*Reynolds v. Spears*, 93 F.3d 428 (8th Cir. 1996).)

Voice Mail

Much business communication these days takes place through messages left on voice mail systems—and the ECPA appears to protect them. It states that an employer may be liable for obtaining, reading, disclosing, deleting, or preventing access to an employee's voice mail messages that are in "electronic storage." But given the true workings of voice mail systems, this clarifies little. It is not yet known, for example, whether the ECPA—widely denounced as an awkward and muddled piece of legislation—prohibits employers from listening to messages that employees have listened to but not deleted from the workplace phone systems.

Perhaps because of the workiness of capturing and listening to employees' voice mail messages, the practice is far less prevalent than tracking their telephone, Internet, and email use, however. In a recent poll by the American Management Association, only 15% of all businesses admitted to reviewing them as a way to route out possible inappropriate behavior on the job.

Computers

Nearly every workplace in America today conducts some part of its business on computers, and many businesses have become slavishly devoted to them. While hailed by many as time-savers and aids to efficiency, computers have lent a new murkiness to workplace privacy laws.

Prying Into a McLove Affair

When Michael Huffcut and Rose Hasset became smitten with each other a few years ago, they also became what many couples in the first throes of romance are: sappy and careless. Huffcut worked as a regional supervisor at a McDonald's in Elmira, New York. Hasset held a management-track position at a McDonald's 60 miles up the road in Binghamton. When the two weren't able to share happy meals together, they kept in touch by phone.

Harry Harvey, another McDonald's manager, intercepted messages the lovers left on each other's voice mail systems at work. He then relayed them to Fred Remillard, operator of a dozen of the fast food franchises, who directed Harvey, an alleged friend of the Huffcut family, to play the torrid tapes to Huffcut's wife, Lisa.

That angered both of the Huffcuts. But when Michael complained that his bosses were wrong to spy on him, he was fired.

Michael and Lisa Huffcut each sued McDonald's for $1 million, claiming, in addition to a violation of privacy rights, that Remillard intentionally inflicted emotional anguish, embarrassment, and loss of reputation and income on them. McDonald's defended that there was a legitimate business purpose behind the monitoring—and that Huffcut had no reasonable expectation of privacy in his voice mail, since he should have known it might have been monitored.

Unfortunately for those hoping for some legal guidance on the boundaries of workplace eavesdropping rights, the case did not make it to court.

The Huffcuts and McDonald's reached an out-of-court settlement in March 1996, the terms of which remain undisclosed. Their lawyer coyly admitted only that: "The case has been resolved to the satisfaction of Mr. and Mrs. Huffcut."

There is no shortage of happy endings to the story. Rose Hasset was recently promoted to store manager.

Computer Files

There still is no specific law controlling whether and when the files you create on a workplace computer are legally protected from others' snooping eyes. In legal battles over the issue, employers who claim a right to rummage through employees' computer files must show they have a valid business purpose for doing so. Employees often counter this by claiming that they had a valid expectation of privacy—a logical, reasonable belief that others would not retrieve and read the files.

A growing number of employers have attempted to clear up the question of what is and is not considered private about workplace computers by writing specific policies spelling out what is and what isn't considered proper business use there.

Email

While it is unclear whether the Electronic Communications Privacy Act applies to voice mail messages, its application to electronic mail, or email, systems is murkier still. The Act, which originally served to limit wire-tapping, took effect in 1986, before business email systems became the commonplace animals they are today.

Questions of legality aside, the truth is that well over half of all employers now routinely monitor email messages that their employees send and receive. This is easy to do. Some email systems copy all messages that pass through them; others create backup copies of new messages as they arrive on the system servers. Workers who logically assume their messages are gone for good when they delete them are painfully surprised to learn they are wrong.

Technology has now turned on itself as more companies buy into the software and electronic surveillance systems that make it easier to monitor email spawned in an earlier age. In some situations, even the most stalwart privacy advocate can see that the forces behind the monitoring are legitimate—motivated by concerns over poor job performance, quality control, loss of trade secrets, and potential liability for sexual harassment and other discrimination claims.

Stories abound of those who abused email privileges at work—and got reprimanded or fired for offensive or overindulgent e-chatting. Courts called upon to decide claims that employers have violated workers' privacy by prying into their email are still asked to weigh the reasonable expectation of privacy against the employer's reasonable business justification.

Again, a growing number of companies—nearly 84% of all larger ones—have taken proactive measures by establishing written policies informing employees of acceptable use of email at work. The policies range from absolutist controls banning personal email on the job completely, to limiting it to reasonable use, to the rare but existing nod that email will not be monitored on the job. While there is still no overarching law on email privacy, bills drafted so far have focused on this notification feature.

 TIP

Beware of leaving electronic tracks. In a tip of the hand to employers that should act as a warning to employees, the American Management Association (AMA) recently noted that "workers' email, Instant Messaging (IM), blog and Internet content create written business records that are the electronic equivalent of DNA evidence." The AMA noted that one in five employers has had email subpoenaed by courts and regulators, and another 13% have battled workplace lawsuits triggered by email sent or received on the job.

Internet Use

The next gasp of complaints about employers monitoring computer use on the job is likely to settle on employees' Internet habits. And some former employees have already felt the sting when hit with evidence of site surfing that is hard to pass off as work-related. For

If You Must Blog, Blog Safely

A blog—a blend of the words Web and log—is a user-generated website in which entries are made in journal style and displayed in reverse chronological order.

Some applaud blogging as an intellectually stimulating way to connect instantaneously with an audience worldwide. Others claim it is the byproduct of people with computers and too much time on their cursors. Whether you laud or abhor blogging, it is undeniably big: In November 2006, a blog search engine tracked more than 57 million blogs.

And dozens of bloggers have already found out that the words they post can land them jobless. Sometimes, they're fired after an employer finds they've logged too many alleged work hours by blogging instead. Sometimes, they are fired for blogging too openly about a company secret or strategy. These firings are often understandable.

But a growing number are fired more obviously because the employer finds the blog, even a blog that is maintained solely after hours, is somehow unacceptable. A Delta flight attendant, for example, was recently fired for including "inappropriate pictures in uniform on the Web" with the blog she claimed she started as therapy after her mother's death. A Washington, D.C., worker with an alleged "glamour job" was fired after her employer discovered her blog giving bawdy details of afternoon trysts and such. Another blogger was fired after an employer noticed his blog extolling the virtues of crystal meth.

The Electronic Frontier Foundation, a group, a group with the slogan "Defending Freedom in the Digital World," claims that when blogging, it's most important for employees to keep their minds on their subject matter. And the group offers the following advice for some sensitive topics that are common game for blogging.

Political opinions. Many states include sections in their labor codes that prohibit employers from regulating their employees' political activities and affiliations, or influencing employees' political activities by threatening to fire them.

Unionizing. In many states, talking or writing about unionizing your workforce is strongly protected by the law, so in many cases blogging about your efforts to unionize will be safe. Also, if you are in a union, it's possible that your contract may have been negotiated in a way that permits blogging. Some states protect "concerted" speech about the workplace, which means that if two or more people start a blog discussing the conditions in their workplace, this activity could be protected under local labor laws.

Whistleblowing. Often there are legal shields to protect whistleblowers—people who expose the harmful activities of their employers for the public good. (See Chapter 9, "Whistleblowing Violations.") Many people have the misconception that if you report the regulatory violations or illegal activities of your employer in a blog, you're protected. But that isn't the case. You need to report the problems to the appropriate regulatory or law enforcement bodies first. You can also complain to a manager at your company. But notify somebody in authority about the sludge your company is dumping in the wetlands first, then blog about it.

If You Must Blog, Blog Safely (continued)

Reporting on government work. If you work for the government, blogging about what's happening at the office is protected speech under the First Amendment. It's also in the public interest to know what's happening in your workplace, because citizens are paying you with their tax dollars. But do not post classified or confidential information.

Legal off-duty activities. Some states have laws that may protect an employee or applicant's legal off-duty blogging, especially if the employer has no policy or an unreasonably restrictive policy with regard to off-duty speech activities. For example, California has a law protecting employees from "demotion, suspension, or discharge from employment for lawful conduct occurring during nonworking hours away from the employer's premises." These laws have not been tested in a blogging context.

Source: Electronic Frontier Foundation, www.eff.org

---

example, one fellow was recently fired on his third day of work at a large CPA firm after being confronted with company records that revealed repeated trips to a pornography website.

A number of employers—about 76% of them, and growing—are taking the draconian step of blocking employees' access to home email and Internet sites they deem frivolous or without a sufficient work-related purpose, such as movie search and retail sites. Such filters are imperfect at best and often counterproductive at worst—barring access to sites the employee needs to complete a job task. But they are currently legal.

Mail

Whether or not an employee has the right to expect privacy in the mail he or she receives at work depends for the most part on company custom and policy. No laws specifically cover it beyond those guaranteeing general privacy rights. In most workplaces, one or more individuals routinely sort and distribute the mail—and most mailings related to work matters range from the boring to the mundane. An employer may inadvertently, or even purposely, open most such mail without incurring any legal liability.

However, sometimes mail arrives addressed to an individual worker that is also marked "Personal" or "Confidential"—or sometimes with the overkilling warning "Personal and Confidential." An employer who opens such mail, or directs or sanctions another person in the workplace to do so, must usually have a compelling business reason to open it. If the employer cannot demonstrate a compelling reason—for example, that there was important, time-sensitive business information in the envelope, and the employee to whom it was addressed was on a month-long vacation—then the employer may be guilty not only of being rude, but of invading the addressee's privacy.

Audiotaping and Videotaping

As the number of lawsuits over workplace disputes has grown, so has an alarming trend: Employers and employees intent on bolstering their claims have begun to record one another in the hope of capturing some wrongdoing on tape. There are a number of legal and practical problems with this approach to gathering evidence, however.

Federal law appears to allow any person involved in a conversation to tape it without the other person's knowledge or permission—as long as the recording is not made for the purpose of committing a crime, such as extortion. But a number of state laws have much stricter controls—generally requiring that everyone involved must consent before a conversation or an action can be taped.

Although our guts might tell us the opposite, audiotapes and videotapes also have questionable value as trial evidence. Before any jury would be allowed to hear or see a tape of a workplace scene, the tape would have to satisfy many picky rules designed to qualify and disqualify trial evidence.

Also, in real life, tapes rarely run to script. They often come out garbled or unclear. And they rarely hold up well out of context. What may feel like a damning conversation in which your boss blatantly admits you were fired because of your age may sound very different to those who do not know your boss or you.

If you have any desire to keep your job, confronting your employer with a tape immortalizing some perceived transgression is not the way to convince him or her that you make a loyal asset to the company.

All warnings said, the fact that you have an incriminating tape may make your employer more likely to quickly settle a complaint you lodge. It may make an investigating agency such as the Department of Labor or Equal Employment Opportunity Commission take a closer look at your file. It may make an attorney more inclined to take on your case. But the tactic is just as likely to backfire. You are in the best position to evaluate whether recording a workplace confrontation or other incident may be your best shot at getting strong evidence for later negotiations or a lawsuit—or is more likely to help you lose your job.

Someone's Reading Over Your Shoulder

The American Management Association (AMA) regularly polls U.S. businesses about their policies and practices in monitoring workplaces. The most recent survey reflects a growing concern with the ease and availability of electronic communication on the job.

In some of the more poignant responses to queries from the 2004 survey, companies reported that:

- Employee email has been subpoenaed by a court or regulatory body—20%.
- They have a written email retention and deletion policy—42%.
- There is a written policy governing email use and content—84%.
- Outgoing and incoming email is monitored—55%.

Searches and Seizures

Most employers would claim a legitimate desire to keep workplaces free of illegal drugs, alcohol, and weapons. And most employees would claim that they have a right to expect that their personal belongings will remain safe from the groping hands of their employers.

The legal truth lies somewhere between. Employers are generally free to search through an employee's personal items kept at work—unless the employee reasonably expects that the spot in which those items are stored is completely private. An employer who searches an employee's private belongings such as a purse, briefcase, pockets, or car must usually meet a higher standard and have a compelling reason to do so—such as the belief that work property is being stolen and hidden inside.

> **EXAMPLE:** Thomas sold household appliances for a department store that provides each employee with a storage cabinet for personal belongings in a room adjacent to the employee lounge. The store's employee manual states that, although the company does not provide locks for the cabinets and does not take responsibility for any thefts from the storage area, employees may bring in a lock of their own to secure their individual cabinet.
>
> One day while at work, Thomas was called to the manager's office, where he was confronted with a letter that had been written to him from his drug rehabilitation counselor. The manager said the letter had been found in his storage cabinet during a routine search by the company's security force, and that he was being fired because he had a history of drug abuse.
>
> Thomas could likely win an invasion of privacy lawsuit against his former employer because, by allowing Thomas to use his own lock to secure his cabinet, the department store had given him a logical expectation of privacy for anything kept in that cabinet. His claim would be somewhat weaker if his former employer had furnished the locks and doled out the keys or combinations to them, because Thomas would then be on notice that others could get into his locker—defeating his claim to an expectation of privacy.

Another fact that weighs heavily in determining whether an employer's search is legal is the reasonableness of its length and scope. For example, an employer who suspected an employee of stealing foot-long copper piping might be justified in searching his or her work locker, but not purse or pockets.

Clothing and Grooming Codes

In general, employers have the right to dictate on-the-job standards for clothing and grooming as a condition of employment. Codes governing employees' appearance may be illegal, however, if they result in a pattern of discrimination against a particular group of employees or potential employees. This type of violation has most often been mounted in companies with different codes for male and female employees.

Dress Codes

Many companies have policies about uniforms to keep their employees looking uniform—a legal goal. There is nothing inherently illegal, for example, about a company requiring all employees to wear navy blue slacks during working hours.

Many employers provide workers with some or all of the clothing that they are required to wear on the job. A few companies even rent attire for their employees to assure that they will be similarly dressed.

Although generally legal, such systems can violate your rights if the cost of the clothing is deducted from your pay in violation of the Fair Labor Standards Act (FLSA). For example, it is illegal under the FLSA for an employer to deduct the cost of work-related clothing from your pay so that your wages dip below the minimum wage standard, or so that the employer profits on the clothing. (For details on the FLSA and how to file a complaint under it, see Chapter 2.)

A few states have attempted to address the concerns of employees who fear their uniform costs will cut into their earnings, and have passed laws that prohibit employers from charging employees for required uniforms. But these laws are very narrow—and often do not apply to workers who need the economic boost the most, such as restaurant employees. Other laws erase the patina of generosity by imposing complicated schemes for when an

employer may charge employees for cleaning a uniform. If you have questions about the legality of uniform charges, ask your state department of labor. (Contact details are in the Appendix.)

And, sometimes, the legal lines on dress restrictions become blurry. Courts have held, for example, that an employer cannot require female employees to wear uniforms if it allows male employees to wear street clothes on the job. And some differences that seem to be gender-based—such as barring men from wearing earrings but allowing them for women—have been allowed to stand. The courts reason that the differences in dress codes are not discriminatory if they do not put an unfair burden on one gender or the other.

Grooming Codes

Most workplace grooming codes simply require that employees be clean and presentable on the job—a reasonable request. And such codes are rarely challenged.

However, several lawsuits challenging workplace grooming codes have been waged by black men with pseudofollicullitis barbae, a race-specific skin disorder making it painful to shave. Several individuals have successfully challenged companies that refuse to hire men with beards or that fire men who do not comply with no-beard rules.

> **EXAMPLE:** Nelson, a black man, was advised by his physician not to shave his facial hair too closely because that would cause his whiskers to become ingrown and infected. Although Nelson took with

him to a job interview a note from his doctor attesting to this problem, he was turned down for employment because the company where he had applied had a no-beard policy.

Nelson filed a complaint against the company under his state's antidiscrimination laws on the basis of racial discrimination. Medical experts testified in his case that the condition which prevented Nelson from shaving usually affected only black men.

The court ruled in Nelson's favor, saying that the company's failure to lift its ban on beards despite Nelson's well-documented medical problem resulted in illegal workplace discrimination against black men. (See Chapter 7 for details on discrimination laws.)

Conduct Codes

Some employers have fashioned comprehensive behavior codes for their employees, setting out the bounds of workplace behavior they consider Professional. The dictate that gets caught in many workers' craws is the prohibition against dating others in the workplace, sometimes quaintly referred to as fraternizing. Others go a step farther and prohibit married couples from working in the same place.

Such attempted controls over workers' personal relationships fly in the face of reality. Workplace experts claim that as many as 70% of all male and female workers have dated someone they met at work. Those are far better odds than you have of meeting

No Paint, No Powder, No Job

Darlene Jespersen toiled for nearly 20 years as a bartender at the sports bar in Harrah's Casino in Reno. Along the way, she garnered rave performance reviews from her supervisors, along with a stack of customer feedback forms praising her excellent service and good attitude.

Then Harrah's served up something new—a Beverage Department Image Transformation Program with new appearance standards for employees, called "Personal Best." It required all women who work in the beverage department to wear makeup—"foundation or powder, blush, lipstick, and mascara applied neatly in complimentary colors"; stockings; colored nail polish; hair "teased, curled, or styled every day" and "worn down at all times, no exceptions."

Men, on the other hand, were simply forbidden by the policy from wearing any makeup of any kind and required to maintain trimmed hair and fingernails.

Jespersen claimed that making up was not her style—and protested that it made her feel "dolled up" like a sexual object and undermined her ability to deal with drunk or rowdy customers on the job. After gamely trying to follow the Personal Best guidelines for a while, she stopped—and was fired.

Jespersen filed a federal lawsuit accusing Harrah's of sex discrimination. But an all-male panel held against her, opining that that there was no proof that Harrah's Personal Best policy imposed unequal burdens on men and women workers.

Jespersen v. Harrah's Operating Co., Inc., 444 F.3d 1104 (2006).

someone at a bar, party, or other social gathering specifically engineered to be a meeting place.

But courts have been painfully slow to recognize the social reality of today's work-places. During the last decade, employees have been fired for having extramarital affairs, for attending out-of-town conventions with someone other than a spouse, and for dating and marrying coworkers. There are no clear guidelines but an appeal to common sense. Where that fails, and an employer's demands truly seem unreasonable, there may be no alternative but to sue.

Policies Against Marrying

Some employers think that nepotism—hiring an employee's spouse or other relative—is an efficient way to recruit new workers and to keep them happy by surrounding them with loved ones. But others adamantly refuse to allow two spouses to be part of their work-force. They reason that married couples will be inconvenient at best, insisting on the same time off for vacations and holidays. At worst, they claim that being married will make workers less stable. For example, some police departments have argued that married troopers would not react objectively if a spouse got injured on the job—or that their credibility would be undermined if called to testify to support one another's actions.

Some such policies, however, may be on shaky legal ground. Nearly half the states explicitly prohibit public and private employers from discriminating based on marital status. (See Chapter 7, "State and Local Antidiscrimination Laws.")

But whether or not your state prohibits marital status discrimination, the legality of no-spouse employment rules is still unclear. Courts called upon to decide the issue have been contradictory. Some have found that there is no business justification for preventing coworkers from marrying or working together. Other courts stick stridently to the letter of workplace policies, reasoning that employees are legally free to ban married workers on their premises.

Policies Against Dating

Where the issue is prohibiting employees from dating rather than marrying, the law is even less clear. Few of the policies banning workers from dating have been challenged in court—most likely because the love-struck workers were surreptitious about their strickenness, or they got annoyed enough to get jobs elsewhere, or their love took a back seat to the stress of a court battle, ending the relationship.

To many, policies prohibiting coworkers from dating seem paternalistic and contrary to a cardinal law of human nature: Proxim-ity Often Breeds Attraction. Those with the gumption to challenge such policies might base a legal claim on their right to privacy, freedom of association, wrongful discharge—or, if the policies are enforced dispropor-tionately against workers of a particular age, gender, or race, they might claim a violation of civil rights.

A number of employers have adopted strict policies prohibiting supervisors from dating people they supervise, although, these days, a growing number give the supervisor the option of being transferred rather than fired on the spot. While these strong antidating policies may be understandable given the relatively low legal threshold for a supervisor's conduct to be considered sexual harassment, they may be just as impossible to enforce. (See Chapter 8.) Consider the practical difficulty, for example, in determining exactly when two people have crossed the line between friendly and involved. Strict policies prohibiting liaisons between bosses and worker bees also seem to encourage a double standard of behavior within the ranks of employees. Far better to remember that since workplace harassment is almost always about an abuse of power—not about romance gone sour—the focus should be on preventing intimidation.

Health and Safety

Workers in the past 20 years have pushed strongly for laws to protect their health and safety on the job. And they have been successful. Several laws, notably the Occupational Safety and Health Act (OSHA), now establish basic safety standards aimed at reducing the number of illnesses, injuries, and deaths in workplaces. Since most workplace safety laws rely for their effectiveness on employees who are willing to report on-the-job hazards, most laws also prevent employers from firing or discriminating against employees who report unsafe conditions to proper authorities.

An invention of the federal government, OSHA, and its policies and priorities, are particularly sensitive to political shifts. In March 2001, for example, one of the first major pieces of legislation signed by President George W. Bush was to repeal the previously hard-fought workplace ergonomics standard. Since then, OSHA has issued three ergonomics guidelines, and only a small handful of ergonomic citations under the Act's "general duty" clause.

The Bush administration largely replaced the process of issuing mandatory regulations with voluntary guidelines and put additional resources into other, previously existing voluntary programs. In 2004, the General Accounting Office issued a report questioning the effectiveness of these programs and warning that their projected growth threatened to take resources away from OSHA's enforcement budget.

Major reform is yet to come. But over the years, OSHA has taken some steps to restructure its complaint and response procedures to battle the cries of its ineffectiveness.

The Occupational Safety and Health Act

The main federal law covering threats to workplace safety is the Occupational Safety and Health Act, or OSHA. (29 U.S.C. §§ 651 to 678.) That law created the Occupational Safety and Health Administration (also called OSHA) under the U.S. Department of Labor to enforce workplace safety. And it created the National Institute for Occupational Safety and Health (NIOSH) to research ways to increase workplace safety. (See the Appendix for contact details.)

OSHA broadly requires employers to provide a safe workplace for employees— one that is free of dangers that could physically harm those who work there. The law implements this directive by requiring employers to inform employees about potential hazards, to train them in how to deal with hazards, and to keep records of workplace injuries.

Sometimes, workplace dangers are caught and corrected during unannounced inspections by OSHA. But the vast majority of OSHA's actions against workplace hazards are initiated by complaints from employees or labor unions representing them.

Still more reform is needed. According to recent estimates, six million Americans are injured at work each year, and more than 5,000 workers actually die as a result of their injuries. In addition, 50,000 Americans die each year from illnesses caused by chemicals they were exposed to while on the job.

CAUTION

States have OSHA laws, too. About half the states now have their own OSHA laws. The legal requirements for workplace health and safety in the state laws are generally similar to the federal law. In some cases, the state laws are more strict. (See "State and Local Health and Safety Laws," below.)

Who Is Covered

Unlike many other laws, which cover only companies with a minimum number of employees, OSHA covers nearly all private employers engaged in interstate commerce. That includes nearly every employer that uses the U.S. Postal Service to send mail to other states or makes telephone calls to other states, or uses the Internet to conduct business. Independent contractors are not specifically covered by the law.

OSHA does not apply to state and local governments. However, these employees have some protection if their state or local government has a safety plan. As an incentive to these employers, OSHA will fund half the cost of operating such a plan. Farms owned and operated by a family are the only significant private employers exempted from OSHA coverage.

RESOURCE

For more information on the basics of the law, see "All About OSHA," a free pamphlet. You can download it from the agency's website at www. osha.gov.

OSHA Requirements

The Occupational Safety and Health Act requires all private employers to maintain a workplace that is as safe and healthy for employees as is reasonably possible. Under OSHA, all employers are charged with this general safety duty. In addition, the law sets specific workplace safety standards for four major categories of work: General Industry, Maritime, Construction, and Agriculture.

Safety regulations are usually concerned with preventing a one-time injury—falling from an unsafe ladder or tripping on an irregular walkway, for example.

The Act's health concerns are in preventing employee illnesses related to potential health dangers in the workplace—exposure to toxic fumes or asbestos, for example—and cumulative trauma such as carpal tunnel syndrome. (See Chapter 12, "Conditions Covered," for more about carpal tunnel syndrome.)

The law quite simply, but frustratingly, requires employers to protect workers from "recognized hazards." It does not specify or limit the types of dangers covered, so hazards ranging from things that cause simple cuts and bruises, to the unhealthy effects of long-term exposure to some types of radiation, are all arguably covered.

But proving the law was violated is not easy. To prove an OSHA violation, you must produce evidence of both of the following:

- Your employer failed to keep the workplace free of a hazard.
- The particular hazard was recognized as being likely to cause death or serious physical injury.

Under OSHA, the definition of a workplace is not limited to the inside of an office or factory. The Act requires that work conditions be safe no matter where the work is performed—even where the workplace is an open field or a moving vehicle.

In addition to the general duty to maintain a safe workplace, employers are required to meet OSHA's safety standards for their specific industries. Depending on the types of hazards and workplaces involved, the employer's responsibility for creating and maintaining a healthy and safe workplace can include such diverse things as informing workers about potentially hazardous substances and labeling them, upgrading or removing machinery that poses a danger, providing employees with special breathing apparatus to keep dust created by a manufacturing process from entering workers' lungs, improving lighting above work areas, providing emergency exits and fire protection systems, vaccinating against diseases that can be contracted at work, or even tracking the effects of workplace conditions on employees' health through periodic medical examinations.

Finally, OSHA requires employers to display a poster explaining workers' rights to a safe workplace in a conspicuous spot. If the workplace is outdoors, the poster must be displayed where employees are most likely to see it—such as in a trailer at a construction site where workers use a time clock to punch in and out.

These posters are supplied to employers by OSHA and commercial publishers. An employer's failure to display such posters is itself a violation of OSHA rules.

Injury and Illness Reports

Within eight hours of any workplace accident that results in the death of a worker or requires hospitalization of four or more workers, employers must report complete details to OSHA, including names of injured workers, time and place of the accident, nature of the injuries, and any type of machinery involved in the accident. All employees and former employees must be given access to this report upon request.

Companies employing ten or more people must also keep records of workers' work-related injuries and illnesses that have caused death or days off work and post a report on those injuries and illnesses.

Enforcing OSHA Rights

If you believe that your workplace is unsafe, your first action should be to make your supervisor at work aware of the danger as soon as possible. If your employer has designated a particular person or department as responsible for workplace safety, inform the appropriate person of the danger.

In general, your complaint will get more attention if you present it on behalf of a group of employees who all see the situation as a safety threat. And, as for filing a complaint, there is safety in numbers. An employer who becomes angry over a safety complaint is much less likely to retaliate against a group of employees than against an individual. (See "Penalties for Retaliation," below.)

When You Suspect a Lurking Health Hazard

A Health Hazard Evaluation, or HHE, is a study of a workplace conducted by representatives at the national Institute for Occupational Safety and Health. It is conducted, free of charge, to learn whether workers are exposed to hazardous materials or harmful conditions. The aim with such inspections is to diagnose a problem whose cause is not obvious rather than to punish an employer for causing it; NIOSH officials do not have any punishment or enforcement authority. Three or more employees, a union rep, or an employer may seek these workplace evaluations.

HHEs are intended to route out systemic health and safety problems in a workplace, rather than an immediate danger or hazard; those should be reported to OSHA by following the steps described below, in "Enforcing OSHA Rights." But it is appropriate to seek an HHE instead if:

- employees in your workplace have an illness from an unknown cause
- employees are exposed to an agent or working condition that is not regulated by OSHA
- employees experience adverse health effects from exposure to a regulated or unregulated agent or working condition,

even though the permissible exposure limit is not being exceeded

- medical or epidemiological investigations are needed to evaluate the hazard
- the incidence of a particular disease or injury is higher than expected in a group of employees
- the exposure is to a new or previously unrecognized hazard, or
- the hazard seems to result from the combined effects of several agents.

Recent HHE investigations were requested, for example, because of an alarming number of cases of cancer, hearing loss, and sickness alleged from workplace exposure to diesel fuel, smoke, and chemicals.

NIOSH responds to an HHE request by writing to you with a referral to another agency that may be able to help, calling to discuss possible solutions to the problem, or visiting the workplace one or more times to talk with affected employees and conduct studies. This process can take from a few months to a few years, depending on the type of evaluation.

For more information on HHEs, call OSHA at 800-321-6742, or visit the agency's website at www.osha.gov.

This Law Swings Both Ways

Although neither federal nor state OSHA laws cite employees for violations of their responsibilities, the laws generally require that workers comply with all standards, rules, regulations, and orders issued under the Act. The unspoken inference here is that workers who do not hold up their end of the safety law bargain may jeopardize their own protections under health and safety laws.

Specifically, according to OSHA, an employee should:

- read the OSHA poster at the job site
- comply with all applicable OSHA standards
- follow all employer safety and health regulations and wear or use prescribed protective equipment while working
- report hazardous conditions to the supervisor
- report any job-related injury or illness to the employer and seek treatment promptly
- cooperate with the OSHA compliance officer conducting an inspection if he or she inquires about safety and health conditions in the workplace, and
- exercise rights under the Act in a responsible manner.

While some of these responsibilities sound a bit nebulous, you should be prepared to show that you did your best to carry them out before claiming protection under any OSHA law.

Filing a Complaint

If you have not been successful in getting your company to correct a workplace safety hazard, you can file a complaint with OSHA.

You can file a complaint online at the OSHA Workers' Page at www.osha.gov/as/opa/worker/index.html. However, be aware that most online complaints are addressed by OSHA's phone/fax system. That means they may be resolved informally over the phone with your employer. In general, file online for less serious complaints, or when you are not interested in an onsite inspection of your workplace.

Written, signed complaints submitted to OSHA offices are more likely to result in onsite OSHA inspections. To follow this approach, download the OSHA complaint form, complete it and then fax or mail it to your local OSHA regional office. Or you may simply contact your local OSHA office to receive a copy of the complaint form. You can find the nearest OSHA office by looking in the federal government section of the telephone book, or by searching for it through the agency's website at www.osha.gov.

However you opt to file, it is wise to make a copy of the paperwork or send it to yourself as an email—and if you mail in the form, send it by certified mail.

If you request it, OSHA must keep confidential your identity and that of any other employees involved in the complaint. If you want your identity to be kept secret, be sure to check the section on the complaint form that states: "Do not reveal my name to the employer." And if you file online, you may want to take the added precaution of using your home computer or one in a library or other public facility.

Upon receiving your complaint, OSHA will assign a compliance officer to investigate your case. The compliance officer will likely talk with you and your employer and inspect the work conditions that you have reported.

 CAUTION

Time off under the FMLA. If your workplace injury requires an extended recovery at home or in a hospital, state and federal leave laws may not only protect your right to take time off work but require that you be returned to your former position with continued insurance benefits. (See Chapter 4.)

How Complaints Are Resolved

There are two ways that OSHA can respond to a complaint. Agency workers can either perform an on-site inspection or an off-site investigation, also quaintly known as a "phone/fax investigation."

OSHA responds more quickly to lower priority hazards using a phone/fax approach. The agency claims that this allows it to concentrate resources on the most serious workplace hazards.

If an off-site investigation is appropriate, the agency telephones the employer, describes the alleged hazards and then follows up with a fax or letter. The employer must respond in writing within five days, identifying any problems found and noting corrective actions

it has taken or is planning to take. If the response is adequate, OSHA generally will not conduct an inspection. The person who filed the original complaint will receive a copy of the employer's response and, if still not satisfied, may then request an onsite inspection.

If the employee or employee representative files a written complaint, then OSHA may conduct an on-site inspection. Those conditions include claims of serious physical harm that have already resulted in disabling injuries or illnesses, or claims of imminent danger situations; written, signed complaints requesting inspections; and situations where the employer provided an inadequate response to a phone/fax investigation.

During an inspection, a compliance officer who finds that the condition about which you complained poses an immediate danger to you and your co-workers can order your employer to immediately remove the danger from the workplace—or order the workers to leave the dangerous environment.

Where the danger is particularly urgent or the employer has a record of violations, OSHA may get tough by asking the courts to issue an injunction—a court order requiring the employer to eliminate workplace hazards.

EXAMPLE: A group of pipeline workers complained to OSHA that the earth walls of the excavation in which they were working were not well supported and could collapse on them. The OSHA compliance officer tried unsuccessfully to talk the employer into improving the situation. OSHA obtained a court injunction forbidding work to continue within the excavation until the walls were shored up with steel supports.

If the danger is less immediate, the compliance officer will file a formal report on your complaint with the director of OSHA for your region. If the facts gathered by the compliance officer support your complaint, the regional director may issue a citation to your employer.

The citation will specify what work conditions must be changed to ensure the safety of the employees, the timetable that OSHA is allowing for those changes to be made—usually known as an abatement plan—and any fines that have been levied against your employer.

> **EXAMPLE:** Leslie is a machine operator in an old woodworking shop that uses lathes that throw a large quantity of wood dust into the air inside the shop. The wood dust appeared to be a hazard to the employees who breathed it, and Leslie was unsuccessful in resolving the problem with the shop's owner. She filed a complaint with OSHA.
>
> OSHA studied the air pollution in the shop and agreed that it was a threat to workers' health. It ordered the shop's owner to install enclosures on the lathes to cut down on the amount of dust put into the air and filter-equipped fans throughout the shop to capture any wood dust that escaped from the enclosures. Because the lathe enclosures and fans needed to be custom-designed and

installed, OSHA allowed the shop's owner six months to correct the situation.

In the meantime, OSHA ordered the shop's owner to immediately provide Leslie and all the other people employed there with dust-filtering masks to wear over their mouths and noses. However, since OSHA regulations generally require employers to make the workplace safe and not just protect workers from an unsafe work situation, the masks were considered merely a temporary part of the long-term abatement plan.

An OSHA inspector who finds a workplace safety hazard or other violation will tell all affected employees about it and post a danger notice before leaving the workplace. This public notice of an unsafe condition is often the impetus an employer needs to take it seriously and correct it.

 CAUTION

The importance of being specific. Like many other government agencies, OSHA is a huge bureaucracy that is organized and operated according to computerized file numbers. The best way to get prompt service and accurate information from OSHA is to be as specific as possible. In your dealings with OSHA, be sure to mention the name of the company, the department of that company, the number assigned to the complaint that you are tracking, and the date on which it was filed.

Jot down the names and numbers of those with whom you speak. And keep detailed notes of your conversations, complete with dates and times.

Preventing Additional Injuries

Workplace hazards often become obvious only after they cause an injury. For example, an unguarded machine part that spins at high speed may not seem dangerous until someone's clothing or hair becomes caught in it. But, even after a worker has been injured, employers sometimes fail—or even refuse—to recognize that something that hurt one person is likely to hurt another.

If you have been injured at work by a hazard that should be eliminated before it injures someone else, take the following steps as quickly as possible after obtaining the proper medical treatment:

- If you believe the hazard presents an immediate life-threatening danger to you and your coworkers, call OSHA's emergency reporting line at 800-321-6742.
- File a claim for workers' compensation benefits so that your medical bills will be paid and you will be compensated for your lost wages and injury. (See Chapter 12.) Workers' compensation claims can cost a company a lot of money; filing such a claim tends to quickly focus an employer's attention on safety problems. In some states, the amount you receive from a workers' comp claim will be larger if your injury was due to a violation of a state workplace safety law.
- Point out to your employer the continuing hazard created by the cause of your injury. As with most workplace safety complaints, the odds of getting action will be greater if you can organize a group of employees to do this.
- If your employer does not eliminate the hazard promptly, file a complaint with OSHA and any state or local agency that you think may be able to help.

Contesting an Abatement Plan

You have the right to contest an abatement plan directed to your employer by OSHA to correct a workplace hazard—for example, if you feel the suggested plan is insufficient. To do so, send a letter expressing your intent to contest the plan to your local OSHA director within 15 days after the OSHA citation and announcement of the plan is posted in your workplace. You need not list specific reasons for contesting the plan in this letter; all you need to make clear is that you think the plan is unreasonable.

TIP

There really is strength in numbers. If other employees feel the abatement plan is unfair or insufficient, encourage them to register their protests with OSHA as well.

Sample Letter

April 10, 20xx

Ms. Mary Official
Regional Director
Occupational Safety and Health
Administration
321 Main Street
Anycity, USA 12345

Dear Ms. Official:

As allowed by 29 U.S.C. Section 659(e), I wish to contest the abatement plan agreed to by your agency and my employer, the Oldtime Mousetrap Company. This abatement program resulted from a complaint that I filed with your office on April 3, 20xx. That complaint was assigned number A-123456 by your office.

I contest this agreement because I believe that it is unreasonable.

Sincerely,

Elmer Springmaker

Elmer Springmaker
456 Central Road
Anycity, USA 12340
123-555-5555

After it receives your letter, OSHA will refer the matter to the Occupational Safety and Health Review Commission in Washington, D.C., an agency independent of OSHA. That commission will send your employer a notice that the abatement plan is being contested.

This notice will order the employer to post in the workplace an announcement that the plan is being contested. It will also require the employer to send a form that certifies the date on which that announcement was made back to the commission—with copies to OSHA, to you, and to other employees who have contested the plan.

Then, everyone involved in the case has ten days from the date the contest notice was posted to file an explanation of their viewpoints on the abatement plan with the commission. Copies must also be sent to all others involved in the case.

Administrative Review

When attempts to reach a resolution are unsuccessful, the commission submits the case to an administrative law judge. These proceedings usually take several months—and sometimes years—depending upon the complexity of the workplace hazards involved.

Hearings before administrative law judges are very much like a trial. Much time and money can be consumed in gathering evidence, and the hearings are usually scheduled during daytime hours, when most employees are at work. You will probably have to hire a lawyer to help if you decide to pursue your safety complaint at this level. (See Chapter 17.)

You also have the right to appeal a decision by an administrative law judge for the Occupational Safety and Health Review Commission to the full commission or in federal court, but you will probably have to hire a lawyer to help you at these levels as well.

Tips on Presenting Your Views

The explanation you file on the abatement plan need not be elaborate. It should be as clear, brief, and precise as possible. For example, if you have made a list of employee injuries that have already resulted from the hazard in your workplace, list the date, time, location, and identity of the worker injured for each incident in your explanation.

Your explanation need not be typewritten, but your odds of communicating your viewpoint effectively will be increased if it is easy to read.

Send your explanation by certified mail to:

Executive Secretary
Occupational Safety and Health Review
   Commission
200 Constitution Avenue, NW
Washington, DC 20010

Be sure to include a cover letter—and to specify in it the name of the company involved, the number assigned to the case by the review commission and OSHA, and your mailing address and telephone number. Send a copy to the OSHA office where you filed your original complaint, to your employer, and to any people identified in the paperwork the commission sent to you as parties in the case. Also, be sure to save a copy of your cover letter, your explanation, and any supporting documents that you send with it for your personal files.

After it has gathered all the statements on the case, the commission will typically turn them over to U.S. Labor Department lawyers, who will attempt to meet with everyone who submitted statements and negotiate a resolution that is agreeable to all. The commission tries to negotiate settlements whenever possible, and by this point everyone involved will have had an opportunity to read and think about each other's viewpoints. So the odds are that your complaint will be resolved at this stage.

Walking Off the Job

OSHA gives you the right to refuse to continue doing your job in extreme circumstances that represent an immediate and substantial danger to your safety.

This right is limited. You cannot walk off the job and be protected by OSHA in just any workplace safety dispute—and this tactic cannot be used to protest general working conditions. But OSHA rules give you the right to walk off the job without being discriminated against later by your employer if the situation is a true workplace safety emergency.

A walk-off will be legally merited only if your situation meets all of the following conditions:

- You asked your employer to eliminate the hazard and your request was ignored or denied. To protect your rights, it would be best to tell more than one supervisor about the hazard or to call the danger to the attention of the same supervisor at least twice—preferably in front of witnesses.

- You did not have time to pursue normal OSHA enforcement channels. In most cases, this means that the danger must be something that came up suddenly and is not a safety threat that you allowed to go unchallenged for days, weeks, or months.
- Staying on the job would make a reasonable person believe that he or she faced a threat of serious personal injury or death because of the workplace hazard. If the hazard is something that you can simply stay away from—such as a malfunctioning machine in a work area that you do not have to enter—it probably would not qualify as creating an emergency.
- You had no other reasonable alternative to refusing to work, such as asking for a reassignment to another area.

EXAMPLE: Mike is a welder in a truck building plant. Shortly after starting work one day, he noticed that a large electrical cable running along the plant's ceiling had broken overnight, was coming loose from the hardware attaching it to the ceiling, and was dangling closer and closer to the plant floor. He and several of his coworkers immediately told their supervisor about the broken cable, but the supervisor did nothing about it. The group also told the supervisor's boss about the danger, but still nothing was done to correct it.

By about 11 a.m., the broken cable had dropped to the point where it was brushing against the truck body that Mike was welding. Sparks flew each time the cable and the truck body touched. Because he had a reasonable fear that an electrical shock transmitted from the broken cable could seriously injure or kill him, Mike walked off the job. His supervisor fired him for leaving work without permission. But, because the danger fit OSHA's definitions of an emergency, OSHA ordered the company to reinstate Mike to his job with back wages—after first repairing the broken and dangling cable.

If you use the extreme option of walking off a job because of a safety hazard, be sure to contact your nearest OSHA office as soon as you are out of danger. Call the agency's emergency reporting number: 800-321-6742. Jot down the name of the OSHA officer with whom you speak—and also note the time that you report the hazard. That will preserve your right to be paid back wages and other losses from the time that the hazard forced you to walk away from work.

Tracking OSHA Actions

Any citation issued by OSHA must be posted for at least three days in a conspicuous place within the workplace it affects. If the hazard specified in the citation is not corrected within three days after the citation is issued, then the citation must remain posted until it is corrected.

Compliance officers are required to advise those who originally filed a complaint of the action taken on it. If you need more information about the outcome of an OSHA investigation that affects your workplace, call, write, or visit your local OSHA office.

If OSHA has given your employer an extended time to remedy a workplace hazard, then you also have a right to request a copy of that abatement plan from your employer. Your other recourse is to obtain a copy from the OSHA compliance officer who handled your complaint.

Penalties for Retaliation

Under OSHA, it is illegal for an employer to fire or otherwise discriminate against you for filing an OSHA complaint or participating in an OSHA investigation. OSHA can order an employer who violates this rule to return you to your job and to reimburse you for damages —including lost wages, the value of lost benefit coverages, and the cost of searching for a new job. A number of state laws also protect against retaliation for reporting work-

place health and safety violations. (See "State and Local Health and Safety Laws," below.)

However, you can not enforce this restriction against retaliation by going directly into court; you must ask OSHA to intercede.

If you suspect illegal retaliation, you have 30 days from the time the illegal action took place to file a complaint about it with your local OSHA office. The outcome of your illegal discrimination complaint may turn on whether you can prove that you were fired or demoted because you contacted authorities, not because your performance slipped or economic cutbacks made the firing necessary. Be sure to back up your complaint with as much documentation for your employer's action as possible. (For details on how to document a dismissal, see Chapter 9, "Getting Documentation.")

Once you have filed a complaint about illegal job discrimination, OSHA has 90 days to respond. If you have shown that you were fired or otherwise punished because of complaining to OSHA, the compliance officer handling your complaint will attempt to convince your employer to take the proper action to remedy the situation. For example, if you were demoted in retaliation for your complaint, the OSHA compliance officer would probably ask your employer to reinstate you to your original position and give you the back pay to which you are entitled.

If OSHA is unsuccessful in talking your employer into reversing the effects of the illegal discrimination, it can sue your employer in federal court on your behalf.

Criminal Actions for OSHA Violations

As noted, the enforcement arm of OSHA has the power in some situations to pursue criminal prosecutions against employers who fail to maintain a safe workplace, but it rarely does.

However, state prosecutors are increasingly bringing criminal charges such as reckless endangerment and even murder against employers whose behavior seriously endangers workers.

You may want to contact your state's attorney general about the possibility of criminal action if your work conditions pose a serious threat of injury or death to you or your coworkers and you are not able to resolve your concerns through OSHA or other civil actions.

While employers can be prosecuted for criminal negligence when an employee dies as a result of violations of OSHA regulations, such convictions are rare. In fact, in the first 20 years the law was in effect, only one employer was convicted and sent to jail for such a death. The main reason for this low conviction rate is that, under OSHA, prosecutors must show that an employer's violation of workplace safety rules was willful—that is, done on purpose—a subjective standard that can be tough to meet.

State and Local Health and Safety Laws

Many states and municipalities have laws that mandate a certain level of safety in the workplace. These laws vary greatly in what they require, how they are enforced, and even which employers they cover.

Early on, California began enforcing the most powerful of these laws: It requires every employer in the state to have a written plan to prevent workplace injuries. A number of states have followed the lead, putting teeth and nails into the laws that protect workplace safety. For example, Texas maintains a 24-hour hotline for telephone reports of violations—and prohibits employers from discriminating against workers who use it.

State OSHA Laws

Most states now have their own OSHA laws—most with protections for workers that are similar to those provided in the federal law. For example, employers in some low-hazard industries, such as retailers and insurance companies with fewer than ten employees, are exempt from some posting and reporting requirements. Most state laws cover all small employers, regardless of the type of business.

A number of states that do not now have OSHA laws in place are presently considering passing them—and many of the states that already have such laws are considering wholesale amendments changing their coverage and content. Check your state's particulars with a local OSHA office—or call the state department of labor to check whether your state has enacted an OSHA law recently. (See the Appendix for contact details.)

A number of state laws specifically forbid employers from firing employees who assert their rights under workplace health and safety

When the Boss Doubles as a Bathroom Monitor

It wasn't big news to many when government health authorities recently slapped a $332,500 fine on Hudson Foods, a poultry processing plant in the town of Noel, Missouri. The plant had been inspected by the Occupational Safety and Health Administration (OSHA) 23 times in 24 years—a healthy number for an agency notoriously backlogged and selective in carrying out its charge of ferreting out workplace health and safety violations.

A number of news sources dutifully recounted the parade of transgressions OSHA inspectors had noted: blocked and restricted fire exits, failure to provide training in and enforce use of eye protective equipment, failure to provide training and issue procedures for handling hazardous chemicals, failure to securely anchor machines.

Less widely reported was one innocuous sounding violation: Insufficient Toilet Facilities. The charge drew at least a few glib jibes: "Let My People Go," trumpeted one legal journal in a headline thumbnailing the inspection.

But few could fathom the human humiliation behind it all. Hudson workers claim they were required to ask permission before being allowed bathroom breaks—and that permission was denied as often as granted. Some say they were forced to urinate in their clothes or wear diapers to absorb the inevitable. Thom Hanson, chief regulatory compliance officer at Hudson, defended the company's position: The workers simply "need to ask supervisors to release them," he explained. "Normally, a relief person comes by and takes their place."

But relief was not always in sight, according to one woman who worked five years as a packer at Hudson. "It matters how good you get along with your supervisor. Sometimes they'll say no," she said. "And it's pretty hard to leave the line when you've got thousands of chickens coming at you."

OSHA regulations have long required that employers provide toilets in the workplace: at least six for the first 150 workers, and one more for each additional 40 workers. But in a twist of semantics that defies logic, the regulations mandate only the presence of toilets on the scene—not employees' rights to use them. In considering the Hudson complaints, OSHA officials found for the first time that the company in effect denied workers toilet facilities when it denied them the right to use them.

In the wake of the *Hudson* case and the ensuing public outcry, OSHA officials dictated at last that employers must give workers prompt and reasonable access to toilet facilities, even though the regulations do not specifically require it.

An official Standards and Compliance Letter issued by OSHA noted: "Toilets that employees are not allowed to use for extended periods cannot be said to be 'available' to those employees."

In other words, employers can no longer hide behind the lacking letter of the law. Employers who do not allow employees reasonable access to workplace toilets may now be cited and sanctioned by OSHA inspectors.

rules. (See Chapter 9, "Violations of Public Policy.") Some states, like OSHA, give workers the right to refuse to work under certain conditions, although the workers may need to report the condition first. And some states protect workers from retaliation not only for exercising their rights under OSHA, but also for using state "right to know" laws—statutes that require employers to give workers information about hazardous substances on the job.

Still another group of state laws extends beyond the workplace to protect employees who report violations of laws and rules that create specific dangers to public health and safety. These laws, commonly referred to as whistleblower statutes, generally protect good eggs—individuals who are attempting to uphold a public policy of the state. For example, typical whistleblower statutes prohibit employees from being fired for reporting toxic dumping or fraudulent use of government funds. (See Chapter 9, "Whistleblowing Violations," for an extensive discussion of these laws.)

Sanitation Laws

Many state and local health and building codes offer guidance in how to keep your workplace safe. While not intended specifically to ensure workplace safety, these laws often include programs designed to ensure good sanitation and public safety in general.

For example, the health department of the city in which you work probably has the power to order an employer to improve restroom facilities that are leaking and causing unsanitary workplace conditions. And your local building inspector typically can order an employer to straighten out faulty electrical wiring that presents a shock or fire hazard to people working near that wiring.

You can find state and local health and building codes at your city hall or county courthouse.

Tobacco Smoke in the Workplace

OSHA rules apply to tobacco smoke only in the most rare and extreme circumstances, such as when contaminants created by a manufacturing process combine with tobacco smoke to create a dangerous workplace air supply that fails OSHA standards. Workplace air quality standards and measurement techniques are so technical that typically only OSHA agents or consultants who specialize in environmental testing are able to determine when the air quality falls below allowable limits. But, when asked to intercede on early workplace complaints about tobacco smoke, Environmental Protection Agency (EPA) officials typically hedge that "exposures to the carbon monoxide or other toxic substances in the tobacco smoke rarely exceed current OSHA permissible exposure limits or PELs." (OSHA Standards Interpretation and Compliance Letter, 10/26/98.)

But the torturous effects of tobacco smoke on human health have now been clearly established and even certified by the government. A recent report by the EPA itself, for example, estimated that secondhand tobacco smoke that emerges from exhaling and burning cigarettes causes approximately 3,000 lung cancer deaths and 37,000 heart disease deaths in nonsmokers each year.

In June 2006, the Surgeon General released a major report on involuntary exposure to secondhand smoke, concluding that secondhand smoke causes disease and death in children and nonsmoking adults. The report finds a causal relationship between secondhand smoke exposure and Sudden Infant Death Syndrome (SIDS), and declares that the home is becoming the predominant location for exposure of children and adults to secondhand smoke.

And later that year, a report contrasting cities with nonsmoking laws in force with the have-nots found that secondhand smoke increases the risk of heart disease in nonsmokers by 30%.

So people who smoke cigarettes, cigars, or pipes at work increasingly find themselves to be an unwelcome minority—and many employers already take actions to control when and where smoking is allowed.

Although there is no federal law that directly controls smoking at work, a majority of states protect workers from unwanted smoke in the workplace. (See the chart summarizing state laws, below.) In addition, hundreds of city and county ordinances restrict smoking in the workplace, but only a few of these local laws ban it outright. (See the Appendix for contact details for organizations with current information on laws that restrict smoking in your workplace.)

In contrast, about half the states make it illegal to discriminate against employees or potential employees because they smoke during nonworking hours. (Also summarized in the state chart, below.) And, because it has much encouragement and financial support from the tobacco industry, this smokers' rights movement appears to be gaining strength.

So the ongoing legal battle boils down to a question of what is more important: one person's right to preserve health by avoiding coworkers' tobacco smoke, or another's right to smoke without the interference of others.

Protections for Nonsmokers

The sentiment against smoking in the workplace and any other shared space has grown so strong that many companies now increase their attractiveness to job seekers by mentioning in their Help Wanted advertising that they maintain a smokefree workplace.

Except in those states that forbid work-related discrimination against smokers or discrimination against employees on the basis of any legal activities outside work, there is nothing to prevent employers from establishing a policy of hiring and employing only nonsmokers.

While most states now protect workers from unwanted smoke on the job, they follow different approaches. As described below, many states have laws that specifically address smoking in workplaces; they live on the books alongside regulations that apply to other areas. A large number of states have smoking control laws that apply to everyone in public places and specified private places; nonsmoking employees in these states are protected only if they happen

Clearing the Air in the Workplace

If your health problems are severely aggravated by coworkers' smoking, there are a number of steps you can take:

- **Ask your employer for an accommodation.** Successful accommodations to smoke-sensitive workers have included installing additional ventilation systems, restricting smoking areas to outside or special rooms, and segregating smokers and nonsmokers.

  EXAMPLE: Carmelita's sinus problems were made almost unbearable by the smoke created by the people who work with her in an insurance claims processing office. Since her job involves primarily individual work on a computer terminal and no contact with people outside the company, Carmelita convinced her employer to allow her to start her workday at 4 p.m., just an hour before her coworkers leave for home.

  When Carmelita needs to discuss something with coworkers or her supervisor, she does so via electronic mail or at occasional one-hour staff meetings that begin at 4 p.m.—and at which smoking is not allowed.

- **Check local and state laws.** As indicated, a growing number of local and state laws prohibit smoking in the workplace. Most of them also set out specific procedures for pursuing complaints. If you are unable to locate local legal prohibitions on smoking, check with a nonsmokers' rights group. (See the Appendix for contact details.)

- **Consider filing a federal complaint.** While OSHA is handling an increasing number of smoking injuries, most claims for injuries caused by secondhand smoke in the workplace are pressed and processed under the Americans With Disabilities Act. (See Chapter 7.) In the strongest complaints, workers were able to prove that smoke sensitivity rendered them handicapped in that they were unable to perform a major life activity: breathing freely.

- **Consider income replacement programs.** If you are unable to work out a plan to resolve a serious problem with workplace smoke, you may be forced to leave the workplace. But you may qualify for workers' compensation or unemployment insurance programs to provide some benefits while you look for a new job. (For details on unemployment insurance and workers' compensation benefits, see Chapters 11 and 12.)

to work in a place that is specifically covered by the statute. A few state laws are all-encompassing—limiting or banning smoking in both public places and workplaces.

Where smoking is limited, some states prohibit it except in a designated area within the workplace. Other states take the opposite approach, requiring employers to set aside pristine areas for the nonsmokers in the work crowd.

There are also common exceptions written into antismoking laws. Often, their protections do not apply to:

- places where private social functions are typically held, such as rented banquet rooms in hotels; presumably, even the most sensitive nonsmoking employees must brave the smoke when they are guests in these places
- private offices occupied exclusively by smokers
- inmates at correctional facilities and hospital patients, who usually must comply with the rules of the institution while they are confined, and
- employers who can show that it would be financially or physically unreasonable to comply with the legal limitations.

 CAUTION

Additional protection under the ADA. Some workers who are injured by smoke on the job have brought successful claims for their injuries under the Americans With Disabilities Act, which prohibits discrimination against people with disabilities. (See Chapter 7, "The Americans With Disabilities Act.") You are entitled to protection under this law only if you can prove that your ability to breathe is severely limited by tobacco smoke, making you physically disabled.

Protections for Smokers

Because of the potentially higher costs of health care insurance, absenteeism, unemployment insurance, and workers' compensation insurance associated with employees who smoke, some companies now refuse to hire anyone who admits to being a smoker on a job application or in prehiring interviews.

Some states protect both smokers and non-smokers by insisting that employers provide a smokefree environment for nonsmokers and by prohibiting discrimination against an employee who smokes—either while off the job or at limited places and times in keeping with a worksite smoking policy.

Protection for smokers may be couched in laws that prohibit discrimination against employees who use "lawful products" outside the workplace before or after workhours. Wisconsin law goes an extra step and forbids employers from discriminating against both workers who use and workers who do not use lawful products.

Several of the state laws that prohibit discrimination against smoking employees do not apply if not smoking is truly a job requirement. In these states it is likely, for example, that a worker in the front office of the American Cancer Society—a group outspoken in its disdain of tobacco—could be fired for lighting up on the job.

And even in those states that offer some protection to smokers, employers are free to charge smokers higher health insurance premiums than nonsmoking employees must pay.

State Laws on Smoking

The chart below summarizes state laws setting out rights and responsibilities for both smokers and nonsmokers. Different rules may apply to workplaces that are also public spaces, such as restaurants, bars, hotels, or casinos; those rules are not covered here. Beware that even if there is no statute regulating smoking in the workplace, there may still be a state administrative regulation or local ordinance that does control it. Call your state labor department for more information. (See the Appendix for contact details.)

Pesticide Laws

Misused and overused pesticides are one of the greatest safety threats to people who work on farms, in other parts of the food industry, and in gardening and lawn care companies,

to name just a few. Heavy exposure to some of these chemicals can cause serious health problems and even death. For people with certain types of allergies, even small doses of some pesticides can cause severe illness.

However, as early as 1975, a federal court ruled that the U.S. Environmental Protection Agency (EPA)—not OSHA—is responsible for making sure that workers are not injured by exposure to pesticides at work. (*Organized Migrants in Community Action, Inc. v. Brennan,* 520 F. 2d 1161.)

There have been some disputes between the EPA and OSHA over this ruling in recent years—and the question of enforcement responsibility remains unsettled decades later. If you believe that you or your coworkers are being exposed to dangerous doses of pesticides at work, the best thing to do is to file complaints with both OSHA and the EPA—and let them decide who gets to regulate you. To find the nearest EPA office, look in the U.S. Government section of the white pages of the telephone book. You can also find a listing of local EPA offices at the agency's website at www.epa.gov under "About EPA."

State Laws on Smoking in the Workplace

Note: The states of Kansas, Michigan, Ohio, and Texas are not included in this chart because they do not have laws governing smoking in private workplaces. Different rules may apply to workplaces that are also public spaces, such as restaurants, bars, hotels, or casinos—we don't cover those rules here. Check with your state department of labor (see Appendix A for contact list) or with your state or local health department if you need more information.

Alabama
Ala. Code §§ 22-15A-3 and 22-15A-5

Workplaces where laws apply: Enclosed places of employment with 5 or more employees.

Where smoking prohibited: Employer may prohibit smoking in all or part of workplace. Individual employee may designate his or her own work area as a nonsmoking area. No smoking in common work areas unless majority of workers in that area agree to designate it as a smoking area.

Where smoking permitted: Majority of workers in an area may decide to designate common work area as smoking area, unless employer prohibits.

Accommodations for nonsmokers: Employers must provide signs to post if an employee designates his or her own work area as nonsmoking.

Employer smoking policy: Written policy must meet minimum requirements and be communicated to all employees.

Alaska
Alaska Stat. §§ 18.35.300 and 18.35.320

Workplaces where laws apply: Any private place of business that posts signs regulating smoking; restaurants serving more than 50; grocery stores.

Where smoking prohibited: Throughout workplace except in designated smoking area. Employer may designate entire site nonsmoking.

Where smoking permitted: Designated smoking area.

Smoking area requirements: Ventilated or separated to protect nonsmokers from active by-products of smoke.

Accommodations for nonsmokers: Reasonable accommodations to protect the health of non-smokers.

Arizona
Ariz. Rev. Stat. § 36-601. 01

Workplace where laws apply: Any enclosed workplace.

Where smoking prohibited: Entire enclosed workplace. Employer may permit smoking outside so long as people entering or leaving the building will not be subject to breathing tobacco smoke and the smoke does not enter the building.

Protection from discrimination: No employer may discharge or retaliate against an employee for exercising rights under this law.

Arkansas
Ark. Code Ann. §§ 20-27-1804 and 20-27-1805

Workplace where laws apply: Any enclosed workplace.

Exceptions: Nonpublic workplaces with fewer than 3 employees.

Where smoking prohibited: Entire enclosed workplace.

Protection from discrimination: No employer may discharge or retaliate against an employee for making a complaint under this law or furnishing information about a violation to an enforcement authority.

State Laws on Smoking in the Workplace (continued)

California
Cal. Lab. Code §§ 96, 98.6, 6404.5

Workplaces where laws apply: Workplaces with more than 5 employees.

Exceptions: Designated lobby areas; meeting and banquet rooms when food is not being served; warehouses over 100,000 sq. ft. with fewer than 20 employees; truck cabs if no nonsmoking employees are present.

Where smoking prohibited: Employer may not knowingly or intentionally permit smoking in any enclosed workplace; must take reasonable steps to prevent nonemployees from smoking. May designate entire site nonsmoking.

Where smoking permitted: Breakrooms designated for smokers.

Smoking area requirements: Breakroom must be in a nonwork area. No employee may be required to enter room as part of job (does not apply to custodial work when room is unoccupied). Air must be exhausted directly outside with a fan and cannot recirculate to other areas of the building.

Accommodations for nonsmokers: If there is a breakroom for smokers, must be enough breakrooms for all nonsmokers.

Accommodations for smokers: None required. However, employers with 5 or fewer employees may permit smoking if:

- all the employees agree
- no minors are allowed in the smoking area, and
- no employee is required to enter smoking area.

Protection from discrimination: Employer may not discharge or discriminate against employee for engaging in lawful activity during nonwork hours away from the employer's premises.

Colorado
Colo. Rev. Stat. §§ 25-14-204 to 25-14-206, 24-34-402.5

Workplaces where laws apply: Any indoor workplace.

Exceptions: Places of employment not open to the public, under the control of the employer, and with 3 or fewer employees.

Accommodations for nonsmokers: Exempted employers must designate a smoke-free area if requested by an employee.

Protection from discrimination: Employee may not be fired for lawful conduct offsite during nonwork hours.

Connecticut
Conn. Gen. Stat. Ann. §§ 31-40q, 31-40s

Workplaces where laws apply: Enclosed facilities.

Where smoking prohibited: Employers with 5 or more employees must prohibit smoking, except in designated smoking rooms. Employer may prohibit smoking throughout the workplace.

Smoking area requirements: Employers with fewer than 5 employees: Existing physical barriers and ventilation systems. Employers with 5 or more employees: Air must be exhausted directly outside with a fan and cannot recirculate to other areas of the building; room must be in a nonwork area where no employee is required to enter.

Accommodations for nonsmokers: Employers with fewer than 5 employees: Employer must provide one or more clearly designated work areas for nonsmoking employees. Employers with 5 or more employees: If there are smoking rooms, employer must provide sufficient nonsmoking breakrooms.

State Laws on Smoking in the Workplace (continued)

Protection from discrimination: Employer may not require employee to refrain from smoking as a condition of employment.

Delaware
Del. Code Ann. tit. 16, §§ 2902 to 2907

Workplaces where laws apply: Indoor areas.

Exceptions: Restaurants serving 50 or fewer.

Where smoking prohibited: Any indoor enclosed area where the general public is permitted or may be invited.

Protection from discrimination: Employer may not discriminate against or retaliate against employee who files a complaint or testifies in a proceeding about violation of workplace smoking laws.

District of Columbia
D.C. Code Ann. §§ 7-1701 to 7-1703.03

Workplaces where laws apply: Any private employer.

Where smoking prohibited: Throughout the workplace except for designated smoking area.

Where smoking permitted: Designated smoking area.

Smoking area requirements: Physical barrier or separate room.

Accommodations for smokers: Employer required to provide smoking area.

Protection from discrimination: Employee may not be fired or discriminated against in hiring, wages, benefits, or terms of employment because of being a smoker.

Employer smoking policy: Must have written policy that designates a smoking area; must notify each employee orally and post policy within 3 weeks after adopting it.

Florida
Fla. Stat. Ann. §§ 386.201 to 386.209

Workplaces where laws apply: All enclosed indoor workplaces (more than 50% covered and surrounded by physical barriers).

Exceptions: Private residences and standalone bars.

Where smoking prohibited: Smoking is prohibited throughout the workplace.

Employer smoking policy: Employer must develop and enforce a policy prohibiting smoking in the workplace. May post "No Smoking" signs to increase awareness.

Georgia
Ga. Code Ann. §§ 31-12A-1 to 31-12A-8

Workplace where laws apply: Any enclosed workplace.

Where smoking prohibited: Entire indoor workplace except for designated smoking area. Employer may designate the entire workplace nonsmoking.

Where smoking permitted: Any designated smoking area.

Smoking area requirements: Smoking area must be in a nonwork area where no employee is required to enter (except to perform custodial and maintenance work when the smoking area is unoccupied). Must

- have ventilation systems that exhausts air outdoors,
- no air recirculating to nonsmoking areas, and
- be only for employee use.

Protection from discrimination: No employer may discharge or retaliate against an employee for making a complaint under this law or furnishing information about a violation to an enforcement authority.

State Laws on Smoking in the Workplace (continued)

Hawaii

Haw. Rev. Stat. §§ 328K-1 to 328k-14

Workplaces where laws apply: Any enclosed area.

Where smoking prohibited: Any area open to the public. Everywhere else, employer decides based on preferences of nonsmokers and smokers. If decision does not satisfy all employees, workers will vote to prohibit or permit smoking in their work area.

Smoking area requirements: Existing ventilation and partitions. No expenditures or structural changes required.

Accommodations for nonsmokers: If nonsmoker complains about smoke, employer must attempt reasonable accommodation between nonsmokers' and smokers' needs. If nonsmokers are not satisfied, a simple majority may appeal to the state director of health for a determination.

Employer smoking policy: Implement and maintain written policy that outlines accommodations for smokers and nonsmokers, procedures for voting and appeal. If employees vote to decide smoking and nonsmoking areas, policy must be announced and posted within 2 weeks after vote.

Idaho

Idaho Code §§ 39-5501 and following

Workplaces where laws apply: Enclosed indoor area used by the general public, including restaurants that seat 30 or more, retail stores, and grocery stores.

Exceptions: Bowling alleys, bars.

Where smoking prohibited: Everywhere except designated smoking area.

Where smoking permitted: Employer or proprietor designates, not required to provide smoking area.

Accommodations for nonsmokers: "Good faith effort" to minimize effect of smoke on nonsmoking areas.

Illinois

410 Ill. Comp. Stat. §§ 80/3 to 80/11; 820 Ill. Comp. Stat. § 55/5

Workplaces where laws apply: Any enclosed indoor workplace.

Exceptions: Offices occupied exclusively by smokers, even if visited by nonsmokers. Factories, warehouses, and other workplaces not visited by the public; bowling alleys; bars.

Where smoking prohibited: Entire workplace except for designated smoking area.

Where smoking permitted: Designated smoking area only.

Smoking area requirements: Existing ventilation systems and physical barriers to minimize smoke in nonsmoking areas.

Protection from discrimination: Employee may not be discriminated against for asserting rights under the clean indoor air laws. May not be refused a job, fired, or discriminated against in terms of compensation or benefits because of using lawful products outside of work. Different insurance rates or coverage for smokers are not discriminatory if:

- difference is based on cost to employer, and
- employees are given a notice of carriers' rates.

Indiana

Ind. Code Ann. § 22-5-4-1

Protection from discrimination: Employer may not require prospective employee to refrain from using tobacco products outside of work in order

State Laws on Smoking in the Workplace (continued)

to be hired or discriminate against employee who uses them in terms of wages, benefits, or conditions of employment.

Iowa

Iowa Code §§ 142B.1, 142B.2

Workplaces where laws apply: Enclosed indoor area at least 250 sq. ft.; restaurants serving more than 50 people.

Exceptions: Offices occupied exclusively by smokers, even if visited by nonsmokers. Factories, warehouses, and other workplaces not visited by the public.

Where smoking prohibited: Entire workplace except for designated smoking area.

Where smoking permitted: Designated smoking area only (may not be entire workplace).

Smoking area requirements: Existing physical barriers and ventilation systems to minimize toxic effect of smoke.

Accommodations for nonsmokers: Employee cafeteria in warehouse or factory must have nonsmoking area.

Kansas

Kan. Stat. Ann. §§ 21-4009 to 21-4011

Workplaces where laws apply: Any workplace open to the public.

Where smoking prohibited: Anywhere other than designated smoking areas.

Where smoking permitted: Designated smoking areas.

Smoking area requirements: Existing barriers and ventilation systems are to be used to minimize the toxic effect of smoke in nonsmoking areas.

Kentucky

Ky. Rev. Stat. Ann. § 344.040(3)

Protection from discrimination: As long as employee complies with workplace smoking policy, employer may not:

- discharge employee or discriminate in terms of wages, benefits, or conditions of employment because of being a smoker or nonsmoker
- require employee to refrain from using tobacco products outside of work as a condition of employment.

Louisiana

La. Rev. Stat. Ann. §§ 40:1300.251 to 40:1300.263, 23:966

Workplaces where laws apply: Any enclosed workplace.

Where smoking prohibited: Any enclosed workplace.

Where smoking permitted: Outdoors, unless employer posts signs prohibiting smoking in the outdoor area.

Protection from discrimination: Employer may not:

- require prospective employee to refrain from using tobacco products outside of work as a condition of employment
- discriminate against smokers or nonsmokers regarding termination, layoffs, wages, benefits, or other terms of employment.

Maine

Me. Rev. Stat. Ann. tit. 22, §§ 1580-A and following; tit. 26, § 597

Workplaces where laws apply: Structurally enclosed business facilities.

State Laws on Smoking in the Workplace (continued)

Where smoking prohibited: Employer may prohibit throughout entire workplace.

Where smoking permitted: Designated smoking area.

Protection from discrimination: Employer may not discriminate or retaliate against employee for assisting with enforcement of workplace smoking laws. As long as employee follows workplace smoking policy employer may not:

- discriminate in wages, benefits, or terms of employment because of use of tobacco products outside of work
- require employee to refrain from tobacco use as a condition of employment.

Employer smoking policy: Written policy concerning smoking and nonsmoking rules. State bureau of health will assist employees and employers with creating policy.

Maryland
Md. Regs. Code 09.12.23.01 to 09.12.23.05

Workplaces where laws apply: Any indoor work area. Includes employee lounges, restrooms, and cafeterias; work vehicle when occupied by more than one employee; conference or meeting room.

Where smoking prohibited: Entire workplace except for designated smoking area.

Where smoking permitted: Designated smoking area. Employer not required to provide one.

Smoking area requirements: May not be in location where any employee required to work (maintenance and cleaning to take place when no one is smoking in area). Must have:

- solid walls and closable door
- ventilation system that exhausts air outdoors
- no air recirculating to nonsmoking areas, and
- negative air pressure to prevent smoke migration.

Massachusetts
Mass. Gen. Laws ch. 270, § 22

Workplaces where laws apply: Any enclosed workspace.

Where smoking is prohibited: Where employees work in an enclosed workspace.

Minnesota
Minn. Stat. Ann. §§ 144.411 to 144.417, 181.938

Workplaces where laws apply: Enclosed indoor workplace.

Exceptions: Offices occupied exclusively by smokers, even if visited by nonsmokers. Factories, warehouses, and other workplaces not visited by the public; however, state commissioner of health will restrict smoking if smoke pollution affects nonsmokers.

Where smoking prohibited: Entire workplace except for designated smoking area.

Where smoking permitted: Designated smoking area (may not be entire workplace, except in bars).

Smoking area requirements: Existing barriers and ventilation systems to minimize toxic effects of smoke.

Protection from discrimination: Employer may not refuse to hire, discipline, or discharge an employee for using lawful products offsite during nonwork hours; employer may restrict nonwork use if it is a genuine job requirement. It is not discrimination to have an insurance plan with different premiums and coverage for smokers if difference reflects actual cost to employer.

Mississippi
Miss. Code Ann. § 71-7-33

Protection from discrimination: Employer may not make it a condition of employment

State Laws on Smoking in the Workplace (continued)

for prospective or current employee to abstain from smoking during nonwork hours, as long as employee complies with laws or policies that regulate workplace smoking.

Missouri

Mo. Rev. Stat. §§ 191.765 to 191.171, 290.145

Workplaces where laws apply: Enclosed indoor workplaces.

Exceptions: Bars or restaurants seating fewer than 50 people, bowling alleys and billiard parlors, and stadiums seating more than 15,000 people.

Where smoking prohibited: Entire workplace except for designated smoking area.

Where smoking permitted: Designated smoking area (may not be more than 30% of workplace).

Smoking area requirements: Existing physical barriers and ventilation systems that isolate area.

Protection from discrimination: Employer may not refuse to hire, discharge, or in any way discriminate against employee for lawful use of tobacco offsite during nonwork hours, unless use interferes with employee's or coworkers' performance or employer's business operations.

Montana

Mont. Code Ann. §§ 50-40-104, 39-2-313

Workplaces where laws apply: Any enclosed indoor workplace.

Where smoking prohibited: Entire workplace.

Protection from discrimination: Employer may not discharge, refuse to hire, or discriminate against employee in regard to compensation, promotion, benefits, or terms of employment because of lawful tobacco use offsite during nonwork hours. Use that affects job performance or other workers' safety or conflicts with a genuine job requirement is not protected. It is

not discrimination to have different insurance rates or coverage for smokers if:

- difference is based on cost to employer, and
- employees are given a written statement of carriers' rates.

Nebraska

Neb. Rev. Stat. §§ 71-5702 to 71-5709

Workplaces where laws apply: Any enclosed indoor workplace.

Exceptions: Offices occupied exclusively by smokers, even if visited by nonsmokers. Factories, warehouses, and other workplaces not visited by the public; however, state health department will restrict smoking if smoke pollution affects nonsmokers.

Where smoking prohibited: Entire workplace except in designated smoking area.

Where smoking permitted: Designated smoking area (may not be entire workplace).

Smoking area requirements: Existing barriers and ventilation systems to minimize toxic effects of smoke.

Employer smoking policy: Employer must make reasonable effort to prevent smoking and minimize secondhand smoke.

Nevada

Nev. Rev. Stat. Ann. § 613.333

Protection from discrimination: Employer may not fail or refuse to hire, discharge, or discriminate in terms of compensation, benefits, or conditions of employment because of employee's lawful use of any product offsite during nonwork hours, unless use adversely affects job performance or the safety of other employees.

State Laws on Smoking in the Workplace (continued)

New Hampshire

N.H. Rev. Stat. Ann. §§ 155:64 to 155.77, 275:37-a

Workplaces where laws apply: Enclosed workplaces where 4 or more people work.

Exceptions: Restaurants that seat fewer than 50.

Where smoking prohibited: Throughout the workplace except for designated smoking area. If smoking area cannot be effectively segregated, smoking will be totally prohibited. Employer may declare entire workplace nonsmoking.

Where smoking permitted: Designated smoking area.

Smoking area requirements: Effectively segregated so that smoke does not cause harm or enter nonsmoking area. It must:

- be located as close as possible to exhaust vents
- have 200 sq. ft. minimum contiguous workspace
- have (1) a continuous, physical barrier at least 56 in. high, or (2) a buffer zone space at least 4 ft. wide separating area from nonsmoking area.

Accommodations for nonsmokers: Special consideration for employees with medically proven conditions adversely affected by smoke, as documented by an occupational physician.

Protection from discrimination: Employer may not require employee or applicant to refrain from using tobacco products outside of work as a condition of employment, as long as employee complies with workplace smoking policy. Employer may not retaliate or discriminate against any employee who exercises rights under smoking laws; however, laws do not give employee right to refuse to perform normal duties, even if duties require entering a smoking area.

Employer penalties and liabilities: For discrimination, misdemeanor with a fine of up to $1,000 and up to one year in prison.

Employer smoking policy: Written policy outlining either smoking prohibition or areas where smoking permitted. Policy must be handed out or posted; employees must receive policy orientation. If there is a designated smoking area, must be written training procedures for:

- enforcing smoking policy
- handling complaints and violations, and
- accommodating employees with medical conditions.

New Jersey

N.J. Stat. Ann. §§ 26:3D-56 to 26:3D-61, 34:6B-1

Workplaces where laws apply: Any indoor workplace.

Where smoking prohibited: Entire workplace.

Protection from discrimination: Employer may not discharge or discriminate in terms of hiring, compensation, benefits, or conditions of employment because employee does or does not smoke, unless smoking or not smoking relates to work and job responsibilities.

New Mexico

N.M. Stat. Ann § 50-11-3

Protection from discrimination: Employer may not:

- refuse to hire, discharge, or disadvantage an employee with respect to compensation, terms, conditions, or privileges of employment because the individual is a smoker or nonsmoker, or
- require that an employee abstain from tobacco products during nonwork hours.

State Laws on Smoking in the Workplace (continued)

Employer may restrict smoking if it relates to a genuine occupational requirement or if it materially threatens a legitimate conflict of interest policy.

New York

N.Y. Pub. Health Law §§ 1399-n to 1399-p; N.Y. Lab. Law § 201-d(2b),(6)

Workplaces where laws apply: Indoor workspaces.

Where smoking prohibited: Smoking is prohibited throughout the workplace, in copy machine and common equipment areas, and in company vehicles.

Protection from discrimination: Employee may not be discharged, refused employment, or discriminated against in terms of compensation or benefits because of lawful use of products offsite during nonwork hours when not using employer's equipment or property. It is not discrimination to offer insurance with different rates or coverage for smokers if:

- difference is based on cost to employer, and
- employees are given a written statement of carriers' rates.

Employer smoking policy: Must post "No Smoking" signs; must make good faith effort to ensure that employees do not smoke.

North Carolina

N.C. Gen. Stat. § 95-28.2

Workplaces where laws apply: Discrimination laws apply to employers with 3 or more employees.

Protection from discrimination: Employer may not discharge, refuse to hire, or discriminate in regard to compensation, benefits, or terms of employment because of employee's use of

lawful products offsite during nonwork hours. Use that affects employee's job performance or other workers' safety or conflicts with a genuine job requirement is not protected. It is not discrimination to offer insurance with different rates or coverage for smokers if:

- difference is based on cost to employer
- employees are given written notice of carriers' rates, and
- employer makes equal contribution for all employees.

Employer penalties and liabilities: For discrimination, employee may sue for lost wages and benefits, reinstatement, or offer of employment. Employer liable for costs and attorney fees.

North Dakota

N.D. Cent. Code §§ 14-02.4-03, 23-12-09 to 23-12-11

Workplace where laws apply: Any enclosed workplace.

Where smoking prohibited: Entire indoor workplace.

Protection from discrimination: Employer cannot discharge, refuse to hire, or retaliate against employee or applicant for exercising rights related to this law.

Protection from discrimination: Employer may not refuse to hire, discharge, or discriminate with regard to training, apprenticeship, tenure, promotion, compensation, benefits, or conditions of employment because of employee's lawful activity offsite during nonwork hours, unless it is in direct conflict with employer's essential business-related interests.

Ohio

Ohio Rev. Code Ann. §§ 3794.01 to 3794.06

State Laws on Smoking in the Workplace (continued)

Workplace where laws apply: Any enclosed workplace.

Exceptions: Family owned and operated business in which all employees are related to the employer and the area is not open to the public, as long as the smoke will not migrate to nonsmoking areas.

Where smoking prohibited: Entire indoor workplace and outside immediately adjacent to entrances or exits to the building. Employer may designate the entire workplace nonsmoking.

Where smoking permitted: Outdoors, including outdoor patios that are physically separate from enclosed areas, as long as windows and doors prevent migration of the smoke into enclosed areas.

Smoking area requirements: Employer must ensure that tobacco smoke does not enter enclosed areas through entrances, windows, ventilation systems, or other means.

Protection from discrimination: No employer shall discharge, refuse to hire, or retaliate against an individual for exercising any rights under this law, including reporting a violation.

Oklahoma

Okla. Stat. Ann. tit. 40, §§ 500 to 503

Workplace where laws apply: Any indoor workplace.

Exceptions: Family owned and operated business in which all employees are related to the employer or where all the employees are nonsmokers, and there is only occasional public access.

Where smoking prohibited: Throughout workplace except in designated smoking area. Employer may designate entire site nonsmoking.

Where smoking permitted: Designated smoking area.

Smoking area requirements: Smoking area must be in a nonwork area where no employee is required to enter (except to perform custodial and maintenance work when the smoking area is unoccupied). Must

- have ventilation systems that exhausts air outdoors at least 15 feet from entrances, exits, or air take
- be fully enclosed
- no air recirculating to nonsmoking areas, and
- under negative air pressure so that no smoke can drift or circulate into a nonsmoking area.

Protection from discrimination: Employer may not:

- discharge or disadvantage employee in terms of compensation, benefits, or conditions of employment because of being a nonsmoker or smoking during nonwork hours, or
- require that employee abstain from using tobacco products during nonwork hours as a condition of employment.

Employer may restrict nonwork smoking if it relates to a genuine occupational requirement.

Oregon

Or. Rev. Stat. §§ 433.835 to 433.850, 659A.315

Workplaces where laws apply: All enclosed areas used by employees.

Where smoking prohibited: Entire workplace unless there are employee lounges designated for smoking.

Where smoking permitted: Employee lounges designated for smoking.

Smoking area requirements:

- Lounge must be inaccessible to minors.
- Lounge must be in a nonwork area.

State Laws on Smoking in the Workplace (continued)

- Air must be exhausted directly to the outside with a fan.
- Air may not recirculate to other areas of building.
- No employee may be required to enter lounge as part of job (does not apply to custodial work when lounge is unoccupied).

Accommodations for nonsmokers: If there is a lounge for smokers, must be enough lounges for nonsmokers.

Protection from discrimination: Employer may not require that employee refrain from lawful use of tobacco products during nonwork hours as a condition of employment, unless there is a genuine occupational requirement.

Pennsylvania

35 Pa. Cons. Stat. Ann. § 1230.1

Workplaces where laws apply: Enclosed indoor workplaces.

Exceptions: Factories, warehouses, and other workplaces not visited by the public.

Where smoking prohibited: Employer designates.

Where smoking permitted: Employer designates.

Employer smoking policy: Must have policy that regulates smoking. Must post and provide copy to any employee upon request.

Rhode Island

R.I. Gen. Laws §§ 23-20.10-1 to 23-20.10-14

Workplaces where laws apply: Smoking shall be prohibited in all enclosed facilities within places of employment. Required signs must be posted.

Exceptions: Certain businesses are exempt from the law: Private homes, unless licensed for child care or adult care; hotel or motel rooms

designated as smoking rooms; tobacco stores and smoking bars; designated parts of assisted living facilities and nursing homes; licensed gaming facilities.

Where smoking permitted: Employer may designate outdoor area.

Smoking area requirements: Must be physically separate from enclosed workspace, to prevent smoke from getting into the workplace.

Protection from discrimination: Employers cannot prohibit the use of tobacco outside of work and cannot discriminate in compensation, terms, or benefits for tobacco use outside of work or retaliate against an employee for reporting or attempting to prosecute a violation of the law.

South Carolina

S.C. Code Ann. § 41-1-85

Protection from discrimination: Employer may not take personnel actions, including hiring, discharge, demotion, or promotion, based on use of tobacco outside the workplace.

South Dakota

S.D. Codified Laws Ann. §§ 22-36-2 to 22-36-4, 60-4-11

Workplaces where laws apply: Any enclosed indoor work area; includes employee cafeterias, lounges, and restrooms; conference and classrooms; hallways.

Where smoking prohibited: The entire workplace.

Protection from discrimination: Employer may not discharge employee because of using tobacco products offsite during nonwork hours, unless not smoking is a genuine occupational requirement. It is not discrimination to have insurance policies with different rates or coverage for smokers.

State Laws on Smoking in the Workplace (continued)

Tennessee
Tenn. Code Ann. § 50-1-304(e)

Protection from discrimination: Employee may not be fired for use of a lawful product during nonwork hours as long as employee observes workplace policy when at work.

Utah
Utah Code Ann. §§ 26-38-2 and 26-38-3

Workplaces where laws apply: All enclosed indoor workplaces unless owner-operated with no employees and not open to the public.

Where smoking prohibited: Entire workplace.

Vermont
Vt. Stat. Ann. tit. 18, §§ 1421 to 1426

Workplaces where laws apply: Enclosed structures not usually open to the public.

Where smoking prohibited: Throughout workplace except for designated smoking area. Employer may prohibit smoking entirely.

Where smoking permitted: Restricted to designated enclosed smoking area. Up to 30% of employee cafeteria and lounge areas may be designated.

Smoking area requirements: Must be area that nonsmokers are not required to visit on a regular basis. Must be enclosed or may be unenclosed, if layout prevents smoke from irritating non-smokers and 75% of employees agree.

Protection from discrimination: Employer may not discharge, discipline, or otherwise discriminate against employee who assists in enforcement of workplace smoking laws.

Employer smoking policy: Written policy that either prohibits smoking entirely or restricts it to designated areas (need be written only if employer has 10 or more employees working more than 15 hours a week). The policy must be posted and copies provided to employees upon request.

Virginia
Va. Code Ann. § 15.2-2807

Workplaces where laws apply: No state laws regulate smoking in the workplace. However, if local ordinance permits, employer may:

- regulate smoking, if smoking and nonsmoking areas are designated by written agreement between employer and employees, or
- totally ban smoking, if a majority of the affected employees vote for it.

Washington
Wash. Admin. Code §§ 296-800-240, 296-800-24005

Workplaces where laws apply: Office environment: indoor or enclosed space used for clerical, administrative, or business work. Includes offices in manufacturing, food service, construction, and agricultural facilities.

Exceptions: Outdoor structures, gazebos, and lean-tos provided for smokers that are at least 25 feet from nonsmoking areas.

West Virginia
W.Va. Code § 21-3-19

Protection from discrimination: Employer may not refuse to hire, discharge, or penalize an employee with respect to compensation, conditions of employment, or other benefits for using tobacco products offsite during nonwork hours. It is not discrimination to have insurance policies with different rates or coverage for smokers if:

- difference is based on cost to employer, and
- employees are given a notice of carriers' rates.

State Laws on Smoking in the Workplace (continued)

Wisconsin

Wis. Stat. Ann. §§ 101.123, 111.35

Workplaces where laws apply: Professional, clerical, or administrative services work offices; retail establishments.

Exceptions: Offices occupied exclusively by smokers, even if visited by nonsmokers. Manufacturing plants.

Where smoking prohibited: Throughout the workplace except in designated smoking area.

Where smoking permitted: Designated smoking area. Employer may not designate entire building a smoking area.

Smoking area requirements: Existing ventilation systems and physical barriers to minimize smoke in nonsmoking areas; no new construction required.

Accommodations for nonsmokers: Employer must post signs designating smoking areas, arrange seating to accommodate nonsmokers if they work adjacent to smoking areas.

Protection from discrimination: Employer may not discriminate against employee who uses or does not use lawful products offsite during nonwork hours. Use that impairs employee's ability to perform job or conflicts with a genuine occupational requirement is not protected. It is not discrimination to have insurance policies with different coverage and rates for smokers and nonsmokers if:

- difference is based on cost to employer, and
- each employee is given a written statement of carriers' rates.

Wyoming

Wyo. Stat. § 27-9-105(a,iv)

Protection from discrimination: Employer may not make use or nonuse of tobacco products outside of work a condition of employment unless nonuse is a genuine occupational qualification. May not discriminate regarding compensation, benefits, or terms of employment because of use or nonuse of tobacco products outside of work. It is not discrimination to offer insurance policies with different rates and coverage for smokers and nonsmokers if:

- difference reflects actual cost to employer, and
- employees are given written notice of carriers' rates.

Current as of February 2007

Hazardous Substances Laws

Most states now have laws that restrict or regulate the use, storage, and handling of hazardous substances in the workplace. These laws vary greatly from state to state. The identification of toxic and otherwise hazardous substances is a very technical matter that most often is the responsibility of the state's labor department.

In some cases, workers detect that they are being exposed to a hazardous substance when one or more of them notices that a health problem—a skin rash or eye irritation are common examples—coincides with work hours.

If you think that you are being subjected to hazardous substances in your workplace, follow your complaint to OSHA with a call to your state's labor department. (See the Appendix for contact details.)

> **EXAMPLE:** Hanchung took a job as a forklift driver in a metal plating plant. After his first few hours at work, his eyes began to water and became badly reddened. On the way home from work, Hanchung visited a walk-in medical clinic, where the doctor used a cotton swab to take samples of skin residues from his face. A few days later, the doctor told Hanchung that the problem with his eyes was a reaction to sulfuric acid that apparently was in the air where he worked and had settled on his skin and eyes.
>
> Hanchung filed a complaint with OSHA and his state's labor department.

As a result of the joint investigation, OSHA ordered his employer to construct an enclosure around processing areas that used sulfuric acid and to provide Hanchung and his coworkers with protective clothing to wear at work while the enclosures were being built.

Violence in the Workplace

The numbers and pronouncements about our chances of being attacked or killed while at work are scary.

Homicide reigns as the leading cause of workplace death among women. In fact, the National Institute for Occupational Safety and Health lists homicide as a leading cause of all work-related deaths in the United States, second only to motor vehicle crashes. More than 800 people are kill annually in American workplaces. And an estimated one million workers suffer nonfatal assaults on the job each year. The U.S. Postal Service alone reported 500 cases of employees being violent toward supervisors in a recent period of 18 months—and an additional 200 cases of supervisors acting violently toward employees. And frightening results of a recent study claim that an employee in California is more likely to be murdered at work than to die in a car accident commuting to or from work.

And a look at more statistics reveals a particularly flummoxing fact: Most employers are doing very little to protect workers from this clear and present danger on the job. A 2005 Survey of Workplace Violence Prevention conducted by the Bureau of

Labor Statistics revealed that nearly 5% of the 7.1 million private industry business establishments in the United States had an incident of workplace violence within the past year. Although about a third of these establishments reported that the incident had a negative impact on their workforce—including increased turnover and absentee rates—the great majority did not change their workplace violence prevention procedures after the incident. Almost 9% had no program or policy addressing workplace violence.

Part of what makes violent behavior difficult to control is that it usually comes unannounced. But most workplace killers are disgruntled former employees who have been laid off or fired, or the obsessed spouse or lover of an employee. And those who kill at work, experts say, usually give off warning signals that typically include:

- following or stalking an employee to or from the place of work
- entering the workplace
- following an employee at work, and
- telephoning or sending correspondence to the employee.

Coworkers describe many individuals who have committed violence in the workplace as: loners, not team players, having a history of interpersonal conflict and displays of anger, having made threats of violence in the past, being withdrawn, showing symptoms of current drug or alcohol abuse, being argumentative and quick to blame others for their own problems and frustrations.

Both employers and employees may be able to help ward off violence by heeding these signals of disturbed souls and taking immediate action. As an employee, you should report threatening coworkers. And encourage your employer to both refer such problem coworkers to a ready source of help and to tell them, in no uncertain terms, that they will be fired if their bad behavior continues.

Legal Developments

Realistically, employers who try to ward off violence often get caught in the conundrum of balancing employees' safety against the rights of the potential perpetrator. On one hand, employers are charged with keeping the workplace safe. Several have been successfully sued for negligent hiring, negligent supervision, and wrongful death because they kept suspicious employees on staff who ultimately maimed or killed others on the job.

Increasingly, the pressure to act comes from victims of workplace violence and their survivors. And an increasing number of courts find employers directly liable for violence when they turn a deaf ear to workers' complaints about inadequate security—or a blind eye to knowledge that a worker's past actions might make him or her likely to attack coworkers and others on the job.

But employers have also felt the sting of lawsuits by employees who claim that overzealous investigations have violated laws protecting them from discrimination or invasions of their privacy.

Of late, scales are tipping in favor of keeping workplaces safe. In one case, for example, a Massachusetts court held that an employer, the U.S. Postal Service, was well within its rights when it fired a worker who screamed obscenities, swept the contents off a supervisor's desk, threw a typewriter and chair, and knocked down several office partitions. The employee defended that he had an explosive personality disorder that entitled him to protection as a disabled employee rather than a pink slip. But the court held that a fundamental requirement of any job is that an employee must not be violent and destructive. (*Mazzarella v. U.S. Postal Service,* 849 F. Supp. 89 (D. Mass. 1994).)

And a Florida court held that an employee— even one diagnosed with a chemical imbalance —could be fired on the spot for bringing a loaded gun to work. (*Hindman v. GTE Data Services,* 4 A.D. Cas. (BNA) 182 (M.D. Fla. 1995).)

Practical Prevention Steps

As reports of violence in the workplace have grown, concerned and conscientious employers and employees alike have turned to OSHA for help. While the agency has not set a specific safety standard for workplaces to follow, it has issued two sets of guidelines to help employers identify and prevent situations in workplaces with high potentials for violence: health care and social service industries and late-night retail establishments. The guidelines, which recommend setting up a violence prevention program, include five elements that may be useful for safety plans in all workplaces. If your workplace does not

yet have a violence prevention program, the guidelines might serve as a starting point.

1. **Management commitment and employee involvement.** All violent and threatening incidents should be taken seriously— and management should develop a plan for workplace security, working with local police and other public safety agencies to improve physical security.

2. **Worksite analysis.** This includes identifying risk factors. For example, in retail establishments, risk factors commonly include contact with the public, exchanging money, working alone or in small numbers, and being located in a high crime area. A worksite analysis should also include a review of any past incidents, a security review, and periodic safety audits.

3. **Hazard prevention and control.** This includes adequate lighting, possible installation of video surveillance, drop safes, and physical barriers.

4. **Training.** All employees, supervisors, and security personnel should be trained to ensure awareness of potential security hazards and procedures for protecting themselves and others in the workplace.

5. **Evaluation.** Methods of hazard control and training needs should be evaluated—including record keeping, incident reports, police recommendations, and notes from safety meetings.

When Domestic Violence Comes to Work

In a recent survey of corporate security directors, 94% ranked the threats and battery associated with domestic violence as a high security risk in the workplace. Their feelings are justified. A full 75% of battered employees are harassed at work by their abusers—a spouse, former spouse, or member of the family or household. And, last year, there were 60,000 incidents of on-the-job violence in which those who were attacked knew their attackers intimately.

Beyond its obvious toll on human psyches, domestic violence has a huge impact on workplace productivity. For every 100 employees suffering the effects of domestic violence, 94 will take at least one extra sick day a year, over 60 will be late by more than an hour five times a month, and nearly 60 will be harassed at work on the phone by their abuser. All of this adds up to a situation where 70% of hurting, afraid, distracted, and otherwise compromised workers will have difficulty performing their jobs. And legislatures have been slow to respond to this reality. A rare exception, a California statute, provides that employers with 25 employees or more must offer domestic violence leave—reasonable time off to deal with related issues including health, counseling, safety, and housing. (Cal. Lab. Code Sec. 230.)

And a recent study of those subjected to domestic violence found that nearly 30% lost their jobs as a direct result of the abuse. Of all the other high costs associated with domestic violence, some of the most insidious from an employer's standpoint are heightened health insurance premiums, increased workers' compensation, and higher unemployment insurance.

The first step toward ending domestic violence is to find out the alternatives and possibilities available. If you or a coworker needs help or information on domestic violence, look in the telephone book under Crisis Intervention for local resources. Or call the National Domestic Violence Hotline for information on nearby shelters, legal help, health care advocacy, and counseling: 800-799-7233 or (TTY) 800-787-3224.

Statistics from DV Initiatives, www.dvinitiative.com.

Illegal Discrimination

CHAPTER 7 | ILLEGAL DISCRIMINATION | 253

It is almost always illegal for employers to discriminate against workers because of their race, skin color, gender, religious beliefs, national origin, disability—or age, if the employee is at least 40 years old. In most situations, it is also illegal for employers to discriminate against workers on the basis of factors such as testing positive for the HIV virus or being pregnant, divorced, gay, or lesbian.

The most powerful antidiscrimination law governing the workplace is Title VII of the federal Civil Rights Act of 1964. It originally outlawed discrimination based on race, skin color, religious beliefs, or national origin, and it created the Equal Employment Opportunity Commission (EEOC) to administer and enforce the legal standards it set.

Today, a number of additional federal laws—several of them amendments to Title VII—are used to fight unfair workplace discrimination:

- The Equal Pay Act of 1963 specifically outlaws discrimination in wages on the basis of gender. (See "Title VII of the Civil Rights Act," below.)
- The Age Discrimination in Employment Act (ADEA) outlaws workplace discrimination on the basis of age. The law has been amended several times since it was passed in 1967, and now applies only to employees who are at least 40 years old. (See "The Age Discrimination in Employment Act, below.)
- The Older Workers Benefit Protection Act is an amendment to the ADEA,

passed in 1990, that specifically outlaws discrimination in employment benefit programs on the basis of employees' age. It too applies only to employees age 40 and older. It also deters employers' use of waivers in which employees sign away their rights to take legal action against age-based discrimination. (See "The Older Workers Benefit Protection Act," below.)

- The Pregnancy Discrimination Act (PDA), which makes it illegal for an employer to refuse to hire a pregnant woman, to terminate her employment, or to compel her to take maternity leave, was passed in 1978 as an additional amendment to Title VII. (See Chapter 4, "The Pregnancy Discrimination Act," for more on family and medical leaves.)
- In 1986, in *Meritor Savings Bank v. Vinson*, the U.S. Supreme Court held that Title VII also protects against sexual harassment, another form of illegal workplace discrimination. (See Chapter 8.)
- The Americans With Disabilities Act (ADA), enacted in 1990, makes it illegal to discriminate against people because of their physical or mental disability. (See "The Americans With Disabilities Act," below.)
- The Labor Management Relations Act and amendments, passed as a patchwork of protections, generally make it illegal to discriminate against workers for belonging to or refusing to join a labor union. (See Chapter 15.)

Title VII of the Civil Rights Act

Most of the workplace laws that broadly protect employees from discrimination in the workplace have been enacted through the years as amendments to the Civil Rights Act, also known as Title VII. (42 U.S.C. §§ 2000 and following.)

Who Is Covered

Title VII applies to all companies and labor unions with 15 or more employees. It also governs employment agencies, state and local governments, and apprenticeship programs.

Title VII does not cover:

- federal government employees—special procedures have been established to enforce antidiscrimination laws for them, and
- independent contractors—those who generally work on specific projects for a number of different employers.

Illegal Discrimination

Under Title VII, employers may not use race, skin color, gender, religious beliefs, or national origin as the basis for decisions on hirings, promotions, dismissals, pay raises, benefits, work assignments, leaves of absence, or just about any other aspect of employment. Title VII covers everything about the employment relationship—from prehiring ads to working conditions, performance reviews, and post-employment references.

Counting Employees: Not As Easy As It Sounds

The Civil Rights Act is clearly written to apply to employers with 15 or more employees. But courts across the nation have been of differing minds when it comes to deciding which employees should stand up and be counted.

Most courts used a counting system in which both hourly and part-time employees were considered in the total, but only on the days they were at work or on paid leave.

However, the U.S. Supreme Court took the issue and ruled that this is a disingenuous shell game. The Court held that employees should be defined and tallied for purposes of Title VII according to the payroll method. Under the payroll method, employers are covered if they have 15 or more employees on the payroll for each working day in 20 or more weeks, regardless of the actual work the workers perform or whether they are compensated for each of those days. (*Walters v. Metropolitan Educational Enterprises, Inc.*, 519 U.S. 202 (1997).)

This judicial clarification can be important if your discrimination claim is dismissed because your employer is too small. You may be able to successfully argue that part-time workers and those on leave should be included in the final tally of employees.

Remedies Available

There are a number of remedies that an employee who suffers the effects of discrimination on the job can obtain.

Reinstatement and promotion. A court can order that the employee be rehired, promoted, or reassigned to whatever job was lost because of the discrimination.

Wages and job-connected losses. A court can award any salary and benefits the employee lost as a result of being fired, demoted, or forced to quit because of discrimination. This can include loss of wages, pension contributions, medical benefits, overtime pay, bonuses, back pay, shift differential pay, vacation pay, and participation in a company profit-sharing plan.

Money damages. A court can award a limited amount of damages for personal injuries, which can include money to cover the actual amount of out-of-pocket losses, such as medical expenses. It can also include other compensatory damages—to compensate or make whole the wronged one—and punitive damages—aimed to punish a wrongdoer. But the amount of such damages is limited to between $50,000 and $300,000—depending on the number of people employed by the business.

Injunctive relief. A court can direct the company to change its policies to stop discrimination and to prevent similar incidents in the future.

Attorneys' fees. If the employee wins a case, a court can order the company to pay attorneys' fees.

Damages That Sneak in Under the Cap

The U.S. Supreme Court recently removed limits on some damages employees may collect from employers who fail to step in and stop discrimination. The decision was heralded as a victory for workers' groups, which have long argued that arbitrary limits on such awards did not reflect the actual harm done by discrimination. (*Pollard v. E. I. DuPont de Nemours & Co.*, 532 U.S. 843 (2001).)

The case involved Sharon Pollard, who worked for 19 years at Tennessee's DuPont chemical plant until she was fired in 1996. Pollard was promoted after ten years on the job to an assistant operator in the coveted hydrogen peroxide area of the plant, which did not sit well with a few of her male coworkers, one of whom placed a Bible passage on her desk that read: "A woman should learn in quietness and full submission. I do not permit a woman to teach or have authority over man. She must be silent."

Pollard, however, spoke up—and was transferred to another shift. Workers there got along amicably—until on Take Your Daughter to Work Day, Dupont asked Pollard to speak to some of the girls touring the plant. This galled one of the male supervisors, who instructed Pollard's coworkers and reports not to eat with,

Damages That Sneak in Under the Cap (continued)

socialize with, or talk with her, nor to follow any instructions she gave them. Pollard was subsequently subjected to behavior on the job ranging from boorish to life-threatening, as several male coworkers regularly:

- called her vile and obscene names
- set off false fire alarms in her work area
- neglected to tell her about actual safety alerts in her department
- altered the chemicals in the tank for which she was responsible, making her appear inept in her job, and
- argued that women workers did not belong in the peroxide portion of the plant.

In addition, Pollard produced evidence that one coworker slashed the tires on her bicycle and that another tried to run her off the road with a car. Pollard's complaints to went unheeded, but for a cursory couple of meetings that resulted in no further investigation, no reprimands, and no discipline.

When Pollard again found the Silent Woman Bible quote pinned to her locker, she requested and was given a medical leave of absence to deal with the stress she suffered in the workplace. Six months later, when she declined DuPont's offer to put her back on the job with the same coworkers, the company fired her.

A Tennessee district court awarded Pollard over $660,000 in back pay, attorneys' fees, and damages. But they denied her claim for front pay—wages lost from the date of judgment until the time a worker is returned to the job or deemed unable to return, most often because of continuing hostilities between the former worker and the former workplace. As Pollard and DuPont had clearly become bad fits, she urged the court to award her front pay to cover her losses—and the U.S. Supreme Court agreed with her.

Gender discrimination has been illegal since 1964, when the Civil Rights Act was adopted. But early on, all that an employee who suffered discrimination on the job could collect was lost wages. In 1990, labor groups pushed a bill through Congress that would have allowed an employee to sue for compensatory damages —that is, money to compensate for the wrong. The first President Bush vetoed that bill.

The issue resurfaced in 1991, in the wake of the hearings alleging Supreme Court nominee Clarence Thomas had sexually harassed his coworker Anita Hill when they worked together at the EEOC. This time, the Bush Administration agreed to allow employees to sue for damages but put a limit on the amount they could recover in compensatory damages—$50,000 to $300,000 based on the number of employees in the company. In *Pollard*, the Supreme Court held that front pay does not constitute compensatory damages, so is not limited by this statutory cap.

Because of the *Pollard* decision, labor law lawyers have predicted two things: more former employees suing for more front pay and still more cases on whether or not an award of front pay would be appropriate. But the case is also a wakeup call for employers: Once a lawsuit is filed, they must act and act quickly to limit the amount of time for which an employee would be able to collect front pay.

Filing a Complaint With the EEOC

Compared to most other government agencies, the EEOC has very well-defined procedures for filing complaints. But the EEOC also operates through a complex hierarchy of offices and has strict time limits for filing complaints, which usually range from a few months to nearly a year. Pay particular attention to timing if you decide to take action against what you believe is illegal workplace discrimination. (See "When to File," below.)

Where to File

Title VII complaints can be filed at:

- Local Equal Employment Opportunity agency offices. These are not federal offices, but state and local agencies that have been designated as representatives of the EEOC. (See "State Agencies That Enforce Laws Prohibiting Discrimination

Who Will Heed the Calls?

The EEOC is the federal agency responsible for evaluating, smoothing over, and pursuing nearly all cases of workplace discrimination. That includes a wide stripe of claims—including those based on disability, age, unequal pay, national origin, pregnancy, race, religion, and gender. And like many enforcement agencies, it is struggling with a strapped budget.

Despite its beleaguered condition, the EEOC has historically vowed to ferret out all reported discrimination on the job. But that might be changing. The EEOC recently quietly issued a new policy setting its sights a little lower: It will deal with the worst cases; the rest are anyone's call.

The dictate will likely make EEOC staff lawyers more prone to cut deals in cases that seem weaker on their merits rather than to insist that the wrongdoers pay large amounts in damages.

As part of its rehaul, the agency will divide claims into three categories:

- A cases—those likely to result in a finding of discrimination
- B cases—those that cannot be immediately assessed one way or the other, and
- C cases—those unlikely to result in a discrimination judgment.

The claims now most likely to get attention are those that affect a large number of employees. And, for better or worse, there is an early indication that the changed policy has made the agency more efficient. By the end of fiscal year 2004, the backlog of charges was reduced substantially from its highest level of languishing charges, reached in 1995. And money awards the EEOC was able to secure nearly doubled.

Bear in mind that even if the EEOC deigns not to take on your case, you are still free to sue your employer in federal court. (See "Filing a Title VII Lawsuit," below.)

in Employment," below, for contact information.)

- State and regional offices of the EEOC. (See the listing below.)

There are EEOC offices throughout the United States. Normally, it is best to file a complaint at the office nearest to you or your place of employment. But, if there is no office nearby or in your state, you can legally file a complaint in any office. If the staff at the office listed below is unable to help, call the EEOC at 800-669-4000 for more assistance.

When to File

If your state has its own equal employment opportunity laws (see "State and Local Antidiscrimination Laws," below), you will typically be allowed 300 days after the act of discrimination occurred to file a complaint. But, if your state does not have its own equal employment opportunity laws, you have only 180 days to file. The safest way to proceed is to assume that 180 days is the limit in your case and file your complaint as soon as possible.

In some cases, you will not be able to recognize illegal discrimination from a single action by an employer. If you discern a pattern of illegal discrimination that extends back more than 180 days, the safest way to proceed is to assume that the EEOC time limit began with the event that caused you to recognize the pattern and file a complaint as soon as possible. Since such cases often require complicated proof, consider consulting a lawyer for help. (See Chapter 17, "Hiring a Lawyer.")

Tips for Dealing With the EEOC

There are a number of things to keep in mind when helping to shuttle your claim through the EEOC bureaucracy most efficiently:

- **Stay vigilant.** Do not assume that the EEOC will do everything and that you don't have to monitor what is going on. Check periodically with the EEOC to find out what is happening with your case.
- **Be assertive.** If some EEOC action—or, more likely, inaction—is causing you serious problems, call that to the attention of the people handling your case.
- **Read—and reread—the fine print.** When you file a charge with the EEOC, a worker there will ask you to read and sign a written statement summarizing your claim. Be sure to scrutinize the form carefully before signing. Some later argue that their words were twisted or misstated on the EEOC charge form—an allegation that's hard to prove once the signed form wends its way into the system.
- **Keep your options open.** Filing a claim with the EEOC does not prevent you from taking other action to deal with your case. You still have a right to try to solve the problem on your own or use a company complaint procedure. You also have the right to hire an attorney to file a lawsuit, if that is appropriate for your situation.

EXAMPLE: A woman who worked with Jan in a pharmaceutical lab was fired in January. Two months later, the lab fired another woman. In June, a third woman was fired.

When the third woman was fired, Jan began to notice that the firings seemed to have nothing to do with job performance. Although the lab employed several men with less experience and whose job performance was not as good as the three women who had been fired, no men had been fired.

After consistently receiving positive performance reviews, Jan's supervisor informed her the lab staff was being reduced and she should start looking for another job. Jan took a few weeks to gather evidence to support her belief that the company was illegally discriminating against women on the basis of gender and then filed a complaint with the EEOC in September.

Organizing Your Evidence

Because illegal discrimination rarely takes the form of one simple event, it is important to organize your evidence of incidents of illegal discrimination before contacting the EEOC to file a complaint.

Whenever possible, keep a log of the date, time, location, people involved, and nature of actions that demonstrate any pattern of illegal discrimination. Keep a file of any documents that your employer gives you, such as written performance reviews or disciplinary notices. (See Chapter 1.)

If you present your evidence to the EEOC in an organized way—without yielding to the temptation to vent your displeasure with your employer's policies and practices—you will raise the chances of your complaint getting full attention and consideration from the EEOC investigators.

How the EEOC Handles Complaints

When you file a complaint, typically an EEOC staff lawyer or investigator will interview you and initially evaluate whether or not your employer's actions appear to violate Title VII. Theoretically, the EEOC has 180 days to act on your complaint. If the interviewer does not feel that the incident warrants a complaint, he or she will tell you so. You may have to think about other options, such as pursuing a complaint through your company's established complaint procedure.

If the interviewer feels you should pursue your complaint with the EEOC, he or she will fill out an EEOC Charge of Discrimination form describing the incident and send it to you to review and sign. After receiving your complaint, the EEOC is supposed to interview the employer that is the subject of the complaint and then try to mediate a settlement of the complaint between you and that employer.

That is what the EEOC's operating regulations provide. And, for the most part, the EEOC does what it is supposed to do. But do not expect every claim to proceed as described. EEOC offices differ in caseloads, local procedures, and the quality of their personnel. Investigations are usually slow, sometimes taking three years or more. The

EEOC takes only a small portion of its cases to court—less than 1% of those that are filed with it. These and other factors can have an impact on how a case is actually handled.

Penalties for Retaliation

It is illegal for your employer to retaliate against you either for filing a Title VII complaint or for cooperating in the investigation of one. But, to take advantage of this protection, you must be able to prove that the retaliation occurred because you filed a complaint. (See Chapter 9, "Retaliation.")

And historically, you were required to prove that the retaliation was work-related. However, in 2006, the U.S. Supreme Court dramatically changed and expanded the scope of such claims by redefining retaliation, holding for the first time that an employer's harmful actions need not be related to employment or the workplace to qualify as Title VII retaliation.

And it also resolved the question of how serious the harm must be before it qualifies as retaliation. In the case, the employer, Burlington Northern, resassigned Sheila White, the only female forklift operator, to a less desirable position and suspended her without pay for more than a month after she complained of workplace discrimination. Burlington then claimed White was not sufficiently harmed, since the new position was within the same work classification and her back pay was eventually reinstated. The justices, however, were persuaded by the reality that the new position was less prestigious and "by all accounts more arduous and dirtier." And they also underscored that

while she was eventually repaid, White and her family had to live for 37 days without income, noting her testimony at trial: "That was the worst Christmas I had out of my life. No money, no income—and that made all of us feel bad." The Court held that as long as "a reasonable employee" finds an action to be "materially adverse," it can qualify as retaliation in a Title VII claim. (*Burlington Northern & Santa Fe Ry. Co. v. White,* 126 S. Ct. 2405 (2006).)

But more often than not, an employer that wants to retaliate against you for filing a Title VII complaint will cite substandard job performance.

> **EXAMPLE:** Hector filed a Title VII complaint because he observed that his employer never promotes anyone of his race above a certain level. To investigate Hector's complaint, the EEOC reviewed documents related to the company's hiring practices to determine whether it is, in fact, using race as the basis for hiring decisions.
>
> Two weeks later, Hector was dismissed from his job because, the company claimed, his performance was below its standards. If Hector decides to file an additional complaint charging the company with illegal retaliation, he will probably have to prove that his performance satisfied or exceeded the company's standards—and that the real reason he was fired was because he filed a Title VII complaint.

State EEOC Offices

Alabama

Birmingham District Office
1130 22nd Street S, Suite 2000
Birmingham, AL 35205
205-212-2100 or 800-669-4000
TTY: 205-212-2112 or
800-669-6820
FAX: 205-212-2105

Mobile Local Office
63 South Royal Street
Suite 504
Mobile, AL 36602
800-669-4000
TTY: 800-669-6820
FAX: 251-690-2581

Arizona

Phoenix District Office
3300 N. Central Avenue,
  Suite 690
Phoenix, AZ 85012
602-640-5000 or
800-669-4000
TTY: 602-640-5072 or
800-669-6820
FAX: 602-640-5071

Arkansas

Little Rock Area Office
820 Louisiana Street
Suite 200
Little Rock, AR 72201
501-324-5060 or
800-669-4000
TTY: 501-324-5481 or
800-669-6820
FAX: 501-324-5991

California

Fresno Local Office
2300 Tulare Street
Suite 215
Fresno, CA 93721
559-487-5837 or
800-669-4000
TTY: 559-487-5837 or
800-669-6820
FAX: 559-487-5053

Los Angeles District Office
255 E. Temple Street
4th Floor
Los Angeles, CA 90012
213-894-1000 or
800-669-4000
TTY: 213-894-1121 or
800-669-6820
FAX: 213-894-1118

Oakland Local Office
1301 Clay Street
Suite 1170-N
Oakland, CA 94612
510-637-3230 or
800-669-4000
TTY: 510-637-3234 or
800-669-6820
FAX: 510-637-3235

San Diego Area Office
401 B Street, Suite 510
San Diego, CA 92101
619-557-7235 or
800-669-4000
TTY: 619-557-5748 or
800-669-6820
FAX: 619-557-7274

San Francisco District Office
350 Embarcadero, Suite 500
San Francisco, CA 94105
415-625-5600 or
800-669-4000
TTY: 415-625-5610 or
800-669-6820
FAX: 415-625-5609

San Jose Local Office
96 N. Third Street
Suite 200
San Jose, CA 95112
408-291-7352 or
800-669-4000
TTY: 408-291-7374 or
800-669-6820
FAX: 408-291-4539

Colorado

Denver District Office
303 E. 17th Avenue, Suite 510
Denver, CO 80203
303-866-1300 or
800-669-4000
TTY: 303-866-1950 or
800-669-6820
FAX: 303-866-1085

District of Columbia

Washington Field Office
1801 L Street, NW, Suite 100
Washington, DC 20507
202-419-0700 or
800-669-4000
TTY: 202-275-7518 or
800-669-6820
FAX: 202-419-0740

State EEOC Offices (continued)

Florida

Miami District Office
One Biscayne Tower
2 S. Biscayne Boulevard
Suite 2700
Miami, FL 33131
305-536-4491 or
800-669-4000
TTY: 305-536-5721 or
800-669-6820
FAX: 305-808-1855

Tampa Area Office
501 E. Polk Street SW
Suite 1000
Tampa, FL 33602
813-228-2310 or
800-669-4000
TTY: 813-228-2003 or
800-669-6820
FAX: 813-228-2841

Georgia

Atlanta District Office
100 Alabama Street, SW
Suite 4R30
Atlanta, GA 30303
404-562-6800 or
800-669-4000
TTY: 404-562-6801 or
800-669-6820
FAX: 404-562-6909

Savannah Local Office
410 Mall Boulevard
Suite G
Savannah, GA 31406
912-652-4234 or

800-669-4000
TTY: 912-652-4439 or
800-669-6820
FAX: 912-652-4248

Hawaii

Honolulu Local Office
300 Ala Moana Boulevard
Room 7-127
P.O. Box 50082
Honolulu, HI 96850
808-541-3120 or
800-669-4000
TTY: 808-541-3131 or
800-669-6820
FAX: 808-541-3390

Illinois

Chicago District Office
500 W. Madison Street
Suite 2800
Chicago, IL 60661
312-353-2713 or
800-669-4000
TTY: 313-353-2421 or
800-669-6820
FAX: 312-886-1168

Indiana

Indianapolis District Office
101 W. Ohio Street, Suite 1900
Indianapolis, IN 46204
317-226-7212 or
800-669-4000
TTY: 317-226-5162 or
800-669-6820
FAX: 317-226-7953

Kansas

Kansas City Area Office
4th & State Avenue
9th Floor
Kansas City, KS 66101
913-551-5655 or
800-669-4000
TTY: 913-551-5657 or
800-669-6820
FAX: 913-551-6957

Kentucky

Louisville Area Office
600 Dr. Martin Luther King Jr.
 Place
Suite 268
Louisville, KY 40202
502-582-6082 or
800-669-4000
TTY: 502-582-6285 or
800-669-6820
FAX: 502-582-5895

Louisiana

New Orleans Field Office
1555 Poydras Street
Suite 1900
New Orleans, LA 70112
800-669-4000
TTY: 800-669-6820
FAX: 504-589-6861

Maryland

Baltimore Field Office
10 S. Howard Street
3rd Floor
Baltimore, MD 21201

State EEOC Offices (continued)

410-962-3932 or
800-669-4000
TTY: 410-962-6065 or
800-669-6820
FAX: 410-962-4270

Massachusetts

Boston Area Office
John F. Kennedy Federal
  Building
475 Government Center
Boston, MA 02203
617-565-3200 or
800-669-4000
TTY: 617-565-3204 or
800-669-6820
FAX: 617-565-3196

Michigan

Detroit Field Office
477 Michigan Avenue
Room 865
Detroit, MI 48226
313-226-4600 or
800-669-4000
TTY: 313-226-7599 or
800-669-6820
FAX: 313-226-4610

Minnesota

Minneapolis Area Office
330 S. Second Avenue
Suite 430
Minneapolis, MN 55401
612-335-4040 or
800-669-4000

TTY: 612-335-4045 or
800-669-6820
FAX: 612-335-4044

Mississippi

Jackson Area Office
Dr. A. H. McCoy Federal
  Building
100 West Capitol Street
Suite 207
Jackson, MS 39269
601-965-4537 or
800-669-4000
TTY: 601-965-4915 or
800-669-6820
FAX: 601-948-8401

Missouri

St. Louis District Office
1222 Spruce Street
Room 8.100
St. Louis, MO 63103
314-539-7800 or
800-669-4000
TTY: 314-539-7803 or
800-669-6820
FAX: 314-539-7894

Nevada

Las Vegas Local Office
333 Las Vegas Blvd. South
Suite 8112
Las Vegas, NV 89101
800-669-4000
TTY: 800-669-6820
FAX: 702-388-5094

New Jersey

Newark Area Office
1 Newark Center
21st Floor
Newark, NJ 07102
973-645-6383 or
800-669-4000
TTY: 973-645-3004 or
800-669-6820
FAX: 973-645-4524

New Mexico

Albuquerque Area Office
505 Marquette Street, NW
Suite 900
Albuquerque, NM 87102
505-248-5201 or
800-669-4000
TTY: 505-248-5240 or
800-669-6820
FAX: 505-248-5239

New York

Buffalo Local Office
6 Fountain Plaza
Suite 350
Buffalo, NY 14202
716-551-4441 or
800-669-4000
TTY: 716-551-5923 or
800-669-6820
FAX: 716-551-4387

State EEOC Offices (continued)

New York District Office
33 Whitehall Street
New York, NY 10004
212-336-3620 or
800-669-4000
TTY: 212-336-3622 or
 800-669-6820
FAX: 212-336-3790

North Carolina

Charlotte District Office
129 W. Trade Street
Suite 400
Charlotte, NC 28202
704-344-6682 or
800-669-4000
TTY: 704-344-6684 or
 800-669-6820
FAX: 704-344-6734 or
 704-344-6731

Greensboro Local Office
2303 W. Meadowview Road
Suite 201
Greensboro, NC 27407
336-547-4188 or
800-669-4000
TTY: 336-547-4035 or
 800-669-6820
FAX: 336-547-4032

Raleigh Area Office
1309 Annapolis Drive
Raleigh, NC 27608
919-856-4064 or
800-669-4000
TTY: 919-856-4296 or
800-669-6820
FAX: 919-856-4151

Ohio

Cincinnati Area Office
550 Main Street
10th Floor
Cincinnati, OH 45202
513-684-2851 or
800-669-4000
TTY: 513-684-2074 or
800-669-6820
FAX: 513-684-2361

Cleveland Field Office
1240 E. 9th Street, Suite 3001
Cleveland, OH 44199
Skylight Office Tower
216-522-2003 or
800-669-4000
TTY: 216-522-8441 or
800-669-6820
FAX: 216-522-7395

Oklahoma

Oklahoma Area Office
215 Dean A. McGee Avenue
Suite 524
Oklahoma City
Oklahoma 73102
405-231-4911 or
800-669-4000
TTY: 405-231-5745 or
800-669-6820
FAX: 405-231-4140

Pennsylvania

Philadelphia District Office
21 S. Fifth Street, Suite 400
Philadelphia, PA 19106
215-440-2600 or

800-669-4000
TTY: 215-440-2610 or
800-669-6820
FAX: 215-440-2606

Pittsburgh Area Office
1001 Liberty Avenue
Suite 300
Pittsburgh, PA 15222
412-644-3444 or
800-669-4000
TTY: 412-644-2720 or
800-669-6820
FAX: 412-644-2664

South Carolina

Greenville Local Office
301 N. Main Street
Greenville, SC 29601
864-241-4400 or
800-669-4000
TTY: 864-241-4403 or
800-669-6820
FAX: 864-241-4416

Tennessee

Memphis District Office
1407 Union Avenue, Suite 621
Memphis, TN 38104
901-544-0115 or
800-669-4000
TTY: 901-544-0112 or
800-669-6820
FAX: 901-544-0111

State EEOC Offices (continued)

Nashville Area Office
50 Vantage Way, Suite 202
Nashville, TN 37228
615-736-5820 or
800-669-4000
TTY: 615-736-5870 or
800-669-6820
FAX: 615-736-2107

Texas

Dallas District Office
207 S. Houston Street
3d Floor
Dallas, TX 75202
214-253-2700 or
800-669-4000
TTY: 214-253-2710 or
800-669-6820
FAX: 214-253-2720

El Paso Area Office
300 E. Main Street
Suite 500
El Paso, TX 79901
915-534-6700 or
800-669-4000
TTY: 915-534-6710 or
800-669-6820
FAX: 915-534-6701

Houston District Office
1919 Smith Street
6th Floor
Houston, TX 77002
713-209-3320 or
800-669-4000
TTY: 713-209-3439 or
800-669-6820
FAX: 713-209-3381

San Antonio Field Office
5410 Fredericksburg Road
Suite 200
San Antonio, TX 78229
210-281-7600 or
800-669-4000
TTY: 210-281-7610 or
800-669-6820
FAX: 210-281-7690

Virginia

Norfolk Local Office
200 Granby Street
Suite 739
Norfolk, VA 23510
757-441-3470 or
800-669-4000
TTY: 757-441-3578 or
800-669-6820
FAX: 757-441-6720

Richmond Local Office
830 E. Main Street, 6th Floor
Richmond, VA 23219
804-771-2200 or
800-669-4000
TTY: 804-771-2227 or
800-669-6820
FAX: 804-771-2222

Washington

Seattle Field Office
909 1st Avenue, Suite 400
Seattle, WA 98104
206-220-6883 or
800-669-4000
TTY: 206-220-6882 or
800-669-6820
FAX: 206-220-6911

Wisconsin

Milwaukee District Office
310 W. Wisconsin Avenue
Suite 800
Milwaukee, WI 53203
414-297-1111 or
800-669-4000
TTY: 414-297-1115 or
800-669-6820
FAX: 414-297-4133

Current as of May 2007

State Laws Prohibiting Discrimination in Employment

State	Law applies to employers with	Private employers may not make employment decisions based on			
		Age (protected ages, if specified)	Ancestry or national origin	Disability	AIDS/ HIV
Alabama Ala. Code §§ 25-1-20, 25-1-21	20 or more employees	✓ (40 and older)			
Alaska Alaska Stat. §§ 18.80.220, 47.30.865	One or more employees	✓ (40 and older)	✓	Physical and mental	✓
Arizona Ariz. Rev. Stat. §§ 41-1461, 41-1463	15 or more employees	✓ (40 and older)	✓	Physical and mental	✓
Arkansas Ark. Code Ann. §§ 16-123-102, 16-123-107, 11-4-601, 11-5-403	9 or more employees		✓	Physical and mental	
California Cal. Gov't. Code §§ 12920, 12940, 12941, 12945, 12926.1; Cal. Lab. Code § 1101	5 or more employees	✓ (40 and older)	✓	Physical and mental	✓
Colorado Colo. Rev. Stat. §§ 24-34-301, 24-34-401, 24-34-402, 27-10-115	One or more employees	✓ (40 to 70)	✓	Physical, mental, and learning	✓
Connecticut Conn. Gen. Stat. Ann. §§ 46a-51, 46a-60, 46a-81	3 or more employees	✓ (40 and older)	✓	Present or past physical, mental, or learning	✓
Delaware Del. Code Ann. tit. 19, §§ 710, 711	4 or more employees	✓ (40 and older)	✓	Physical or mental	✓

[1] Employees covered by FLSA.

	Gender	Marital status	Pregnancy, childbirth, and related medical conditions	Race or color	Religion or creed	Sexual orientation	Genetic testing information	Additional protected categories
	✓	✓ (Includes changes in status)	✓ Parenthood	✓	✓			Mental illness
	✓			✓	✓		✓	
	✓			✓	✓		✓ [1]	
	✓	✓	✓	✓	✓	✓	✓	• Gender identity • Medical condition • Political activities or affiliations
	✓		✓	✓	✓			• Lawful conduct outside of work • Mental illness
	✓	✓	✓	✓	✓	✓	✓	Mental retardation
	✓	✓	✓	✓	✓		✓	

State Laws Prohibiting Discrimination in Employment (continued)

State	Law applies to employers with	Private employers may not make employment decisions based on				
		Age (protected ages, if specified)	Ancestry or national origin	Disability	AIDS/HIV	
District of Columbia D.C. Code Ann. §§ 2-1401.01, 2-1401.02, 7-1703.03	One or more employees	✓ (18 and older)	✓	Physical or mental	✓	
Florida Fla. Stat. Ann. §§ 760.01, 760.02, 760.10, 760.50, 448.075	15 or more employees	✓	✓	"Handicap"	✓	
Georgia Ga. Code Ann. §§ 34-6A-1 and following, 34-5-1,34-5-2	15 or more employees (disability) 10 or more employees (gender)			Physical or mental		
Hawaii HI Const. Art. 1, § 3 Haw. Rev. Stat. §§ 378-1 and 2	One or more employees	✓	✓	Physical or mental	✓	
Idaho Idaho Code §§ 39-8303, 67-5902, 67-5909	5 or more employees	✓ (40 and older)	✓	Physical or mental		
Illinois 775 Ill. Comp. Stat. §§ 5/1-102, 5/1-103, 5/2-101 to 5/2-103, Ill. Admin. Code tit. 56, § 5210.110 775 ILCS 5/1-103	15 or more employees One or more employees (disability)	✓ (40 and older)	✓	Physical or mental	✓	

2 Wage discrimination only.

Gender	Marital status	Pregnancy, childbirth, and related medical conditions	Race or color	Religion or creed	Sexual orientation	Genetic testing information	Additional protected categories
✓	✓ (includes domestic partnership)	✓ Parenthood	✓	✓	✓	✓	• Enrollment in vocational, professional, or college education • Family duties • Source of income • Place of residence or business • Personal appearance • Political affiliation • Smoker • Gender identity or expression • Any reason other than individual merit
✓	✓		✓	✓			Sickle cell trait
✓[2]							
✓	✓	✓	✓	✓	✓	✓	Arrest and court record (unless there is a conviction directly related to job)
✓		✓	✓	✓		✓	
✓	✓	✓	✓	✓	✓	✓	• Citizen status • Military status • Unfavorable military discharge • Gender identity • Arrest record

		Private employers may not make employment decisions based on				
State	**Law applies to employers with**	**Age (protected ages, if specified)**	**Ancestry or national origin**	**Disability**	**AIDS/ HIV**	
Indiana *Ind. Code Ann. §§ 22-9-1-2, 22-9-3, 22-9-2-1, 22-9-2-2*	6 or more employees	✓ (40 to 70) (One or more employees)	✓	Physical or mental (15 or more employees)		
Iowa *Iowa Code §§ 216.2, 216.6, 729.6*	4 or more employees	✓ (18 or older)	✓	Physical or mental	✓	
Kansas *Kan. Stat. Ann. §§ 44-1002, 44-1009, 44-1112, 44-1113, 44-1125, 44-1126, 65-6002(e)*	4 or more employees	✓ (18 or older)	✓	Physical or mental	✓	
Kentucky *Ky. Rev. Stat. Ann. §§ 344.010, 344.030, 344.040, 207.130, 207.150, 342.197*	8 or more employees	✓ (40 or older)	✓	Physical or mental	✓	
Louisiana *La. Rev. Stat. Ann. §§ 23:301 to 23:352, 23:368*	20 or more employees	✓ (40 or older)	✓	Physical or mental		
Maine *Me. Rev. Stat. Ann. tit. 5, §§ 19302, 4552, 4553, 4571- 4576*	One or more employees	✓	✓	Physical or mental		
Maryland *Md. Code 1957 Art. 49B, §§ 15, 16, 17*	15 or more employees	✓	✓	Physical or mental		
Massachusetts *Mass. Gen. Laws ch. 149 § 24A, ch. 151B, §§ 1, 3A, 4*	6 or more employees	✓ (40 or older)	✓	Physical or mental	✓	

State Laws Prohibiting Discrimination in Employment (continued)

Gender	Marital status	Pregnancy, childbirth, and related medical conditions	Race or color	Religion or creed	Sexual orientation	Genetic testing information	Additional protected categories
✓			✓	✓			
✓		✓	✓	✓		✓	
✓			✓	✓		✓	Military status
✓			✓	✓			• Smoker or nonsmoker • Occupational pneumoconiosis with no respiratory impairment resulting from exposure to coal dust
	✓	✓ (Applies to employees with 25 or more employees)	✓	✓		✓	Sickle cell trait
✓		✓	✓	✓	✓	✓	• Gender identity or expression • Past workers' compensation claim • Past whistleblowing
✓	✓	✓	✓	✓	✓	✓	
✓	✓		✓	✓	✓	✓	• Military service • Arrests

		Private employers may not make employment decisions based on				
State	Law applies to employers with	Age (protected ages, if specified)	Ancestry or national origin	Disability	AIDS/HIV	
Michigan *Mich. Comp. Laws §§ 37.1201, 37.1202, 37.2201, 37.2202, 37.1103, 750.556*	One or more employees	✓	✓	Physical or mental	✓	
Minnesota *Minn. Stat. Ann. §§ 363A.03, 363A.08, 181.81, 181.974*	One or more employees	✓ (18 to 70)	✓	Physical or mental	✓	
Mississippi *Miss. Code Ann. § 33-1-15*						
Missouri *Mo. Rev. Stat. §§ 213.010, 213.055, 191.665, 375.1306*	6 or more employees	✓ (40 to 70)	✓	Physical or mental	✓	
Montana *Mont. Code Ann. §§ 49-2-101, 49-2-303, 49-2-310*	One or more employees	✓	✓	Physical or mental		
Nebraska *Neb. Rev. Stat. §§ 48-1101, 48-1102, 48-1001 to 48-1003, 20-168, 48-1111, 48-1104*	15 or more employees	✓ (40 to 70) (Applies to employers with 25 or more employees)	✓	Physical or mental	✓	
Nevada *Nev. Rev. Stat. Ann. §§ 613.310 and following*	15 or more employees	✓ (40 or older)	✓	Physical or mental		

The table title spans the top: **State Laws Prohibiting Discrimination in Employment (continued)**

Gender	Marital status	Pregnancy, childbirth, and related medical conditions	Race or color	Religion or creed	Sexual orientation	Genetic testing information	Additional protected categories
✓	✓	✓	✓	✓		✓	• Height or weight • Arrest record
✓	✓	✓	✓	✓	✓	✓	• Gender identity • Member of local commission • Perceived sexual orientation • Receiving public assistance
							• Military status (all employers) • No other protected categories unless employer receives public funding
✓		✓	✓	✓		✓	
✓	✓	✓	✓	✓			
✓	✓	✓	✓	✓		✓ All employers	
✓		✓	✓	✓	✓	✓	• Lawful use of any product when not at work • Use of service animal

		Private employers may not make employment decisions based on				
State	**Law applies to employers with**	**Age (protected ages, if specified)**	**Ancestry or national origin**	**Disability**	**AIDS/ HIV**	
New Hampshire N.H. Rev. Stat. Ann. §§ 354-A:2, 354-A:6, 354-A:7, 141-H:3	6 or more employees	✓	✓	Physical or mental		
New Jersey N.J. Stat. Ann. §§ 10:5-5 to 10:5-12, 10:5-29.1, 34:6B-1, 43:21-49	One or more employees	✓ (18 to 70)	✓	Past or present physical or mental	✓	
New Mexico N.M. Stat. Ann. §§ § 24-21-4, 28-1-2, 28-1-7	4 or more employees	✓ (40 or older) (Applies to employers with 20 or more employees)	✓	Physical or mental		
New York N.Y. Exec. Law §§ 292, 296; N.Y. Lab. Law § 201-d	4 or more employees	✓ (18 and over)	✓	Physical or mental	✓	
North Carolina N.C. Gen. Stat. §§ 143-422.2, 95-28.1, 127B-11, 130A-148, 168A-3, 168A-5	15 or more employees	✓	✓	Physical or mental	✓	
North Dakota N.D. Cent. Code §§ 14-02.4-02, 14-02.4-03, 34-01-17	One or more employees	✓ (40 or older)	✓	Physical or mental		

Title row: **State Laws Prohibiting Discrimination in Employment (continued)**

Gender	Marital status	Pregnancy, childbirth, and related medical conditions	Race or color	Religion or creed	Sexual orientation	Genetic testing information	Additional protected categories
✓	✓	✓	✓	✓	✓	✓	
✓	✓ (Includes domestic partner)	✓	✓	✓	✓	✓	• Predisposing genetic characteristics • Military service or status • Smoker or nonsmoker • Accompanied by service or guide dog • Gender identity (effective June 17, 2007)
✓	✓ (Applies to employees with 50 or more employees)	✓	✓	✓	✓³	✓	• Gender identity (employers with 15 or more employees) • Serious medical condition
✓	✓	✓	✓	✓	✓	✓	• Lawful use of any product when not at work • Military status • Observance of Sabbath • Political activities • Accompanied by service dog
✓			✓	✓		✓	• Lawful use of any product when not at work • Military service • Sickle cell trait
✓	✓	✓	✓	✓			• Lawful conduct outside of work • Receiving public assistance

State Laws Prohibiting Discrimination in Employment (continued)

State	Law applies to employers with	Private employers may not make employment decisions based on			
		Age (protected ages, if specified)	Ancestry or national origin	Disability	AIDS/ HIV
Ohio Ohio Rev. Code Ann. §§ 4111.17, 4112.01, 4112.02	4 or more employees	✓ (40 or older)	✓	Physical, mental, or learning	
Oklahoma Okla. Stat. Ann. tit. 25, §§ 1301, 1302; tit. 36, § 3614.2; tit. 40, § 500; tit. 44, § 208	15 or more employees	✓ (40 or older)	✓	Physical or mental	
Oregon Or. Rev. Stat. §§ 659A.001 and following, 659A.303	One or more employees	✓ (18 or older)	✓	Physical or mental (Applies to employers with 6 or more employees)	
Pennsylvania 43 Pa. Cons. Stat. Ann. §§ 954-955	4 or more employees	✓ (40 to 70)	✓	Physical or mental	
Rhode Island R.I. Gen. Laws §§ 28-6-18, 28-5-6, 28-5-7, 23-6-22, 12-28-10, 28-6.7-1	4 or more employees One or more employees (gender-based wage discrimination)	✓ (40 or older)	✓	Physical or mental	✓
South Carolina S.C. Code §§ 1-13-30, 1-13-80	15 or more employees	✓ (40 or older)	✓	Physical or mental	
South Dakota S.D. Codified Laws Ann. §§ 20-13-1, 20-13-10, 60-12-15, 60-2-20, 62-1-17	One or more employees		✓	Physical, mental, and learning	
Tennessee Tenn. Code Ann. §§ 4-21-102, 4-21-401 and following, 8-50-103, 50-2-201, 50-2-202	8 or more employees One or more employees (gender-based wage discrimination)	✓ (40 or older)	✓	Physical or mental	

[3] Employers with 15 or more employees.

Gender	Marital status	Pregnancy, childbirth, and related medical conditions	Race or color	Religion or creed	Sexual orientation	Genetic testing information	Additional protected categories
✓		✓	✓	✓			
✓			✓	✓		✓	• Military service • Smoker or nonsmoker
✓	✓	✓	✓	✓		✓	
✓		✓	✓	✓			• Familial status • GED rather than high school diploma • Use of guide or service animal
✓		✓	✓	✓	✓	✓	• Domestic abuse victim • Gender identity or expression
✓		✓	✓	✓			
✓			✓	✓		✓	Preexisting injury
✓			✓	✓			Refer to chart on Family and Medical Leave

State Laws Prohibiting Discrimination in Employment (continued)

State	Law applies to employers with	Private employers may not make employment decisions based on			
		Age (protected ages, if specified)	Ancestry or national origin	Disability	AIDS/ HIV
Texas *Tex. Lab. Code Ann. §§ 21.002, 21.052, 21.101, 21.402*	15 or more employees	✓ (40 or older)	✓	Physical or mental	
Utah *Utah Code Ann. §§ 26-45-103, 34A-5-102, 34A-5-106*	15 or more employees	✓ (40 or older)	✓	Follows federal law	✓
Vermont *Vt. Stat. Ann. tit. 21, § 495, 495d; tit. 18, § 9333*	One or more employees	✓ (18 or older)	✓	Physical or mental	✓
Virginia *Va. Code Ann. §§ 2.2-3900, 2.2-3901, 40.1-28.6, 40.1-28.7:1, 51.5-41*	Law applies to all employees	✓	✓	Physical or mental	
Washington *Wash. Rev. Code Ann. §§ 38.40.110, 49.60.040, 49.60.172, 49.60.180 to 210, 49.12.175, 49.44.090; Wash. Admin. Code § 162-30-020*	8 or more employees One or more employees (gender-based wage discrimination)	✓ (40 or older)	✓	Physical, mental, or sensory	✓
West Virginia *W.Va. Code §§ 5-11-3, 5-11-9, 21-5B-1, 21-5B-3, 21-3-19*	12 or more employees	✓ (40 or older)	✓	Physical or mental	✓
Wisconsin *Wis. Stat. Ann. §§ 111.32 and following*	One or more employees	✓ (40 or older)	✓	Physical or mental	✓
Wyoming *Wyo. Stat. §§ 27-9-102, 27-9-105, 19-11-104*	2 or more employees	✓ (40 or older)	✓	Not specified	

[4] Equal pay laws apply to employers with one or more employers

Gender	Marital status	Pregnancy, childbirth, and related medical conditions	Race or color	Religion or creed	Sexual orientation	Genetic testing information	Additional protected categories
✓		✓	✓	✓		✓	
✓		✓	✓	✓		✓	
✓			✓	✓	✓	✓	Place of birth
✓	✓	✓	✓	✓		✓	Use of a service animal
✓	✓	✓	✓	✓	✓	✓	• Hepatitis C infection • Member of state militia • Use of a trained guide dog • Gender identity
✓[4]			✓	✓			• Smoking away from work
✓	✓	✓	✓	✓	✓	✓	• Arrest or conviction • Lawful use of any product when not at work • Military service or status
✓			✓	✓			• Military service or status • Smoking off duty

Current as of February 2007

Filing a Title VII Lawsuit

While you file your discrimination claim with the EEOC, be aware that the agency pursues only a small fraction of the charges it receives. In the very likely event that the EEOC does not act on your complaint within 180 days, you then have the right to request a right-to-sue letter that authorizes you to file a lawsuit in federal court against the offending employer. This type of lawsuit is complex and, in cases involving an employee dismissal, is often packaged with other claims. You will probably need to hire a lawyer to help you file a lawsuit under Title VII. (See Chapter 17, "Hiring a Lawyer.") A number of specialized organizations offer legal referrals and advice on workplace discrimination. (See the Appendix for contact details.)

Once you receive a right-to-sue letter, you have only 90 days to file a lawsuit, so deadlines are very important at this point of the Title VII process. The EEOC has the right to file a lawsuit on your behalf, but do not expect that to happen unless your case has a very high political or publicity value—a very small percentage of the claims filed. The EEOC's out-of-pocket expenses are limited by law to $5,000 per lawsuit—many thousands of dollars less than it typically costs to take an employment discrimination case to court.

Class Actions

For some employees, the most likely way to succeed in a Title VII case is to become part of a class action lawsuit. The courts allow lawsuits to be pursued as class actions when a number of people have been injured by the same unlawful act. Because the potential damages from a Title VII class action lawsuit are much larger than in an individual lawsuit, some attorneys will take those cases on a contingency basis—which means that their fees will not be paid up front but will be taken as a percentage of the total amount recovered. (See Chapter 17, "Class Action Lawsuits.") The rest will then be divided among those certified as class members.

State and Local Laws

In general, employment-related lawsuits filed under state or local laws are easier to win than those filed under Title VII. And, unlike most Title VII cases, state and local antidiscrimination laws often offer the possibility of a larger judgment in favor of the worker who files the lawsuit.

State and Local Anti-Discrimination Laws

Nearly all state and local laws prohibiting various types of discrimination in employment echo the federal antidiscrimination law in that they outlaw discrimination based on race, color, gender, age, national origin, and religion. But the state and local laws tend to go into more detail, creating categories of protection against discrimination that are not covered by federal law.

In Florida, Louisiana, and North Carolina, for example, it is illegal to discriminate in employment matters on the basis of a worker's sickle cell trait. In Minnesota, it is illegal to discriminate against people who

BFOQs: Jobs That Require Discrimination

Under Title VII and many state and local antidiscrimination laws, an employer may intentionally use gender, religious beliefs, or national origin as the basis for employment decisions only if the employer can show that the job has special requirements that make such discrimination necessary.

When an employer establishes that such a special circumstance exists, it is called a bona fide occupational qualification (BFOQ).

EXAMPLE: A religious denomination that employs counselors who answer telephone inquiries from those interested in becoming members of that religion would typically be allowed to limit its hiring of counselors to people who believe in that religion. Being a member of that denomination would be a BFOQ.

In general, the courts, the EEOC, and state equal employment opportunity agencies prohibit the use of BFOQs except where clearly necessary. They typically require any employer using a BFOQ in employment decisions to prove conclusively that the BFOQ is essential to the successful operation of the company or organization. Typically, this type of permissible discrimination turns on gender. The classic example is the job of a wet nurse, who must be female. But theaters, cosmetic companies, and modeling agencies have also succeeded in arguing that workers hired needed to be of a particular gender to get the job done.

You are most likely to encounter a BFOQ on a job application, in which case the employer must state on the application that the employment qualification covered by the questions would otherwise be illegal but has been approved by the EEOC.

are collecting public assistance. California's anitdiscrimination measures apply to independent contracts as well as employees. And in Michigan, employees cannot be discriminated against because of their heights or weights.

Many state antidiscrimination laws also provide faster and more effective procedures for pursuing complaints about illegal workplace discrimination than the EEOC process.

State laws prohibiting discrimination in employment are listed in the chart above. Agencies responsible for antidiscrimination laws in those states are listed in the chart below. You can research municipal antidiscrimination laws at the headquarters of your community's government, such as your local city hall or county courthouse.

How to Take Action

If you wish to consider filing a complaint under your state's employment discrimination laws, you must first find out if your state has an agency empowered to process such a complaint. (The chart below provides this information.) There are several states that

Keeping the Faith at Work

In the last few years, there has been a notable increase in the number of religious discrimination lawsuits. In 2006, the EEOC received 2,541 such claims—the highest number ever tallied. Theologians hail this burst in litigation as a sign that Americans are returning to the fold. Pessimists say that workers are just looking for another excuse to work less. And politicians point to politics.

Title VII of the Civil Rights Act and most state laws prohibit employers from discriminating on the basis of religious beliefs. Where workers articulate a need to express their religious beliefs and practice in the workplace, employers are generally required to accommodate them—unless doing so would cause the employer undue hardship.

As in all other claims where the term comes up, the meaning of undue hardship in this context gives employers and courts cause for pause. The U.S. Supreme Court has pronounced twice on the issue.

In *Trans World Airlines Inc. v. Hardison* (432 U.S. 135 (1977), an airline employee claimed that his religion, the Worldwide Church of God, forbade him from working on Saturdays. In subsequent meetings, TWA union officials argued that allowing the employee to change shifts would violate a collective bargaining agreement that banned the arrangement for workers without sufficient seniority. The Court agreed, holding that the union agreement was more sacrosanct than the religious practices.

Nearly a decade later, the Court again heard the pleas of a member of the Worldwide Church of God—this time arguing that he needed six days off per school year for religious observance. The sticking point again was a collective bargaining agreement providing only three days of paid leave for religious observation. The Court waffled some in its opinion, holding that the court below could decide whether providing unpaid leave to make up the balance was a reasonable accommodation. (*Ansonia Board of Education v. Philbrook*, 479 U.S. 60 (1979).)

Since then, the lower courts that have faced the issue have reached grandly differing conclusions about what is an undue burden for employers. A Florida police officer's request for Saturdays off was denied "for public safety reasons." A Tennessee jury denied a number of Muslim factory workers' request to take a break for sunset prayers—when that would mean temporarily shutting down a production line. But a New Mexico court ruled that a truck driver was illegally denied a job because of his practice of smoking peyote during a Native American ritual. And a California court shot down an employer's order that banned religious artifacts in all workers' cubicles and prevented them from any type of "religious advocacy" on the job.

For now, employers and employees grappling with the issue would be best served to work together to reach an accommodation—and keep the issue out of the uncharted territory of court decisions.

have discrimination laws but no state agency to enforce them. In these states, you must rely on the federal law or a private lawsuit to enforce your rights.

Time Limits for Filing

Ordinarily, a charge with the EEOC must be filed within 180 days of the date of the action about which you are complaining. State laws have their own separate time limits. And, if your state has an agency that enforces its own age discrimination law, you must file your EEOC complaint within 30 days after you receive notice that the state is no longer pursuing your case, even if the normal 180-day period is not up.

These time limits are counted from the date you get notice from your employer or union of the action that you think is discriminatory—a demotion, layoff, forced retirement. If there is no specific date you can pinpoint, file your charge as soon as you have gathered enough information to convince yourself that you have been subjected to discrimination.

State Laws and Enforcing Agencies

See the chart, "State Laws Prohibiting Discrimination in Employment," below, for a synopsis of factors that may not be used as the basis for employment discrimination under state laws. Keep in mind that it is only a synopsis, and that each state has its own way of determining such factors as what conditions qualify as a physical disability. Many state antidiscrimination laws apply only to employers with a minimum number of employees, such as five or more.

You can find your state's enforcement agency in the chart "State Agencies That Enforce Laws Prohibiting Discrimination in Employment," below. In states where no special agency has been designated to enforce antidiscrimination laws, your state's labor department or attorney general's office or the closest office of the federal Equal Employment Opportunity Commission should direct you to the right agency or person with whom to file a complaint over illegal discrimination in employment.

In certain states or circumstances, you may have no way to pursue your complaint over illegal discrimination other than to file a lawsuit or to hire an attorney to file one for you. (See Chapter 17, "Hiring a Lawyer.")

State Agencies That Enforce Laws Prohibiting Discrimination in Employment

Alabama
EEOC District Office
Birmingham, AL
205-212-2100
800-669-4000
www.eeoc.gov/birmingham/
index.html

Alaska
Commission for Human Rights
Anchorage, AK
907-274-4692
800-478-4692
http://gov.state.ak.us/aschr

Arizona
Civil Rights Division
Phoenix, AZ
602-542-5263
877-491-5742
www.azag.gov/civil_rights/index.
html

Arkansas
Equal Employment Opportunity
Commission
Little Rock, AR
501-324-5060
www.eeoc.gov/littlerock/index.
html

California
Department of Fair Employment
and Housing
Sacramento District Office
Sacramento, CA
916-445-5523
800-884-1684
www.dfeh.ca.gov

Colorado
Civil Rights Division
Denver, CO
303-894-2997
800-262-4845
www.dora.state.co.us/Civil-Rights

Connecticut
Commission on Human Rights
and Opportunities
Hartford, CT
860-541-3400
800-477-5737
www.state.ct.us/chro

Delaware
Office of Labor Law Enforcement
Division of Industrial Affairs
Wilmington, DE
302-761-8200
www.delawareworks.com/
industrialaffairs/welcome.shtml

District of Columbia
Office of Human Rights
Washington, DC
202-727-4559
http://ohr.dc.gov/ohr/site/default.
asp

Florida
Commission on Human Relations
Tallahassee, FL
850-488-7082
http://fchr.state.fl.us

Georgia
Atlanta District Office
U.S. Equal Employment
Opportunity Commission
Atlanta, GA
404-562-6800

800-669-4000
www.eeoc.gov/atlanta/index.html

Hawaii
Hawai'i Civil Rights Commission
Honolulu, HI
808-586-8636
www.hawaii.gov/labor/hcrc/

Idaho
Idaho Commission on Human
Rights
Boise, ID
208-334-2873
www2.state.id.us/ihrc

Illinois
Department of Human Rights
Chicago, IL
312-814-6200
www.state.il.us/dhr

Indiana
Civil Rights Commission
Indianapolis, IN
317-232-2600
800-628-2909
www.in.gov/icrc

Iowa
Iowa Civil Rights Commission
Des Moines, IA
515-281-4121
800-457-4416
www.state.ia.us/government/crc

Kansas
Human Rights Commission
Topeka, KS
785-296-3206
www.khrc.net

State Agencies That Enforce Laws Prohibiting Discrimination in Employment (cont'd)

Kentucky
Human Rights Commission
Louisville, KY
502-595-4024
800-292-5566
www.kchr.ky.gov

Louisiana
Commission on Human Rights
Baton Rouge, LA
225-342-6969
www.gov.state.la.us/HumanRights/
humanrightshome.htm

Maine
Human Rights Commission
Augusta, ME
207-624-6050
www.maine.gov/mhrc

Maryland
Commission on Human Relations
Baltimore, MD
410-767-8600
www.mchr.state.md.us

Massachusetts
Commission Against
Discrimination
Boston, MA
617-994-6000
www.state.ma.us/mcad

Michigan
Department of Civil Rights
Detroit, MI
313-456-3700
www.michigan.gov/mdcr

Minnesota
Department of Human Rights
St. Paul, MN
651-296-5663
www.humanrights.state.mn.us

Mississippi
Department of Employment
Security
Jackson, MS
601-321-6000
www.mdes.ms.gov

Missouri
Commission on Human Rights
Jefferson City, MO
573-751-3325
www.dolir.state.mo.us/hr

Montana
Human Rights Bureau
Employment Relations Division
Department of Labor and
Industry
Helena, MT
406-444-2884
800-542-0807
http://erd.dli.state.mt.us/
HumanRight/HRhome.asp

Nebraska
Equal Opportunity Commission
Lincoln, NE
402-471-2024
800-642-6112
www.neoc.ne.gov

Nevada
Equal Rights Commission
Reno, NV
775-688-1288
http://detr.state.nv.us/nerc/NERC_
index.htm

New Hampshire
Commission for Human Rights
Concord, NH
603-271-2767
www.nh.gov/hrc

New Jersey
Division on Civil Rights
Newark, NJ
973-648-2700
www.state.nj.us/lps/dcr

New Mexico
Human Rights Division
Santa Fe, NM
505-827-6838
800-566-9471
www.dol.state.nm.us/dol_hrd.
html

New York
Division of Human Rights
Bronx, NY
718-741-8400
www.dhr.state.ny.us

North Carolina
Employment Discrimination
Bureau
Department of Labor
Raleigh, NC
919-807-2796
800-NC-LABOR
www.nclabor.com/edb/edb.htm

North Dakota
Human Rights Division
Department of Labor
Bismarck, ND
701-328-2660
800-582-8032
www.nd.gov/labor

State Agencies That Enforce Laws Prohibiting Discrimination in Employment (cont'd)

Ohio
Civil Rights Commission
Columbus, OH
614-466-5928
888-278-7101
www.crc.ohio.gov

Oklahoma
Human Rights Commission
Oklahoma City, OK
405-521-2360
www.hrc.state.ok.us

Oregon
Civil Rights Division
Bureau of Labor and Industries
Portland, OR
971-673-0761
www.oregon.gov/BOLI/CRD

Pennsylvania
Human Relations Commission
Harrisburg, PA
717-787-4410
www.phrc.state.pa.us

Rhode Island
Commission for Human Rights
Providence, RI
401-222-2661
www.richr.state.ri.us/frames.html

South Carolina
Human Affairs Commission
Columbia, SC
803-737-7800
800-521-0725
www.state.sc.us/schac

South Dakota
Division of Human Rights
Pierre, SD
605-773-4493
www.state.sd.us/dol/boards/hr

Tennessee
Human Rights Commission
Knoxville, TN
865-594-6500
www.tennessee.gov/humanrights

Texas
Commission on Human Rights
Austin, TX
512-463-2642
www.twc.state.tx.us

Utah
Anti-Discrimination and Labor
   Division
Labor Commission
Salt Lake City, UT
801-530-6801
800-222-1238
http://laborcommission.utah.gov/
   Utah_Antidiscrimination_Labo/
   utah_antidiscrimination_labo.
   htm

Vermont
Attorney General's Office
Civil Rights Division
Montpelier, VT
802-828-3657
www.atg.state.vt.us

Virginia
Council on Human Rights
Richmond, VA
804-225-2292
http://chr.vipnet.org

Washington
Human Rights Commission
Seattle, WA
206-464-6500
800-233-3247
www.hum.wa.gov

West Virginia
Human Rights Commission
Charleston, WV
304-558-2616
888-676-5546
www.wvf.state.wv.us/wvhrc

Wisconsin
Equal Rights Division
Madison, WI
608-266-6860
www.dwd.state.wi.us/er

Wyoming
Department of Employment
Cheyenne, WY
307-777-7261
http://wydoe.state.wy.us

Current as of February 2007

The Equal Pay Act

A federal law, the Equal Pay Act (29 U.S.C. § 206), requires employers to pay all employees equally for equal work, regardless of their gender. It was passed in 1963 as an amendment to the Fair Labor Standards Act. (See Chapter 2, "Rights Under the FLSA.")

While the Act technically protects both women and men from gender discrimination in pay rates, it was passed to help rectify the problems faced by women workers because of sex discrimination in employment. And, in practice, this law almost always has been applied to situations where women are being paid less than men for doing similar jobs.

The wage gap has narrowed slowly since 1980, when women's weekly earnings were only 64% of men's; the 2005 figure had women earning about 77%. But the Equal Pay Act likely had little to do with either the advances or setbacks. The law's biggest weakness is that it is strictly applied only when men and women are doing the same work. Since women have historically been banned from many types of work and have had only limited entree to managerial positions, the Equal Pay Act in reality helps very few women.

To successfully raise a claim under the Equal Pay Act, you must show that two employees, one male and one female:

- are working in the same place
- are doing equal work, and
- are receiving unequal pay.

You must also show that the employees in those jobs received unequal pay because of their genders.

Who Is Covered

The Equal Pay Act applies to all employees covered by the Fair Labor Standards Act, which means virtually all employees are covered. (See Chapter 2, "The Fair Labor Standards Act.") But, in addition, the Equal Pay Act covers professional employees, executives, and managers—including administrators and teachers in elementary and secondary schools.

Concerned About Equal Pay—For Good Reason

According to a recent nationwide survey by the AFL-CIO, money is foremost in the minds of America's working women. Asked to cite their top workplace concerns, about 94% of the women polled rated equal pay for equal work; 33% noted child care; 78% cited sexual harassment; 72% mentioned downsizing.

The math supports the mindset. On average, according to the National Committee on Pay Equity, women earn $31,858 annually—much less than men's $41,386 yearly average.

Determining Equal Work

Jobs do not have to be identical for the courts to consider them equal. In general, the courts have ruled that two jobs are equal for the purposes of the Equal Pay Act when both require equal levels of skill, effort, and responsibility and are performed under similar conditions.

Equal Pay Versus Comparable Worth

The Equal Pay Act covers only situations where men and women are performing jobs that require equal skill, effort, and responsibility and are performed under similar circumstances. Often, however, men and women are doing different jobs at different pay rates, despite the fact that the value of their work to the employer is equal. Disputes over this type of situation are typically lumped under the term comparable worth.

When Congress passed the Equal Pay Act, legislators squirmed to choose their words carefully. Representative Goodell (R-NY), one of the Act's sponsors, explained: "We went from 'comparable' to 'equal,' meaning that the jobs should be virtually identical—that is, that they would be very much alike or closely related to each other."

A comparable worth case typically is not covered by the Equal Pay Act. Because they are broader in scope, Title VII or the state antidiscrimination laws (discussed above) are better routes to use for pursuing comparable worth complaints.

There is a lot of room for interpretation here, of course. But the general rule is that, if there are only small differences in the skill, effort, or responsibility required, two jobs should still be regarded as equal. The focus is on the duties actually performed. Job titles, classifications, and descriptions may weigh in to the determination but are not all that is considered.

The biggest problems arise where two jobs are basically the same, but one includes a few extra duties. It is perfectly legal to award higher pay for the extra duties, but some courts have looked askance at workplaces in which the higher-paying jobs with extra duties are consistently reserved for workers of one gender.

Determining Equal Pay

In general, pay systems that result in employees of one gender being paid less than the other gender for doing equal work are allowed under the Equal Pay Act if the pay system is actually based on a factor other than gender, such as a merit or seniority system.

EXAMPLE: In 1990, the Ace Widget Company was founded and initially hired 50 male widget makers. Many of those men are still working there. Since its founding, the company has expanded and hired 50 more widget makers, half of them female. All of the widget makers at Ace are doing equal work, but because the company awards raises systematically based on seniority or length of employment, many of the older male workers earn substantially more per hour than their female coworkers. Nevertheless, the pay system at Ace Widget does not violate the Equal Pay Act because its pay differences between genders doing equal work are based on a factor other than gender.

Top 10 Reasons for the Wage Gap

Not nearly as funny as a Letterman Show opener—but here they are.

Reason 1: Wage Secrecy Hurts Women

Wage data are largely kept secret in America, so women and minorities can be underpaid without knowing it. Employers frequently have policies that forbid workers from discussing their salaries, even though these policies are unfair and sometimes unlawful. Yet corporate cultures continue to intimidate workers by making it taboo to discuss salary, even among trusted coworkers. And, because a woman often doesn't know what a job truly pays, she can undervalue herself when negotiating a new salary—and that can label her as an underachiever. So not knowing about wage discrepancies can perpetuate them.

Reason 2: Suing Is Not Always Practical

Taking an employer to court under the Equal Pay Act, Title VII of the Civil Rights Act, or appropriate state laws is an option out of reach for many women. Because awards are severely limited in Equal Pay Act cases, there is a lack of incentive for attorneys to accept cases. In addition, pursuing an equal pay case can wreak havoc on the personal lives and finances of the plaintiffs. Employers often fight back aggressively and ruin an employee's credibility as they seek to defend the company.

Reason 3: When You Stay Home More,
You Take Home Less

Given their lower earnings, women are usually the parent who takes time off to raise small children.

That means they are out of the workforce for a few years, which lowers their earnings when they return.

Reason 4: Women's Job Pay Less

Sometimes the jobs dominated by women in a company are not valued in the same way that men's jobs are. Studies have shown that the more women and people of color fill an occupation, the less it pays. Using a point factor job evaluation system, the state of Minnesota recently found that the "women's jobs" paid 20% less on average than male-dominated jobs, even when their jobs scored equally on the job evaluation system.

Reason 5: Market Forces Are Not
Eliminating Discrimination

Some say market forces will eliminate salary inequities, yet it has been several decades since the Equal Pay Act and the Civil Rights Act were signed into law. Still, discrimination exists. If we had relied on market forces to implement fairness, we never would have needed the Civil Rights Act, the Family and Medical Leave Act, or the Americans With Disabilities Act. Market forces do not overcome bias in the workplace. Bigoted employers will pay more to work with white people, for example.

Reason 6: Discrimination Is
Intangible, But It Exists

Discrimination is almost never found in the form of a smoking gun. Instead, it takes a more subtle yet pervasive form. For example, in the recent class action sex discrimination suit filed against

Top 10 Reasons for the Wage Gap (continued)

Merrill Lynch, female employees complained that the accounts of retiring employees, walk-ins, and other lucrative networking opportunities were steered toward the men in the company. Another typical concern is that women are not offered career-shaping assignments or spots on important committees. When women have trouble advancing in a company, they can't gain the experience needed to lead.

Reason 7: Old Stereotypes Die Hard

Women are not working for pin money. They are supporting America's families. As one plaintiff recounted, a manager told her, "You don't need pay equity, you're married." There are also stereotypes about what kind of work is appropriate for women that hinder women's advancement in some fields currently dominated by men.

Reason 8: Not All Jobs Are Open to Women

Over half of all women are concentrated in the broad categories of sales, clerical, and service jobs. Women can have a hard time breaking into the male-dominated jobs, as evidenced through Department of Labor audits of federal contractors. When women do break into male-dominated jobs, sometimes they experience hostile work environments and find little support for their presence there.

Reason 9: Companies Aren't Addressing the Problem

Why won't employers address the issue on their own? Perhaps they are worried about future liability. Part of it may be psychological—many employers don't want to believe they are discriminating or that they have tolerated discrimination. Private sector compensation experts can help to develop a fair pay system that is phased in over time. A written pay policy will show workers that the system is based on objective criteria.

Reason 10: Current Laws Are Not Strong Enough

Put simply, current laws prohibiting wage discrimination need to be strengthened. The Equal Pay Act and Title VII of the Civil Rights Act are important laws, but they are hard to enforce, and legal cases are extremely difficult to prove and win. Because enforcement of the laws is complaint-driven and most of the information needed to prove a complaint is held by employers, these laws lack the ability to completely rid America of discriminatory pay practices.

Adapted from: National Committee on Pay Equity, www.pay-equity.org

How to Take Action

The Equal Pay Act (EPA) was passed one year before Title VII of the Civil Rights Act. Both laws prohibit wage discrimination based on gender, but Title VII goes beyond ensuring equal pay for equal work, as it also bars discrimination in hiring, firing, and promotions. In addition, Title VII broadly prohibits other forms of discrimination, including that based on race, color, religion, and national origin. (See "Title VII of the Civil Rights Act, above, for a detailed discussion of how to take action.)

> **EXAMPLE:** Suzanne works as a reservations agent for an airline, answering calls on the company's toll-free telephone number. About half of the other reservations agents in her office are men, who are typically paid $1 per hour more than Suzanne and the other female agents. What's more, the company has established a dress code for female reservations agents, but not for the male agents.
>
> If Suzanne decides to file a discrimination complaint against her employer, the EPA would apply to the pay difference between females and males. Title VII would apply to both the pay difference and the fact that only the female employees in her office are held to a dress code.

In cases where both Title VII and the Equal Pay Act apply, the EPA offers one big advantage: You can file a lawsuit under the EPA without first filing a complaint with the EEOC.

To Get a Bad Job, Get a Good Education

A recent national study concluded that while women have made remarkable strides in education during the past three decades, these gains have yet to translate into full equity in pay—even for college-educated women who work full time. A typical college-educated woman working full time earns $44,200 a year, compared to $61,800 for college-educated male workers—a difference of $17,600.

The top five—those with the smallest gender gap in pay were:

1. Nevada
2. District of Columbia
3. Hawaii
4. New York
5. Alaska

And the five bringing up the rear with the largest gender gap were:

48. Utah
49. Oklahoma
50. South Carolina
51. Mississippi
52. Puerto Rico

Source: "Women's Educational Gains and the Gender Earnings Gap," by the American Association of University Women, 2005

There is also a longer statute of limitations for claims under the EPA, which means that you have a longer period of time after you were mistreated to file a claim—two years for unpaid damages or three years for a willful violation—as opposed to Title VII's requirement that you file anywhere from a few months to a year after you were wronged.

However, you also stand to gain less in an EPA claim. Damages are limited to back pay—and an additional sum equal to your back pay award for willful violations—plus attorneys' fees and court costs. You are entitled to no additional damages as compensation or to punish the wrongdoing employer.

The Age Discrimination in Employment Act

The federal Age Discrimination in Employ-ment Act, or ADEA (29 U.S.C. §§ 621 to 634), is the single most important law protecting the rights of older workers. Basically, it pro-vides that workers over the age of 40 cannot be arbitrarily discriminated against because of age in any employment decision. Perhaps the single most important rule under the ADEA is that no worker can be forced to retire.

The Act also prohibits age discrimination in hiring, discharges, layoffs, promotion, wages, health care coverage, pension accrual, other terms and conditions of employment, referrals by employment agencies, and membership in and the activities of unions. It requires that there must be a valid reason not related to age —for example, economic reasons or poor job performance—for all employment decisions, but especially firing.

Of all the possible claims of workplace discrimination, age discrimination has the broadest potential reach; most workers will live to be over 40. And the protection is likely to become even more important. We live in a time where the life expectancy is increasing, the older population is expanding rapidly, and many older workers stay in the workforce for a long time—a growing number of them past age 70.

Generally, to win a claim under the ADEA, you must be able to prove all of the following:

- You are 40 years old or older.
- You have been discharged, demoted, or denied a benefit.
- When you were discharged or demoted, you were performing your job in a way that met your employer's legitimate expectations.

Some courts used to require that you also prove that after you were discharged or demoted, your position was filled by someone younger than 40 years. Ohio now seems to stand alone in adhering to this standard. (*Pichy v. Medical Mut. of Ohio*, 2000 Ohio App. Lexis 5118.) The U.S. Supreme Court, setting the current standard for all other states, recently held that you need not be replaced by a whippersnapper to make your case. In one of the briefest opinions on record, the Court held that what is important is that a worker is discriminated against because of age; who takes over the job is irrelevant. The Court held that "there can be no greater inference of age discrimination when a 40-year-old is replaced by a 39-year-old than when a 56-year-old is replaced by a 40-year-old." (*O'Connor v. Consolidated Coin Caterers Corp.*, 517 U.S. 308 (1996).)

An amendment to the ADEA, the Older Workers Benefit Protection Act, discussed below, sets out specifics of how and when ADEA protections can be waived.

The End of Mandatory Retirement

No one fought so hard or did so much to shape the law for the poor and the elderly as Claude Pepper, the Democratic Congressman from Florida. He promoted, and many say created, legal rights for the elderly—backing legislation to fight crime in housing projects for the elderly, to cut Amtrak fares for senior citizens, and to provide meals for home-bound older Americans. He was also widely recognized as the primary congressional advocate of Social Security and Medicare.

Elected to the House of Representatives for 14 terms, Pepper was appointed chair of the Select Committee on Aging in 1977. In that role, he orchestrated dramatic parades of witnesses to testify about the plight of the aging elderly, some of them wheeled in on hospital beds and hooked to oxygen tanks.

But the legislative reform of which Pepper was proudest was the 1978 bill abolishing the federally mandatory retirement age of 65. True to form, Pepper packed the congressional hearing room when the bill was being debated. This time, he filled it with vibrant and able-bodied septuagenarians—politicians, actors, and businesspeople, including Colonel Harlin Sanders, the fried chicken magnate. That bill did away with the mandatory retirement limit for federal government workers; the retirement age for nonfederal employees was raised from 65 to 70 years.

Pepper died on May 30, 1989. He was 88 years old. On September 7, 2000, the U.S. Postal Service honored the congressman by issuing a stamp bearing his likeness.

The ADEA is enforced, along with other discrimination complaints, by the EEOC. (See "Title VII of the Civil Rights Act," above, for more on procedure.) A number of national organizations will also provide legal referrals and help in evaluating age discrimination complaints. (See the Appendix for contact information.)

Who Is Covered

The ADEA applies to employees age 40 and older—and to workplaces with 20 or more employees. Unlike several other federal workplace laws, the ADEA covers employees of labor organizations and local and federal governments. State workers are protected by the law but are limited to having the EEOC act to enforce it on their behalf.

There are a number of exceptions to the broad protection of the ADEA in addition to workers employed by companies which have fewer than 20 employees.

- Executives or people "in high policy-making positions" can be forced to retire at age 65 if they would receive annual retirement pension benefits worth $44,000 or more.
- There are special exceptions for police and fire personnel, tenured university faculty, and certain federal employees having to do with law enforcement and air traffic control. If you are in one of these categories, check with your personnel office or benefits plan office for details.
- The biggest exception to the federal age discrimination law is made when

age is an essential part of a particular job—referred to by the legal term of bona fide occupational qualification (BFOQ). An employer that sets age limits on a particular job must be able to prove the limit is necessary because a worker's ability to adequately perform that job does in fact diminish after the age limit is reached.

State Laws

Most states have laws banning age discrimination in employment. (See the chart, "State Laws Prohibiting Discrimination in Employment," above.) An individual working in a state with such a law can choose to file a complaint under either state law or the federal law (ADEA), or both.

In many cases, the state law can provide greater protection than the federal law. For example, several states provide age discrimination protection to workers before they reach age 40, and other states' laws apply to employers with fewer than 20 employees. Even if the protection offered by your state law is the same as that provided by the federal law, you may get better results pursuing your rights under state law. A state agency entrusted with investigating and enforcing its own age discrimination law may provide easier, quicker, and more aggressive prosecution of your complaint than the overburdened Equal Employment Opportunity Commission does in enforcing the ADEA. (See "State and Local Anitdiscrimination Laws," above, for specific information on how to enforce your rights under state law.)

The Older Workers Benefit Protection Act

The main purpose of the Older Workers Benefit Protection Act (29 U.S.C. §§ 623, 626, and 630), passed in 1990, is to make it clearly illegal:

- to use an employee's age as the basis for discrimination in benefits, and
- for companies to target older workers for their staff-cutting programs.

Most of the effects of this law are very difficult for anyone but a benefits administrator who is immersed in the lingo to understand. However, one provision of the law that you are most likely to run into—regulating the legal waivers that employers are increasingly asking employees to sign in connection with so-called early retirement programs—is relatively clear and specific.

By signing a waiver—often called a release or covenant not to sue—an employee agrees not to take any legal action, such as an age discrimination lawsuit, against the employer. In return for signing the waiver, the employer gives the employee an incentive to leave voluntarily, such as a severance pay package that exceeds the company's standard policy.

This type of transaction was very popular in the early 1990s among large corporations that wanted to reduce their payroll costs. Because older workers who have been with a company a long time typically cost more in salary and benefits than younger workers, most staff-cutting programs were directed at older workers. But cutting only older workers constitutes illegal age discrimination, so companies commonly induced the older workers to sign away their rights to sue their former employers. In colloquial parlance, these deals are often referred to as Golden Handshakes—as in Thank-You-Very-Much-for-Your-Hard-Years-of-Service-and-If-You-Retire-Right-Now-This-Grand-Bunch-of-Benefits-Will-Be-Yours. This cruel squeeze play is now somewhat limited.

Under the Older Workers Benefit Protection Act, you must be given at least 21 days to decide whether or not to sign such a waiver that has been presented to you individually. If the waiver is presented to a group of employees, each of you must be given at least 45 days to decide whether or not to sign. In either case, you have seven days after agreeing to such a waiver to revoke your decision.

Who Is Covered

The Older Workers Benefit Protection Act applies to nonunion employees in private industry who are at least 40 years old.

Restrictions on Agreements Not to Sue

There are a number of other key restrictions the Older Workers Benefit Protection Act places on agreements not to sue.

- Your employer must make the waiver understandable to the average individual eligible for the program in which the waiver is being used.
- The waiver may not cover any rights or claims that you discover are available after you sign it, and it must specify that it covers your rights under the ADEA.

- Your employer must offer you something of value—over and above what is already owed to you—in exchange for your signature on the waiver.
- Your employer must advise you, in writing, that you have the right to consult an attorney before you sign the waiver.
- If the offer is being made to a class of employees (as part of an early retirement incentive program, for example), your employer must inform you in writing how the class of employees is defined, the job titles and ages of all the individuals to whom the offer is being made, and the ages of all the employees in the same job classification or unit of the company to whom the offer is not being made.
- You must be given a reasonable time in which to make a decision on whether or not to sign the waiver.

Employers are allowed no room to hedge on any one of these requirements—and a waiver that does not comply with all the absolute requirements is the same as no waiver at all. The U.S. Supreme Court reaffirmed this in a case decision—and pointedly held that an employee who signed a deficient waiver could not only sue for age discrimination, but also did not have to return the severance pay she received from her former employer for signing the invalid waiver. *(Oubre v. Entergy Operations, Inc.,* 522 U.S. 422 (1998).)

Negotiating a Better Deal

The Older Workers Benefits Protection Act gives additional legal protections if your employer offers you the opportunity to participate in a staff reduction program. The Act indirectly puts you in a position to negotiate the terms of your departure.

The fact that your employer has offered an incentive tells you that the company wants you gone and is worried that you might file a lawsuit for wrongful discharge. (See Chapter 9, "When a Firing May Be Illegal.") Although company heads may say that you have only two choices—accept or reject the offer—there is nothing preventing you from making a counteroffer.

For example, after taking a week or two to think, you might go back to your employer and agree to leave voluntarily if your severance pay is doubled. There is power in numbers, so this type of negotiating is even more likely to be effective if done on behalf of a group of employees who are considering the same offer.

As in all employment transactions, it is wise to advise your employer of your decision in writing and to keep a copy of that letter—along with copies of all documents given to you by your employer as part of the staff reduction program. If you refuse to accept such an offer and are later dismissed, you may be able to allege illegal age discrimination as a basis for challenging your dismissal.

How to Take Action

If you believe that an employer has violated your rights under the Older Workers Benefit Protection Act, you can file a complaint with the EEOC just as you would against any other

workplace discrimination prohibited by Title VII, discussed above. Note, however, that money damages are limited to back pay—and an additional sum equal to your back pay award for willful violations—plus attorneys' fees and court costs.

If the EEOC does not resolve your complaint to your satisfaction, you may decide to pursue your complaint through a lawsuit. (See "Filing a Title VII Lawsuit," above.) This additional avenue is not available for state workers, however, who are constrained to having the EEOC enforce the OWBPA for them.

The Americans With Disabilities Act

The Americans With Disabilities Act, or ADA (42 U.S. Code §§ 12102 and following), prohibits employment discrimination on the basis of workers' disabilities. While debated, haggled over, and honed by both employees and employers before it was passed, the law is not a panacea for either group. It is widely criticized as poorly drafted.

Generally, the ADA prohibits employers from:

- discriminating on the basis of any physical or mental disability
- asking job applicants questions about their past or current medical conditions
- requiring job applicants to take pre-employment medical exams, and
- creating or maintaining worksites that include substantial physical barriers to the movement of people with physical handicaps.

The Act requires that an employer must make reasonable accommodations for qualified individuals with disabilities, unless that would cause the employer undue hardship. But those dictates are frustrating. It is unclear what disabilities qualify individuals for coverage under the law. (See "Definition of Disabled," below.) And the meanings of "qualified workers," "reasonable accommodations," and "undue hardship" remain elusive. (See "Who Is Covered" and "Accommodations by Employers," below.)

A precursor of the ADA, the Vocational Rehabilitation Act (29 U.S.C. § 794), prohibits discrimination against handicapped workers in state and federal government. Its narrow protections are generally usurped by the more extensive ADA.

Who Is Covered

The ADA covers employers with 15 or more employees. Its coverage broadly extends to private companies, employment agencies, labor organizations, and state and local governments. State workers, while covered by the Act, cannot sue on their own behalf; they must rely on the EEOC to enforce their rights.

The Act protects workers who, although disabled in some way, are still qualified for a particular job—that is, they would be able to perform the essential functions of a job, either with or without some form of accommodation. Whether a disabled worker is deemed qualified for a job depends on whether he or she has appropriate skill, experience, training, or education for the position.

Modest Progress for People With Disabilities

A recent poll found that Americans with disabilities are at a critical disadvantage compared to other Americans in several key areas of life. But continuing a hopeful trend, the survey found slow and modest progress in the last decade.

The most recent poll found that:

- Although 22% of employed people with disabilities report encountering job discrimination, this is a dramatic drop from 36% four years ago.
- Only 35% of people with disabilities reported being employed full or part time, compared to 78% of those who do not have disabilities.
- Three times as many live in poverty with annual household incomes below $15,000 (26% versus 9%).
- People with disabilities remain twice as likely to drop out of high school (21% versus 10%).
- They are twice as likely to have inadequate transportation (31% versus 13%), and a much higher percentage go without needed health care (18% versus 7%).
- People with disabilities are less likely to socialize, eat out, or attend religious services than their nondisabled counterparts.
- Not surprisingly, given the persistence of these gaps, life satisfaction for people with disabilities also trails, with only 34% saying they are very satisfied compared to 61% of those without disabilities.

Source: National Organization on Disability, 2004

To determine whether a particular function is considered essential for a job, look first at a written job description. If a function is described there, it is more likely to be considered an essential part of the job. But an employer's discretion and the reality of an individual workplace enter the fray, too. For example, if other employees would likely be available to take over some tangential part of a job, only a small portion of the workday is spent on the function, or the work product will not suffer if the function is not performed, that function may not be deemed essential to the job.

Definition of Disabled

The ADA's protections extend to the disabled—defined as a person who:

- has a physical or mental impairment that substantially limits a major life activity
- has a record of impairment, or
- is regarded as having an impairment.

This list makes clear why the new law provides just cause for consternation. Many of the terms used in the Act are broad—and not well defined. Some of their intended meanings were hinted at during the congressional debates on the legislation, but many will simply have to be hammered out in the courts over time.

Impairments Limiting a Life Activity

Impairment includes both physical disorders, such as cosmetic disfigurement or loss of a limb, and mental and psychological disorders. Physical disabilities that can be easily seen are those most often protected, presumably

for the simple reason that they are easiest to prove to others.

Many of the conditions the ADA is intended to cover are specifically listed—a list that is sure to grow over time. In fact, the ADA requires that, every year, the Secretary of Health and Human Services must provide a list of infectious and communicable diseases, as well as information on how they are transmitted.

Note, however, that several state and local public health departments have passed regulations that allow some forms of discrimination in the food handling industry. For example, several state laws provide that, if a communicable disease can be transmitted through handling food, and if the risk cannot be eliminated by reasonable accommodation, then an employer may refuse to hire an individual for a food handling job. For more information on these types of laws, contact your local public health department.

In addition, testing applicants and employees for the possibility of infectious diseases raises a number of privacy issues, commonly addressed in local and state laws. (See Chapter 5.)

Several courts, including the U.S. Supreme Court, have recently ruled that it is not the diagnosis but the effects of a condition that control. However, the ADA likely protects workers with Acquired Immune Deficiency Syndrome (AIDS) and the Human Immuno-deficiency Virus (HIV) (see Chapter 5, "Workplace Testing"), alcoholism, cancer, cerebral palsy, emotional illness, epilepsy, hearing and speech disorders, heart disorders, learning disabilities such as dyslexia, mental retarda-

CHAPTER 7 | ILLEGAL DISCRIMINATION | 299

tion, muscular dystrophy, and visual impairments.

A number of other conditions can be protected under the ADA upon proper proof that they are limiting in some way. To be covered, an individual's condition must restrict a life activity—broadly defined as the ability to walk, talk, see, hear, speak, breathe, sit, stand, reach, reason, learn, work, or care for himself or herself. However, the ADA does not cover conditions that impose short-term limitations, such as pregnancy or broken bones.

And the U.S. Supreme Court recently held that health conditions that can be limiting, but may be treated through drugs or accouterments—such as diabetes and poor eyesight—are not protected disabilities under the ADA. (*Sutton v. United Air Lines*, 527 U.S. 471 (1999) and *Murphy v. United Parcel Serv., Inc.*, 527 U.S. 516 (1999).)

And, in its most recent pronouncement on the issue, the Court held that a Kentucky auto worker, Ella Williams, was not disabled by carpal tunnel syndrome, which limited her work activities, because she was able to care for herself off the job. While Williams was unable to do the repeated lifting, carrying, and arm extensions required for the auto line job, the Court held that had limited relevance in determining whether she qualified as disabled under the ADA. What matters most, according to the unanimous Court, is "whether the claimant is able to perform the variety of tasks central to most people's daily lives," not the tasks associated with a specific job. In this case, the Justices seemed particularly taken with the fact that

Williams could perform personal chores such as brushing her teeth, gardening, sweeping, and doing the laundry. (*Toyota Motor Mfg v. Williams*, 534 U.S. 184 (2002).)

This last decision will likely limit the type and number of conditions that will qualify as legally disabling. Those claiming a disability protected by the ADA will no longer be able to cherry-pick the major life activities in which they are limited; their lists must pass muster as necessary for the average individual. As backlash, some legal experts warn that the decision will serve as a full employment bill for private investigators—who will doggedly tail those claiming disabilities to track whether they really can trek to the grocery store and take Spot on his daily constitutionals.

These Court decisions will also be tied to the larger new wave of controversy in ADA claims based on conditions some workers contend limit them but are murky for outsiders to detect. For example, some workers claim that Multiple Chemical Sensitivity, or MCS, caused by carpet, glue, or furniture fumes makes them dizzy, tired, and headachy. Other workers claim that mold and mildew on the job aggravate or cause respiratory problems. And some claim latex gloves and chemical coatings have given them asthma. Where the symptoms can be traced to poor ventilation in workplaces, they are commonly dubbed Sick Building Syndrome.

But linking the Syndrome to a successful ADA claim is still a gamble. A few complaints have resulted in money awards from employers—but, paradoxically, most workers have had to prove they were unable to work to collect. The greater success stories come from employees and employers who work together to come up with a solution to a complaint before it produces a disabling condition—often as simple as improving ventilation or setting up an office with air filtration and without carpeting.

Records of Impairment

Because discrimination often continues even after the effects of a disability have abated, the ADA prohibits discrimination against those who have had impairments in the past. This includes workers such as former cancer patients, rehabilitated drug addicts, recovering alcoholics, and even those misclassified as having a condition, such as someone misdiagnosed as being HIV-positive.

This type of ADA claim is perhaps most difficult to plead and prove, because the discrimination often takes the form of subtler ostracization. One recent case which succeeded in this way involved an anesthesiologist who was hospitalized for panic disorder and depression, then took a medical leave of absence to deal with side effects of his medication. Although he was later released to work without restrictions, the hospital administration subjected him to more rigorous observation and discipline than appeared to be warranted. After he was fired, an appellate court held that he made out a valid claim for discrimination based on "a record of impairment in the major life activities of sleeping, eating, thinking, and caring for himself" during his earlier bout with depression. (*Mattice v. Memorial Hospital of South Bend*, 249 F.3d 682 (7th Cir. 2001).)

Regarded as Impaired

In recognition of the fact that discrimination often stems from prejudice or irrational fear, the ADA protects workers who have no actual physical or mental impairment but may be viewed by others as disabled—for example, someone who is badly scarred, deaf, or epileptic. An employer cannot refuse to hire a person because of the perception that others will react negatively to him or her.

So far, this legal requirement has drawn the most questions. But there has been increased focus on it as public debate over the use of genetic testing in the workplace becomes louder, with critics arguing that such testing could too easily run roughshod over workers' privacy rights and subject them to this form of discrimination. (See Chapter 5, "Workplace Testing.") The House Labor Committee Report that originally considered the ADA attempted to provide some guidance by stating that, if an employer fires someone "because of the employer's perception that the person has an impairment which prevents that person from working, that person is covered" under the Act. In truth, the guidance has not been great enough. And judges called upon to decide ADA cases have refused to follow what guidance this offers: Most blatantly hold that a perceived limitation is simply not a handicap under the Act.

Illegal Discrimination

The ADA prohibits employers from discriminating against job applicants and employees who have disabilities in a number of specific situations.

All in the Mind? The ADA and Mental Disability Claims

In the newest wave of ADA complaints, workers claim that post-traumatic stress makes them hyperactive or short tempered. Others claim that Attention Deficit Disorder, or ADD, makes it difficult for them to concentrate and be productive on the job. Even where diagnosed and treated with drugs, some argue that mental conditions such as these are not true disabilities within the meaning of the law.

The EEOC issued guidelines on mental illness in March of 1997, mostly reiterating that the ADA protects workers who have mental impairments that limit "a major life activity" such as learning, thinking, concentrating, interacting with others, caring for himself or herself, or performing manual tasks. The EEOC opined that protected conditions may include major depression, bipolar disorder, anxiety disorders such as panic, and obsessive-compulsive disorders. But the agency also emphasized that the impairment must be lasting; while a serious depression lasting a year or more might qualify under the ADA, a down spell of a month probably would not.

Despite this gentle nudge from the EEOC to heed mental disability claims, many judges and juries around the country continue to reject them out of hand. The discrepancy may be due to the problem of definition. The lack of objective criteria for assessing mental diseases often makes their diagnoses murky—and the most skeptical observers claim that some employees seek out a finding of mental disability as an excuse to shirk work.

And workers who claim mental disabilities are often faced with a catch-22 when proving their cases: The ADA covers only those who are still able to perform their jobs; a worker who makes a convincing case of mental disability may have a tough time persuading others that he or she is still fit to work.

Finally, there may be problems getting an accommodation that realistically meets the needs of worker and workplace. Some accommodations may be effective and easy to provide—for example, moving an employee away from noisy machinery or allowing beverages in the workplace to combat a dry mouth caused by medication. But other accommodations, such as allowing more time to complete a work activity, may smack of favoritism in the hearts and minds of other workers. And, in the meanest workplaces, doctors' orders not to startle or ridicule a particular employee may cause coworkers to escalate the bad behavior.

Screening Tests

Employers may not use preemployment tests or ask interview questions that focus on an applicant's disabilities rather than skills related to the job. Although these questions used to be routine, employers can no longer ask, for example: Have you ever been hospitalized? Have you ever been treated for any of the following listed conditions or diseases? Have you ever been treated for a mental disorder? (See Chapter 5, "Workplace Testing," for a discussion of privacy issues related to testing.)

However, in screening applicants to find the best match to fill a job opening, employers are free to ask questions about an individual's ability to perform job-related tasks, such as: Can you lift a 40-pound box? Do you have a driver's license? Can you stand for long periods of time?

Insurance Benefits

Employers cannot deny health coverage or other fringe benefits to disabled workers. Before the ADA was passed, many employers railed that their insurance costs would skyrocket if they were forced to provide coverage for the special medical needs of disabled workers. The ADA does not require that all medical conditions be covered; workplace policies can still limit coverage for various treatments or design exclusions for preexisting conditions. However, employers must provide the same coverage for workers with disabilities as they do for workers without disabilities. (See Chapter 3 for a discussion of health insurance.)

Is Obesity a Disability? Still Too Soon to Tell

Courts that have been called upon to decide whether overweight people are disabled within the meaning of state disability laws and the ADA have split on the issue.

Some courts have held that all overweight workers are physically impaired—and entitled to be protected from discrimination under disability laws. Some courts have opined that overweight workers are protected by disability laws only if there is some medical evidence showing that the weight gain is due to a physiological condition. And a third line of legal reasoning holds that only obese workers—those 100% or more over normal weight or, by some definitions, those who weigh twice the normal weight for their height—are entitled to the law's protections.

When asked to provide some guidance, the EEOC was noncommittal—stating only that obesity claims would be considered "on a case by case basis." It added, however, that because of the ADA requirement that a disability must substantially limit a major life activity, few individuals can meet the burden.

Disabled Relatives and Friends

The ADA also attempts to clamp down on the invidious effects of taint by association. Employers are banned from discriminating against people who are not disabled but are related to or associated with someone who is disabled. For example, an otherwise qualified worker cannot be denied employment because a sibling, roommate, or close friend has AIDS.

Segregation

On the job, employers cannot segregate or classify disabled workers in a way that limits their opportunities or status—for example, by placing them in jobs with different pay, benefits, or promotion opportunities from workers who are not disabled.

Accommodations by Employers

The core of the ADA is what initially got employers up in arms over its passage; some of them felt the law wrested important workplace decisions from them. It requires employers to make accommodations— changes to the work setting or the way jobs are done—so that disabled people can work. The law also specifies what employers must do in the sticky situation where two equally qualified candidates, one of whom is disabled, apply for a job. An employer cannot reject the disabled worker solely because he or she would require a reasonable accommodation— a reserved handicapped parking space, a modified work schedule, a telephone voice amplifier—to get the job done.

In reality, a disabled individual who wants a particular job must become somewhat of an activist. Since the law does not require an employer to propose reasonable accommodations—only to provide them—the onus of suggesting workable and affordable changes to the workplace that would allow him or her to perform a job is on the employee who wants the accommodation.

What Is a Reasonable Accommodation

The ADA points to several specific accommodations that are likely to be deemed reasonable—some of them changes to the physical set-up of the workplace, some of them changes to how, when, or where work is done. They include:

- making existing facilities usable by disabled employees—for example, by modifying the height of desks and equipment, installing computer screen magnifiers, or installing telecommunications for the deaf
- restructuring jobs—for example, allowing a ten-hour/four-day workweek so that a worker can receive weekly medical treatments
- modifying exams and training material— for example, allowing more time for taking an exam, or allowing it to be taken orally instead of in writing
- providing a reasonable amount of additional unpaid leave for medical treatment (see also Chapter 4, "Family and Medical Leave.")
- hiring readers or interpreters to assist an employee
- providing temporary workplace specialists to assist in training, and
- transferring an employee to the same job in another location to obtain better medical care.

These are just a few possible accommodations. The possibilities are limited only by an employee's and employer's imaginations— and the reality that one or more of these accommodations might be financially impossible in a particular workplace.

It Helps to Beat Them to the Punch

As one might imagine, the ADA has spawned yet another crop of Workplace Experts, all eager to give tips to employers on what they must do to comply with the convoluted law. Most offer some type of checklist or list of steps to take to help meet the ADA's provisions.

In truth, the checklists are most valuable for disabled employees who want to get or keep a job. If you have a disability, you will be in the best possible bargaining position if you approach a potential employer with answers to the questions.

Here are some things to ponder:

- Analyze the job you want and isolate its essential functions.
- Write down precisely what job-related limitations your condition imposes and note how they can be overcome by accommodations.
- Identify potential accommodations and assess how effective each would be in allowing you to perform the job.
- Estimate how long each accommodation could be used before a change would be required.
- Document all aspects of the accommodation—including cost and availability.

What Is an Undue Hardship

The ADA does not require employers to make accommodations that would cause them an undue hardship—a weighty concept defined in the ADA only as "an action requiring significant difficulty or expense." To show that a particular accommodation would present an undue hardship, an employer would have to demonstrate that it was too costly, extensive, or disruptive to be adopted in that workplace.

The Equal Employment Opportunity Commission (EEOC), the federal agency responsible for enforcing the ADA, has set out some of the factors that will determine whether a particular accommodation presents an undue hardship on a particular employer:

- the nature and cost of the accommodation
- the financial resources of the employer—a large employer, obviously, may reasonably be asked to foot a larger bill for accommodations than a mom and pop business
- the nature of the business, including size, composition, and structure, and
- accommodation costs already incurred in a workplace.

It is not easy for employers to prove that an accommodation is an undue hardship, as financial difficulty alone is not usually sufficient. Courts will look at other sources of money, including tax credits and deductions available for making some accommodations and the disabled employee's willingness to pay for all or part of the costs.

How to Take Action

Title I of the ADA is enforced by the Equal Employment Opportunity Commission. (See "Filing a Complaint With the EEOC," above, for specifics on how to file a complaint.) How

When Money Isn't Everything

According to ergonomic and job accommodation experts, the amount of money employers would need to pay to accommodate a particular worker's disability is often surprisingly low.

- 31% of accommodations cost nothing.
- 50% cost less than $50.
- 69% cost less than $500.
- 88% cost less than $1,000.

The following is a list of the problems that recently surfaced—and their inexpensive solutions:

Problem: A person had an eye disorder. Glare on the computer screen caused fatigue.

Solution: The employer purchased an antiglare screen for $39.

Problem: An individual lost the use of a hand and could no longer use a camera. The company provided a tripod, but that was too cumbersome.

Solution: A waist pod, such as is used in carrying flags, enabled the individual to manipulate the camera and keep his job. Cost? $50.

Problem: A seamstress could not use ordinary scissors due to pain in her wrist.

Solution: The business purchased a pair of ergonomically designed springloaded scissors for $18.

Problem: A receptionist, who was blind, could not see the lights on her telephone that indicated whether the telephone lines were ringing, on hold, or in use at her company.

Solution: The company bought a light probe, a penlike product that detected a lighted button, for $45.

Problem: A medical technician who was deaf could not hear the buzz of a timer, which was necessary for specific laboratory tests.

Solution: An indicator light was attached for $26.95.

Problem: A person who used a wheelchair could not use a desk because it was too low and his knees would not go under it.

Solution: The desk was raised with wood blocks, allowing a proper amount of space for the wheelchair to fit under it. Cost? Nothing.

Source: The Job Accommodation Network, www.jan.wvu.edu

efficient and responsive the agency will be and what kinds of lines it will draw in the cases it investigates remain to be seen as the relatively new law makes its presence felt in workplaces and courts.

In addition, many state laws protect against discrimination based on physical or mental disability. (See "State and Local Antidiscrimination Laws," above, for a list of laws and enforcing agencies.) An individual working in a state with such a law can choose to file a complaint under either state law or the federal law (ADA), or both.

Where to Get More Information

For additional information on the ADA, contact:

Disability Rights Section
Civil Rights Division
U.S. Department of Justice
950 Pennsylvania Avenue, NW
Washington, DC 20530
800-514-0301
TDD: 800-514-0383

The Disability Rights Section operates a Web page devoted to the ADA at www.usdoj. gov/crt/ada/adahom1.htm. There are also a number of national organizations that offer guidance and referrals in dealing with ADA problems. (See the Appendix for contact details.)

RESOURCE

For detailed information on Title VII, the Equal Pay Act, the ADEA, the Older Workers' Benefits Protection Act, and the ADA—including the text of each law—see *Federal Employment Laws:*

A Desk Reference, by Amy DelPo and Lisa Guerin (Nolo).

Discrimination Against Workers With HIV or AIDS

Government tallies place more than one million Americans as having been infected by HIV, the virus believed to cause Acquired Immune Deficiency Syndrome (AIDS). And the epidemic has hit workplaces hard. In some communities with high-risk populations, such as New York City, Los Angeles, and San Francisco, the infection rate is reported to be as high as one in every 25 workers. Additional recent polls reveal that even these high estimates are unrealistically low.

More than half of our nation's workers are in the age group of those most likely to be infected in the future—adults between 25 and 44 years old.

A growing number of employers have attempted to smooth over real and perceived problems with HIV-infected and AIDS-infected workers by holding training sessions and adopting written policies specifically prohibiting discrimination.

Nevertheless, some employers and employees have reacted to the spread of AIDS with panic—and a strong prejudice against working with people who are infected with HIV. Some insurance companies have made that panic worse by restricting health care coverage or dramatically raising premiums for those infected. (See Chapter 5, "Workplace Testing," for a discussion of privacy rights connected with AIDS testing.)

While prejudice and skittishness remain, the legal picture for workers with HIV and AIDS is more clear since the passage of the Americans With Disabilities Act, or ADA, discussed above. Under the ADA, it is clearly illegal for any company employing 15 or more people to discriminate against workers because they are HIV-infected or have AIDS. Employers covered by the ADA must also make reasonable accommodations to allow employees with AIDS or HIV to continue working. Such accommodations include extended leave policies and reassignment to vacant positions that are less physically strenuous or that have flexible work schedules.

In addition, many state and local antidiscrimination laws make it illegal to discriminate in employment-related matters on the basis of HIV infection or AIDS. (See "State and Local Administrative Laws," above.)

RESOURCE

A number of organizations offer publications and specific information on the HIV virus, AIDS, and resources on AIDS in the workplace. The organizations often provide sources of counseling and legal referrals. (See the Appendix for contact details.)

Discrimination Against Gay and Lesbian Workers

Gay men and lesbians have historically been subjected to painful measures that would legalize discrimination: initiatives barring them from teaching in public schools, local ordinances allowing private clubs to bar them from their doors, loud and heavy lobbying against same-sex marriage laws. On the job, the discrimination often continues—with homophobic comments and jokes, lectures about upholding The Company Image, promotions denied, and jobs lost.

Although women, minorities, people older than 40, and people with disabilities now enjoy an umbrella of state and federal protections from discrimination in the workplace, gays and lesbians have, for the most part, been left out in the rain, at least at the national level. There is no federal law that specifically outlaws workplace discrimination on the basis of sexual orientation—in either the public or the private sector.

At the state level, however, there is more cause for hope. As of January 2007, 18 states had laws prohibiting sexual orientation discrimination in employment: California, Connecticut, District of Columbia, Hawaii, Illinois, Maine, Maryland, Massachusetts, Minnesota, Nevada, New Hampshire, New Jersey, New Mexico, New York, Rhode Island, Vermont, Washington, and Wisconsin. States that ban employment discrimination based on gender identity include California, Illinois, Maine, Minnesota, New Jersey, New Mexico, Rhode Island, and Washington.

If you are gay or lesbian and your state does not have a law that protects you from workplace discrimination, you may still be protected by city and county ordinances. Hundreds of cities and counties now prohibit discrimination based on sexual orientation in the workplace—from Albany, New York, to Ypsilanti, Michigan. In addition, some companies have adopted their own policies prohibiting such discrimination.

According to the National Gay and Lesbian Taskforce, the hodgepodge of laws and ordinances means that the glass is half full. About 47% of the U.S. population now lives in a jurisdiction that bans discrimination on the basis of sexual orientation.

However, in states and cities that do not have laws forbidding workplace discrimination on the basis of sexual orientation, you can often take action against an employer who fires or otherwise discriminates against you because you are gay or lesbian by filing a lawsuit claiming invasion of privacy.

> **EXAMPLE:** Janet worked at a small law firm specializing in patents. After 15 years of work filled with consistent promotions, pay raises, and good performance reviews, Janet was fired the day after her supervisor saw her holding hands with her lover at a weekend movie. Janet would have a good shot at winning a lawsuit against the law firm based on invasion of privacy, because the firing amounted to the employer exerting undue control over her private life.

Finally, a growing number of more enlightened employers have included a clause that they will not discriminate against workers based on sexual orientation.

With sufficient documentation, you may also be able to prove in specific instances that your demotion or firing was due to:

- illegal discrimination under the ADA (discussed above) based on a perceived fear of HIV infection
- one of the other wrongful discharge strategies (discussed in Chapter 9, "When a Firing May Be Illegal"), or
- illegal discrimination prohibited by a specific workplace policy.

TIP

Damned either way. Deciding whether to be openly identified at work as gay can be a grueling choice. Courts have split on whether there is legal protection for workers who do not openly identify themselves as gay but who are discriminated against because an employer believes they are gay.

RESOURCE

For more information on the legal rights of gay and lesbian couples, see *A Legal Guide for Lesbian & Gay Couples*, by Hayden Curry, Denis Clifford, and Frederick Hertz (Nolo). A number of organizations offer publications, counseling, advice, and research on issues gay and lesbian workers face on the job. (See the Appendix for contact details.)

Sexual Harassment

In legal terms, sexual harassment is any unwelcome sexual conduct on the job that creates an intimidating, hostile, or offensive working environment. Simply put, sexual harassment is any offensive conduct related to an employee's gender that a reasonable woman or man should not have to endure while at work.

The laws prohibiting sexual harassment are gender-blind; they prevent women from harassing men, men from harassing other men, and women from harassing other women. However, the vast majority of cases involve women workers who have been harassed by male coworkers or supervisors.

The forms that sexual harassment can take range from offensive sexual innuendoes to physical encounters, from misogynist humor to rape. An employee may be confronted with sexual demands to keep a job or obtain a promotion, known in the earliest cases as a quid pro quo form of harassment—literally, do this for that. In other forms of sexual harassment, the threat—or the trade-off—is not as blunt. When sexually offensive conduct permeates the workplace, an employee may find it difficult or unpleasant to work there. The term hostile environment was frequently used in the cases and literature to describe this form of sexual harassment.

The definition of sexual harassment is evolving as it passes through courts and legislatures. The most authoritative refinements come from the U.S. Supreme Court, which has issued a number of pronouncements on the subject.

For example, the Court held that a worker need not show psychological injury to prove a case of sexual harassment; it also intimated that one or two offensive remarks are not enough to make a case. (*Harris v. Forklift Sys., Inc.*, 510 U.S. 17 (1993).)

And, in additional recent cases, the Court has offered some uncharacteristically homespun advice for both employers and employees entangled in harassment issues: Act reasonably. Use your common sense.

- The Court recognized that illegal harassment can occur between people of the same gender. It implied that drawing the line between horseplay or flirtations and discrimination on the job is not as hard as some pretend, even while acknowledging that men and women may play differently. (*Oncale v. Sundowner Offshore Services, Inc.*, 523 U.S. 75 (1998).)

- The Court also acknowledged that the jargony labels of quid pro quo and hostile environment may be more confusing than helpful in defining sexual harassment, although many lower courts continue to cling to them to this day. It held that an employer may be liable for sexual harassment even when an employee did not succumb to sexual advances or suffer diverse job consequences. But the employer can defend itself against liability and damages by showing that it used reasonable care in stopping harassment—for example, that it had a strong written antiharassment policy or an investigation procedure. An employee who does not take advantage of the workplace policy by reporting the harassment has a considerably weaker case. (*Burlington Industries, Inc. v. Ellerth,* 524 U.S. 742 (1998).)

- And the Court resolved the question of whether an employer could be held liable for a supervisor's harassing behavior when it had no knowledge of it. It held again that an employer could defend itself against a sexual harassment charge by showing it acted reasonably to prevent it. The Court intimated that, at a minimum, acting reasonably includes establishing a policy prohibiting sexual harassment and establishing a procedure for dealing with it. (*Faragher v. City of Boca Raton, Florida,* 524 U.S. 775 (1998).)

The fervor over sexual harassment has cooled somewhat in the last decade, and the number of claims alleging it has decreased—partially due to laws that mandate regular training on the topic. But the workplace problem is far from solved. In 2006, the EEOC received 12,025 charges of sexual harassment and recovered $48.8 million in monetary benefits for those affected—and many millions more were collected in private lawsuits.

The Effects of Sexual Harassment

Sexual harassment on the job can have a number of serious consequences, both for the harassed individual and for other workers who experience it secondhand and become demoralized or intimidated

at work. (See "Federal Law," below, for a discussion of legal remedies.)

Loss of Job

Sometimes the connection between sexual harassment and the injuries it causes is simple and direct: A worker is fired for refusing to go along with the sexual demands of a coworker or supervisor. Usually the management uses some other pretext for the firing, but the reasons are often quite transparent.

Sometimes the firing technically occurs because of some other event, but it is still clearly related to sexual harassment. For example, if a company downgrades an employee's job and assignments because of a harassment incident and then fires him or her for complaining about the demotion, that injury is legally caused by sexual harassment.

If an employee is temporarily unable to work as a result of the harassment and the management uses that as an excuse to fire him or her, that is also considered legally related to the harassment.

Loss of Wages and Other Benefits

An employee who resists sexual advances or objects to obscene humor in the office may suffer work-related consequences including:

- being denied a promotion
- being demoted, or
- suffering various economic losses.

That employee may also suffer harm to his or her standing within the company,

Hollywood's Latest: 'The Vulgar Necessity Defense'

While working as a writers' assistant for the popular television sitcom "Friends," Amaani Lyle says she got a close-up of the show's writers in action: making sex-related jokes, discussing blow job story lines, discussing the actresses' sexuality, writing sex-related words on scripts, and pantomiming masturbation. After four months, Lyle was fired for her poor typing skills and for her failure to accurately record important jokes and dialogue in her notes.

She sued Warner Bros. Television Production and three individual comedy writers under California's Fair Employment and Housing Act for harassment based on race and gender.

The case itself had impeccable timing—first wending its way through the courts during the season finale of the popular "Friends," a show about ageless 20/30-somethings coming of age. And it coincided with initial tabloid reports of actor Brad Pitt canoodling with Angelina Jolie—a woman not his wife. His wife was Jennifer Aniston, one of the stars on "Friends."

And on the legal front, it attracted briefs from writers, employer groups, and unions, pitting the television industry and free speech advocates against some women's rights advocates.

The Los Angeles County Superior Court initially dismissed Lyle's complaint as frivolous. But the appellate court held that the case presented triable issues of fact regarding sexual harassment. It also noted that the court could consider the nature of the defendants' work in determining if their conduct amounted to true harassment—thus fostering The Creative Necessity Defense.

The California Supreme Court agreed, reasoning that while sexual language may constitute harassment, the "Friends" writers' language did not reach that level, as it was not aimed directly at Lyle or at other women because of their gender. In reaching its unanimous decision, the court famously noted: "The FEHA is 'not a civility code' and is not designed to rid the workplace of vulgarity," nor does it "outlaw sexually coarse and vulgar language that merely offends." (*Lyle v. Warner Brothers Television Production*, 38 Cal. 4th 264 (2006).) And the court reiterated that a harassing remark must be "objectively and subjectively offensive, one that a reasonable person would find hostile or abusive."

The case quickly garnered camps of supporters and opponents. Those favoring it noted that it would cut off frivolous claims from fired workers eager to construct a sexual harassment claim. Opponents voiced the fear that Lyle would too easily allow harassing workers to claim their bad behavior was "necessary" in their own "creative workplaces."

So far, the holding has been put to the test once—in a case in which a male maintenance mechanic claimed he was harassed by sexual and racial taunting from male coworkers on the night shift. The California appellate court, apparently finding the manufacturing plant not "creative" enough, held that the conduct was arguably sexual harassment, and set aside the ruling in the employer's favor. (*Singleton v. U.S. Gypsum Co.*, 140 Cal. App. 4th 1547 (2006).)

which could jeopardize future pay increases and opportunities for promotion.

A loss of wages usually entails a loss of other job benefits as well, such as pension contributions, medical benefits, overtime pay, bonuses, sick pay, shift differential pay, vacation pay, and participation in any company profit-sharing plan.

Forced Reassignment

Sometimes a company responds to an employee's complaint of sexual harassment by transferring that individual somewhere else in the company and leaving the harasser unpunished. This forced reassignment is another form of job-connected injury, and it may be compounded if it results in a loss of pay or benefits or reduced opportunities for advancement.

Constructive Discharge

Sometimes the sexual harassment is so severe that the employee quits. If the situation was intolerable and the employee was justified in quitting, sexual harassment caused him or her to be constructively discharged—that is, forced to leave. While often difficult to prove, courts treat this as an illegal firing.

> **EXAMPLE:** A woman who worked for a film editing company received frequent threats as well as blatant sexual solicitations from the owner of the company, which culminated when he posed the ultimatum: "Fuck me, or you're fired." The owner told the woman he was leaving for a brief business trip, but his

parting words were, "I'll see you when I get back." A federal court hearing the case ruled that the sexual ultimatum, combined with the explicit threat, made her working conditions so intolerable that a reasonable person in her position would be compelled to resign—the very definition of a constructive discharge. (*Stockett v. Tolin*, 791 F. Supp. 1536 (S.D. Fla. 1992).)

Penalties for Retaliation

Employees are frequently fired or penalized for reporting sexual harassment or otherwise trying to stop it. Such workplace reprimands are called retaliation. In such cases, the injury is legally considered to be a direct result of the sexual harassment.

Personal Injuries

In addition to job-connected losses, a sexually harassed worker often suffers serious and costly personal injuries—ranging from stress-related illnesses to serious physical and emotional problems.

Sexual harassment also causes a great many other types of physical, mental, and emotional injuries. Some of these injuries are stress-related, but others are caused by physical pranks or violent acts directed at the harassed worker.

Federal Law

Sexual discrimination in employment became illegal in the United States when

Yes, Virgil. Men Get Harassed, Too

A few years after sexual harassment against women came out of workplace closets across America, a new whisper emerged: "I've been harassed, too. And I'm a man." At first, many people—particularly women—took a dim view of this development. Sexual harassment on the job, after all, had been diagnosed as a social ill stemming from an abuse of power, and men had long dominated the powerful positions in most workplaces. It was harder to sympathize with The Harassed Man than to see him as the poor lunk who failed to duck as the pendulum was swinging.

The popular press and the silver screen seemed titillated by the thought of the role reversal. Michael Crichton was inspired to pen yet another novel on the theme, *Disclosure*. Still, when the book surfaced inevitably in a film version, even the threat of a besuited Demi Moore pinning a hapless male underling against her mahogany desk seemed less scary than, say, being passed over for a promotion.

The reality is, of course, that abusive behavior in the workplace is not limited by stereotypes of Bad Boys and Good Girls. Sexual harassment on the job is not about sex; it's about unwanted, abusive behavior—usually repeated and often in the face of requests to cut it out. Women as well as men dish out the discriminatory behavior that

is sexual harassment, and they'll do it to harass men they want to intimidate, humiliate, or drive out of their workplaces.

Some believe it's worse than we fear, that nearly as many men as women are harassed on the job, but few of them are willing or able to speak up about it—as if that extra chromosome reared up and got caught in their collective throats.

Recent statistics show a steady increase in the percent of claims that men have filed with the EEOC—up from 7.5% in 1991 to about 15.4% in 2006.

The exciting development is that gender may not matter in the eyes of the law. Many judges who have considered sexual harassment issues recently—including the U.S. Supreme Court justices, who took on a blockbusting number of four such cases during the 1998 term—have edged toward making them gender neutral. For example, most have stopped taking up space in their decisions over whether incidents of alleged harassment should best be viewed from the eyes of a reasonable woman or a reasonable man.

For a growing number of courts these days, the vantage point is common sense, the guiding premise that most workers, men and women, simply want to come to work and do their jobs.

the Civil Rights Act of 1964 was adopted. That Act established the Equal Employment Opportunities Commission (EEOC), which later issued regulations and guidelines on the subject of sexual harassment. (See Chapter 7, "Title VII of the Civil Rights Act," for a discussion of the EEOC.)

It was not until a long time later, however, that the agency began enforcing the law as written. In late 1991, in the wake of the well-publicized hearings to confirm Clarence Thomas as a U.S. Supreme Court Justice, Congress amended the Civil Rights Act to allow employees to sue for money damages for sex discrimination, including harassment.

Behind Open Doors: How the Battle Was Accidentally Waged

As introduced in Congress, the Civil Rights Act of 1964 only prohibited employment discrimination based on race, color, religion, or national origin. Discrimination on the basis of sex was not included. It was attached to the bill at the last moment by conservative Southern opponents of the bill. They hoped that adding sexual equality was so obviously preposterous that it would scuttle the entire bill when it came to a final vote.

The very idea of prohibiting sex-based discrimination engendered mirth on the floor of Congress and on the editorial pages of major newspapers: Men, it was laughingly argued, could now sue to become Playboy bunnies. The Lyndon Johnson administration, however, wanted the Civil Rights Act passed badly enough that it decided not to oppose the amendment. The Civil Rights Act, including the ban on sex discrimination, became law. Only one of the congressmen who had proposed the sex discrimination amendment actually voted for the bill.

They'll Be Watching You, Too

Keep in mind that an important part of the definition of sexual harassment is that it is unwelcome behavior. Realistically, it is up to you, as the harassed person, to make clear that you find it objectionable.

Giving mixed signals can defeat your claim. For example, courts have suggested that telling sexual stories, engaging in sexual gestures, initiating sexual talk, or soliciting sexual encounters with coworkers may imply that sexual conduct was welcome.

You will also have a tougher time making out a claim of sexual harassment if you do not report the unwelcome behavior to others.

Who Is Covered

As discussed in Chapter 7, The Civil Rights Act extends protection against sexual harassment to employees of all public and private employers in the United States, including U.S. citizens working for a U.S. company in a foreign country. The Act also applies to labor unions—both to the workers they employ and to their members.

For several years, the EEOC took no action against sexual discrimination in employment.

However, there is one major exception: The Civil Rights Act does not apply to any company that has fewer than 15 employees.

Remedies Available

Remedies that the courts can provide under the Civil Rights Act to a sexually harassed employee include reinstatement and promotion in a job, an award of wages and job-connected losses, money damages to compensate the worker or punish the wrongdoer, and injunctive relief—including a court order to the employer to fashion a written sexual harassment policy and to pay attorneys' fees to the harassed employee.

State Laws

Some states have passed their own laws and regulations making sexual harassment illegal—usually called Fair Employment Practices (FEP) laws. But whether a harassed worker has good protection under state law depends on where he or she lives.

On the key issue of compensation for personal injuries, some states, such as New York and Massachusetts, have enacted relatively good remedies that allow an employee to recover full compensation. Unfortunately, most state laws have no provision for awarding compensatory damages for personal injuries an employee suffers.

To find out about your state's law, contact your state's fair employment practices agency. (See Chapter 7, "State Agencies That Enforce Discrimination in Employment," for contact details.)

Taking Steps to End Sexual Harassment

The alternatives described here can be viewed as a series of escalating steps you can take to stop sexual harassment. If a particular tactic does not end the objectionable behavior, you can switch to increasingly formal strategies until you find one that is effective.

Confront the Harasser

Often the best strategy for the employee sounds the simplest: Confront the harasser and tell him or her to stop. This is not appropriate or sensible in every case, particularly when you have suffered injuries or are in some physical danger. But surprisingly often—most workplace experts say up to 90% of the time—it works.

Confronted directly, harassment is especially likely to end if it is at a fairly low level: off-color jokes, inappropriate comments about appearance, repeated requests for dates, sexist cartoons tacked onto the office refrigerator. Clearly saying no does more than assert your determination to stop the behavior. It makes clear that you find the behavior unwelcome—a critical part of the definition of sexual harassment. It is also a crucial first step if you later decide to take more formal action against the harassment.

Tell the harasser to stop. It is best to deal directly with the harassment when it occurs. But, if your harasser surprised you with an obnoxious gesture or comment that caught you completely off guard—a common tactic—you may have been too flabbergasted to respond at once. Or, if you did respond, you may not have expressed yourself clearly. Either way, talk to the harasser the next day.

Here are some tips for telling the harasser to back off:

- **Keep the conversation brief.** Try to speak privately, out of the hearing range of supervisors and coworkers.

- **Do not use humor to make your point.** Joking may be too easily misunderstood —or interpreted as a sign that you don't take the situation seriously yourself.

- **Be direct.** It is usually better to make a direct request that a specific kind of behavior stop than to tell your harasser how you feel. For example, saying "I am uncomfortable with this" may be enough to get the point across to some people, but the subtlety may be lost on others. And, of course, making you uncomfortable may be just the effect the harasser was after.

- **Offer no excuses.** Keep in mind that you're not the one whose behavior is inexcusable. Simply make the point and end the conversation. There is no need to offer excuses, such as: "My boyfriend wouldn't like it if we met at your apartment to discuss that new project."

Put it in writing. If your harasser persists, write a letter spelling out the behavior you object to and why. Also specify what you want to happen next. If you feel the situation is serious or bound to escalate, make clear that you will take action against the harassment if it does not stop at once. If your company has a written policy against harassment, attach a copy of it to your letter.

CAUTION

Beware of retaliation. Do not overlook the possibility that some company witnesses may be blackmailed with the threat—often unspoken—that they will lose their jobs or be demoted if they cooperate with you in documenting or investigating a sexual harassment complaint. While retaliation is illegal, it is difficult to prove. If possible, try to document the harassment by talking with witnesses both inside and outside the company.

Use a Company Complaint Procedure

A court sometimes requires a company to write a comprehensive policy if it finds there has been a problem with sexual harassment. Many businesses are also adopting sexual harassment policies on their own, to foster a better atmosphere for employees.

If you are harassed at work, a sexual harassment policy can help you determine what behavior you can take action against and how to ensure the harassment is stopped.

And, in fact, it is essential for you to heed these policies. The U.S. Supreme Court has recently ruled in a number of cases that employees can no longer be coy: If a workplace has a policy or a complaint procedure in place, workers must follow it to complain about or take other action against the bad behavior. Workers who don't take advantage of company procedures for complaining about harassment may lose the legal right to sue the employer.

Find out whether your employer has a sexual harassment policy by contacting the human resources department or the person who handles employee benefits. If there is no policy, lobby to get one.

File a Complaint With a Government Agency

If the sexual harassment does not end after face-to-face meetings or after using the company complaint procedure, consider filing a complaint under the U.S. Civil Rights Act with the U.S. Equal Employment Opportunities Commission (EEOC) (see Chapter 7, "Title VII of the Civil Rights Act") or filing a complaint under a similar state law with a state Fair Employment Practices (FEP) agency. (See "State Laws," above.)

Filing a complaint with these agencies does two important things:

- It sets in motion an investigation by the EEOC or the state FEP agency that may resolve the sexual harassment complaint.
- It is a necessary prerequisite under the U.S. Civil Rights Act and under some state FEP laws if you want to file a lawsuit under the Civil Rights Act or under a state FEP law.

Sometimes the EEOC or a state FEP agency can resolve a sexual harassment dispute at no cost to the employee and with relatively little legal involvement. Almost all of these agencies provide some sort of conciliation service—a negotiation between the employer and employee to end the harassment and restore peace in the workplace. And most agencies protect the employee against retaliation for filing the complaint. Most agencies have the power to expand their investigation to cover more widespread sexual harassment within

the company. A few state FEP agencies also provide an administrative hearing panel that can award money to compensate a harassed employee for personal injuries, although the EEOC and most state agencies do not have this important power.

The EEOC and state FEP agencies can resolve a lot of cases, but not all of them. Investigations sometimes drag on longer than the harassed employee is prepared to wait. Not all cases will yield to the conciliation efforts of such agencies; this is particularly true in severe cases of sexual harassment with significant personal injuries.

File a Private Lawsuit

If investigation and conciliation by the EEOC or a state FEP agency do not produce satisfactory results, your next step may be to file a lawsuit under the U.S. Civil Rights Act or under one of the state FEP statutes.

Even if you intend right from the beginning to file such a lawsuit, you generally must first file a claim with a government agency, as described above. An employee must file a claim with the EEOC before bringing a lawsuit under the U.S. Civil Rights Act. Some states also require that the employee first file a claim with the state FEP agency before suing under state law. At some point after such claims are filed and investigated, the agency will issue you a document—usually referred to as a right-to-sue letter—that allows you to take your case to court. Going to court in such lawsuits requires getting legal advice from an attorney who is experienced in these types of cases. (See Chapter 17, "Hiring a Lawyer.")

Generally speaking, suing under the U.S. Civil Rights Act is potentially more lucrative than relying on state law. Most state FEP laws allow you to win lost wages and benefits, but not compensation for physical and mental injuries such as stress and anxiety caused by the harassment. By contrast, the Civil Rights Act allows the employee to recover some money—out-of-pocket losses plus $50,000 to $300,000, depending upon the number of employees in the company. Its coverage, however, is limited to employers with 15 or more employees.

However, some states, such as New York and California, do better. They allow an employee to be compensated up to the full amount of damages proven, without any artificial limits. Employees in those states will probably want to pursue their rights under state law or maybe a combination of state and federal law.

File a Tort Lawsuit

Bringing a tort action (that is, a lawsuit for personal injuries) is often the last legal resort for sexually harassed workers. These legal actions provide a wider range of possible remedies than those available under the Civil Rights Act. You can sue both for compensatory damages for the emotional and physical distress you suffered because of the workplace harassment, and for potentially large punitive damages aimed at punishing the wrongdoer.

These lawsuits, which will usually require help from a lawyer, are based on traditional legal theories such as assault and battery,

intentional infliction of emotional distress, interference with contract, and defamation. These actions, called torts, are civil wrongs—and are filed in state courts like any other lawsuit based on a personal injury.

Can You Collect If You Win?

Even a multimillion dollar court award will be worth only the paper it's written on unless the person or company found liable is able to pay. In most sexual harassment cases, collecting what is due and owing to you is not a problem, because your employer and the harasser are both liable—and either or both are likely to be solvent. Some larger employers also purchase a form of specialized insurance that covers attorneys' costs and sometimes damages awards in a harassment lawsuit.

As a general rule, employers are responsible for sexual harassment by supervisors and managers who work there. And they may even be held financially responsible for harassment you suffer at the hands of a coworker if a supervisor either knew or should have known about the wrongful behavior.

Where a coworker commits one act of harassment with no prior history or workplace pattern of such treatment, the employer may not be liable. When the employee alone is liable, it will probably be difficult to collect. And if the employer is small, has a limited cash supply, and has no insurance to cover attorneys' fees for defending a sexual harassment lawsuit, it may be impossible to collect a large judgment.

At least in theory, tort actions allow unlimited dollar verdicts for some of the most severe injuries wrought by harassment: emotional and physical harm. These tort actions are particularly appropriate where a worker has suffered severe trauma from the psychological remnants of harassment—embarrassment, fright, or humiliation—which can cause a permanent loss of self-esteem and take a heavy toll on emotional and physical health.

While a tort lawsuit may be the best option for some harassed workers, it is the only possible remedy for others. As mentioned, if your employer has 14 or fewer employees, you are not covered by the U.S. Civil Rights Act and cannot file an EEOC complaint or a federal lawsuit for money.

Where to Get More Information

Contact the local office of the EEOC and your state FEP agency. Many will send you written materials on sexual harassment and can provide information on local training programs, support groups, and attorneys. A growing number also operate websites listing this information.

Some states and larger cities also have a Commission on the Status of Women or a state or local agency dealing specifically with women's issues; these agencies often offer help to sexually harassed workers. The services these groups provide range from referrals to local groups, to advice and counseling, to legal referrals. Check your telephone book to see if there is such a group in your area.

Many unions and groups for union members are especially active in the fight against sexual harassment. Contact your local to find out if it offers any special services or guidance.

Also, some law schools have clinics that deal with sexual harassment or employment law. These clinics are usually staffed by students, who are assisted by experienced attorneys. Many provide in-person or telephone counseling and legal advice, and some will even represent you in court. Their services are low-cost, often free. Call law schools in your area and ask if they have such a clinic.

Finally, a number of organizations offer specialized information and guidance on evaluating sexual harassment in the workplace, and many also offer legal referrals. (See the Appendix for contact details.)

Losing or Leaving a Job

The truth will surprise you: No law gives you an automatic right to keep your job. In fact, most of the legal principles and practices of the workplace are indisputably on the side of the employer who fires you.

You can be fired for a host of traditional and obvious reasons: incompetence, excessive absences, violating certain laws or company rules, or sleeping or taking drugs on the job. And other reasons for firings are gaining in popularity—most notably, because of economic need occasioned by a downturn in company profits or demands. In most cases, an employer does not need to provide any notice before giving an employee walking papers.

Still, there are limits. The laws do guarantee you some rights on the way out the door. And, because of the grand importance of job security to the majority of Americans, employees are increasingly fighting for and slowly garnering more rights in the workplace. In fact, when a case in which a former employee challenges a firing makes it to court, jurors of late are apt to concentrate not on whether the worker committed a wrong and deserved to be fired; they look at whether the employer treated the fired soul fairly and reasonably.

Even at the tail end of your work relationship, employers do not have the right to discriminate against you illegally (see Chapter 7) or to violate state or federal laws, such as those controlling wages and hours (see Chapter 2). And there are a number of other, more complex reasons that may make it illegal for an employer to fire you—basically boiling down to the Golden Rule that an employer must deal with you fairly and honestly.

If you lost your job—or have good reason to think you are about to lose it—it may behoove you to become familiar with the various situations in which it may be illegal to fire an employee, discussed in this chapter, and with the services and benefits that may be of assistance if you do lose your job. (See Chapter 10, "Collecting Fringe Benefits" and "Replacing Your Income.")

At the very least, understanding how and when laws may protect job security and other workplace rights should help you determine whether your job loss may justify taking legal action, in which case you may want to consult a lawyer. (See Chapter 17, "Hiring a Lawyer," for advice on this.)

The Doctrine of Employment at Will

Once again, for the value of its shock: People employed in private industry have no automatic legal right to their jobs.

That is because of the long-established legal doctrine of employment at will—a term you are most likely to hear cited by your boss or your company's lawyers if you speak up and protest your dismissal. An employer's right to unilaterally determine whether or not you should stay on the payroll stems from an 1894 case (*Payne v. Western & Atlantic RR*, 81 Tenn. 507), in which the court ruled that employers do not need a reason to fire employees; they may fire any or all of their workers at will—that is, at any time and for any reason that is not illegal. Even if the reason for dismissal is morally wrong, the court held, no legal wrong has occurred and the government has no basis to intervene.

The management of America's factories was still in the experimental stage in the 1890s when that case was decided. The business community successfully argued then, and in cases that followed, that factories could not be operated profitably unless employers were free to hire and fire as they chose. The employment at will doctrine has been reinforced over and over again by subsequent court rulings—and expanded to include not only factories but also virtually all other types of private industry jobs.

But don't fall prey to the common misconception that the hidebound doctrine means that employees simply have no ground to stand on to fight back against pink slips. If that were true, there would be no wrongful termination lawsuits, which is hardly the case. There would be no call for mediating or arbitrating employment cases—which is, in fact, a burgeoning industry. There would be no need for employment lawyers, of which there are many breathing examples. And there would be no need for books about employees' rights—perish the thought.

Employment at will has been weakened substantially since the 1970s by rulings in wrongful discharge suits in which former employees question the legality of their firings (discussed below)—and by some new laws that are more favorable to employees. For example, in Montana, employees who have completed a probationary period can only be fired for good cause. (Mont. Code Ann. § 39-2-904.) And a federal law, the Uniformed Services Employment and Reemployment Rights Act, or USERRA, protects those who have served in the uniformed services from being fired for any reason but good cause up to a year after they return to the job. And some states have made it illegal to fire employees for taking time off to care for a sick child (discussed in Chapter 4, "State Laws on Family Leave") or because they are gay or lesbian (discussed in Chapter 7, "State and Local Antidiscrimination Laws").

When a Firing May Be Illegal

There are a few important exceptions to the employment at will doctrine—and some additional legal theories about unfair treatment on the job—that may make it possible for employees to hang onto their jobs or to sue their former employer for wrongful termination. And, as anxieties deepen over job security, more employees are taking the time and effort to contradict their employers' assertions that it is time for them to go—and more workers seem willing to do battle in court over unfair treatment.

Written Promises

If you have a written employment contract setting out the terms of your work, pay, and benefits, you may be able to get it enforced against an employer who ignores any one of its provisions.

A legal contract—covering employment or anything else—is created when three things occur:

- An offer is made by one person to another.
- That offer is accepted.
- Something of value is exchanged based on the agreement.

You have the best chance of arguing that you are not an employee at will (and, therefore, that you are entitled to keep your job) if there is a strong written statement signifying that you are excepted from the employment at will doctrine.

For example, most collective bargaining agreements (contracts that set out union members' rights) state that union members can be fired only "for good cause." So, while union members are still technically employees at will, their agreements often make them exceptions to the general rule, requiring employers to have a specific, legally valid reason before firing them. (See Chapter 15.)

And some employees negotiate and sign detailed contracts with their employers—contracts that set out the specific terms of their employment, including salary, relocation rights, and beginning and ending dates of work. Employment contracts have become more rare since the rise and fall of the dot-com companies—and are now usually reserved for notables such as professional athletes and for the top executives at larger companies; about 55 chief execs at the 100 biggest companies have signed one by current count. Those holding employment contracts are usually not subject to the employment at will doctrine; their contracts spell out the length of their employment and specifically note when and how the employment relationship can end.

Implied Promises

Claiming that you and your employer have an implied contract is one more way employees can chip away at the doctrine of employment at will. But the chipping won't be easy. An implied contract assumes that words and things of value exchanged between a former employer and employee created a legal contract governing their relationship.

Until legal challenges to employee dismissals began to be filed with fervor in the early 1980s, many employers used terms such as "permanent employment" in their employee manuals, on job application forms, or orally when offering a position to a prospective employee. Today, employees who challenge their firings sometimes argue that, when an employer referred to permanent employment in the hiring process, that created an implied contract between them. They claim that this implied contract means that the company can only fire them for just cause, such as bad behavior on the job. An employer who fires for less than that, the theory goes, has breached the implied contract. And sometimes, when bolstered by strong evidence, that theory holds up in court.

In addition to making the foolhardy promise of permanent employment, employee handbooks may also offer other fertile grounds for exceptions to employment at will.

A few courts have held, for example, that where company manuals state that employees must be given specific forms of progressive discipline before being fired, employers must deliver on those promises. However, most savvy businesses these days are well acquainted with this legal loophole, so few of them now include such promises in their employee manuals.

And courts have become more circumspect about when they will find an implied employment contract in an employee manual, most opining that the manuals must be very specific and detailed—more than general statements of policy—to constitute a contract.

Outside of employee manuals, courts have also found implied contract exceptions to employment at will where employers overtly agree to continue employment for a specific time period, for example: "until the company relocates its main office." And, less commonly, such implied contracts have also been found where employers offer persuasive job negotiations along with letters of reassurance or job offers promising stability.

In determining whether you have a binding implied employment contract with a former employer, courts will look at a number of factors that might have led you to believe your employment was rooted in solid ground, including:

- the duration of your employment
- whether you received regular promotions
- whether you consistently received positive performance reviews
- whether you were assured that you would have continuing employment

- whether your employer violated a usual employment practice in firing you—such as neglecting to give a required warning, or
- whether promises of permanence were made when you were hired.

EXAMPLE: In 1980, Marguerite took a job as an accountant with EZ Ink Printing. EZ Ink's employee manual stated that employees were not considered permanent until they completed a 90-day probationary period.

For many years, Marguerite built her life around EZ Ink—assuming that she would be able to keep her job there until she reached retirement age. However, after she toiled more than two decades there, the head of EZ Ink unexpectedly fired Marguerite, claiming her quarterly reports were incomplete.

Marguerite would likely be able to win a lawsuit against EZ Ink based on breach of an implied contract. The three elements required to create an implied employment contract were there:

- an offer—the employee manual's implication that all employees who remained with the company more than 90 days were permanent employees
- an acceptance of that offer— Marguerite's many years of employment by the company, and
- an exchange of value—the wages that EZ Ink had paid Marguerite and her labor for them.

Beware of Job Loss Insurance Policies

As the concept of long-term job security fades, some businesses are trying to exploit employees' fears of job loss by offering insurance policies that claim to cover certain bills during periods of unemployment.

Flyers urging you to buy job loss insurance are often included with your monthly credit card statement. The glitzy ads usually offer to make the payments on that worrisome credit card account should you lose your job. And mortgage companies frequently offer job loss insurance as a part of the process of closing the purchase of a home, arguing that your mortgage payments would be made by the insurance company should you become unemployed.

Such insurance usually is not a wise buy for most people. Look closely at the fine print of most job loss insurance policies and you will see a long list of situations in which benefits are not available. Typical exceptions: you are out of work for less than several weeks, you volunteered for an early retirement program, you were fired because of something you did at work, or you were involved in a labor dispute.

Most job loss policies only provide coverage in limited situations—for example, if your employer suddenly went bankrupt.

And a closer look at the fine print on such policies usually reveals any number of defeating caveats.

- Self-employed workers, independent contractors and retired or active military personnel typically aren't eligible for the coverage.
- There's a moratorium of a month or more after the policy begins before a homeowner can actually file a claim. After the moratorium, the owner typically must be out of work 30 days before the first benefit is paid.
- Benefits are paid to the mortgage company or its servicer, not to the policy owner.
- Insurers can choose not to write policies for employees of certain industries or in regions hit hard by layoffs.
- And most unexpectedly, premiums may be adjusted without warning.

Breaches of Good Faith and Fair Dealing

While it is an uphill battle to prove that a written or implied promise tantamount to a contract ever existed, it's even tougher to prove that one has been violated. And, barring discrimination or some other egregious wrongdoing in the process, your best hope of fighting a firing may be to claim that your former employer breached what is referred to as a duty of good faith and fair dealing.

Courts have held that employers have committed breaches of good faith and fair dealing by:

- firing or transferring employees to prevent them from collecting sales commissions
- misleading employees about their chances for future promotions and wage increases
- fabricating reasons for firing an employee on the basis of on-the-job performance when the real motivation is to replace that employee with someone who will work for lower pay
- soft-pedaling the bad aspects of a particular job, such as the need to travel through dangerous neighborhoods late at night, and
- repeatedly transferring an employee to remote, dangerous, or otherwise undesirable assignments to coerce him or her into quitting without collecting the severance pay and other benefits that would otherwise be due.

While their rulings may be subject to change, some courts do not appear to recognize this exception to at-will employment at all. And some states allow employees to sue for breach of good faith and fair dealing only if they have a valid employment contract.

Violations of Public Policy

The employment at will doctrine won't protect an employer from a wrongful discharge claim if a worker is fired for complaining about illegal conduct or a wrong an employer committed, such as failing to pay workers a minimum wage or overtime pay when it is required. Indeed, it is illegal to violate public

policy when firing a worker—that is, to fire for a reason that harms not only the fired worker, but also the interests of the public in general.

Figuring out whether a court would decide that a particular firing fits into this category can, of course, be an exasperating exercise. Before allowing an action for a violation of public policy, most courts strictly require that there be some specific law setting out the policy. Many state and federal laws oblige and take some of the guesswork out of this issue by specifying employment-related actions that clearly violate public policy, such as firing an employee for:

- disclosing a company practice of refusing to pay employees their earned commissions and accrued vacation pay (see Chapter 2, "Rights Under the FLSA")
- taking time off work to serve on a jury (see Chapter 2, "Time Off for Jury Duty")
- taking time off work to vote (see Chapter 2, "Time Off for Voting")
- serving in the military or National Guard (see Chapter 2, "Time Off for Military or National Guard Duty"), or
- notifying authorities about some wrong-doing harmful to the public—generally known as whistleblowing (discussed below).

In addition, a number of state laws protect employees from being fired for asserting a number of more arcane rights—including serving as an election officer, serving as a volunteer firefighter, having certain political opinions, appearing as a witness in a criminal case, or even being elected to the general assembly. Many of these laws, passed as knee-jerk reactions to assuage particular workplace disputes, have become all but dead letters. Few people know they exist. And very few workers attempt to claim their protections. Still, if you feel that your firing may have violated one of these prohibitions, double check the laws in your state. (See Chapter 17, "Legal Research," for detailed guidance.)

Courts have also held that it violates public policy for an employer to fire you because you took advantage of some legal remedies or exercised a legal right. And some states will not recognize this exception unless there is a specific statute conferring a particular right. For example, it is illegal for your employer to fire you because you:

- file a workers' compensation claim (see Chapter 12)
- file a complaint under the Fair Labor Standards Act (see Chapter 2)
- report a violation of the Occupational Safety and Health Act or state safety law (see Chapter 6)
- claim your rights under Title VII of the Civil Rights Act (see Chapters 7 and 8)
- exercise your right to belong or not to belong to a union (see Chapter 15)
- exercise your right to take a leave from work that was available under state or federal law (see Chapter 4)
- refuse to take a lie detector test or refuse to take a drug test given without good reason (see Chapter 5, "Workplace Testing"), or
- have your pay subject to an order for child support or a wage garnishment order (see Chapter 2).

In a few states, this exception for violating public policy is nearly sacrosanct, but not quite. When a terminated employee's wrongful termination claim raises an important public policy interest, a court will consider whether the employer violated that policy by firing the worker. For example, an Arizona appellate court recently found that a former employee might have been fired as a scapegoat after complaining about possible violations of his employer's internal antitrust policy. (*Murcott v. Best Western International,* 9 P.3d 1088 (2000).)

Just one year later, however, another Arizona court rejected an employee's wrongful discharge claim based on the public policy exception to employment at will. The former employee claimed he was fired for refusing to copy Bible study software onto another employee's computer, an illegal act. The court held that the plaintiff's "good faith belief" in the illegality of the Bible software copying was not enough; he had to prove the actual illegality of the act. The case serves as yet another reminder of the need to collect and preserve good documentation to succeed with such legal claims. (*Cummins v. Mold-in-Graphic Sys.,* 200 Ariz. 335 (2001).)

Retaliation

Various types of laws—notably, those protecting whistleblowing (see "Whistleblowing Violations," below) and prohibiting discrimination (see Chapter 7)—specifically forbid employers from retaliating against employees who avail themselves of legal protections. But a lawsuit alleging retaliation need not always be pegged to a specific statute. An increasing number of cases are now based on the time-tested ban against getting even, legally known as retaliation.

The broad claim of retaliation is a little more complicated, but somewhat easier to prove, than a charge of workplace discrimination. The reason is that evidence supporting retaliation claims is usually less subjective and more obvious than for cases of discrimination. To make out a case of retaliation, you must prove all of the following:

- You were engaged in a legally protected activity—such as filing a complaint with the Equal Employment Opportunity Commission or formally complaining to your own company officials about harassment or discrimination.
- Your actions were the cause of your employer's actions—for example, you were demoted just after your employer found out that you filed a charge of sexual harassment.
- Your employer then took adverse action against you—by firing you, denying you a promotion, giving you an unwarranted bad performance review, increasing your job duties or responsibilities, overscrutinizing your work, or giving you an inaccurate poor reference. However, the U.S. Supreme Court recently ruled that in a Title VII discrimination claim, the employer's action need not be related to employment or to the workplace. And legal experts predict this broader standard may soon apply in other types of retaliation claims as well. (See Chapter 7, "Penalties for Retaliation.")

The employer or former employer is then free to show that there was some legitimate reason—other than retaliation—for its actions. If such evidence is presented, you get one more shot at winning by showing that the employer would not have acted—that is, fired or demoted you—if you had not acted first. This last is a tad tricky. In seeing whether this link exists, courts are most likely to look at:

- who made the job decision against you—he or she must have known about the action you took
- your prior work record—especially important if you were fired, demoted, or given poor job performance evaluations following your action, and
- the timing of your actions and the employment decision—the shorter the time between them, the more likely a court is to find that they are related.

Fraud

In extreme cases, an employer's actions are so devious and wrong-hearted that they constitute fraud. Fraud can be found at various stages of an employment relationship—most commonly in the recruiting process, where promises are made and broken, or in the final stages, such as when an employee is induced to resign.

By dint of its devious nature, fraud is tough to track and expose—and harder still to prove in court. To win, you must show all of the following:

- The employer made a false representation.
- Someone in charge knew of the false representation.

Dream Job Delivers Rude Awakening

Native New Yorker Andrew Lazar uprooted his family to take a California dream job only after a long and agonizing courtship instituted by Rykoff, a restaurant supply and equipment firm.

When Rykoff first set its eyes on Lazar in 1990, he was working in the same family-owned restaurant in which he had worked for more than 18 years—and bringing home about $120,000 each year to help cover living expenses for himself, his wife, and their two teens. Rykoff promised him more: a $130,000 salary to start, ample chances for bonuses and increases, a sure shot at becoming department head in a few years, a job with a lifetime guarantee.

Lazar bit—after being assured that Rykoff was fiscally strong and growing. The company resisted entering a written contract, however, assuring Lazar that "in the Rykoff family, our word is our bond."

But Rykoff's financial picture was not as rosy as painted. While wooing Lazar, it had just experienced its worst year in a long time and was planning to merge with another company—a move that would mean cutting many employees from its staff.

Lazar worked hard and well, exceeding sales goals, increasing sales, and lowering operating costs. But after two years on the job, he was shown the door. Out of work, out of money for home payments, out of touch with New York job contacts, Lazar sued. He claimed that Rykoff never intended to make him a permanent part of the staff, never intended to pay the wages and bonuses it promised—and so was guilty of fraud. The court agreed. (*Lazar v. Superior Court of Los Angeles County*, 12 Cal. 4th 631 (1996).)

- Your employer intended to deceive you or induce you to rely on the representation.
- You relied on the representation as the truth.
- You were harmed in some way by your reliance.

The hardest part of proving fraud is connecting the dots to show that the employer acted badly on purpose, in an intentional effort to trick you. That requires good documentation of how, when, to whom, and by what means the false representations were made. If your employer is a large corporation, the task of collecting and proving this information is all the more difficult, since you must usually work through layers of bureaucracy and many individuals. You must be able to name the people who made the fraudulent representations, their authority to speak, to whom they spoke, what they said or wrote, and why you relied on it.

If you are sufficiently lucky and resourceful to present this cogent puzzle after your employer defrauds you, you may be entitled to reimbursement for a surprising array of costs, including the costs of uprooting your family to take the job and the loss of income and security that resulted from leaving your former employer.

Defamation

Defamation is a legal action with the chivalrous-sounding intent of protecting a person's reputation and good standing in the community. There are a lot of opportunities in the typical firing process for an employer to sully an employee's reputation, so it is increasingly common for former employees to bring a defamation charge when they are fired.

A defamation claim is not a challenge to the legitimacy of an employee's dismissal. Rather, it is a way of getting monetary revenge on the employer who was sloppy, insensitive, or downright mean in firing you or in dealing with your need for references in obtaining a new job.

Defamation is usually difficult to prove. Typically, you must show that, in the process of dismissing you from your job or subsequently providing references to potential new employers, your former employer significantly damaged your good name and, usually, that this jeopardized your chances for gaining new employment.

This commonly entails much legal hairsplitting over the facts surrounding a firing. Most disputes involve whether the employer may legitimately communicate the facts surrounding a dismissal to other people. And a number of defamation claims center on whether or not the distribution of the damaging information was intentional and malicious—that is, meant to harm you.

To sue for defamation, you must show that your former employer:

- made a false statement about you
- told or wrote that statement to at least one other person
- was negligent or intentional in communicating the statement, and
- harmed you in some way by communicating the statement, such as by causing others to shun you or causing you to lose a job or promotion.

To win a case of defamation, you must prove that the hurtful words were more than petty watercooler gossip. The words must also be more than a personal opinion. It is ordinarily legal for anyone to voice an opinion, no matter how unflattering. True defamation must be factual information—or imply a fact—and it must be false.

Statements that have been ruled to sufficiently harm a worker and qualify as defamation are false claims that he or she:

- committed a crime
- performed job duties incompetently
- improperly used drugs or alcohol, or
- acted in some other way that clearly implied unfitness for a particular job.

Because a few unflattering comments or even a small dose of mean-spiritedness does not usually qualify as defamation, it is extremely important to scrupulously document cases where false statements are made. You can do this by writing down not only the exact offensive words that were said and who said them, but also when and where they were said and whether there were any witnesses. Securing this type of documentation may be difficult if you have lost your job and are no longer in the workplace.

Company Makes a Very Expensive Call

Don Hagler had just finished a shift at a Dallas office of Proctor & Gamble Co. when a burly security guard stopped him at the front gate, searched a bag he was toting, and confiscated a telephone inside it.

Hagler, who had worked at the detergent plant for 41 years, claimed he had paid for the phone out of his own pocket. But P&G management members saw the phone as their own. They began an intensive investigation, which included posting notices on 11 bulletin boards throughout the plant and over the company email system that read: "It has been determined that the telephone in question is Proctor & Gamble's property and that Don had therefore violated Work Rule #12 concerning theft of company property."

Then Hagler was fired.

He sued for defamation, claiming that P&G used him as an example to stem a tide of property pilfering. At trial, a coworker testified that he was with Hagler at a mall when he bought the phone. Hagler testified that he had applied for more than 100 jobs, but no employer would take him on after learning he was fired for theft.

After deliberating for five hours, the jury returned a verdict for Hagler—and awarded him $15.6 million in damages.

Hagler became richer, but wistful. "I'm not proud of the fact that I had to sue the company I was dedicated to for 41 years," he told *The Wall Street Journal* just after the verdict. "I sued because they called me a thief and put it on 11 bulletin boards in the plant. I think P&G's a good company. But I think they've changed. They're not as nice to people as they used to be."

Keep in mind that courts will generally be most persuaded by words that clearly damage your work reputation. For example, a former employer's false statement that you stole money would probably qualify as defamation, because most people would probably not hire you because of it. But a false statement that you had stayed on your last job only two months would probably be defamatory only if you could prove that it damaged you severely—such as by preventing you from getting a new job, causing a landlord to refuse to rent an apartment to you, and otherwise causing you social embarrassment and emotional distress.

Whistleblowing Violations

Whistleblowing is a sort of subset of the public policy violations discussed above. While states differ in the details, whistleblowing laws generally protect individuals who report to proper authorities activities that are unlawful or harm the public interest. One unique feature about whistleblowing is its foul-crying aspect. The whistleblower is protected for doing the civic duty of pointing out the misdeeds of powers that be. To merit this protection, the whistleblower must avoid crying wolf: Generally, whistleblowers are protected from retaliation only if they act in good faith and have some good reason to believe that the information they report to authorities is accurate.

Some states protect whistleblowers who complain of any legal violation—that is, who complain that the employer has violated any law, regulation, or ordinance. Others limit whistleblower status to those who report violations of particular laws, such as labor laws or environmental protections. A play fair provision in a number of state laws requires employees to tell their employer about the wrongdoing first—to allow him or her an opportunity to fix the problem. These rules are summarized in the chart below.

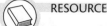

RESOURCE

For more information on whistleblowing cases and legislation, contact:

National Whistleblower Center
P.O. Box 3768
Washington, DC 20027
202-342-1903
FAX: 202-342-1904

The organization also maintains a robust website at www.whistleblowers.org.

The U.S. Department of Labor also recently instituted a website, the Whistleblower Program, that combines information and links in one spot. It's located at www.osha.gov/dep/oia/whistleblower/index.html.

The High Cost of Blowing the Whistle

The story of one of the most famous whistle-blowers, Karen Silkwood, was the inspiration for hundreds of articles, several books—and a heavily bankrolled motion picture.

In the early '70s, Silkwood worked as a lab analyst in an Oklahoma Kerr-McGee plant which manufactured plutonium pins used as fuel for nuclear reactors. Plutonium, a radioactive chemical element, is known to be highly toxic and carcinogenic. Silkwood, an elected union official and outspoken critic of Kerr-McGee's health and safety practices, began collecting and recording information to substantiate her charges that employees at the plant were dangerously exposed.

In early November 1974, Silkwood was found to be contaminated with the chemical. Nine days later, while enroute to meet with a *New York*

Times reporter and union leader to turn over her documentation of Kerr-McGee's unsafe work conditions, Silkwood was killed in a car accident with suspicious overtones. The damning documentation she was alleged to have had with her was not recovered from the accident scene.

Silkwood's estate sued Kerr-McGee for the injuries caused by the escaping plutonium. After several appeals involving esoteric issues of state and federal legal authority, the U.S. Supreme Court affirmed the award to the Silkwood estate of $10 million in punitive damages—damages designed to punish the wrongdoer and act as a deterrent—and an additional $5,000 in property damages to cover the cost of sanitizing her contaminated apartment. (*Silkwood v. Kerr-McGee*, 464 U.S. 238 (1984).)

State Whistleblower Laws

The following chart summarizes state whistleblowing laws that apply to private employers. Other laws, such as those protecting employees from retaliation, may also apply.

State	Statutes protecting whistleblowers	Statutes protecting employees who report health and safety violations	Notes and exceptions
Alabama	Ala. Code § 25-8-57		Whistleblower statues apply to Alabama child labor laws.
Alaska	Alaska Stat. § 08.68.279	Alaska Stat. § 18.60.089, 08.68.279	Whistleblower protections apply to nurses.
Arizona	Ariz. Rev. Stat. § 23-1501	Ariz. Rev. Stat. §§ 3-376, 23-425	
Arkansas	Ark. Code Ann. § 16-123-108		
California	Cal. Lab. Code § 1102.5; Cal Bus. 8c Prof. code § 7583.46	Cal. Lab. Code §§ 6310 to 6312, 6399.7	Employer may not have policy that prevents employee from disclosing information to agency enforcing law.
Colorado	Colo. Rev. Stat. § 8-4-120		Whistleblower protections may be specific to wage claims.
Connecticut	Conn. Gen. Stat. Ann. §§ 31-51m, 16-8a	Conn. Gen. Stat. Ann. §§ 31-40d, 31-40o	
Delaware	Del. Code Ann. tit. 19, § 1703	Del. Code Ann. tit. 16, § 2415	
Dist. of Col.		D.C. Code Ann. § 32-1117	
Florida	Fla. Stat. Ann. §§ 68.088, 448.101 to 448.105		Whistleblower laws do not apply to employers with fewer than ten employees. Employee must report unlawful activity in writing to supervisor or employer and allow reasonable opportunity to correct.
Georgia		Ga. Code Ann. § 45-22-7	
Hawaii	Haw. Rev. Stat. § 378-62	Haw. Rev. Stat. § 396-8(e)	
Illinois	210 Ill. comp. Stat. § 86/35; 740 Ill Comp. Stat. § 174/15	820 Ill. Comp. Stat. § 255/14; 210 Ill. Comp. Stat. § 86/35	
Indiana	Ind. Code Ann. § 22-5-3-3	Ind. Code Ann. § 22-8-1.1-38.1	Employee must first report violation or misuse to employer; if employer is violator, must report to appropriate agency. If employer or agency does not make good faith effort to correct, employee may then make written report to any organization, person, or agency.

State Whistleblower Laws (continued)

State	Statutes protecting whistleblowers	Statutes protecting employees who report health and safety violations	Notes and exceptions
Iowa		Iowa Code § 88.9(3)	
Kansas	Kan. Stat. Ann. § 44-615	Kan. Stat. Ann. § 44-636(f)	Whistleblower laws apply to Kansas labor and industry regulations. Employee protected when notifying Secretary of Human Resources about an employer-employee controversy.
Kentucky		Ky. Rev. Stat. Ann. § 338.121(3)	
Louisiana	La. Rev. Stat. Ann. §§ 23:964, 30:2027, 22:13		Whistleblower laws apply to Louisiana labor and insurance laws, and to environmental laws, rules, and regulations, including lead hazard laws.
Maine	Me. Rev. Stat. Ann. tit. 26, § 833	Me. Rev. Stat. Ann. tit. 26, §§ 570, 833	Employee must notify employer or supervisor and allow reasonable opportunity to correct violation or condition (not required when there is good reason to believe employer will not make correction).
Maryland		Md. Code Ann. [Lab. & Empl.] § 5-604	
Massachusetts		Mass. Gen. Laws ch. 111F, § 13; ch. 149, §6D	
Michigan	Mich. Comp. Laws § 15.362	Mich. Comp. Laws §§ 408.1029(10), 408.1031, 408.1065	
Minnesota	Minn. Stat. Ann. § 181.932	Minn. Stat. Ann. § 182.654(Subd. 9, 11)	Employee must inform employer of reason before refusing to work. Government agency must keep employee's identity private.
Montana	Mont. Code Ann. § 39-2-904	Mont. Code Ann. § 50-78-204	
Nebraska	Neb. Rev. Stat. § 48-1114	Neb. Rev. Stat. § 48-443	Whistleblower laws apply to employers who receive state funding or employ 15 or more employees. Whistleblower laws apply to federal and state law and to the Nebraska Fair Employment Practice Act.

		State Whistleblower Laws (continued)	
State	Statutes protecting whistleblowers	Statutes protecting employees who report health and safety violations	Notes and exceptions
Nevada	Nev. Rev. Stat. §§ 630.293, 633.505	Nev. Rev. Stat. Ann. §§ 618.445, 630.293, 633.505	Whistleblower protections apply to employees of physicians who report conduct to state health board that could result in disciplinary action or relate to physician's competence.
New Hampshire	N.H. Rev. Stat. Ann. § 275-E:2	N.H. Rev. Stat. Ann. §§ 277:35-a, 277-A:7	Employee must notify employer or supervisor and allow reasonable opportunity to correct violation (not required when there is good reason to believe employer will not make correction).
New Jersey	N.J. Stat. Ann. § 34:19-3, 34:19-4	N.J. Stat. Ann. § 34:5A -17	Before disclosing violation, employee must make written report to supervisor and allow reasonable opportunity for employer to correct (not required in an emergency or if employee fears physical harm or is reasonably sure violation is known to supervisor).
New Mexico		N.M. Stat. Ann. § 50-9-25	
New York	N.Y. Lab. Law §§ 740, 215	N.Y. Lab. Law § 215	Whistleblower laws apply to federal, state, and municipal law and to New York labor laws. Before disclosing violation to government agency, employee must make written report to supervisor and allow reasonable opportunity for employer to correct.
North Carolina		N.C. Gen. Stat. §§ 95-196, 95-241	
North Dakota	N.D. Cent. Code § 34-01-20		Employee must have objective factual basis for believing that work order violates law and inform employer of reasons for refusing to carry it out.
Ohio	Ohio Rev. Code Ann. § 4113.52	Ohio Rev. Code Ann. § 4113.52	Employee protected when making an inquiry to ensure that information reported is correct. Before reporting violation to authority, employee must first notify supervisor and file written report and then give employer 24 hours to correct or make good faith effort to correct violation.
Oklahoma		Okla. Stat. Ann. tit. 40, § 403(B)	

State Whistleblower Laws (continued)

State	Statutes protecting whistleblowers	Statutes protecting employees who report health and safety violations	Notes and exceptions
Oregon	Or. Rev. Stat. §§ 659A.230 to 233	Or. Rev. Stat. § 654.062	Whistleblower laws apply to federal, state, and municipal law and to Oregon unemployment insurance law.
Pennsylvania	43 Pa. Cons. Stat. Ann. §§ 1423, 1431	35 Pa. Cons. Stat. Ann. §§ 7305(d), 7313	Whistleblower laws apply to federal, state, and municipal law; codes of ethics or conduct that protect public interest; and federal or state motor carrier safety standards, laws, or regulations. Employee protected when refusing to operate a commercial motor vehicle that does not comply with safety laws or when there is danger of serious injury to the public or employee.
Rhode Island	R.I. Gen. Laws § 28-50-3	R.I. Gen. Laws §§ 23-1.1-14, 28-20-21, 28-21-8	
South Carolina		S.C. Code Ann. § 41-15-510	
Tennessee	Tenn. Code Ann. § 50-1-304	Tenn. Code Ann. §§ 50-3-106(7), 50-3-409	Whistleblower laws apply to federal and state law and to regulations that protect public health, safety, and welfare.
Texas		Tex. Lab. Code Ann. §§ 411.081 to 411.083	
Utah		Utah Code Ann. § 34A-6-203	
Vermont	Vt. Stat. Ann. tit. 21, §§ 494d, 495, 507; tit. 3, § 961(4)	Vt. Stat. Ann. tit. 21, §§ 231, 232	Whistleblower laws apply to Vermont health care employees lie detector testing laws, and to unfair labor practice and workplace discrimination laws.
Virginia	Va. Code Ann. § 54.1-515	Va. Code Ann. § 40.1-51.2:1	Whistleblower laws apply to Virginia asbestos and lead worker and contractor laws. Employee is protected when cooperating with a board or agency to enforce or administer laws.
Washington	Wash. Rev. Code Ann. § 49.60.210	Wash. Rev. Code Ann. §§ 49.17.160, 49.70.110	Whistleblower laws apply to Washington workplace discrimination laws.
West Virginia		W. Va. Code § 21-3A-13	
Wisconsin		Wis. Stat. Ann. §§ 101.595, 146.997	Whistleblower protections apply to employees of health care facilities, health care providers, and residential care facilities.
Wyoming		Wyo. Stat. § 27-11-109(e)	

Current as of March 2007

Tips for Figuring Out Whether You Are Protected

Whistleblower statutes attempt to protect against the too-common occurrence of employees getting fired just after speaking to authorities about some wrongdoing.

Coincidence? Maybe.

What makes the firing questionable—and possibly covered by a whistleblower statute—is often the timing. Pay strict attention to when you were fired. Note whether it was soon after your employer found out that you reported the wrongful behavior. The shorter the time, the more likely that you are protected by a whistleblower statute.

There are also a number of other questions you should ask to help determine whether you may be covered by a whistleblower statute:

- Did you complain to anyone at your own workplace about the wrongful behavior before going outside? If so, what was the response? Were you threatened? Were you offered special benefits for not filing a complaint?

- If your company has a policy of progressively disciplining employees—reprimand, probation, suspension, dismissal—was it speeded up or ignored in your case?
- Were your whistleblowing activities specifically mentioned to you by your supervisor? By company management? By other employees?
- Have other employees been fired for whistleblowing?
- Did you notice management or coworkers treating you differently after you complained about the illegal behavior? Were you suddenly ostracized or ignored, passed over for promotions, given a less-attractive job assignment?

The more documentation you can produce—memos from management, dated notes summarizing conversations with coworkers, signed statements from other former employees—the stronger your case will be. (For other advice on documenting your dismissal, see "Getting Documentation," below.)

Employees' Rights

The other side of the employment at will logic is that employees are also free to leave a job at any time; an employer cannot force you to stay in a job you no longer wish to keep. And, while it is customary to give an employer notice before leaving a job, it is not usually required by law. The right to leave a job at any time feels like small recompense for most

workers. Obviously, most legal battles are fought by former employees who want their jobs back, not employers demanding that employees stay on.

Finding Out the Reason

Few job losses—or even disciplinary actions —come as complete surprises. You may disagree with the thought process behind the decision—or the complete lack of thought. But the first step to avoiding termination and deciding whether to take action against a firing is the same: You must delve into the inner workings of your employer's mind to find out the reason. Often this is simple: You are put on probation for missing four deadlines last month. You are being fired for grossly mishandling the company's biggest account. And you are told just so.

But sometimes, discerning the reason or ostensible reason for a disciplining or firing takes more sleuth work.

If You Have Been Disciplined

Although an employer has the right to fire you on the spot for substandard performance or stealing from the company coffer, most employers proceed more gingerly these days—beginning with a verbal warning and progressing to a written warning to probation to suspension, then to dismissal.

There are a number of steps you can take when you suspect the end is near. You are not legally entitled to any progressive warning system unless your employee handbook or other document guarantees it without exception.

But, if you find yourself on the receiving end of a disciplinary notice, there are several steps you should take that might actually save your job:

- Be sure you understand exactly what work behavior is being challenged. If you are unclear, ask for a meeting with your supervisor or human resources staff to discuss the issue more thoroughly.

- If you disagree with allegations that your work performance or behavior is poor, ask for the assessment in writing. You may want to add a written clarification to your own personnel file—but you should do so only if you feel your employer's assessment is inaccurate. First, take some time to reflect and perhaps discuss your situation with friends and family. If your clarification is inaccurate or sounds vengeful, your words could be twisted against you as evidence of your inability to work as a team player or take constructive criticism, or some other convenient company slang.

- Look for a written company policy on discipline procedures in the employee handbook or a separate document. If the policy says certain measures "must," "will," or "shall" be followed before an employee will be dismissed, then you have more clout in demanding that they be followed to the letter. Point out the rules and ask why they are being bent in your situation. That may help buy you more time so that you can change your work habits—or allow you to wait until a workplace controversy dies down or the situation improves in some other way.

- Read behind the lines to see whether your disciplining or firing may be discriminatory or in other ways unfair. Pay particular attention to the timing: Were you put on probation shortly before your rights in the company pension plan vested? Look also at uneven applications of discipline: Are women more often given substandard performance reviews or they are more likely to be fired before being elevated to supervisor?

If You Have Been Fired

Unless you are the unfortunate heir to a sudden unforeseen cutback in the workforce, you are likely to have seen the end of your employment coming well before it arrived. This is particularly true if you are fired because your employer claims your work was below par or that you violated a particular workplace rule. Still, it almost always behooves you to Get It In Writing.

Before any holes had been punched in the employment at will doctrine, companies often refused to give employees any reasons for being fired. Since a company had the legal right to hire and fire without any justification, most opted not to invite trouble by stating a reason for firing.

Today, many companies have reversed their policies on giving reasons for dismissals. Because courts throughout the country are gradually establishing more rights for fired employees, many companies, particularly large corporations that are attractive targets for wrongful discharge lawsuits, now are careful to provide at least the appearance of fair and evenhanded treatment of employees who are fired. Company owners and managers typically do this by carefully documenting the employee's allegedly unacceptable work performance. Then, the employer can provide the employee—and a court, should it come to that—with specific and tangible documentation of the cause of firing.

If you are fired, make your best effort to obtain a clear statement of the employer's reasons for doing so. Office or factory rumors, your suspicions, or your spouse's hunches just will not suffice. If you eventually decide to challenge your dismissal, the reasons that your former employer stated for firing you will almost certainly become a major point in any legal battle that may develop.

Whatever They Call It, It Still Feels Bad

People tend to think that getting fired means that you did something wrong on the job, and that when other terms are used—such as dismissal, discharge, layoff, staff cut, reduction in force, downsizing, and the all-too-sane-sounding rightsizing—it somehow means something less onerous. In hopes of preventing bad community relations and wrongful discharge lawsuits, many companies use these gentler words to describe firings.

Some companies have gone so far as to announce the firing of large groups of employees by using sterile, institutional terms such as Reorganizational Incentives or Activity Analysis and Review. Still other companies have described the process of firing groups of employees as early retirement—even where the people being dismissed are not being given anywhere near enough money to continue to live the rest of their lives without working.

Whenever you are permanently dismissed from a job without being given sufficient income to continue living without working, all these terms mean the same thing: You've been fired. (For more information on layoffs, see "Plant Closings," below.)

Getting Documentation

Securing the supporting paperwork behind the decision is most important if you have been fired and are considering taking legal action. But, even if you decide not to challenge the legality of your firing, you will be in a much better position to enforce all of your workplace rights if you carefully document the circumstances. For example, if you apply for unemployment insurance benefits and your former employer challenges that application, you will typically need to prove that you were dismissed for reasons beyond your control. (See Chapter 11, "Filing a Claim.")

There are a number of time-tested ways to document the circumstances leading to your firing.

Keeping a Paper Trail

Long before being fired, you may sense that something has gone wrong in the relationship between you and your employer, even if there has been no formal disciplinary action against you. Perhaps your first clue will be that your pay has been stuck at one level with no raises for an unusually long time. Or you may notice that none of your work assignments extend more than a few weeks. Whatever the sign that your job may be in jeopardy, use it as a reason to begin keeping a log of your interactions with your employer.

Record and date each work-related event, such as performance reviews, commendations or reprimands, salary increases or decreases,

and even informal comments that your supervisor makes to you about your work. Note the date, time, and location for each event; which members of management were involved; and whether or not there were witnesses. Whenever possible, back up your log with written materials your employer has issued, such as copies of the employee handbook, memos, brochures, and employee orientation videos.

In addition, ask to see your personnel file. (See Chapter 5, "Your Personnel Records," for information on your right to see your file.) Make a copy of all reports and reviews in it. Because personnel administrators are notoriously covetous of employee files, you may have to make repeated requests to see your file or pay a certain amount of money to copy each page in the file. It will be money well spent.

Many former employees are startled to learn that their personnel files have been tampered with by unscrupulous former employers. If you fear this might happen, make an additional copy of your file or of relevant reports or performance reviews, and mail them to yourself by certified mail. Then, should matters heat up later—or should a court battle become necessary—you will have dated proof of how the documents looked before any tampering took place.

Getting Written Explanations

There are a number of reasons you might want to get a written explanation of why you were fired from a former employer: to see whether the reason your former employer gives meshes with your own hunches and, in the hardest situations, to use as documentation if you feel your dismissal was discriminatory or otherwise illegal. Written explanations may also help you in a later job search, as you will be better able to assess whether a soon-to-be-former employer is likely to give a good recommendation to your prospective employers. (See Chapter 10, "Getting References," for more on employer references.)

In a rare but possible scenario, you may receive an explanation of your firing that is so shocking, so wrongheaded, and so mean-spirited that it seems that its purpose is to keep you from being hired again. It may indicate that your employer is blacklisting you—a practice that is illegal in many states. (See Chapter 10, "Blacklisting.")

Information From Former Employers

Many states regulate what an employer may say about a former employee—for example, when giving a reference to a prospective employer. In some states, employers may provide information about a former employee only with the employee's consent. And, to protect employers from defamation lawsuits (see discussion above), some states give employers who provide this information immunity—which means that the former employee cannot sue the employer for giving out the information as long as the employer acted in good faith.

Some states have laws, sometimes known as service letter laws, that require employers to provide former employees with letters describing certain aspects of their employment—for example, their work histories, pay rates, or reasons for their termination. These laws vary greatly from state to state and are summarized in the chart below.

CAUTION

You don't get it both ways. When asking a former employer for a service letter, you are asking for the truth, the whole truth, and nothing but the whole truth as to why you were fired. But reasons for firing are subjective. And, chances are, you may not like what you read. As noted above, a number of states specifically protect employers from being sued for defamation because of what they have written in a service letter. Most laws require a former employer to provide a statement that is "truthful" or "in good faith" to take advantage of this protection.

CAUTION

Additional laws may apply. If the chart below indicates that your state has no statute, this means there is no law that specifically addresses the issue. However, there may be a state administrative regulation or local ordinance that does control information from former employers. Call your state labor department for more information. (See the Appendix for contact details.)

State Laws on Information From Former Employers

Alaska

Alaska Stat. § 09.65.160

Information that may be disclosed

- job performance

Who may request or receive information

- prospective employer
- former or current employee

Employer immune from liability unless

- Employer knowingly or intentionally discloses information that is false or misleading or that violates employee's civil rights.

Arizona

Ariz. Rev. Stat. Ann. § 23-1361

Information that may be disclosed

- job performance
- reasons for termination or separation
- performance evaluation or opinion
- knowledge, qualifications, skills, or abilities
- education, training, or experience
- professional conduct

Who may request or receive information

- prospective employer
- former or current employee

Copy to employee required

- Copy of disclosures must be sent to employee's last known address.

Employer immune from liability

- employer with less than 100 employees who provides only the information listed above
- employer with at least 100 employees who has a regular practice of providing information requested by a prospective employer

No employer immunity if

- Information is intentionally misleading.
- Employer provided information knowing it was false or not caring if it was true or false.

Arkansas

Ark. Code Ann. § 11-3-204

Information that may be disclosed

- reasons for termination or separation
- length of employment, pay level, and history
- performance evaluation or opinion
- job description and duties
- eligibility for rehire
- attendance
- drug and alcohol test results from the past year
- threats of violence, harassing acts, or threatening behavior

Who may request or receive information

- prospective employer (employee must provide written consent)
- former or current employee

Employer immune from liability unless

- Employer disclosed information knowing it was false or not caring if it was true or false.

Other provisions

- Employee consent required before employer can release information.
- Consent must follow required format and must be signed and dated.
- Consent is valid only while employment application is still active, but no longer than six months.

California

Cal. Civ. Code § 47(c); Cal. Lab. Code §§ 1053, 1055

Information that may be disclosed

- job performance
- reasons for termination or separation
- knowledge, qualifications, skills, or abilities based upon credible evidence
- eligibility for rehire

State Laws on Information From Former Employers (continued)

Who may request or receive information
- prospective employer

Employer required to write letter
- public utility companies only

Colorado
Colo. Rev. Stat. § 8-2-114

Information that may be disclosed
- job performance
- reasons for termination or separation
- knowledge, qualifications, skills, or abilities
- eligibility for rehire
- work-related habits

Who may request or receive information
- prospective employer
- former or current employee

Copy to employee required
- Upon request, a copy must be sent to employee's last known address.
- Employee may obtain a copy in person at the employer's place of business during normal business hours.
- Employer may charge reproduction costs if multiple copies are requested.

Employer immune from liability unless
- Information disclosed was false, and employer knew or reasonably should have known it was false.

Connecticut
Conn. Gen. Stat. Ann. § 31-51

Information that may be disclosed
- "truthful statement of any facts"

Who may request or receive information
- prospective employer
- former or current employee

Delaware
Del. Code Ann. tit. 19, §§ 708 to 709

Information that may be disclosed
All employers
- job performance
- performance evaluation or opinion
- work-related characteristics
- violations of law

Health or child care employers
- reasons for termination or separation
- length of employment, pay level, and history
- job description and duties
- substantiated incidents of abuse, neglect, violence, or threats of violence
- disciplinary actions

Who may request or receive information
- prospective employer (health or child care employers must provide signed statement from prospective applicant authorizing former employer to release information)

Employer immune from liability unless
- Information was known to be false, was deliberately misleading, or was disclosed without caring whether it was true.
- Information was confidential or disclosed in violation of a nondisclosure agreement.

Employer required to write letter
- Letter required for employment in health care and child care facilities.
- Letter must follow required format.
- Employer must have written consent from employee.
- Employer must send letter within 10 days of receiving request.

State Laws on Information From Former Employers (continued)

Florida

Fla. Stat. Ann. §§ 768.095, 435.10, 655.51

Information that may be disclosed

Employers that require background checks

- reasons for termination or separation
- disciplinary matters

Banks and financial institutions

- violation of an industry-related law or regulation, which has been reported to appropriate enforcing authority

Who may request or receive information

- prospective employer
- former or current employee

Employer immune from liability unless

- Information is known to be false or is disclosed without caring whether it is true.
- Disclosure violates employee's civil rights.

Employer required to write letter

- only employers that require background checks

Georgia

Ga. Code Ann. § 34-1-4

Information that may be disclosed

- job performance
- qualifications, skills, or abilities
- violations of state law

Who may request or receive information

- prospective employer
- former or current employee

Employer immune from liability unless

- Information was disclosed in violation of a nondisclosure agreement.
- Information was confidential according to federal, state, or local law or regulations.

Hawaii

Haw. Rev. Stat. § 663-1.95

Information that may be disclosed

- job performance

Who may request or receive information

- prospective employer

Employer immune from liability unless

- Information disclosed was knowingly false or misleading.

Idaho

Idaho Code § 44-201(2)

Information that may be disclosed

- job performance
- performance evaluation or opinion
- professional conduct

Employer immune from liability unless

- Information is deliberately misleading or known to be false.

Illinois

745 Ill. Comp. Stat. § 46/10

Information that may be disclosed

- job performance

Who may request or receive information

- prospective employer

Employer immune from liability unless

- Information is truthful.
- No employer immunity if information is knowingly false or in violation of a civil right.

Indiana

Ind. Code Ann. §§ 22-5-3-1(b),(c), 22-6-3-1

Information that may be disclosed

- reasons for termination or separation
- length of employment, pay level, and history
- job description and duties

State Laws on Information From Former Employers (continued)

Who may request or receive information
- former or current employee (must be in writing)

Copy to employee required
- Prospective employer must provide copy of any written communications from current or former employers that may affect hiring decision.
- Prospective employee must make request in writing within 30 days of applying for employment.

Employer immune from liability unless
- Information was known to be false.

Employer required to write letter
- Must have written request from employee.
- Must state nature and length of employment and reason, if any, for separation.
- Employers that don't require written recommendations do not have to provide them.

Iowa
Iowa Code § 91B.2

Information that may be disclosed
- "work-related information"

Who may request or receive information
- prospective employer
- former or current employee

Employer immune from liability unless
- Information violates employee's civil rights.
- Information is not relevant to the inquiry being made.
- Information is disclosed without checking its truthfulness.
- Information is given to a person who has no legitimate interest in receiving it.

Kansas
Kan. Stat. Ann. §§ 44-808(3), 44-199a

Information that may be disclosed

Does not have to be in writing
- length of employment, pay level, and history
- job description and duties

Must be in writing
- performance evaluation or opinion (written evaluation conducted prior to employee's separation)
- reasons for termination or separation

Who may request or receive information
- prospective employer (written request required for performance evaluation and reasons for termination or separation)
- former or current employee (request must be in writing)

Copy to employee required
- Employee must have access to reasons for termination or separation and performance evaluations.
- Employee must be given copy of written evaluation upon request.

Employer immune from liability
- employer who provides information as it is specified in the law

Employer required to write letter
- Upon written request, must give former employee a service letter stating the length of employment, job classification, and rate of pay.

Louisiana
La. Rev. Stat. Ann. § 23:291

Information that may be disclosed
- job performance
- performance evaluation or opinion
- knowledge, qualifications, skills, or abilities
- job description and duties
- attendance, attitude, and effort
- awards, demotions, and promotions
- disciplinary actions

State Laws on Information From Former Employers (continued)

Who may request or receive information
- prospective employer
- former or current employee

Employer immune from liability unless
- Information is knowingly false or deliberately misleading.

Maine

Me. Rev. Stat. Ann. tit. 26, §§ 598, 630

Information that may be disclosed
- job performance
- work record

Who may request or receive information
- prospective employer

Employer immune from liability unless
- Employer knowingly discloses false or deliberately misleading information.
- Employer discloses information without caring whether or not it is true.

Employer required to write letter
- Employer must provide a discharged employee with a written statement of the reasons for termination within 15 days of receiving employee's written request.

Maryland

Md. Code Ann. [Cts. & Jud. Proc.] § 5-423

Information that may be disclosed
- job performance
- reasons for termination or separation
- information disclosed in a report or other document required by law or regulation

Who may request or receive information
- prospective employer
- former or current employee
- federal, state, or industry regulatory authority

Employer immune from liability unless
- Employer intended to harm or defame employee.

- Employer intentionally disclosed false information, or disclosed without caring if it was false.

Massachusetts

Mass. Gen. Laws ch. 111, § 72L 1/2

Information that may be disclosed (applies only to hospitals, convalescent or nursing homes, home health agencies, and hospice programs)
- reasons for termination or separation
- length of employment, pay level, and history

Employer immune from liability unless
- Information disclosed was false, and employer knew it was false.

Michigan

Mich. Comp. Laws §§ 423.452, 423.506 to 423.507

Information that may be disclosed
- job performance information that is documented in personnel file

Who may request or receive information
- prospective employer
- former or current employee

Employer immune from liability unless
- Employer knew that information was false or misleading.
- Employer disclosed information without caring if it was true or false.
- Disclosure was specifically prohibited by a state or federal statute.

Other provisions
- Employer may not disclose any disciplinary action or letter of reprimand that is more than 4 years old to a third party.
- Employer must notify employee by first class mail on or before the day of disclosure (does not apply if employee waived notification

State Laws on Information From Former Employers (continued)

in a signed job application with another employer).

Minnesota

Minn. Stat. Ann. § 181.933

Employer immune from liability

- Employer can't be sued for libel, slander, or defamation for sending employee written statement of reasons for termination.

Employer required to write letter

- Employer must provide a written statement of the reasons for termination within 10 working days of receiving employee's request.
- Employee must make request in writing within 15 working days of being discharged.

Missouri

Mo. Rev. Stat. §§ 290.140, 290.152

Information that may be disclosed

- reasons for termination or separation
- length of employment, pay level, and history
- job description and duties

Who may request or receive information

- prospective employer (request must be in writing)

Copy to employee required

- Employer must send copy to employee's last known address.
- Employee may request copy of letter up to one year after it was sent to prospective employer.

Employer required to write letter

- Law applies only to employers with 7 or more employees, and to employees with at least 90 days service.
- Letter must state the nature and length of employment and reason, if any, for separation.
- Employee must make request by certified mail within one year after separation.

- Employer must reply within 45 days of receiving request.

Other provisions

- All information disclosed must be in writing and must be consistent with service letter.

Montana

Mont. Code Ann. §§ 39-2-801, 39-2-802

Information that may be disclosed

- reasons for termination or separation

Who may request or receive information

- prospective employer

Employer required to write letter

- Upon request, employer must give discharged employee a written statement of reasons for discharge.
- If employer doesn't respond to request within a reasonable time, may not disclose reasons to another person.

Nebraska

Neb. Rev. Stat. §§ 48-209 to 48-211

Employer required to write letter

- Law applies only to public utilities, transportation companies, and contractors doing business with the state.
- Upon request from employee, must provide service letter that states length of employment, nature of work, and reasons employee quit or was discharged.
- Letter must follow prescribed format for paper and signature.

Nevada

Nev. Rev. Stat. Ann. § 613.210(4)

Employer required to write letter

- Upon request of an employee who leaves or is discharged, employer must provide a written statement listing reasons for separation and

State Laws on Information From Former Employers (continued)

any meritorious service employee may have performed.

- Statement not required unless employee has worked for at least 60 days.
- Employee entitled to only one statement.

New Mexico

N.M. Stat. Ann. § 50-12-1

Information that may be disclosed

- job performance

Who may request or receive information

- no person specified ("when requested to provide a reference ...")

Employer immune from liability unless

- Information disclosed was known to be false or was deliberately misleading.
- Disclosure was careless or violated former employee's civil rights.

North Carolina

N.C. Gen. Stat. § 1-539.12

Information that may be disclosed

- job performance
- reasons for termination or separation
- knowledge, qualifications, skills, or abilities
- eligibility for rehire

Who may request or receive information

- prospective employer
- former or current employee

Employer immune from liability unless

- Information disclosed was false, and employer knew or reasonably should have known it was false.

North Dakota

N.D. Cent. Code § 34-02-18

Information that may be disclosed

- job performance

- length of employment, pay level, and history
- job description and duties

Who may request or receive information

- prospective employer

Employer immune from liability unless

- Information was known to be false or was disclosed without caring whether it was true.
- Information was deliberately misleading.

Ohio

Ohio Rev. Code Ann. § 4113.71

Information that may be disclosed

- job performance

Who may request or receive information

- prospective employer
- former or current employee

Employer immune from liability unless

- Employer disclosed information knowing that it was false or with the deliberate intent to mislead the prospective employer or another person.
- Disclosure constitutes an unlawful discriminatory practice.

Oklahoma

Okla. Stat. Ann. tit. 40, §§ 61, 171

Information that may be disclosed

- job performance

Who may request or receive information

- prospective employer (must have consent of employee)
- former or current employee

Employer immune from liability unless

- information was false, and employer knew it was false or didn't care whether or not it was true

Employer required to write letter

- Law applies only to public utilities,

State Laws on Information From Former Employers (continued)

transportation companies, and contractors doing business with the state.

- Upon request from employee, must provide letter that states length of employment, nature of work, and reasons employee quit or was discharged.
- Letter must follow prescribed format for paper and signature.

Oregon

Or. Rev. Stat. § 30.178

Information that may be disclosed
- job performance

Who may request or receive information
- prospective employer
- former or current employee

Employer immune from liability unless
- Information was knowingly false or deliberately misleading.
- Information was disclosed without caring whether or not it was true.
- Disclosure violated a civil right of the former employee.

Rhode Island

R.I. Gen. Laws § 28-6.4-1(c)

Information that may be disclosed
- job performance

Who may request or receive information
- prospective employer
- former or current employee

Employer immune from liability unless
- Information was knowingly false or deliberately misleading.
- Information was in violation of current or former employee's civil rights under the employment discrimination laws in effect at time of disclosure.

South Carolina

S.C. Code Ann. § 41-1-65

Information that may be disclosed
- length of employment, pay level, and history
- reasons for termination or separation
- job performance
- performance evaluation or opinion (evaluation must be signed by employee before separation)
- knowledge, qualifications, skills, or abilities
- job description and duties
- attendance, attitude, and effort
- awards, demotions, and promotions
- disciplinary actions

Who may request or receive information
- prospective employer (written request required for all information except dates of employment and wage history)
- former or current employee

Copy to employee required
- Employee must be allowed access to any written information sent to prospective employer.

Employer immune from liability unless
- Employer knowingly or thoughtlessly releases or discloses false information.

Other provisions
- All disclosures other than length of employment, pay level, and history must be in writing for employer to be entitled to immunity.

South Dakota

S.D. Codified Laws Ann. § 60-4-12

Information that may be disclosed
- job performance (must be in writing)

State Laws on Information From Former Employers (continued)

Who may request or receive information
- prospective employer (request must be in writing)
- former or current employee (request must be in writing)

Copy to employee required
- upon employee's written request

Employer immune from liability unless
- Employer knowingly, intentionally, or carelessly disclosed false or deliberately misleading information.
- Information is subject to a nondisclosure agreement or is confidential according to federal or state law.

Tennessee

Tenn. Code Ann. § 50-1-105

Information that may be disclosed
- job performance

Who may request or receive information
- prospective employer
- former or current employee

Employer immune from liability unless
- Information is knowingly false or deliberately misleading.
- Employer disclosed information regardless of whether it was false or defamatory.
- Disclosure is in violation of employee's civil rights according to current employment discrimination laws.

Texas

Tex. Lab. Code Ann. §§ 52.031(d), 103.001 to 103.003; Tex. Civ. Stat. Ann. Art. 5196

Information that may be disclosed
- reasons for termination or separation (must be in writing)
- job performance
- attendance, attitudes, and effort

Who may request or receive information
- prospective employer
- former or current employee

Copy to employee required
- Within 10 days of receiving employee's request, employer must send copy of written disclosure or true statement of verbal disclosure, along with names of people to whom information was given.
- Employer may not disclose reasons for employee's discharge to any other person without sending employee a copy, unless employee specifically requests disclosure.

Employer immune from liability

employer who makes disclosure based on information any employer would reasonably believe to be true

Employer required to write letter
- Employee must make request in writing.
- Employer must respond within 10 days of receiving employee's request.
- Discharged employee must be given a written statement of reasons for termination.
- Employee who quits must be given a written statement, including all job titles and dates, that states that separation was voluntary and whether employee's performance was satisfactory.
- Employee entitled to another copy of statement if original is lost or unavailable.

Utah

Utah Code Ann. § 34-42-1

Information that may be disclosed
- job performance

Who may request or receive information
- prospective employer
- former or current employee

State Laws on Information From Former Employers (continued)

Employer immune from liability unless

- There is clear and convincing evidence that employer disclosed information with the intent to mislead, knowing it was false, or not caring if it was true or false.

Virginia

Va. Code Ann. § 8.01-46.1

Information that may be disclosed

- job performance
- reasons for termination or separation
- performance evaluation or opinion
- knowledge, qualifications, skills, or abilities
- job description and duties
- attendance, effort, and productivity
- awards, promotions, or demotions
- disciplinary actions
- professional conduct

Who may request or receive information

- prospective employer

Employer immune from liability unless

- Employer disclosed information deliberately intending to mislead, knowing it was false, or not caring if it was true or false.

Washington

Wash. Admin. Code 296-126-050

Employer required to write letter

- Within 10 working days of receiving written request, employer must give discharged employee a signed statement of reasons for termination.

West Virginia

W.Va. Code § 31A-4-44

Information that may be disclosed

- violation of an industry-related law or regulation, which has been reported to appropriate enforcing authority (applies only to banks and financial institutions)

Wisconsin

Wis. Stat. Ann. §§ 134.02(2)(a), 895.487

Information that may be disclosed

- job performance
- reasons for termination or separation
- knowledge, qualifications, skills, or abilities

Who may request or receive information

- prospective employer
- former or current employee
- bondsman or surety

Employer immune from liability unless

- Employer knowingly provided false information in the reference.
- Employer made the reference without caring whether it was true or permitted by law.
- Reference was in violation of employee's civil rights.

Wyoming

Wyo. Stat. § 27-1-113

Information that may be disclosed

- job performance

Who may request or receive information

- prospective employer

Employer immune from liability unless

- Information was knowingly false or deliberately misleading.
- Disclosure was made with no concern for whether it was true or permitted by law.

Current as of March 2007

Did They Say Merge or Squeeze Out?

The economic uncertainty of our times has forced many formerly hardy employers to scuttle about for funds. Some pressed companies decide that the best route out of their woes is to restructure the business completely. Many of them opt to merge with or acquire other companies. This can leave all employees involved in the lurch—unsure of their rights, unsure of the security of their jobs.

The law is lurching to keep up with these corporate gyrations, too. Legal questions are just now beginning to emerge that may help shape employees' rights during mergers and acquisitions.

A few hot spots are already clear.

Imperiled personnel information. When two companies merge, the negotiation process leaves all the transitory employees vulnerable: Their salaries are disclosed to potential buying companies, and their personnel files are often laid bare as part of full disclosure before the deal gets closed.

Robbed of negotiation rights. Employees who are left over after a merger are most often handed a Take It or Leave It package: They can accept the position available at the reconstituted company—or walk. The deal their employer strikes may rob them of the chance to negotiate a severance package.

Noncompete rights and wrongs. A number of employees sign noncompete agreements when they come on board, in which they typically agree not to go into the same type of business within a certain geographical region for a specified number of years. This is to prevent workers from running off with trade secrets and established clients by setting up a competing business. (See Chapter 10, "Agreements Not to Compete.") But, as more of the specialized companies merge to become conglomerates, this will mean that employees who quit or are fired will have fewer places to look for work.

Stay tuned for developments.

Requesting an Explanation

If you live in a state that has a service letter law requiring explanations of dismissals, and the employer who fired you does not provide you with one, request one in writing. Use the following sample letter as a starting point for drafting your request.

Sample Letter

June 10, 20xx

Ellen Ullentine
President
Tasteless Frozen Pizzas Inc.
123 Main Street
Anywhere, MO 54321

Dear Ms. Ullentine:

As required by Missouri Statutes Section 290.140, I request from you a letter stating the length of my employment with Tasteless Frozen Pizzas Inc., the nature of my work there, and the reason I was dismissed from employment.

Please note that this law requires you to provide me with such a letter within 45 days of when you receive this request.

Sincerely,

Paul Smith

Paul Smith
321 Front Street
Anywhere, MO 54321
234-555-6666

Some laws specify a time limit for requesting service letters. But, if possible, you should make your request within a day or two of your dismissal to make sure that you meet any such deadlines and to prevent the passage of time from affecting people's memories. Send your request for a service letter by certified mail so that you can prove, if necessary, that you made your request within any time limits specified.

States Without Laws or Explanations

If you live in a state that does not have a service letter law, there is a chance that your employer might not offer you any written explanation for your firing. This is particularly likely if the company dismissing you is small or does not know much about workplace law and current legal techniques for firing employees. If no written explanation of your dismissal is given, ask the person who officially informs you of your firing for a written explanation of the company's decision to dismiss you. Be firm but polite; keep in mind that having to fire someone is an extremely stressful assignment for even the most experienced managers.

Companies usually want dismissed employees out of their buildings and away from their remaining employees as quickly as possible to prevent vengeful sabotage or spreading anticompany sentiment. Therefore, a person being fired exercises a substantial amount of negotiating power by merely sitting in place in front of the person doing the firing, quietly insisting on written documentation until the request is satisfied. Remember, however, that in some companies, using your posterior as a negotiating tool, if pushed too far, can get you escorted out forcibly by the corporate security force or local police.

Letters of Understanding

If you have done everything within the limits of civility and your employer still refuses to give you written documentation of the reasons for your dismissal, you may be in for a wait—and some extra work—before you get it. If your state is among the majority that have no laws requiring such documentation, there is not much else you can do to force the issue at the time of your dismissal. Later, you may obtain documentation through some of the laws granting employees access to their personnel files (see Chapter 5, "Your Personnel Records"), or by filing a wrongful discharge lawsuit (see "Taking Action Against Your Dismissal," below) and demanding the company's internal documents concerning your employment during the course of the lawsuit.

But, before that, you might want to write a letter of understanding to the person who fired you—similar to the sample letter, below. This is especially important if you received some mixed messages upon being fired. Of course, it is to your advantage to get your employer to specify the reason for your firing that makes you seem the least culpable—and the most attractive to prospective employers.

Although you should mail your letter of understanding promptly, it is usually best to let it sit for a day or two after writing it. Then, read it over again to make sure you have kept it businesslike and to the point. Getting fired is a very emotional event—one that often generates more than a little anger and desire for revenge in even the most saintly people.

Correspondence between you and your former employer may eventually become the basis of future negotiations or even courtroom evidence, and you do not want its credibility to be tainted by ink from a poison pen.

Send your letter of understanding by certified mail so that you will be able to prove that the company received it. Using certified mail in this case may also help drive home to your former employer that you are serious about enforcing your rights concerning your dismissal.

Sample Letter

August 2, 20xx

Aggie Supervisor
XYZ Company
2222 Lake Street
Anytown, CA 12345

Dear Ms. Supervisor:

I'm writing to clarify the reasons for my dismissal from employment at XYZ Company on July 29, 20xx.

My understanding is that I was dismissed because there was a sharp decline in the market for our product, seamless rolled rings, due to the recent cutback in government military spending.

If you feel that my understanding is incorrect, please advise me in writing by August 16, 20xx.

Sincerely,

John Employee

John Employee
123 Any Street
Anytown, CA 12345
234-555-6666

If the company responds to your letter, you have obtained at least one piece of documentation of its reason for firing you. If the company does not respond to your letter after a month or so, you can probably assume that the reason stated in your letter of understanding is correct.

Additional Documentation

Other important forms of documentation for your firing may come your way in the weeks following your dismissal. For example, if you file a claim for unemployment compensation, your former employer will have to respond to that claim. That response will eventually be translated into a document that the local unemployment insurance office will provide to you. (See Chapter 11.)

Store all such documents in a file folder, a shoebox, or some safe place where they will not get lost or destroyed—and where you can find and organize them easily.

Waiving Your Right to Sue

In some companies, the firing process may work like this: A member of the human resource management staff hands you a formal written notice that you are fired. You are then asked to sign a statement indicating that you have read the documents and that you accept what is written in them. You are given a check for a few extra months of severance pay, although this is beyond the company's legal obligations. (See "When a Firing May Be Illegal," above.) You will then

be told that the check will be released to you immediately if you sign a waiver of any rights to take legal action against the company as a result of your dismissal.

This method of firing can seem cruel or unfair. But, in the past, it was effective for some companies in discouraging wrongful discharge lawsuits.

It is no longer a foolproof tactic. An increasing number of employees who have signed waivers of their rights to file a lawsuit over their firing have later succeeded in having the courts throw out the waivers by arguing, for example, that the waivers were signed under duress. Whether signing such a waiver will prevent you from suing your former employer depends on the circumstances of each individual case, however, so there is no way of predicting the power of a waiver in advance.

Going along with the firing will typically mean that you get immediate severance pay. However, if you have doubts about the validity of your dismissal, withhold your signature on any waiver of your right to sue while you think over the company's offer, obtain more information, and perhaps hire a lawyer. (See Chapter 17.) You take the chance of not getting the money that the company waves in front of you, but you will reduce the risk of signing away essential rights.

 CAUTION

Beware of the early retirement waiver. If you are asked to sign a waiver of your right to sue in return for participation in an early retirement program offered by your former employer, the Older Workers Benefit Protection Act may give you the right to consider the company's offer for 45 days before you accept or reject it, and seven more days to revoke a decision to accept the company's offer. (See Chapter 7, "The Older Workers Benefit Protection Act.")

Taking Action Against Your Dismissal

Once you become familiar with how employee dismissals are successfully challenged, compare those legal strategies to your firing and decide:

- which legal principle used to challenge a job loss best fits your situation
- whether you are willing to expend the effort, money, and time it usually takes to fight a firing, and
- whether or not you will need additional legal help to challenge your firing.

Look first to local specialized resources for affordable help. For this, your telephone book can be a godsend. Check the topic index in the Yellow Pages under Community Services, Employment, or similar headings. You are likely to find a number of listings for groups that deal with specialized workers: younger workers, older workers, immigrants, blue collar workers. Steel your nerves and give them a call. Many organizations now offer legal counseling or referrals. A growing number also offer the invaluable help of support groups or workplace counselors—

people in like situations or with specialized training who can help you discover what your options might be.

Also check the Appendix to this book; it lists a number of specialized organizations that may offer advice, publications, or referrals.

If you were fired for reasons that appear to violate public policy (discussed earlier in the chapter) or were discriminated against in some way (see Chapter 7), you may be able to get government help in challenging your dismissal. For example, if you were fired for filing a complaint under the Fair Labor Standards Act, you can ask the Labor Department to help you fight that dismissal. But be forewarned: These agencies are swamped with complaints—and are able to pursue only a fraction of the claims that have merit.

Look into possibilities less drastic and usually cheaper and more satisfying than going to court—such as arbitration or mediation. (See Chapter 17.)

Finally, consider getting a lawyer's help in filing a lawsuit to challenge your dismissal. (Also discussed in Chapter 17.) If you do consult a lawyer, he or she will likely urge you to package two or more legal claims in a single lawsuit. This may be your strongest bet in a wrongful discharge case because, if a judge or jury decides against you on one of the claims, you still have another leg to stand on. It is especially difficult to base an entire successful case on a breach of contract theory, because there are limits on what you can collect even if you do win such cases.

For example, damages awarded in a lawsuit based only on a breach of an implied employment contract would typically be limited to:

- reinstatement to the job—not a desirable thing, in many cases, because there are often bad feelings between the employee and employer, and
- lost wages, which do not often amount to much—particularly if you find a new job soon after being fired.

In contrast, some states consider a breach of good faith and fair dealing to be a tort: an intentional or careless act of a person or institution that directly harms another person or institution. And, in tort actions, you typically can ask for actual damages based on such things as emotional suffering, and for punitive damages: an amount of money that the wrongdoer is ordered to pay as a form of punishment and as a deterrent to repeating the behavior that gave birth to the lawsuit.

Punitive damages are usually based not on the size of the injury, but on the court's estimate of how large a financial penalty would be needed to make a former employer feel the sting. In the case of many large corporations, the size of the penalty needed to make the company hurt can be quite large.

EXAMPLE: Elmer was a salesperson for a building supply company whose employee manual stated that employees were considered permanent after completing a 90-day probation period. Elmer had been employed by the company for 14 years and was about to qualify for more than $50,000 in commissions from accounts he had sold years before.

He was fired just a week before qualifying for those commissions—but he found an equivalent new job just a few weeks later. Elmer sued the company that had fired him for breach of implied contract (the employee manual's statement on permanent employment) and breach of good faith and fair dealing (the company's use of dismissal as a way to avoid having him qualify contractually for the commissions).

On the breach of implied contract count, the court awarded him only the wages he lost while unemployed—which, because he quickly found a replacement job, totaled less than $5,000. But on the breach of good faith and fair dealing claim, the court awarded Elmer the $50,000 in commissions that he would have qualified for had he not been fired, $250,000 for the emotional stress he suffered because of the ordeal of being fired, and another $250,000 in punitive damages to deter his ex-employer from using that commission-avoidance trick again.

Using Other State Laws

Even if the reason for your dismissal is not specifically outlawed by a public policy law in your state or a provision within one of your workplace laws, you may have another convincing legal argument to raise. Courts often play Follow the Leader—adopting the public policy holdings from other states. If you can point to a well-reasoned opinion with facts similar to yours, you may be able to convince a court that conduct that was against public policy in another state should be illegal in your state, too.

EXAMPLE: Horatio, a salesperson in a clothing store in Virginia, was fired because he reported to police that the manager of the store was buying stolen wristwatches and selling them to customers on the sly. Virginia does not have a law that specifically prohibits firing an employee who reports a crime. Nevertheless, Horatio might be able to argue successfully in court that his firing violated public policy because other states, such as South Carolina, have laws that specifically forbid such firings.

Plant Closings

Sometimes, a job is lost through no fault of the employer or the employee; economics or changing marketplace demands simply make a job superfluous or extinct. Even in such situations, however, plant closing laws may give employees some rights as the workplace doors close.

The statutes typically known as plant closing laws apply only to mass dismissals of employees. They are the poor cousins of wrongful discharge lawsuits.

These laws sometimes offer a way to challenge a job loss that is much quicker, easier, and less expensive than filing a lawsuit. But the amounts of money and other relief that workers can seek under plant closing laws typically are minuscule compared with the recoveries available via the wrongful discharge lawsuit route.

Also, keep in mind that neither the federal plant closing law nor the state and local laws in the same category actually forbid closing worksites and dismissing the people who work there. All these laws really do is require that companies give employees a little advance notice that their jobs are going to go away, like it or not.

At most, plant closing laws can provide some income between jobs for employees of companies that fail to provide a warning that they're going to make a mass staff cut—and some punishments that might persuade a company that does not comply with the advance notice requirements of the plant closing laws not to repeat that behavior.

Federal Law

The federal plant closing law—torturously acronymed the Worker Adjustment and Retraining Notification, or WARN Act (29 U.S.C. §§ 2101, 2102 to 2109)—requires employers with 100 or more full-time employees to provide 60 days of advance written notice that they are going to lose their jobs before closing a facility—and before putting into effect any other mass staff reduction that will last six months or more.

Employers are also required to provide 60 days of notice of the staff reduction to the chief local elected official, such as the mayor of the city in which the cut will take place, and to the Dislocated Worker Unit of the state in which the cut will occur. The agency designated as the Dislocated Worker Unit varies from state to state, but your state's labor department should be able to direct you to the agency responsible for assisting workers who lose their jobs in mass dismissals. (See the Appendix for contact information.)

Exceptions

The federal plant closing law does not apply if any of the following are true:

- Fewer than 50 workers are cut from the payroll.
- The cut takes away the jobs of fewer than 500 workers and represents less than one-third of the employer's workforce.
- The workers affected are part time; this law defines part-time workers as those who average fewer than 20 hours of work per week, or who have been employed by the company for less than six of the 12 months preceding the staff cut.

- The employees left voluntarily or were discharged for good cause, such as performance that does not meet the company's standards.
- The plant closing or mass layoff was due to an economic strike or lockout.
- The staff cut is the result of a natural disaster.
- The employees affected were working on a project that was considered temporary and were told that when they were hired.
- Waiting 60 days to let the workers go would put the company in danger of going out of business.
- The employer could not have foreseen the circumstances that make the staff cut necessary.
- The employer offers the workers being cut new jobs at another site within reasonable commuting distance, and the new jobs start within six months of when the old ones ended, or the workers being cut are offered new jobs at another site anywhere and they agree to the transfers within 30 days of when the employer offers them.
- The employer voluntarily offers severance pay, not required under any contract or other agreement, that is equal to or greater than the number of days that the company is short on the 60-day notice requirement.
- More than 90 days pass between two mass dismissals that would require advance notice if added together but that

fall under the minimum size rules when counted separately.

Penalties for Violations

Obviously, the plant closing law has almost as many holes as fabric. But employers who manage to violate it despite all the exceptions can be made to pay the following penalties:

- back pay to each employee affected by the violation, up to a maximum of 60 days of pay
- reimbursement of the employees' benefit costs that would have been paid by the company had the illegal staff cut not occurred
- a fine of up to $500 per day for each day of the violation, up to a maximum of $30,000 (this fine is paid to the state, not to the workers who were laid off), and
- any attorneys' fees incurred.

This last penalty—requiring that legal fees be paid—is important because, if you have received your walking papers as part of a mass firing that violates the federal plant closing law and the government refuses to go to bat for you, you and your coworkers will probably have no recourse but to file a lawsuit to enforce your rights.

CAUTION

The math may be tricky. Counting the days may be more difficult than you would assume. Several courts have ruled recently that back pay was based on 60 workdays rather than calendar days.

Help From Your Uncle Sam

Before you hire a lawyer to take action under the federal plant closing law, you may want to write or call the highest elected official of the municipality where the staff cut took place and ask him or her to pursue your complaint. The federal plant closing law specifies that a unit of the local government aggrieved may sue the employer involved in the federal district court where the incident occurred or in any district where the employer does business.

In general, governmental bodies are not very aggressive in pursuing complaints against businesses. But, because large-scale staff cutting may be a high profile political issue, your local mayor may surprise you by suddenly becoming your legal advocate.

State Plant Closing Laws

A growing number of states have their own plant closing laws. (See the chart below.) Even a few cities, such as Vacaville, California, and Philadelphia, Pennsylvania, have laws restricting companies that order mass dismissals. Most of these laws merely add a minor restriction or two to the rules of the federal plant closing law, such as requiring that the corporation planning a mass staff cut notify another level of government of its plans in advance.

However, some of the state plant closing laws do provide substantial benefits for the workers they cover. For example, Hawaii's version requires an employer, under certain conditions, to make up the difference between a worker's regular pay and the unemployment compensation the worker will receive for up to four weeks after the staff cut. Employers who shirk this legal duty must pay a high price: three months of compensation to every former worker. (Haw. Rev. Stat. §§ 394B 10-12.)

Each of these laws specifies different restrictions, penalties, and methods of enforcement. You can usually learn the details of any state or local law governing mass dismissals by calling your state's labor department.

> **CAUTION**
>
> **Additional laws may apply.** If the chart below indicates that your state has no statute, this means there is no law that specifically addresses the issue. However, there may be a state administrative regulation or local ordinance that does control plant closings. Call your state labor department for more information. (See the Appendix for contact details.)

State Plant Closing Laws

Alabama
Ala. Code § 25-3-5

When law applies: Substantial layoff or closing of any plant or industry.

State assistance for employees: Commissioner of labor to provide seminars to unemployed or underemployed employees on legal rights regarding debts. To lessen the financial burden of closure or layoffs, commissioner may meet with management and with labor or other organizations, may facilitate communication with creditors, and may set up programs to provide financial assistance. No employer or employee group may be required to contribute to or participate in these programs.

Alaska
Alaska Stat. § 23.15.635

State assistance for employees: Department of Labor offers employment and training programs to workers who are liable to be displaced within 6 months because of reductions in workforce or job elimination.

California
Cal. Lab. Code § 1401

When law applies: Mass layoff, relocation or closing of any industrial or commercial facility with at least 75 employees.

Notification requirements: Employer must give employees at least 60 days' advance notice in writing before mass layoff, relocation, or termination. Employer must also notify the Employment Development Department, the local workforce investment board, and the chief elected official of each city and county government within which the termination, relocation, or mass layoff occurs. Notice shall include the elements required by the federal WARN Act.

Colorado
Colo. Rev. Stat. § 23-60-306

When law applies: Plant closings; workers displaced by technological changes.

State assistance for employees: Workers who have lost their previous jobs because of plant closings are eligible for retraining for new jobs through customized training programs provided by the State Board for Community Colleges and Occupational Education.

Connecticut
Conn. Gen. Stat. Ann. §§ 31-51n, 31-51o

When law applies: Permanent shutdown or relocation of facility out of state.

Employers affected by requirements: Employers with 100 or more employees at any time during the previous 12-month period.

Severance requirements: Employer must pay for existing group health insurance coverage for terminated employee and dependents for 120 days or until employee is eligible for other group coverage, whichever comes first.

Exceptions: Facility closure due to bankruptcy.

District of Columbia
D.C. Code Ann. §§ 32-101, 32-102

When law applies: When a new contractor takes over a service contract.

Employers affected by requirements: Contractors and subcontractors who employ 25 or more nonprofessionals as food service, health service, or janitorial or building maintenance workers.

State Plant Closing Laws (continued)

Severance requirements:
- Within 10 days after a new contract is awarded, previous contractor must give new contractor names of all employees. New contractor must hire all employees who have worked for past eight months for a 90-day transition period. After 90 days must give each employee a written performance evaluation and retain all employees whose performance is satisfactory.
- Contractor whose contract is not renewed and who is awarded a similar contract within 30 days must hire at least 50% of the employees from the former sites.

Florida
Fla. Stat. Ann. §§ 288.972, 370.27, 446.60

When law applies: Job loss or displacement due to industry changes.

State assistance for employees:
- Department of Labor and Employment Security establishes Workforce Florida, which provides counseling, training, and placement services to displaced workers in the defense industry and local telecommunications exchange workers.
- State agencies must give priority hiring to anyone who loses full-time employment in the commercial saltwater fishing industry because of the constitutional amendment limiting the use of nets to harvest marine species.

Hawaii
Haw. Rev. Stat. §§ 394B-1 to 394B-13

When law applies: Permanent or partial closing of business; relocation of all or substantial portion of business operations out of state.

Employers affected by requirements: Employers with 50 or more employees at any time during the previous 12-month period.

Severance requirements: Employer must provide 4 weeks' dislocated worker allowance as a supplement to unemployment compensation; amount is the difference between the weekly former wage and the unemployment benefit. Employers who do not follow notice and severance requirements are liable to each employee for three months of compensation.

Notification requirements: Employer must provide each employee with written notice 60 days in advance of closing or relocation.

State assistance for employees: Dislocated workers' program in Department of Labor and Industrial Relations provides assistance and training for workers who have lost their jobs or received a notice of termination.

Illinois
820 Ill. Comp. Stat. 65/1 to 65/99

When law applies: Mass layoff, relocation, or employment loss.

Employers affected by requirements: Any business enterprise that employs 75 or more full-time employees or 75 or more employees who in the aggregate work at least 4,000 hours per week (not counting overtime).

Notification requirements: Employer must give 60 days' written notice to affected employees and representatives of affected employees, and to both the Department of Commerce and Economic Opportunity and the chief elected official of each municipal and county government within which the employment loss, relocation, or mass layoff occurs.

Exceptions: Employer seeking capital in good

State Plant Closing Laws (continued)

faith; completion of explicitly temporary project; unforeseen circumstances; strike or lockout; physical calamity or war.

Penalties: Up to 60 days of back pay and the value of benefits for that time. Up to $500 per day civil penalty, unless employer pays the back pay within three weeks of announced layoffs; federal penalty payments count toward state penalty.

Kansas

Kan. Stat. Ann. §§ 44-603, 44-616

When law applies: Employers involved in:

- manufacture, transportation, or preparation of food products or clothing
- fuel mining or production
- public utilities, or
- transportation

must apply to state Secretary of Labor for approval before limiting or discontinuing business operations.

Louisiana

La. Rev. Stat. Ann. §§ 23:1842 to 23:1846

When law applies: Job loss related to state environmental protection laws.

State assistance for employees: Workers who have lost jobs because employer has relocated to another state to avoid compliance with state environmental protection laws or instituted technological changes because of laws are eligible for services through the Displaced Worker Retraining Program administered by the Department of Workforce Development.

Maine

Me. Rev. Stat. Ann. tit. 26, § 625-B

When law applies: Discontinuation or relocation of business operations at least 100 miles from original location.

Employers affected by requirements: Employers with 100 or more employees at any time during the previous 12-month period.

Severance requirements: Employer must give severance pay of one week for each year of employment to all employees who have worked for at least three years; pay due within one regular pay period after employee's last full day of work.

Notification requirements: Employer must give employees at least 60 days' advance notice in writing before relocating a plant. Employer must also notify the director of the Bureau of Labor Standards and municipal officials where the plant is located.

Maryland

Md. Code Ann. [Lab. & Empl.] §§ 11-301 to 11-304

When law applies: Shutdown of workplace or a portion of the operations that results in layoffs of at least 25% of workforce or 15 employees, whichever is greater, over any three-month period.

Employers affected by requirements: Employers with 50 or more employees who have been in business at least one year.

Severance requirements: Employers are encouraged to follow Department of Labor voluntary guidelines for severance pay, continuation of benefits, and notification.

Notification requirements: 90 days whenever possible.

Exceptions: Bankruptcy, seasonal factors common to industry, labor disputes, temporary workplaces, or construction sites.

State assistance for employees: Department of Labor will provide on-site unemployment insurance bulk registration (when more than 25 workers are laid off), retraining, job placement, and job-finding services.

State Plant Closing Laws (continued)

Massachusetts

Mass. Gen. Laws ch. 149, §§ 179B, 182, 183; ch. 151A, §§ 71A to 71H

When law applies:
- Permanent cessation or reduction of business operations which results or will result in the permanent separation of at least 90% of the employees within six months.
- Sale or transfer of ownership of a business with 50 or more employees.

Employers affected by requirements:
- Employers receiving assistance from state business financing or development agencies.
- Employers with 50 or more employees who sell or transfer control of a business.

Severance requirements:
- Employers receiving state agency assistance must make a good faith effort to provide 90 days' group health insurance coverage for employees and dependents, at the same payment terms as before plant closing.
- When a company with 50 or more employees is sold or changes hands, new owner must give severance pay of two weeks' compensation for every year of service to employees who have worked at least three years. Employees terminated within two years of the sale are due severance within one regular pay period after last day of work; employees terminated within one year of sale are due severance within four pay periods after the sale.

Notification requirements:
- Employers receiving state agency assistance are expected to provide 90 days' notice.
- Employers with 12 or more employees must notify the Director of Labor and Workforce Development when business changes location.

- New owner of business with 50 or more employees must provide written notice of rights to each employee and to any collective bargaining representative within 30 days of completion of sale.

State assistance for employees:
- Reemployment assistance programs which provide counseling, placement, and training are available through the employment and training division of the Department of Workforce Development.
- Employees who have worked for a company for at least one year are eligible for up to 13 weeks of reemployment assistance benefits.

Michigan

Mich. Comp. Laws §§ 450.731 to 450.737

When law applies: Permanent shutdown of operations at any establishment with 25 or more employees.

Notification requirements: Department of Labor encourages businesses that are closing or relocating to give notice as soon as possible to the Department, the employees and any organization representing them, and the community.

State assistance for employees: Department of Labor may study the feasibility of the employees establishing an employee-owned corporation to continue the business.

Minnesota

Minn. Stat. Ann. §§ 116L.17, 116L.976

When law applies:
- Plant closing: Announced or actual permanent shutdown of a single site.
- Substantial layoff: Permanent reduction in workforce (not due to plant closing) at a single site which results in job loss for at least

State Plant Closing Laws (continued)

50 full-time employees during any 30-day period.

Notification requirements: Employers are encouraged to give 60 days' notice to the Department of Trade and Economic development. If federal WARN Act requires notice, then employer must report to state commissioner of employment and economic development the occupations of workers being terminated.

State assistance for employees: Department of Trade and Economic Development offers rapid response assistance to employees and businesses through the dislocated worker program. May include on-site emergency assistance, information about state and other agency resources, and help in setting up an employee-management committee.

Missouri

Mo. Rev. Stat. § 409.516(5)

When law applies: Any company making a business takeover offer.

Notification requirements: Company making offer must file a registration statement with the state securities commission disclosing any plans to liquidate, merge, or consolidate the target company; sell its assets; or make any other major change to its business, corporate structure, management, or employment policies.

New Hampshire

N.H. Rev. Stat. Ann. § 421-A:4(IV)

When law applies: Any company making a business takeover offer.

Notification requirements: Company making offer must file a registration statement with the secretary of state and with the target company disclosing any plans to liquidate,

merge, or consolidate the target company; sell its assets; or make any other major change to its business, corporate structure, management, or employment policies.

New Jersey

N.J. Stat. Ann. §§ 34:1B-30, 52:27H-95

When law applies: Potential plant closings.

State assistance for employees: Department of Labor and other agencies mandated to assist workers who want to establish employee ownership plans to save jobs threatened by plant closure. If plant closure would cause significant employment loss to an economically distressed municipality, the commissioner of commerce may fund a profitability study of an employee stock ownership plan.

New York

N.Y. Lab. Law §§ 835 to 849, Pub. Auth. Law §§ 1836-a to 1836-g; Bus. Corp. Law § 1603(5)

When law applies:
- Plant closing: Permanent or temporary shutdown of a single site or one or more facilities or operating units within a single site which results in job loss for at least 25 full-time employees during any 30-day period. (If shutdown causes job losses at other sites, they also count toward the 25.)
- Substantial layoff: Reduction in workforce (not due to shutdown) at a single site which results in job loss for at least 33% full-time and 50 part-time employees or 500 full-time employees during any 30-day period.
- Any company making a business takeover offer.

Notification requirements: Company making offer must file a registration statement with the attorney general's New York City office and

State Plant Closing Laws (continued)

with the target company disclosing plans for plant closures or major changes in employment policies.

State assistance for employees:

- The Department of Labor, in coordination with the Department of Economic Development and the dislocated worker unit, provides rapid response services after a plant closure, including: on-site intervention within 48 hours; basic emergency readjustment services; information about retraining, unemployment insurance, and technical assistance.
- The Job Development Authority encourages employees of plants that are about to be closed or relocated to continue to operate them as employee-owned enterprises; state assistance is available.

Ohio

Ohio Rev. Code Ann. §§ 122.13 to 122.136

When law applies: Permanent shutdown of operations at a business with at least 25 employees; relocation of all or substantial portion of operations at least 100 miles from original location.

State assistance for employees: Department of Development has an employee ownership assistance program that provides technical assistance and counseling; will conduct a feasibility study for workers who want to establish employee ownership plans to continue running a business threatened by plant closure.

Oklahoma

Okla. Stat. Ann. tit. 71, § 453(F)(3)

When law applies: Any company making a business takeover offer.

Notification requirements: Company making

offer must file a registration statement with the state securities commission disclosing plans to close or relocate facilities or to make major changes in employment policies.

Oregon

Or. Rev. Stat. §§ 285A.510 to 285A.522, 657.335 to 657.340

When law applies

- Plant closing: Permanent or temporary shutdown of a single site or one or more facilities or operating units within a single site which results in job loss for at least 50 full-time employees during any 30-day period.
- Mass layoff: Reduction in workforce at a single site not due to shutdown which results in job loss for at least 33% of the workforce and 50 full-time employees, or for 500 full-time employees during any 30-day period.

Employers affected by requirements: Employers with 100 or more full-time employees.

Notification requirements: Employers must notify the Department of Community Colleges & Workforce Development of plant closings or mass layoffs.

State assistance for employees: State assistance and professional technical training available to dislocated workers. Workers who are in training are entitled to unemployment compensation and related benefits.

Pennsylvania

43 Pa. Cons. Stat. Ann. §§ 690a.1 to 690a.6; 70 PCSA §§ 74; 75(4)

When law applies:

- Current or projected plant closures.
- Any company making a business takeover offer.

State Plant Closing Laws (continued)

Notification requirements: Company making offer must file a registration statement 20 days in advance with the state securities commission, the target company, and the collective bargaining agent. Must disclose plans for closing down the target company, making major changes in employment policies, or changing any collective bargaining agreements.

State assistance for employees: Workers dislocated by plant closures are eligible for customized job training program through the Department of Labor & Industry and are eligible for assistance to support them while in training.

Rhode Island

R.I. Gen. Laws § 27-19.1-1

When law applies: Involuntary layoff; permanent reduction of workforce.

Severance requirements: Employees and dependents are entitled to at least 18 months' continuation of health care coverage at own expense; premium rate must be the same as the one offered under the group plan. (Length of coverage cannot exceed time of continuous employment.)

South Carolina

S.C. Code Ann. § 41-1-40

Employers affected by requirements: Employers who require employees to give notice before quitting work.

Notification requirements: Employers must give same amount of notice they require of employees or at least two weeks' warning. Notice must be in writing and posted in every room of the work building. Employers who do not comply are liable to every employee for any damages that result from failure to give notice.

Tennessee

Tenn. Code Ann. §§ 50-1-601 to 50-1-604

When law applies: Closing, modernization, relocation, or new management policy of a workplace or a portion of the operations which permanently or indefinitely lays off 50 or more employees during any three-month period.

Employers affected by requirements: Employers with 50 to 99 full-time employees within the state.

Notification requirements: Employer must first notify employees who will lose their jobs due to a reduction in operations and then notify the Commissioner of Labor and Workforce Development. Must give circumstances of closing and number of employees laid off. Toll-free telephone line established to encourage employer compliance.

Exceptions: Construction sites; seasonal factors common to industry.

Texas

Tex. Gov't. Code Ann. §§ 2310.301 to 2310.308; Tex. Util. Code Ann. § 39.906

When law applies: Industry restructuring or plant or facility closing.

Employers affected by requirements: Private employers who contract with Department of Defense or whose business is directly affected by defense-related economic factors.

State assistance for employees:

- Through defense readjustment projects, state provides funding to communities, programs, and businesses that assist or hire dislocated defense workers.
- Public Utility Commission allows employers to recover reasonable transition costs for severance, retraining, early retirement,

State Plant Closing Laws (continued)

outplacement, and related expenses for employees affected by electric utility industry restructuring.

Utah

Utah Code Ann. § 67-1-12

When law applies: Defense industry layoffs.

State assistance for employees: Workers in defense or defense-related jobs who are laid off may apply to the Office of Job Training for assistance in retraining or reeducation for job skills in demand.

Washington

Wash. Rev. Code Ann. §§ 50.04.075, 50.12.280, 50.20.042, 50.20.043, 50.70.030 to 50.70.050

When law applies: Employees who have been terminated or received a notice of termination and are unlikely to return to work at their principal occupations or previous industries.

State assistance for employees: The Department of Employment Security offers special training and counseling programs for dislocated workers in aerospace, thermal electric generation, and forest products industries in addition to any regular unemployment compensation.

Wisconsin

Wis. Stat. Ann. §§ 106.15, 109.07

When law applies:
- Business closing: Permanent or temporary shutdown of an employment site or of one or more facilities or operating units at a site or within one town that affects 25 or more employees.
- Mass layoff: Reduction in workforce that is not the result of a business closing and that affects at least 25% or 25 employees,

whichever is greater, or at least 500 employees.
- Employees who have worked at least six of the previous 12 months and who work at least 20 hours/week.

Employers affected by requirements: Employers with 50 or more employees in the state.

Notification requirements: An employer who has decided upon a business closing or mass layoff in Wisconsin must give at least 60 days' written notice to:
- the Dislocated Worker Committee in the Department of Workforce Development
- every affected employee
- the employees' collective bargaining representative, and
- the highest official of the municipality where the business is located.

Employer who does not comply is liable to employees for pay and for the value of benefits employee would have received if closing or layoff did not take place, from the day that notice was required to the day notice was actually given or business closing or mass layoff occurred, whichever is earlier.

Wyoming

Wyo. Stat. §§ 27-13-101 to 27-13-103

When law applies: Workers unemployed due to plant closings or substantial plant layoffs.

State assistance for employees: Department of Employment, in conjunction with the Department of Education, the University of Wyoming, and the Community College Commission, offers occupational transfer and retraining programs and services for displaced workers.

Current as of February 2007

After a Job Loss

I t is often hard to put on a perky face when your livelihood—and the identity often attributed to a job—are shaken or taken.

But, if you have lost your job or think you may soon lose it, do not despair. There are some laws that may protect you against suddenly joining the ranks of the unemployed without money or other help to ease the impact.

Depending on your situation, you may have the legal right to:

- fair treatment during and after you are fired
- severance pay
- a truthful reference from your former employer to help in future job hunting, or
- continuing coverage under your former employer's benefit programs.

You may even be able to get some compensation if the firing causes you severe economic hardship, or to win a court judgment against your former employer in a wrongful discharge lawsuit. (See Chapter 9.)

This chapter also outlines other income replacement programs that may be available to you. And it explains how and whether to take action if you feel your former employer's bad actions are preventing you from getting a job in your new life.

Your Final Paycheck

Most state laws specify when a final paycheck must be issued to employees who are fired or resign, and some of those laws require your employer to pay you in fairly short order. (See the chart below.) For example, the laws in several states require that an employee who is fired be paid that same day. The chart below also indicates which states require employers to include accrued vacation pay in the final paycheck.

CAUTION

If you have a contract, you're outside the law. If you are one of the rare breed who have an employment contract (see Chapter 9, "When Firing Is Illegal") you may be specifically excluded from the protections of the laws listed below. Your rights to pay are dictated by the terms of the employment contract you signed.

Additional laws may apply. If the chart below indicates that your state has no statute, this means there is no law that specifically addresses the issue. However, there may be a state administrative regulation or local ordinance that does control final paychecks. Call your state labor department for more information. (See the Appendix for contact details.)

Severance Pay

Many people assume that when they leave a job they have a legal right to severance pay. This is yet another bit of workplace lore that builds false hope in the newly unemployed.

Most employers do offer severance in the form of a month's or more worth of salary to employees who are laid off or let go for some reason other than misconduct. The old general rule was that where severance was offered, a reasonable amount was one month's pay for every year of service—up to 24 months.

State Laws That Control Final Paychecks

Note: The states of Alabama, Florida, Georgia, and Mississippi are not included in this chart because they do not have laws specifically controlling final paychecks. Contact your state department of labor for more information. (See Appendix A for contact list.)

State	Paycheck due when employee is fired	Paycheck due when employee quits	Unused vacation pay due	Special employment situations
Alaska *Alaska Stat.* *§ 23.05.140(b)*	Within 3 working days.	Next regular payday at least 3 days after employee gives notice.	No provision.	
Arizona *Ariz. Rev. Stat.* *§ 23-353*	Next payday or within 3 working days, whichever is sooner.	Next payday.	Yes, if company has policy or practice of making such payments.	
Arkansas *Ark. Code Ann.* *§ 11-4-405*	Within 7 days from discharge date.	No provision.	No provision.	Railroad or railroad construction: day of discharge.
California *Cal. Lab. Code* *§§ 201 to 202, 227.3*	Immediately.	Immediately if employee has given 72 hours' notice; otherwise, within 72 hours.	Yes.	Motion picture business: next payday. Oil drilling industry: within 24 hours (excluding weekends & holidays) of termination. Seasonal agricultural workers: within 72 hours of termination.
Colorado *Colo. Rev. Stat.* *§ 8-4-109*	Immediately. (Within 6 hours of start of next workday, if payroll unit is closed; 24 hours if unit is offsite.) Employer decides check delivery.	Next payday.	Yes.	
Connecticut *Conn. Gen. Stat.* *Ann. § 31-71c*	Next business day after discharge.	Next payday.	Only if policy or collective bargaining agreement requires payment on termination.	

State Laws That Control Final Paychecks (continued)

State	Paycheck due when employee is fired	Paycheck due when employee quits	Unused vacation pay due	Special employment situations
Delaware *Del. Code Ann. tit. 19, § 1103*	Next payday.	Next payday.	No provision.	
District of Columbia *D.C. Code Ann. § 32-1303*	Next business day.	Next payday or 7 days after quitting, whichever is sooner.	Yes, unless there is express contrary policy.	
Hawaii *Haw. Rev. Stat. § 388-3*	Immediately or next business day, if timing or conditions prevent immediate payment.	Next payday or immediately, if employee gives one pay period's notice.	No.	
Idaho *Idaho Code §§ 45-606, 45-617*	Next payday or within 10 days (excluding weekends & holidays), whichever is sooner. If employee makes written request for earlier payment, within 48 hours of receipt of request (excluding weekends & holidays).	Next payday or within 10 days (excluding weekends & holidays), whichever is sooner. If employee makes written request for earlier payment, within 48 hours of receipt of request (excluding weekends & holidays).	No provision.	
Illinois *820 Ill. Comp. Stat. § 115/5*	At time of separation if possible, but no later than next payday.	At time of separation if possible, but no later than next payday.	Yes.	
Indiana *Ind. Code Ann. §§ 22-2-5-1, 22-2-9-2*	Next payday.	Next payday. (If employee has not left address, (1) 10 days after employee demands wages or (2) when employee provides address where check may be mailed.)	Yes.	Does not apply to railroad employees.
Iowa *Iowa Code §§ 91A.4, 91A.2(7)(b)*	Next payday.	Next payday.	Yes.	If employee is owed commission, employer has 30 days to pay.

State Laws That Control Final Paychecks (continued)				
State	**Paycheck due when employee is fired**	**Paycheck due when employee quits**	**Unused vacation pay due**	**Special employment situations**
Kansas *Kan. Stat. Ann. § 44-315*	Next payday.	Next payday.	Only if required by employer's policies.	
Kentucky *Ky. Rev. Stat. Ann. §§ 337.010, 337.055*	Next payday or 14 days, whichever is later.	Next payday or 14 days, whichever is later.	Yes, if employer has policy or practice of making such payments.	
Louisiana *La. Rev. Stat. Ann. § 23:631*	Next payday or within 15 days, whichever is earlier.	Next payday or within 15 days, whichever is earlier.	Yes.	
Maine *Me. Rev. Stat. Ann. tit. 26, § 626*	Next payday or within 2 weeks of requesting final pay, whichever is sooner.	Next payday or within 2 weeks of requesting final pay, whichever is sooner.	Yes.	
Maryland *Md. Code Ann., [Lab. & Empl.] § 3-505*	Next scheduled payday.	Next scheduled payday.	Yes, unless employer has contrary policy.	
Massachusetts *Mass. Gen. Laws ch. 149, § 148*	Day of discharge.	Next payday. If no scheduled payday, then following Saturday.	Yes.	
Michigan *Mich. Comp. Laws §§ 408.471 to 408.475; Mich. Admin. Code R. 408.9007*	Next payday.	Next payday.	Only if required by written policy or contract.	Hand-harvesters of crops: within one working day of termination.
Minnesota *Minn. Stat. Ann. §§ 181.13, 181.14; 181.74*	Immediately.	Next payday. If payday is less than 5 days from last day of work, then following payday or 20 days from last day of work, whichever is earlier.	Only if required by written policy or contract.	Migrant agricultural workers who resign: within 5 days.
Missouri *Mo. Rev. Stat. § 290.110*	Day of discharge.	No provision.	No.	

State Laws That Control Final Paychecks (continued)

State	Paycheck due when employee is fired	Paycheck due when employee quits	Unused vacation pay due	Special employment situations
Montana *Mont. Code Ann. § 39-3-205; Mont. Admin. Code § 24.16 7521*	Immediately if fired for cause or laid off (unless there is a written policy extending time to earlier of next payday or 15 days).	Next payday or within 15 days, whichever comes first.	Yes.	
Nebraska *Neb. Rev. Stat. §§ 48-1229 to 48-1230*	Next payday or within 2 weeks, whichever is earlier.	Next payday or within 2 weeks, whichever is earlier.	Yes.	
Nevada *Nev. Rev. Stat. Ann. §§ 608.020, 608.030*	Immediately.	Next payday or 7 days, whichever is earlier.	No provision.	
New Hampshire *N.H. Rev. Stat. Ann. §§ 275:43(III), 275:44*	Within 72 hours. If laid off, next payday.	Next payday, or within 72 hours if employee gives one pay period's notice.	Yes.	
New Jersey *N.J. Stat. Ann. § 34:11-4.3*	Next payday.	Next payday.	No provision.	
New Mexico *N.M. Stat. Ann. §§ 50-4-4, 50-4-5*	Within 5 days.	Next payday.	No provision.	If paid by task or commission, 10 days after discharge.
New York *N.Y. Lab. Law §§ 191(3), 198-c(2)*	Next payday.	Next payday.	Yes, unless employer has a contrary policy.	
North Carolina *N.C. Gen. Stat. §§ 95-25.7, 95-25.12*	Next payday.	Next payday.	Yes, unless employer has a contrary policy.	If paid by commission or bonus, on next payday after amount calculated.
North Dakota *N.D. Cent. Code § 34-14-03; N.D. Admin. Code R. 46-02-07-02(12)*	Next payday, or 15 days, whichever is earlier.	Next payday.	Yes.	

State Laws That Control Final Paychecks (continued)				
State	Paycheck due when employee is fired	Paycheck due when employee quits	Unused vacation pay due	Special employment situations
Ohio Ohio Re. Code Ann. § 4113.15	First of month for wages earned in first half of prior month; 15th of month for wages earned in second half of prior month.	First of month for wages earned in first half of prior month; 15th of month for wages earned in second half of prior month.	Yes, if company has policy or practice of making such payments.	
Oklahoma Okla. Stat. Ann. tit. 40, §§ 165.1(4), 165.3	Next payday.	Next payday.	Yes.	
Oregon Or. Rev. Stat. §§ 652.140, 652.145	End of first business day after termination (must be within 5 days if employee submits time records to determine wages due).	Immediately, with 48 hours' notice (excluding weekends & holidays); without notice, within 5 business days or next payday, whichever comes first (must be within 5 days if employee submits time records to determine wages due).	Yes.	Seasonal farm workers: fired or quitting with 48 hours' notice, immediately; quitting without notice, within 48 hours or next payday, whichever comes first.
Pennsylvania 43 Pa. Cons. Stat. Ann. §§ 260.2a, 260.5	Next payday.	Next payday.	Only if required by policy or contract.	
Rhode Island R.I. Gen. Laws § 28-14-4	Next payday.	Next payday.	Yes, if employee has worked for one full year and the company has agreed verbally or in writing.	
South Carolina S.C. Code Ann. §§ 41-10-10(2), 41-10-50	Within 48 hours or next payday, but not more than 30 days.	No provision.	Only if required by policy or contract.	
South Dakota S.D. Codified Laws Ann. §§ 60-11-10, 60-11-11, 60-11-14	Next payday (or until employee returns employer's property).	Next payday (or until employee returns employer's property).	No.	

		State Laws That Control Final Paychecks (continued)		
State	**Paycheck due when employee is fired**	**Paycheck due when employee quits**	**Unused vacation pay due**	**Special employment situations**
Tennessee Tenn. Code Ann. § 50-2-103	Next payday or 21 days, whichever is later.	Next payday or 21 days, whichever is later.	Only if required by policy or contract.	Applies to employers with 5 or more employees.
Texas Tex. Lab. Code Ann. §§ 61.001, 61.014	Within 6 days.	Next payday.	Only if required by policy or contract.	
Utah Utah Code Ann. §§ 34-28-5; Utah Admin.Code 610-3	Within 24 hours.	Next payday.	Only if required by policy or contract.	
Vermont Vt. Stat. Ann. tit. 21, § 342(c)	Within 72 hours.	Next regular payday or next Friday, if there is no regular payday.	No provision.	
Virginia Va. Code Ann. § 40.1-29(A.1)	Next payday.	Next payday.	No provision.	
Washington Wash. Rev. Code Ann. § 49.48.010	End of pay period.	End of pay period.	No provision.	
West Virginia W.Va. Code §§ 21-5-1, 21-5-4	Within 72 hours.	Immediately if employee has given one pay period's notice; otherwise, next payday.	Yes.	
Wisconsin Wis. Stat. Ann. §§ 109.01(3), 109.03	Next payday or 1 month, whichever is earlier. If termination is due to merger, relocation, or liquidation of business, within 24 hours.	Next payday.	Yes.	Does not apply to managers, executives, or sales agents working on commission basis.
Wyoming Wyo. Stat. Ann. §§ 27-4-104, 27-4-507(c)	5 working days.	5 working days.	Yes.	

Current as of February 2007

In the last couple years, the amount of severance pay has been less likely to be tied to the length of time an employee has worked with a company. Rates have also become less generous—averaging from 30 weeks of pay for nonexempt employees to 39 weeks for those classified as executives.

And the cut-rate severance comes with an additional price tag, as more companies demand that departing employees sign broad severance agreements before getting a red cent. The agreements typically include provisions requiring a former employee to waive the right to file a number of legal claims against the company. And, increasingly, severance agreements include confidentiality and "non-disparagement" clauses aimed at preventing employees who leave from complaining about the company to other employees, talking to the media about negative experiences while on the job, and sometimes even telling their friends how much money the company gave them in severance.

Some employment experts are quick to disparage such so-called nondisparagement clauses, fearing that disgruntled workers are being unjustly paid to zip their lips rather than shed light on larger workplace wrongs.

There is no grand guidance on the issue. If presented with the option of either signing a nondisparagement clause and getting a hefty severance sum or losing the right to vent and getting nothing, you are the only one who can evaluate which is more important.

But keep in mind that no law requires an employer to pay severance. Whether it is given at all now varies drastically from employer to employer, region to region, industry custom to industry custom.

However, an employer may be legally obligated to pay you some severance if you had good reason to believe you had it coming, as evidenced by:

- a written contract stating that severance will be paid
- a promise or policy that employees would receive severance pay as documented in an employee handbook
- a history of the company paying severance to other employees in your position, or
- an oral promise that the employer would pay you severance—although you may run into difficulties proving the promise existed.

If your employer refuses to pay you severance or offers an amount that you find unacceptable, you have nothing to lose by asking, or asking again. Request a meeting with a company representative to discuss the issue. Remain calm and polite; do not threaten. Explain why you need the money—to support yourself or your family while finding another job is the usual reason. In the last few years, employers' building fear of lawsuits has meant that more of them are willing to grant severance pay to departing employees and to be flexible in the amount they will award.

If you meet with no success, take another hard look at the legal reasons listed above that may entitle you to severance pay. If you feel you may have a valid claim, collect as much evidence as you can to back up your position. (See Chapter 9, "Getting Documentation.")

Then think again. A breach of contract action, which is what you can bring against an employer that has reneged on a promise to pay severance, will likely require the help of an attorney. If the amount involved is not substantial, you could be facing more in legal fees than you would stand to gain by collecting the severance money. If you consult with an attorney about handling your case, that calculation should be one of the first questions you ask. (See Chapter 17, "Hiring a Lawyer.")

Getting References

As soon as you are ready, you should put your best foot and face forward and prepare for a new job. For many, that means glancing backward—to secure references from past employers.

Sometimes, that task is not as simple as it sounds. It might help you to understand why: Employers contacted for references about former employees often find themselves caught between the desire to be truthful and the fear that if they say anything unflattering they will be sued. The number of costly defamation lawsuits filed in the last decade over negative references makes this fear a real one. And the U.S. Supreme Court added fuel to the fire when it ruled that former employees can sue their employers under the Civil Rights Act for retaliatory negative job references. (*Robinson v. Shell Oil Co.,* 519 U.S. 337 (1997).)

These days, conventional legal wisdom cautions all employers to stick to the barest bones. Many companies have steel-clad policies to supply only the dates of employment, job title, and amount of final salary to prospective employers.

So when seeking references from a former employer, you may run into hesitancy fueled by these lawsuits, case decisions, and watercooler wisdom. But depending on where you live, your efforts may also be helped or hampered by your state law that spells out information that may be disclosed to current and former employees. Be sure to check those requirements—and point to them and lobby for them if they are in your favor. (See Chapter 9, "State Laws on Information From Former Employers.")

Some cautious companies require employees who leave to sign releases allowing the companies to give reference information in the future—and in some states, the law requires this, as noted above. And some employers ask even prospective employees to sign the same sort of release. Courts have upheld these releases of late, holding that employees who sign away rights to this information have also signed away their rights to bring a lawsuit for defamation based on what beans get spilled. In some states, employers are protected by law from defamation lawsuits if they answer questions about former employees truthfully. (See Chapter 9, "Defamation.")

The broad warning for employers giving references is that they should give out only easily documented facts—your attendance record or production record, for example.

But this closed approach seems to unfairly penalize prize employees, who may depend on good references to snag their next jobs. And many employers who think that an employee has done a poor job or has blatantly violated company rules feel that they have a responsibility to let prospective employers know about the problem. There is nothing inherently illegal about this, unless you can prove that an employer told a bald-faced lie about you—for example, that you raided the company till when you did not. However, gathering proof of an intentional lie is nearly impossible. And a seemingly noncommital "no comment" in response to a prospective employer's probe about your strengths and weaknesses may be the most damaging of all—yet its evasiveness makes it a poor candidate for the basis of a defamation lawsuit.

If you suspect your former employer might give a negative review of your work, it is best

---

Sometimes, It's Better to Remain Mum

A California court recently turned the tables and sent out a warning signal to employers who are inclined to leave an important element—the truth—out of letters of recommendation. While the full impact of the case is yet to be felt, it may signal to workers that they can expect less-glowing letters of recommendation from former employers.

When Robert Gadams went looking for a job with the Livingston Union School District, he came armed with letters of recommendation from former employers—all of them painting him in no uncertain glowing terms.

One letter effused: "He is a 'perfectionist' and concentrates on 'getting the very best' from everyone. I wouldn't hesitate to recommend Mr. Gadams for any position!"

"Considering his experience at the elementary, high school, and adult education levels," wrote another former employer, "I would recommend him for almost any administrative position he wishes to pursue."

Still a third letter described Gadams as "an upbeat, enthusiastic administrator who relates well to the students."

In fact, Gadams left all three of these positions after being investigated for sexual misconduct with female students.

Failing to read between the lines of the enthusiastic letters, Livingston hired Gadams as vice principal at once. Shortly after that, he was accused of sexually molesting a 13-year-old student in his new office.

The student sued, claiming that school authorities who failed to disclose their former employee's propensity for sexually molesting students were liable for the harm he caused her. The court agreed that the school districts had a duty not to misrepresent Gadams's suitability for the job as vice principal. It held that the student could base claims of negligent misrepresentation and fraud on the disingenuous letters. (*Randi W. v. Livingston Union School District,* 14 Cal. 4th 1066 (1997).)

to have a strategy worked out ahead of time. Try to secure a letter of recommendation from someone in the company who would praise your work. Perhaps you can persuade your employer to keep certain employment matters confidential—such as the reason for your dismissal. If not, it might be best not to list the employer as a reference. But have a ready reason to explain the circumstances that has no acrimonious ring to it—for example, that it was time for you to move on to new challenges.

Collecting Fringe Benefits

Employers are generally not required by law to provide workplace benefits, formerly known by the quaint title of "fringe benefits." However, most employers do—at least to full-time employees. Fringe benefits include retirement plans, group health insurance, and paid days off for vacations, holidays, personal, and medical leave. (See Chapters 2, 3, and 4 for a more in-depth discussion of these topics.)

Keep in mind, however, that if your employer does have a policy of offering some or all of these job benefits, it cannot discriminate in offering them. The question that most often arises about these discretionary benefits when employees quit or are fired from a job is whether they are entitled to be paid for time that was accrued—or earned and owing—but not taken.

There is no easy answer.

First of all, just as the benefits are discretionary with each employer, so is the policy of how and when they accrue. Employers are free to apply conditions on fringe benefits. For example, it is perfectly legal for employers to require a certain length of employment—six months or a year are common—before an employee is entitled to any fringe benefits. It is perfectly legal for employers to prorate—or deny—fringe benefits for part-time employees. Employers are also free to set limits on how much paid time off employees may accrue before it must be lost or taken.

Getting the Benefits You Are Due

In evaluating whether your former employer has given you all accrued fringe benefits you are due, you have two allies: documentation and history. First, search for any written policy on benefit accrual in an employee manual, personnel package, or company memo. If the rights have been promised to you, you can enforce them just like any other contract. If the promise is in writing, you have an even better chance of succeeding.

Look, too, to how other employees were treated in the past. If it has become company custom to pay employees accrued fringe benefits when they leave, you may be legally entitled to them, too. You must compare apples with apples. Look to other employees who worked in jobs similar to yours and who worked the same hours.

Finding out what others were paid when they left may take some brave sleuthing on your part: You may have to hunt down past employees and ask them some uncomfortable questions, point blank. But the effort may be worth it. If other former workers with jobs similar to yours were given benefits you were denied, you may be able to claim that your employer discriminated against you when it denied them. (See Chapter 7.)

Continuing Health Care Coverage

Most workplace disputes and misunderstandings over fringe benefits concern health care coverage. Ironically, workers have more rights to health care insurance coverage after they lose their jobs than while employed, because of a 1986 law, the Consolidated Omnibus Budget Reconciliation Act, or COBRA. Under COBRA, employers must offer former employees the option of continuing to be covered by the company's group health care insurance plan at the workers' own expense for some time after employment ends. Family coverage is included.

In general, COBRA gives an employee who quits or is dismissed for reasons other than gross misconduct the right to continue group health care coverage for 18 months. In some other circumstances, such as the death of the employee, that employee's dependents can continue coverage for up to 36 months. (See Chapter 3, "Coverage for Former Employees.")

Outplacement Programs

Each year, many thousands of workers are permanently dismissed by corporations that are shrinking or dying. And, as they bid adieu, some former employers offer outplacement services to workers to help ease the sting of being out of work.

Outplacement services are not employment agencies. They are not executive search firms. They are not employee leasing companies. They do not find a new job for you, but they do help and encourage you in finding one for yourself.

Although some outplacement firms offer packages of services that can be purchased by individuals, outplacement counselors are most often brought in and paid for by employers who want to diminish their risks of being sued for wrongful discharge. Outplacement benefits have even been negotiated into union contracts.

The theory underlying the popularity of outplacement in the corporate world is that fired employees who move quickly and smoothly into a new job typically do not sustain grudges against the company that fired them. Nor do they experience the kind of financial problems that can inspire job-related lawsuits. If a person goes through outplacement, cannot find a replacement job, and decides to file a wrongful discharge lawsuit, the company can show a court that it has done all it can to limit the financial damage done to the employee by the firing.

An outplacement program typically begins with classes or individual counseling on how to take an inventory of your marketable job skills. Then, you are assigned a furnished office space from which to launch your search for a new employer. These offices are usually equipped with a telephone, a computer, and an extensive library of business directories, and some of them include services that will pump out resumes and letters for you.

Many outplacement firms even provide the people passing through them with business cards that carry only the person's name and a daytime telephone number, but no business title. Outplacement offices are frequently equipped with a switchboard operator to answer telephone calls in a corporate style, but without indicating any company affiliation. These props typically get a lot of use, because many outplacement participants are required to turn in daily or weekly logs of potential employers they have contacted to inquire about possible job openings.

Periodic counseling and encouragement sessions with the outplacement firm's staff continue until you have found a new job or until your former employer's willingness to pay for the outplacement services runs out.

Two Wrongs May Mean No Rights

Many jobseekers inflate their resumes by exaggerating their experience or credentials. A recent study revealed that:

- 9% of job applicants falsely claimed they had a college degree, listed false employers, or identified jobs that didn't exist
- 4% listed incorrect job titles
- 11% misrepresented why they left a former employer, and
- nearly 33% listed dates of employment that were off by more than three months.

Employers have always been free to fire employees who lie about a significant qualification. Now they may be able to use this misinformation to defend against lawsuits for wrongful termination or discrimination. Courts reason, in essence, that employees who lied to get a job cannot later come to court and claim that the employer did them wrong.

The emerging tactic even has a name: the After-Acquired Evidence Theory. Conduct that has been held sufficiently serious to be admitted as after-acquired evidence has included:

- 150 instances of falsifying company records
- failing to list a previous employer on a resume
- failing to admit being terminated for cheating on timecards
- failing to reveal a prior conviction for a felony
- lying about education and experience on a job application
- fabricating a college degree during an interview, and
- removing and copying the company's confidential financial statements.

If you did lie on your job application or resume, however, you may not be completely out of luck. Your employer can use the mis information as a defense only if it was truly related to your job duties or performance. The employer must be able to show that you would have been fired—or not hired in the first place—if he or she had known the truth. Proving this type of second-guessing may not be easy.

There is no standard duration. Some people spend only a few days in outplacement, but some stay for a year or more. Because some people have a difficult time finding a new job even with the support of an outplacement firm, some of these firms now offer programs that teach new work-related skills.

An employer cannot force you to participate in an outplacement program. However, most large employers will continue to pay your salary and benefits for at least a few weeks or months after you are fired on the condition that you actively participate in the outplacement services provided. If you drop out, you are on your own financially.

Your refusal to participate in an outplacement program might also weaken any lawsuit you might later file against your former employer, because you could be depicted as contributing to your loss of employment income. Your participation in outplacement might, on the other hand, provide additional verification that you were competent and professional while at the job from which you were fired.

Replacing Your Income

When your employment is interrupted, it is important to act quickly to replace as much of your income as you can. Each day that passes without money earned puts you and those who rely on you for financial support in greater risk of running into money troubles. In some states, for example, the gap between the time that a person files for unemployment insurance and the time he or she receives the first unemployment check averages six weeks. And applying for the wrong income replacement program can waste many more precious days, weeks, or even months.

Here is a brief breakdown of what is covered by each of the three major income replacement programs;

- **Unemployment insurance.** This program provides some financial help if you lose your job, temporarily or permanently, through no fault of your own. (See Chapter 11.)
- **Workers' compensation.** When you cannot work because of a work-related injury or illness, this is the program that is most likely to provide you with replacement income promptly. It may also pay the medical bills resulting from a workplace injury or illness; compensate workers for a permanent injury, such as the loss of a limb; and provide death benefits to the survivors of workers who die from a workplace injury or illness. (See Chapter 12.)
- **Social Security disability insurance.** This is intended to provide income to adults who, because of injury or illness, cannot work for at least 12 months. Unlike the workers' compensation program, it does not require that your disability be caused by a workplace injury or illness. (See Chapter 13.)

Once you have decided which of these programs fits your situation, read the more detailed description of that program in the chapters noted, and then apply for the appropriate benefits without delay.

Dual Payments for Disabled Workers

Many disabled employees qualify for benefits under both workers' compensation and Social Security disability insurance. There is nothing illegal about collecting from both at the same time if the claims you file are valid.

However, if you qualify for benefits from both programs, the total benefits you receive from both programs cannot equal more than 80% of your average earnings prior to becoming disabled.

Some states also allow disabled workers to collect both unemployment and workers' compensation benefits at the same time. When in doubt, file truthful claims for any program for which you might logically qualify and let the system decide if you are eligible for benefits.

Although the government insurance programs covering unemployment, workplace injuries, and permanent disability are the most substantial sources of replacement income for people who are out of work, there are other options.

Private Disability Insurance

While you were working, you or your employer may have been paying into a private disability insurance program. If you were paying for it through payroll withholdings, or if all the premiums were being paid by your employer, you may have forgotten that you even have this coverage.

Coverage and eligibility for benefits differ among policies and companies. Review the employee policy manual or packet that your employer gave you when you took the job to see whether any private disability coverage is described there. If not, the people who handle benefits for your employer should be able to help you determine whether you have such coverage.

State Disability Programs

A few states—including California, Hawaii, New Jersey, New York, and Rhode Island—offer disability benefits as part of their unemployment insurance programs. Typical program requirements mandate that you submit your medical records and show that you requested a leave of absence from your employer. Some may also require proof that you intend to return to your job when you recover. Call the local unemployment insurance and workers' compensation insurance offices to determine whether your state maintains this kind of coverage. (See Chapters 11 and 12.)

Withdrawals From Retirement Plans

Some retirement plans allow withdrawals prior to retirement for emergency purposes. The administrator of your plan can advise you on whether you have this option. (For more on pensions, see Chapter 14, "Private Pensions.")

Food Stamps

Although many people incorrectly think that the federal food stamp program is a form of welfare, it is actually financed by the

U.S. Department of Agriculture as a way of increasing the demand for food products. You do not have to be receiving welfare to qualify for food stamps. In fact, the eligibility formula for food stamps makes them available to many people who are not all that poor. If your income is eliminated or significantly reduced for several months because you are not working, check on whether you are eligible for food stamps.

To locate the agency in your area that issues food stamps, scan the county government offices listings in the telephone directory. Typically, you will find a listing for food stamp information under a category such as Human Services. If not, call your local office of the U.S. Department of Agriculture. Or get more information about the USDA's Food and Nutrition Service online at www.fns.usda.gov.

Veterans' Benefits

There are programs that provide income to veterans of the U.S. military who become unable to work because of a disability, even if that disability is not a result of military service. Additional specialized laws also provide veterans returning from service with the right to return to their jobs without losing seniority or benefits.

However, laws protecting veterans' rights, particularly their job rights, are passed and repealed with the changing of the political winds—making it tough to keep current. Your local Department of Veterans Affairs office, listed in the federal government agency section of the telephone directory, can give

you details. Local offices are also listed on the VA's website at www.vba.va.gov.

Supplemental Social Security Income

Usually known as SSI, this program provides money to disabled people who have low incomes and very few assets. Unlike Social Security disability insurance, it does not require you to have worked under and paid into the Social Security program. If the circumstances surrounding your inability to earn income are so unusual that you have fallen between the cracks of the larger programs, SSI may be the one program that provides you with some income.

You can get details and file a claim at your local Social Security Administration office. Look in the federal government section of the telephone directory for contact details. Or look for information and contact details at www.ssa.gov.

Black Lung Benefits

The U.S. Department of Labor also runs a federal program that provides money benefits to victims of anthracosilicosis—an occupational disease often suffered by miners. Typically known as Black Lung, the disease is caused by long exposure to coal particles in the air. It frequently leaves miners unable to work because they cannot breath properly.

The benefits under this program are also payable to dependents of Black Lung victims, so the best way to research your eligibility for those benefits is to investigate details of the program at your labor department office.

(See the Appendix for contact details.) Or look for information and contact details at www.dol.gov.

Disaster Unemployment Assistance

Disaster Unemployment Assistance (DUA), also referred to as Disaster Relief and Emergency Assistance, is a federal program that provides temporary financial assistance to individuals unemployed as result of a major disaster declared by the president.

For example, as of September 28, 2005, a federal disaster was declared due to Hurricanes Katrina and Rita in selected counties located in Alabama (declared August 28), Mississippi (selected counties declared August 29, extended to all counties on September 6), Louisiana (declared August 29, and extended in selected counties on September 24 due to Hurricane Rita), Florida (declared August 28), and Texas (selected counties declared on September 24). For a current list of the states and counties, see the Federal Emergency Management Agency's website at www.fema.gov/news/disasters.fema.

To qualify for DUA, you must meet two major requirements. You must be out of work as a "direct result" of a major disaster. And you must not qualify for regular unemployment insurance (UI) from any state. Once found to be eligible for DUA, workers must actively look for work and accept suitable work offered them, not unlike UI recipients—unless the state opts to temporarily suspend their work search requirements for some workers, as some did in the aftermath of the 2005 hurricanes.

In addition, a person must show that for every week he or she is collecting DUA, his or her unemployment continues to be the direct result of the disaster, not other factors.

Medicare

Like Social Security, most people think that Medicare is reserved solely for elderly people. But, in fact, it also covers disabled people and can be a good way of coping with medical bills when an injury or illness prevents you from working. For more details on this program, call the Medicare information line: 800-952-8627.

However, you should be aware that the federal government has been tightening the restrictions for Medicare for those less than 65 years old, so this type of coverage may be difficult to secure.

Agreements Not to Compete

A growing number of employers are straining to expand their control beyond the office by asking employees to sign noncompete agreements promising that they will not work for a direct competitor.

These concerns and attempts to control the future are more understandable and more often enforced where workers have access to sensitive business information or trade secrets. A trade secret is information that gives a competitive advantage because it is not generally known and cannot be readily learned by other people who could benefit from it. It can be a formula, pattern, compilation, program, device, method, technique, or process that an employer has made reasonable efforts to keep secret.

When employees with access to trade secrets leave—because they either quit or have been fired—their former employers may be concerned that they will use the information gleaned on the job to their personal advantages. For example, a former employee may open a competing business or may go to work for a competitor and unwittingly or wittingly divulge hard-won keys to success.

Whether a judge will enforce a covenant not to compete is always an iffy question. The legal system puts a high value on a person's right to earn a living. California, for example, has taken a hard-line stance against noncompetes—a state statute makes them unenforceable in most circumstances. And a few states, such as Colorado, set out very narrow circumstances in which noncompetes will be enforced—if the agreement accompanies the sale and purchase of a business, for example.

But the rule in most states is that covenants not to compete will be enforced only if they're reasonable. A covenant may be held unreasonable—and therefore invalid—if it:

- lasts for too long a time
- covers too wide a geographic area

- does not cover information that requires legal protection, such as a trade secret
- is too broad in the types of business it prohibits, or
- imposes an undue hardship on the worker.

The biggest and most often raised bone of contention with noncompete agreements is how long they last—that is, for how long can an employee be restrained from competing in a similar business. While there is no dyed-in-the-wool guidance on what will and will not pass muster, courts and legislatures are beginning to set out some bounds as to what is reasonable. A good example is Florida's statute (Fla. Stat. § 542.335), which sets out specific guidance as to the type and length of business matters that can be restrained after an employee leaves.

A covenant may also be held unreasonable if the information revealed to the worker isn't all that sensitive, so the restriction doesn't serve a valid business purpose.

Judges are more likely to enforce restrictive covenants against high-level managers who truly are given inside information, on the theory that such former employees are in a position to do real harm.

If pressed, a judge may order an employee not to use the information even if he or she

Florida's Statute § 542.335			
Subject Matter of Agreement	**Reasonable**	**Iffy**	**Unreasonable**
Trade secrets	Up to 5 years	5-10 years	10 years
Sale of a business	Up to 3 years	3-7 years	7 or more years
Other	Up to 6 months	6 months to 2 years	2 or more years

Next Time, I'll Know Better

When initially faced with signing a non-compete agreement, your first best step may be to negotiate some of the finer print with your employer:

There are a few pointers for crafting your arguments.

- If you are promoted to a new job that carries with it a new request to sign a noncompete agreement, it is not too cheeky to ask for money to compensate you for signing. Keep in mind, though, that this will almost certainly prevent you from later claiming that the clause should not be enforced against you. Courts will likely point to your fattened wallet and conclude that you should not collect money for agreeing to do something, then claim that your agreement is invalid.
- If presented with a noncompete clause, demand that it take effect only if you leave the job voluntarily. This may make a job search less daunting for an employee who is fired or laid off.
- Ask for the prohibited competition to be clearly specified. Many employers, for example, will fear competition with only one or two specific companies—and will readily name their names in your agreement.

didn't sign a secrecy agreement—if the former employer can show that what the employee took is truly a trade secret. This often involves establishing two things: that the information was not readily obtainable elsewhere, and that precautions were taken to keep it secret. For example, an employer who put together a valuable customer list that includes customers' buying history and buying habits must also be able to show that the list was painstakingly built up over several years and that only a limited number of employees were allowed to see it.

Former employees who have signed noncompete agreements may face special hardships, as their job searches will be even more limited. And even those with solid job offers may face lawsuits by former employers—often accompanied by a damaging court order forbidding them from working until the case is resolved.

Blacklisting

As archaic and barbaric as it may seem, there are still some companies, labor unions, and people working within them that are not content to merely fire you or force you out of your job. They seem unwilling to rest until they have squelched all hope that you will ever work again.

The danger of losing a defamation lawsuit does not seem to dissuade some vengeful people from trying to put former employees on a list of people that no one else will hire. So some states have passed laws that expressly allow former employees to take legal action—criminal, civil, or both—against those who try to sabotage their efforts to secure new employment. (See the chart below for state blacklisting laws.)

Although, in many cases, you could sue for defamation instead, the advantage of using the blacklisting statute is that you do not have to prove that you were harmed—often a difficult task at trial. (See Chapter 9, "Defamation.")

Detecting Blacklisting

The mere fact that you have to work hard at finding a new job usually is not sufficient evidence to suggest blacklisting. But a strong signal would be a series of situations in which potential new employers seem to be on the verge of hiring you, then suddenly lose all interest. This indicates that, when a prospective employer checks your references just before hiring you, the blacklister is tipped off to where you have applied for work and is able to ding you.

State Laws on Blacklisting

The chart below is a synopsis of state laws prohibiting blacklisting. Note that these laws define blacklisting in varying ways—some prohibit employers from maintaining an actual blacklist, some prohibit employers from making false statements about an employee, and some simply prohibit employers from using any means to prevent an employee from finding a job.

CAUTION

Additional laws may apply. If the chart below indicates that your state has no statute, this means there is no law that specifically addresses the issue. However, there may be a state administrative regulation or local ordinance that does control blacklisting. Call your state labor department for more information. (See the Appendix for contact details.)

State Blacklisting Laws	
State and Statute	**Employer actions prohibited (if intended to prevent a former employee from obtaining other employment)**
Alabama *Ala. Code §§ 13A-11-123*	Maintaining a blacklist. Notifying others that an employee has been blacklisted. Using any other similar means to prevent a person from obtaining employment.
Arizona *Ariz. Rev. Stat. Ann. § 23-1361 to 23-1362*	The knowing exchange, solicitation, or gift of a blacklist. A blacklist is any understanding or agreement which communicates a name, or list of names, or descriptions between two or more employers, supervisors, or managers in order to prevent an employee from engaging in a useful occupation. A blacklist can be spoken, written, printed, or implied.
Arkansas *Ark. Code Ann. § 11-3-202*	Writing, printing, publishing, or circulating false statements in order to get someone fired or prevent someone from obtaining employment. Publishing that someone is a member of a secret organization in order to prevent that person from securing employment.
California *Cal. Lab. Code §§ 1050 to 1053*	Preventing or attempting to prevent former employee from getting work through misrepresentation. Knowingly permitting or failing to take reasonable steps to prevent blacklisting. In a statement about why an employee was discharged or left employment, implying something other than what is explicitly said, or providing information that was not requested.
Colorado *Colo. Rev. Stat. §§ 8-2-110 to 8-2-114*	Publishing or maintaining a blacklist. Conspiring or contriving to prevent a discharged employee from securing other employment. Notifying another employer that a former employee has been blacklisted. Any employer that provides written information to a prospective employer about a current or former employee, shall, upon that employee's request, send a copy to the employee's last known address. The subject of such a reference may also obtain a copy by appearing at the employer or former employer's place of business during normal business hours.
Connecticut *Conn. Gen. Stat. Ann. § 31-51*	Blacklisting, publishing, or causing to be published the name of any employee with the intent and for the purpose of preventing that person's engaging in or securing other employment. Conspiring or contriving to prevent an employee from procuring other employment.

State Blacklisting Laws (continued)

State and Statute	Employer actions prohibited (if intended to prevent a former employee from obtaining other employment)
Florida *Fla. Stat. Ann. § 448.045*	Agreeing or conspiring with another person or persons in order to get someone fired or prevent someone from obtaining employment. Making threats, whether verbal, written, or in print, against the life, property, or business of another in order to get someone fired or prevent the procurement of work.
Hawaii *Haw. Rev. Stat. § 377-6(11)*	Making circulating, or causing the circulation of a blacklist.
Idaho *Idaho Code § 44-201*	Maintaining a blacklist. Notifying another employer that a current or former employee has been blacklisted.
Indiana *Ind. Code Ann. § 22-5-3-1*	Using any means to prevent a discharged employee from obtaining employment. Upon written request, prospective employers shall provide job applicant with copies of any written communication from the applicant's current or former employers that may affect the possibility of employment.
Iowa *Iowa Code §§ 730.1 to 730.3*	Preventing or trying to prevent, either verbally or in writing, a discharged employee from obtaining other employment. Authorizing or permitting blacklisting. Making false statements about an employee's honesty. If a company, partnership or corporation authorizes or allows blacklisting of a former employee, it shall be liable for treble damages.
Kansas *Kan. Stat. Ann. §§ 44-117 to 44-119*	Using words, signs, or any kind of writing to prevent or attempt to prevent a discharged employee from obtaining other employment. Any person, firm, or corporation found guilty of blacklisting shall be liable to the injured employee for treble damages and attorney's fees.
Maine *Me. Rev. Stat. Ann. title 17, § 401*	Maintaining or being party to a blacklist, either alone or in combination with others. Preventing or attempting to prevent an employee from entering, leaving, or remaining in employment by threats of injury, intimidation, or force. Preventing or attempting to prevent anyone from obtaining employment by means of a blacklist. Any person who violates this law can be found guilty regardless of whether he or she intended to cause the employee harm.

State and Statute	State Blacklisting Laws (continued)
	Employer actions prohibited (if intended to prevent a former employee from obtaining other employment)
Massachusetts *Mass. Gen. Laws ch. 149 § 19*	Using intimidation or force to prevent or attempt to prevent someone from obtaining or continuing in employment.
Minnesota *Minn. Stat. Ann. § 179.60*	Combining or conferring with another or other employers to interfere with or prevent a person from obtaining employment. Using threats, promises, blacklists, or any other means to get someone fired. Blacklisting any discharged employee. Verbally or in writing attempting to prevent a former employee from obtaining employment elsewhere.
Montana *Mont. Code Ann.* *§§ 39-2-801 to 39-2-804*	Refusing to respond to a former employee's demand for a written statement of the reasons for discharge while providing a statement of those reasons to any other person. Blacklisting by word or writing of any kind, or authorizing or allowing a company's agents to blacklist. Attempting, by written, verbal or any other means, to prevent a discharged or former employee from obtaining employment elsewhere.
Nevada *Nev. Rev. Stat. Ann. § 613.210*	For an employer or employer's representative: Blacklisting or causing any employee to be blacklisted; publishing any employee's name or causing it to be published with the intent to prevent that person from getting work. Conspiring or contriving in any manner to prevent discharged employee from procuring other work.
New Mexico *N.M. Stat. Ann. § 30-13-3*	For an employer or employer's agent: Preventing or attempting to prevent a former employee from obtaining other employment.
New York *N.Y. Labor Law § 704(2) and (9)*	Making, maintaining, distributing, or circulating a blacklist to prevent an employee from obtaining or continuing employment because employee exercised rights to organize, unionize, or bargain collectively. Informing any person of an individual's membership in a labor organization or exercise of protected labor rights in order to prevent them from obtaining or retaining employment.
North Carolina *N.C. Gen. Stat. § 14-355*	Preventing or attempting to prevent, by word or writing of any kind, a discharged employee from obtaining other employment.
North Dakota *N.D. Cent. Code § 34-01-06*	Maliciously interfering or in any way hindering a person from obtaining or continuing other employment.

	State Blacklisting Laws (continued)
State and Statute	**Employer actions prohibited (if intended to prevent a former employee from obtaining other employment)**
Oklahoma *Okla. Stat. Ann. tit. 40, § 172*	Blacklisting or causing an employee to be blacklisted. Publishing or causing employee's name to be published with the intent to prevent the employee from getting work. Requiring employee to write a letter of resignation with the intent to prevent or hinder other employment.
Oregon *Or. Rev. Stat. § 659.805*	Blacklisting or causing any discharged employee to be blacklisted; publishing or causing the name of any discharged employee to be published with the intent to prevent the employee from getting or keeping work. Conspiring or scheming by correspondence, or by any other means, to prevent a discharged employee from obtaining employment.
Rhode Island *R.I. Gen. Laws § 28-7-13(2)*	Making, maintaining, distributing, or circulating a blacklist to prevent an employee from obtaining or continuing in employment because employee exercised rights to organize, unionize, or bargain collectively. Informing any person of an individual's membership in a labor organization or exercise of protected labor rights in order to prevent them from obtaining or retaining employment.
Texas *Tex. Civ. Stat. Ann. Art. 5196(1) to (4)* *Tex. Lab. Code Ann. § 52.031*	Blacklisting or causing to be blacklisted. Preventing or attempting to prevent by word, printing, sign, list or other means, directly or indirectly, a former employee from obtaining other work. Communicating, directly or indirectly, information about an applicant without giving the applicant a copy of the communication, and the names and addresses of those to whom it was made, within ten days of demand. Receiving a request, notice or communication preventing, or calculated to prevent, the employment of an applicant without giving a copy of the communication to the applicant, and the names and addresses of those to whom it was made, within ten days of demand.
Utah *Utah Code Ann. §§ 34-24-1 to 34-24-2* *Utah Const. Art. 12, § 19; Art. 16, § 4*	Blacklisting or causing any former employee to be blacklisted, or publishing or causing the name of any former employee to be published, with the intent or purpose of preventing the employee from obtaining or retaining similar employment. Exchanging blacklists with or among railroads, corporations, associations or persons. Maliciously interfering with any person's obtaining or continuing in employment with another employer.

	State Blacklisting Laws (continued)		
State and Statute	**Employer actions prohibited (if intended to prevent a former employee from obtaining other employment)**		
Virginia *Va. Code Ann. § 40.1-27*	Willfully and maliciously preventing or attempting to prevent, verbally or in writing, directly or indirectly, a former employee from obtaining other employment.		
Washington *Wash. Rev. Code Ann. § 49.44.010*	Willfully and maliciously sending, delivering, making, or causing to be made, any document, signed, unsigned or signed with a fictitious name, mark, or other sign; publishing or causing to be published any statement, in order to prevent someone from obtaining employment in Washington or elsewhere. Willfully and maliciously blacklisting or causing a person to be blacklisted, by writing, printing, or publishing their name, or mark or sign representing their name, in a paper, pamphlet, circular, or book, along with a statement about that person for the purpose of preventing employment. Willfully and maliciously publishing or causing to be published that a person is a member of a secret organization in order to prevent them from obtaining employment. Willfully and maliciously making or issuing any statement or paper in order to influence or prejudice the mind of an employer against a person seeking employment, or to cause someone to be discharged.		
Wisconsin *Wis. Stat. Ann. § 134.02*	Any two or more employers joining together to: • Prevent any person seeking employment from obtaining employment • Cause the discharge of an employee by threats, promises, circulating blacklists, or causing blacklists to be circulated • Prevent or attempt to prevent, by blacklist or any other means, a former employee from obtaining other employment • Authorize or allow any of their agents to blacklist a former employee. Giving any statement of the reasons for an employee's discharge with the intent to blacklist, hinder, or prevent the discharged employee from obtaining other work.		

Current as March 2007

Unemployment

Unemployment insurance, often called UI or unemployment compensation, is intended to provide you with regular financial support when you are out of work.

Unemployment insurance programs are run jointly by the federal government and the states and are paid for primarily by a tax on employers. There are differences among the states in how the programs are administered, who qualifies to receive benefits—and, perhaps most important, how much is available in benefits.

This chapter discusses unemployment insurance in general and explains some specific state nuances. For more information on your state's program, check with the nearest Unemployment Insurance Office or Employment Security Division, usually part of the state department of labor. (See the Appendix for contact details.)

Who Is Covered

Unemployment insurance covers nearly 97% of the workforce—employees of nearly every stripe, including part-timers and temporaries.

To be covered, you must meet a number of qualifications:

- You must have worked as an employee for a substantial period and earned a minimum amount in wages before becoming unemployed. In most states, you must have been employed for at least six months during the year before your job loss. The amount you are required to have earned to qualify for unemployment insurance benefits varies by state and is frequently changed to reflect inflation and the cost of living.

- You must be a U.S. citizen or have the documents required by the U.S. Immigration and Naturalization Service to legally work in the United States. (See Chapter 16.)

- You must be available for work. For example, you may become ineligible if you take a new job or if you take a long vacation during which you cannot be reached by your former employer or a new one.

- You must be physically and mentally able to perform your old job or a similar one. The requirement that workers must be physically able to work can be confusing when applied to pregnant women. In general, the courts have ruled that unemployment insurance benefits cannot be denied simply because an employee is pregnant, but can be denied if the pregnancy makes the employee physically unable to perform her normal job or one similar to it.

Workers who are physically unable to perform their jobs usually have to apply for financial help under workers' compensation or Social Security disability insurance programs. (See Chapters 12 and 13.) However, a few states pay unemployment insurance benefits during periods of temporary disability. Your local unemployment insurance agency should help you determine whether your state is one of them.

Being Disqualified for Benefits

A few categories of employees are specifically ineligible to receive unemployment insurance benefits. And a great many more employees are disqualified because of their own behavior or actions—such as quitting a job without a legally recognized reason.

Employees Excluded

The categories of employees not covered by unemployment insurance usually include people employed by small farms, those who are paid only through commissions, casual domestic workers and babysitters, newspaper carriers under age 18, children employed by their parents, adults employed by their spouses or their children, employees of religious organizations, some corporate officers, and elected officials.

Disqualifying Behavior

Even if you are covered by unemployment insurance and otherwise eligible, you may be disqualified from receiving benefits. The reasons for disqualification vary from state to state, but the most common ones are:

- You were fired from your job for deliberate and repeated misconduct, such as chronic absence or tardiness without a good explanation, sleeping on the job, or violating clear and reasonable workplace rules. Note that it is not enough that you were careless or negligent on the job, that you arguably used poor judgment, or that you accidentally damaged some of your

employer's property. Your misconduct must have been purposeful and, unless it is very serious, must usually have happened more than one time.

- You refused to accept a similar job without good reason. In these economically strapped times, courts have been especially unlikely to find that you had legally sufficient grounds to reject a valid job offer. The few arguments that have succeeded are that the employee was not physically able to do the work required, that the job was too far from his or her home and family, or that the job would have required the employee to violate a firmly held religious belief, such as working on days when his or her religion prohibits work.

- You are unemployed because you went on strike or because you refused to cross a picket line. In some states, you will be entitled to unemployment benefits if there is a lockout at work—that is, if your employer closes down because there is a contract dispute or refuses to let you work until you agree to accept changed work conditions.

- You quit your job without a good reason. (See the discussion below.)

Acceptable Reasons for Quitting

The last reason you might be denied benefits —quitting your job—is particularly troublesome. Disputes over unemployment insurance claims often occur when the employee believes that his or her reason for quitting a job was a good one, and the employer disagrees.

Independent Contractors: A Gray Area

Independent contractors are not usually eligible for unemployment insurance. But, in some cases, people treated as independent contractors by companies are found to be legal employees—and therefore eligible for unemployment benefits. If you have questions about your legal work status, contact your local department of labor. (See the Appendix for specifics.)

In fact, the legal controls are somewhat relaxed in allowing independent contractors to be covered by unemployment benefits. If your employment status is somewhat uncertain, you may need to provide proof that you qualified as an employee of a company rather than as an independent contractor before you can collect benefits from your state's unemployment system.

Persuasive proof would be evidence showing any of the following:

- Your work was supervised by employees of the company.
- Your work was considered a normal part of the company's course of business—for example, an integral part of the quarterly financial review, rather than a one-time consulting job.
- You worked in the company office, rather than from your own home, workshop, or studio.
- You used company-owned equipment—computers, machining tools, construction equipment—to get the work done.

Of course, the definition of a good reason to quit a job varies with each person and each circumstance. In most situations, you must first have informed your employer that there was a change in the job or working conditions that made it impossible for you to stay on. These reasons are usually considered good enough for you to quit your job and still be eligible for unemployment insurance:

- Some form of fraud was involved in recruiting you for the job. For example, employers sometimes offer a certain level of wages and benefits, then try to cut back on that offer once the employee shows up for work.
- Your life or health was endangered by the employer's failure to maintain workplace safety. You will need to have some evidence that a doctor has examined you and confirmed that your health was jeopardized by the chemical discharge or other condition in the workplace. (See Chapter 6 for additional workplace safety concerns.)
- The nature of your work was changed dramatically from what you had originally been hired to do, or your wages and benefits were substantially reduced without your consent. Keep in mind that you may have to tolerate small changes in your job duties or conditions due to work restructuring or simple economics. However, if your job changes so substantially that it begins to look and feel different from the position you were offered originally, that may mean you are legally allowed to quit and still collect unemployment benefits.

- You were subjected to some intolerable or illegal condition on the job, such as discrimination or sexual harassment, and your employer refused to correct the situation after learning of it.
- A change in the location of your work made it impractical for you to continue in the job. A change of only a few miles would not likely be sufficient. But, if the move is so far that it adds a substantial increase to your commuting time—several hours—or the company relocates to another state, that may be considered sufficient reason for you to leave the job and collect unemployment benefits.
- Your spouse had to relocate to take a new job. Not all states recognize this as a good reason, however. In a number of cases, former employees argued that, because women most often leave their jobs when a spouse gets transferred, it is discriminatory to deny unemployment benefits to them. The courts so far have disagreed and held that because men could be affected, too, there is no sex discrimination in denying benefits to workers who must move to stay with their mates.

Several states may also award you unemployment benefits if you can prove you quit for a compelling personal reason. But beware that you must usually back such claims with substantial evidence. For example, if you quit your job to care for a sick spouse, you will probably be asked to show that no alternative care arrangements were feasible and that your employer was unwilling to grant you a paid or unpaid leave of absence.

If you have the luxury, do a little research on your eligibility for benefits before you leave your job. You can quit your job for other reasons and still file a claim for unemployment insurance benefits. Filing for unemployment benefits often requires perseverance, time, wading through paperwork, and waiting in lines to speak with—and sometimes be berated by—unemployment office personnel. But you have little to lose by filing a claim you consider to be valid and hoping for a favorable decision.

And the recent economic downturn with large numbers out of work forced local unemployment offices to turn to computers and automated phone systems to help field applications—perversely making processing more efficient as those intake workers are at least partially replaced by machines.

As the system is set up, employees who file for unemployment benefits are presumed to be entitled to them. If your former employer challenges your claim, however, you will need to prove through the appeal process described below that your reason was good enough.

Calculating Your Benefits

Each state sets its own maximum and minimum limits on the amount of benefits you can collect. Hawaii currently has the lowest minimum at $5 weekly—and Massachusetts has one of the highest maximum amounts at $551–$826 weekly, depending on whether an individual has dependents. Whether you are entitled to the high end or the low end of the benefit range depends on how much money you earned in your last position.

You must meet the state requirements for wages earned or time worked during a one-year period referred to as a base period. In most states, this is the first four out of the last five calendar quarters completed just before you file your claim, In general, benefits are based on a percentage of the earnings you took in during this time. Benefit formulas change with the economy and with individual state coffers.

To find out your state's current benefit scheme, go to the Employment and Training Administration link at the U.S. Department of Labor's website at www.dol.gov. It will

---

Severance Pay: It May Not Compute

As protection against wrongful discharge lawsuits, employers increasingly offer an unearned severance payment—usually several months' worth of the employee's normal pay—to get an employee to quit a job rather than be fired. (See Chapter 9, "Waiving Your Right to Sue.") In such situations, severance pay can delay the start of unemployment insurance benefits—or even make a worker ineligible for them.

EXAMPLE: Raj worked for a company that wanted to economize by cutting 500 employees. He accepted the company's offer of six months' severance pay—four months more than the two months' severance pay he had earned through the benefits program—in return for a signed statement that he had not been dismissed but had volunteered to quit his job.

When Raj filed a claim for unemployment insurance benefits, he was shocked and disappointed when it was turned down. His former employer contested the claim, arguing that Raj had made a decision to quit voluntarily.

Raj appealed the denial of his claim, and he won because he proved that he was coerced into quitting. But the appeal office also ruled that Raj could not begin collecting unemployment insurance benefits until the four months covered by the unearned severance package had expired.

Regulations and rulings covering the effects that severance pay has on unemployment insurance vary greatly from state to state, and are changing rapidly. In some cases, groups of workers who have been cut from company payrolls through offers of severance packages have created enough political pressure to have the rules in their state changed in their favor.

If you quit your job in exchange for severance pay, protect your rights by filing a claim for unemployment insurance benefits. If that claim is denied, you will then have the right to explain during the appeals process what really happened—or to benefit from any changes in your state's unemployment insurance rules covering severance pay.

in turn link you to the appropriate state organization—and some sites even have helpful calculators that will help you do the math to estimate your benefit amount.

Under normal circumstances, unemployment insurance benefits are paid for only 26 weeks. However, this period is extended by legislative whim—especially during periods of high unemployment. In most states during most times, you will be entitled to an additional 13 weeks of benefit payments on top of the 26 weeks you already have coming.

Part-Time Work: Throwing It Into the Mix

Unemployment benefits are based on the amount you used to earn. If your former job was part time, you still may be eligible to collect unemployment benefits if you lose that job. This is true even if you hold down several part-time jobs—and lose only one of them. Keep in mind, however, that the amount to which you are entitled in unemployment benefits will be offset by the amount you still earn—and by any amounts you receive from workers' compensation and other sources.

The same is true if you secure a part-time job after losing other work. Your unemployment benefits will be reduced by the amount of income you earn in the new part-time job. You will have to weigh the drawbacks of this income loss against the benefits the part-time work may afford: a boost to your confidence, camaraderie of coworkers, increased visibility and contacts in the work world, and added work experience.

Filing a Claim

Claims for unemployment insurance benefits are accepted and paid by the states through thousands of offices throughout the country. Tales of difficult dealings with the unemployment office are legion—long waits, surly office workers, piles of paperwork—all coming your way at what is likely to be an emotionally shaky time for you. Keep in mind that you are merely pursuing your legal right. And cloak yourself with the mantle of patience.

As mentioned earlier, the upside to the recent downturn in the economy is that many beleaguered unemployment offices stepped up to streamline the application process. In many locales, you can apply for benefits over the telephone, online, or by mailing or faxing a form; you need not apply in person. And, not to put too fine a point on it, but the recession generally caused unemployment offices to become kinder, gentler places. Most now offer beefed-up job search services, such as employment fairs and websites, in addition to seminars on topics ranging from improving resumes and interviewing skills to career planning and skill training.

But finding the right office can still be a daunting first hurdle. The names of the agencies that handle the claims vary but are typically something that sounds more upbeat than unemployment—such as Bureau of Employment Security, Job Service Office, or State Employment Service.

Whatever your local version is called, you can locate the office closest to you by checking the state government section of your local telephone directory. There are also links to all of the state unemployment offices' websites through the U.S. Department of Labor's website at www.dol.gov; check under the Employment and Training Administration.

In most states, there is a waiting period of one week between the time you file for unemployment benefits and the time you can collect them. But it is a good idea to contact the nearest unemployment office as soon after you lose your job as possible. You can then supply all required information, complete the necessary paperwork, and convince agency representatives to begin investigating your claim—all the initial steps needed to get the bureaucratic ball rolling.

Required Documentation

Your claim will get processed more quickly if you bring the proper documentation when you visit the local office or have it handy if you are able to apply over the telephone. You will need:

- recent pay stubs and other wage records, such as the W-2 form on which your employer reports your income to the Internal Revenue Service
- your Social Security card, or another document that shows your Social Security number, and
- any documentation you have that proves you are unemployed, such as a layoff or dismissal notice from your employer, and your employer's unemployment insurance account number, if you know it. (For more on how to document a job loss, see Chapter 9, "Getting Documentation.")

Typically, the unemployment insurance claims office will invite you to attend some type of orientation—ranging from simple explanatory pamphlets to sophisticated video productions to live group seminars. Attendance is mandatory.

The Taxman Will Cometh

Unlike workers' compensation benefits (discussed in Chapter 12), unemployment insurance benefits are taxed as income. Because the benefit amounts paid are often below the taxable annual earning level, however, many states will not take the automatic step of deducting any taxes from your unemployment benefit check.

However, the state will—almost unfailingly— take the leap of reporting the unemployment benefit amount you were paid to the Internal Revenue Service and to your state taxing authority.

If you were receiving unemployment benefits during a year in which you got a new job, you may want to increase the amount your employer withholds in taxes from your paycheck. Otherwise, you may be unpleasantly surprised at tax time when you either owe more tax or receive less of a refund than anticipated.

What to Say, and What Not to Say

When completing your unemployment forms, one of the first questions posed will be something like: Explain in your own words the reason for leaving your last job. You will see first that there is little room for long-worded explanations. Take the clue and keep your responses simple and noncommittal.

Unless you were clearly dismissed from your job because of something you did wrong, avoid using the word "fired" in filing out any forms or answering any interview questions at the unemployment insurance office. There are many unspecified words thrown around concerning the end of employment, but fired is the one most often taken to mean that you did something wrong and were dismissed because of it.

If you lost your job because business was slow, note that you were laid off. "Laid off" is an equally vague term, but it is less likely to raise questions about the validity of your claim.

If you were discharged by your employer, take pains to note: "Discharged without any misconduct" or "Quit for good cause personal reason." Leave out any qualifying details, such as: "My supervisor never liked me from the first day I walked in, so naturally I was the first to be laid off."

The Investigation

Once you have handed in your completed forms, the rituals that follow vary somewhat from state to state. You may be interviewed the same day, told to come back for an interview, or simply sent a check in the mail. If a second visit is required, be sure to take your employment document collection with you.

Whatever the procedure is in your locale, the goal of the unemployment insurance claim filing process is to determine whether you are entitled to benefits, and what the amount of those benefits should be. The interviewer will likely concentrate on why you left your last job. Keep your explanations helpful but as brief and objective as possible.

In some states, you may be approved to receive benefits immediately. If your employer later challenges the award, you should continue to get those benefits during the time the appeal is processed.

But, in most states, the clerks at the unemployment insurance office will use your first interview to launch an investigation of your claim by sending inquiries to your former employer. The employer then must respond, either verifying or disputing your version of the circumstances surrounding your unemployment, the wages you received, and other relevant information. The process usually takes at least a few weeks, and sometimes more.

While waiting for your claim to go through this verification process, you will probably be required to visit the unemployment insurance office once each week or two or sign a statement that will be mailed to you affirming that you still meet all the legal requirements of the program—and that you are looking for a new job. It is important to comply with this reporting requirement even before receiving unemployment insurance checks. If you have not yet received a cent in unemployment benefits, once your claim is verified, you will usually be paid after the fact for all the weeks for which you did qualify.

If your claim is approved, you will typically receive your unemployment benefit check in the mail every two weeks after your claim is verified and your benefit level is determined.

Continuing Your Benefits

Once you have qualified for unemployment insurance benefits, you are not free to simply sit back and welcome the checks each week. You must continue to comply with the state program's rules and rituals to keep them coming.

You must visit the unemployment insurance office or complete specific paperwork as frequently as your state requires it. Periodically, you must verify that you remain unemployed but available for work, that you remain physically able to work, and that you are actively looking for work. The documents you sign will typically ask you to certify that you continue to meet these requirements, and it is usually a criminal offense to lie about any of your answers.

In some states, you are also required to list a minimum number of potential employers to whom you have applied for work since the last time you signed for benefits. This requirement may vary according to economic conditions.

The unemployment insurance program cannot require you to take a job that varies much from your normal field of work and your normal wage level. But these ranges are subject to interpretation, so exercise care in deciding where to apply for a new job. Some unemployment insurance offices maintain and post listings of jobs that are available locally. Apply only for jobs that are similar to your normal type of work and wage levels so that you will not run the risk of having your unemployment insurance claim discontinued because you refused to accept substitute employment.

Where to File If You Move

If you become unemployed in one state and then move to another, you can file your claim in your new state. However, your benefits will be determined by the rules of your former state. Although your new state administers your claim, the cost of your benefits is charged back to the state in which you became unemployed. A move will also add time to processing your claim—usually increasing the delay by several weeks.

Keep in mind that, even when you relocate, you still must meet all the requirements of the unemployment insurance program to qualify for benefits. Your new location must be one to which you were required to move by family circumstances, or in which it is logical for you to expect to find a new job. For example, you cannot decide to move to a small seacoast town with virtually no business activity because you like the countryside there, quit your old job for no other reason, then expect to be eligible for unemployment insurance when you get to your new home and cannot find work.

Appealing Benefit Decisions

If your claim is approved, your former employer will have the right to appeal it. If you are denied benefits, you are legally entitled to appeal the decision.

If Your Employer Appeals

There are cases, of course, where some former employees begin to collect unemployment insurance benefits to which they are not legally entitled—and the employer justifiably appeals the decision.

However, some employers have an outrageous policy of appealing all unemployment insurance claims filed against them. Typically, they use tactics such as claiming that workers quit when, in fact, they were fired because business became slow.

These employers often hire lawyers or agencies that specialize in frustrating unemployment insurance claims—hired gunslingers who make a living by fighting employees' claims until the employees find new jobs and drop their complaints. Money is usually their motivation: The more unemployment claims filed against a company, the higher the company's unemployment premiums.

If your claim is approved but your employer appeals it, you will be notified of that appeal in writing. In general, an appeal by your former employer will be conducted in the same way as your appeal of a denied claim. (See the discussion below.)

You will be able to continue collecting your benefits until a decision is issued on your former employer's appeal. You may, however, be required to repay all or part of the benefits if your ex-employer wins the appeal. Typically, your ability to repay is the deciding factor in such circumstances.

Appealing a Denied Claim

If your claim is denied, you will be notified in writing of the reasons for that decision, and the procedure and time limits for filing an appeal. Depending on your state, you will have from one to four weeks to file an appeal after the notice of denial of an unemployment insurance claim is mailed to you.

A hearing will likely be scheduled within a few weeks after you advise the unemployment insurance office of your intention to appeal its decision. You will have the option of representing yourself or hiring a lawyer for help. If you want a lawyer but cannot afford one, check with your local Legal Aid Society or a clinic at a nearby law school to see if someone there can represent you. If you are unemployed and without benefits, chances are good that they will help. (See the Appendix for additional contacts for legal help.)

Your former employer also has the option of being represented by a lawyer or an agency that specializes in challenging unemployment insurance claims. Typically, the appeal hearing will be conducted informally before a hearing examiner, referee, or administrative law judge. At the hearing, you and your former employer will be allowed to bring witnesses, such as coworkers and medical experts—and most of the formal rules of evidence that apply to formal courtroom proceedings will not apply or will be only loosely enforced.

CAUTION

Mind the time. Most states have strict rules about the time limits within which appeals must be filed—and they are doggedly enforced. You should find the appeal limit clearly marked on the notice of the determination or ruling. And late appeals will be accepted only if you can show that you have extremely good cause for being late: that unanticipated circumstances beyond your control caused your tardiness. Excuses such as you forgot or did not note the filing due date will not pass legal muster.

RESOURCE

Many Unemployment Insurance Appeals Boards publish pamphlets or other publications explaining the state's appeal process. These publications vary in comprehensiveness and helpfulness. But, if you plan to appeal, it is certainly worth your while to call the local UI office and ask whether a publication is available.

Representing Yourself

If you can clearly document the reasons that you are unemployed and present them in an organized manner, you can do a good job of representing yourself in all but the most complex situations. At this level, the appeal process is intended to resolve disputes rather than to take on the look of a formal court action, so do not be afraid to ask questions at the unemployment insurance office or at your hearing.

Well before the hearing is scheduled to begin, write down the reasons that you feel you are entitled to unemployment insurance benefits in as few words as possible; then practice presenting those reasons to a friend or family member. Do not give in to the human temptation to use the hearing as an opportunity to insult or get revenge on your former employer.

Do a thorough and thoughtful job of researching, organizing, documenting, and presenting your case. Keep your argument focused, because it is at this level that you are most likely to win a decision that will quickly start your benefit checks flowing. (For details of how to document your job loss, see Chapter 9, "Getting Documentation.")

If you win this appeal, you will soon begin receiving benefits, typically including back payments from the date on which you first became eligible.

Both you and your former employer will have the option of appealing the ruling on your appeal to the state courts. However, only a tiny percentage of unemployment insurance cases continue up into the state courts or higher. Those that do typically require help from a lawyer. (See Chapter 17, "Hiring a Lawyer.")

Workers' Compensation

The workers' compensation system provides replacement income and medical expenses to employees who are injured or become ill as a result of their jobs. Financial benefits may also be paid to workers' dependents and to the survivors of workers who are killed on the job. In most circumstances, workers' compensation also protects employers from being sued for those injuries or deaths.

The benefits paid by workers' compensation are almost always relatively modest. The system is financed primarily by insurance premiums paid by employers. In some states, employers may opt to self-insure—meaning that they can pay any claims themselves.

Contrary to popular misconception, filing a workers' comp claim does not involve suing the employer. Unless the employer has committed some serious wrong or is illegally uninsured or underinsured, filing for workers' comp is more like submitting a claim to a car insurer following an accident.

The purpose of the workers' comp system is to allow employers and employees to settle their potential differences over money and liability privately and quickly. Injured employees are compensated for the costs of workplace injuries and illnesses. In return, employers can run their businesses free from the constant threat of negligence lawsuits filed by their employees. In reality, however, the system is fraught with difficulties: high premiums for employers and grindingly slow claim processing for injured employees. Doctors and lawyers are often thrown into the fray to make the system painfully costly and complicated.

Other Laws on Work-Related Illness and Injury

Workers' compensation covers some aspects of work-related injuries, illnesses, and deaths. But injured workers should be aware of other laws that may give them rights or entitle them to compensation. Some laws work in tandem, providing individuals with different options; some provide the exclusive remedy for a workplace wrong.

- Social Security disability insurance provides some income for people who are unable to work because of a physical or mental disability. (See Chapter 13.)
- Unemployment compensation provides individuals with some financial benefits when they are out of work. (See Chapter 11.)
- The Americans With Disabilities Act prohibits discrimination against workers who have some types of physical limitations or illnesses. (See Chapter 7.)
- The Family and Medical Leave Act allows an employee to take up to 12 weeks of unpaid leave in a year due to a serious health condition that makes the employee unable to do his or her job. (See Chapter 4.)

Other lawsuits for injuries or job loss may help redress some additional workplace injuries, particularly where workers have lost their jobs. For example, workers' comp claims filed by workers who have been fired are often paired with wrongful termination actions.

Similar to unemployment insurance (discussed in Chapter 11) and Social Security disability insurance (discussed in Chapter 13), the workers' compensation system is national but is administered by the states. The laws and court decisions governing it follow a pattern throughout the country but vary significantly from state to state on everything from eligibility for benefits to the proper process for filing claims.

Who Is Covered

In general, anyone who qualifies as a part-time or full-time employee is covered by workers' compensation insurance. There are a few exceptions to this rule—notably harbor workers, seafarers, railroad employees, and federal employees—all of whom must file lawsuits to get payment for their injuries rather than going through the workers' comp system.

But coverage details vary from state to state, so certain categories of employees may be excluded from coverage in some locales. For example, in some states, companies with fewer than five employees are not required to carry workers' compensation coverage, and many states exclude volunteers, farmworkers, federal employees, and domestic workers from coverage.

Workers who are not covered by workers' comp but who suffer work-related illnesses or injuries are usually relegated to getting compensation from their employers through:

- a company-backed policy, such as paid time off for sick days
- a settlement reached through arbitration or mediation (see Chapter 17), or
- a lawsuit filed against an employer or former employer—for negligence or breach of contract, for example.

Many states require employers to post an explanation of workers' compensation coverage in a prominent place within the work area. If your employer keeps such a notice on your workplace bulletin board, you are probably covered. If you are unsure whether your employer is covered, your state workers' compensation agency should tell you. (See the listing of "State Worker's Compensation Offices," below, for contact details.)

 CAUTION

Independent contractors lose out. Independent contractors are not covered under the workers' comp systems in most states. However, workers who are categorized as independent contractors may in reality be employees. If you are unclear about your status as a worker, file a workers' comp claim for your injuries anyway. It will then be up to your employer to prove that you are not eligible because you qualify legally as an independent contractor rather than an employee. For guidance on whether you should be classified as an employee or independent contractor, consult your local department of labor. (See the Appendix for contact details.)

Conditions Covered

Workers' compensation provides a claim and benefit system for workers who become ill, are injured, or die on the job.

Injuries

To be covered by workers' compensation, an injury need not be caused by a sudden accident such as a fall. Equally common claims are for injuries due to the repeated physical motions—backstrain from lifting heavy boxes, for example. Also covered may be a physical condition that was aggravated by workplace conditions—such as emphysema made worse by airborne chemicals. And, increasingly, workers are being compensated for the effects of psychological stress caused by the job.

With a few exceptions, any injury that occurs in connection with work is covered. The legal boundary is that employees are protected by workers' comp as long as the injury happened "in the course of employment." For example, a computer repair technician would be covered by workers' comp while making service calls on customers, but not while traveling to and from work or going to a purely social dinner later that evening.

From the employee's standpoint, workers' comp is a no-fault system. It does not matter whether a worker was careless when injured— although claims from employees hurt while drunk or fighting have traditionally been rejected as outside the bounds of "work-related activity." Some states restrict coverage for injuries caused by employees' own "willful

misconduct"—a term given differing spins by differing courts. And a number of states expressly restrict or deny benefits when an employee's claim is based on injuries caused by the use of nonprescription, illegal drugs.

Injuries that can be shown to have been intentionally self-inflicted by the employee, or to have been caused by substance abuse, generally are not covered. However, courts have often sided with the injured worker when such cases are disputed—ruling that the injury is covered as long as the employee's behavior was not the only thing that caused the injury. Another questionable area is injuries caused by a coworker's violent behavior—although the workers' comp laws in a few states, including California, specifically cover them.

The legal definition of when you are working, for workers' compensation purposes, also has expanded in recent years to cover a greater number of injuries. For example, employees who were injured playing baseball or football on a company-affiliated team have been allowed to collect workers' compensation benefits for those injuries.

Illnesses

An illness becomes an occupational illness—and is covered under the workers' compensation system—when the nature of a job increases the worker's chances of suffering from that disease. In fact, in some states, certain illnesses (such as heart attacks and hernias) are presumed to be covered for high-stress jobs such as police work and firefighting. There must, however, be a clear

Avoiding Injuries Cased by Repetitive Motion

In a typical year, more than six million work-related injuries and illnesses occur in the United States. The most rapidly growing category of workplace injuries is caused by repetitive motions of the body. These occupational pains go by many names and acronyms: Repetitive Stress Injuries (RSIs), Cumulative Trauma Disorders (CTDs), Repeated Motion Injuries (RMIs).

When they primarily afflict the wrists, hands, and forearms, these injuries are called Carpal Tunnel Syndrome—the bane of office workers who spend their days in front of computer terminals. Many other parts of the body are susceptible to injury when used repeatedly to perform motions beyond the specifications for which nature designed them. Our bodies were simply not made to withstand the demands of making the same motion thousands of times in a short time period. Especially if we don't want to: A recent study found that employees who were dissatisfied with their jobs were most likely to develop repetitive stress injuries.

Typical symptoms of repetitive stress injuries include swelling and redness near bone joints; extreme sensitivity to movement and external touch; pain, both sharp and dull, in the overused area that may radiate into other parts of the limb, abdomen, head, or back; and numbness of the affected body part or those near it. If detected early, injuries caused by repeated motions can often be cured by a short period of rest, light medication, and rehabilitative exercise. The most serious cases, however, can escalate to a lifelong physical disability.

Work-related cumulative motion injuries are typically covered by workers' compensation insurance. But the best workers' compensation claim is the one that you never have to file, so here are a few of the steps that health experts recommend to avoid these injuries:

- Take frequent, short breaks from repetitive, physically stressful work whenever possible. This allows your muscles and joints to recover a bit from unnatural tensions that may result from your work.
- Do gentle stretching exercises at work regularly, paying particular attention to the parts of your body that you use most often. This reduces the muscle tightening that contributes to the problem.
- Watch for early symptoms, such as stiffness or other discomfort in heavily used body parts. Complete recovery is much more likely if the symptoms are recognized early.
- Redesign your work tools or your work position and movements—or ask your employer to help do so. Good redesign examples are wrist rests for use with personal computer keyboards and ergonomic office furniture.
- Remember that heart-pounding physical exertion is not necessary for dangerous body stress to occur. Just as you can wake up with a sore shoulder after sleeping all night, you can suffer a muscle or tendon injury even in jobs that involve very limited exertion. (For more on preventing workplace injuries, see Chapter 6, "Enforcing OSHA Rights.")

connection between the job and the illness. Also, in examining a claim, investigators will look into nonwork factors—such as diet, exercise, smoking and drinking habits, and hobbies—that may affect or aggravate a particular condition.

Illnesses that are the gradual result of work conditions—for example, emotional illness and stress-related digestive problems—increasingly are being recognized by the courts as covered by workers' compensation insurance. Perhaps not coincidentally, such stress injury claims are on the rise, too.

The American medical profession, traditionally slow to acknowledge the interworkings of mind and body, no longer ignores the effects of job-related stress on general health. According to the American Institute for Preventative Medicine, stress is at the root of nearly two-thirds of all office visits and plays a major role in heart disease and cancer. Currently, only about half the states recognize stress as a valid basis for workers' comp claims. But, in every state, if you show that stress has disabled you from doing your job, employers must accommodate your work to your condition—by reducing work hours or providing a quieter atmosphere, for example. (See Chapter 7, "The Americans With Disabilities Act.")

Deaths

Dependents of workers—usually a spouse, children, or other family members—who are killed on the job or die as a result of a work injury or illness are almost always eligible to collect workers' compensation benefits.

The Expanding and Shrinking Compensation World

One of the most dramatic expansions of the definition of work-related illness occurred in a 1990 Michigan appeals court ruling. In that case, a brewery worker was found eligible for workers' compensation benefits because his tendency toward alcoholism—he typically drank 15 to 20 bottles of beer at work each day, and more at home—had been made worse by the fact that his employer gave employees free beer to drink during their breaks. (*Gacioch v. Stroh Brewery Co.*, 466 N.W. 2d 302.)

However, the courts do set some limits, as demonstrated by a California case. There, a workers' compensation claim was filed by a lawyer who fell off his bicycle while pedaling to a weekly meeting of workers' compensation attorneys. He argued that, because he is a lawyer, much of his work involves thinking and analyzing. And because "his office is in his head," he claimed he should remain covered by workers' comp around the clock.

In rejecting the claim, the workers' comp board referee injected a bit of common sense: "Would claimant be covered if he woke in the middle of the night with an idea regarding a case and injured himself falling out of bed to write it down?" he asked. "Common sense tells me that the employment relationship, no matter how all-consuming it may appear to the claimant, must have limits. When claimant fell from his bicycle ... while thinking of client calls to be made, he was pedaling beyond those limits." (WCB Case No. 90-18674.)

Even if an employee is found dead in the workplace, no one witnessed the death, and no cause of death is obvious, the death is usually covered by workers' compensation. The possibilities of suicide or murder are usually ignored by courts unless there is strong evidence that the death qualifies as one or the other.

The Right to Medical Care

When you are injured at work, the workers' comp system usually entitles you to receive immediate medical care.

Treating Physician

If you have a regular doctor, inform your employer in writing that you wish to be treated by that doctor if you are injured at work. Keep a copy of that letter should problems arise later.

If you make no such written request—and you intend to have an injury claim handled under the workers' comp system—either your employer or the insurance company will usually be free to dictate which doctor will treat you for the first 30 days after your injury or work-related illness. After that time, you may be free to receive treatment from the doctor of your choice. But, by that time, the company-referred doctor, who is likely to give a conservative diagnosis of the extent of your injury, may have already jeopardized your benefit claim (or your health).

Laws Regulating Work Injuries: Both a Blessing and a Curse

Most employers make every effort to get injured workers back on the job as soon as possible. In some situations, this may mean modifying an employee's job somewhat—eliminating the requirement of hand-delivering hourly reports, for example, until a broken leg heals.

Making such accommodations is sanctioned and may even be required by the Americans With Disabilities Act, a federal workplace law that protects most workers who are disabled by injuries. (See Chapter 7.)

However, these well-meaning plans may conflict with yet another workplace law, the Family and Medical Leave Act. (See Chapter 4.) The FMLA allows employees to take up to 12 weeks of unpaid leave in a year due to a serious health condition that makes them unable to do their jobs.

Legal experts fret that the FMLA serves as a disincentive for workers to come back to a modified job while they heal completely—and an incentive to keep them out of work until their allotment of leave time expires. What the experts might be forgetting is that FMLA leave is unpaid time off—a luxury many workers cannot afford.

Continuing Treatment

The insurance company is responsible for paying for all treatment you are diagnosed to require, even if that treatment must continue after you return to work. Your ongoing treatment should be paid for life, but you can trade away future medical payments for cash when you settle your case.

If you are uncertain about whether settling makes good financial sense for you more likely if your work-related illness or injury is quite severe—you may want to consult an experienced workers' comp attorney. (See Chapter 17, "Hiring a Lawyer.")

Filing a Workers' Compensation Claim

Get immediate medical care if your injury requires it. You must then inform your employer of your injury as soon as possible. This is a tricky part of processing a workers' comp claim, since states have wildly different limits on the number of days you have to notify your employer; in most states, the limit is one month, but the range is from a few days to two years.

In the unlikely event that your employer refuses to cooperate with you in filing a workers' compensation claim, a call to your local workers' compensation office will usually remedy the situation.

Typically, your employer will have claim forms for you to fill out and submit or can obtain a form quickly. It then becomes your employer's responsibility to submit the paperwork to the proper insurance carrier. Depending on state law, you—rather than your employer—may need to file a separate claim with your state's workers' compensation agency. There is a time limit on this, too—often a year after injury. But your state may have a shorter limit.

If your claim is not disputed by your employer or its insurance carrier, it will be approved and an adjuster for the insurance company will typically contact you or your employer with instructions on how to submit your medical bills for payment. But be prepared; things do not always go smoothly. The employer, in an attempt to keep workers' comp rates from skyrocketing, may fight your right to benefits. The best way you can counteract such disputes is by producing good documentation, including complete medical records, of your injury and treatment.

If your injury is not permanent and does not cause you to lose income, getting payment for your medical bills will probably be the extent of your claim, and there will not be much else for you to do. If you are temporarily unable to work because of your injury, you will also begin receiving checks to cover your wage loss—typically within a week or two after your claim is approved. Your employer will notify the insurance company to stop sending you wage-replacement checks as soon as you recover and return to work.

Calculating Benefits

Your workers' compensation benefits may take several forms. The following are the most common, although some states may provide additional benefits.

Costs of Medical Care

The bills for your medical care will be paid. Theoretically, at least, there is no limitation on medical coverage for illnesses and injuries that are covered. Medical coverage includes costs of:

- doctors
- hospitals
- nursing services, including home care
- physical therapy
- dentists
- chiropractors, and
- prosthetic devices.

Temporary Disability

This is the most common disability compensation paid under workers' compensation, awarded if you are unable to work but are expected to recover and return to work.

You will receive tax-free temporary disability payments that substitute for the income you would have earned had you not been injured. If you cannot work at all, typically you will be paid two-thirds of your average wages, with state-set minimums and maximums. People with unusually low incomes may actually experience an income increase while receiving workers' compensation—and those with high incomes will probably experience an income cut.

In most states, workers become eligible for wage loss replacement benefits as soon as they have lost a few days of work because of an injury covered by workers' compensation. The number of days required to qualify varies by state—and some states allow the payments to be paid retroactively to the first day of wage loss if the injury keeps the employee out of work for an extended period.

Vocational Rehabilitation

If your injury prevents you from returning to your job but you are physically able to do some work, you may be entitled to vocational rehabilitation, which may include additional job training or schooling. Since the early '90s, when workers' comp costs skyrocketed, most states have put severe limits on the sensible benefit of rehabilitation. At a minimum, your treating physician and a workers' comp board staffer or judge must agree that you need vocational rehabilitation. Injured workers who qualify for state-sponsored rehabilitation programs will usually be entitled to receive temporary disability payments—at a somewhat reduced rate.

Permanent Disability

If you have a partial or complete disability, you may receive a lump sum payment in workers' compensation benefits. The lump sum payments that you are eligible to receive will vary greatly with the nature and extent of your injuries. If your injuries fall into one of the following categories, you may qualify for lump sum benefits:

- **Permanent total disability.** You are unable to work at all, and you are not expected to be able to work again.

- **Permanent partial disability.** Although you are able to perform some types of work, you are not expected to be able to fully regain your ability to earn money. This type of disability is usually divided into two groups, schedule and nonschedule injuries:

  - **Schedule injuries.** These are injuries for which a set lump sum payment has been prescribed by law in your state. It is the injury that is assigned a value, not the employee, so your former earnings levels are irrelevant.

  - **Nonschedule injuries.** These are injuries for which no such lump sum amount has been specified, so a settlement must be negotiated. In Florida, for example, there is no law specifying the benefit to be paid to an employee who loses a foot in a work-related accident.

Death Benefits

Weekly compensation benefits are paid to surviving dependents (usually children and spouses) of workers who are killed in the course of employment or as the result of a work-related injury or occupational disease. The amounts paid typically equal about two-thirds of the deceased worker's weekly salary. About a third of the states limit the total amount of the death award given; a few states limit the number of weeks or years survivors may receive death benefits.

Death benefits to surviving spouses usually come to an end if they remarry—and some states provide for a lump sum to a former spouse upon remarriage. Death benefits for surviving children usually end when they reach majority—or somewhat later for full-time students.

In addition, if an employee dies from a workplace accident, then the employee's estate receives burial expenses in the amount specified by law in the state where the accident occurred.

Complex Cases Require Expertise

If your workers' compensation claim is denied, you have the right to appeal it at several levels. If your work-related injury is a permanent or long-term one, then pursuing your claim for workers' compensation benefits to its fullest extent will likely be a complicated task.

If your claim falls into these categories, you will probably need to hire a lawyer who specializes in workers' compensation cases to help. (See Chapter 17, "Hiring a Lawyer.")

State Workers' Compensation Offices

The listings below will enable you to contact the agency handling workers' compensation claims in your state. And as noted, many states also operate dedicated hotlines and websites. While they vary in comprehensiveness, they should provide the basic information you'll need to decide whether to pursue a claim.

State Workers' Compensation

Alabama
Workers' Compensation Division
Department of Industrial Relations
Industrial Relations Building
649 Monroe Street
Montgomery, AL 36131
334-353-0990
800-528-5166
FAX: 334-353-8262
http://dir.alabama.gov/wc

Alaska
Department of Labor
Division of Workers' Compensation
P.O. Box 115512
Juneau, AK 99811
907-465-2790
FAX: 907-465-2797
http://labor.state.ak.us/wc/home.htm

Arizona
State Compensation Fund
3030 N. 3rd Street
Phoenix, AZ 85012
602-631-2000
800-327-9726
FAX: 602-631-2213
www.statefund.com

Arkansas
Workers' Compensation Commission
324 Spring Street
P.O. Box 950
Little Rock, AR 72203
501-682-3930
800-622-4472
TDD: 800-285-1131
www.awcc.state.ar.us

California
Department of Industrial Relations
Division of Workers' Compensation
455 Golden Gate Avenue
San Francisco, CA 94102
415-703-5070
www.dir.ca.gov

Colorado
Department of Labor and Employment
Division of Workers' Compensation
633 17th Street, Suite 400
Denver, CO 80202
303-318-8700
888-390-7936
FAX: 303-318-8710
www.coworkforce.com/dwc

Connecticut
Workers' Compensation Commission
21 Oak Street
Hartford, CT 06106
860-493-1500
FAX: 860-247-1361
http://wcc.state.ct.us/index.html

Delaware
Office of Workers' Compensation
4425 N. Market Street
3rd Floor
Wilmington, DE 19802
302-761-8200
FAX: 302-761-6601
www.delawareworks.com/industrialaffairs/services/workerscomp.shtml

District of Columbia
Office of Workers' Compensation
64 New York Avenue, NE
2nd Floor
Washington, DC 20002
202-671-1000
http://does.dc.gov/does/cwp/view,a,1232,q,537428.asp

State Workers' Compensation (continued)

Florida

Division of Workers'
Compensation
200 E. Gaines Street
Tallahassee, FL 32399
850-413-1601
800-742-2214
www.fldfs.com/WC

Georgia

State Board of Workers'
Compensation
270 Peachtree Street, NW
Atlanta, GA 30303
404-656-2048
www.sbwc.georgia.gov

Hawaii

Department of Labor &
Industrial Relations
Disability Compensation
  Division
830 Punchbowl Street
Room 211
P.O. Box 3769
Honolulu, HI 96813
808-586-8842
FAX: 808-586-9099
www.hawaii.gov.labor

Idaho

Industrial Commission
317 Main Street
P.O. Box 83720
Boise, ID 83720
208-334-6000
FAX: 208-334-2321
www.iic.idaho.gov

Illinois

Workers' Compensation
Commission
100 W. Randolph Street
Suite 8-200
Chicago, IL 60601
312-814-6611
866-352-3033
www.state.il.us/agency/iic

Indiana

Workers' Compensation Board
402 W. Washington Street,
  Room W-196
Indianapolis, IN 46204
317-232-3809
www.in.gov/workcomp

Iowa

Division of Workers'
Compensation
1000 E. Grand Avenue
Des Moines, IA 50319
515-281-5387
800-562-4692
www.iowaworkforce.org/wc

Kansas

Division of Workers'
Compensation
800 SW Jackson Street
Topeka, KS 66612
785-296-2996
800-332-0353
www.dol.ks.gov/wc/html/
  wcinjwkr_EMP.html

Kentucky

Office of Workers' Claims
657 Chamberlin Avenue
Frankfort, KY 40601
502-564-5550, ext. 4423
www.labor.ky.gov/workersclaims

Louisiana

Office of Workers'
Compensation
Administration
1001 N. 23rd Street
P.O. Box 94040
Baton Rouge, LA 70804
225-342-7555
FAX: 225-342-5665
www.laworks.net/wrk_owca.asp

Maine

Workers' Compensation Board
27 State House Station
Augusta, ME 04333
207-287-3751
TTY: 207-287-6119
FAX: 207-207-7198
www.maine.gov/wcb

Maryland

Workers' Compensation
Insurance
8722 Loch Raven Boulevard
Towson, MD 21286
410-494-2000
800-264-4943
www.iwif.com

State Workers' Compensation (continued)

Massachusetts

**Workers' Compensation
Advisory Council**
600 Washington Street
Boston, MA 02111
617-727-4900, ext. 378
FAX: 617-727-7122
www.state.ma.us/wcac

Michigan

**Workers' Compensation
Agency**
7150 Harris Drive
1st Floor, B Wing
Lansing, MI 48909
517-322-1106
888-396-5041
www.michigan.gov/wca

Minnesota

**Department of Labor &
Industry**
Workers' Compensation Division
443 Lafayette Road N
St. Paul, MN 55155
651-284-5005
800-342-5354
TTY: 651-297-4198
www.doli.state.mn.us/
workcomp.html

Mississippi

**Workers' Compensation
Commission**
1428 Lakeland Drive
Jackson, MS 39216
601-987-4247
866-473-6922
www.mwcc.state.ms.us

Missouri

**Division of Workers'
Compensation**
3315 W. Truman Boulevard
P.O. Box 58
Jefferson City, MO 65102
573-751-4231
800-775-2667
www.dolir.mo.gov/wc

Montana

Workers' Compensation Court
1625 11th Avenue
Helena, MT 59624
406-444-7798
FAX: 406-444-7798
http://wcc.dli.mt.gov/whoweare.
asp

Nebraska

Workers' Compensation Court
Capitol Building
P.O. Box 98908
Lincoln, NE 68509
402-471-6468
800-599-5155
www.wcc.ne.gov

Nevada

Division of Industrial Relations
400 W. King Street
Suite 400
Carson City, NV 89703
775-684-7260
FAX: 775-687-6305
http://dirweb.state.nv.us

New Hampshire

**Workers' Compensation
Division**
95 Pleasant Street
Concord, NH 03301
603-271-3176
800-272-4353
www.labor.state.nh.us/workers_
compensation.asp

New Jersey

**Division of Workers'
Compensation**
P.O. Box 381
Trenton, NJ 08625
609-292-2515
FAX: 609-984-2515
www.nj.gov/labor/wc/wcindex.
html

New Mexico

**Workers' Compensation
Administration**
2410 Centre Avenue, SE
P.O. Box 27198
Albuquerque, NM 87125
505-841-6000
800-255-7965
http://workerscomp.state.nm.us

New York

Workers' Compensation Board
20 Park Street
Albany, NY 12207
866-750-5157
877-632-4996
FAX: 518-473-9166
www.wcb.state.ny.us

State Workers' Compensation (continued)

North Carolina

Industrial Commission

4340 Mail Service Center

Raleigh, NC 27699

919-807-2500

FAX: 919-715-0282

www.comp.state.nc.us

North Dakota

Workforce Safety & Insurance

1600 E. Century Avenue

Suite 1

Bismarck, ND 58503

701-328-3800

800-777-5033

TDD: 701-328-3786

www.workforcesafety.com

Ohio

Bureau of Workers'
Compensation

30 W. Spring Street

Columbus, OH 43215

800-644-6292

FAX: 800-520-6446

www.ohiobwc.com

Oklahoma

Workers' Compensation Court

1915 N. Stiles Avenue

Oklahoma City, OK 73105

405-522-8776

800-522-8210

www.owcc.state.ok.us

Oregon

Workers' Compensation
Division

350 Winter Street, NE

P.O. Box 14480

Salem, OR 97309

503-947-7810

800-452-0288

TTY: 503-947-7993

www.cbs.state.or.us/external/
wcd/index.html

Pennsylvania

Bureau of Workers'
Compensation

Department of Labor & Industry

1171 S. Cameron Street

Room 324

Harrisburg, PA 17104

717-772-4447

800-482-2383

TTY: 800-362-4228

www.dli.state.pa.us/landi/cwp/
view.asp?a=138&Q=58929

Rhode Island

Division of Workers'
Compensation

1511 Pontiac Avenue

Building 69, 2nd Floor

P.O. Box 20190

Cranston, RI 02920

401-462-8100

TDD: 401-462-8006

www.dlt.ri.gov/wc

South Carolina

Workers' Compensation
Commission

1612 Marion Street

Columbia, SC 29201

803-737-5700

FAX: 803-737-5768

www.wcc.state.sc.us

South Dakota

Division of Labor and
Management

Department of Labor

Kneip Building

700 Governors Drive

Pierre, SD 57501

605-773-3681

FAX: 605-773-4211

www.state.sd.us/dol/dlm/dlm-
home.htm

Tennessee

Workers' Compensation
Division

Andrew Jackson State Office

Building

9th Floor

Nashville, TN 37243

615-741-2734

www.treasury.state.tn.us/wc

State Workers' Compensation (continued)

Texas

Division of Workers'
Compensation
7551 Metro Center Drive
Suite 100
Austin, TX 78744
512-804-4400
FAX: 512-804-4401
www.tdi.state.tx.us/wc/index.
html

Utah

Industrial Accidents Division
160 E. 300 S, 3rd Floor
Salt Lake City, UT 84111
801-530-6800
http://laborcommission.utah.
gov/indacc/indacc.htm

Vermont

Workers' Compensation
Division
Department of Labor and
Industry
National Life Building Drawer 20
Montpelier, VT 05620
802-828-2138
FAX: 802-828-2195
www.labor.vermont.
gov/Business/
WorkersCompensation/
tabid/114/Default.aspx

Virginia

Workers' Compensation
Commission
1000 DMV Drive
Richmond, VA 23220
877-664-2566
FAX: 804-367-9740
www.vwc.state.va.us

Washington

Department of Labor and
Industries
P.O. Box 44000
Olympia, WA 98504
360-902-5800
TDD: 360-902-5797
FAX: 360-902-6690
www.lni.wa.gov/ClaimsIns/
Claims/default.asp

West Virginia

Workers' Compensation
4700 MacCorkle Avenue, SE
Charleston, WV 25304
304-926-3470
866-452-7425
FAX: 304-926-5372
www.brickstreet.com/Pages/
BrickStreetHome.aspx

Wisconsin

Workers' Compensation
Division
201 E. Washington Avenue
Room C100
Madison, WI 53703
608-266-1340
FAX: 608-267-0394
www.dwd.state.wi.us/wc

Wyoming

Workers' Safety &
Compensation Division
1510 Pershing Boulevard
Cheyenne, WY 82002
307-777-7441
FAX: 307-777-6552
http://wydoe.state.wy.us/doe.
asp?ID=9

Current as of June 2007

Related Lawsuits for Work Injuries

The workers' compensation system is the normal remedy for work-related injuries and illness. But, in a growing number of situations, an injured worker will have the option of filing a lawsuit against another responsible person or company in addition to filing a claim for workers' compensation. For example, an injured worker might sue the manufacturer of a defective machine for negligence.

Employers who fail to maintain the workers' compensation coverage required in their state or who otherwise violate the laws of the workers' compensation system generally can be sued over work-related injuries. You will probably need to hire a lawyer to help with this type of lawsuit. (See Chapter 17, "Hiring a Lawyer.")

Nearly half the states also allow employees to sue employers who fired them in retaliation for filing a workers' compensation claim or for testifying on someone else's behalf in a workers' compensation case.

Social Security Disability Insurance

Social Security disability insurance is one component of the federal Social Security system. The benefits it provides are intended to prevent people from becoming paupers because an injury or illness has left them completely unable to earn a living—something that happens to a surprisingly large portion of the population. In fact, according to the Social Security Administration, a 20 year-old worker has a 3-in-10 chance of becoming disabled before retirement age. And over 7.2 million workers and their families currently draw Social Security disability benefits.

When you and your employer pay into the Social Security program, you are buying long-term disability insurance coverage. Once you have paid into the program for a period specified by the government, you are eligible for benefits should you become unable to earn a living.

Disability program payments are not intended to cover temporary, short-term, or partial disability. The benefits were sanctioned by Congress with the assumption that working families have other support resources during short-term disabilities—such as workers' compensation, insurance, savings, and investment income.

RESOURCE

For a complete explanation of the Social Security system and more detail on filing and appealing Social Security disability insurance claims, see *Social Security, Medicare, & Government Pensions: Get the Most Out of Your Retirement & Medical Benefits*, by Joseph L. Matthews with Dorothy Matthews Berman (Nolo).

Workers' Comp and Social Security: Separate and Unequal

In contrast to the workers' compensation program (see Chapter 12), the Social Security disability insurance system does not recognize degrees of wage-earning capability. Under Social Security eligibility rules, you are either able to work (in which case you do not qualify for its benefits) or you are not able to work (in which case you may qualify). Also, unlike workers' comp eligibility requirements, a disability need not be work-related to be covered under the Social Security benefit system.

However, if you receive workers' comp payments, your Social Security benefit may be reduced. The law states that the sum of all your disability payments cannot exceed 80% of your earnings averaged over a period of time shortly before you became disabled. (See "Other Disability Benefits," below.)

Who Is Covered

Disability benefits are paid only to workers and their families if the worker has enough work credits to qualify.

What is required to earn a work credit changes over time. Currently, workers accumulate credits based on income and length of time worked, but only for jobs covered by Social Security. You can earn up to four work credits per year. The number of work credits needed to qualify for disability

Age of Disability and Work Credits Required			
If you were born before 1930, and you became disabled before age 62 in:	You need this many work credits:	If you were born after 1929, and you became disabled at age:	You need this many work credits:
1980	29	42 or younger	20
1981	30	44	22
1982	31	46	24
1983	32	48	26
1984	33	50	28
1985	34	52	30
1987	36	54	32
1989	38	56	34
1991 or later	40	58	36
		60	38
		62 or older	40

benefits depends on your age when you become disabled.

Timing of the work you put in is important, too. You must have earned at least 20 credits of the required amount within the ten years immediately before you became disabled—unless you qualify under one of the special rules explained below. The amount of your monthly disability check is based on your age and earnings record. (See "Calculating Benefits," below.)

Young Workers

If you were disabled when still young, you need fewer work credits to qualify for benefits. The Social Security formula recognizes that you obviously did not have the opportunity to acquire many quarters of work.

Blind Individuals

If your vision is not better than 20/200 even with glasses, or if your field of vision is limited to 20 degrees or less, you are considered blind under Social Security rules.

If you are disabled by blindness, you are not required to have earned your work credits within the years immediately preceding your disability. Your work credits can be from any time after 1936—the year the Social Security law went into effect. The only requirement is that you have enough cumulative work credits, based on your age, as shown in the chart above.

Widows and Widowers

If you are a widow or widower, age 50 or over, and disabled, you may receive disability benefits even though you do not have enough work credits of your own to qualify—as long as your deceased spouse had enough work credits for his or her age at the time of death.

The rules are as follows.

- You must be disabled. Your age, work experience, and training are not considered in determining whether you are disabled.
- You must be age 50 or older.
- Your spouse must have been fully insured at death—meaning he or she had enough work credits based on his or her age.
- Your disability must have begun before your spouse's death or within seven years after the death.
- If you already receive Social Security benefits as a surviving widow or widower with children, you will be eligible for disability benefits if you are age 50 or older and you become disabled before those payments end or within seven years after they end.
- Even if you were divorced before your former spouse died, you may still be eligible for these benefits if you had been married to him or her for at least ten years.

The amount of benefits you receive will depend entirely upon your spouse's work record and average earnings. And these special disability benefits may end if you remarry.

Disabilities Covered

Many injuries and illnesses are obviously disabling. There are others, however, such as chronic illnesses that become acute with age, or residual conditions that deteriorate over time, which become disabling even though they were not initially too severe. For example, a worker may have had a previous injury that is aggravated through the years to the point where work is extremely difficult or impossible. He or she may become eligible for disability benefits even though the original illness or injury was not disabling.

Because Social Security disability is a government program, its features include a grand amount of qualifying rules and regulations. To receive Social Security disability benefits:

- You must have a physical or mental impairment.
- The impairment must prevent you from doing any substantial gainful work.
- The disability must be expected to last, or have lasted, at least 12 months, or must be expected to result in death.

Of course, these terms are subject to different interpretations. There are guidelines developed by Social Security and the courts regarding qualifications for disability. But proving a disability is often a difficult task. In preparing your claim for a disability, examine these guidelines carefully, discuss the matter with your doctor or doctors, and plan your claim accordingly.

Physical or Mental Impairments

The basic rule regarding disability is that the condition preventing you from working must be a medical one—meaning that it can be discovered and described by doctors. To prove this, when you file your disability claim, you should bring letters from doctors, or from hospitals or clinics where you have been treated, describing the medical condition that prevents you from doing any substantial gainful work. The letters should also state that your disability is expected to last for 12 months or to result in your death.

Substantial Gainful Work

Social Security will first consider whether your condition prevents you from doing the job you had at the time you became disabled, or the last job you had before becoming disabled. If your disability prevents you from performing your usual job, Social Security will next decide whether you are able to do any other kind of substantial gainful work—defined as any job that pays $900 per month or more.

Your age, education, training, and work experience will be considered in making this determination—as will the practicality of learning new job skills for another work position. Social Security will evaluate whether you are able to perform any kind of work for pay, whether or not there are actually any such jobs available in the area in which you live. However, it is up to Social Security to prove that there is gainful employment you can perform. You need not prove there is no work you can do.

EXAMPLE: Arnold has been a longshoreman for 40 of his 58 years. Weakened by an early injury, Arnold's back has grown slowly but steadily worse over the past decade, causing him to miss several months of work in the past two years. His doctor has told him that his back will not get better, and Arnold decides to apply for disability benefits.

As Arnold's back prevents him from standing for long periods of time and restricts the movement of his arms, Social Security determines he is unable to do any physical labor. The next question would be whether he is able to do any other kind of work. It is possible that his back would be too bad for him to do even a job which required him to sit at a desk; if so, and if Arnold proved this to Social Security through his doctor or by trying and being unable to do a desk job, he would probably get his disability payments. On the other hand, if his back were not quite that bad, he might be forced to at least try other work.

Disability Must Be Lasting

No matter how serious or completely disabling your illness or injury is, you will not qualify for disability benefits unless your condition has lasted, or is expected to last, for 12 months—during which time you are unable to perform substantial gainful work. The disability will also qualify if it is expected to result in your death. Even though the disability must be expected to last 12 months, you do not have to wait for 12 months to apply.

Are You Disabled? How the Social Security Administration Decides

To decide whether you are disabled and able to receive benefits based on that condition, the Social Security Administration uses a step-by-step process involving five questions.

Step 1: Are you working?

If you are working and your earnings average more than $900 a month—the base amount set by Social Security for 2007—you generally cannot be considered disabled. If you are not working, go to Step 2.

Step 2: Is your disability severe?

Your condition must interfere with basic work-related activities for your claim to be considered. If it does not, the Social Security Administration will find that you are not disabled. If your condition does interfere with basic work-related activities, go to Step 3.

Step 3: Is your disability found in the list of disabling conditions?

The Social Security Administration maintains a list of medical conditions that are so severe they automatically mean that you are disabled. If your condition is not on the list, the Social Security

Administration will have to decide if it is of equal severity to a medical condition that is listed. If it is, the Social Security Administration will find that you are disabled. If it is not, go to Step 4.

Step 4: Can you do the work you did previously?

If your condition is severe but not at the same or equal level of severity as a medical condition on the list, then the Social Security Administration must determine if your condition interferes with your ability to do the work you did previously. If it does not, your claim will be denied. If it does, proceed to Step 5.

Step 5: Can you do any other type of work?

If you cannot do the work you did in the past, the Social Security Administration will see if you are able to adjust to other work. The Social Security Administration considers your medical conditions and your age, education, and past work experience and any transferable skills you may have. If you cannot adjust to other work, your claim will be approved. If you can adjust to other work, your claim will be denied.

Source: Social Security Administration, *Disability Planner*, 2007, www.ssa.gov

As soon as the condition is disabling and a doctor can predict that it is expected to last a year, you may qualify for disability benefits. And if, after you begin receiving benefits, it turns out that your disability does not last 12 months, Social Security cannot ask for its money back. You are not penalized for recovering sooner than expected, as long as the original expectation that the illness would last 12 months was a legitimate one.

Timing May Be Everything

Social Security disability benefits may be discontinued if you are able to earn your own living. If you are legally disabled but are earning too much money to qualify for Social Security benefits, you may still be able to claim something if your earnings are significantly lower than they were before the onset of your disability.

You may qualify because, in some circumstances, the Social Security Administration can put a disability freeze on your earnings record. The amount of your ultimate retirement benefits or of your disability benefits if you later qualify is determined by your average income over the years. If, after your disability, you are earning considerably less than you were before, the years of those earnings would pull your average income lower, which could result in a lower ultimate Social Security payment. The disability freeze permits you to work and collect your lower income without having it figured into your lifetime average earnings.

Dependents Entitled to Benefits

If you are disabled, your spouse and children under age 18 may also be eligible for dependents' benefits. If so, your combined family benefits—the total amount you, your spouse, and your children receive—will be limited to between 150% and 180% of what your monthly individual benefit would have been, depending on their ages and whether they worked in jobs covered by Social Security. (See "Calculating Benefits," below.)

> **EXAMPLE:** Juan Menendez was making $2,200 a month when he was disabled. At the time he became disabled, Juan's total Social Security earnings record would have given him an individual disability benefit of $600 a month. But Juan's wife, Theresa, and their two teenage children, Angela and Bobby, were also eligible to collect dependents' benefits. Their total family benefits would be the lower of 85% of Juan's $2,200 monthly salary, which comes out to $1,870, or 150% of what Juan's individual disability benefit ($600) would be, which comes out to $900. The Menendez family would receive $900 a month, the lower of the two amounts.

In addition, certain family members may qualify for benefits if a disabled worker dies. They include:

- a disabled widow or widower who is at least 50 years old, and
- a disabled ex-wife or ex-husband who is at least 50 years old, if the marriage lasted ten years or longer.

Filing a Social Security Claim

It is extremely important to file your claim for Social Security disability benefits as soon as you become disabled, because there is a waiting period of five months after you file before you can begin receiving payments. The Social Security Administration imposes this waiting period to ensure that your disability is a lasting one, as required. If you wait a long time to file, you will be disappointed to learn that back payments are limited to the 12 months before the date on which you file.

You must file your claim at one of the Social Security Administration offices located in most cities, listed in the government section of the telephone book or through the ZIP Code search feature of the Social Security website at www.ssa.gov. If your disability prevents you from visiting a Social Security office, you can usually file your claim by mail or over the telephone.

Documentation Required

Social Security staff will complete the forms and other paperwork necessary to file a disability claim. You will need to provide as much documentation as you can, including:

- medical information: names, addresses and phone numbers of all doctors, hospitals and clinics; patient ID numbers; dates you were seen; names of medicines you are taking; and medical records you have
- an original or certified copy of your birth certificate; if you were born in another country, proof of U.S. citizenship or legal residency
- if you were in the military service, the original or a certified copy of your military discharge papers (Form DD 214) for all periods of active duty
- if you worked, your W-2 Form from last year, or if you were self-employed, your federal tax return (IRS 1040 and Schedules C and SE)
- workers' compensation information, including date of injury, claim number and proof of payment amounts
- Social Security Numbers of your spouse and minor children
- your checking or savings account number, if you have them
- name, address, and phone number of a person to contact if the agency is unable to get in touch with you, and
- kinds of jobs and dates you worked in the 15 years before you became unable to work.

Admittedly, this is a fairly comprehensive list. Do the best you can—and do not put off applying or cancel a planned visit to the Social Security office if you don't have it all in hand.

If you have dependents who may be eligible for benefits under your Social Security disability insurance claim, you will have to present similar documentation for them when you file your claim. Some people may also be able to complete the application process online. To see whether you qualify, go to www.ssa.gov and click on "Qualify and Apply" under the heading Disability and SSI.

The Social Security Administration will then investigate your claim—and will pay for any examinations and reports it requires to verify your claim. The Social Security staff will also help you with the paperwork and procedures required for payment if needed.

The results of those examinations and reports will usually be sent to your state's vocational rehabilitation agency, which is responsible for determining whether or not you are considered sufficiently disabled to qualify for benefits. In some cases, the vocational rehabilitation office will conduct its own examination, tests, and personal interviews as well before giving the Social Security Administration a decision on your case.

The Social Security Administration provides emergency funds for disabled people who need financial help during the long waiting period while their claims are being processed. The Social Security employees handling your claim can give you details on how to qualify for emergency funds.

Calculating Benefits

Like other Social Security benefits, the amount of your monthly disability check is determined by your age and earnings record. The amount of your benefits will be based upon your average earnings for all the years you have been working—not just on the salary you were making most recently. Although the amount will be substantial, it alone will not equal your pre-injury income.

Trial Runs at Returning to Work

Social Security disability insurance is more friendly than other income-replacement programs because it allows you to try going back to work without canceling your claim. You can participate in a total of nine months of trial work without losing any benefits—and the nine months need not be consecutive or in one job. Of course, you must still technically qualify as disabled to take advantage of this trial period.

You could, for example, continue to receive Social Security disability checks while trying different jobs for a week or two every few months, until you find one you can do with your disability. Any months in which you do not earn more than $390—or spend more than 40 hours in self-employment—do not count as trial months.

After a trial work period, Social Security will review your case to see whether you have become able to work gainfully. The first test is whether you are able to earn $900 per month in gross wages. (See "Earned Income," below.)

If you succeed in returning to work after qualifying for Social Security disability benefits, the checks will keep coming for two months after your period of disability has ended, to help ease your transition back into the workforce.

Monthly payments for individuals qualifying for disability benefits average about $1,044. The average disability payment for a disabled worker's spouse is $518 monthly and, for a child, also $518. There is also a yearly cost of living increase if the Consumer Price Index rises over 3% for the year. For those who first became disabled in 1982 or later, there is no minimum benefit amount.

Some people—generally only those with high total incomes—may have to pay federal income taxes on their Social Security disability benefits. At the end of the year, you will receive a Social Security Benefit Statement showing the amount of benefits you received.

RESOURCE

Contact the Internal Revenue Service's toll-free number for forms and publications, 800-829-3676, and ask for IRS Publication 907, *Tax Highlights for Persons With Disabilities*, if you need additional information on the tax. You can also download the publication from the IRS website at www.irs.gov.

Your monthly check will be based entirely on your earnings record, with no consideration given to a minimum amount you may need to survive. If you receive only a small disability benefit, however, and you do not have a large amount of savings or other assets, you may be eligible for some other benefits in addition to your Social Security disability benefits. (See "Collecting Other Benefits," below.)

Help With Estimating Benefits

Unlike many of the more sluggish government agencies, the Social Security Administration has taken full advantage of evolving computer technology—and it provides a comprehensive website at www.ssa.gov that includes calculators that you can use to estimate your potential benefit amounts using different retirement dates and levels of future earnings.

The calculators will show your retirement benefits as well as disability and survivor benefit amounts if you should become disabled or die.

There are three types of benefits calculators available:

A quick calculator: This gives you a simple, rough estimate when you input your date of birth and this year's earnings.

An online calculator: You can input your date of birth and your complete earnings history to get a benefit estimate. You may project your future earnings until your retirement date.

A detailed calculator: This calculator provides the most precise estimates. It must be downloaded and installed on your computer before you can use it.

All of these helpful calculators are available on the Social Security Administration's website at: www.ssa.gov/planners/calculators.htm.

Continuing Your Claim

Although many people who suffer total disabilities remain disabled for life, that is not always the case. So the Social Security disability insurance program includes various efforts to rehabilitate workers and get them back to work.

RESOURCE

If at first you don't succeed, try again. Some disabilities experts estimate that only about 35% of all Social Security disability claims are approved the first time they are submitted. Another 13% of applicants win benefits after appealing.

They'll Be Keeping Tabs

If your medical condition improves and you go back to work, your disability eligibility will end. Even if you do not go back to work voluntarily, Social Security will review your case periodically—or at least once every three years—to determine whether, in its opinion, your condition has improved enough for you to go back to work. From time to time, therefore, Social Security may ask for updated medical evidence from your doctor or may even require that you be examined by another doctor or undergo additional medical tests arranged and paid for by Social Security.

You must cooperate with these periodic reviews or run the risk of losing your disability benefits. You have the right, however, to insist on being given enough time to gather necessary information from your doctor, and enough notice to meet the appointment for the examination or test. If you are unable to keep an appointment scheduled for you by the Social Security office, do not hesitate to ask for a rescheduling.

Appealing a Denied Claim

The greatest number of Social Security disability claims are denied because an individual is deemed to be able to do some kind of work, in spite of a disability. If your claim is denied, there are four levels of appeal available to you. At each step of the appeal process, you have 60 days from the date of the previous decision to take action to move up to the next appeal level.

With the exception of the fourth option, filing a lawsuit in federal court, the staff at the Social Security Administration office will supply you with the proper forms for pursuing an appeal and will assist you in completing them.

Request for reconsideration. After your claim is denied, you can ask to see the Social Security Administration's files concerning your claim, then submit corrections or additional information that you hope will cause the agency to reconsider your claim and approve it.

Administrative hearing. You can request a hearing by an administrative law judge who has never looked at your case before. You can ask to have the judge issue a ruling based on the evidence you have already submitted, or you can ask the judge to rule without a hearing after considering additional written evidence. You can also request a hearing at which new or more detailed evidence can be presented. These hearings are usually informal and held in the same locale where you filed your claim.

Review by appeals council. If the judge doesn't find in your favor, you can ask to have the Social Security Appeals Council, based in

Washington, D.C., consider your claim. If the council decides to hear your appeal, you can submit a written argument in support of your evidence. Or you can elect to appear before the council to argue your case. In an attempt to streamline its appeals process, the SSA has randomly selected several thousand cases to study—and those participants must appeal directly to federal court from an unsatisfactory decision at the hearing level.

Federal court. If you do not win approval of your claim at any of the previous levels, or if the appeals council refuses to hear your appeal, you can file a lawsuit in federal court to try to get the courts to order the Social Security Administration to approve your claim. You will probably have to hire a lawyer to help you at this appeal level. (See Chapter 17, "Hiring a Lawyer.")

Collecting Other Benefits

Since disability payments are often not enough to live on, it will be important for you to collect all the other benefits to which you may be entitled and even try to supplement your income by working a little, if you are able.

CAUTION

You may qualify for state benefits. Note that a few states—including California, Hawaii, New Jersey, New York, and Rhode Island—offer disability benefits as part of their unemployment insurance programs. (See Chapter 11.) Call your local unemployment insurance and workers' compensation insurance offices to determine whether your state maintains this kind of coverage. (See Chapters 11 and 12.)

Earned Income

If you earn any regular income, you might not be considered disabled any longer, and you could lose your disability eligibility altogether. You are only officially disabled if you are unable to perform any substantial gainful work.

However, Social Security usually permits you to earn up to about $900 a month, or $1,500 if you are blind, before you will be considered to be performing substantial gainful work—its buzzword for disability eligibility. But this income limit is not an absolute rule; other facts will be considered—including your work duties, the number of hours you work, and, if you are self-employed, the extent to which you run or manage your own business. In deciding how much you are earning, the Social Security office can deduct from your income the amounts of any impairment-related work expenses such as medical devices or equipment—a wheelchair, for example—attendant care, drugs, or services you require to be able to work.

Other Social Security Benefits

You are not permitted to collect more than one Social Security benefit at a time. If you are eligible for more than one monthly benefit—disability and retirement, for example, or disability based on your own work record and also as the disabled spouse of a retired worker—you will receive the higher of the two benefit amounts, but not both.

For the purposes of this rule, though, Supplemental Security Income (SSI)—a program jointly run by federal and state governments to guarantee a minimum income to elderly, blind, and disabled people—is not considered a Social Security benefit. You may collect SSI in addition to a Social Security benefit.

Other Disability Benefits

You are permitted to collect Social Security disability payments and, at the same time, private disability payments from an insurance policy or coverage from your employer. You may also receive Department of Veterans Affairs disability coverage at the same time as Social Security disability benefits. And you may collect workers' compensation benefits at the same time as Social Security disability benefits.

However, the total of your disability and workers' compensation payments cannot be greater than 80% of what your average wages were before you became disabled. If they are, your disability benefits will be reduced to the point where the total of both benefits is 80% of your earnings before you became disabled. If you are still receiving Social Security disability benefits when your workers' compensation benefits run out, you can again start receiving the full amount of your Social Security benefits.

EXAMPLE: Minnie became disabled while working for the telephone company in the computer analysis department. At that time, she was making $1,400 a month. Her Social Security disability benefits were $560 a month; she also applied for and began receiving workers' compensation benefits of $625 a month. Because the total of the two benefits was more than 80% of her prior salary (80% of $1,400 is $1,120, and she would be getting $1,185), her disability benefits were reduced by the extra $65 down to $495 a month.

If Minnie were still disabled when her workers' compensation benefits ran out, her Social Security disability benefits would go back up to $560 a month, plus whatever cost of living increases had been granted in the meantime. If Minnie also had private insurance which paid disability benefits, she could receive those benefits as well as all of her Social Security.

Medicare

After you have been collecting disability benefits for 24 months—not necessarily consecutive months—you become eligible for Medicare coverage even if you are not old enough to be covered by Medicare under the regular rules of the program. Medicare Part A hospitalization coverage is free after you pay a deductible. Like everyone else, though, you must pay a monthly premium if you want to be covered by Medicare Part B medical insurance that partially covers doctor bills, lab work, outpatient clinic care, and some drugs and medical supplies.

For more information on Medicare, contact the Medicare information line: 800-952-8627. Or go to the Medicare website at www.medicare.gov.

Retirement Plans

No law requires private employers to offer their employees retirement plans. In fact, only about half of the workers in this country's private workforce are employed by companies that have some kind of pension plan.

Those employers that do offer pension plans are not required to pay any minimum amount of money—and an increasing number of individuals who invested in saving for their futures are disappointed and disillusioned to learn that their retirement plans simply do not deliver what they promised.

The old standby, Social Security—the government's income system for people 55 and over created by the passage of the Social Security Act in 1935—was not meant to be a pension program as much as insurance against extreme poverty in the later years of life. Although Social Security benefit checks for retirees have increased some in recent years, they still do not provide enough income for most people to maintain their preretirement lifestyles. Consequently, many people rely on some form of private pension—however small—to enhance their incomes after they retire.

This chapter cannot begin to cover all aspects of pension law, which has evolved into a complex morass of legal exceptions, exemptions, and loopholes and is controlled by the terms of individual pension plans. It discusses the most important laws concerning your right to collect the pension benefits you have earned and provides resources for more help.

Social Security Retirement Benefits

There are many ins and outs to the Social Security retirement benefit system—most of them dependent on factors such as the type of job you hold, the length of time you work, and the age at which you retire.

RESOURCE

For more information on Social Security programs and benefits and how to file for them, see *Social Security, Medicare, & Government Pensions: Get the Most Out of Your Retirement & Medical Benefits*, by Joseph L. Matthews with Dorothy Matthews Berman (Nolo).

Who Is Qualified

As with other Social Security benefits, you will be eligible for retirement benefits only if you have accumulated enough work credits. Work credits are measured in quarters (January through March, April through June, and so on) in which you earned more than the required amount of money. The number of work credits you need to be eligible for benefits depends on your age when you apply.

In addition, certain dependents of retired workers are eligible for monthly benefits if the worker has amassed enough work credits to qualify for benefits. Dependents who may qualify for these derivative benefits include:

- a spouse age 62 or older
- a spouse under age 62 who cares for the worker's young or disabled children
- a divorced spouse age 62 or older, if the marriage lasted at least ten years and if at least two years have passed since the divorce
- unmarried children under 18 or who are severely disabled, and
- grandchildren under the care and custody of the worker.

Work Credits Required for Social Security Retirement Benefits	
If you reach age 62 in:	You need this many quarters of employment:
1980	29
1981	30
1982	31
1983	32
1984	33
1985	34
1990	39
1991 or later	40

Maybe They Should Rename It 'Social Insecurity'

There is currently much heated debate about the relative security of the Social Security system. Some say the coffers are quickly running dry; others denounce that as overheated hooey.

Interestingly, the Social Security Administration itself recently posted the following pessimistic prognostication on its website—and included the message on the annual Social Security Statement sent out to workers and former workers over age 25.

Social Security is a compact between generations. For more than 70 years, America has kept the promise of security for its workers and their families. But now, the Social Security system is facing financial problems, and action is needed to make sure that the system is sound when today's younger workers are ready for retirement.

Here is why the level of benefits that Social Security will be able to pay in the future is uncertain. Today there are about 38 million Americans age 65 or older. Their Social Security retirement benefits are funded by today's workers and their employers, who jointly pay Social Security taxes—just as the money they paid into Social Security was used to pay benefits to those who retired before them.

Unless action is taken to strengthen Social Security, in just 10 years we will begin paying more in benefits than we collect in taxes. Without changes, by 2040 the Social Security trust funds will be exhausted. By then, the number of Americans 65 or older is expected to have doubled. There will not be enough younger people working to pay all of the benefits scheduled for those who are retiring. At that point, there will be enough money to pay only about 74 cents for each dollar of benefits that retirees are scheduled to receive.

We will need to resolve these issues to make sure Social Security will provide a foundation of protection for future generations as it has done in the past.

Calculating Your Benefits

Note that when the term "retire" is used by the Social Security Administration, it only refers to the date when you claim your retirement benefits. It does not necessarily mean you have reached a particular age or that you have stopped working.

The average benefit for a person who retires at age 65 is about $1,044 per month. Whatever the amount of your retirement benefit, you will receive an automatic cost of living increase on January 1 of each year. This increase is tied to the rise in the Consumer Price Index—the cost of basic goods and services.

Even if you have not worked for many years and you did not make much money in the years you did work, check your earnings record. You may be surprised to find you have quite a few quarters of credit from years gone by.

If you want to estimate the amount of Social Security benefits you are entitled to receive after you have retired from your job, complete and submit the Social Security Administration's Form SSA-7004, "Request for Social Security Statement." You can obtain one from the Social Security Administration office closest to you or download one, or calculate your own retirement benefit on the SSA website at www.ssa.gov.

Taxes on Your Benefits

Most Social Security retirement benefits are not considered taxable income by the Internal Revenue Service—although you do have to pay income tax on any interest you earn from saving your benefits. But, if your adjusted gross annual income—from a part-time job, for example—plus one-half of your year's Social Security benefits adds up to $25,000 or more, then you must pay income tax on one-half of your Social Security benefits.

In January of each year, you will receive a statement from the Social Security Administration showing the amount of benefits you received in the previous year and an IRS form explaining how to report this income, if necessary.

Medicare and Disability: Not-So-Distant Cousins

The Social Security system wears many hats. One of them is Medicare—a federal government program run by the Department of Health and Human Services, set up to assist seniors and some disabled people in paying for some hospital and medical costs. If you become sick or disabled and unable to work, you and your dependents may qualify for additional benefits that are part of the broader Social Security system. (See Chapter 13, "Collecting Other Benefits.")

Timing Your Retirement

You can start your Social Security retirement benefits as early as age 62, but, if you do decide to jump that gun, the benefit amount you receive will be less than your full retirement benefit amount. If you start your benefits early, they will be permanently reduced based on the number of months before you reach what Social Security defines as your full retirement age.

What is considered full or normal retirement age has traditionally been age 65. However, beginning with people born in 1938 or later, that age will gradually increase until it reaches 67 for people born after 1959. For example, if you were born in 1955, the SSA currently clocks your full retirement age as 66 years and two months.

If your full retirement age is 65, but you begin to claim benefits at 62, they will be reduced by 20%; at age 63, the reduction would be about 13⅓%; and at age 64, it is about 6⅔%.

If your full retirement age is older than 65, you can still start your retirement benefits at 62. But the reduction in your benefit amount will be greater—up to a maximum of 30% at age 62 for people born in 1960 and later.

On the opposite side of the sloth or financial necessity scale, however, a good many people these days are opting to continue working full time beyond retirement age. These industrious souls can increase their Social Security benefit in two ways:

- Each additional year a person works adds another year of earnings to their Social Security record. Higher lifetime earnings may result in higher benefits at retirement.
- In addition, a person's benefit will be increased by a certain percentage if he or she delays retirement. These increases, called delayed retirement credits, will be added in automatically from the time one reaches full retirement age until that individual starts taking benefits or reaches age 70.

Private Pensions

According to many workplace experts, pensions are a good idea run amok.

Pension plans became popular during the Second World War, when there were more jobs than workers. Employers used fringe benefits such as pensions to attract and keep workers without violating the wartime wage freeze rules. Since the early 1950s, unions and employers have both recognized pension plans as crucial elements in labor negotiations.

But, until the mid-1970s, having a pension plan and actually collecting a pension benefit check were two different things. Many people were promised a pension as part of the terms of their employment, and many workers contributed to pension funds through payroll deductions, but relatively few actually received much in the way of benefits at retirement. There were several reasons for the failure of pensions to deliver what they promised: People changed jobs and had to leave their pension rights behind; workers were not-so-mysteriously let go just before they reached retirement age; and pension plans, or whole companies, went out of business.

Legal Controls on Pensions

Since the passage of a federal law, the Employee Retirement Income Security Act of 1974 (29 U.S.C. §§ 301 and following), commonly called ERISA, at least some of the worst sorts of disappearing pension acts have been halted. ERISA sets minimum standards for pension plans, guaranteeing that pension rights cannot be unfairly denied or taken from a worker. ERISA also provides some protection for workers if certain types of pension plans cannot pay all the benefits to which workers are entitled. But, while ERISA provides the protection of federal law for certain pension rights, its scope is limited.

The Incredible Shrinking Pension Check

Inflation is an old enemy of your right to receive a decent retirement pension. The figures an employer shows you as your potential pension benefit may seem decent when you are hired, and may even pay a reasonable amount when you first retire. But, because few private pension plans are indexed to the rising cost of living, the amount you receive when you retire will seem smaller and smaller as inflation cuts into the value of your pension dollar. In other words, the cost of living will go up, but your pension check will not. Unfortunately, ERISA does not require pension plans to respond to inflation's bite into your retirement benefits.

Eligibility for Pension Coverage

There is no law that requires an employer to offer a pension plan. However, if a company chooses to do so, ERISA requires that the pension plan spell out who is eligible for coverage. Pension plans do not have to include all workers, but they cannot legally be structured to benefit only the top executives or otherwise discriminate—for example, by excluding older workers. The plan administrator for your company's pension program can tell you whether you are eligible to participate.

If you are eligible to participate in your employer's pension program, the administrator must provide you with several documents to help you understand the plan:

- **A summary plan description.** Explains the basics of how your plan operates. ERISA requires that you be given the summary plan within 90 days after you begin participating in a pension plan, as well as any updates issued.

  This document will also tell you the formula for vesting in the plan (if it is a plan that includes vesting), the formula for determining your defined benefits or the defined contributions that your employer will make to the plan, and whether or not your pension is insured by the Pension Benefit Guaranty Corporation or PBGC. (See "Mismanaged Plans," below.)

- **A summary annual report.** A yearly accounting of your pension plan's financial condition and operations.

- **Survivor coverage data.** A statement of how much your plan would pay to any surviving spouse should you die first.

Your plan administrator is also required to provide you with a detailed, individual statement of the pension benefits you have earned, but only if you request it in writing or are going to stop participating in the plan because, for example, you change employers. Note, however, that ERISA gives you the right

Pension Terms Defined

Jargon dominates the pension industry. The following definitions will get you on the road to understanding pension rights and wrongs.

Defined benefit plan. The employer promises to pay the employee a fixed amount of money, usually monthly, after the employee retires. Although a defined benefit plan is what usually comes to mind when people think about pensions, this plan has become less common than the defined contribution type.

Defined contribution plan. The employer promises to pay a certain amount into the employee's retirement account while the employee is working but does not promise a specific amount of income for the employee after retirement. Your employer may promise to pay $50 per month per employee into the company's pension plan, for example, but the size of the monthly pension check you receive after retirement would vary according to the interest rate paid on your pension account and other economic factors.

Defined contribution plans can take several different forms, including 401(k) plans, through which your employer and you can contribute jointly to retirement savings. (See "401(k) Deferred Compensation Plans," below.) Defined contribution pension plans are individual savings accounts that usually have some tax advantages—but also some limitations on withdrawals and reinvestment—that regular savings accounts do not have.

Integrated plan. When a pension plan is integrated with Social Security, the actual monthly or yearly pension benefit is reduced by some—or all—of your Social Security check.

This approach allows employers who sponsor their own pension plans to take credit for the fact that their FICA contributions on behalf of lower-income workers buy proportionately more generous benefits than their contributions for higher-income workers. Pension benefits are thereby lowered for all workers, and total retirement benefits—that is, pensions plus Social Security—replace a more uniform percentage of final pay for all employees. Both defined benefit and defined contribution plans may operate as integrated plans.

Employee Retirement Security Act (ERISA). Administered by the U.S. Department of Labor, the Internal Revenue Service, and the Securities and Exchange Commission, ERISA sets minimum standards for pensions and attempts to guarantee that pension rights cannot be unfairly taken from or denied to workers.

Pension Benefit Guaranty Corporation. An organization that insures many pension plans in the United States, the PBGC is half private and half public. It is supposed to get its money from insurance premiums paid by the pension plans it covers, but it regularly turns to the federal government for money when it runs short.

Plan administrator. The person or organization with the legal authority and responsibility for managing your pension program.

Vesting. Getting a legal right to collect from a benefit program. Some pension plans require you to work a certain number of years for a company before you have a right to a pension. Once you are "vested," you continue to have rights to the pension plan even if you no longer work there.

to only one such statement from your plan per year.

Early Retirement and Pension Benefits

Each pension plan has its own rules on the minimum age for claiming benefits. Most private pension plans still consider 65 to be the normal retirement age. However, some private pensions also offer the option of retiring early, usually at age 55. If you elect early retirement, however, expect your benefit checks to be much smaller than they would be if you waited until the regular retirement age.

Many corporations now use the early retirement option of their pension plans to cut staff. By making a temporary offer to increase the benefits available to those who opt to retire early, these corporations create an incentive for employees to voluntarily leave the company's payroll before turning age 65. Sometimes companies make the early retirement offer even more attractive by throwing in a few months of extra severance pay.

Some early retirement offers are very lucrative and some are not. Before accepting one, study the details carefully, keeping in mind that the offer you accept may have to serve as your primary income for the rest of your life. (See Chapter 7, "The Older Workers Benefit Protection Act.")

Because pension law is so specialized and complex, you may also consider consulting a lawyer who specializes in it if the terms of your employer's early retirement offer are not clear. (See Chapter 17, "Hiring a Lawyer.")

When Retirement Does Not Mean Retirement

If your benefits have vested when you reach the retirement age established by your pension plan—usually 65—you are free to leave a job with the employer who pays your pension and work for someone else, or open your own business, while collecting your full pension.

However, if you return to work for the employer that is paying your pension benefits, ERISA permits the employer to suspend payment of your pension for as long as you continue working for that employer. Some workers are covered by a multi-employer pension plan, such as those through an industry-wide union contract. If you are covered by this type of plan, your pension benefits can be suspended if you return to work for a different employer whose employees are covered by the same plan.

Filing for Benefits

Although ERISA does not spell out one uniform claim procedure for all pension plans, it does establish some rules that must be followed when you retire and want to claim your benefits. All pension plans must have an established claim procedure, and all participants in the plan must be given a summary of the plan that explains the plan's claim procedure. When your claim is filed, you must receive a decision on the claim, in writing, within a "reasonable time." The decision must state specific reasons for the denial of any claimed benefits and must explain the basis for determining the benefits that are granted.

From the date you receive a written decision on your pension claim, you have 60 days to file a written appeal of the decision. The rules on where and how this appeal should be filed must be explained in the plan summary. In presenting your appeal, the claim procedures must permit you to examine the plan's files and records and to submit evidence of your own. ERISA does not, however, require the pension plan to actually give you a hearing regarding your appeal. Within 60 days after you file your appeal, the pension plan administrators must file a written decision on your appeal. If your claim is still denied, in whole or in part, you then have a right to press your claim in either state or federal court.

Appealing a Denial of Benefits

Each pension plan has its own system for appeals. If your pension plan denies you benefits to which you are entitled, its administrator is required to tell you how to appeal that decision. You will have 60 days to request such an appeal, and the group that reviews your appeal will, in most cases, have 120 days after you file it to issue its decision. ERISA requires that you be given a plain-English explanation of the decision on your appeal.

If your pension plan's internal review system also rules against you, you are entitled to appeal that decision by contacting:

Employee Benefits Security Administration
200 Constitution Avenue, NW
Washington, DC 20210
866-444-3272
TTY: 877-889-5627
www.dol.gov/ebsa

In addition, the rules of ERISA permit you to file a specific ERISA enforcement lawsuit in federal court to enforce any rule or provision of the ERISA law or of a pension plan covered by ERISA rules. In particular, you may file a federal court lawsuit under ERISA to:

- recover benefits which have been unfairly denied
- challenge a ruling by the pension plan that would affect your future benefits— such as a ruling regarding eligibility, accrual, or vesting
- force the plan to provide information required by ERISA
- correct improper management of the plan or its funds, and
- protect any other right established by the rules of your particular pension plan or by ERISA itself.

Terminated Plans

Your employer may simply decide to terminate your plan, even if it is financially sound. About 10,000 firms do just that every year, mostly in the name of cutting back on corporate costs. If your employer terminates your pension plan, your plan administrator is required to notify you of the approaching termination, in writing, at least 60 days before the plan ends.

If the termination is a standard one, that means that your plan has enough assets to cover its obligations. Your plan administrator is required to tell you how the plan's money will be paid out and what your options are during the payout period.

If the termination happens under distress, the Pension Benefit Guaranty Corporation may become responsible for paying your pension benefits. (See "Mismanaged Plans," below.) If your plan is not insured by the PBGC and it is terminated, your pension rights may be reduced—or lost entirely.

Mismanaged Plans

In recent years, a number of pension funds have gone broke, because of mismanagement, fraud, or overextended resources. The future is likely to bring an increasing number of pension plan failures. Under ERISA, there is some insurance against pension fund collapses. ERISA established the Pension Benefit Guaranty Corporation, a public, nonprofit insurance fund, to provide protection against bankrupt pension funds. Should a pension fund be unable to pay all its obligations to retirees, the PBGC may, under certain conditions, pick up the slack and pay much of the pension fund's unfulfilled obligations.

However, the PBGC does not cover all types of pension plans and does not guarantee all pension benefits of the plans it does cover. Only defined benefit plans are covered—through insurance premiums they pay to the PBGC—and only vested benefits are protected by the insurance. Also, PBGC insurance normally covers only retirement

pension benefits; other benefits, such as disability, health coverage, and death benefits, are not usually covered.

If you have a question about termination of benefits because of the failure of your pension plan, contact:

> Pension Benefit Guaranty Corporation
> Case Operations and Compliance
> 1200 K Street, NW
> Washington, DC 20005
> 202-326-4000
> 800-400-7242
> TDD: 800-877-8339
> www.pbgc.gov

If you think you can prove that the people managing your pension plan are not handling your pension money in your best interests—for example, they are making questionable investments—ERISA gives you the right to file a lawsuit against them in federal court. You will probably need to hire a lawyer to help you with this type of lawsuit. (See Chapter 17, "Hiring a Lawyer.")

 RESOURCE

If you want more details on your rights to receive benefits from a private pension plan, there are a number of free brochures available from:

American Association of Retired Persons (AARP)
601 E Street, NW
Washington, DC 20049
202-434-2277
888-687-2277
TDD: 202-434-6554
FAX: 202-434-2320
www.aarp.org

Another organization that offers a number of publications relating to pensions is:

The Pension Rights Center
1359 Connecticut Avenue, NW
Suite 206
Washington, DC 20036
202-296-3776
FAX: 202-833-2472
www.pensionrights.org

401(k) Deferred Compensation Plans

Many employers that offer retirement benefits do so through a 401(k) deferred compensation plan—the name taken from the number of an IRS regulation that provides the plan with its tax-deferred status. 401(k) plans are deferred compensation programs in which employees invest part of their wages, sometimes with added employer contributions, to save on taxes; they are not actually pension programs that establish a right to retirement benefits. This section explains the basics of 401(k) plans.

Structure of 401(k) Plans

In a 401(k) plan, an employee contributes part of his or her salary to one of several retirement investment accounts set up by the employer and administered by a bank, brokerage, or other financial institution.

Depending on the rules of the particular plan, the employer often makes a contribution in addition to the amount the employee sets aside. However, unlike traditional pension plans, the employer has no obligation to contribute anything and can change the contribution amounts from year to year.

These plans are cheaper for the employer than more traditional pension plans, because employees make the primary contributions from their salaries, the employer has no fixed obligation to contribute, and, when the employer does contribute, it does so as a tax-deductible business expense.

Investment Choices

401(k) plans do not require either the employee or the employer to contribute any set amount each year. The IRS limits how much an employee can contribute each year. The maximum permissible contribution amount goes up each year with the rise in the cost of living. There is no legal limit on the amount an employer may contribute, but most employers contribute a percentage of the amount of the employee's contribution.

A 401(k) plan usually offers the employee a choice among different investments for the deferred income. Some plans offer a selection of preapproved savings accounts, money market funds, stocks and bonds, and mutual funds. Other plans permit employees to select their own investment funds or even to buy individual stock shares on the open market. However, there are usually some limits on the number of investments offered and on the frequency and number of changes in investments that can be made in a given period of time.

For Most Americans, Retirement Looks Cheesy

Researchers analyzing results from a recent survey of American workers concluded that for most people, "retirement expectations are like a piece of Swiss cheese—full of holes." Many have accumulated only modest retirement savings, have underestimated how much income they are likely to need in retirement, and haven't estimated how much they will need to live comfortably once they retire.

- **Savings.** Of the current workers polled, 68% said they and their spouses have accumulated less than $50,000 in retirement savings. This modest level of saving is more prevalent among younger workers: 88% of workers ages 25 to 35 have less than $50,000 saved for retirement, compared with 52% of workers ages 55 and older.

- **Health care costs.** Nearly 58% of current workers said they and their spouses do not expect to receive any health insurance from their employers when they retire. Recent research showed that individuals age 55 who live to age 90 would need to have accumulated $210,000 by age 65 to pay for insurance to supplement Medicare and out-of-pocket medical expenses in retirement—far more than all but about 10% of workers currently have saved for all retirement expenses. Older workers are more likely to have the retirement assets to pay those costs. But 25% of workers age 55 and older say they have accumulated more than $250,000 in retirement savings, compared with 12% for those 45 to 54 and 4% of workers ages 25 to 34.

- **Longevity.** About 66% of current workers think they have some chance of living to be 90, which means they will spend about 25 years in retirement. Furthermore, 41% of current workers think that they have some chance of living until at least age 95—or 30 years of retirement. However, 58% of current workers think they will have less than 25 years of retirement and another 19% are unable to estimate how long their retirement will last. These findings suggest many workers may not be planning and saving enough to finance their retirement years, increasing the odds that they will outlive their retirement savings.

- **Income replacement:** Just 14% of current workers said they thought they would need less than half of their preretirement income to live comfortably in retirement, and another 36% expected to need 50% to 70%. However, 62% of current retirees say their income is 70% or more of their preretirement income.

- **Planning:** Nearly 6 in 10 current workers said they hope to have a retirement standard of living equal to or higher than in their working years. But when current workers were asked if they or their spouse have calculated how much money they will need to retire comfortably, nearly 6 in 10 said no. And of those who did do a retirement calculation, 8% said they arrived at an answer by guessing.

Source: *The 16th Retirement Confidence Survey*, by the Employee Benefit Research Institute, 2006

Tax Advantages of 401(k) Plans

401(k) plans have two tax advantages for the employee.

First, income taxes on the amount of wages invested in the plan are not paid in the year you earn them but are deferred until you withdraw the money from the plan after retirement. Most people have significantly lower income tax brackets after they stop working, so the total tax paid on the income is lower.

Second, taxes on income earned by the investments of the 401(k) plan are likewise deferred until the money is withdrawn after retirement.

CAUTION

401(k) investments may be risky. Along with a choice of investments for the employee comes the risk of poor returns. Unlike traditional pension plans that sink or swim on the total pension fund's portfolio and are backed up by the government's Pension Benefit Guaranty Corporation, the amount of an employee's 401(k) plan fund at retirement depends entirely on how well the plan's individual investments do over the years. An employee who makes particularly risky investments could wind up with less in 401(k) funds than he or she invested.

Withdrawing Money

One of the advantages of most 401(k) plans is that they permit you to withdraw your deferred compensation earlier than pension plans. Most 401(k) plans permit withdrawal without any tax penalty at age 59½, or at age 55 if you have stopped working. Funds may be withdrawn in a lump sum or in monthly allotments. Money that remains in the account, including future earnings, will not be taxed until withdrawal. 401(k) plans also allow your beneficiaries to withdraw the 401(k) funds without tax penalty if you die at any age.

If you withdraw funds before the age permitted by the rules of your plan, you will pay a 10% penalty on the amount withdrawn, plus all income taxes at your current tax rate. And IRS rules require that you begin withdrawing funds by age 70½ at the latest. The amount you must withdraw to avoid a tax penalty is determined by the IRS based on your age and the year you were born. The administrator of your plan can tell you your minimum withdrawal amount.

Some 401(k) plans also permit you to withdraw funds without penalty if needed for a family emergency, such as for medical expenses or for investment in a home. And, in some plans, you can take out a loan from your own 401(k) funds, up to 50% of the total in the account or $50,000, whichever is less, if you have sufficient collateral and you repay it within five years. There are strict rules applying to such withdrawals and loans. Check with your 401(k) plan administrator or a financial adviser.

RESOURCE

For an explanation of how to take money out of your retirement plan, see *IRAs, 401(k)s, & Other Retirement Plans: Taking Your Money Out*, by Twila Slesnick and John C. Suttle (Nolo).

10 Warning Signs of 401 (k) Fraud: When All the Gold Loses Its Glitter

Increasingly employees are asked to make voluntary or mandatory contributions to pension and other benefit plans. This is particularly true for 401(k) savings plans—which allow you to deduct from your paycheck a portion of pretax income every year, invest it, and pay no taxes on those contributions until the money is withdrawn at retirement. But as these plans have become more common, so have incidents of 401(k) fraud.

A recent antifraud campaign by the Department of Labor uncovered a number of employers who abused employee contributions by either using the money for corporate purposes or holding on to the money too long.

Here are 10 warning signs that your pension contributions are being misused:

1. Your 401(k) or individual account statement is consistently late or comes at irregular intervals.

2. Your account balance does not appear to be accurate.

3. Your employer failed to transmit your contribution to the plan in the time it was required to do so.

4. There is a significant drop in account balance that cannot be explained by normal market ups and downs.

5. Your 401(k) or individual account statement shows your contribution from your paycheck was not made.

6. Investments listed on your statement are not what you authorized.

7. Former employees are having trouble getting their benefits paid on time or in the correct amounts.

8. Unusual transactions, such as a loan to the employer, a corporate officer, or one of the plan trustees, are made to the account.

9. There are frequent and unexplained changes in investment managers or consultants.

10. Your employer has recently experienced severe financial difficulty.

Source: U.S. Department of Labor, Employee Benefits Security Administration, 2007

Labor Unions

L abor unions are organizations that deal with employers on behalf of a group of employees. Their best-known role is negotiating group employment contracts for members that spell out workplace essentials such as mandatory procedures for discipline and firing. But unions also often perform other workplace chores such as lobbying for legislation that benefits their members and sponsoring skill training programs.

Today, about 12% of all American workers are union members—and their numbers have steadily declined since 1983, when union membership was first accurately tracked.

If you belong to a union, the specifics of your work relationship are probably covered in a collective bargaining agreement. That means nearly everything—work schedules, wages and hours, time off, discipline, safety rules, retirement plans—is spelled out in that contract. If you have a workplace problem, the process available to resolve it is spelled out in your collective bargaining contract, too.

Usually, you are required to discuss your problem first with a designated union representative, who will then take it up with union officials. If your complaint is found to be a reasonable one, the union reps will guide you through a complaint or grievance procedure. If you disagree with the union's assessment of your situation, you can follow the steps provided for appealing the decision.

Some labor unions also operate benefit programs, such as vacation plans, health care insurance, pensions, and programs that provide members with discounts on various types of personal needs, such as eyeglasses and prescription drugs.

Most unions are operated by a paid staff of professional organizers, negotiators, and administrators, with some help from members who volunteer their time. In general, the money to pay unions' staffs and expenses comes from dues paid by their members— which typically total about $50 per member per month. There is no law that specifically regulates the amount of money that unions can charge their members—but it may not be excessive. Courts have provided little guidance in defining this but have held that a union initiation fee equal to one month's salary would likely be considered excessive.

The laws and court decisions governing labor unions and their relationships with employers are so complex and separate from the rest of workplace law that this chapter can give you only an overview.

If you are already a member of a labor union and want to continue as one, the information provided here can help you double-check on the performance of your union's leaders.

If you are not represented by a union and would like to be, or if you are a member of a union and want out, this chapter will help you become familiar with the basic laws labor unions must follow and alert you to your rights in dealing with unions.

Federal Laws

The federal laws broadly regulating unions— and the copious amendments to those laws— have dramatically changed the look and function of unions over time. The changing laws have also acted as political mirrors—alternately protecting employees from unfair labor practices and protecting employers from unfair union practices as unions' influence in the workplace has ebbed and flowed. Several of the most important federal controls are discussed here.

A Closer Look at the Union Label

The number of American workers who belong to a union fell by 326,000 in 2006, to 15.4 million. The membership rate has steadily declined from 20.1% of the worksheet in 1983, the first year for which comparable union data are available.

Some highlights from the 2006 data are:

- Workers in the public sector had a union membership rate nearly five times that of private sector employees.
- Education, training, and library occupations had the highest unionization rate among all occupations: 37%.
- The unionization rate was higher for men than for women.
- Black workers were more likely to be union members than were white, Asian, or Hispanic workers.

Source: U.S. Department of Labor, Bureau of Labor Statistics, 2007

The National Labor Relations Act

Labor unions secured the legal right to represent employees in their relationships with their employers when the National Labor Relations Act, or NLRA (29 U.S.C. §§ 151 and following), was passed in 1935. That federal act also created the National Labor Relations Board (NLRB) to police the relationships among employees, their unions, and their employers.

Under the NLRA, an employer may not:

- interfere with or restrain employees who are exercising their rights to organize, bargain collectively, and engage in other concerted activities for their own protection
- interfere with the formation of any labor organization—or contribute financial or other support to it
- encourage or discourage membership in a labor organization by discriminating in hiring, tenure, or employment conditions
- discharge or discriminate against employees who have filed charges or testified under the NLRA, or
- refuse to bargain collectively with the employees' majority representative.

The NLRA requires most employers and unions to negotiate fairly with each other until they agree to a contract that spells out the terms and conditions of employment for the workers who are members of the union. The agency enforces this requirement by using mediators, negotiators, administrative law judges, investigators, and others.

Who Is Covered

With the few exceptions mentioned below, the NLRA applies to all employers involved in interstate commerce—which broadly implicates most of those in business.

Who Is Excluded

Certain groups of employees are not covered by the NLRA. They include:

- managers, supervisors, and confidential employees such as company accountants
- farmworkers
- the families of employers
- government workers
- most domestic workers, and
- certain industry groups, such as railroad employees, whose work situations are regulated by other laws.

The NLRA also contains some special exemptions for specific groups of workers within industries that are otherwise covered. Contact your local NLRB office for more information on whether your job is covered by the NLRA.

The Labor Management Relations Act

In the dozen years following enactment of the NLRA, Congress was progressively bombarded with pleas to rein in the unions' power in the workplace. Both employers and employees contended that they needed protection from union overreaching, such as coercing workers to join by using threats and violence. The public joined in the outcry—complaining about work stoppages that increasingly threatened health, safety, and the food supply.

In 1947, the Labor Management Relations Act, popularly known as the Taft-Hartley Act (29 U.S.C. §§ 141 and following), was passed. It was aimed at preventing unfair union practices and banned unions from:

- restraining or coercing employees who were exercising their rights under the NLRA, including the right to select a bargaining representative
- causing or influencing an employer to discriminate against an employee because of membership or nonmembership in a union
- refusing to bargain in good faith with an employer if a majority of employees have designated a union bargaining agent
- inducing or encouraging employees to stop work to force special treatment of union matters, and
- charging excessive fees to employees and employers.

The Labor Management Reporting and Disclosure Act

In a third attempt to right the balance among employees, employers, and unions, Congress passed the Labor Management Reporting and Disclosure Act of 1959. (29 U.S.C. §§ 153 and following.) The most important contribution of that law is that it imposes a code of conduct for unions, union officers, employers, and management consultants—holding each to a standard of fair dealing.

Enforcing Your Rights

You can take action against unions and employers over violations of the NLRA, including unfair labor practices such as threatening workers who join or do not join a union and problems with union elections in the workplace. To begin the process, you must file a charge with a local office of the NLRB. (Get contact information from the agency's website at www.nlrb.gov or check the Federal Government section of your telephone directory.)

NLRB staff will investigate your charge to determine whether there has been a legal violation. If it finds merit, it will attempt to settle the matter—or pursue a complaint. If it finds no merit to the claim, you may appeal that decision. However, you will probably need a lawyer's help to do so. (See Chapter 17, "Hiring a Lawyer.")

Also, there are a number of organizations that may provide free or low-cost help in pursuing union problems and complaints. (See "Where to Get More Help,"below, and the Appendix for contact information.)

State Laws

Section 14(b) of the NLRA authorizes each state to pass laws that require all unionized workplaces within their boundaries to be open shops—and nearly half the states have passed such laws. (See the chart below.) In each of these states, you have the right to hold a job without joining a union or paying any money to a union. These are usually called right to work laws.

One boon for employees in right to work states is that the NLRA requires that a union give fair and equal representation to all members of a bargaining unit, regardless of whether they are union members. If you are employed in a right to work state and are a member of a bargaining unit represented by a labor union, you can refuse to join the union or to pay any dues—and the union still must represent you the same as your union co-

workers. However, you can be required to pay the union's costs for any grievances it brings on your behalf.

If the union representing your bargaining unit fails or refuses to represent you in such situations, you can file an unfair labor practices charge against it with the NLRB.

The states listed below have right to work laws—which prohibit making union membership or nonmembership a condition of employment.

CAUTION

Additional laws may apply. If the chart below indicates that your state has no statute, this means there is no law that specifically addresses the issue. However, there may be a state administrative regulation or local ordinance that does control right to work issues. Call your state labor department for more information. (See the Appendix for contact details.)

The Bargaining Unit

The basic union building block under the NLRA is the bargaining unit: a group of employees who perform similar work, share a work area, and could logically be assumed to have shared interests in such issues as pay rates, hours of work, and workplace conditions.

A bargaining unit may be only a part of a larger union, or it may constitute a whole union itself. And a bargaining unit is not always limited to people who work in one

State Rights to Work Laws

Alabama....................Ala. Code §§ 25-7-30 to 25-7-36

Alaska ....No right to work law.

Arizona....................Ariz. Const. art. 25; Ariz. Rev. Stat. §§ 23-1301 to 23-1307

Arkansas..................Ark. Const. amend. 34; Ark. Code Ann. §§ 11-3-301 to 11-3-304

California.................No right to work law.

Colorado..................No right to work law.

Connecticut ....No right to work law.

Delaware ....No right to work law.

Dist. of Col. ....No right to work law.

Florida ....Fla. Const. art. 1, § 6; Fla. Stat. Ann. § 447.17

Georgia ....Ga. Code Ann. §§ 34-6-20 to 34-6-28

Hawaii ....No right to work law.

Idaho ....Idaho Code §§ 44-2001 to 44-2012

Illinois ....No right to work law.

Indiana ....No right to work law.

Iowa ....Iowa Code § 731.1 to 731.9

Kansas ....Kan. Const. art. 15 § 12; Kan Stat. Ann §§ 44-808(5), 44-831

Kentucky ....No right to work law.

Louisiana ....La. Rev. Stat. Ann. §§ 23:981 to 23:987 (all workers) and 23:881 to 23:889 (agricultural workers)

Maine ....No right to work law.

Maryland ....No right to work law.

Massachusetts .....No right to work law.

Michigan ....No right to work law.

Minnesota ....No right to work law.

Mississippi ....Miss. Const. Art. 7, § 198-A; Miss. Code Ann. § 71-1-47

Missouri ....No right to work law.

Montana ....No right to work law.

Nebraska ....Neb. Const. art XV, §§ 13 to 15; Neb. Rev. Stat. § 48-217 to 48-219

Nevada ....Nev. Rev. Stat. Ann. §§ 613.230 to 613.300

New Hampshire....No right to work law.

New Jersey ....No right to work law.

New Mexico ....No right to work law.

New York ....No right to work law.

North Carolina ....N.C. Gen. Stat. §§ 95-78 to 95-84

North Dakota ........N.D. Cent. Code §§ 34-01-14 to 34-01-14.1

Ohio ....No right to work law.

Oklahoma ....Okla. Const. Art. 23, § 1A

Oregon ....No right to work law.

Pennsylvania ....No right to work law.

Rhode Island ....No right to work law.

South Carolina .....S.C. Code Ann. §§ 41-7-10 to 41-7-100

South Dakota ........S.D. Const. art. VI, § 2; S.D. Codified Law Ann. §§ 60-8-3 to 60-8-8

Tennessee ....Tenn. Code Ann. §§ 50-1-201 to 50-1-204

Texas ....Tex. Lab. Code Ann. §§ 101.001 to 101.004, 101.051 to 101.053, 101.111

Utah ....Utah Code Ann. §§ 34-34-1 to 34-34-17

Vermont ....No right to work law.

Virginia ....Va. Code Ann. §§ 40.1-59 to 40.1-69

Washington ....No right to work law.

West Virginia ....No right to work law.

Wisconsin ....No right to work law.

Wyoming ....Wyo. Stat. §§ 27-7-108 to 27-7-115

Current as of February 2007

building or for one company. For example, the workers in several small, independent sheet metal shops in a specific city will often be members of the same union bargaining unit.

On the other hand, a bargaining unit may include only part of a company. So it is possible—and quite common—for only a small portion of a company's workforce to be unionized, or for various departments in one company to be represented by different unions.

Something that is frequently misunderstood about bargaining units is that they are composed of jobs or job classifications—not of individual workers. For example, if Wilda Samano retires, and her former position as machinist is then filled by Sam Alvarez, the bargaining unit does not change—only the personnel.

Types of Union Work Situations

If you take a job that is covered by a contract between the employer and a labor union, a representative of the union will typically approach you about membership requirements shortly after you are hired.

Unionized work situations generally fall into one of three categories: open shop, agency shop, and union shop. The type of shop that exists within a unionized bargaining unit will be spelled out in the contract between the union representing that unit and the employer. Ask the union representative for a copy of the contract governing your job before you sign up for union membership.

The Open Shop

Here, a union represents the bargaining unit of which you are a member—but you are not required to join the union or pay dues to it. Open shops are most commonly found in states that have passed right to work laws. (See "State Laws," above.)

The Agency Shop

You can make your own decision about whether to join the union. But, whether you join or not, you will have to pay the union the same dues and other fees that other members of your bargaining unit are required to pay. In return for your dues, the union must represent you if labor problems develop, just as it protects members of a bargaining unit. However, you will not be able to take advantage of the broader protections and disciplinary processes included in union contracts. This type of arrangement is legal in any state that has not passed a right to work law. (See "State Laws," above.)

The Union Shop

Although you are not required to be a union member when you take the job, the contract covering your bargaining unit may require you to join after a specified grace period— usually within 30 days after starting your new job. Such contract language is called a "union shop clause."

The law specifies that it is legal for a contract to require an employee to join a union within 30 days of starting a job. However, an employer may fire you because of your lack of union membership only if the union rejected or expelled you for not paying the union's regular fees and dues. This means that, as long as you pay fees and dues, you cannot be required to join the union.

If you take a job in a company in which the union contract calls for a union shop but you refuse to join the union, the employer and the union will usually overlook your refusal to join as long as you pay the union's fees and dues. You can, however, expect to be subjected—at the very least—to cold shoulder treatment by union officials and members.

Union Elections

When a union files a petition with the NLRB to be recognized as the representative of a bargaining unit, the petition includes the union's description of what group of workers it would like to have included in that bargaining unit. The employer usually contests these descriptions and tries to have the size of the bargaining unit trimmed down. Negotiations follow, and, if the union and the employer cannot agree on the exact shape and size of a bargaining unit, the NLRB decides.

Bargaining units are little democracies, in which the majority rules and the minority must comply. For example, if you work in an office and more than half of the people who work there vote to be represented by a union, the entire office is likely to be designated as a bargaining unit. You will be represented by that union. Even if you do not want to be.

Except in a few circumstances, the NLRB generally will conduct an election for a bargaining unit to decide whether or not it wants to be represented by a certain union whenever at least 30% of the members of that bargaining unit indicate they want an election to be held. The members of the bargaining unit may express their wishes for an election by signing a group petition—or by signing individual cards that state, in essence, the same thing—and presenting that evidence of their wishes to their local NLRB office.

Types of Union Elections

NLRB-supervised elections generally fall into three categories:

- certification elections, in which employees in a bargaining unit vote on whether to have a union begin representing them
- decertification elections, in which employees in a bargaining unit vote on whether to end their representation by a specific union, and
- situations where the employees who make up a bargaining unit want to switch unions. The existing union must be voted out through a decertification election and the new union voted in through a certification vote.

Restrictions on Union Elections

The courts have reached different conclusions about when and under what circumstances a union-related election can be held. But there are three NLRB policies on union-related elections that you can usually count on. The NLRB will not conduct an election:

- during the first year that a bargaining unit is represented by a particular union
- within a year of the last election held for that bargaining unit, or
- during the period covered by a union contract.

If the contract lasts more than three years, the NLRB will conduct an election at the end of the first three years of the contract if that is what the bargaining unit's members want.

The Right to Unionize

Sections 7 and 8 of the National Labor Relations Act guarantee employees the right to create, join, and participate in a labor union without being unfairly intimidated or punished by their employers.

Employee Rights

Generally, the courts have ruled that Section 7 of the NLRA gives employees the right to:

- discuss union membership and read and distribute union literature during nonwork time in nonwork areas, such as an employee lounge
- sign a card asking your employer to recognize your union and bargain with it, sign petitions and grievances concerning employment terms and conditions, and ask your coworkers to sign petitions and grievances, and
- display your pro-union sentiments by wearing message-bearing items such as hats, pins, and T-shirts on the job.

Religious Objections to Unions

Some employees are members of religions with beliefs that conflict with membership in a labor union. If your religion prohibits you from taking oaths, for example, having to swear allegiance to a labor union might force you to violate your religious beliefs.

In general, the courts have recognized an employee's right to refuse to join a union on religious grounds. However, you can still be required to pay union dues and fees —or to donate their equivalent to a nonreligious charity—if you work in an agency or union shop in a state that has not passed a right to work law. (See "State Laws," above.)

Employer Limitations

Most courts have also ruled that Section 8 of the NLRA means that an employer may not:

- grant or promise employees promotions, pay raises, desirable work assignments, or other special favors if they oppose unionizing efforts
- close down a work site or transfer work or reduce benefits to pressure employees not to support unionization, or
- dismiss, harass, reassign, or otherwise punish or discipline employees—or threaten to—if they support unioniza-tion. (See Chapter 10, "Blacklisting," for a related discussion of these laws.)

How Unions Are Born

If a group of employees wishes to campaign for unionization of their jobs, the best place to begin is by contacting a union that might be interested and proposing the idea.

Unions are usually listed in the Yellow Pages of your local telephone directory under Labor Organizations. Don't let their names discourage you. It is not unusual for meat packers to belong to the United Steel Workers, for example, or for office workers to belong to the Teamsters union, which originally represented freight drivers. The only practical way to determine which unions might be interested in unionizing your workplace is to call and ask.

If the union you approach is interested, it will assign professional organizers who will guide you through the rest of the process. If it is not interested—perhaps because your employer is too small or because you work in an industry with which it is not comfortable—that union should be able to suggest another one that would be more appropriate for you to contact. If not, contact:

> The American Federation of Labor and
> Congress of Industrial Organizations
> (AFL-CIO)
> 815 16th Street, NW
> Washington, DC 20006
> 202-637-5000
> FAX: 202-637-5058
> www.aflcio.org

The National Labor Relations Act allows you to form your own, independent union to represent only the workers at your place of employment without affiliating with any established union. Such unions exist, but the complexities of labor law and the cost of running an independent union typically make them unfeasible in all but the largest companies.

Deducting Union Dues From Paychecks

One thing on which labor unions and the government agree is that it is easier to get money from people who never get to touch that money in the first place. To ease their operations, many union contracts include a dues check-off clause.

Much like income tax withholding, the check-off clause requires your employer to withhold your union dues from your pay and then forward the money to the union.

By voting to approve a contract between your union and your employer, you also signify approval of any check-off clause in that contract. So, unions' practice of having employers withhold dues from a paycheck is generally legal.

The Right to De-Unionize

Just as it gives employees the right to unionize, the NLRA also gives them the right to withdraw from union membership.

How to De-Unionize

There are two basic ways to de-unionize.

One way is to conduct a campaign among the members of your bargaining unit to get them to petition the NLRB to conduct a decertification election. You generally have to show the NLRB that at least 30% of the bargaining unit wants to get rid of the union before the NLRB will hold an election. If you are able to bring about an election, you will probably also have to campaign hard against the union for the votes of other members of the bargaining unit.

Another way to de-unionize is simply to re-sign your individual membership. The courts have ruled that informing your employer that you want check-off deductions for union dues and fees stopped is not sufficient to quit a union; you must advise the union in writing of your decision to quit.

In right to work states, such a resignation leaves you free and clear of the union altogether—no membership, no dues, no fees. In other states, you may be required to continue paying fees and dues to your bargaining unit's union if the contract there calls for a union or agency shop, as described in "Types of Work Situations," above.

Limitations on Unions

The NLRA also prohibits unions from interfering with your right to reject or change union membership. Unions may not:

- restrain or coerce employees from exercising their rights under the NLRA; this includes the violence and threats of violence that some unions use against people who reject union membership
- cause or encourage an employer to discriminate against an employee or group of employees because of their deunionization activities
- interfere in any way with an employee's right to freely express opinions on union membership
- fail or refuse to bargain in good faith with an employer on behalf of a bargaining unit that has designated the union as its bargaining agent, even if the union and the bargaining unit are at odds, or
- prevent you from going to work by using such tactics as mass picketing.

Where to Get More Help

It is easier to get free legal advice and help with labor union matters than with any other aspect of workplace law.

The place to start is your local office of the National Labor Relations Board (NLRB), listed in the Federal Government section of your telephone directory. The NLRB also maintains a list of local offices on its website at www.nlrb.gov. If the NLRB considers your union-related problem to be a serious one, it will pay for all the costs of the investigations and hearings required to take your complaint through the legal process.

If the NLRB cannot or will not help, you can turn to several other sources. If you consider yourself to be pro-union, contact AFL-CIO headquarters:

The American Federation of Labor and
    Congress of Industrial Organizations
815 16th Street, NW
Washington, DC 20006
202-637-5000
FAX: 202-637-5058
www.aflcio.org

If you consider yourself to be anti-union, contact:

The National Right to Work Committee
8001 Braddock Road
Suite 500
Springfield, VA 22160
703-321-9820
800-325-7892
FAX: 703-321-7342
www.nrtwc.org

If you are unsure about what your opinion on unions is, call both places. These organizations maintain legal staffs to answer union-related questions. They may even provide you with free legal representation.

Immigration Issues

Many immigrants, even those with the documentation required to stay in the United States, may incorrectly believe they have fewer legal rights than American-born citizens. In fact, the Constitution of the U.S. protects everyone, regardless of citizenship or immigration status. It guarantees the same freedoms: to practice religion, to say what you want, to get due process of law, and to live and work free from discrimination.

Federal Law

The Immigration and Naturalization Act of 1990, also known as the Immigration Act (8 U.S.C. §§ 1323a and b), marked the most comprehensive overhaul of employment related immigration law since legal controls were passed in the early 1900s. It sets out a complex system of quotas and preferences for determining who will be allowed to permanently live and work in the United States.

RESOURCE

For a complete explanation of immigration laws, including step-by-step guidance and forms required to enter and stay in the United States legally, see:

- *How to Get a Green Card: Legal Ways to Stay in the U.S.A.*, by Ilona Bray (Nolo),
- *U.S. Immigration Made Easy*, Ilona Bray (Nolo), and
- *Becoming a U.S. Citizen: A Guide to the Law, Exam, & Interview*, by Ilona Bray (Nolo).

The Immigration Act covers all employers and all employees hired since November 6, 1986, except employees who provide occasional, irregular domestic services in private homes. Independent contractors are not covered. If you have a question on your work status, consult your local department of labor. (See the Appendix for contact details.)

Under the Immigration Act, it is illegal for an employer to:

- hire or recruit a worker who the employer knows has not been granted permission by the U.S. Citizenship and Immigration Services (USCIS) to be employed in the United States
- hire any worker who has not completed an INS Form I-9, the Employment Eligibility Verification Form, proving the worker's identity and legal right to work in the United States, or
- continue to employ an unauthorized worker—often called an illegal alien or undocumented alien.

Employers may continue to employ workers who were on their payrolls before November 6, 1986—regardless of their immigration status—as long as those workers continue in essentially the same jobs they had before the law went into effect.

Your employer is not required to fire you if you lack employment authorization from the USCIS but have been in the same job since before the law took effect. However, this provision does not exempt employees from complying with other requirements of U.S. immigration law.

Documentation Required to Work in the U.S.

Only legally authorized employees may work in the United States. When you take a new job, you are required to fill out the employee's section of immigration Form I-9 by the end of your first day on the job. You then have three business days to present your new employer with documents that prove:

- that you are who you say you are, and
- that you are legally authorized to work in the United States.

If you use forged, counterfeit, or altered documents to prove your identification or authorization to work, you may be fined and imprisoned.

When One Document Is Sufficient

USCIS recently revised its list of documents sufficient to prove both identity and eligibility to be employed in the United States. The following will now be accepted:

- a United States passport—either expired or unexpired
- an unexpired foreign passport with an I-551 stamp
- an alien registration receipt card or permanent resident card
- an unexpired employment authorization card
- an unexpired employment authorization document, issued by USCIS, which contains a photograph, or
- an unexpired foreign passport with Form I-94 containing an endorsement of nonimmigrant status.

When Two Documents Are Required

An employee who does not have any of that evidence must produce two documents: one establishing that he or she is authorized to work in the United States and another verifying identity.

As documents proving employment authorization, USCIS will accept:

- a Social Security card
- a U.S. birth or birth abroad certificate
- a Native American tribal document
- a U.S. citizen ID card
- a resident citizen ID card, or
- unexpired employment authorization documents issued by USCIS.

As documents proving identity, USCIS will accept:

- a current U.S. or Canadian driver's license
- a federal, state, or local identification card with a photograph on it
- a school ID card with a photograph
- a voter's registration card
- a U.S. military card or draft record
- a military dependent's ID card
- a U.S. Coast Guard Merchant Mariner card, or
- a Native American tribal document.

For workers age 16 and younger, USCIS considers a school report card or a hospital record such as a birth certificate acceptable as proof of identity.

Time Limits

New employees have three days to complete the I-9 Form. However, if you require some extra time to pull together the documents proving your identity and authorization—for example, if you need to obtain a certified copy of a birth certificate from another state—your employer can give you an additional 18 business days to produce the required documents. To get an extension of time, you must show proof that you have applied for the documents by producing, for example, a receipt for fees charged for a certified birth certificate.

 CAUTION

Your employer may copy and keep the forms. Your new employer is required to note the type of documents you produce and any expiration dates on your Form I-9. Although employers are not required to photocopy such documents, they have the right to do so. If they do, the copies must be kept on file with your Form I-9.

Illegal Discrimination

The Immigration Act makes it illegal for an employer with three or more employees to:

- discriminate in hiring and firing workers—other than unauthorized immigrant workers, of course—because of their national origin
- discriminate in hiring and firing workers because of their citizenship, or
- retaliate against employees for exercising any rights under immigration laws.

To be successful in charging an employer with a violation of the Immigration Act, you must prove that the employer knowingly discriminated against you because of your citizenship or national origin, or that the employer had a pattern of committing the same offense against others.

Enforcing Your Rights

If a prospective or current employer violates your rights under the Immigration Act, you have 180 days from the date of the violation to file a complaint with the Office of the Special Counsel for Unfair Immigration-Related Employment Practices. The most common violation of the antidiscrimination laws protecting immigrants occurs when employers refuse to hire someone because they suspect—incorrectly—that the person is not legally authorized to work in the United States.

The Complaint Process

To begin the complaint process, you can write a letter summarizing the situation to the following address:

Special Counsel
Immigration-Related Unfair Employment
  Practices
950 Pennsylvania Avenue, NW
Washington, DC 20530

If you need legal advice, call the special counsel office to discuss your situation with a staff attorney: 202-616-5594; there is also a hotline at 800-255-7688. And you can get basic background information at the website: www.usdoj.gov/crt.osc.

The special counsel has 120 days from the day it receives your complaint to investigate and decide whether it will pursue a charge against the employer before an administrative law judge.

If the special counsel does not bring a charge against the employer within the 120 days or notifies you that it has not found sufficient evidence to support your charges, you have the right to plead your case directly before an administrative law judge. But you must request your hearing within 90 days of the end of the original 120-day period allowed for the special counsel to take action.

Immigration law is a world all its own. You will probably need the help of an attorney with experience in immigration law if you decide to pursue an antidiscrimination complaint after the special counsel has failed to do so. (See Chapter 17, "Hiring a Lawyer.")

The Appendix of this book also contains contact information for a number of groups that may provide advice and legal referrals. Since the Immigration Act specifically outlaws immigration-related discrimination only in hiring and firing decisions, but not in other employment-related actions such as promotions and wage increases, you may want to file your immigration-related complaint under Title VII of the Civil Rights Act or your state's antidiscrimination laws. (For details on those laws and how to take action under them, see Chapter 7.)

English-Only Rules

The U.S. Census Bureau predicts that, by the year 2050, 24% of the population of the United States will be Hispanic—and Asians and Pacific Islanders will make up nearly 10%. Facing this future, American workplaces will need better direction on the legality of rules that limit or prohibit employees from speaking languages other than English on the job.

The debate about English-only rules is already boiling.

Supporters of English-only rules claim they are essential so that employers can assure that workers are obeying company rules and being polite and respectful to coworkers and clients. Opponents denounce the rules as punishing and demeaning to workers who are not fluent in English, and they claim the rules are a thinly veiled method to target and discriminate against immigrant workers. Some also point out that in parts of the country (such as Southern California) that have a workforce rich in immigrants, it is a boon to businesses to train new hires or deal with customers in their native languages.

The Equal Employment Opportunity Commission has found many English-only workplace rules to be wrongful discrimination on the basis of national origin under the Civil Rights Act. (See Chapter 7, "Title VII of the Civil Rights Act.")

In most situations, employees must be allowed to speak among themselves in their own language while working or during breaks. In fact, EEOC guidelines issued to clarify the suspicion with which courts must approach English-only rules expound that such rules are presumed to be illegal—unless there is a clear business necessity for speaking only English.

The same skepticism applies to workplace screening tests that seem to exclude or disqualify a disproportionate number of applicants of a specific national origin.

Exceptions have been allowed only in cases where there is a clear business necessity, such as for air traffic controllers or for those who must deal with company customers who speak only English. Whenever there is some stricture requiring that employees speak only English on the job, employers must first:

- notify all employees of the rule
- inform all employees of the circum-stances under which English is required, and
- explain the consequences of breaking the rule.

Some states are pioneering their own limits on English-only rules in workplaces. In California, for example, employers with five or more employees must have a "business necessity" to justify imposing employee language restrictions—and must notify all employees about when any restrictions apply and about the consequences of violations. And, in Illinois, employers may not prohibit workers from talking in any language they choose as long as their communications are not related to employment duties.

This is the law of the land. But, in recent years, courts and a number of employers have been pushing the bounds of these guidelines—or ignoring them altogether. The tug and pull in these cases is over whether the English-only policy has a valid business purpose or is downright discriminatory. And, while there is a theoretical difference between rules that ban languages other than English altogether and those that have bans under limited circumstances, that line is not always clear.

In recent legal challenges, courts have upheld some form of English-only rules when they were passed:

- so that supervisors could better manage employees' work, or because customers might object to hearing conversations in a language they could not understand, and
- to promote racial harmony after non-Spanish-speaking employees claimed that hearing Spanish spoken distracted them.

Courts in many of the cases have intimated, however, that employers must exempt employees who do not speak any English from the requirements of English-only rules—or provide training in English so that they may learn to speak it.

Now You Say It, Now You Don't

The war of the words that has developed over English-only rules prompted the Equal Employment Opportunity Commission to issue examples of when it might and might not be permissible to require that only English be uttered on the job. Even this guidance might appear to offer some distinctions without differences.

Possibly Permissible

- A chemical refining plant requires English for employees working directly with dangerous chemicals.
- All workers on the deck of an oil rig are required to speak English because they need to communicate quickly and respond effectively to emergencies.

- A factory requires English of workers who must share tools on an assembly line and are paid according to the number of components they assemble.

Possibly Not Permissible

- A chemical refining plant requires English for clerical workers who do not work directly with dangerous chemicals.
- A retailer requires English at all times during the workday because its customers object to employees speaking Spanish.
- An insurance company orders English only after employees argue in Spanish and are openly insubordinate to their supervisor.

Source: Compliance Manual for EEOC investigators

Lawyers and Legal Research

I f you are facing a workplace dispute, there are specialized agencies to advise and assist you. If your problem is a matter of wage and hour law, for example, you can call the Labor Department's investigators directly for assistance. If your problem involves illegal discrimination, you can call the Equal Employment Opportunity Commission and talk over your case with a compliance officer or staff attorney. A number of specialized agencies are noted throughout the book—and a list of additional resources and contact information is contained in the Appendix.

With some types of workplace problems, however, you are on your own. If you need help getting your former employer to continue your health care benefits after you have lost your job, for example, no one is quite sure where to turn for help. If you have been denied workers' compensation benefits, you may want to double-check your rights before deciding whether to file an appeal.

In some unsettled legal areas, you may need to decide the best course of action: using an alternative to court such as mediation, going to small claims court, hiring a lawyer to help you through, or doing some of your own legal research. This chapter gives you guidance in using and choosing among your options.

Mediation and Arbitration

Because of how the legal world is portrayed on television and in movies, some people think that a courtroom is the best—and only—place to resolve any legal dispute.

In fact, mediation and arbitration can be faster, less expensive, and more satisfying alternatives than going to court. Workplace experts are hailing these less-confrontational methods of solving workplace disputes as the hallmark of forward-thinking companies. And many employers are jumping on the bandwagon by adding clauses to their written employment agreements and employee manuals requiring that workplace disputes be resolved by arbitration or mediation.

Although mediation and arbitration are often lumped together under the general heading of alternative dispute resolution, there are significant differences between the two.

Mediation. Two or more people or groups get a third person—a mediator—to help them communicate. The mediator does not represent either side or impose a decision but helps the disagreeing parties formulate their own resolution of their dispute.

Arbitration. Both sides agree on the issue but cannot resolve it themselves. They agree to pick an arbitrator who will come up with a solution. Essentially, the arbitrator acts as an informal judge, but at far less cost and expense than most legal proceedings require.

Mediation and arbitration are sometimes used to help work out the terms of an agreement to end a work relationship, but they are most effective when those involved have a continuing relationship and want to find a mutually acceptable way to work together.

When Mediation Works Best

Mediation offers benefits to many employers and employees, since the resolution to a particular problem is reached quickly and creatively. And, because all involved feel they have a stake in fashioning the agreement, they are more likely to abide by the solution.

Mediation is not the best solution for all types of disputes, however, because success depends on both sides being willing to meet in the middle and deal directly with one another. Many workplace experts have found that mediation is particularly effective in resolving these workplace conflicts:

- **Disputes between employees.** Many disputes fester because two people are not able to talk with one another. By setting up a nonjudgmental, nonconfrontational way for them to air their differences, mediation may offer a way for them to change their behavior so they can work together more effectively.
- **Deteriorating performance.** Good employees may stop performing well for any number of reasons. By encouraging judgment-free discussion, mediation can help remove the dynamics of browbeating and defensiveness that often result when a supervisor confronts an employee about a slipping work record.
- **Sexual harassment complaints.** Many such problems involve an initial misperception about what is and is not considered acceptable workplace behavior—and are made worse by an inability to discuss the differences openly. Mediation can open communication and help ease the hostility that may pollute a work environment.
- **Termination.** While a firing is usually unpleasant for both employers and

employees, mediation can help an employee receive a fair hearing of differences when that deck is so often stacked in favor of the company. For the employer, mediation can offer hope for a peaceful parting, free from the threat of future litigation.

 RESOURCE

The Appendix of the book lists some good resources for finding professional mediators and arbitrators—and the websites for those organizations include some helpful information about understanding the processes involved in alternative dispute resolution.

And for more information about how to choose a mediator, prepare a case, and go through the mediation process, see *Mediate, Don't Litigate: Strategies for Successful Mediation*, by Peter Lovenheim and Lisa Guerin (Nolo).

Small Claims Court

Some disputes over workplace law, such as whether wages are owed to you by a former employer, involve only small amounts of money. In many of those cases, you can file your own lawsuit in small claims court to collect the money are owed.

The hallmark of small claims court is simplicity: It is inexpensive and easy to file a case there, and court procedures are streamlined. You do not need to hire a lawyer to represent you; in some states, lawyers are not even allowed. The small claims hearing is held before a judge, magistrate, commissioner, or volunteer attorney, who will usually decide the case on the spot or within a few days.

The amount you can sue for is limited—usually to between $2,000 and $5,000, depending on your state. But these limits increase regularly, so check first with the local court clerk if you decide to use small claims court.

RESOURCE

For more information on using small claims court, see *Everybody's Guide to Small Claims Court,* by Ralph Warner (Nolo).

Class Action Lawsuits

The federal courts sometimes allow lawsuits to be filed jointly by groups of people who have all been injured by the same or similar conduct by an employer. These are called class actions. Because they spread the legal costs among many people who are injured, class actions can make it feasible to sue an employer or former employer where the expense would be too great for an individual. Of course, all those who join in the lawsuit will also share in any judgment.

The legal requirements for pursuing a class action are complex and almost always require a lawyer's help. But keep this option in mind if a number of other workers suffered similar wrongs or injuries to yours.

Your local office of the American Civil Liberties Union (ACLU) should be able to direct you to lawyers who specialize in

civil rights class action lawsuits. (See the Appendix for contact details of the national headquarters.)

Hiring a Lawyer

If your workplace problem involves a complex or ambiguous area of law—negotiating a complicated settlement, filing a claim of blacklisting, or a violation of public policy—you will probably need to hire a lawyer for help. Depending on your circumstances and location, a number of places may provide referrals to lawyers with special expertise in workplace law.

- Try local legal clinics. Some may only make referrals to lawyers with appropriate knowledge and experience. And some may have lawyers on staff who will handle your case for a low cost or free of charge. Locate your community's legal aid clinics by looking in the telephone directory under Legal Aid Society or Legal Services—or check with the nearest law school.
- Organizations in your area that serve as advocates for the legal rights of minority groups, such as gay rights coalitions and local chapters of the National Association for the Advancement of Colored People (NAACP), may also make lawyer referrals.
- National organizations that deal with specific types of workplace rights, such as the National Association of Working Women, may know of competent lawyers for referrals.

Class Actions Wipe the Smile From Wal-Mart's Faces

Betty Dukes first learned about Sam Walton, founder of the Wal-Mart empire, in a sociology class. "I learned in that class that Sam Walton had a profound vision and started Wal-Mart on a faith venture. I have always deeply appreciated his visionary spirit and his efforts to reach for the stars." But once she became employed there, she learned something else: Wal-Mart, the allegedly family friendly retail giant whose corporate logo is a yellow smiley face ball, was doing her wrong.

Dukes and a few of her coworkers became the catalysts for the largest private civil rights case in history—charging Wal-Mart with discriminating against women in pay and promotions.

According to the 1.25 million pages of evidence and 200 sworn depositions in the early discovery stages of the lawsuit:

- Six women initially filed the lawsuit; about 1.7 million women who worked at Wal-Mart since December of 1998 may belong to the class now suing the store.
- $8.44 per hour was the rate longtime female employees earned, versus an average of $9 hourly for male new hires.
- About 50% of the female Wal-Mart workers qualify for the federal food stamp program.
- 57% of the managers are female at other large retailers; at Wal-Mart, only 33% rise to that rank—although 72% of its sales force is female.
- 90% of the store managers are male.
- There is one woman among the twenty top officers.

Depositions of male managers revealed strong policies against filling many of the higher-paid positions—which required handling guns in Sporting Goods or dealing with live crickets in the Bait Shop—with women, who were considered constitutionally unfit for the tasks. And several uttered quotes which are the stuff that can sink lawsuits, including:

> "Women have shown little interest in management positions."

> "Men are here to make a career and women aren't."

> "Retail is for housewives who just need to earn a little extra money."

And this query from a male manager to women employee: "You're a girl. We need you in toys. Why do you want to work in the Hardware Department?"

Wal-Mart contested the class certification. But on February 6, 2007, the Ninth Circuit Court of Appeals upheld the decision certifying a class consisting of all women employed at Wal-Mart's U.S. facilities any time since December 26, 1998 to the present. The court described the case as "the largest certified class in history."

As the world awaits the final legal word in this lawsuit, other class actions against the box store behemoth rage on, including a $172 million verdict and injunction for Wal-Mart's violation of wage and labor laws in a California. In that case, Wal-Mart claimed that workers voluntarily gave up their meal and rest breaks to stay on the job. And at least 30 other class actions await resolution in the courts.

You could conclude that Wal-Mart is simply one of the nation's largest employers—so a sitting duck for large-scale lawsuits alleging unfair treatment. Or you could conclude that its policies and actions are so wrongheaded that the mega-corporation deserves whatever is coming to it. Either way, you might be right.

- Groups of specialized employees may have access to legal help offered by special interest groups. Union workers, for example, can contact the Coalition for Labor Union Women for legal guidance and referrals to experienced attorneys.

See the Appendix for listings of organizations that provide legal referrals and for additional information on specialized workplace problems.

CAUTION

Beware of lawyer-run referral services. Bar associations and other lawyer groups often maintain and advertise lawyer referral services. Usually, there is little or no screening before a lawyer can get listed in these services. While it is always possible you will find a good lawyer through one of these services, your chances are hit or miss.

Comparison Shopping for a Lawyer

If you take detailed notes on each lawyer mentioned during your research, you should soon have your own small directory of lawyers with employment-related expertise from which to choose.

Be careful that people do not merely give you the names of lawyers they have heard of—or one who handled an entirely different kind of case, such as a divorce or a house closing. Any lawyer can become well known just by buying a lot of advertising time on television or a large block in the Yellow Pages. Beware that in many states, lawyers can advertise any area of specialization they choose—even if they have never before handled a case in the area.

Questions to Ask

Keep in mind that individual preferences for a particular lawyer are guided by intangibles such as personality or your comfort level with the person. Here are a few questions you may want to ask a person who gives you a glowing review of a particular employment law lawyer:

- Did this lawyer respond to all your telephone calls and other communications promptly?
- Did the lawyer take the time to listen to your explanation and understand your situation fully?
- Were all the bills you received properly itemized and in line with the cost projections you got at the start of your case?
- Did this lawyer personally handle your case, or was it handed off to a younger, less-experienced lawyer in the same firm?
- Did the lawyer deliver what he or she promised?

It may be slightly more difficult to evaluate a lawyer referral you get from an agency or special interest group. Reputable organizations will strike from their referral lists the names of lawyers about whom they have received negative reviews. You can help groups that make referrals keep their information accurate and useful to others if you let them know of both your good and bad experiences with a particular individual.

Deciding on a Lawyer

Once you have a referral to a lawyer—or even better, several referrals—contact each one and see whether he or she meets your needs.

Come forearmed with some inside knowledge.

Most lawyers are guided by the principle that Time Is Money. And time and money should also be your guiding concerns in deciding whether to hire a lawyer to help with your workplace claim.

Even the simplest problems can take a long time to be resolved through the legal system. And potential legal problems in the workplace do not often present themselves in straightforward issues. Unless a case is settled (most cases are), a court proceeding can take from five to eight years before a final judgment is reached.

A lawyer's help rarely comes cheap. Legal organizations estimate that workplace rights cases eat up an average of between $8,000 to $30,000 in lawyers' time and other legal costs such as court filings and witness interviews.

Lawyers often take on workplace cases for little or no money up front. They depend on court-ordered fees and often a percentage of your recovery, or a contingency fee. (See "Paying a Lawyer," below.) This means that a lawyer will be assessing whether your case is likely to pay off so that he or she will be compensated.

Given these hapless circumstances, you will want to be as certain as possible that any lawyer you hire will be doing the utmost to represent you fairly and efficiently—and that you are comfortable with his or her representation.

The Initial Interview

Start by calling for an appointment. Some lawyers will try to screen you over the phone by asking you to discuss the basics of your case. A little of this can be helpful to you both. You can begin to assess the lawyer's phoneside manner; he or she can begin to assess whether you truly need expert legal advice.

Many lawyers will agree not to charge you for an initial consultation to decide whether your situation requires legal action. But be prepared to pay a reasonable fee for legal advice. A charge of between $75 and $250 for a one-hour consultation is typical. Organize the facts in your case well before going to your consultation, and be clear about what you are after—whether it is a financial settlement or reinstatement to your old job. Bring any important documents (such as an employment contract, disciplinary warning, or proposed severance agreement) with you to the meeting. An hour should be more than enough to explain your case and obtain at least a basic opinion on how it might be approached and what it is likely to cost. If you find the right lawyer and can afford the charge, it can be money well spent.

Keep in mind that very few employment law disputes actually end up in a courtroom. Most are settled or resolved in some other way. So you need not be swayed by a lawyer's likely effect on a jury alone. A good lawyer may also offer the valuable advice that you do not have a good case—or may suggest a good strategy for negotiating a settlement.

Paying a Lawyer

Some words to the wise about legal bills: Get Them in Writing.

After you have interviewed a few lawyers and decided which one can best handle your case, do not just turn the case over to the lawyer of your choice. Most disagreements between lawyers and clients involve fees, so be sure to get all the details involving money in writing—including the per-hour billing rate or the contingency fee arrangement, the frequency of billing, and whether you will be required to deposit money in advance to cover expenses.

Most workplace cases are handled under some form of contingent fee arrangement in which a lawyer agrees to handle a case for a fixed percentage of the amount finally recovered in a lawsuit. If you win the case, the lawyer's fee comes out of the money awarded to you. If you lose, neither you nor the lawyer will get any money.

A lawyer's willingness to take your case on a contingent fee is a hopeful sign of faith in the strength of your claim. A lawyer who is not firmly convinced that your case is a winner is unlikely to take you on as a contingency fee client. Be very wary of a lawyer who wants to take your case on an hourly payment basis. That usually signals that he or she does not think your case is very strong in terms of the money you might be able to recover. It could also mean financial disaster for you, as your legal bills are likely to mount up with no useful results. At the very least, insist that the lawyer write down some specific objectives

to be accomplished in your case—and put a limit on how high the fees can accumulate.

Although there is no set percentage for contingency fees in most types of cases, lawyers demand about a third if the case is settled before a lawsuit is filed with the courts, and 40% if a case has to be tried. Keep in mind that the terms of a contingency fee agreement may be negotiable. You can try to get your lawyer to agree to a lower percentage—especially if the case is settled quickly—or to absorb some of the court costs.

Sometimes, a lawyer working for you under a contingency agreement will require that you pay all out-of-pocket expenses, such as filing fees charged by the courts and the cost of transcribing depositions—interviews of witnesses and others involved in a lawsuit who may provide additional information about the facts and circumstances. If this is so, the lawyer will want you to deposit a substantial amount of money—a thousand dollars or more—with the law firm to cover these expenses. From your standpoint, it is a much better arrangement for the lawyer to advance such costs and get repaid out of your recovery. A commonsense arrangement might involve you advancing a small amount of money for some costs, with the attorney advancing the rest.

In some types of workplace lawsuits, such as Civil Rights Act violations, the court may award you attorneys' fees as part of the final judgment. However, this award may not be large enough to cover the entire amount owed to your attorney under the legal fee contract. Therefore, the contingency fee contract should spell out what happens to a court award of attorneys' fees.

One approach is to have the fees paid to the attorney in their entirety—and subtract that amount from the contingency fee to which you have agreed. Another common approach is to add the awards for fees and damages, then subtract the attorney fee as a cut of that total. Attorneys are apt to angle for this approach if they disagree with the amount a court awards in legal fees.

Managing Your Lawyer

Most complaints against lawyers have to do with their failure to communicate with their clients. Your lawyer may be the one with the legal expertise, but the rights that are being pursued are yours—and you are the most important person involved in your case. You have the right to demand that your lawyer be reasonably available to answer your questions and to keep you posted on your case.

You may need to put some energy into managing your lawyer.

Carefully check every statement. Each statement or bill should list costs that the lawyer has paid or that you are expected to pay. If you question whether a particular bill complies with your written fee agreement, call your lawyer and politely demand that a new, more detailed version be sent before you pay it. Don't feel as though you are being too pushy: The laws in many states actually require thorough detail in lawyers' statements.

Do your homework. Learn as much as you can about the laws and decisions involved in your case. By doing so, you will be able to monitor your lawyer's work and may even be able to make a suggestion or provide information that will move your case along faster. Certainly if the other side offers a settlement, you will be in a better position to evaluate whether or not it makes sense to accept it.

Keep your own calendar of dates and deadlines. Note when papers and appearances are due in court. If you rely on your lawyer to keep your case on schedule, you may be unpleasantly surprised to find that an important deadline has been missed. Many a good case has been thrown out simply because of a lawyer's forgetfulness. Call or write to your lawyer at least a week before any important deadline in your case to inquire about plans to meet it.

Maintain your own file on your case. By having a well-organized file of your own, you will be able to discuss your case with your lawyer intelligently and efficiently—even over the telephone. Being well informed will help keep your lawyer's effectiveness up and your costs down. Be aware that if your lawyer is working on an hourly basis, you will probably be charged for telephone consultations. But they are likely to be less expensive than office visits.

Disagreeing on a Settlement Offer

In many cases, your employer may offer a cash amount to settle the case. The problem is that you and your lawyer may have different interests at heart.

If your lawyer is rushed or needs money, he or she may be ready to settle your case quickly for an inadequate amount. You, on the other hand, may want to hold out for an amount that you consider to be more adequate. At this critical juncture, you may wish to get a second legal opinion as to whether the amount offered is realistic given the facts of your situation.

Firing a Lawyer

If your relationship with a particular lawyer does not seem to be working out for some reason, or if you truly believe your case is not progressing as it should, consider asking another lawyer to take over. Beware, however, that if you are in the midst of a lawsuit, the judge may need to approve the switch—and has the discretion to refuse the request if he or she believes change would cause an unreasonable delay or prejudice the other side.

If you are able and anxious to change lawyers, be clear with the first one that you are taking your business elsewhere, and send him or her an immediate written notification of your decision. Otherwise, you could end up receiving bills from both lawyers—both of whom might claim that they handled the lion's share of your case, complicating the matter of who is owed what.

Before you pay anything, be sure that the total amount of the bills does not amount to more than you agreed to pay. If you have a contingency fee arrangement, it is up to your new lawyer and former lawyer to work out how to split the fee.

Take prompt action against any lawyer whose behavior appears to be deceptive, unethical, or otherwise illegal. A call to the local bar association, listed in the telephone directory under Attorneys, should provide you with guidance on what types of lawyer behavior are prohibited and how to file a complaint.

Most state attorney regulatory bodies are biased toward lawyers. Unless the lawyer's conduct is plainly dishonest or he or she has abandoned your case, you will probably not get much satisfaction. However, sometimes the threat of filing a complaint can move your lawyer into action. And, if worse comes to worst, filing a formal complaint will create a document that you will need if you later file a lawsuit against a lawyer for malpractice.

RESOURCE

For detailed information on hiring and working with a lawyer—and commonsense explanations of every stage of a lawsuit—see *The Lawsuit Survival Guide: A Client's Companion to Litigation* by Joseph L. Matthews (Nolo).

Legal Research

This book gives you a general understanding of the legal principles involved in common workplace disputes. However, in negotiating with your employer, presenting your workplace problem to government investigators, preparing for mediation or arbitration, or working with a lawyer you hire, you may gain additional power and speed the resolution of your dispute by having detailed and specific legal knowledge.

In these situations, you may want to do some legal research of your own. If you have been laid off or fired, you likely have some time on your hands—and may even find it surprisingly therapeutic to get to work doing your own research.

This book explains the more traditional form of legal research—using books and law libraries—and the newer-fangled method of research through online services.

 CAUTION

Don't start from scratch. For more general information about specific workplace issues, check the Appendix. Many legal and special interest groups publish helpful bibliographies and pamphlets on the legal aspects of workplace issues such as sexual harassment and age discrimination. Before you do extensive research on your own, take a look at what others have done.

Library Research

The reference sections in most larger public libraries contain a set of local and state laws, as well as a set of the federal statutes. The reference librarian should be able to help you look up any laws that might affect your situation. However, if you want to look up a court case or a ruling by a government agency such as the Equal Employment Opportunity Commission, you will probably have to visit a law library.

In many states, county law libraries are free and open to the public. You can also try the library of the nearest law school, particularly if it's affiliated with a public university funded by tax dollars. Law school libraries offer one big advantage: They are usually open from early in the morning until late at night—even on weekends and some holidays. Whatever library you choose, you will find that most librarians are not only well versed in legal research techniques, but are also open to helping you through the mazes of legal citations.

Where to Begin

There are several types of research materials concentrating on employment law that you may find useful: secondary sources such as books and law review articles, and primary sources such as statutes and cases. These resources serve different purposes.

Secondary sources—general books and scholarly articles—are usually used to get an overview of a particular topic. If you find a good article or chapter on a topic you're interested in, it will give both an explanation of the law and citations to other materials—especially cases—that may prove helpful.

Primary sources—statutes (state and federal laws) and cases (published decisions of state and federal courts)—tell you the current status of the law. Very often, your goals in doing legal research are first to find the statutes that apply to you, and then to find the court cases that interpret the statutes in situations similar to yours. There may be cases with similar facts—for example, a supervisor who persistently asked a female employee to go out with him after she repeatedly said no. Or there may be a court case that raises a similar issue or legal question—for example, whether an employer is legally responsible for paying for an independent contractor's commuting costs. These court decisions may give you some indication of how a government agency or court is likely to decide your case.

The best place to begin your research depends on your situation. If you want some additional general information about a particular workplace issue, or an update on the law since this book was published, you will probably find a recent book or article more than adequate. However, if you want very specific legal information—for example, whether wrongful discharge is a valid legal theory in your state—you will probably need to look at both your state fair employment practice law and any judicial decisions dealing with the issue. The sections that follow describe how to find and use several types of resources to learn about the law that applies to your situation.

RESOURCE

For more on the specifics of legal research, see *Legal Research: How to Find & Understand the Law*, by Stephen Elias and Susan Levinkind (Nolo).

Statutes

When people refer to The Law, they are usually talking about statutes—the written laws created by state and federal legislatures.

Federal statutes are contained in the United States Code. For example, if you are looking for the Civil Rights Act, 42 U.S.C. § 2000, locate Title 42 of the United States Code and turn to Section 2000.

Finding state statutes is a bit trickier, because states use slightly different systems to number and organize their statutes. Most states use one of the following methods:

- **By topic.** California uses this type of organization. To find Cal. Gov't. Code § 12900, locate the volumes that contain the state's government code and turn to Section 12900.
- **By title.** Vermont, for example, divides its statutes into titles, similar to the federal citation system. To find 21 Vt. Stat. § 495, locate Title 21 of the Vermont Statutes— and turn to Section 495.

Inside the back cover of the volume, you will find an unbound supplement called a pocket part. This material updates the information in the main volume, including any amendments or changes to the law that have happened since the main volume was published. It is organized just like the main volume, using the same numerical system. Be sure to check the pocket part every time you use a statute. If you forget this crucial step, you may be relying on law that is no longer valid.

The Two Research Tracks: Federal and State

Two separate sets of laws control the workplace—federal law and state law. Each has separate statutes, regulations, and court cases, so you must decide which law you are relying on before you start to research.

The U.S. Civil Rights Act, for example, is a federal law, and the court decisions which interpret it—including those involving the EEOC—are federal cases. However, not all federal decisions carry equal weight. The cases which will be most persuasive in federal court are those from the highest court in that jurisdiction: the United States Supreme Court. On the second level in the hierarchy are the federal courts of appeal. You should look first for cases in the same judicial circuit or geographical region as yours, since these will be more likely to control the outcome of your particular case. And, finally, on the lowest level are the federal district courts—again, look first for cases in your geographical area.

If you are researching your state's laws, you will be looking at state court cases. Most state court systems are similar to the federal system, in that there are three hierarchical levels of courts. The most authoritative cases will be those from your state's highest court —usually called the supreme court—followed by decisions issued by your state appellate court, followed by decisions issued by your state trial court.

Regulations

In some situations, you may also want to consult the regulations that pertain to a statute. Regulations are the rules created by administrative agencies for carrying out legislation. If, for example, a statute requires an agency to investigate complaints about workplace safety hazards, there will probably be regulations that give more detail about what form the investigation will take, who will conduct it, and how it will be done.

Federal regulations can be found in the Code of Federal Regulations—usually abbreviated as CFR.

RESOURCE

Don't forget local laws. Many major cities and some counties also have their own laws on illegal workplace practices, such as discriminating against gay and lesbian workers, and regulations detailing how these laws should be carried out. Do not neglect these in your research. Sometimes a local law will contain the best protections against workplace problems or provide the best remedies. Ask your law librarian how to find and use your city or county code.

Cases

Sometimes, you will find all the information you need in the statutes and regulations. However, laws can be deceptively straightforward, impossibly complex—or somewhere in between. To be sure you get the point, it is wise to also look at court cases that involve the statute and see how the courts apply and interpret it. Courts have been known to take a law with an apparently obvious meaning and turn it on its head.

And, sometimes, you will need to turn to case law because there is no statute that applies to your situation. For example, when you are researching whether a legal theory such as the intentional infliction of emotional distress applies to your situation, you will absolutely need to look at some court decisions, since these issues are decided on a case-by-case basis.

Many court cases are cited throughout this book. Be sure to look at them as possible leads. If the discussion here makes a case seem similar in some way to your situation, you might want to look up the case and read the court's ruling. For information on how to interpret case citations, see "How to Read a Case Citation," below.

Finding a case interpreting a statute. If you want to track down how a certain statute has been referred to by the courts in a case, your research task will be fairly simple: All you have to do is consult an annotated code. An annotated code is a version of the state or federal statutes that contains summaries of cases that have interpreted various provisions of a statute. There are two sets of federal annotated codes: the United States Code Service and the United States Code Annotated. Most states also have annotated codes. Ask the law librarian where you can find them.

To use an annotated code, look for the numbered section of the statute that is relevant to your situation. If there have been any court cases interpreting that statute,

they will be listed after the specific section of the statute, along with a sentence or two describing the case. If the summary of the case leaves you wanting to know more about it, you can track down the case and read it by following the citation given there.

Finding a case using secondary sources. In some situations, you will want to find court decisions on a particular topic without referring to a statute. For example, if you want to find out whether some uncomfortable situation at work might form the basis of a tort action in your state, you should probably not begin your research with a statute. Common law tort actions were developed almost exclusively by case decisions. Sometimes these torts are also written into code—such as a state criminal statute defining and setting out the punishment for assault—but, more likely, you will have to hunt down a few cases.

One good way to find relevant cases is through secondary sources (discussed below). Quite often, a law review article or book—including this one—will discuss key cases and give citations for them. If you find a source that analyzes an issue that is important in your case, you will likely get some good leads there.

Digests. Another good resource for finding cases is the digest system. These digests, published by the West Publishing Company, provide brief summaries of cases organized by topic. There are many sets of digests, divided by geographic region.

To use the digest system to find cases, first choose the relevant volumes—regional, state, or federal. Next, look in the descriptive word

How to Read a Case Citation

There are several places where a case may be reported. If it is a case decided by the U.S. Supreme Court, you can find it in either the United States Reports (U.S.) or the Supreme Court Reporter (S.Ct.). If it is a federal case decided by a court other than the U.S. Supreme Court, it will be in either the Federal Reporter, Second Series (F.2d) or the Federal Supplement (F. Supp.).

Most states publish their own official state reports. All published state court decisions are also included in the West Reporter System. West has divided the country into seven regions—and publishes all the decisions of the supreme and appellate state courts in the region together. These reporters are:

A. and A.2d. Atlantic Reporter (First and Second Series), which includes decisions from Connecticut, Delaware, the District of Columbia, Maine, Maryland, New Hampshire, New Jersey, Pennsylvania, Rhode Island, and Vermont.

N.E. and N.E.2d. Northeastern Reporter (First and Second Series), which includes decisions from Illinois, Indiana, Massachusetts, New York,* and Ohio.

N.W. and N.W.2d. Northwestern Reporter (First and Second Series), which includes decisions from Iowa, Michigan, Minnesota, Nebraska, North Dakota, South Dakota, and Wisconsin.

P. and P.2d. Pacific Reporter (First and Second Series), which includes decisions from Alaska, Arizona, California,* Colorado, Hawaii, Idaho, Kansas, Montana, Nevada, New Mexico, Oklahoma, Oregon, Utah, Washington, and Wyoming.

S.E. and S.E.2d. Southeastern Reporter (First and Second Series), which includes decisions from Georgia, North Carolina, South Carolina, Virginia, and West Virginia.

So. and So.2d. Southern Reporter (First and Second Series), which includes decisions from Alabama, Florida, Louisiana, and Mississippi.

S.W. and S.W.2d. Southwestern Reporter (First and Second Series), which includes decisions from Arkansas, Kentucky, Missouri, Tennessee, and Texas.

A case citation will give you the names of the people or companies on each side of a case, the volume of the reporter in which the case can be found, the page number on which it begins, and the year in which the case was decided. For example:

Smith v. Jones Internat'l, 123 N.Y.S.2d 456 (1994)

Smith and Jones are the names of the parties having the legal dispute. The case is reported in volume 123 of the New York Supplement, Second Series, beginning on page 456; the court issued the decision in 1994.

*All California appellate decisions are published in a separate volume, the California Reporter (Cal. Rptr.), and all decisions from New York appellate courts are published in a separate volume, New York Supplement (N.Y.S.).

index. You will find a number of categories listed under each heading. Look in the digest under topics that are relevant to your search —for example, Wrongful Discharge, Employer Negligence, Blacklisting. Under each topic, there will be short summaries of cases, arranged chronologically. If a case interests you, you can find the complete decision in the state or regional reporter by using the case citation.

The digests have a handy feature: the key number system. All of the digests use the same headings to categorize cases. Topics are divided into subtopics; each subtopic is given a number. If you find a topic in the state digest that seems relevant and want to find federal cases on the same point, look in the federal practice digest under the same key number.

Finding similar cases. Once you find a case that seems relevant to your situation, you can determine if there are more by using a publication called Shepard's Citations. Shepard's collects and lists every reference to a particular case. In other words, you can look up any case—state or federal—in the Shepard's volumes and get a list of every case decided after it that has mentioned your case. This is very valuable for finding cases on the same subject, as well as for determining whether the original case you found has been influential or discredited.

Treatises

There are hundreds of books—sometimes called treatises—that cover workplace issues. The drawback of most treatises is that nearly all of them are written by and for lawyers—with little effort made to translate legalese into English. Also, these books oftentimes devote many pages to lawyerly concerns, such as how to plead and prove picayune points of law. Still, these volumes will often provide you with helpful background information— and will also often lead you to cases that pertain to your situation. When using a legal treatise, be sure to check the back inside cover; most publishers update the books periodically by issuing pocket parts, bound pamphlets noting changes and additions to the text.

If you are interested in pursuing your legal research through such a treatise, your best bet is to go to a law library and ask the research librarian for some steering on your particular topic. Or peruse the shelves and trust your own instincts about the usefulness of a tome based on a quick scan.

Law Review Articles

Law reviews are periodicals containing articles written by lawyers, law professors, and law students—usually covering a unique or evolving legal topic. Since workplace law is of great current interest, you will find lots of articles about it. The inside joke about law review articles is that they are made up mostly of footnotes. While annoying to many readers, these footnotes—which contain references or citations to other relevant cases, statutes, and articles—can be gold mines for researchers. Look especially for articles that are published in law reviews from schools in your state, since these will be most likely to discuss your state's law and court decisions.

There are two tools in every law library that can help you find law review articles on topics that interest you: the *Current Law Index* and the *Index to Legal Periodicals*. These volumes are published annually, except for the most recent listings, which are published every month. Both list articles by subject, by author, and by the cases and statutes referred to in the article. If you don't have a case name or a specific statute in mind to guide you, turn to the index and peruse the listings of articles there.

How to Read Law Review Citations

Both the *Current Law Index* and the *Index to Legal Periodicals* will give you the author, title, and citations of law review articles. The citations will give the title of the publication and the volume and page numbers of the articles you want to look at. For example, if you look under Sexual Harassment—Analysis, you will see a listing for Susan Estrich's article "Sex at Work." The citation reads:

43 Stan. L. Rev. 813 (1991)

This article can be found in volume 43 of the *Stanford Law Review*, beginning on page 813; 1991 is the year of publication. If you have trouble deciphering the law review names, check the listing of abbreviations in the index—or ask a law librarian for help.

Online Resources

There are currently many websites—maintained by the government, law schools or libraries, law firms, and individuals—that can be useful to employees. They may have just what you are looking for—and they certainly are convenient.

 RESOURCE

Useful internet sites:

- **AHI's Employment Law Resource Center**
  www.ahipubs.com
  Aimed at managers and human resource personnel, this site offers common sense packaged as frequently asked questions about many aspects of employment, from benefits to safety and health concerns. Of course, the information is helpful to Just Plain Workers, too.

- **Nolo**
  www.nolo.com
  Sorry to toot our own horn too loudly, but this one is tootable. Under "Rights and Disputes—Employee Rights," loads of free information is available for consumers interested in finding out more about rights in the workplace. Topics covered under Employment Law include discrimination, sexual harassment, fair pay and time off, health and safety, independent contractors, losing or leaving a job, and privacy.

- **Workplace Fairness**
  www.workplacefairness.org
  Click on the tab titled "Your Rights" to find a wealth of information explaining your basic workplace rights, from be hired to coping with a job loss.

Resources

The organizations listed here can give you additional information or assistance on specific workplace issues. Some groups offer a wide variety of services—including publications and written materials, telephone counseling and hotlines for advice, support groups or in-person counseling, attorney referrals, and training resources. Some organizations offer only limited services or restrict services to their members or to a limited geographic area, so be sure to ask about possible limitations. Also, ask for an additional, more appropriate referral if the group you contact is not able to help.

Advocacy, Generally

Workplace Fairness
2031 Florida Avenue, NW; Suite 500
Washington, DC 20009
202-243-7660
FAX: 202-282-8801
Nonprofit organization providing information, education, and assistance to individual workers and their advocates. Focus is on workplace concerns including hiring, discrimination, wages and hours, working conditions, and termination.

AIDS-HIV
See also organizations listed under Gay and Lesbian.

AIDS Action
1730 M Street, NW; Suite 611
Washington, DC 20036
202-530-8030
FAX: 202-530-8031
www.aidsaction.org

National advocacy organization with the slogan "Until It's Over," working for more effective AIDS policy, education, and funding. No direct service for individuals. Promotes and monitors legislation on AIDS research and education and on related public policy issues.

American Foundation for AIDS Research (AmFAR)
1150 17th Street, NW; Suite 802
Washington, DC 20036
202-331-8600
800-392-6327
FAX: 202-331-8606
www.amfar.org
Nonprofit public foundation funds programs for AIDS research, education for AIDS prevention, and public policy development.

Centers for Disease Control
National Prevention Information Network
Post Office Box 6003
Rockville, MD 20849
800-458-5231
FAX: 888-282-7681
www.cdcnpin.org
The CDC National Prevention Information Network (NPIN) provides information about HIV/AIDS, sexually transmitted diseases, and tuberculosis to people and organizations working in prevention, health care, and research and support services.

National AIDS Fund
729 15th Street, NW; 9th Floor
Washington, DC 20005
202-408-4848
888-234-2437
www.aidsfund.org

A philanthropic organization providing funding for education, advocacy, and research efforts in local communities. Also acts as a clearinghouse for information on HIV and AIDS, youth involvement in prevention, nutrition programming, and return to work efforts.

National Association of People With AIDS

8401 Colesville Road, Suite 750
Silver Spring, MD 20910
240-247-0880
FAX: 240-247-0574
www.napwa.org
Policy advocates for people living with HIV and AIDS.

National Minority AIDS Council

1931 13th Street, NW
Washington, DC 20009
202-483-6622
FAX: 202-483-1135
www.nmac.org
Encourages leadership within minority communities responding to the HIV and AIDS epidemic. Monitors legislation and provides AIDS programs with technical assistance. Distributes information on AIDS—especially information concerning the impact of the disease on minorities.

Civil Rights

American Civil Liberties Union (ACLU)

125 Broad Street, 18th Floor
New York, NY 10004
212-607-3300
www.aclu.org
Advocates individual rights through litigation and public education on a broad range of issues affecting individual freedom, from genetic testing to wrongful discharge. Legal advice and counseling, as well as attorney referrals, provided by state offices.

Human Rights Watch

350 Fifth Avenue, 34th Floor
New York, NY 10118
212-290-4700
FAX: 212-366-1300
www.hrw.org
International activist group dedicated to preventing discrimination and upholding political freedom.

Disabled Workers

ABLEDATA

8630 Fenton Street, Suite 930
Silver Spring, MD 20910
800-227-0216
TTY: 301-608-8912
FAX: 301-608-8958
www.abledata.com
A consumer referral service sponsored by the U.S. Department of Education's National Institute on Disability and Rehabilitation Research that maintains a database of more than 30,000 adaptive devices from white canes to voice output programs.

Job Accommodation Network (JAN)

P. O. Box 6080
Morgantown, WV 26506
800-526-7234
TTY: 877-781-9403
www.jan.wvu.edu
Provides free consulting services to people with disabilities seeking accommodation information under the Americans With

Disabilities Act (ADA) and to employers seeking to accommodate employees with disabilities. Maintains a database of companies nationwide that have accommodated workers and organizations, support groups, government agencies, and placement agencies that assist the disabled.

National Organization on Disability

910 16th Street, NW; Suite 600
Washington, DC 20006
202-293-5960
TTY: 202-293-5968
FAX: 202-293-7999
www.nod.org

Administers the Community Partnership and National Partnership programs, which address educational, employment, social, and transportation needs of people with disabilities. Provides members with information and technical assistance, makes referrals, monitors legislation.

Office on the Americans With Disabilities Act

Civil Rights Division
U.S. Department of Justice
950 Pennsylvania Avenue, NW
Washington, DC 20530
800-514-0301
TTY: 800-514-0383
FAX: 202-307-1198
www.usdoj.gov/crt/ada/adahom1.htm

Government agency specialists answer questions about the ADA—except on federal government holidays. Publishes a number of free booklets, including information on how to file a complaint under the ADA. Publications are also available in alternate formats for the disabled: Braille, computer disk, audiocassette, and large print.

Social Security Administration

Disability Office
6401 Security Boulevard
Baltimore, MD 21235
800-772-1213
TTY: 800-325-0778
www.ssa.gov

Administers and regulates the disability insurance program and disability provisions of the Supplemental Security Insurance (SSI) program.

Discrimination

4era

4355J Cobb Parkway, #233
Atlanta, GA 30339
678-793-6965
www.4era.org

A national, nonpartisan, single issue organization working to finish ratification of the Equal Rigths Amendment to the U.S. Constitution.

Equal Employment Opportunity Commission

1801 L Street, NW
Washington, DC 20507
800-669-4000
TTY: 800-669-6820
www.eeoc.gov

Government agency that enforces federal laws prohibiting employment discrimination and sexual harassment through investigation, conciliation, litigation, coordination, education, and technical assistance.

National Committee on Pay Equity

555 New Jersey Avenue, NW; Suite 402

Washington, DC 20001

703-920-2010

FAX: 703-979-6372

www.pay-equity.org

Provides information and technical assistance to those interested in eliminating wage discrimination based on gender and race. Members receive updates and mailings on pay equity activity, NCPE's newsletter, discounts on NCPE publications, and access to pay equity networks.

Gay and Lesbian

ACLU National Lesbian and Gay Rights Project

See American Civil Liberties Union under Civil Rights.

Gay and Lesbian Advocates and Defenders (GLAD)

30 Winter Street, Suite 800

Boston, MA 02108

617-426-1350

800-455-4523

www.glad.org

Publishes information and provides general advice on sexual orientation and HIV status. Provides lawyer referrals.

Human Rights Campaign

1640 Rhode Island Avenue, NW

Washington, DC 20036-3278

202-628-4160

FAX: 202-347-5323

TTY: 202-216-1572

800-777-4723

www.hrc.org

Lobbies Congress, provides campaign support to fair-minded candidates, and works to educate the public on a wide array of topics affecting gay, lesbian, bisexual and transgender Americans, including relationship recognition, workplace, family, and health issues. The affiliated HRC Foundation engages in research and provides public education and programming.

Lambda Legal Defense and Education Fund

120 Wall Street, Suite 1500

New York, NY 10005

212-809-8585

FAX: 212-809-0055

www.lambdalegal.org

Provides publications, advice, and legal information on gay, lesbian, bisexual, and transgender job discrimination and HIV discrimination issues. Phone-in service for lawyer referrals.

National Center for Lesbian Rights

870 Market Street, Suite 370

San Francisco, CA 94102

415-392-6257

FAX: 415-392-8442

www.nclrights.org

Offers publications, advice, counseling, and lawyer referrals to promote the rights and safety of lesbians and their families.

National Gay and Lesbian Task Force Policy Institute

1325 Massachusetts Avenue, NW; Suite 600

Washington, DC 20005

202-393-5177

TTY: 202-393-2284

FAX: 202-393-2241

www.thetaskforce.org

Political advocacy group for lesbian, gay. bisexual, and transgender individuals. Publishes organizing manual for implementing domestic partnership benefit plans and nondiscrimination policies. Provides referrals for counseling and lawyers.

Immigration

Bureau of U.S. Citizenship and Immigration Services
800-375-5283
TTY: 800-767-1833
www.uscis.gov
Federal agency responsible for overseeing citizenship, asylum, and employment authorization and enforcing visa and lawful permanent resident applications and procedures.

Labor Departments

U.S. Department of Labor
200 Constitution Avenue, NW
Washington, DC 20210
866-487-2365
TTY: 877-899-5627
www.dol.gov
You can find a list of regional offices of the Wage and Hour Division at the Department of Labor's website at: www.dol.gov/esa/contacts/whd/america2.htm and a comprehensive list of state labor resources at: www.dol.gov/dol/location.htm.

State Labor Departments

Note: Phone numbers are for department headquarters. Check websites for regional office locations and numbers.

Alabama
Department of Industrial Relations
Montgomery, AL
334-242-8990
www.dir.state.al.us

Alaska
Department of Labor and Workforce Development
Juneau, AK
907-465-2700
www.labor.state.ak.us

Arizona
Industrial Commission
Phoenix, AZ
602-542-4411
www.ica.state.az.us

Arkansas
Department of Labor
Little Rock, AR
501-682-4500
www.state.ar.us/labor

California
Department of Industrial Relations
San Francisco, CA
415-703-5050
www.dir.ca.gov

Colorado
Department of Labor and Employment
Denver, CO
303-318-8000
www.coworkforce.com

Connecticut
Labor Department
Wethersfield, CT
860-263-6000
www.ctdol.state.ct.us

Delaware
Department of Labor
Wilmington, DE
302-761-8085
www.delawareworks.com

District of Columbia
Department of Employment Services
Washington, DC
202-724-7000
www.does.ci.washington.dc.us

Florida
Agency for Workforce Innovation
Tallahassee, FL
850-245-7105
www.floridajobs.org

Georgia
Department of Labor
Atlanta, GA
404-232-7300
www.dol.state.ga.us

Hawaii
Department of Labor and Industrial Relations
Honolulu, HI
808-586-8842
www.hawaii.gov/labor

Idaho
Department of Commerce & Labor
Boise, ID
208-332-3570
www.labor.state.id.us

Illinois
Department of Labor
Chicago, IL
312-793-2800
www.state.il.us/agency/idol

Indiana
Department of Labor
Indianapolis, IN
317-232-2655
www.in.gov/labor

Iowa
Labor Services Division
Des Moines, IA
515-281-5387
www.iowaworkforce.org/labor

Kansas
Department of Human Resources
Office of Employment Standards
Topeka, KS
785-296-4062
www.dol.ks.gov

Kentucky
Department of Labor
Frankfort, KY
502-564-3070
www.labor.ky.gov

Louisiana
Department of Labor
Baton Rouge, LA
225-342-3111
www.ldol.state.la.us

Maine
Department of Labor
Augusta, ME
207-624-6400
www.state.me.us/labor

Maryland
Division of Labor and Industry
Baltimore, MD
410-767-2236
www.dllr.state.md.us/labor

Massachusetts
Department of Workforce Development
Boston, MA
617-626-7122
www.mass.gov/dol

Michigan
Department of Labor and Economic Growth
Lansing, MI
517-373-1820
www.cis.state.mi.us *or* www.michigan.gov/cis

Minnesota
Department of Labor and Industry
St. Paul, MN
651-284-5005
www.doli.state.mn.us

Mississippi
Department of Employment Security
Jackson, MS
601-321-6100
www.mdes.ms.gov

Missouri
Department of Labor and Industrial Relations
Jefferson City, MO
573-751-4091
www.dolir.mo.gov/lirc

Montana
Department of Labor and Industry
Helena, MT
406-444-2840
www.mt.gov

Nebraska
Department of Workforce Development
Lincoln, NE
402-471-2275
www.nebraskaworkforce.com

Nevada
Office of the Labor Commissioner
Carson City, NV
775-687-6409
www.laborcommissioner.com

New Hampshire
Department of Labor
Concord, NH
603-271-3176
www.labor.state.nh.us

New Jersey
Department of Labor and Workforce Development
Trenton, NJ
609-292-2323
www.state.nj.us/labor

New Mexico
Department of Labor
Albuquerque, NM
505-222-4600
www.dol.state.nm.us

New York
Department of Labor
Albany, NY
518-457-9000
www.labor.state.ny.us

North Carolina
Department of Labor
Raleigh, NC
919-807-2796
800-625-2267
www.nclabor.com

North Dakota
Department of Labor
Bismarck, ND
701-328-2660
www.state.nd.gov/labor

Ohio
Division of Labor and Worker Safety
Columbus, OH
614-644-2239
www.com.state.oh.us/ohio/agency.htm

Oklahoma
Department of Labor
Oklahoma City, OK
405-528-1500
www.state.ok.us/~okdol

Oregon
Bureau of Labor and Industries
Portland, OR
971-637-0761
www.oregon.gov/boli

Pennsylvania
Department of Labor and Industry
Harrisburg, PA
717-787-5279
www.dli.state.pa.us

Rhode Island
Department of Labor and Training
Cranston, RI
401-462-8000
www.dlt.state.ri.us

South Carolina
Department of Labor, Licensing, and Regulation
Columbia, SC
803-896-4300
www.llr.state.sc.us/labor

South Dakota
Department of Labor
Pierre, SD
605-773-3101
www.state.sd.us/dol/dlm/dlm-home.htm

Tennessee
Department of Labor and Workforce Development
Nashville, TN
615-741-6642
www.state.tn.us/labor-wfd

Texas
Texas Workforce Commission
Austin, TX
512-463-2222
www.twc.state.tx.us

Utah
Labor Commission
Salt Lake City, UT
801-530-6801
www.laborcommission.utah.gov

Vermont
Department of Labor and Industry
Montpelier, VT
808-828-4000
www.labor.vermont.gov

Virginia

Department of Labor and Industry

Richmond, VA

804-371-3104

www.doli.virginia.gov

Washington

Department of Labor and Industries

Tumwater, WA

360-902-5800

www.lni.wa.gov

West Virginia

Division of Labor

Charleston, WV

304-558-7890

www.labor.state.wv.us

Wisconsin

Department of Workforce Development

Madison, WI

608-266-3131

www.dwd.state.wi.us

Wyoming

Department of Employment

Cheyenne, WY

307-777-7672

http://wydoe.state.wy.us

Legal Referrals

National Employment Lawyers Association

44 Montgomery Street, Suite 2080

San Francisco, CA 94104

415-296-7629

FAX: 415-677-9445

www.nela.org

National directory of employment law attorneys.

Mediation and Arbitration

American Arbitration Association

1633 Broadway, Floor 10

New York, NY 10019

212-716-5800

800-778-7879

FAX: 212-716-5905

www.adr.org

National nonprofit organization offering mediation and arbitration services through local offices across the country. Also conducts neutral investigations of workplace disputes. General information about out-of-court settlements, negotiation opportunities, rules and procedures of mediation.

JAMS Resolution Centers

1920 Main Street, Suite 300

Irvine, CA 92614

800-352-5267

www.jamsadr.com

International nonprofit organization providing mediation and arbitration services, largely through retired judges.

Mediate.com

Post office Box 51090

Eugene, OR 97405

541-345-1629

www.mediate.com

National database of mediators searchable by name, location, or type of practice.

Older Workers

American Association of Retired Persons
601 E Street, NW
Washington, DC 20049
202-434-2277
888-687-2277
TDD: 202-434-6554
FAX: 202-434-2320
www.aarp.org
Nonprofit membership organization of older Americans open to people age 50 or older. Wide range of publications on retirement planning, age discrimination, and employment-related topics, and a "National Employer Team" listing employers seeking mature workers. Networking and direct services available through local chapters.

National Senior Citizens Law Center
1101 14th Street, NW; Suite 400
Washington, DC 20005
202-289-6976
FAX: 202-289-7224
www.nsclc.org
Litigates on behalf of legal services and elderly poor clients. Focus includes retirement income and security issues—including Social Security and Supplemental Security Income (SSI) and age discrimination.

Older Women's League
3300 N. Fairfax Drive, Suite 218
Arlington, VA 22201
703-812-7990
FAX: 703-812-0687
www.owl-national.org
Organization concerned with the social and economic problems of middle-aged and older women. Interests include health care, Social Security, pension rights, employment, and effects of budget cuts.

Retirement Plans and Pensions
See also listings under Older Workers.

Pension Benefit Guaranty Corporation
1200 K Street, NW
Washington, DC 20005
202-326-4000
TDD: 800-877-8339
www.pbgc.gov
Government agency established to protect pension benefits. Collects premiums from participating companies. Provides insolvent multi-employer pension plans with financial assistance to enable them to pay guaranteed benefits.

Pension Rights Center
1350 Connecticut Avenue, NW; Suite 206
Washington, DC 20036
202-296-3776
FAX: 202-833-2472
www.pensionrights.org
Nonprofit organization and service network providing pension advice and information.

Safety and Health Issues

American Psychological Association
750 First Street, NE
Washington, DC 20002
202-336-5500
800-374-2721
TDD/TTY: 202-336-6123
FAX: 202-336-5708
www.apa.org

Information on career training, stress and well-being at work, counseling and psychotherapy for work dysfunctions.

Americans for Nonsmokers' Rights

2530 San Pablo Avenue, Suite J
Berkeley, CA 94702
510-841-3032
FAX: 510-841-3071
www.no-smoke.org
Nonprofit advocacy group that campaigns for legislation to assure that nonsmokers can avoid involuntary exposure to secondhand smoke in the workplace, restaurants, public places, and public transportation.

National Institute for Occupational Safety and Health (NIOSH)

200 Independence Avenue, SW
HHH Building, Room 715-H
Washington, DC 20201
202-401-6997
800-356-4674
www.cdc.gov/niosh/homepage.html
Research institute offering publications on various workplace health and safety issues. Maintains database on indoor air quality, carpal tunnel, workplace homicide, and other current topics. Conducts evaluations of individual worksites. Also makes available training programs, materials, and videos.

National Safety Council

1121 Spring Lake Drive
Itasca, IL 60143
630-285-1121
FAX: 630-285-1315
www.nsc.org

Conducts research and provides education and information on occupational safety; encourages policies that reduce accidental deaths, injuries, and preventable illnesses; monitors legislation and regulations affecting safety.

Occupational Safety and Health Administration

200 Constitution Avenue, NW
Washington, DC 20210
202-693-1999
800-321-6742
www.osha.gov
Federal agency responsible for establishing and overseeing workplace health and safety standards.

White Lung Association

Post Office Box 1483
Baltimore, MD 21203
410-243-5864
www.whitelung.org
National nonprofit organization of asbestos victims. Teaches consequences and effects, removal and disposal of asbestos. Provides literature and legal information.

Unions

American Federation of Labor and Congress of Industrial Organizations (AFL-CIO)

815 16th Street, NW
Washington, DC 20006
202-637-5000
FAX: 202-637-5058
www.aflcio.org
Voluntary federation of unions on all aspects of union employment. Provides information and assistance for union-related issues at local levels.

American Federation of State, County and Municipal Employees (AFSME)

1625 L Street, N.W.

Washington, DC 20036-5687

202-429-1000

TTY: 202-659-0446

FAX: 202-429-1293

www.afsme.org

The largest union for workers in the public service, AFSCME organizes for social and economic justice in the workplace and through political action and legislative advocacy.

Association for Union Democracy

104 Montgomery Street

Brooklyn, NY 11225

718-564-1114

www.uniondemocracy.com

Nationwide attorney referrals, legal advice, counseling, and organizational assistance for union members.

Coalition of Labor Union Women (CLUW)

815 16th Street, NW, 2nd Floor South

Washington, DC 20006

202-508-6969

FAX: 202-508-6968

www.cluw.org

National organization with local chapters. Provides education, organizes conferences and workshops, lobbies for legislation, supports strikes and boycotts. Newsletter and written materials. Provides referrals to attorneys and legal rights groups for union workers.

National Right to Work Committee

8001 Braddock Road, Suite 500

Springfield, VA 22160

800-325-7892

FAX: 703-321-7342

www.nrtwc.org

Citizens' lobbying organization supporting right to work legislation and opposing compulsory unionism.

Women's Issues

Business and Professional Women/USA

1900 M Street, NW; Suite 310

Washington, DC 20036

202-293-1100

FAX: 202-861-0298

www.bpwusa.org

Seeks to improve the status of working women through education, legislative action, and local projects. Sponsors Business and Professional Women's Foundation, which awards grants and loans, based on need, to mature women reentering the workforce or entering nontraditional fields.

Equal Rights Advocates

1663 Mission Street, Suite 250

San Francisco, CA 94103

415-621-0672 (General information)

800-839-4372 (Advice and counseling hotline)

FAX: 415-621-6744

www.equalrights.org

Nonprofit public interest legal advocacy organization providing legal advice and counseling in both English and Spanish.

Federally Employed Women, Inc.

1666 K Street, NW; Suite 440

Washington, DC 20006

202-898-0994

www.few.org

Membership group for women who work for the federal government. Focuses on eliminating sex discrimination in government employment and increasing job opportunities for women. Offers training programs, monitors legislation and regulations.

Feminist Majority Foundation

1600 Wilson Boulevard, Suite 801

Arlington, VA 22209

703-522-2214

FAX: 703-522-2219

www.feminist.org

Political organization that lobbies to increase the number of feminists running for public office. The Foundation with which it is associated is a nonprofit research organization, which provides information about battered women, sexual harassment, and international women's issues.

9to5, National Association of Working Women

207 E. Buffalo Street, #211

Milwaukee, WI 53202

414-274-0925

800-522-0925 (Hotline)

FAX: 414-272-2870

www.9to5.org

National grassroots nonprofit membership organization for working women. Provides counseling, information, and referrals for problems on the job—including family leave, pregnancy disability, termination,

compensation, and sexual harassment. Publishes legal guides, factsheets, and videos. Local chapters throughout the country.

National Partnership for Women and Families

1875 Connecticut Avenue, NW; Suite 650

Washington, DC 20009

202-986-2600

FAX: 202-986-2539

www.nationalpartnership.org

A nonprofit, nonpartisan membership organization that uses public education and advocacy to promote fairness in the workplace, quality health care, and policies that help women and men meet the dual demands of work and family.

National Women's Law Center

11 Dupont Circle, NW; Suite 800

Washington, DC 20036

202-588-5180

FAX: 202-588-5185

www.nwlc.org

Works to expand and protect women's legal rights through litigation, advocacy, and public education. Interests include child and family support, health education, employment discrimination, sexual harassment, and income security.

National Organization for Women

1100 H Street, NW, 3rd Floor

Washington, DC 20005

202-628-8669

TTY: 202-331-9002

FAX: 201-785-8576

www.now.org

A nonprofit advocacy organization that strives to eliminate discrimination and harassment in the workplace. NOW pursues its goals through direct mass actions including marches, rallies, pickets, counter-demonstrations, nonviolent civil disobedience, lobbying, grassroots political organizing, and litigating.

U.S. Department of Labor, Women's Bureau
200 Constitution Avenue, NW, #S3002
Washington, DC 20210
800-827-5335
202-219-6611
FAX: 202-693-6725
www.dol.gov/wb
Monitors employment issues and promotes employment opportunities for women. Sponsors workshops, job fairs, demonstrations, and pilot projects. Offers technical assistance, conducts research, and provides publications on issues that affect working women.

Women in Community Service
1900 N. Beauregard Street, Suite 103
Alexandria, VA 22311
703-671-0500
800-442-9427
FAX: 703-671-4489
www.wics.org
Contracts with the Labor Department for outreach, support services, and job placement for women with low incomes. Sponsors the Lifeskills Program, which assists at-risk women in such areas as job training and money management.

Women Work!
The National Network for Women's Employment
1625 K Street, NW; Suite 300
Washington, DC 20006
202-467-6346
FAX: 202-467-5366
www.womenwork.org
Fosters development of programs and services for women to enter, re-enter, and advance in the workforce, and provides information about public policy issues that affect displaced homemakers.

Work/Life Issues

See also organizations listed under Women's Issues.

A Better Balance
West Village Station Box 20206
New York, NY 10014
888-595-9390
www.abetterbalance.org
Provides legal support and technical assistance for legislative and voter initiatives around the country aimed at obtaining guaranteed paid sick leave that workers can use for themselves and their families. Also works with state and local officials and the business community to promote flexibility in the workplace, and with local community groups to assess how work/family conflict affects low income workers.

Center for Work/Life Law

University of California

Hastings College of the Law

200 McAllister Street

San Francisco, CA 94102

415-565-4640

Hotline: 800-981-9495

www.worklifelaw.org

Works with employees, employers, attorneys, legislators, unions, journalists, and researchers, providing guidance and technical assistance to help eliminate discrimination based on family responsibilities.

Families and Work Institute

267 Fifth Avenue, 2nd Floor

New York, NY 10016

212-465-2044

FAX: 212-465-8637

www.familiesandwork.org

Operates a national clearinghouse of information on work and family life; advises business, government, and community organizations, and conducts management training on work and family issues.

MomsRising

www.momsrising.org

Online effort mobilizing mothers and providing grassroots support to leaders and organizations addressing key issues such as paid family leave, flexible work options, after-school programs, healthcare for all kids, quality childcare, and living wages. Website includes an extensive list of allied organizations that offer information and engage in lobbying on these issues.

New Ways to Work

103 Morris Street, Suite A

Sebastopol, CA 95472

707-824-4000

FAX: 707-824-4410

www.nww.org

Educational and advocacy organization devoted to promoting flexible work arrangements and in training youth for work. Serves as a clearinghouse for information, has an extensive publications list, and offers seminars and training to companies.

Work/Family Directions

55 Chapel Street

Newton, MA 02458

800-447-0543

www.wfd.com

Consulting company offering services to companies, including workplace surveys and help with planning and implementing work and family programs.

Workplace Options

4020 Capital Boulevard, Suite 100

Raleigh, NC 27604

800-699-8011

FAX: 919-833-9888

www.workplaceoptions.com

Corporate consulting firm specializing in helping employers design and deliver work and family benefits. Offers training workshops, needs assessment, and resource and referral services.

Index

workplace fairness®

it's everyone's job

*"If you're getting a raw deal at work,
turn to Workplace Fairness."*

–PC Magazine

Thousands of people turn to us every day.

- Comprehensive information on employee rights in all 50 states

- Complete listings of resources for further information and help

- Practical tips on handling job problems and taking legal action

- Daily coverage of news and issues

- Powerful tools for grassroots action

www.workplacefairness.org

44 Montgomery Street, Suite 2080 San Francisco, CA 94104

Get the Latest in the Law

1 **Nolo's Legal Updater**
We'll send you an email whenever a new edition of your book is published!
Sign up at **www.nolo.com/legalupdater**.

2 **Updates at Nolo.com**
Check **www.nolo.com/update** to find recent changes in the law that
affect the current edition of your book.

3 **Nolo Customer Service**
To make sure that this edition of the book is the most recent one, call us at
800-728-3555 and ask one of our friendly customer service representatives
(7:00 am to 6:00 pm PST, weekdays only). Or find out at **www.nolo.com**.

4 **Complete the Registration & Comment Card ...**
... and we'll do the work for you! Just indicate your preferences below:

Registration & Comment Card

NAME _____ DATE _____

ADDRESS _____

CITY _____ STATE _____ ZIP _____

PHONE _____ EMAIL _____

COMMENTS _____

WAS THIS BOOK EASY TO USE?   (VERY EASY)   5   4   3   2   1   (VERY DIFFICULT)

☐ Yes, you can quote me in future Nolo promotional materials. *Please include phone number above.*

☐ Yes, send me **Nolo's Legal Updater** via email when a new edition of this book is available.

Yes, I want to sign up for the following email newsletters:

   ☐ **NoloBriefs** (monthly)
   ☐ **Nolo's Special Offer** (monthly)
   ☐ **Nolo's BizBriefs** (monthly)
   ☐ **Every Landlord's Quarterly** (four times a year)

☐ Yes, you can give my contact info to carefully selected
   partners whose products may be of interest to me.

YRW 8.0

NOLO

Nolo
950 Parker Street
Berkeley, CA 94710-9867
www.nolo.com

YOUR LEGAL COMPANION